Praise for

RADICAL SEPARATION OF POWERS

'Hallaq has already authored definitive books on how Islamic civilization articulated law and how both Western scholarship and many Islamist movements have grossly misunderstood Islamic law and the premodern state. Now this latest, fascinating volume draws on a career of expertise to bring these studies together, laying out how the Sharīʿa and state fit together and should be understood today.'

Jonathan A. C. Brown, author of *Justice and Islamic Law*

'The breadth of Hallaq's analysis of Islamic constitutionalism and the philosophical depth that he brings to it open new vistas on political thought in premodern Islam. His brilliant readings of key texts in Islamic political theory serve to peel off thick layers of misrepresentation, bringing those texts to life and allowing us to view them with fresh eyes. Along the way, he offers a trenchant critique of both Orientalism and liberalism. This book will have a transformative impact on the study of Islamic political thought, but its arguments speak to a much wider audience, which, too, will be in Hallaq's debt.'

Muhammad Qasim Zaman, author of *Islam in Pakistan: A History*

'This is Wael Hallaq at his provocative and erudite best. He reimagines Arabic philology as an empathetic praxis, shows how modern scholars must reintegrate the fields of Islamic learning artificially separated by Orientalism, and in the process rewrites the history of Islamic political thought to make a powerful case for a distinctive Islamic constitutionalism rooted in prophethood, ethics, and above all the Sharīʿa. His reassessment of Islamic constitutional structures, from the Qur'an to the Ottomans, aims also to lay the groundwork – in ways likely to be equally controversial and generative – for a sober appraisal of the constitutional disappointments and dilemmas that we confront today.'

Joseph E. Lowry, translator of *The Epistle on Legal Theory*

'Hallaq offers a much-needed corrective to the Orientalist narratives, which do not provide a viable foundation for historical inquiry nor serve as building blocks for new scholarship. In their place, he presents a panoramic account of constitutionalism and the separation of powers, giving readers a fine-grained perspective on the primacy of law in curbing, limiting, and guiding executive authority. Spanning the millennium from the tenth to the eighteenth century, Hallaq not only presents a historical account of constitutional practice but also offers a narrative infused with theoretical inquiry and multidimensional critique. The reader will appreciate the book's explication of a Sharīʿa-oriented, ulema-led mode of political thought in relation to recent scholarly interventions on the secular *adab al-siyasa* discourses of good governance in Islamic history.'

Hayrettin Yücesoy, author *of Disenchanting the Caliphate*

Radical Separation of Powers

A History of Islamic Constitutionalism

WAEL B. HALLAQ

ONEWORLD
ACADEMIC

A Oneworld Academic Book

First published by Oneworld Publications Ltd in 2026

A CIP record for this title is available from the British Library

ISBN 978-1-83643-117-6
eISBN 978-1-83643-118-3

Typeset by Geethik Technologies
Printed and bound in Great Britain by Clays Ltd, Elcograf S.p.A.

The authorised representative in the EEA is eucomply OU,
Pärnu mnt 139b–14, 11317 Tallinn, Estonia
(email: hello@eucompliancepartner.com / phone: +33757690241)

Oneworld Publications Ltd
10 Bloomsbury Street
London WC1B 3SR
England

For Carmen

Contents

List of Abbreviated Titles

The following list represents the treatises that are discussed in great detail. Works analyzed less extensively or briefly are cited in the form of the author's last name and a short title.

ADD = Māwardī, *Adab al-Dīn wal-Dunyā* (2013 ed.)
AS = Māwardī, *Al-Aḥkām al-Sulṭāniyya*
FB = Ghazālī, *Faḍā'iḥ al-Bāṭiniyya*
GU = Juwaynī, *Ghiyāth al-Umam*
IK = Ibn ʿArabī, *al-Insān al-Kāmil*
ITSS = Ibn Taymiyya, *al-Siyāsa al-Sharʿiyya*
OCC = Ottoman Criminal Code (10th/16th c.)
RMI = Ibn ʿĀbidīn, *Radd al-Muḥtār*
SAQ = Qalqashandī, *Ṣubḥ al-Aʿshā fī Ṣināʿat al-Inshā*
SM = Niẓām al-Mulk, *Siyar al-Mulūk*
SSD = Dede Jöngi Efendī (Ar. Dāda Afandī), *al-Siyāsa al-Sharʿiyya*
TAB = Ibn Farḥūn, *Tabṣirat al-Ḥukkām*
TAJ = Ibn Jamāʿa, *Taḥrīr al-Aḥkām fī Tadbīr Ahl al-Islām*
TH = Ibn Qayyim al-Jawziyya, *al-Ṭuruq al-Ḥukmiyya*
TM = Ghazālī, *Al-Tibr al-Masbūk fī Naṣīḥat al-Mulūk*
TMH = Ṭarābulsī, *Muʿīn al-Ḥukkām*
TN = Mawardı, *Tashıl al-Naẓar wa-Taʿjıl al-Ẓafar*

Preface and Acknowledgments

There usually arise in the course of inquiry and research a number of questions that urge themselves on scholars as worthy of further investigation. Even a first book tends to raise a number of such questions, generating answers that may culminate in an article, a monograph, or even a sizable tome. The present book, however, did not come about this way. In fact, although the subject matter has interested me since my late teens, writing a book on constitutional questions was not on my radar until the appearance of *The Impossible State*, published in 2013 by Columbia University Press, and translated thereafter into several languages, beginning with its rendering into Arabic in 2014.

In *The Impossible State*, I made the argument that under the hegemony of our current state system, it is inconceivable to establish a Muslim polity that takes the fundamental Islamic norms and values as its foundation, values known to have governed Muslim communities for the twelve centuries that preceded European colonialism. The book advanced several arguments, only one of which, covered in chapter 3, pertained to constitutionalism. It was titled "Separation of Powers: Rule of Law or Rule of the State?" In it, I argued that, first, the liberal constitutional model, in theory and in practice, is engulfed in multiple irresolvable problems, to an extent that the theory of separation of powers can be said to have already collapsed (I expand on this argument in chapter 12 here.) Second, that the Islamic constitutional model was significantly more robust than its liberal counterpart and that, therefore, Muslims have little to borrow or even to learn from it as an example to follow (although learning from the pitfalls of problematic phenomena remains, in my judgment, mandatory).

Now, when I wrote that book and chapter, I had drawn on more than three decades of reading in the Islamic primary sources that pertained to politics, "constitutional" theory and practice, as well as to law, theology, ethics, and much else. And as any experienced author knows, when scholars with many years behind them write, they do not – and in fact cannot – comprehensively and meticulously detail every aspect of every argument they make in a single book, much less in a single chapter. Scholars read much more than they eventually manage to register in their index cards, publications, or footnotes.

The genesis of the book thus began right after the initial reactions to *The Impossible State* appeared in print media, TV talk shows, social media, and internet debates. The reactions from the Arab and Muslim world were particularly intense, with many criticisms directed at chapter 3. Chief among these was the allegation that my account idealizes Islamic constitutional history. The present book emerged out of the conviction that much more needs to be said about the issues raised in chapter 3 of *The Impossible State* and that a structural and more wide-ranging constitutional history of Islam must therefore be written.

It has been my practice ever since I started my professional career in academia to wed teaching to research. It is my belief that good teaching and good research stand in a dialectical relationship. I usually teach what I research and often research the subjects I teach, which explains the transmutations in my graduate course offerings every few years. Right after the appearance of the reactions to *The Impossible State*, I began teaching, at Columbia University, a graduate seminar in which my students read with me a dozen or so of what usually are considered important Islamic primary sources on "political thought." The course, continuing to be offered as I write these lines (autumn 2024), aimed to achieve several goals, one of which is to militate against the very idea that the works we were reading represented, or were limited to, "political thought" or even intellectual history. As I explain in the Introduction, the notion that these works were merely "a collection" of ideas on politics is a function of the Orientalist stance that for long avoided the acknowledgement that there is a cogent constitutional conception in Islam. For the recognition that there is such a thing as an Islamic constitutional history would necessarily instigate a further investigation, one likely to compel the conclusion that there was indeed a constitutional structure that was not only functional, viable, and successful, but even respectable.

Such a discovery would have put Orientalist scholarship in a major predicament, because the narrative would then have to explain away the dominant discourses that have been produced by Orientalism in justification of modernization and the massive colonialist reforms that Europe directly or indirectly imposed on Muslims since the middle of the nineteenth century. In other words, to uncover "Islamic constitutionalism" in meaningful detail and as a structure is to disrupt and contradict the colonialist and thus Orientalist narrative of the *mission civilisatrice*. This consideration, incidentally, also explains why Orientalism, in its nearly two centuries of prolific production, has never come up with a single book on Islamic constitutional history, although promising attempts on usually smaller scales have been coming to light.

The second goal of the seminar was organically connected to the first. In order to tap into and tease out the "constitutional" contents of the sources we were reading, a new method of textual analysis had to be developed. The need for an alternative approach stemmed from the realization that the Orientalist philological method was utterly defective and that its defects are not haphazard or incidental but are rather the necessarily attendant function of the epistemological and conceptual structure of Orientalism as the handmaiden of colonialism, not to mention secularism, materialism, print capitalism, sovereignty, and much else. In other words, Orientalist philology is structurally tied up with the colonialist narrative as integral to the colonialist project, if not with coloniality across the board. In the Introduction, I outline a new conception of philology that has emerged from my pedagogical deliberations for researching this book, although my philological discomfort with the prevailing methods had begun to arise decades earlier. It is my hope to take up the elaboration of this conception in a separate writing.

The preceding comments about the connections between teaching and research entail a decade-long register of indebtedness to the successive generations of students who participated in my seminar. While all students contributed meaningfully to the rich discussions of the classroom, I would like to acknowledge the following participants in particular: Omar Abdel-Ghaffar, Nadia Abdulrahman, Sundus Al Ameen, Ruwa Alhayek, Nourah Alohali, Thaer AlSheikh Theeb, Jealool Amari, Toqa Badran, Jenna Barhoush, Muhammet Emin Canli, Alaa El-Shafei, Wajdi Ben Hammed, Doha Tazi Hemida, Yosra Hussein, Amir Izadpanahi, Nur Jabarin, Jaehoon Jung, Rami Koujah, Abdul Latif, Karim Malak, Antonio Musto, Laura Sani, Furkan Şentürk, Aseel Sharawneh, Lama Suleiman, and Toha Toriq. I am also deeply indebted to the efficient help of my research assistants, particularly Aseel Najib, Furkan Şentürk, Aneka Kazlyna, Mariel Povolny, Hasene Esma Ozgun, and Aziza Ben Abdallah.

Dr. Asım Cüneyd Köksal, to whom I am deeply grateful, generously provided me with microfilms of numerous Ottoman manuscripts dealing with politics and governance. Necmettin Kızılkaya has for years been a rock of support and an ideal colleague without whom my scholarly and research engagements in Turkey would not have been so productive and painless. I owe him a large debt, as I owe Recep Şentürk and Abed Awad the generosity of valuable help they have extended over the years.

The book benefited from critical readings and constructive engagements offered by Humeira Iqtidar, Omar Farahat, and Doha Tazi Hemida. I am immensely grateful to them. I likewise acknowledge with gratitude the useful comments and valuable suggestions made by my publisher's readers, one of whom, I have later come to know, was Hayrettin Yücesoy. I also record my gratitude to Ahmad Khan, visiting professor at Columbia during the year 2022-23. His interventions in my graduate seminars were always productive, having raised significant questions and stimulated rich discussions. Rida Vaquas, Oneworld's Commissioning Editor, and Tom Feltham, the book's copy-editor, were exemplary in getting the volume ready for print and in offering invaluable editorial assistance. Last but not least, I was blessed to receive the loving support and unwavering encouragement of Carmen Mihai, to whom this book is dedicated.

A Note on Footnotes

It is in the nature of revisionist scholarship to encounter opposition and suspicion. The unfamiliar has few friends. When Orientalists write, they can take much for granted, not only because their outputs represent the politically and culturally dominant narrative, but also because they speak with a sense of sovereignty that has proven throughout the last two centuries to possess performative powers. To go against this hegemonic and powerfully colonizing knowledge is no easy task. It would seem that every step of the way is an uphill battle, struggling against the odds. The reader will therefore find that many of my footnotes consist of heavy citations of the Arabic sources, so that it is clear to the reader how I chose to interpret the language of the relevant passages; in doing so I also did my best to be as consistent as I can be with the ways in which Muslim intellectuals understood and used their terms. This is why I also recover the lexical and technical meaning of terms from the old lexicons, another practice populating my footnotes. It would be a fatal error to see this practice as pedantic. The great effort and investment in this aspect of the work is intended to provide as rigorous an argument as possible in favor of its theses, and to avoid to the utmost extent possible the translatability problems I discuss in the Introduction. It is hoped that the readers who are proficient in classical Arabic will take the time to indulge themselves in these textual citations, since no matter how well I tried to convey the habitus behind these texts, a translation remains a translation: "Lost in Translation" is a monumental axiom.

Introduction

I

The notion of Islamic constitutionalism before the emergence of the modern nation-states has only recently emerged as a research priority,[1] after a century and a half of relative neglect. Our first two queries must then be about why we should take up the study of this subject in the first place and then why it is that this field of inquiry has suffered such prolonged neglect.

---

1 Some of the most noteworthy writings on constitutional matters (including those on the modern period) are: Sherman Jackson, *Islamic Law*, an important and competent study that addresses the constitutional writings of the distinguished Mamlūk-era jurist al-Qarāfī; being a study of a specific context – or perhaps of a "constitutional moment" – Jackson makes no claim to mapping out either the general Islamic constitutional *structures* or their history and evolution. Another general but useful article is Abou El Fadl, "Centrality of Sharīʿah." See also Quraishi-Landes, "Islamic Constitutionalism," 553-79, esp. at 564-78; this article is concerned with modern possibilities rather than a study of premodern constitutional history, and much less of constitutional structures. So is Azizah al-Hibri's "Islamic Constitutionalism and the Concept of Democracy," where constitutionalism is seen through the prism of the question of Islam's compatibility with modern forms of democracy. Similarly, Emon's essay "Shariʿa and the Rule of Law" is essentially preoccupied with modern issues. For aspects of constitutional checks and balances during the peak of the Ottoman Empire, see the useful article of Yilmaz, "Containing Sultanic Authority." On political thought during the Ayyūbid and Mamlūk periods (with intermittent attention to constitutional issues), see El-Merheb, *Political Thought*. Frank Vogel's "Tracing Nuance in Māwardī's *Al-Aḥkām al-Sulṭāniyyah*" is to date the best study of Māwardī's constitutional thought in *al-Aḥkām al-Sulṭāniyya*, but it hardly goes beyond this ambition. A dated and problematic reading of Māwardī's *al-Aḥkām al-Sulṭāniyya* and other political works is Gibb's "Constitutional Organization," discussed in due course. For a general survey, see March, "Constitutional Authority." In addition, see Bibliography for works by Afsaruddin, Anjum, Atçıl, Ayoub, Baldwin, Fadel, Hassan, Rapoport, Siddiqui, Stilt, Tezcan, Yücesoy, and Zaman, among others.

Every student of Islam knows that Muslims who inhabited the premodern (or should we say extra-modern) world never spoke of their own system of governance or political experiences in constitutional terms. Neither the conceptual categories nor the vocabulary signifying them existed. And if this is the case, one might well ask why bother writing about constitutions or constitutional history in Islam at all? Yet, considering the enormous body of dynamic discourse on constitutions and constitutional matters around the globe nowadays, the answer, I think, is necessarily at hand. For if writing history inevitably means writing the history of the present, then we are naturally bound to think of the past both in terms of present concerns and within the boundaries of our linguistic imagination. Our discourse has on a global scale been preoccupied with questions about good governance, democratic rule, separation of powers, and various concepts of similar stripes. These political and constitutional concepts, along with the scholarly output, political discourse, and "culture talk" surrounding them, have become the proverbial air we breathe. In fact, we cannot think about politics and governance without or outside of these concepts. Yet, I am aware of the risks involved in cultural translation, for no lesser reason than the danger of rendering the Islamic constitutional experience as a replica, a mirror image, of our own. This book is therefore as much an exercise in method and theory as it is an attempt to offer a structural historical account.

There are at present two major contingents of scholars whose thinking and discourse cannot escape the conceptual repertoire of "Islamic constitutionalism," for – despite their different perspectives and teleologies – they are both entangled with it to their bone. First, it is by now well-known that modern Europe has partly defined its own identity through a juxtaposition with Islamic culture, historically the most important and formidable neighbor it had. The West's obsession with Islam probably has no parallel. Islamic history and culture were and continue to be at the forefront of the Orientalist machinery that Europe deployed in its bid to colonize Muslim lands. Among the countless areas of research, a few command this level of particular attention. Nothing is as sensitive in the Western political imagination as to speak of *jihād*, for instance. Issues pertaining to women and sexual and other personal forms of freedom rank as high. And joining this select menu is the large question of democratic rule, an emblem of which is the perpetual question "Is Islam compatible with democracy?" This question is of course inseparable from the question "What is Islam?" in the first place. And since Islam was not born yesterday, the long and short histories of this culture and "religion"[2] are crucial for answering the question about its democratic potential. Whether Muslims of premodernity had spoken the language of constitutionalism and separation of powers or not does not therefore matter – the "problem" of Islam's compatibility with democracy is as much on the West's mind as it is on its tongue. To say that this discourse needs to be set aright is an understatement. To say that we must speak the language of constitutionalism whether we want to or not is to state the most obvious. Yet, for this contingent and for the community of constitutional scholars, this book offers a radically different model of separation of powers and constitutional structure.

The other colossal contingent speaking in these terms are modern Muslims themselves, whose stakes in the matter are the highest of all. Having been massively liberalized, the talk of democracy, constitutions, separation of power, and the rule of law has dominated their political imagination and public and private discourses, as anyone familiar with the local scenes around the Muslim world knows well. Exiting what they see as their political nightmare and the general state of authoritarian rule constitutes one of their major aspirations and goals. And since their own history, near and distant, continues to be important, if not central, for their sense of their own identity as Muslims, the challenge of leaving the current conditions behind is compounded by the difficult considerations of maintaining their cultural legacy and simultaneously adopting Western forms of government. Needless to say, questions about West-inspired constitutionalism, separation of powers, sovereignty, and the like not only abound in their midst but define the very discourse in which they are so heavily engaged. The question therefore is not whether or not the West and Muslims are interested in the political history of premodern Islam and its modes of governance – they categorically are.[3] Rather, the question

2 Throughout this book, when I speak of things Islamic, I often use the term "religion" to indicate the indigenous meaning of *dīn*. As this Introduction shows, the reader will approach this *translation* with extreme caution, since, strictly speaking, what "religion" signifies in Christian Western cultures does not in any unproblematic way correspond to *dīn*. On the substantive translation problematics of *dīn*/religion, see Anidjar, "Idea of an Anthropology."

3 As evidenced in the vast literature on the subject. For example, see Baldwin, *Islamic Law*; Black, *History*; Bosworth, "Political and Dynastic History;" Broadbridge, *Kingship and Ideology*; Burak, *Second Formation*; Butterworth, "Prudence Versus Legitimacy;" Crone and Hinds, *God's Caliph*; Darling, *History*; El-Merheb, *Political Thought*; Gibb, "Constitutional Organization;" Ginio, "Administration of Criminal Justice;" Goitein, "Birth-Hour;" Heyd, *Studies*; Imber, *Ebu's-Su'ud*; Irwin, "Privatization of 'Justice';" Jennings, "Kadi, Court;" Lambton, "Justice;" Lange, *Justice*; Nagel, *Staat und Glaubensgemeinschaft*; Peters, *Crime and Punishment*; Rapaport, "Royal Justice." See also sources listed in n. 58, below.

which should occupy us is how do we embark on the study of these issues in an extinct culture that never spoke the language of constitutions, democracy, rule of law, separation of powers, or the like? But before we address such matters, we turn to the second query pertaining to the near silence of Orientalist scholarship on Islamic constitutional history, silence that persisted till the very end of the twentieth century.

Given the scholarly work cited so far, my meaning of neglect must be understood in structural terms. Several scholars have done admirable work on aspects of Islamic constitutionalism or themes related to it,[4] but that does not make the neglect any less remarkable. During the last century and a half, entire scholarly narratives were developed about, say, "Islamic law." There is a whole subgenre on early borrowings, another on the middle-period (mostly about "stagnation" of the law), and yet another on modern "reform," and much else in between and beyond. In other words, a sizeable body of writings and a robust field of legal Orientalism had been in place even before the 1980s. The same can be said of literary studies, *falsafa* ("philosophy"), military history, political history, social history, and many more. Each of these fields has developed a *narrative* that can be analyzed in terms of *structure*.[5] But this is not the case for Islamic constitutionalism, which cannot be said to have developed a *narrative structure* (the Orientalist account notwithstanding). This area of research remains patchy at best.

There are a number of reasons for the stunted development of this history, but none more important than the nature of the conception of what constitutes governance and politics in the Islamic tradition, a tradition that effectively stretched from the first/seventh century to the early thirteenth/nineteenth. To date, the general conception continues to be that Islam is authoritarian through and through, anti-democratic, and even fanatical about its own doctrines and dogmas. These widespread stereotypes and latent prejudices, tenacious in scholarship till the very end of the twentieth century, precluded the need to study a history that has been identified with a severe lack of a reasonably steady rule of law or so-called democratic government. The conception, furthermore, has a long and complex genealogy whose structure is drawn from medieval Christian attitudes and phobias that were in time gradually transformed into secularized forms of modern historical and colonial discourse.[6] This is to

4 See n. 1, above.

5 For the Orientalist narrative structure of "Islamic legal history" as an example, see sec. II, below, and main text in ch. 3, at n. 42.

6 This argument encounters the familiar objection that not all European thinkers thought

say that the narrative does not only reflect bias and dogmatically negative depictions of Islam, considerably driven by strategic and immediate political interests, but also functions as a structured ideological prop and justification for colonization.[7] From the nineteenth-century's conquests and domination of Muslim lands and until the American-led Iraq-Syria wars of this century, the narrative has served distinct political purposes, and has throughout continued its robust association with the doctrine of *mission civilisatrice*.

One of the most prevalent and powerful modernist[8] assumptions and ideas about the way Muslims ruled themselves politically over the centuries is captured by the powerful epithet "Oriental Despotism." This was an Orientalist descriptor of choice, having travelled in time – when Orientalizing performativity[9] had been consummated by its Oriental object – to the Muslim repertoire of concepts and convictions of late modernity. Oriental despotism emerged out of Europe's fear of itself,[10] of its own tyrannies that were perpetrated by an exceptionally oppressive Church, feudalism and, later, absolute monarchies that deepened the oppression to intolerable limits. It is this intolerability that violently pushed Europe to jettison the Church and the political tyrant, replacing them with what has become modernity, with its distinct structural components of secularism, notions of popular will, deep bureaucracy, an administrative state, and a trenchant materialism, among others. Because to Europe Islam was profoundly "religious," it came – by traumatic elision – to see in Islam and its ways of life everything it hated and despised about itself. The study of Islamic political history by Orientalism

the same about Islam, and that some even admired certain features of Islamic governance (and opposed colonialism to boot). While true, these "voices," I have argued elsewhere, are not paradigmatic and in fact constitute the exception to the rule. See *Restating Orientalism*, 33-41, and n. 28 (p. 282).

7 For an example of a structured historiographic narrative designed as part of a colonialist telos, see Hallaq, "Quest for Origins or Doctrine?" On Orientalism as the handmaiden of colonialism and as integral to the structure of modern knowledge, see Hallaq, *Restating Orientalism*.

8 In my usage, "modernist" refers to distinctly modern forms of thought, rationality, and modern conceptions of reality, emphasizing the referent as a quality rather than as a temporality or an epoch of time.

9 On performativity and Orientalist discourse, see Hallaq, *Restating Orientalism*, 61-63.

10 On the history of the concept as internal to Europe's fantasy and its domestic political anxieties, see Rubiés, "Oriental Despotism." This article alone convincingly showcases the crucial fact that the emergence of the concept has nothing to do with Europe's scientific observation of Muslim cultures and their histories, and that it is wholly related to Europe's fabrication of an ideology that served its political discourses about what was thought as good governance. To similar effects, see also Kaiser, "The Evil Empire?"

merely came to confirm this presupposition, even enhance and embellish it. Similarly, by sheer mimesis, this narrative has become integral to the Muslims' view of their own history. On behalf of colonialism and empire, Orientalism has finally accomplished its goal.

The narrative of Oriental Despotism emerged within a context of presences and absences,[11] both of which must raise our curiosity. I have already noted the relatively scant attention given to constitutional questions in Islam.[12] The presences, however, come to confirm the absences. As early as the 1950s, the once highly influential H. A. R. Gibb wrote that in Islam "there can be no sovereign state, in the sense that the state has the right of enacting its own law," because "the Law precedes the State, both logically and in terms of time; and the State exists for the sole purpose of maintaining and enforcing the law."[13]

---

11 See n. 60, below. Speaking of yet another absence, Lambton, "Justice," 92, says: "[P]olitical science did not exist as an independent discipline in Islam; and so far as it existed at all it was a department of theology." An equally benighted narrative is that of Goitein. Mostly consisting of erroneous generalizations if not outright historical blunder, Goitein's essay, "Attitudes Toward Government," offers a story in which the Qur'ān "says nothing" about "political regime," that is, how Muslims ought to govern themselves (cf. ch. 4, below). Citing the hyper-modern thesis of ʿAlī ʿAbd al-Rāziq, Goitein in effect argues that caliphate itself was not a requirement in Islam and that it is a sort of an imposition on Muslims. Caliphs and sultans were nothing but "autocratic," ruling an "amorphous mass of Muslims" who "had little opportunity to develop interest in the conduct of the state." (198, 200).

12 See n. 1, above. The only scholar noting the absence of scholarly interest in the Islamic rule of law (but no mention of separation of powers or constitutional history) is Anver Emon, "Shariʿa and the Rule of Law." Emon entirely misses the hegemonic Orientalist bias and its involvement in a larger colonialist narrative, and instead explains the neglect of this subject in terms of segregated academic expertise, lack of interdisciplinarity, and, "perhaps more to the point," the problematics of "bringing together Shariʿa and rule of law" when "each term of art remains highly contested and thereby subject to dispute" (37-38). The first two reasons are obviously unconvincing, since there have been scholars, since Joseph Schacht, Emile Tyan, and many others, who studied law and Sharīʿa and who remained entirely silent on these issues. If the third explanation were true, no more than a handful of concepts would have been studied in academia's departments.

Furthermore, it would be imprudent to interpret absences and blind spots as individual and autonomous occurrences, taking place as micro-events in different factual contexts. Indeed, in their totality, absences in Orientalist discourse reflect structures of thought that manifest themselves in reality as performative acts, producing colonial effects of devastating consequences. The claim that the Sharīʿa did not formulate a theory of contract (an absence) is not very different from the absence of a constitutional history of Islam (bearing the clear implications of absence of rule of law or of "democracy"), nor, at the end of the day, is it different from the ideological claim that "Palestine is a land without people." These three absences, located in different fields of inquiry, are in fact structurally connected with each other by a programmatic narrative structure, one that culminates in a single effect: to render Islam and Muslims colonizable.

13 Gibb, "Constitutional Organization," 3.

Gibb's "Law" is of course the Sharīʿa which, by virtue of being accepted by "all Muslims" as "God's Will, supplies the authority, sanctions, and moral basis for the unity and constitution of the *Umma* as a political entity."[14] Yet, page after page, Gibb proceeds with his exposition of "political theory" in order to finally conclude that the "caliph is an absolute ruler"[15] who effectively commands both the Community and its Law, precisely because he rules in absolute terms. His initial proposition that the "law precedes the State" and that it is "the expression of God's will" does not seem to have any consequence, making his later findings in the article a *non sequitur*.

Despite the acknowledgement that the Sharīʿa is supreme, the theme of the rule of law and the separation of powers in Islam was never picked up by the field of Islamic studies as a subject worth pursuing.[16] In fact, Gibb's work seems to have given a new push for later scholarship to refine its narratives of "Oriental despotism." The realization that Islam may possess a system of rule of law would have contradicted not only the overwhelmingly negative stereotypes of Islam but would more importantly contravene the basis of the colonialist project, which, when Gibb was writing, was at its peak (as it continues unabetted in mutating forms into the present). As I have argued in more than one writing in regard to several aspects of the European academic field called "Islamic studies,"[17] "Islamic law" and its associated, but never fully acknowledged, constitutional structures were rarely ever depicted as possessing meritorious qualities, that is, qualities that are meritorious by European standards.[18] How would the energetic projects of "legal reform" in the Muslim

14 Gibb, "Constitutional Organization," 4.

15 Gibb, "Constitutional Organization," 17. This notion of absolutism populates Gibb's writings. See Gibb, "Schools of Law," 57, 59, 61 and passim.

16 The concept is at times claimed to be absent altogether. See ch. 5, n. 73.

17 E.g., *Restating Orientalism*; Hallaq, "The Quest for Origins;" Hallaq, "On Orientalism, Self-Consciousness and History."

18 Immensely relevant to this context are the writings of the influential Joseph Schacht, the so-called "Father of Islamic law," whose characterizations of this law and its relationship to what he called the "state" and governance were consistently negative. Schacht effectively regarded the Sharīʿa as suffering from an incurable incompetence to deal with reality and "practice." Its "nature is to a great extent determined by its history, and its history is dominated by the contrast between theory and practice." It is at times "irrational" while at others it displays forms of "magic." It possesses "an impressive number of legal concepts, both special and generic, but they are generally speaking broad and lacking in positive content" (Schacht, *Introduction*, 199-205). This implacable negativity pervades through and through, traveling as far as the borders of constitutional discussions (but stopping there). In the very last paragraph of his *Introduction*, 210-11, and describing the tenth feature that is supposed to constitute "the nature of Islamic law" (the title of the chapter), he says this:

world, much less its patron colonialism itself, be justified should the Sharīʿa in scholarly and public discourse appear superior even to Western law, this latter being ultimately a law of the modern nation-state, and an inherently colonialist state no less?[19]

Assuming that a historian is fully aware of these ideological biases and colonial historiographies, narratives of constitutional doctrines and constitutional

---

> Islamic law provides the unique phenomenon of legal science and not the state playing the part of a legislator, of scholarly handbooks having the force of law (*to the extent to which Islamic law was applied in practice*). This depended on two conditions: that legal science guaranteed its own stability and continuity, and that the place of the state was taken by another authority, high enough to impose itself on both the government and the governed. The first condition was met by the doctrine of consensus which led to a cumulative elimination of differences of opinion… The second condition was met by the fact that Islamic law claimed to be based on divine authority. This claim was reinforced by the *progressive reduction of the human element of personal opinion*, until only the mechanical method of reasoning by analogy remained, and even the use of this method was put out of reach of the later generations by the doctrine of the 'closing of the gate of independent reasoning' (*ijtihād*). The traditionalism of Islamic law, which is perhaps its most essential feature, is typical of a 'sacred law' (italics mine).

Note here how Schacht contextualizes the "unique" phenomenon of the rule of law, a contextualization that manages at the end of the day to drown this phenomenon in a maze of intractable negativities. Like "Islamic law" itself, what would have been a rule of law was simply ink on paper, because whatever the "handbooks" of the law said, this unnamed "rule" remained subject to the question of the "extent to which [it] was applied in practice." And since the relationship between "theory and practice" remained at best tenuous, then there effectively was no such thing as a rule of law. And in a move of a double-kill, Schacht wants to ensure that this rule had no means of asserting itself as a historical reality. The first of the "two conditions" he stipulated is also drowned by a host of qualifications and diminutions of the importance of consensus as a means of reducing difference of opinion, when "Islamic law" is in fact famously known for its juristic difference which evolved into the formidable science of *ikhtilāf* (best translated as "the Science of Juristic Difference"); the second condition is drowned by another false "reduction," this time of "the human element of personal opinion" that devolves into the use of mere analogy. This "reduction" could lead to nothing less than a dead-end, due to the now well-known myth of the "closure of the gate of ijtihad," which presumably signals the rigidity of the law and its inability to bridge "theory and practice." Schacht's commentary here captures the Orientalist structure of thought about the fact of supremacy of the law in Islam, a fact that is transformed into a failure and descension into useless, self-exhausting complexities. On how consensus functioned through the *madhhab* to ensure the neuralization of the executive power vis-à-vis the legislative, see ch. 4, sec. III; on the misconception that analogy is the only form of legal reasoning in Islam, see Hallaq, "Non-Analogical Arguments in Sunni Juridical *Qiyās*;" on the myth of the closure of the "gate of ijtihad," see Hallaq, "Was the Gate of Ijtihad Closed?" as well as Hallaq, "On the Origins of the Controversy about the Existence of *Mujtahids*."

19 Hallaq, *Restating Orientalism*.

histories – especially those concerned with non-Western polities – would still pose a formidable conceptual challenge as well as a linguistic straightjacketing of the first order. It would not have been inevitable to view Islamic history in such terms of "constitutionalism" had it not been for Europe's own historical experiences and experiments with constitutional forms, experiences that were crisis-driven, having been closely associated with church and monarchical oppression and tyranny.

As in all other domains of hegemonic discourse, Euro-American constitutional narratives have created and thus far permanently defined the conceptual limits, even the very vocabulary, of politics, political association and nearly all modes of governance. While the Islamic tradition over a millennium has possessed robust and highly articulate forms of rule of law, unsurprisingly it did not define itself along the conceptual lines dictated by the modern political coinage. Muslim jurists and constitutional scholars simply and all too obviously did not speak the language of constitutionalism that is second nature to us today. Which is to say that our modern discourse on constitutionalism has emerged as a "legislated language," to invoke Nietzsche's perceptive formulation. Legislated within an intense and long political experiment and dominated by a common intra-European dialectic,[20] Europe's political discourse was then exported to the colonies and made to rule over the precolonial forms of political expression. Creating thus truths of its own, and driven by its specific historical context, evolution, and nuance, the legislated language does not only exclude by the mere fact of assertion and inclusion, but also establishes concepts that become commonly accepted as "fixed, canonical, and binding," when in fact truths themselves "are metaphors" that represent "the duty to lie according to a fixed convention."[21] We thus find ourselves perforce corralled into a discursive terrain in which a particular European convention produced particular truths, where "every word is a prejudice,"[22] yet we ironically have no way but to operate from within the domain of this prejudice. Our formidable challenge therefore is to try to exit this domain, or at least reduce its deleterious effects to a minimum. But the fact remains that we are operating from within a fixed category, from which we ourselves cannot possibly exit, and into which we must corral, indeed lock up, a rich and complex history of a culture that defined itself in vastly dissimilar ways.

20 For intra-European influences of political ideas, see Skinner's important work, *Foundations*, vols. 1-2.

21 Nietzsche, "On Truth and Lies in a Nonmoral Sense," 80–86, at 81, 83-84.

22 Nietzsche, *Human, All Too Human*, 323.

It is of course not enough to be aware of this prejudice and its imminent dangers, though crystal awareness is a first important step. One must in addition construct an operative conceptual system, a methodology to first subvert this "legislated" conceptual repertoire, and then replace it with a methodology that befits the subject (not object) being studied. But before attempting to construct this methodology, we must understand the nature of the problem we are facing. We must therefore begin with the realization that our "legislated" conceptual world squarely places us in the heart of the dilemma of translatability. How do we access a political and constitutional repertoire of concepts hailing from a vastly different premodern context, and an Islamic one, to boot?

This epistemic "foreignness" consists of a double distance of perpendicular measure: one travelling across different and "foreign" cultural boundaries and forms of living in the present, while the other is a crossing line taking us back to a chronological remoteness created by now extinct life-forms. In an intensely globalized world, the historian and philologist does not move from, say, a New York moment *directly* to an eleventh-century Baghdad moment, because there is a complex of cultural, political, and linguistic concepts that have formed in the contemporary Muslim world and that intervenes between these two moments. Our first line of travel in perpendicular remoteness is confined to the modern, the outer wall in the fortification that must be demolished. It is only after the way has been cleared through the first wall that we begin to encounter the Baghdadian moment with some clarity. And if accessing the first line on its own makes for a challenge, then retrieving the second would double and triple that challenge. This is because perpendicular remoteness is a conceptually layered and compounded problem, where the gateway to accessing the Muslim past is complicated by not only modern language in general, but also by the interplay, and indeed hegemonic sway, between modern languages themselves. Specifically, and insofar as this particular book is concerned (being written in the English language), we must consider the relationship of English as a colonizing language – and thus as a system of thought – to colonized Arabic, or for that matter, to the other major Islamic languages, such as Persian and Turkish. The intervention that, say, modern Arabic makes under the spell of colonialist English is to be seen as yet another barrier that compounds the problematics that inevitably arise from the English thought-system in accessing the constitutional terrains of premodern Islam.

What does all this mean in concrete terms?

The schema of the division of powers into legislative, judicial, and executive has often been implicit in and fundamental to discourses about governance, and, needless to say, rule of law and constitutional organization. As I intimated earlier, the Islamic tradition prior to the nineteenth century never spoke this language, nor did it articulate its legal and political concerns through concepts that can map onto our modern modes of expression. Yet, as we will see in exquisite detail, the tradition possessed a robust system of constitutional divisions, structured and practiced differently from what is familiar to us in secular-liberal democracies. It emerged from a drastically different genealogy and was articulated for goals and purposes that are more complex in structure and "political" and ethical nuance than the modern forms have come to possess.

With its genealogy and teleology, this tradition possessed a range of norms and values that were not only equivalent to the power of culture as we have come to know it in modernity but also constituted a complex and powerful habitus of socio-political, metaphysical, cosmological, and, significantly, ethical dimensions. That Orientalist and modern scholarship is often unequipped to evaluate such a phenomenon does in no way deprive this tradition of its force, be it political or ethical.[23] The reader of this book must therefore reckon with robust presences in the Islamic constitutional map that are missing or absent from its Euro-American counterpart. As I have suggested in detail elsewhere[24] and as I continue to insist here, it is of the essence for reforming Orientalism to begin to engender psycho-epistemic technologies that are indispensable

23 It must be said that while much of the Orientalist and modernist understanding is the function of subliminal, and perhaps the unconscious, operations of the mind, there are also plain modes of ignorance that are precipitated by willful disregard for the weight of certain human values, just because the Orientalist or secular scholar disagrees with them. The religious/secular divide is perhaps the most prominent of them, and some of the staunchest critics of Orientalism have failed precisely on account of being not only entrenched in secularist values and ideology but also – and perhaps as an inevitable result – antipathetic toward traditional religion. The reference here is of course to Edward Said and his *Orientalism*, but also to the vast bulk of what is called postcolonial studies. Likewise, many Muslim scholars could not see in the ethical thrust of the works we study anything but "moralism," an unwarranted cynical dismissal that is analytically problematic. My linguistic ontological discussion in this Introduction is not concerned with such crude scholarly attitudes, for I take them to be obvious even to the layperson. For a critique of Said on these accounts, see my *Restating Orientalism* and relevant sources cited therein. For a view of Islamic political ethics as moralism, see Yilmaz, *Caliphate Redefined*, 160, but also passim.

24 Hallaq, *Restating Orientalism*, 229-67; Hallaq, *Reforming Modernity*, 257-72, to be read together.

for appreciating the crucial role and significance of these absences, i.e., Orientalism's blind spots.

The first challenge of translatability arises with the encounter with the term "constitution" itself, as well as with its derivatives. In modern parlance, the term emerged out of the concept of the nation and its history as associated with nationalism. "Constitution" both describes and inscribes the process of *constituting* the modern state, how a society or a group *constitutes* itself as a nation and a *nation-state*. This definition, foundational as it is, already intrudes on our historiographical task of describing and speaking about a polity and culture that formed itself almost a millennium before the modern project of the nation-state started. The slippery slope of anachronism already seeps, in an *a priori* fashion, into our procedures of philological dissections even before these dissections begin.

What do "constitution," "constitutional," "constitutionalism," and "constitutionalization," among other associated terms, mean in the case of a philologist embarking on the study of constitutive political organization in Islam? How can one speak of even the generic notion of the "*constitutional*" while being fully cognizant of the problematics of translatability? What does it mean to speak of the associated notions of politics, justice, tyranny, sovereignty, rule of law, and the like given a context and a discursive field saturated with perpendicular remoteness?

Consider just two instances of the distorting effects of perpendicular remoteness, one related to the concept of sovereignty, the other to that of politics.[25] The first concept has an exquisitely rich history in Europe since the seventeenth century, if not earlier. Notwithstanding its multiple definitions and shades of meaning, the concept has become most central in political discourse. The young scholar who was raised within an environment in which this term was naturalized in the modern Islamic languages might take it as a classical Arabic term, since "*siyāda*" has become the term *par excellence* to describe

25 I take it for granted that the concepts of sovereignty and politics are both correlatives of, and overlapping with, central questions of constitutionalism. It matters much what type of sovereignty dominates a constitutional or a political system, since in a modern state system, for instance, the state's sovereignty decides the very quality of the relationship between the legislative and executive branches, not to mention the quality of biopower that forms the subjectivity of both the citizen and the "population" (on this latter see ch. 12; for distinctions between sovereignty and reason of state, see Foisneau, "Sovereignty and Reason of State," 333 ff.). Likewise, the concept of politics – homonymous in the extreme – creates various effects on constitutional structures by virtue of its own constitution. The politics of *raison d'état* yields a different concept of the rule of law (and thus relationship between the legislative and all else, including "society," "citizenship" or the executive) than, say, one that did not regard itself as the highest ontological modality of rule.

what we mean by sovereignty.[26] The fact of the matter is that this latter term is a relatively recent coinage. One is hard pressed to find it in use even during the last quarter of the nineteenth century. Thus, working from Western and modern Islamic political imagination – effectively the exclusive cultural and conceptual backgrounds available – would constitute a significant barrier for the philologist and historian who is looking to uncover the premodern Islamic concept and practice of *so-called* "sovereignty."

Yet, this awareness of the dangers of perpendicular remoteness remains insufficient in the project of describing the Islamic political imagination related to sovereignty. The prison of "legislated language" here is made of thick walls. Given the neologism and its foreignness to Islamic political terminology and imagination, *how does one describe the perpendicularly remote political culture* without reference *to the conceptual and terminological repertoire of modern sovereignty*? What are the conceptual inclusions and exclusions conducted by the very act of speaking about a past tradition from the vantage point of the twenty-first century, one that is saturated with categories without which we cannot even speak?

Like Gottlob Frege and Bertrand Russell, Ludwig Wittgenstein took seriously the problematics residing in the very use of terms, concepts, and names, even within one and the same cultural-linguistic tradition. Perpendicular remoteness multiplies the problem threefold, meaning that Wittgensteinian diagnostics no more than just begin to untangle the vexed questions entailed in our project, though this initial step is exceedingly auspicious.

Wittgenstein deliberately avoided, or wanted to avoid, defining what a name or term is, or the functions it performs.[27] For a name is always used in very different ways, being constantly reshaped, by every use, by intention, context, interest, focus, and inclusions, which by definition entail exclusions. To precisely understand a term, it must be studied on its own, individually, in the particular and specific context in which it is used, not merely as a member of a class. Terms are commonly viewed as subject to rules that govern their use, but this is a deceptive way of using language and thus a faulty approach to engaging with thought or argument. Wittgenstein, I think, holds the founding assumption that objects or particulars in the world, to which names refer, are

26 On sovereignty in modern Islamist political discourse, including Mawdūdī's concept of *ḥākimiyya*, see Iqtidar et al., "Divine Sovereignty;" Iqtidar, "Theorizing Popular Sovereignty." A good representation in modern Arabic writings is Khalidi, *Qawa'id Niẓām al-Ḥukm*, 21 ff.

27 These concerns are the subject of his *Brown Book* in *The Blue and Brown Books*.

unique. As much as individual trees or individual humans or individual frogs are unique within their species, so are concepts coined by the human mind.

In our case, "constitution" and "sovereignty" would be meant by the speaker and understood by the listener in different ways: Is "sovereignty" meant to include command over life and death by a monarchical ruler, or by a corporate entity like the modern state? Is it domestic or international, referring to Westphalian conceptions? Is it entirely emanating from a secular source or is it associated, to one degree or another, with a religious form or rule (think of France and the Islamic Republic of Iran)? What does it mean to speak of sovereignty in the latter case? What does it mean to speak of sovereignty during the ʿAbbāsid dynasty, where politico-military rule, the so-called executive, had no legislative prerogatives? Does a Muslim ruler become a sovereign just because he declared himself or his rule "sacred"?[28] Can we speak of the Sharīʿa as sovereign when executive power was out of its hands? Can we speak of the entirety of Islamic governance, in all its "branches" as sovereign when Muslims consensually regarded God as the ultimate and true sovereign? Does it make sense to speak of a sovereign entity when that entity shares sovereignty with other partial "sovereigns"? What does the speaker mean by sovereignty if his or her referent is divisible, and if the concept is assumed by his or her audience to be indivisible? Can one speak of legal sovereignty and political sovereignty when, in that particular system, one domain of sovereignty *structurally* encroaches upon the other, even delimiting and constraining it? For there is the powerful conception, often tacitly assumed in political discourse, that an entity is either a sovereign or not a sovereign; a partial sovereign, it may convincingly be argued, is no sovereign at all.[29]

But things get more complicated as we proceed in our inquiry. Can an atomized "political" entity be regarded as sovereign in its collectivity? What quality of sovereignty is associated with each of the parts that altogether make

---

28 In his otherwise commendable book, *The Millennial Sovereign*, Moin describes the Safavid and Mughal emperors as sovereigns due to their claims to divine right of rule, but there is nothing in his work about law, other than the fact that Akbar claimed himself to be a *mujtahid* (that is, a jurist qualified to reinterpret the law on the basis of evidence derived, *inter alia*, from the Qur'an and/or the Sunna). What were the juristic effects of this claim, Moin does not say. Nor does he say a word about whether these emperors legislated. Did they play by rules of judicial organization that differed from those of other Muslim empires and kingdoms? This he does not ask. Yet, these emperors are described as sovereign, an index of the problem of translatability. One danger that ensues from this description is the equation of, or analogical comparison between, European absolutist rulers and those Safavid and Mughal emperors that Moin describes.

29 Maritain, "Concept of Sovereignty," 349.

up the whole? If many parts are sovereign, then who is the object of their sovereignty, and what are the boundaries within which that sovereign power is exercised? And when I use the term in the context, say, of the ʿAbbāsid dynasty, who exactly do I mean, which office or function, and how do I define the constitutional and other boundaries of what I have included in my concept? How do I translate my own "terms" or "names" into the Islamic conceptual and terminological terrains? Or how do I translate terms the other way around? Where do I look for "sovereignty" when we today mean by it different things, and when the Islamic tradition never used the term or any specific equivalent to it, it being the case that the very notion of sovereignty was the result of a uniquely European experience, generated as it were by quite specific and certainly non-universal (and thus un-universalizable) political and religious events and processes? In other words, how do I legitimately map my terminological and conceptual repertoire – assuming I am aware of exactly what it consists of – onto the conceptual repertoire of a bygone reality in which none of the concepts and categories correspond to anything that I factually and normatively know?

The move from "sovereignty" to "*siyāda*" is already charged with a thick conceptual dissonance that makes the move from "*siyāda*" to its supposed equivalent, say in the ʿAbbāsid constitutional and political experience, seem impossible. With all its genealogical Eurocentricity, bastardization, and cognitive emulation, *siyāda* is often (because it depends on who you ask) meant to refer, at least in part, to God's sovereign power. Therefore, on account of the presence of God in any formulation of "sovereignty," whether the account is imparted by the speaker or received by the listener, there is a great conceptual confusion. When a Muslim individual speaks of the "sovereignty of the people" (*siyādat al-shaʿb*), the sovereignty of the state (*siyādat al-dawla*), and that of God, often in one and the same sequence, conceptual coherence becomes highly problematic, if not impossible.

Catholic philosopher Jacque Maritain's formulation, raised to an exponential power in the Islamic context, sums up this conceptual dilemma, whether for contemporary political purposes or, as I harness it, for historiographical-philological ambition. Sovereignty, he says, is one thing in one context, and another thing in a different context. It loses its pernicious power (which he calls "poison") when it is transplanted from politics to metaphysics. "In the spiritual sphere there is a valid concept of Sovereignty. God, the separate Whole, is Sovereign over the created world ... But with respect to the men or agencies in charge of guiding peoples toward their earthly destinies in the political sphere, there is no valid use of the concept of Sovereignty." This is because, Maritain argues, there is no earthly power that can be a "deputy of God," by which he means a totalistic delegation of divine powers to men. If modern sovereigns are the "vicars" of the people, then they "cannot be divided from the people by any superior essential property."[30] If there is a genuine paradox, if not insoluble contradiction, of sovereignty in modern Islam, it is this coexistence of political rule and God's sovereignty. While Maritain's is a minority position in modern European thought, and a tiny one at that, the paradox he articulates is much more real to modern Muslims than it is to their Christian counterparts.

The problem is not merely conceptual, where we are stopped short at terminological confusion. The problem, as Wittgenstein insisted, is rather richly ontological,[31] because in each use of the term there is a unique abstraction that is also relatively subjective, an abstraction that is meant to refer to a concrete object, with a given composition of potency, power, and weakness, all of which expand and contract according to changing circumstance. And once we face the reality of our use of concepts that refer to both abstract and concrete objects, then it becomes necessary to clarify what is common to them. In other words, the problematic would require the explication of the modalities of existence of both the concept and its referent.

If we accept Wittgenstein's argument that all philosophical problems are ultimately linguistic-ontological problems (and not just strictly linguistic as many think), then we must insist that all translation problems are premier philological problems that engulf our understanding of the Other, any Other, be it our Other or the Other's Other. Our central task in resolving all these multi-layered problems is therefore the philological excavation of ontology, deciphering the forms of existence of the concrete particular to which our abstract, and thus general, concept refers. (This is why studying history in the way I intend to do here cannot content itself with the study of "thought" as we naively conceive it within the domain of intellectual history. If thought is made of concepts, then concepts have a double dialectical relationship with social and political realities. The first dialectical move is this: that concepts emanate and reflect social and political structures as much they are the effects of these structures. The second move is that the reality – which I delimit here in terms of habitus and discursive tradition – that produces its

30 Maritain, "Concept of Sovereignty," 355.
31 Henry, "Wittgenstein and Contemporary Linguistics," 5-6.

own concepts is itself, with the passage of time, affected by these concepts, and so on and so on.)

Now, with this in mind, we can approach the notion of "constitution" and its derivatives with a different eye, one that transcends the simple problematics of finding proper terminological equivalences in the Islamic tradition. In the search for constitutional forms in this tradition, which never defined itself in the ways a liberal state now does, we can no longer ignore the fact that a merely sensitive approach to our linguistic and conceptual impositions on history is utterly insufficient. We must therefore recognize that the problematics embedded in the concept of sovereignty underlie our search for these constitutional forms. "Sovereignty" and "sovereign" represent only one instance among a multiplicity of terms involved in the study of these forms, each of which terms or concepts invoke a cluster of investigations that decipher the forms of existence, even the ontological structure, of the concrete particular within the Islamic tradition to which our abstract modern (and thus essentially anachronistic) concepts refer. Alongside "sovereignty" we list a host of associated terms and concepts, including but not limited to "justice," "tyranny," "authority," "power," "representation," "branches of government," "executive," "judiciary," "legislative," and not least of all, "state," among many others. Each of these terms must be subject to an ontological scrutiny as an essential requirement of philological inquiry.

But note that not all terms have the same complexity. In their translatable capabilities, some seem deceptively less "remote" than others. The more sensitive historian or philologist may realize that some of our abstract concepts may have equivalents in the tradition, while others appear as clear intrusions, foreign, and patently anachronistic. "Justice" can easily be taken to exemplify the first case, while "popular representation," the second. The term "*ʿadl*," for instance, is commonly associated with its supposed "equivalent" of "justice," while "popular representation," like "constitution," finds no parallel. The problems entailed by the untranslatability of the latter are too salient to rehearse, or to escape the attention of even the novice philologist and historian. But the former case is delicate, if not deceptively simple.

Many, I suspect, would consider the term "*ʿadl*" a proper equivalent to "justice," but this is the farthest from the truth as seen from a "Wittgensteinian" perspective (note, however, that I am claiming here that Wittgenstein, a Eurocentric, did not attend to the amplified philological problem of what I have called perpendicular remoteness because his philosophy does not address the vexing problems of translatability between and among distinctly different cultural logics). In today's standard Arabic of the educated, *'adl* is likely to be saturated with liberal or Rawlsian connotations. But as we will see in due course,[32] what seems to be a straightforward equivalent is far from being so. "*'Adl*" turns out to be not only a hypersensitive form of our abstract term "justice," but one that is undergirded and enveloped by a sociological and anthropological matrix of attitudes that constitute a very particular form of habitus.[33]

'Adl's meaning, having a fixed core, manifests itself in the habitus variably, because it has a malleable and adaptable periphery.[34] But in all cases, it is subordinated to, and at once assumes, both the signifiers and "fields" of the habitus. And it is only an understanding of the inner dynamics of this historical habitus that can inform the complex and subtle meanings of "*'adl*." For the habitus underlying "*'adl*" is not as much a political landscape or a procedural concept[35] as it is a politico-theological, social, and customary discursive tradition, understood in its best anthropological sense. The ontological referents of this concept, once understood in their precolonial fullness, would therefore culminate in a nuanced and localized meaning of "justice," one that would alter our conception of the latter term, disturbing its Western forms of usage as well as genealogical purity (all this being applicable to the term's variants: the French "*justice*," the Italian "*giustizia*," and the Spanish "*justicia*," among others).

The question then is this: How do we speak of constitutionalism and constitutional history in Islam without sliding into the range of problematics I have just registered, or at least approach these problematics with a view to minimizing their adverse effects? It is my conviction that a total escape from this essentially philosophical-philological difficulty is impossible, hence why the challenge is to minimize, not to eradicate. This is because escaping our ontological and epistemological conditions of modernity entirely would

32 See, for instance, discussion in main text in ch. 2, at n. 44.

33 On habitus and the ways in which it relates to tradition, see also ch. 1, 2, and 10 (sec. IV).

34 On the concept in various contexts, see the general but useful survey of Khaṭīb, *al-'Adl fī al-Tafkīr al-Islāmī*.

35 On the different notions of justice in the Greek and Kantian traditions, including the procedural and substantive, see Korsgaard, *Self-Constitution*, 148-50. Korsgaard's deliberate conflation of the two kinds of justice (p. 150) does not hold in the Islamic conception, which did not recognize procedure as an exclusive venue to establishing just action. Because of its hypersensitivity, the Islamic conception deemed a breach of *'adl* to occur in any act that deviated from custom and basic, agreed-upon, social behavior, where no procedural rules whatever would be needed to prove it. On its own, this is enough to pose to us a major challenge of translatability.

require a totalistic extraction of our subjectivity from these conditions, an evident impossibility. This is precisely what it means for us to be arrested by our "legislated language." It seems to me that this essentially ontological-linguistic problematic represented for the philologist-historian Nietzsche virtually the same challenge as it did for Wittgenstein.

Yet, despite the truism that all history is the history of the present, this history, the act of thinking and writing the past, must be regulated by a technique of the self, for it is only in reimaging and *disciplining our subjectivity as historians* that we can access a world which spoke different languages and which articulated reality in its own unique ways. The fundamental assumption here is that engaging in history takes much more than a cerebral method or a "scientific" methodology of interpretation. The very forms of reason that generally structure our lives in the modern condition will not do, since these forms have proven to be wholly saturated with an epistemic sovereignty[36] that created dogmatic and perniciously ideological narratives that thus far served the causes of political power and destruction.[37]

The foundations of the techniques of the historian's and philologist's *self* demand the cultivation of epistemic humility. Epistemic humility is antithetical and diametrically oppositional to epistemic sovereignty, a sense that the text's reader, the so-called historian or philologist, stands above the texts, freely deciding what is and is not significant and meaningful in it, and judging it by his or her own criteria of value. Epistemic sovereignty in the historian exhibits itself as philological narcissism, privileging the scholar with an inflated sense of self-importance, while allowing the satisfaction of gaining unfettered dominance over his or her object, represented in the totality of the text as well as

36 It is to be noted here that my use of the concept of epistemic sovereignty is at once separate and similar to the common use of the term, which was formulated in the context of political and modern state-based notions of sovereignty. In my usage, epistemic sovereignty is always individual, expressing the quality of the individual's subjective formation, but one that at the same time pervades the collective psyche and collective thought structure of which the individual is a part. The similarity, on the other hand, ensues from the fact that due to the *formative and performative* social power of modern state formation (through biopower, among other things), epistemic (individual) sovereignty is also the individualized expression of the larger political forces that enjoy political sovereignty. In other words, and to contextualize the matter within our concerns, political sovereignty does not directly decide on the modalities of philology used by the citizen-subject. Rather, these modalities are determined by the sovereign subject of the state, the individual possessor of the overarching *political* sovereignty. To say that these two forms of sovereignty stand in a dialectical relationship to each other is to state the obvious.

37 As I have argued in detail in *Restating Orientalism.*

the human formations that produced it in bygone eras. Epistemic sovereignty, marking much of Orientalist writings – especially on matters of Islamic political forms – is a pathology that has been normalized into a rational method of inquiry. Its narcissistic impulse of exerting power and control over the text through manipulative tactics yields knowledge that disregards the concerns, priorities, and cherished values of the "object" of inquiry, while highlighting and prioritizing the interests of the philologist. Epistemic sovereignty therefore by definition lacks epistemic humility, an indispensable attribute of deep and critical philology.

To be cultivated, epistemic humility does not merely demand a significant reduction in the inflated narcissistic self.[38] It in fact presupposes the near eradication[39] from the philologist's self of a historical-ideological habitus. For the "legislated language" of modernity contains in its inner layers a dogmatic theology of progress,[40] which holds the pervasive assumption that history is linear and that as time passes, human society advances and acquires an increasingly sophisticated form in a deterministic fashion. The presumptive thrust of this theology is that humanity is always heading toward betterment and improvement, refusing to acknowledge any structural problems in the imagined reality it is articulating.

The implications of this omnipresent attitude are grave, for here, while the text is being read and interpreted, we stand in the midst of a relationship in which the interpreter structurally (and unconsciously) assumes that he or she possesses a truth-making power over "less developed" and "less enlightened" human constellations, including their ways of life, traditions, authors, commoners, thinkers, and even towering intellectuals. This explains the astonishing fact

38 Narcissism is of course a complex and multi-faceted phenomenon. In my usage, it does not only refer to a strong sense of self-importance and feelings of superiority over others (here not to be dissociated from racism). Narcissism also refers to living in a false reality or a reality that is perceived to be different, indeed superior, to that of others. The narcissist's reality is also designed to create a fantasy of uniqueness and self-importance that is detached from verifiable reality. This explains why Orientalism has overall interpreted Islamic (and other) texts on European terms, pointing in the objects of study to absences and lacunae or to an overwhelming outlook of negativity and pessimism that were to emerge out of these objects. For a useful survey on narcissism, readily adaptable to the Orientalist context, see Levy, "A Historical Review of Narcissism," 3 ff.

39 "Near eradication" rather than total eradication is the function of the impossibility of entirely exiting the modern condition.

40 On the theology of progress and its malevolent effects, see Hallaq, *Impossible State*, 12-18; Hallaq, *Restating Orientalism*, 107-112, 150-54, 157-58, 194-95, and ch. 12, n. 129.

that many Orientalists – including those with pedestrian minds – confidently and often superficially judge the texts, arguments, doctrines, and theories of bygone Muslim writers whose distinguished intellects and remarkable erudition otherwise immeasurably dwarf the very best intellects in the Orientalist population.

Epistemic humility thus requires, indeed presupposes, the full and genuine recognition on the part of the philologist and historian that bygone people and social formations deserve full and sincere respect as equals, that is, as humans who lived and dealt with their realities as equally competent rational agents, however "rational" and "reason" are defined. The transition from epistemic sovereignty to epistemic humility thus presupposes the cultivation of a host of techniques of the self that cannot all be discussed here.[41] Yet, we can speak of a distinctly relevant technique that results in a genuine appreciation for what I call internal logic.

The attention to internal logic as a human reality first demands the treatment of that reality by the philologist and historian as one equally legitimate and equally respectable to his own. This is clearly a derivative and a historiographical expression of Kant's Categorical Imperative, and so it must be considered as a necessary ethical intrusion upon, even a crucial disruption of, epistemic sovereignty.[42] Internal logic demands intimate attention to the concerns and manners of thinking and action of people who lived before or outside us. It demands a recognition of their preferences *and reasons* for their likes, dislikes, decisions, and choices; for their emotive and cerebral inclinations; and for ordering their lives the way they did.[43]

---

41 For these techniques, see Hallaq, *Reforming Modernity*, 151-75, 257-72; Hallaq, *Impossible State*, 110-38.

42 The Categorical Imperative cannot be dissociated from the concept of majority as outlined in Kant's "What is Enlightenment?" The Categorical Imperative has perforce to derive its ethical power from a particular concept of reason and rationality, which in Kant has been divorced from the discursive tradition of Christian duty. Being a system of praxis, this notion of duty defined the limits and contents of reason but in Kant it has broken out of any – and indeed all – regulative and technological modes of ethical self-formation. On majority, see Kant, "What is Enlightenment?"; for a critique of the concept of duty in Kant's thought, see Anscombe, "Modern Moral Philosophy;" on the problematics of Kant's concept of majority, see Foucault, "What is Critique?" It should also be noted, after Anscombe, that the Categorical Imperative is *in substance* of Christian pedigree, having rich parallels in Judaism and Islam, if not all other major religions.

43 These concerns are also shared by the discipline of conceptual history (*Begriffsgeschichte*). "Conceptual history does not take the haughty position that has all too long characterized Oriental studies: It does not 'measure the past according to the yardstick of the present,' attempting to demonstrate the flaws and deficiencies of historical concepts. Quite to the

But this is not all. The study of internal logic is at once an archeological, architectural, and genealogical excavation of the first order, one in which the study of structures of life and living matters most. It recognizes as a given and out of deep conviction that people of the past did their best under the conditions in which they lived, conditions that constrained them and imposed on them certain limits of awareness. They cannot be judged by the standards of our awareness, not because it is "more advanced" – in most senses it is not – but rather because our awareness is wholly the result of the specific conditions that govern our lives. Our awareness answers to our needs, these being finite and quite specific to our life circumstance. Inasmuch as there are inclusions in it, there are perhaps even more exclusions, making it extraordinarily subjective, even one-sided. Other than axiomatic and mathematical truths, and basic survival, primordial instincts for the preservation of the human species, there are no transhistorical or universal laws of thought and action, and if epistemic sovereignty assumes them to exist and to be valid, it is because this sovereignty is a pathology of some sort.[44]

A constructive approach to the study of internal logic therefore presupposes empathy in the study of historical habitus (to be defined in its proper context in later chapters).[45] What matters for us now is the initial and presupposed recognition that in the very act of deciding to engage with historical texts – that is, with evidence of the way people of the past lived their lives and governed themselves individually and governed the other collectively – we have already embarked on an unequal project of historical judgment, where the past cannot represent itself. In undertaking the project of representing the past, we are engaging in an unfair game of power. We, plaintiffs, sit in the court of judgment without a defendant, who can speak to us as equals. In the court of epistemic sovereignty, the past has no power of argument against our reasons, arguments, biases, and pathologies.

---

contrary, it traces their very logic and plausibility, even necessity, by relating them to the socio-historical milieu that generated them. It is for this very reason that conceptual history cannot be dissociated from social history. It proceeds from the tenet that concepts do not arise and persist accidentally or by mistake but only as an integral part of social reproduction. However unreasonable they may appear from a researcher's perspective, they can be plausibly explained by reference to their social context." See Vogelsang, "Conceptual History," 17.

44 This stands in sharp contrast with the way Muslim "philologists" and authors viewed their texts, including the *uṣūlīs*. On this, see Farahat, "Generality and Exception in Islamic Legal Theory."

45 See ch. 2. On habitus as it relates to tradition, see also ch. 1 and 2, and especially ch. 10 (sec. IV).

It is precisely in combating the inequality of power relationship between us and the past that we are bound by the demands of democratic rules, fair play, and equitable representation. Internal logic and its power of discovery provide the remedy for, or at least our sincere effort to minimize, the hegemonic power we exercise in the study of history. It cannot therefore be overemphasized that epistemic humility as a technique of the self must be present before we embark on our projects of historical excavations.[46]

Toward unraveling the internal logic of Islamic "constitutional" structures, we therefore must assume the terms "constitution" and its variants to be devoid of any specific architectural composition, prior systemic constitution, or a preconceived mapping. The approach must start at the most basic level, meaning that we shall not assume by the term anything other than a way in which Muslims *constituted* and *organized* themselves politically, asking how they arranged their political life so as to govern themselves in the best way *they* saw fit. It is often said that for life to proceed in some orderly fashion, every society must possess a certain law, legal system, or a code of conduct. From family groupings to tribal associations, from clubs and civic associations to larger political structures of dynastic rule, empires, and states, law, in one form/quality or another, must exist. We therefore shall take this simple but apparently axiomatic truth for granted. And so, the question of who or what legislates must be asked in every case. Customarily, and in the only language we have come to know in modernity, this law and its *constructive* origins is known as "legislative," taken here with a grain of salt. When we use it in our context, we shall understand by it simply this: that it is the law – in its multiplicity, pluralistic layers and components, and customary origins – that is *chosen by Muslims* to rule over their lives, including the mechanisms and ways through which this law was brought into existence *by their own* decisions and methods of reasoning.

46 Hallaq, *Reforming Modernity*, 257-72. An interlocutor may argue that in classifying Islamic political and constitutional systems as history (whereas a study of a Kant or a Nietzsche is not), I am entrenching the same "legislated" language of what is hegemonic and what is remote, thereby adopting the same conception of epistemic sovereignty that I am working against. My response is the following: Kant, for one, is both our present and a part of history. Kant can be studied as history, if we inquire, say, into the effect he had on German academia, or the influence that David Hume had on his philosophy. These are historical concerns. But Kant is also a philosopher who captured what Foucault called the fundamental question of "Who are we now?", a foundational inquiry whose import continues to reverberate in our midst as we approach the middle of the twenty-first century. This is precisely why Foucault himself, among others, focused his gaze on this philosopher, for our age remains, in crucial respects, an expression of what might be called the Kantian Moment. See Foucault, "Subject and Power."

Likewise, we shall assume no more than the fact that a law must perforce be applied, an assumption that requires two elements: personnel that interpret the law for the purposes of such application and a *power* that executes the judgement of that personnel. Despite any possible objections to this approach, it remains on the whole exceedingly minimalistic in its assumptions and thus as close as one can get to epistemic humility. By contrast, to depart from the assumption that the Other's system – from another place and time – must consist of certain qualities or features against which it is to be judged would display anything but humility, of any stripe.

With these basic assumptions in mind, we travel back in time through the channels of perpendicular remoteness with a view to making the habitus, at the other end of the line, as intimately familiar as possible. In order to gain intimacy, an empathetic engagement with the voices populating the habitus becomes a priority of the first order.[47] It is in the nature of habitus to be complex and multivalent. The challenge of multivalency is further compounded by another layer of complexity that demands our attention, namely, the presence in the habitus of a discursive tradition. In my usage (that is, in the way I employ habitus in this book, and not necessarily how Bourdieu saw it in all its dimensions), the theory of habitus is largely a synchronic category of description and analysis, while a theory of discursive tradition emphasizes much that constitutes the habitus in diachronic ways.[48] As a concept and a tool of description and analysis, habitus tends to emphasize certain aspects of social existence while discursive tradition tends to emphasize other aspects: habitus encompasses elements and "fields" that transcend and lie outside the domain of discursive tradition,

---

47 Some critics may object that a fair and balanced account requires extending to modernity – clearly the object of our critique – the same courtesy. The courtesy, I respond, has already been extended by dint of the fact that we, even those demanding critics of it amongst us, are already enmeshed in its values and cannot do nearly enough to extricate ourselves of its narcissistic ideological baggage. We are already located in a modernistic habitus that – as I have been insisting – is severely biased against and prejudicial to those who lived before us, to what they did and how they thought. The severity, it must be stressed, stems from the fact that the bias is structural, embedded deeply in the cerebral, emotive, and constitutive layers of modernistic beliefs and practices. For more on this, see ch. 12, sec. II; Hallaq, *Impossible State*, 12-18; Hallaq, *Restating Orientalism*, 107-112, 150-54, 157-58, 194-95.

48 My conception of habitus and discursive tradition refers to the work of Pierre Bourdieu for the former and that of Edward Shils, Alasdair MacIntyre, and Talal Asad for the latter. For more on these concepts and relevant citations, see ch. 1, 2, and 10 (sec. IV).

while the latter offers the analytical category of *long durée* that the former largely lacks.[49]

Now, to acquire intimate familiarity with habitus and discursive tradition, the researcher must, again empathetically (meaning the placement of one's self [not just oneself] as much as possible within the sensibilities, priorities, concepts, emotive structures, and practices of the habitus), absorb as a second nature the elements of life within the tradition and its enveloping habitus, including ideas, conceptions of the world, cosmology, theological beliefs, modes of existence, histories, legal conceptions, political ideas, and practice. In our specific case, to uncover and internalize the values and conceptions of the habitus that undergird constitutional arrangements and modes of governance, one must be intimately familiar with Qur'ānic cosmology and Qur'ānic discourse, works of theology and metaphysics, Qur'ān commentary, various Ḥadīth disciplines and compilations, historical annals, biographical works, legal history, *fiqh*, legal theory, *adab* genres, Ṣūfī classics, anecdotes and stories populating various genres, dream literature, mythology and legend, philosophical and logical treatises, literary production and poetry, writings on astronomy and other scientific fields, language and linguistics, economic and commercial life, and much more. Familiarity with all these fields, or at least those that are broadly relevant to one's historical inquiry, also entails familiarity with their performativity, the way they effect and form subjectivities and engender modes of existential apprehension and views of the world. These cultural expressions must also ground and envelop the various political writings at the heart of, or surrounding, the research hypothesis, these ranging from advice to the ruler to the administrative and juridico-political treatises.

A thorough immersion in this textual world makes not only for background preparation, in terms of academic training and readiness (as in erudition), *but also, and chiefly, as a habituating technology that instills epistemic empathy in the researcher's subjective constitution.* One must reach the point of absorbing and internalizing the emotive structures that lay beneath the worldviews of the humans one studies, trying to see, to the utmost extent possible, the world through their eyes.[50] Empathy, strictly speaking, is a psycho-epistemic process of discovery and

49 "Largely lacks" because much work is needed to tease out the historical implications of Bourdieu's theory of habitus, Bourdieu being the chief exponent of this theory. See George Steinmetz's effortful argument in this regard, in "Bourdieu, History, and Historical Sociology," 45–66.

50 A promising step has recently been made in the historical profession where a subfield focusing on the history of emotions has emerged. Bodice, "History of Emotions;" Dodman, "Theories and Methods."

acquiescing internalization. It demands of the philologists to place themselves in the shoes of the humans they study, to acquire the same technologies of the self the latter developed and on the basis of which they conducted their lives.

With this background preparation and subjectivation, the researcher is ready to begin his or her specific and concrete work. Having reduced perpendicular remoteness to a minimum, care must now be given to the problem of language, especially in the manner I have formulated above through Wittgensteinian philosophical caveats.

Every research question presupposes what I call a "terminological field," that is, a constellation of terms and concepts through and around which the authors of "the primary works" weave their narratives, concerns, aspirations, and arguments. And every term or concept has a core meaning, denotation, or content that is largely fixed and immutable, but one that also has a mutable denotative periphery, allowing each author to use the same concept or term in different contexts. Strictly speaking, without this mutable periphery, no single term can possibly be used in more than one context. The core meaning of *ʿadl*, now a familiar term, is a general notion of "justice." But this core meaning, persisting in all contexts, encompasses multiple variants that give the term a specific and highly nuanced denotation. *ʿAdl* is one thing in the context of adjudication in the Sharīʿa court, and yet somewhat another in a field of meaning referring to the required (or expected?) help for members of the community in need. It is one thing in the context of protecting the religious minorities and to some degree another when used to uphold the Qurʾānic penalties or to refrain from consuming alcohol and other prohibited substances. All these usages and more are variants of *ʿadl*. Indeed, the ninth-/fifteenth-century Ibn al-Mibrad, aware of the multivalent constitution of the concept, proffers as many as twenty shades of meaning of the term, an explication that occupied four pages in his work.[51]

Yet, none of this philological preparation would be considered satisfactory or sufficient without corollary lexical and technical excavations. Etymology in Arabic is of the essence, and no term should be taken for granted – that is, leaving it without an inquiry as to how it is explicated, in its fine shades of meaning, in lexical dictionaries. Yet, while foundational, etymology in certain instances gives way to further technical usage, in which case consulting technical dictionaries becomes, *in addition*, indispensable.[52]

---

51 Ibn al-Mibrad, *Īḍāḥ*, 146-50. See further on this term in ch. 2, n. 44.

52 Among the most important lexical dictionaries are: Ibn Manẓūr, *Lisān al-ʿArab*; and Zabīdī, *Tāj al-ʿArūs*. Two valuable technical dictionaries are Aḥmadnagarī, *Jāmiʿ al-ʿUlūm*; and Tahānawī (Thānavī), *Kashshāf Iṣṭilāḥāt al-Funūn*. Also Abū al-Baqāʾ, *Kulliyyāt*; Jurjānī, *Taʿrīfāt*.

These procedures of philological dissection *and subjective immersion* through epistemic empathy safeguard against at least two fallacies. The first is entirely avoidable while the second is only largely so. The first fallacy is the transposition of a modern Arabic term into its premodern double, it being the same word with a meaning that has gone through changes in connotation, mainly due to the change in the quality of the referent. An excellent and exquisitely telling example is the word "*ḥurriyya*," in modern standard Arabic being the term par excellence to connote "freedom." Since the middle of the nineteenth century, "*ḥurriyya*" has come to carry a variety of meanings, many of which reflected local Muslim adaptations of the evolving European notions of freedom and liberty.[53] By the middle of the twentieth century, if not before, the term increasingly came to acquire the entire spectrum of what Isaiah Berlin dubbed as "negative liberty." In today's popular Muslim conception (that is, "Islam on the street"), the term is nearly identical to its Western liberal equivalents.

In lexical non-technical usage, the notion of "*ḥurr*" refers to an object that is "unadulterated" or "free of impurities" (as in "pure gold" or "pure olive oil"), "independent," "unrestrained," etc. In common and modern popular usage, it refers to political freedom, elections, democracy, the free market economy, freedom of choice, including sexual freedom and much else of the same. *But none* of the latter connotations came under the semantics of *ḥurriyya* in premodern classical Arabic. Its basic technical meaning had referred to the state of not being enslaved, mainly a legal category. When applied to women or men, it also indicated a high social status or belonging to "noble" upbringing.[54] In political conception, and as a political process of subjectivation, the term connoted a decidedly thick meaning of the Berlinian concept of "positive liberty" (in stark contrast to negative liberty), referring to fulfillment of the self through freedom from want, from worldly things, and from materialistic subjection.

The influential popular movement of Ṣūfism saw in *ḥurriyya* the process of inner liberation that engenders contentment (*qanāʿa*). Qushayrī, a Ṣūfī master who represented the mainstream ascetic ethos in both Sharīʿa and Ṣūfism, even went further, equating the freedom residing in *ḥurriyya* to submission (*ʿubūdiyya*) to the world of divinity. To shed wealth and

53 For a history of the modern concept of freedom, see Abu-ʿUksa, *Freedom in the Arab World.*

54 Zabīdī, *Tāj al-ʿArūs*, VI, 264-65: "*Al-ḥurra [hiya] al-karīma min al-nisāʾ.*" For men, the equivalent adjective is "*ashrāf*" or "*min al-ashrāf.*"

material possession was seen to be tantamount to giving, charity, and service to others. This is why he quotes one adage after another to the effect that service to the community and the poor are the emblems of freeing the self.[55] The political semantics of this concept of *ḥurriyya* not only stands as a diametrical opposite of the liberal meaning in current usage but also – effectively and substantively (i.e., as a matter of ethical technologies of the self) – runs it aground.[56]

The term *ʿadl* is another good case in point, illustrating a complex problem of translatability (the second fallacy), because the change in the quality of referent is not a mere description of status or position or state. *ʿAdl* as a rendering of "justice" illustrates the crucial difference in the very content of the term, a content that can quite possibly refer to the characteristics of more than one type of rule or governance. As I intimated earlier, the modern conceptions of "*ʿadl*"/"justice" are essentially liberal, because the hegemonic political system of modernity is saturated with liberal conceptions, values, and institutions, even in so-called totalitarian countries. Arguably, the conception of *ʿadl*, like freedom/*ḥurriyya*, partakes in the very constitution of the modern habitus. The premodern Islamic content of *ʿadl* obviously cannot partake in the formation or substance of the modern concept because modern Muslims obviously do not have the sensory experience or knowledge of the internal logic of, say, ʿAbbāsid or Mamlūk systems of rule, nor even of the social values and living traditions of those communities – these being essential in determining the multifaceted and multilayered meanings of *ʿadl*.

I have indicated above the different connotations and aspects of *ʿadl* as expounded in detail by a Mamlūk-era jurist. And none of these connotations maps onto the modern term. The liberal conception is preoccupied by "the fundamental rights of the individual," for if violated, they would constitute injustice, in one way or another. Other components of liberal justice[57] are freedom of speech, right to vote, as well as a number of others. But none of the

55 In fact, Qushayrī dedicates a chapter to the *praxis* of *ḥurriyya*. See his *Al-Risāla*, 378-80: "*Wa-ʿlam anna ḥaqīqata al-ḥurriyyati fī kamāli al-ʿubūdiyya*" ("know that the true essence of *ḥurriyya* lies in total servitude"); "*Wa-ʿlam anna muʿẓama al-ḥurriyyati fī khidmati al-fuqarā*'" ("know that the greater part of *ḥurriyya* lies in serving the poor").

56 The basic term *ghanī* is another example in point. In modern Arabic, it means exclusively a "rich" or "wealthy" person, whereas in premodern Arabic, it referred as well, if not more so, to a person who is "self-sufficient," who is "not poor." For the premodern connotation, see Tahānawī, *Kashshāf*, III, 404, and *al-Mawsūʿa al-Fiqhiyya*, XXXI, 278 ff.; for modern usage, see Salmoné, *An Advanced Learner's Arabic-English Dictionary* (1889), available at: http://arabiclexicon.hawramani.com/?p=16904#d38cad

57 Lewin, "Liberal Conception of Justice."

rights listed here enters into the substantive content of the Islamic concept of *ʿadl*, just as many of those subsumed in the latter do not have equivalents in the former – hence Wittgenstein's ontological challenge: an abstract concept applied to concrete and quite specific reality creates the problem of conceptual dissonance.

The abstract concept perforce must have an immutable signification at its core, but the periphery of the concept's core comprises a multiplicity of different meanings and nuanced connotations that cannot possibly be present in every concrete case of application. At times, as we saw in the comparison with the liberal concept, the majority of the periphery does not correspond at all, in which case we commonly call this an acute case of anachronism (though still not as acute as that entailed by the use of the concept of *siyāda*=sovereignty). At times, the periphery's denotational possibilities create a major dissonance because the combination of the connotations surrounding the core may be multiple. Assuming liberalism has a dozen variant connotations of justice, we would be at a loss trying to make them map onto Ibn al-Mibrad's twenty definitions. Therefore, the mere invocation of the term *ʿadl* leaves us bewildered as to which of these, or what combination thereof, the speaker includes – or means to include – when they use the term. My point in conclusion is this: that to understand the structure of the workings of a system, one must attend to these potential hazards by employing not only philological acumen but also a subjective empathy combined with epistemic humility.

II

In Search of Structures. Nearly every study of Islamic political thought gives central attention to the Islamic mode of transition of rule.[58] The latent assump-

58 See, for example, Gibb, "Constitutional Organization"; Goitein, "Attitudes Toward Government," 203 and passim; Rosenthal, *Political Thought*, 22-23, 30-35, 41, 52, 60, 153; Lambton, *State and Government*, 73-74, 80-81, 89, 93, 105, 112, 171; Crone, *God's Rule*, 36-39, 65-66, 108, 226-27, 235-36. By contrast, Sherman Jackson captures better, and accurately, what was important to the Muslim juristic and political leadership. Speaking of the constitutional concerns of seventh-/thirteenth-century al-Qarāfī, he states that politics "was not al-Qarāfī's focal point. He appears in fact little concerned with the issue of formal legitimacy and who ruled or what his qualifications were. Nor was he concerned with establishing mechanisms for ensuring smooth and orderly transfers of power from one régime to the next. In this his attitude might be described as conspicuously passive. The issue, however [and this is Jackson's judicious corrective, W.H.], of *how* a ruler ruled

tions about the absence of elections and modes of electoral representation usually dominates the discursive scene, if not directly then by implication.[59] The premodern discourse about "elections" of caliphs and about political devolution of offices is read against the backdrop of technical and formal procedures operative in modern bureaucratic systems. Which is to say that the dryness of the Weberian bureaucratic rationality is effectively mapped onto the discursive landscapes of Islamic political thought and constitutional structures, leaving out of the latter much that was central to it. As we have seen in section I, Islamic constitutional history by implication becomes a history of absence and lack, just as legal history was rendered before it.[60] Total disregard

---

was a different question. For, this had implications that reached deeper down into society affecting more directly that class to which al-Qarāfī belonged." Jackson, *Islamic Law*, 71. In ch. 12, we will see that the prime value placed on the quality of rule was not limited to considerations of class (a concept that did not exist in the first place) but went further down beyond what a social or economic analysis could reveal. For a critique of Orientalist works on the caliphate/sultanate insofar as situating and interpreting Ibn Jamāʿa's thought, see El-Merheb, *Political Thought*, 2-3, 17-18.

59 Much of modern Islamic discourse of course mimics these obsessions, as evidenced, for example, in Khālidī, *Niẓām al-Ḥukm fil-Islām*, 99 ff.

60 See, for instance, one of the most revealing passages in Patricia Crone's *God's Rule*, 281, where she paradoxically argues that "although one could well characterize the Sharīʿa as a constitution, it does not follow that government based on it was constitutional. The Sharīʿa was, or rather included, a constitution, in the broadest sense of the word: a set of rules that allocated functions, powers, and duties among the various agencies and offices of government and defined the relationship between them and the public. Al-Māwardī's *aḥkām sulṭāniyya* [sic.] is a collection of such rules. But a constitution in this sense of the word is simply a frame of government or political order: a set of rules which organize, but do not restrain, the exercise of power. In order for the rules to yield constitutional government they have to include restraints, normally identified as a bill of rights and institutional devices for securing their observance. The Sharīʿa does not include a bill of rights, let alone of rights perceived as common to all mankind, but it could still be said to guarantee personal freedoms for Muslims and people under their protection, and to seek to restrain arbitrary power."

Needless to observe here that Crone's Eurocentrism is quite powerful. The Sharīʿa, it seems, would have met the conditions of a "constitution" had it not been for the fact that it did not possess a bill of rights, nor did it develop institutional devices for securing their observance. This is like saying that you are not eating properly because you are not using a fork and a knife. Crone does not even bother to reflect about the possibility that Muslims developed their own ways to govern and be governed. She admits that the Sharīʿa "included" a constitution, but the problem is that the government that Muslims chose to adopt was not constitutional; and this is because the Sharīʿa did not develop "restraints" on the exercise of power. But then four lines later, there seems to be a reversal of claims. "It could still be said," Crone seems to concede, that the Sharīʿa does after all *guarantee* personal freedoms and to even "restrain arbitrary power." For those readers unfamiliar with Crone's writings, this is a most remarkable admission. She tries hard to demolish the Sharīʿa as a constitutional force but ends up embracing the very thesis she is attempting to refute. Furthermore, as we will see, Māwardī's *AS* is not a "mere collection of ... rules," but rather, for the discerning and nuanced eye, a systematic constitutional treatise, if looked at from the perspective of what I have just called "internal logic."

Nor is it tangential here to remark about at least one of the implications in Crone's language of rights. From my personal experience with Western lawyers, and in some liberal writings in the field, it is almost inevitable that the issue of minorities in Islam (the so-called *dhimmī*s) is raised in the context of Islamic constitutional governance. As I assert more than once in this book, the quality of governance is to be distinguished from the question of constitutionalism. Some modern systems of rule of law and separation of powers have engaged in deep forms of structural racism, genocide, or Apartheid, and at times in all of these at once. In *Restating Orientalism*, I make the argument that modern states are inherently genocidal, when the circumstances arise. But this fact is not intended to justify the status of the *dhimmī*s in Islam but rather to assert the fundamental analytical principle that the quality of governance cannot be always judged by constitutionalization, separation of powers, or rule of law. Crone's insinuations of course go to the matter of the *dhimmī* status in Islam, as an area where rights are claimed by Orientalism to have been abridged. It is my argument that the history of *dhimmism* and *dhimmī* life under the Sharīʿa has not been written yet and that current scholarship has plainly erred in its methodology and approach to this sub-field (see, notably, Emon ["Shariʿa and the Rule of Law," 56 ff.], who regards his scholarship as a revision to the conventional Orientalism wisdom). The *dhimmī*s are invariably assumed to be minorities in the liberal sense, equivalent to the Muslims, Jews, Sikhs, and others living in Western liberal states. But this is a false analogy. The relationship between these minorities and their Western states is based on national considerations, not religious affiliation. A Keralan Indian Christian is a minority in Canada or the US not by virtue of his or her religion, for if this was the basis of status, then they would be equal to white Christians, the dominant and ruling group. The Keralan individual is a minority by dint of his racially ethnic and political affiliation, namely, as a Keralan Indian of brown color. By the same logic, a "blue-eyed" Buddhist German individual immigrating to the North American countries would not be deemed to belong to a minority. Be that as it may, the criterion of belonging is ultimately nationalist, that is, belonging to the nation, as defined and conceived by liberal democracies. This is why the first elements of the Naturalization Oath of Allegiance taken by new immigrants to the USA, for instance, is to renounce loyalty to other countries, to be loyal to the United States, to support and defend the Constitution, and obey the law of the land. (See https://www.uscis.gov/citizenship/learn-about-citizenship/the-naturalization-interview-and-test/naturalization-oath-of-allegiance-to-the-united-states-of-america.) Belonging and being absolutely loyal to the nation are thus elements that define membership in ranks of citizenship; which explains why spying for the enemy, for instance, is generally considered high treason, and punished as such (many countries continue to implement capital punishment and most states sentence convicts to life imprisonment). In liberal states and many others, converting from one religion to another, on the other hand, is of no political consequence whatever. Now, a proper study of minorities in Islam must reckon with the analytical structure of political loyalty. Since Islam did not know the nation or nationalism until the nineteenth century, we cannot analytically, nor factually, consider it within the liberal calculus of minority status. The equivalent of modern national loyalty in Islam was belonging to the Umma, where so-called "religion" constitutes the ultimate criterion. To be a full "citizen" in Islam is to belong to the faith, just as an American is deemed American by virtue of having been born in America or naturalized as American on the conditions stipulated in the Pledge. In other words – and this is the gold standard in any sound analytical study of the *dhimmī*s – in Islam religious affiliation is almost entirely

for the internal logic of the system is the hallmark of this Orientalist approach. Not only the ethical habitus is disregarded (because secular Orientalism lacks the analytical, not to mention the foundational psycho-epistemic, tools to appreciate its significance), but also the intricate dynamics in the relationships that exist between the executive leadership and the largely autonomous powers operating alongside it, including these powers' total command of what Foucault called biopower (the concern of the last chapter). The same is true of interpreting the role of military power in the rotation and replacement of sultanic executives (*imārat al-istīlā'*), taking "Islamic law's" discourse on the matter as a subservient legitimation of raw power and a brute reality lying entirely beyond its control.[61] The artificial knots that Orientalism has tethered to Islamic constitutional history would automatically dissolve themselves once the habitus, structure, and ecology of this history are properly understood.

Added to these pervasive themes is a common portrayal of political rule as harsh and punitive, this being an indication of the rulers' brutality and sense of tyrannical power. This is akin to and no better than the sensationalism that portrays modern Muslims as hand-choppers and stone-killers, in reference to the harsh punishments inflicted on some thieves and adulterers, respectively, in some modern Islamic countries.

The Orientalist historical narrative is almost always shot through the structure of modern taste, sensibility, and expectation. Harsh punishments of the premodern Islamic executive become, quite anachronistically, the

---

equivalent to national affiliation in the modern liberal state. Apostatizing in Islam is therefore equivalent to, if not synonymous with, shedding loyalty to the American nation in favor of an enemy nation (say the Soviet Union during the Cold War). It is akin to high treason. This is so because the relationship of Islam to other faiths is of the same kind that ruled between two political entities like the United States/Western Europe and the Soviet Bloc. Although the foundations of the difference in the Islamic view are robustly moral and ethical, this morality and ethics cannot be separated from their political constitution. To belong to another political entity that is not Islamic is to belong to an entity that is significantly lacking in its moral constitution. The relevant comparison therefore must be between morality/religion, on the one hand, and nationalism/politics, on the other. These categories must be seen as equivalent and as the sources of loyalty, each in its own context: analytically, nationalism *is* a form of religion and religion *is* a form of nationalism. Accordingly, the *dhimmīs* in Islam were more akin to Permanent Residents ("Green Card" holders) than to full citizens. Permanent Residents acquire their full citizenship when they uphold the Pledge. Analogically, the *dhimmīs* can attain that full membership in the Umma when they convert to Islam. For a general but excellent survey of the status of minorities in Islam, see *al-Mawsūʿa al-Fiqhiyya*, VI, 234-35; VII, 121 ff.

61 For these themes in Orientalist scholarship, see, as examples, sources cited in n. 58, above. For the premodern meanings of the term, see ch. 6, n. 37.

evidence and proof of tyranny. The considerations that these punishments were the rule of the day all around the world, especially in Europe, until modernity and that, in Islam, they fell in their vast majority within the prescriptions of the law, are not accounted for. Here, Foucault's analysis of the punitive ruptures that were exemplified by spectacle of Damiens' flaying – as a punishment for the crime of regicide – and then by the modern electric-chair execution behind prison walls does not seem relevant in the least. Premodern forms of punishment were anachronistically judged by modern sensibilities and sensitivities. Nor is there a proper constitutional understanding among Orientalist historians of the complex field of *taʿzīr*, a domain of punishment that the Sharīʿa legislated for the ruler to follow, deliberately leaving for him certain powers of discretion. When put together, these considerations would severely undercut the Eurocentric and anachronistic narrative of Orientalism.

Yet, the narrative operated at many other levels, standing at the bottom of it a conception of law in Islam that has been problematic ever since its inception, when Islam started formulating its "law" during the first century of the Hijra. Operating within a secular conceptual framework, Orientalists took it for granted that "Islamic law" is a project of fabrications and effective theft, a modernist "scholarly" translation of the old Catholic dogma that makes of Muhammad an imposter prophet, a phony whose claims to prophethood were baseless. This dogma was rendered within a palatable, if not sophisticated, transformation of cultural imagination into a law and legal system that cannot pretend to legal or cultural originality, this latter concept being central to European values. The "fraudulence" of the Prophet Muhammad, a theological-dogmatic stance that stood in respectability well below the now "objective" secular and "scientific" approach to knowledge, has come to be replaced by a conception of impoverished mimesis. As evidenced in bookshelves of Orientalist writings on the so-called "origins" of "Islamic law," this law was replete with "borrowings" and "debts" to various legal systems that invariably reflect "Western" cultural sources, i.e., Roman law, Byzantine law, Canon law, and Jewish law. Sassanid law, however important it may have been within the context of cultural exchange, influence, and transplantation, does not appear to Orientalists to be significant in any way. Thus far, to my knowledge, "Islamic studies," in its long life, boasts a single substantial article on the subject of possible Zoroastrian influence on Islamic law.[62]

62 János, "Four Sources of Law in Zoroastrian and Islamic Jurisprudence."

The narrative of borrowings and debts was bolstered by the sub-narrative of large-scale fabrications of the sources of the law, as evidenced by the most influential and enduring writings of Ignaz Goldziher and particularly his successor, Joseph Schacht.[63] Prophetic Ḥadīth, quantitatively the most significant source of "Islamic law," is said to have been forged in a massive, mendacious project in order to rationalize and authorize, *ex post facto*, Muslims' "borrowings" from these old "Western" sources. The upshot of this narrative was to prepare the grounds for what was happening in the twentieth century, which the same Schacht articulated well: Just as Muslims appropriated "Western law" (Roman, Byzantine, etc.) in the seventh century and clothed the project with an Islamic "veneer," they can do the same in their project of "modern reform," another euphemist way of speaking of colonization.[64] My point is this: that Orientalist scholarship was deeply colonialist, in the sense that it constructed, in the name of objective scholarly mission, a narrative in which Islam – in all of its concepts and institutions – always stands in a state of lack, needing Western assistance but also giving expression to the realization of its benevolent *mission civilisatrice*. Europe and its products and services were always needed to civilize Islam, even from as early as the seventh century AD. And integral to this magnanimity, a narrative of absences and impoverished mimesis had to be created. Islam was and remains a failing and failed attempt at becoming Europe and its sublime culture. It failed in its law and legal system, and it failed even more so in its mission to be democratic and to promote a concept and practice of the rule of law. Without such failures, neither Orientalism nor its colonial parent could find the necessary ideological basis to justify their predatorial onslaught on Muslim peoples, their lands and resources.

In its venture to construct the narrative of "Oriental Despotism," Western academia had therefore to focus its energies not on the necessary implications and concomitants of such arguments as Gibb had rudimentarily advanced, but instead to capitalize on largely sketchy accounts of atomized instances of individual sultanic reigns, almost invariably yielding depictions of tyrannical or abusive power. It makes for no surprise therefore that any claim to a robust rule of law in Islam would meet with the counterargument citing such abuses, even by Muslim interlocutors who have now become fully formed within a collective colonized and Orientalized subjectivity.

---

63 The seminal yet highly problematic *textus receptus* is Schacht's *Origins of Muhammadan Jurisprudence*.

64 Schacht, "Problems of Modern Islamic Legislation."

And it is at this juncture where the present book takes leave of the ideological construction of so-called scholarship. No constitutional history of Islam can be written as an account of the totality of individual instances of Muslim sultanic reigns. Such an account will inevitably be impressionistic, lacking, as it were, a convincing methodological basis. In other words, the Orientalist paradigm is not only colonialist in the extreme but also methodologically deficient to the core. An inductive survey of individual sultanic reigns or an impressionistic collection of political ideas – that lacks method and theoretical sophistication[65] – cannot lead to a genuine understanding of how Muslims *constituted* themselves as a polity, how they organized their governing bodies and separated them from each other within an intelligible structure.

This kind of Orientalist history cannot be meaningfully written for two simple but potent reasons: First, that it is impossible to obtain a satisfactory account of all or most sultanic reigns in Islamic history, these posing two insurmountable impediments, namely, that the sheer number of the longer, let alone shorter, sultanic reigns is staggering, reaching the extent of hundreds, if not more. In order to study just these (long or longer) individual sultanic reigns, the effort would consume the energies of a multitude of scholars, who will, furthermore, inevitably disagree on the characterization of these individual sultanic regimes. Therefore, the immense detail of what might be called micro-history will navigate the spectrum between infeasibility and inconclusive judgment. Second, and more importantly, no synthetic account can be derived from such an inductive approach, for no single reign can tell us about how the constitutional structures of Islam manifest themselves, in the way, for instance, the American constitutional structure can be described and analyzed. And if no single reign can perform this task, then the totality of the reigns, even studied to the full, will fail by the same reason.

The inductive approach having failed, the quest for unraveling the "constitutional" structure of Islam persists. Whether we like it or not, the only window we have into understanding what happened in Islam, constitutionally speaking, is that which lies within our "legislated language." For without this "language," which maps out our thought, we would not be asking questions about "Islamic constitutionalism" in the first place. It is precisely from the prison of this language that we must chart a new philology that breaks through the walls of this prison and that allows us to listen attentively to the concerns and aspirations of those humans who lived and struggled on Earth long before we arrived here.

65 As writings listed in n. 58, above, exhibit.

The challenge of studying "Islamic constitutional history" stems from the fact that this kind of inquiry falls within the category customarily labelled "unwritten constitutions."[66] Unwritten constitutions seem more difficult to scrutinize, to describe, and to pin down than written ones, for these latter are more deliberate, concrete, limited, and discernible. In fact, it is not farfetched to argue that the two types have little in common with each other and should therefore not be listed as two species of the same genus. Written constitutions have a well-marked historical point of beginning and are explicable, as expressions of the Paradox of Sovereignty,[67] as self-authorizing originations of polity. Unwritten constitutions emerge out of a protracted and cumulative historical experience, unfolding in time and with practice, and often lacking a meta-theory of constitutional organization. Contrary to modern constitutions, they are "real world constitutions,"[68] the *effect rather than the cause* of the legal and political system at work, synchronically and diachronically.

This difference of effect and cause should alone differentiate the two types qualitatively and as different genera. Unwritten constitutions are arguably more organic than their counterpart. And unlike modern constitutions, which necessarily are written, they are not originary, consciously and intentionally constituting national polities, in the aftermath of a revolution, but rather come into existence through being stable modalities of governance over time. This is not to say, however, that unwritten constitutions do not abide by pre-existing principles; indeed, to the contrary, they do so more than written constitutions, since their very existence over time as unwritten is precisely evidence that they stubbornly insist on higher constitutive principles. If anything, modern constitutions are on the whole less determined than unwritten ones, this being evidenced by the frequent iterations in the form of amendments and frequency of suspensions.

If the concept of written constitution is patently modern, having initially emerged out of the European experience of struggle against absolute monarchical rule, then anything that appears to correspond to this modern category but is not modern would then pose several questions about identity. Is the historical experience that produces a constitutional structure identical to that which emerged in Europe out of popular representation and popular will? Do the conceptual categories of the governing structures in the unwritten type map

66 This is not to say that the category of written/unwritten constitutions is the only typology. Constitutions are classified variously. See Barendt, *Introduction to Constitutional Law*, 8-13.
67 Agamben, *Homo Sacer*, 40-41.
68 Gee and Webber, "What is a Political Constitution?" 273, 275.

onto our modernist conception of constitutionalism and constitutionalization? If Islam, specifically, did not have a written constitution, then where do we look for the latter's equivalent in the Islamic political experience? What problems can emerge out of that historicist exercise? What makes for a definition of the "constitutional" in this experience? What are this experience's substantive components and its conceptual and institutional limits?

In addressing these and similar questions, and with a view to providing a substitute for the resultant deficiencies of the inductive study of sultanic reigns, a viable alternative must be sought. The alternative model would thus seek to identify *the structures* of Islamic governance in terms of constitutionality – that is, the way political and legal governance constituted itself *as a structure*.[69] A constitutional structure refers to the framework or system of fundamental principles, rules, values, institutions, dispositions, and norms that govern a polity *constitutionally*, including the often-complex relationships between and among them. Unwritten constitutions rely heavily on established and longstanding conventions – unwritten and implicit norms and practices that guide the behavior of political actors and institutions as a matter of political and legal culture, as a matter of habitus. These conventions are foundational, in that they govern crucial aspects of governance, such as the formation of governments, the exercise of executive authority, and the relationship between the various powers within the government – powers we must assume to exist perforce everywhere.

Integral to structure, the political, legal, as well as generally cultural conventions carry significant moral – and in our case, ethical – weight, these being essential for maintaining the legitimacy of both the political and legal system. Of profound importance for our concerns, in Islam as in other systems, is the fact that legal precedent (generally so defined) plays a pivotal role in shaping the structure of unwritten constitutions.[70] This is so because unwritten constitutions perforce emerge from centuries of historical evolution, cultural traditions, and legal customs. They reflect the collective experiences, values, and aspirations of a nation, a political community, an *Umma*, thereby encapsulating its political heritage and societal ethos. By imposing order, organization, and a relatively stable continuity onto intricate systems or ideas, structures enable us to discern patterns, identify relationships, and comprehend underlying principles

69 On structures and structural history in general, see Christopher Lloyd, *Structures of History*. On events as they relate to structure, see Koselleck, *Futures Past*.

70 For more on this, see the discussion (below) of the role of analogical devolvement in structures.

that eventually percolate into varying forms of practice. Structures mean that the actions of individuals, political and legal actors, even groups, are always conditioned by an overriding frame of reference, even when these actors, severally or aggregately, violate the imperatives and norms of the system. For it is precisely the structure that enables a judgment to be made about infractions and violations, for general political practice and exercise of power are measured against the norms of the structure. In the case of Islam, this feature is particularly applicable since the concept of *ethical benchmark*[71] plays a pivotal role in this judgment.

I have been trying to define structure within the context of the constitutional problems that Orientalism precipitated. But what do I precisely mean by the word? Anthony Giddens has assiduously attempted a definition in a number of works. What he has to say is no doubt of profound importance to my venture

---

71 On the concept of "ethical benchmark," see Hallaq, *Restating Orientalism*, 73–84:

> "Both Sharīʿa and Ṣūfism, being constituted by an ethical and moral subject matter – down from their epistemological foundations and up to their social dispensations – strove toward the realization of moral ends. Being central paradigms and performative discourses, they may be characterized by what I call a persistent moral benchmark. Benchmarks do not always fully succeed in implementing their desiderata in the real world, but rather stand as reminders and standards against which reality is not only measured but pressured. A persistent benchmark is one whose pressure is greater than those possessed by other benchmarks, especially if its matrix and source of authority stem from a central domain. [For example], the Sharīʿa held itself short of developing any concept of limited liability. And it is easy to see why it did so. One of the central benchmarks of the Sharīʿa was the notion of Sharʿī subject, one constituted by moral technologies of the self, technologies in which ethical and moral liability of the individual believer, the subject, stood supreme. This benchmark was not only operative but performative; which is to say that it was not only applied without reticence, but in the process of its operation, it produced subjects. The premium value in this configuration was moral accountability, not profit. Money and wealth were of such secondary status (despite the great importance Islam and its Sharīʿa placed on business, profit and material wealth) that they could hardly compete with the fundamental, if not constitutive, concept of ethical duty, moral responsibility, and general accountability of the private, individual person. There was no financial or material consideration in the world, however tempting and important, that could alter or mitigate the benchmark of individual and personal accountability, responsibility and liability. This type of accountability and responsibility was irreducible and constituted the most stubborn feature of the entire culture."

Evidence of all of this is the fact that the substantive law of the Sharīʿa possessed the technical legal tools to construct the company/corporation but chose, *due to the benchmark*, not to pursue that path.

here, but I am uncertain that his definition[72] is entirely relevant to my project, or that I accept all its elements. What I offer here briefly draws from his work but later veers in a somewhat different direction. I define "structure" as *a bundle of interconnected heteronomous principles*[73] *constitutively implicated in the reproduction of systems*, be they social, political, legal, or economic. Because they are principles, they (1) exist as non-tangible and virtual phenomena, and (2) are constituted as fields of knowledgeability that shape actual attitudes in the form of social practices. Social practices are what a social system, with all its deliberate and rational agents, routinely does as a reflection of the effect of the principles. Social systems, and here I agree with Giddens, have therefore no "existence apart from the practices that constitute them, for these practices are reproduced by the recursive [i.e., repetitive] enactment of structures."[74]

Now, because they are heteronomous, the principles carry within themselves sources of power that maintain a pattern of practices that constantly binds the rational actors to a negotiated systemic continuity over time. Negotiated, because the practices and effects of the principles' applications are in an *organic* flux, changing while preserving their systemic connections to principles. This of course presupposes that structures are populated by these rational actors who are, in the language of Giddens, "knowledgeable." Hence, structures are mediated by knowledgeable actors who in turn maintain what MacIntyre called rational tradition.[75]

But what does it mean to speak of principles as heteronomous? Instead of "heteronomous principles," Giddens employed the language of "rules and resources,"[76] a language dictated to him by the realities of a "secular age." And it is here where I break away most from his definition. Historian William Sewell has convincingly shown the problems to which Giddens' concept of "resources" gives rise.[77] My objection to "rules" is that they do not account for a thick layer of meaning that the concept of "heteronomous principles" allows

72 In *Logics of History*, 127 ff., William Sewell offers a synthesis of Gidden's definitions scattered in the latter's works. Sewell also offers persuasive revisions to Gidden's theory, but they too seem distant from my concerns.

73 Instead of my "heteronomous principles," Giddens employs "rules and resources," while Sewell's proposed emendation is "schemas." Giddens, *Constitution of Society*, 17, 24-25; Sewell, *Logics of History*, 131.

74 As formulated by Sewell, *Logics of History*, 129. Giddens, *Constitution of Society*, 16-17, 24. On Gidden's concept of structuration (continuity and reproduction of systems), see Giddens, *Central Problems*, 69 ff.

75 MacIntyre, *After Virtue*; MacIntyre, *Whose Justice? Which Rationality?* For more on MacIntyre and tradition, see ch. 10, sec. III.

76 Giddens, *Central Problems*, 64 ff., 100 ff., and passim.

77 Sewell, *Logics of History*, 131-36.

for, namely, sovereign origins of knowledge from which the very principles (and rules) derive; in fact, one can say that the principles are the reflection and expression of this sovereign knowledge. By sovereign here I mean an epistemic (and in our case *epistemoral*)[78] power of disposal that transcends the competence of the ever-changing secular. Structures that ground themselves in neither metaphysics nor ethics are nonetheless governed by heteronomous principles, this being exemplified in the political theology of secular modernity and no less economic theology, the "metaphysical" foundations of modern materialism and capitalist philosophies. My argument here rests on the larger premise that secularism itself is a brand of theology.

In concrete terms, structure is a reflection, perhaps even an emanation, of sovereign knowledge that translates itself, within the confines of the sources available, as principles so commanding and imposing that they control the continual reproduction of social systems. In abstract Kantian terms, it is the transformation of noumena to phenomena in its fullest form. It is the supremacy and force of these principles that explain the endurance of the structure over long stretches of time. This book is a lengthy annotation of the foregoing propositions.

Yet, this conception of structure, so it is argued, leaves us with a legacy of doubt with regard to the ability of structure to change. Doubt is also said to spill over to other concepts that I employ later in this book, such as discursive tradition and particularly habitus. The argument from stasis claims that conceptions of structure and habitus are over-determinative, leaving no agency for the actors populating the systems to effect change or to manipulate the conditions imposed by the structure or habitus to their advantage.

Much ink has been spilled over this seeming predicament, but as a longtime student of Islamic legal history, I am not persuaded that the claims for stasis are valid. A system can be bound by fixed higher principles, by overarching metaphysical structures, and by corralling systemic and even systematic forces and still undergo change. Even under the unprecedentedly hegemonic forces of modernity, change occurs every day, and at a high speed to boot. But even on the most basic level, there is the axiomatic argument – what might be dubbed as *argumentum naturalis* – which runs in fact diametrically opposite to the claim for immutability of structure (or for that matter anything else),

78 Like earlier, neologist amalgamations in my work (such as "psychoepistemic"), "epistemoral" is another term that is intended to avoid the separations and fragmentations in the modern conceptual project. Morality, epistemology, and ethics were never separated as discrete "fields" of knowledge, as evidenced in our detailed and central discussion of *ʿaql* in ch. 1, sec. II.

namely, that no existent whatever is capable of stasis and immutability in the first place, even if it consciously strives to do so. To be is to change. If we accept this basic law of nature, then we must conclude that this recognition alone throws the burden of proof on the shoulders of those who claim that structure and habitus are engulfed by a problematic of immutability. One can furthermore claim that it is our modern obsession with the concept of change (a near-homonymous term)[79] that is behind such exaggerated claims. This is not to mention the theological idea of progress which portrays our modernity as exceptionally agential, and as such pitted as the diametrical opposite of those times and societies that passed.[80] Yet, the *argumentum naturalis* may not satisfy the change-enthusiasts, nor does it in fact explain *how* change occurs, and so further explanation, however briefly, is in order.

Structures are always a part of larger bodies, which I shall call here, for the purposes of my present argument, systems. The legal structure, for example, sits side by side, and in fact overlaps, with the economic structure, and this latter with the social, political, and other structures, which in their totality make up the system.[81] Each structure operates by its own internal logic, principles, and rules that are peculiar to it, as clearly exemplified in the economic and legal structures (though they may share much as well). Because these structures are part of one system, it is inevitable that one structure may generate pressure points against the other, as when rapid economic growth or severe economic crisis spill over into the legal structure, at times inundating it. Inevitably, and at a minimum, these pressure points nudge the legal structure toward adjustment, especially over time. In fact, this is exactly what happened in the *fiqhī* structure.[82]

---

79 A near-homonym term because earlier cultures conceived and articulated a concept of change that is organic and therefore non-disruptive, such as the Islamic concept of legal change. See Hallaq, *Authority*.
80 Note that I do not see a contradiction between my position here on agency and that I expressed in *Restating Orientalism*, 107-112, 150-54, 157-58, 194-95, where I argued that modern colonialism, in its highest moments of trial, deprived the subject of any agency. The civil Jewish and Palestinian populations of Germany and Gaza, respectively, were admittedly denuded of any agency when they suffered such an *existentially* horrible fate. These acts of agential deprivation occurred outside of the structures of the victims' normal lives and in fact precisely *because* these structures were either destroyed or seceded from the victims.
81 My argument for agency and change in structures owes much to Sewell, *Logics of History*, 139 ff. See also Giddens, *Central Problems*.
82 See Hallaq, *Authority*, for general pressure-points. Johansen, "Legal Literature," addresses legal change as the consequence of land rent developments.

Change is likewise effected through what might be called analogical devolvement. In Bourdieu's definition of habitus, as we will see later,[83] and as common sense requires, the transmission and transposition of dispositions, customs, habits, perceptions, and, generally, behavior is achieved mainly through analogical channels, and as any student of the Sharīʿa knows, this is a paradigmatic method of reasoning *and thought* in that culture. And as any logician knows, analogy is never an exact science, this bearing the implication of the countless forms the transpositions can take. There are at least two major causes for this: First, the facts of life requiring transposition within the structure are never exactly identical to the newly emerging facts; and second, the knowledgeable agents inhabiting the habitus inevitably entertain different interpretations of these facts from the manner in which those agents who had operated on the transposed facts had reasoned. This is also why knowledgeability in structure is an essential feature, for it is this fundamentally hermeneutical exercise (and solidly so in the Islamic context) that permits the change to be a legitimate component of the structure. If we take interpretation to be integral to the multiple components and varieties of practice, then as much as structure shapes people's practices, practices themselves also shape structure. In a different context, I have called this very dynamic the "dialectical wheel," where the higher principles fashion dispositions, attitudes, and the practical application of these principles on the ground, only for these applications to be subjected to scrutiny in the process of modifying the higher principles.[84] This, as I have argued, has been shown in the legal domain in Islam, and it will again be demonstrated to be the case in the constitutional arena in this book.

It will be noticed that throughout my explanation of structure, the concepts of habitus and discursive tradition come into view. This is because the three concepts overlap at the center of my concern. I have already remarked that in my usage I conceive habitus as a largely synchronic category of analysis, which perhaps explains in part why it was subjected – I think unfairly – to the critique of stasis. I believe that inasmuch as the answer to this critique remedies the charge against the Bourdieusian concept of habitus, it renders the theory of discursive tradition ever more robust. The latter, on the other hand (and as I explain in chapter 10), proved itself remarkably successful as a diachronic category of analysis, although it does not account for the range of social practices that habitus brings under its purview. Structure thus locates

83 See main text in ch. 10 at n. 159.
84 Hallaq, "Model *Shurūṭ* Works."

itself right in the heart, in the *center*, of the intersection between habitus and discursive tradition, combining the *central* components of each as the matrix of constitutional analysis.

Finally, a word about differentiating structures from events. Orientalist history, as well as its modern Islamic replica, has been preoccupied with events as opposed to structure, or at best with "political thought" as a collection of ideas about politics, government, and "state,"[85] a term that is not only acutely anachronistic, but its use indicates an utter lack of understanding of what modern states are, and how they function and govern. Almost never has this study of "political thought" been articulated as a statement about constitutional divisions and allocation of powers, or at least as a step toward the study of structures. There has thus been a high level of methodological confusion about the analytical function of event, "thought," and structure. No analysis of an event (meaning, in essence, the actions of a sultan regarding a particular matter, or even the actions of a sultan throughout his reign) can teach us about how Muslims conceived the constitution of their government, for the elements that make up the structure cannot be systematically gleaned from, or reflected in, that sultan's deeds or policies or modes of governance throughout his reign. The same can be said of "thought," conceived by Orientalist scholarship as an assortment of segregated ideas about politics and rule (elections, loss of caliphal power, sectarian "ideological" fragmentation, ethnic hierarchy in politics, minorities, etc.). At best, the constitutional structure may be implied, but getting to understand the implications of the event would require the test of consistency, which circularly presupposes knowledge of what the structure is.

Structure, within itself, is a systemic network, which is to say that it embodies systemic relational connections between the parts making it up, this set of relations being itself a central feature of the structure's constitution. Events in themselves – or units of "thought" – are never intelligible for a reading of structure because they lack not only proper contextual placement in the

85 This is most evident in the latest and, by Orientalist standards, credible work of Crone, *God's Rule*. But I may add here that on almost every page, the work exhibits skewed understanding precipitated by what I have called epistemic arrogance, smacking of underlying and markedly racist attitudes. Crone also constantly walks tightropes trying to corral the meaning of powerful evidence (which speaks to a system of a robust rule of law and constitutional restraints) into conventional Orientalist narrative, causing her to fall into contradictions and absurd descriptions of thought and reality. For an example of paradoxical analysis, see n. 60, above. For Crone's general attitude to Islam and its history, see Hallaq, "Use and Abuse of Evidence," 79-91.

structure but also because they are always partial, often lacking the necessary elements that tie the parts of the structure altogether. Being so partial and *structurally incomplete*, they are unequipped to manifest the structure's features, unless, that is, the structure is deduced from some other source or sources. As Koselleck has argued,

> the temporal constants of ... structures transcend the chronologically ascertainable space of experience available to the specific subjects involved in an event. While events are caused or suffered by specific subjects, structures as such are supra-individual and intersubjective. They cannot be reduced to individual persons and seldom to exactly determinable groups. Methodologically, therefore, they demand functional determinants. Structures do not in this way become entities outside of time, but rather gain a processual character, which can then enter into everyday experience.[86]

III

Teleology. In *The Impossible State: Islam, Politics, and Modernity's Moral Predicament*, published in 2013, I argued that under modern conditions it is impossible for Muslims to establish an Islamic state, primarily due to the fact that any recognizably Islamic form of governance – that is consistent with the general tenor of Islamic values as have been known *in practice* for the twelve centuries before colonialism – would contradict the very premises on which the modern state, the only political form we know, is based. My argument was and continues to be that a "recognizably Islamic form of governance" has particular and distinctive foundations, modalities, structure, and teleology. If Islam can be anything, then it is nothing, standing without identity and without a particular character.

True, in its long and extensive history, Islam exhibited multiplicity and astounding diversity, as evidenced in the rich experiences of the juristic schools, differences in and between them, the multifarious Ṣūfī orders and discursive teachings and forms of praxis, a wide range of economic and social institutions, an endless array of local forms of knowledge, a colossal assembly

86 Koselleck, *Futures Past*, 107-8.

of intellectual disciplines and genres, and much else of nearly countless variety and pluralistic constitution. Yet, in all these multiple phenomena, Islam exhibits a coherent overarching structure that is made possible by an appeal to specific and identifiable high order principles (expressed in what we might call cosmology, metaphysics, law, and theology). And it is precisely these principles, governing Islam's astounding variety, that constituted the source for the multiple interpretations which gave rise to Islam's countless forms of life and living. While these principles are akin to those of other complex "religions" and "civilizational" constellations, they stand, like most of these, apart from the fundamental and foundational bases of liberalism and the modern state.

As I have shown in the abovementioned work and others,[87] and as I discuss in this book, the Islamic legal and political conception of the *human* itself stands at odds with the modern liberal conception. Put differently, Islam constitutes the self – that which defines what kind of human subject one is – in ways *qualitatively different* from the materialist, instrumentalist, social, and political liberal subject. In fact, as I argue throughout and as I sum the matter up in the concluding chapter, the very concept of Islamic reason and rationality is at odds with its secular counterpart. The study of rationality and reason is not just a matter of indulging philosophy and elaborations of abstract ideas. It rather has an immediate bearing on concrete political ideas, political practice, and constitutional formation, among many other fields of human activity.

In chapter 3 of *The Impossible State*, I specifically argued that while the constitutional structure of Islam and that of the modern liberal state may appear similar, they in fact are not. This is partly so because the modern liberal state suffers from a host of constitutional problems that are unique to it.[88] More broadly, I argued that the Islamic form of rule of law is more robust than its liberal counterpart, having been grounded in solid and constant cosmological, theological, and socio-cultural foundations. And as chapter 12 of this book details, these foundations' telos was the well-being of the human who is an end unto itself and who is not instrumentalized as a useful object of the state, to be *perpetually* made and remade.

87 Particularly in *Reforming Modernity* and *Restating Orientalism*.

88 An interlocutor may argue that I am not noting the constitutional problems that Islam may have also encountered. My reply is that we need first to understand what the general standing structure of Islamic constitutionalism is before we can judge it and assess its problems. So far we have not attained this understanding and any attempt to critique it before then would not only be premature but unjustifiably reckless or else imperious.

The Impossible State has generated considerable controversy and debate, about more than one of its main arguments. The constitutional argument received the main criticism of depicting the Islamic constitutional system from an idealistic perspective, not attending to "facts" and considerations which might reduce the positive image I was alleged to have accorded to it. This book, among other things, addresses this criticism. It is the result of a deep exploration of the subject, involving much philological work (as described and defined above) that was mostly done after *The Impossible State* was published. It constitutes both a distension and an expansion of the thesis I have advanced in that regrettably short work.

The criticism directed at the constitutional arguments of *The Impossible State* came from various quarters, both Western and Muslim. What is remarkable about this critical attitude, once deciphered and analyzed, is that it shares a single common denominator, namely, an Orientalist-liberal substrate. This substrate, I must emphasize, also underlies the Islamists' criticisms. For it is true, I think, that with the passage of time, contemporary Muslim subjectivity is becoming increasingly liberal, this meaning not only a particular way of living economically, socially, psychologically, and politically, but a way of writing and reading history as well. As I have argued in the preceding parts of this Introduction, Islamic history as a modern form of historiographical narrative is almost wholly the creation of the Western academy. The narrative has been hegemonic, if for no other reason than the fact that the Islamic form of *ta'rīkh*, a discipline of moral import, had no chance whatever in winning the competition against the dominant, if not domineering, "scientific" and "source-critical" methodology of the secular European university. The hegemonic judgment of modern history and historiography could never accord *ta'rīkh*, its ethical premises and their application, a hearing in their courts. The military, political, and economic/financial onslaught of nineteenth-century European colonialism had already demolished the foundations of the Muslim institutions' capabilities of resistance to the intellectual and academic domination of Orientalism.[89]

To write the constitutional history of Islam from a truly postmodern perspective[90] (as intimated in my linguistic- and philological-philosophical

89 For a detailed history of these incursions, see Hallaq, *Sharīʿa*, 357-499, especially at 396-429.

90 For an idea of how I define "postmodern," see my lecture "What is Post-Orientalism?" delivered at Hamad Bin Khalifa University, Qatar (January 10, 2023). Available at: https://www.youtube.com/watch?v=klZ5yybdZJI

approach to what I have called above perpendicular remoteness) amounts to engaging in a project of archeological excavation of significant proportions. An archeologist must first remove the sediments and accumulations of debris, soil, and rock, before reaching the historical artifacts, which themselves represent semiotic signs that tell of the ways certain human groups lived. In our case, the debris, with all of its grime, is the Orientalist narrative that covers and masks the artifacts and their true semiotics. Yet, this is only half the problem. Now that the earth has been dug and debris cleared, the artifacts must be removed and perforce reclassified and re-catalogued, so that they can be re-placed to where they originally belonged, so that we can reevaluate their semiotics, their connections and re-establish the relationships between and among them. The order in which any group of signifiers are placed and classified considerably affects their signification, and thus the way their history is narrated. An integral part of Orientalist misrepresentation is the canny ability to keep much of the artifacts ("facts") in view, making conclusions deriving from their study seem "scientific" and logically compelling, yet the signification that results from their *particular ordering* and *organization* in relation to each other has proven itself to be not only skewed but also pernicious.[91] Orientalism is masterful in the art of reorganizing and reordering facts and data.

91 An example of a twisted logic of ordering facts is to be found in Crone's work, *God's Rule*, 322. There, she argues that "state and society" in the first two centuries of Islam "had parted ways," a typical claim that legal Orientalism had long applied to Sharīʿa as well (see n. 18, above). Instead of seeing this parting of ways as the crucial separation between the legislative and executive powers, it was for Crone a disconnection or a dissonance of sorts. It is presented as a pathology, since it does not fit into her conception of "normal" polities. The seemingly few exceptions to this "parting of ways" occurred "above all in holy war against infidels, when they [i.e., "state and society"] pursued the same aim, on the basis of the same religious law. But by and large," she continues, "people had to accept that the Sharīʿa was only the constitutional law of everyday life, not *of the* government appointed for its protection" (emphasis mine). Note here how Crone teases no implication whatsoever of the fact that the law was not of the "state's" making, and that Muslims lived by a Sharīʿa over which the "state" had no control. The separation was so alien to this prominent Orientalist that she could not make any sense of it because, as the paragraph in question makes crystal clear, she does not recognize the normal unless it conforms to the Western model. The point I am making here is that this prejudice and narrow vision of the world has allowed the Orientalists to acknowledge the facts as they have been *dictated* to them by the primary sources (because as "bare" facts, they are undeniable), yet they ordered and interpreted these facts in ways that are utterly contorted. On the analogous "divorce" that the legal Orientalists claimed to have existed between "state and society," especially in the conception of Joseph Schacht ("the Father of Islamic law"), see n. 18, above, as well as my critique in "Model *Shurūṭ* Works," 109-112, and sources cited therein.

Orientalism also systematically engaged in what I have elsewhere called "topical selection,"[92] emphasizing and deemphasizing at will the significance of the "facts" on the ground. In reading so-called Islamic "political thought," Orientalism attributed to these individual "facts" a host of meanings that accorded with its own Eurocentric hierarchy of values, thereby emphasizing, and in the process detracting from, their original significance and relevance. In almost all cases, Islamic "political thought," distinct in its perpendicular remoteness, was consistently and persistently measured against modernist schemata of so-called democracy, so-called freedom, and so-called popular representation, with their concomitant institutional forms of so-called democratic, electoral change of government. This involved a double fallacy.

First, as already intimated, the Orientalist reading entirely ignores the internal logic of the Muslim political discursive tradition, the negligence being mostly the function of poor scholarship and/or rash and sovereign judgment (not that the three factors are always distinct). This latter, sovereignty, is merely another way of indicating the generalized lack of what I have called above empathetic epistemology.

Second, in this book, I read Islamic constitutional history from a perspective usually unfamiliar to constitutional scholars. Modern constitutional scholarship is preeminently preoccupied with the study of juridico-political institutions and values of *political* culture. There is of course no surprise here, since this approach is consistent with the rational bureaucratic order that "Weberian" modernity has perfected so well. In this scholarship, and this lies at the heart of the second fallacy, the constitution of the subject, the bearer of a particular subjectivity, is at best relegated to insignificance, and at worst, to nullity. The key terms of modern constitutional discourse are "parliaments," "elections," "suffrage," "rights," "branches of power" ("legislative," "judicial," "executive"), "checks and balances," "judicial review," "judicial activism," "constitutional amendment," "originalism," and the like.[93] Note that none of these institutional and conceptual categories is preoccupied with the subjectivities or the ethical formation of the human beings without whom the very constitutional system would be impossible to conceive. While subjectivity in constitutional interpretation is duly recognized by this scholarship as the product of various ethical positions, the subject as the bearer of ethical subjectivity is never deemed crucial for the study (or, for that matter, operation) of constitutional

92 Hallaq, "On Orientalism, Self-Consciousness and History," 409-21.

93 For an average but brief narrative of modern constitutional concerns (as focused on the US), see Chemerinsky, *Constitutional Law*, 1-29.

structures. Nor indeed for the citizen's political life. The idea of the individual *self* as a repository of techniques of ethical formation is almost entirely absent, predictably consistent with the paradigmatic and hegemonic Weberian formal rationality.

This book, propelled by the ethical imperatives of Muslim subject matter, dwells at length on the structure of subjectivity as an integral part of constructing the unwritten history of Islamic constitutional structures. The approach also indirectly unmasks theories of human nature that undergird the Islamic conception of constitutional actors, thereby exposing the difference between these theories and those undergirding their modern constitutional counterparts.[94]

Yet another difference in approach to writing Islamic constitutional history is the special attention paid to the fundamental theories and doctrines that envelop the constitutional worldview in Islam. In modern constitutional scholarship, because our conceptions of politics and the political have been structured by secularism and nationalist ideologies, considerations external to the state, the nation, or, for that matter, science, are not in order. But this is not the case in the Islamic constitutional tradition. Because Islam viewed the world as a unity, created from beginning to end by a single Omnipotent and Omniscient Designer, constitutional structures are consequently conceived as locating themselves comfortably within the Whole. In this worldview, there are no two elements in the universe that can exist without a relationship, however indirect. Every existent is always assumed to be connected to another by *at least* one relationship, one thread; namely, that they are both created, perhaps the most significant fact about their existence.

Yet, it must be stressed that this is not merely an abstract theoretical, theological, or doctrinal conception. These theologies, cosmologies, and metaphysical doctrines are pregnant with practical implications and outright political effects. Which is to say that they do not only entail political effects that determine constitutional structures, but also fashion and maintain the constitutional habitus, and therefore law and living. Perhaps the most central of these tenets is the idea that God is the Owner of the world (*Malik*), since

94 Consistent with my methodological, linguistic, and theoretical cautions expressed here, it must be said that most modern interpretations of Muslim theories of human nature are superficial and easily tend to equate these theories with a Hobbesian conception. There is a severe lack of understanding of the philosophies of the self (*nafs*) as prevalent in Islam which were (and continue to be) the foundations without which no such theories can be properly understood. For example, I find Yilmaz's presentation in *The Caliphate Redefined*, 154 (despite the merits of the work), somewhat insensitive to the deeper considerations germane to the differentiation between the Hobbesian theory and *any* of its Islamic counterparts.

He created it. This notion of ownership might appear to the secularist mind merely as a theological reverie, but in Islam it acquires monumental constitutional power *and practical effect.*[95] In fact, in this political tradition, God's ownership of the world stood as the most central and foundational concept, for it determined the outer limits and much of the inner content of Islamic political and constitutional structures. As significant, it encased and permeated the operational habitus of these structures. In sum, the Islamicist constitutional historian must reckon with a discursive space much wider than is necessary for his or her colleague who studies modern constitutions.

Finally, in the nature of things, this study has produced another unintended effect. Modern scholarship on so-called Islamic law has long been preoccupied with this law's capacity for change. Until the late 1970s, Orientalism propounded the historical doctrine that by the fourth/tenth century or a little thereafter, the Sharīʿa began to suffer from stagnation, where a condition of "ossification" had set in. This phenomenon was captured by the emblematic expression "the closure of the gate of *ijtihād*."[96] It is not difficult nowadays to understand the reasons for the Orientalist invention of this colonialist narrative. As of the 1980s, however, revisionist scholarship has questioned this narrative and effectively overhauled it in its entirety.[97] This book may be added to the existing literature. As we will see throughout the second half of this book, Muslim jurists of the Mamlūk and Ottoman eras implemented juristic and constitutional changes that testify to the adaptability of both the Sharīʿa and the political constitutional structure.

If Islamic constitutional history is to be divided into eras and epochs that manifest evolution and change, then this book offers a narrative that assumes four periods:[98] (1) the formative, extending with constant mutation from the beginning until the second half of the fourth/tenth century. This is when *siyāsa* begins, as an autonomous sphere of political management, but ends, by the end of said century, contained within the Sharʿī grid. In other words, due to the full formation of the Sharīʿa by then,[99] *siyāsa* comes under the latter's regulative sway, but continues to enjoy a wide array of discretionary powers *within its own, now delimited, domain*; (2) the next three and a half to four

95 See Tazi Hemida, "Problem of God's Sovereignty."
96 On this matter, see Hallaq, "Was the Gate of Ijtihad Closed?"; Hallaq, "On the Origins of the Controversy about the Existence of Mujtahids."
97 See Hallaq, "Was the Gate of Ijtihad Closed?"; Baber Johansen, "Legal Literature and the Problem of Change;" Hallaq, "From *Fatwās* to *Furūʿ*;" Hallaq, *Authority.*
98 The focus of this book is limited to the second and third, with "flashbacks" to the first.
99 A history of the first four centuries of the Sharīʿa may be found in Hallaq, *Origins.*

centuries, which generally preserve this arrangement; (3) the emergence of *siyāsa shar'iyya* beginning with the decline of Mamlūk rule, a phenomenon that led to a marked change in the legal, political, and constitutional arrangements. This period, like all others, can be further subdivided, but its mark remains the subsumption of *siyāsa* under Sharī'a more than ever before; and (4) the collapse of the system under the weight of colonialism and the rise, as of 1800, of a new, increasingly secularized, system of rule (see Conclusion).

Before outlining the arguments of the book, I must note two exclusions from its purview. First, there is a notable absence of discussion of the Greek political-philosophical legacy that had seeped into the Islamic soil between the second/eighth century and middle of the fourth/tenth. The exclusion should in no way suggest that this genre, especially the work of Fārābī (d. 340/951) and his like, is unimportant.[100] The exclusion is rather motivated by the fact that this is a book about constitutional structures, modalities of governance, and the juridico-political life of Islam in the post formative and middle periods and until the colonialist incursions into the Muslim world during the nineteenth century. It is not a book on philosophy, the Virtuous City,[101] or intellectual history; nor, as I already stated, is it a book on just "Islamic political thought," as many scholars have made this subject their concern. Our interest rather lies in the actualities of constitutional organization, divisions of powers, and the boundaries between and among them. The Greek-inspired tradition is largely irrelevant to these concerns.[102] There is thus a fundamental difference between political thought, political philosophy, or intellectual history, on the one hand, and constitutional history, on the other.

Second, this book leaves out a long and complex constitutional history of Islam in South Asia, which in some important respects differed from that which dominated in the so-called central lands of Islam (which here I designate as West Asia). Again, this deliberate omission does not reflect a lack of appreciation for the importance of that history. In fact, it is of such weighty significance that it deserves to be studied on its own, for it is my considered opinion that it raises its own set of problems that require a separate treatment, one that my energies do not permit me to undertake in a single work. Nor is it, at any rate, advisable for me to do so, since that region and its history require

100 See Conclusion, n. 5.

101 See Ibn Khaldūn, *Muqaddima*, 238, who makes a clear distinction between the Islamic practice of government and what he calls the "hypothetical" virtuous "city"; "*Wa-innama yatakallamūna 'alayhā 'alā jihati al-farḍi wal-taqdīr.*"

102 But see ch. 2, n. 4.

linguistic and other historical skills that I do not possess. But I am also of the belief that that history cannot be written before we have arrived at an adequate understanding of the constitutional structures of historical Islamic West Asia, which preceded it in point of time and in effect laid down its foundations. Our Māwardī and his like were relevant not only to the much later Mamlūks, Ottomans, and other West Asian empires but continued to resonate in the political and constitutional discourses of Islamic South Asia.[103]

IV

Contents and Layout. There are at least two ways to describe the contents, arguments, and layout of this book. One is the traditional narration of consecutive chapters, which will follow shortly. The other way is to offer a description of the book that proceeds from stating its core concerns and arguments, thereafter moving into larger circles that prop and scaffold the priorities of the core. Think of this core as an argument that sits at the center of a circle and that extends itself in multifarious ways over other expanding circles. Accordingly, the core concern of this book, as intimated earlier, revolves around delineating the boundaries between and among the various organs that, in their totality, constituted the governing body in the Islamic polities of West Asia.

The *basic* argument that will unfold in the course of this book aims to show that the separation of powers, especially between the legislative and executive, was a radical separation, which here means that it was *qur'ānically,* and thus genealogically, constituted as an integral part of the architecture and original design of Islam; that it was not, as the modern system is, the result of a colossal attempt to resolve the problem of oppressive, absolutist monarchical rule; that the Sharīʿa, since its full formation in the fourth/tenth century, represented the dominating law of the land and thus imposed a system of rule of law until the beginning of the nineteenth century; and that, as a consequence of all of the above, Islam and its polities were never exposed to anything like the Paradox of Sovereignty. Yet this basic argument sits under layers of other developments that will also unfold as the book progresses in its narrative.

---

103 See, for instance, Alam, *Languages of Political Islam in India*; Alam, "Shariʿa and Governance in the Indo-Islamic Context."

Since everything we know about constitutionalism and separation of powers is of a distinctly modern conceptual and cognitive stock, the originary research question I have adopted was thus laden with the consciousness that if there happened to be a certain separation of powers in Islam, the genealogies of these "branches" of power – located in another continent, culture, and millennium – would have had very little to do with their modern counterparts. This much is common sense. Thus, the ambition of this core argument was to construct a basic map of (1) the various organs that constituted parts of a whole that governed Islamic polity; and (2) excavating the genealogies of these organs with a view to shedding light on their dispositions, modalities of operation, and their relationships to each other as constitutional powers. The end result of the core argument is that what amounted to the legislative and executive powers in West Asian Islamic polities were so radically separate that they never threatened each other, either existentially or by overreach. The modern constitutional problems existing between these two powers was unknown to Islam. However, the constitutional grind lay in between, in the arena of judicial enforcement.

The second, larger circle added to this basic mapping of constitutional divisions is the question of diachronic accretions: Did this map of the fundamentals of constitutional power change over time and, if it did, how and why? This explains my forays into Mamlūk and Ottoman political management, two dynasties that dominated the political and cultural scene of West Asia and Egypt for well over seven centuries. Considering that the core circle takes for its field of play the late Būyid and Saljūq dynasties, the two circles together can thus be said to cover about a millennium's worth of constitutional mapping.

The third and largest circle superadds a methodological and theoretical web that holds the two inner circles in place, and together. The reader will discover that this work is not a straightforward history of a constitutional system, but rather a narrative laced with a theoretical thrust and a multifaceted critique. As this Introduction has shown, I do not take any assumption or form of modern historiographic knowledge for granted, and this for at least two reasons: First, as I have already advocated in many books and dozens of articles, we can no longer use, much less build on Orientalist narratives. It is a fundamental assumption of my scholarship – as I think it should be for all rising scholars in the field – that the Orientalist narrative as a form of knowledge is *structurally*[104] distortive and false, even outright pernicious, until proven

104 I think it is profoundly important to understand the distinction between narratives of knowledge in general and these narratives as *structures*. To give a well-known example, I may find credible support for my work in writings that revise the history of Prophetic Ḥadīth

otherwise. Being the handmaiden of colonialism and a derivative of modern knowledge, Orientalism is as responsible for the deteriorating state of our world as any other cognate force in modernity.[105] Yet, this is not a dogmatic attitude that is politically motivated (in the way Edward Said, for instance, navigated his critical project in *Orientalism*). Rather, the attitude derives from deeply epistemic considerations that implicate Orientalism as a form of knowledge in a larger destructive project driven by a particular cogito.[106] Thus, with the rejection of the only historiographical narrative we know, we are left – happily I would say – with an empty space to be filled by new and hopefully indigenous narratives.

The second reason lies in the way I probe my sources. I do not assume that I understand words and even common terms unless they have been subjected to lexical and technical excavations, accompanied and supported by inquiries into the internal logic that gives them their premodern meaning. This latter is not used metaphorically. The only real meaning that words and terms have is that given them by their original users, those who effectively either coined these terms or used them organically in their discourse. And it is our ethical responsibility and moral mission to identify with the *subjectivities* authoring the texts we read with the view of accessing to the utmost extent possible their internal logic and the way they saw the world. But then I have said enough of this problem of translatability in what is already a very long Introduction.

Now, the second way of telling what this book offers is to say that it consists of three parts, each dedicated to exploring certain aspects of chronologically contextualized constitutional life in the Islamic lands of West Asia. To

within Orientalism (notably, for example, the writings of Harald Motzki), but I cannot accept as legitimate scholarship the narrative structure of Orientalism about this foundational issue. On Motzki and others, see Hallaq, "Authenticity of Prophetic *Ḥadîth*." The same goes for Orientalist discourse about "Islamic law's debt" to "foreign influences" and the structural connections between the "origins" of law in Islam and modern legal reform, seen, as stated above, as replicating the Muslim pattern of dependence on Europe. Again, I may accept scholar X's findings that a specific rule, legal maxim, or juridical practice was transmitted to Islam from a previous legal system or systems, but the structure of Orientalist narrative is ultimately endowed with – even *structured* as – a colonialist justification. On this, see Hallaq, "The Quest for Origins or Doctrine?"; Hallaq, "On Orientalism, Self-Consciousness and History." As a general rule, therefore, whenever I refer to an Orientalist's writings, it is because I could read them as shining a light on a particular issue (say, modalities of elementary education under the Mamlūks), but I am always wary of the larger structured narratives.

105 This is the fundamental, though initial, argument of my *Restating Orientalism*.

106 Here I am thinking of Enrique Dussel's work. See, e.g., his "Anti-Cartesian Meditations."

prepare for such an account, and to give it the meaning that Muslims thought belonged to it, Part I begins with an exposition of the philosophical foundations of Islamic governance, essentially answering the questions: Why does government and politics and rule in the first place? What are their functions and *raison d'être*? How is the Community as a political body sociologically formed? On what grounds? What kind of rationality must undergird these grounds? How does this rationality lead to a particular form of knowledge, one that decides *what* agencies govern and *how*? This inquiry naturally discloses parallels with what we know in modernity as the theory of social contract; yet more significantly, the import of this discussion obliquely goes into the Islamic theory of human nature. In the second section of this chapter, I offer an account of Māwardī's concepts of reason and knowledge to highlight the stark fact that the Muslim conception of rationality and the knowledge that this rationality generates are distinctly different from their modern counterparts. This account is essential for making better sense of how the Muslim (not just Islamic) *raison politique* worked, how it was embedded in a cosmology and ethical epistemology (also the concern of chapter 4), and how, by implication, a constitutionalized system of governance could thrive in the total absence of *raison d'état*.

Chapter 2 continues the exploration of an ethically-based political and constitutional conception by focusing on the functional boundaries of the caliphate, sultanate, and their wellspring, the prophethood. Read with a constitutional eye, so-called "religious" works of various stripes come across as wholly congruous in defining the Prophetic province as a bundle of functions intended to protect the logically pre-established normative structures. Here, as in various junctures in the book, I enlist the theories of habitus and discursive tradition with a view to bringing out what has been called the worldliness of the texts I am expounding.

I argue that the texts I am reading do much more considerable analytical work than being an expression of high-floating ideas ("political thought") and idealized "religious moralism." Implicit in this chapter (as in chapters 1, 4 and 12) is an attempt to bring the field into the recognition that it has missed the cultural turn altogether, and that the study of subjectivation must take front seat. With this in mind, the chapter further outlines the conception of politics in the Islamic tradition in an attempt to underscore two inextricably interrelated points. The first goes to the problem of (un)translatability we began exploring earlier in the Introduction, since one of the most complex linguistic, epistemic, and ontological problems of translatability lies in the very word "politics." In this chapter, I prepare the grounds for a more complex inquiry to be undertaken in chapter 12, where I wind up the discussion by arguing – and this is the second point – that the modern meaning of politics drastically differs from its premodern denotations, especially in Islam (but also in Greece and, I suspect, Sassanid Iran, among others). The import of this finding is this: that we cannot evaluate premodern conceptions of politics and constitutional effect with the same tools we use to assess the modern forms of politics – forms that bred unprecedented conceptions of sovereignty, *raison d'état*, and the Schmittian political. If the carpenter's saw knows only wood, then cutting diamond calls for another tool.

With this background in mind, chapter 3 begins to delineate the architecture of Islamic constitutionalism by framing the boundaries of the executive, the constellation of agencies that carried out the rules and enforced the law. The reason for beginning with this constellation is the confusion that reigns in modern scholarship about the nature of powers enshrined in the office of the caliphate/imamate. The argument of this chapter will be that other than the spiritual and religiously symbolic significance of the caliphate – which are irrelevant to constitutional determination – the caliphate was a strictly executive function whose powers, as executive, could be delegated to any agency competent to carry out this function. It is also the argument of this chapter, as of the book at large, that the caliphate – being an extension of the Prophetic functions minus the reception of revelation – is the vessel through which executive powers flowed. The powers and their agents may come and go, but the vessel as an enveloping tissue, if you will, was the guarantee that these powers are corralled into what it means to have Islamic/Muslim governance. Otherwise, the executive would look, and be, like any Byzantine, Sassanid, or other "profane" mode of government.

Chapter 4 takes us back to the Qur'ānic revelation in order to probe into the genealogy of the matrix that produced the substantive law of Islam, the law by which executive powers – operating from within the enveloping tissue of the vessel – were bound. This chapter argues that the genesis of the legislative power (that which *discovers* the law)[107] is parallel to the Prophethood and does not stem from it, making the very sources and roots of the executive and the legislative in Islam *genealogically* separate – that is separate from the roots. This monumental

107 It should be elementary knowledge that in Islam the jurists neither make law nor legislate but merely do their best to discover it (through *ijtihād*). In this book, any reference to "legislation" or "legislative" in Islam should be understood with this in mind. See chapter 4, n. 2.

fact, stamping the title of this work, marks the decisive and categorical difference from liberal, and in fact all modern constitutional systems. Whereas the perennial historical struggle of emerging Western polities has been to segregate the legislative from the domineering and authoritarian executive, in Islam this segregation was already predetermined at the time of Qur'ānic revelation.

The interplay between the Sharʿī legislative power and the caliphal-sultanic executive produced the common project of the judiciary, the concern of chapter 5. Common because the judiciary was a division of labor whereby the legislative Sharʿī culture, with its educational institutions and apprenticeship, prepared the judicial personnel, while the executive enlisted them in an administrative system with a view to adjudicating disputes and running the affairs of the Community. The chapter also focuses on the training that the legislative culture provided to produce a secretarial class who ran the executive's system of *dīwāns*. The sultanic executive, rising and vanishing with a regular rhythm, fell, rather automatically, into this all-important and self-standing *dīwān*ic structure.

Now, at variance with the European anxiety about executive overreach, Muslim constitutional scholars insisted on the juridical and political need to have as strong an executive as possible. The problem for Muslims was not too much power residing in the executive but rather too little of it. If tyranny was and remains the impending nightmare of liberal political thinking, in Islam it was the prospect of a weak executive and the threat of civil war.[108] The crux of chapter 6, as of the book at large, is precisely to demonstrate this truth. There was no anxiety about a strong executive because everyone knew that everyone knew that no matter how strong an executive is, it will always be bound by the principle of legislative autonomy and supremacy of the Sharīʿa. Violating the Sharīʿa was not only violating the law of the land but also the very will of God. If there was an anxiety about executive power, it was about possible infractions in the exercise of mundane administration of justice, especially in the penal domain of *taʿzīr* (the chief concern of Part II).

It might be worthwhile at this juncture to caution against confusing the infractions and abuses of executive officials with the ontological modalities of a constitutional structure. We can take it for granted that executive violations of the law occurred, and, indeed, at multiple junctures and contexts in Islamic history. I have no illusions about humans' capacity to engage in wrongdoing and

108 Known in Arabic as *fitna*, civil war was a central motif in Islamic political writings, emerging with time as a genre. For an example of this genre, see Marwazī, *Kitāb al-Fitan*. For the array of Ḥadīths, see Muslim, *Ṣaḥīḥ*, IV, 536 ff.

even cruelty. Nor are such transgressions the exclusive property of Muslims. All governments past and present engaged in one sort of abuse or another, at times brutishly. In fact, it is my argument – elaborated on epistemological grounds in my *Restating Orientalism* – that modern states are by definition able to inflict both legitimate and illegitimate violence on a scale and intensity unseen before modernity, and not only because of the efficient modern technology available to them.

But these interrogations into executive wrongdoing are to be distinguished from questions of constitutional modalities. To take a prominent example, no one can doubt the enduring constitutional edifice of the United States, yet abuses of the US executive abound.[109] However, this is not an argument against the goals of having such constitutional edifices as elaborated in Islam and the USA. In these systems, as in all similar others, executive abuses and violations can be measured and evaluated according to a benchmark, and some political, legal, or cultural calculus of a remedy tends to be effected. Abuses on their own do not entail the absence of an operative constitutional structure, nor does the existence of constitutional structures entail, or for that matter, guarantee the absence of violations.

Throughout the book, but especially in chapters 3, 6, 7, and 12, we have kept an eye on the prominent idea of a coveted strong executive, especially in light of the Islamic discourse to the effect that "an unjust ruler is preferable to a day of civil war." This kind of maxim was and remains a favorite in Orientalist writings, if only to show how the jurists, at least, justified tyranny. But this interpretation, exhibiting European anxiety more than a good scholarly judgement, could not have been farther from the truth. As we will see across these chapters, the limited nature of Islamic executive oversight, in terms of penetration of the social order and biopower, could in no way have had the ill-effects that have effectively accrued in the modern state, or even in the Age of Absolutism, and so Muslim scholars were understandably less worried about a wing-clipped tyranny than about civil war.

Part II of the book moves to the intervening period, between the decline of the ʿAbbāsid House in the fifth/eleventh century and the rise of the Ottomans toward the end of the ninth/fifteenth, increasing the focus of the last (eleventh) chapter of Part II on the middle Ottoman Empire, that is, the eleventh/

109 A few, among many more, examples should suffice: American Civil Liberty Union, "Unleashed and Unaccountable;" Amnesty International, "Fatal Flaws;" Chevigny, *Edge of the Knife*; U.S Government, "Executive Overreach in Domestic Affairs;" DPIC Special Report: "The Innocence Epidemic."

seventeenth and twelfth/eighteenth centuries. Opening Part II, chapter 7 aims to delineate the limits and boundaries of constitutional powers in a Mamlūk-era treatise, authored by the leading Shāfiʿī jurist Ibn Jamāʿa. The argument of this chapter is that this work is an "update" of the *aḥkām al-sulṭāniyya* genre we have discussed in Part I, an update that reflected the particular conditions of Islamic governance under the Mamlūk *dawla* (this latter term being understood exclusively as an executive power). The processes involved here were recognizably juristic and find parallels in modes of generational change in the law.[110]

Taking into consideration the realities of Mamlūk rule, Ibn Jamāʿa's work accounted for the exceptional pressures that this dynasty faced, from both outside and inside its borders. Yet Ibn Jamāʿa's update must be seen as a reaffirmation of the constitutional configuration that had become deeply rooted in Islamic West Asia by his time, a configuration that reflected the tenacity of the political tradition that had reached a level of maturity at least a century before his predecessor and constitutional articulator, Māwardī, was writing. By all indications, including Qalqashandī's massive archival testimonials of administrative-executive practice on the ground, we can speak of Ibn Jamāʿa's work as a fairly accurate constitutional mapping of Islamic West Asia around the 700s/1300s.

In chapters 8 and 9, I trace the developments, modifications, and adjustments that occurred within the established constitutional divisions and boundaries as outlined by both Māwardī and Ibn Jamāʿa, among others, with the hope of showing that while these divisions and boundaries were solidly maintained within what I call an Islamic constitutional ecology, change, and pliable adjustments effectively occurred within the next four or five centuries. It so emerges that the focal point of the constitutional grind and anxiety revolved around criminal law, for it was here where the Sharīʿa embarked on a bid to define, more sharply than ever, the prerogatives and boundaries of the executive in the criminal domain. Furthermore, these chapters tell the story of the rise of a new sub-genre, one that is unprecedented in Islamic legal and political-constitutional history. The genre originally arises from within the contours of *adab al-qāḍī* (rules and procedures of the law court) discourse, only to transcend it by creating a new generation of works that not only rein in executive *siyāsa* within the imperatives of law's empire but also deploy the judiciary as an adjudicator and enforcer virtually equal to those men of the sword who

110 On these modes of legal change, see Hallaq, *Authority*.

had for centuries commanded *siyāsa* for themselves.[111] If the ruler and his men can adjudicate in the law through *maẓālim* (extra-judicial tribunals) and *siyāsa*, then the jurists and their deployed *qāḍī*s (Sharīʿa judges) can decide the course of *siyāsa* through the paradigmatic law. And if it is true that *siyāsa* is an integral part of the Sharīʿa, as standard doctrine suggests, then the men of the Sharīʿa can dispense *siyāsa* as well.

In sum, then, chapters 7-9 cover the main constitutional doctrines of the Shāfiʿīs, Ḥanbalīs, and Mālikīs. Chapter 10 in part attends to the Ḥanafī doctrine as it evolved from the ninth/fifteenth century down to the Ottoman eighteenth century. The focus on criminal law throughout is necessitated by the nature of the constitutional questions that posed themselves in the course of our inquiry. We will see that the discourses emanating from these schools were not neatly divided and segregated from each other along *madhhab* lines, as the study of *fiqh* doctrine usually involves. The rich *madhhab*ic intertextuality with regard to constitutional questions therefore means that the schools fed on each other and were heavily involved, often as a collectivity, in the articulation of the constitutional domain in its various stages of development. This study shows that when it came to governance and constitutional boundaries and overreach, *all schools* were proactive and heavily involved. The schools' equidistance from the common cause of governance stood parallel to their equidistance from *uṣūl al-fiqh*, the foundational legal theory and hermeneutical methodology that not only sustained the operational logic of the jurisprudence but also defined Sunni constitutional structures as a byproduct of the law (as opposed to the Shīʿī model of infallible imamic rule [see ch. 4, sec. II]).

In chapter 10, I trace the rise of a Ḥanafī-Ottoman constitutional accommodation that reflected a change that started in effect with the Mamlūk-era Ḥanbalīs and Mālikīs of the eighth/fourteenth and ninth/fifteenth centuries, and that reached a zenith with the Ottoman-Ḥanafī political writings in the tenth/sixteenth century and beyond. It was on the basis of this accommodation that the Ottoman dynasty constructed its characteristic system of government. In this chapter, I also revert to the last century of Mamlūk rule in Egypt and Syria – the forerunner of the Ottomans in these domains – in order to set

111 On *siyāsa* and its autonomous power during the formative period, see Yücesoy, *Disenchanting the Caliphate*. Yücesoy's general narrative, it must be said, is a necessary background for my own narrative here, if only to show the extent of constitutional transformations that took place between the Early ʿAbbāsid practices and those of the Mamlūks and the Ottomans. For a macro-narrative of the relationship between the ulama and ʿAbbāsid ruling class, see Zaman, *Religion and Politics*; Zaman, "Caliphs, the Ulama, and the Law."

straight a major misconception in the field, namely, that this period can be taken to be representative of larger Mamlūk rule or even beyond. Rather, my argument is that the events making up that century of constitutional upheaval were transient and that they constitute an exception in the constitutional practices of West Asia. This correction amounts to a significant methodological intervention that should be taken into consideration when drawing on the later Mamlūk period when combing for "constitutional pieces of evidence" or even when writing legal history. This chapter suggests that it would be a theoretical and methodological mistake to view Islamic constitutional history in linear terms; instead, this book's narrative suggests that a cyclical conception that permits mutations and variations around an unwavering set of fundamental principles (that is, supremacy of the law) is a more accurate approach to this emerging field.

Chapter 11 continues chapter 10's investigation into the question of Ottoman constitutional arrangements, now paying special attention to the modern historians' claims for what has become known in the field as "Ottoman exceptionalism." The chapter aims to critically assess certain writings in the most advanced scholarship bearing on the constitutional issues we have pursued, if only to show that this scholarship's conclusions on the constitution of Islamic governance are not tenable. These writings are confronted head-on first by means of *streamlining their concerns in constitutional terms* and then by subjecting them to critique. The immediate argument of this chapter is that the Ottomans preserved the rule of law as well as any other dynasty had done, and that their *qānūn*ic intervention – effectively, sultanic administrative regulations – was largely deployed to serve this end. When all is said and done, the Ottomans and their *qānūn*ic intervention remained within the constitutional boundaries that Māwardī had drawn half a millennium earlier.

A necessary further implication of this chapter is that legal change does not have a relationship of *logical entailment or concurrence* with constitutional structures, that not every legal change amounts to a constitutional change, and that modern scholarship has on the whole confused the two (as it has confused, among other things, regal paraphernalia with actual constitutional practices and functional constitutional divisions).[112] The chapter will further argue, in

112 Much of Orientalist scholarship on royal power and executive authority unduly rely on regal titles and royal descriptors (on coins and in annals) to analyze actual configurations of political claims to authority and power. It must be said that this is a risky exercise since titles may not have a necessary relationship with the weight of these claims. For a study that allots excessive importance to titles and the like, see Patricia Crone and Martin Hinds,

preparation for chapter 12, that even constitutional structures have no necessary relationship with the quality of the law. Which is to say that when we study the law it is not necessarily the same thing as when we study constitutional arrangements, although elements of one field may be organically connected with elements in the other. Within this distinction, the present book locates its interests squarely in the constitutional domain. Finally, and in connection with the narrative of "Ottoman exceptionalism," chapter 10, and indirectly chapter 11, attempt to show that the Ottoman conception of constitutional organization was continuous with its Mamlūk counterpart, an argument that weighs heavily against the theories of Mongol dynastic (i.e., executive) overreach.

Constituting on its own Part III of the book, chapter 12 delves into the questions of sovereignty and biopower, attempting to transcend the conventional limitations in the study of constitutionalism, and the more limited and narrow questions that have traditionally inhabited the field. Neither a full account of the rule of law nor a robust narrative of the separation of power, nor even both together, can afford a proper, sufficient understanding of governance or of the quality of it – the quality of governance being the essence and *raison d'être* of erecting constitutional structures in the first place.[113] We know all too well that rule of law can easily become not only rule by law but also a regime of genocide or Apartheid, or, in certain cases, both. This basic truism has escaped the recognition of Orientalist scholarship, which continues to pick at the rudiments of Islamic constitutional and political phenomena, without asking the analytical questions that matter most. The defining parameters of this scholarship involve the question of whether or not sultanic administrative law complemented, revised, or superseded Sharīʿa's law. There has so far been no interrogation of the quality of this supposed intervention, of its sources, intentions, social effects, or distinctive modus vivendi. This quality is all the more important given the dominance of the Sharīʿa as the supreme law of the land.

At the heart of constitutional structures and rule of law stands the ultimate question of sovereignty. For this is the highest category of thought and action which determines the form and content, the quality and quantity, the meaning and even teleology of what it means to have, or to speak of, a constitutional structure in a polity, of a law that rules. Sovereignty is the foundation and vision that bestows on the modalities of rule and governance their existential meaning

God's Caliph; for a study that focuses on royal rituals of inauguration to describe "sacral power," see Marsham, *Rituals of Islamic Monarchy*. In regard to titles and regal appellations and paraphernalia, see also Yilmaz, *Caliphate Redefined*; Al-Azmeh, *Muslim Kingship*.

113 See n. 60, above.

and their quality of life. Chapter 12 therefore delves into these themes, and interrogates, inter alia, the Islamic system in terms of the Foucauldian theory of biopower in order to widen the scope of constitutional inquiry. The chapter is also as much *heuristic and methodological, since it aims to show the extent to which the investigation of Islamic constitutional forms in modern scholarship are shackled by cultural biases and liberal political anxieties.* Yet, the substantive thrust of the chapter must not be underestimated. It compares the liberal and Islamic constitutional orders with a view to assessing their weaknesses and strengths, each on its own terms. Woven into but implicit in this discussion is a rejection of one of the fundamental premises of modern scholarship on Islamic governance, namely, what I have called the theology of progress.[114] The idea that we know better than those who preceded us how to do things, including how to govern ourselves, is assuredly not taken for granted.

Before concluding, a word about the best way to read this book, a word by now familiar to my readers. It is clear from the foregoing that this book is an expansion and deepening of one of the most central themes that my last four books[115] dealt with, but did not offer the kind of extensive constitutional argument necessary to put to rest the ideological and highly flawed scholarship that has dominated the field for over a century. And it is in the nature of ongoing projects to be self-referential, in the specific sense that different parts of the larger argument must often be connected together and be made to support each other for the whole to make sense. The present book demands knowledge of a rich background expounded in these earlier books, especially *Sharīʿa* (2009), *The Impossible State* (2013), and *Restating Orientalism* (2018). For example, of particular importance is the explicatory device of Muslim/Islamic habitus that inhabits the present work from start to finish. However much I tried to articulate the nature of this habitus, it remains the case that much more can be said of it, despite the length of the present volume.

Finally, the reader will note that this book is laden with theoretical discussions, without which no critical history can be written. I have opted to offer a general theoretical account in this Introduction, followed, throughout the book, by more specific accounts that are relevant to the particular discussions raised in the various chapters. Lumping all theoretical discussions in one chapter, one discrete place, would sever the analytical and critical connections

---

114 On this theology, see Hallaq, *Impossible State*, 14-1; Hallaq, *Restating Orientalism*, 34, 88, 107-12, 150-58, and passim (see Index under "progress"). See also ch. 12, n. 129.

115 Namely: (1) *Sharīʿa: Theory, Practice, Transformation*; (2) *The Impossible State*; (3) *Restating Orientalism*; and (4) *Reforming Modernity*.

between textual analysis and the immediacy of these theoretical considerations. The reader who opts to peruse the various chapters without a particular order should be aware that the chapters are theoretically – and substantively[116] – interdependent. The best reading therefore is one that follows the sequential order of the book.

116 In terms of substantive (not theoretical) interdependence, it is particularly advisable to read chapters 9-11 in an orderly sequence.

Part I

CONSTITUTIONALISM IN THE POST-FORMATIVE PERIOD

Chapter 1

The Philosophical Foundations of Governance

I

For months during the year 421/1035, the fifty-seven-year-old ʿAlī b. Ḥabīb al-Māwardī listened to a junior scholar read back to him his own book *Adab al-Dīn wal-Dunyā* (*ADD*).[1] This was a method of simultaneously authenticating and authorizing the transmission of what must have been a new composition by Māwardī. True, the process of authoring a text, teaching it, and engaging in the pedagogical modalities of transmission and authentication represented educational acts, but such acts also constituted modes of worship (*taʿabbud*), a technology of the self that involved routinized praxis. The effect of such intentional, methodical, and iterated performance was the production of embodiment, a set of practices whose purpose is to align the body and mind and make them work in tandem, as a single unit. The idea was not only to align practice with knowledge and theory but also to allow practice and praxis to inform and deepen theoretical knowledge.[2]

1 "Reading back" to a scholar his own book was a form of textual certification that bestowed on the "reader" or the student the authority to transmit the work to others. *ADD* was published twice, with different titles and editions: Māwardī, *Adab al-Dunyā wal-Dīn* (2005); Mawardi, *Adab al-Dīn wal-Dunyā* (2013). I have used the latter edition as my standard reference, although, when suspecting a problem in my edition, I have consulted the other for comparative purposes. See *ADD*, 18, 37. It must be the case that *Adab al-Dīn wal-Dunyā* is the proper word-order of the title, as the exposition in the book of matters of *dīn* always comes before that of *dunya*. It is also the case that this is the order that Māwardī employs when speaking of the two concepts in conjunction, and when all things are equal; this is in addition evident in other works of his, e.g., *TN*, 44.

2 Mauss, "Techniques of the Body."

The connections between so-called theory and practice were entirely dialectical; each was deemed both cause and effect of the other.[3] This technological habituation in turn defined what was known as *adab*, a matrix of disciplined human behavior that enveloped and shaped not only the legal and political fields, but also social groupings at large.[4] Put more concisely, *adab* constituted the rules and modalities of conduct that governed the self and others. *Adab* served as both the foundation and the organizing structure of sociality and knowledge of the Happy Middle, where extremes are used to locate the context-specific, relative, moderate yet ideal middle ground. At the same time, *adab* was also eminently political; it did not just encompass the domain of institutional political management, but also undergirded the entire social psychology of governance. *Adab* was not only indispensable for rulers in their political management (*tadbīr*), but also a reflection of their reason and rational competence.[5] A ruler without rational competence will not last long. *Adab* thus has a concurrent and necessary relationship not only to the faculty of reason but also to the success and longevity of rule, to the ability to develop the capacity for just rule (*ʿadl*) and compassion, and to avert harmful acts towards oneself and the others.[6]

Māwardī's *ADD* is therefore as much a political treatise as it is *adab*-grounded, "religious" or "spiritual." *It is in fact a positive account*[7] *of the foundations and workings of Muslim society, sociology, economy, and polity, with extensive and intensive attention to the formation of individual subjectivity as the foundation for all the elements listed above, those that made Islam during his era what it was.* It is also, strictly speaking, of a wider political significance than his celebrated *al-Aḥkām al-Sulṭāniyya* (*AS*), effectively a technical work of political and legal administration intended to outline the separate yet constitutionally interconnected units of government. It would even be correct, I think, to characterize the latter as derivative of

3 On this dialectic, see Hallaq, *Reforming Modernity*.

4 For an informative background, see Kia, "Lingering with Adab"; for the range of *adab* practices, see Ghazālī, *al-Adab fil-Dīn*, 152 ff.

5 Shayzarī, *Nahj*, 80.

6 Shayzarī, *Nahj*, 80: "*Iftaqara al-maliku ilayhi [i.e., adab] ḍarūratan, li-taṣdura ʿanhu taṣārīfa al-tadbīri fī al-mamlakati ʿalā qānūni al-ʿadli al-ladhī bi-hi dawāmu al-mamlakati.... wa-qīla al-adabu ṣūratu al-ʿaqli, fa-man lā adaba la-hu lā ʿaqla la-hu, wa-man lā ʿaqla la-hu lā siyāsata la-hu, wa-man lā siyāsata la-hu lā mulka la-hu....*"

7 On positive statements as compared to factual and normative propositions, see the conclusion to this chapter.

the former, just as it is equally a derivative of *Tashīl al-Naẓar* (*TN*), another work of Māwardī on politics and governance. To put the matter differently, *AS* should be subsumed under *TN*, and both should in turn be subsumed under *ADD*. This subsumption is justified by the fact that *AS* is substantively, methodologically, and philosophically derivative of *TN*, while the latter is a derivative, on the same grounds, of *ADD*.

On yet another level, we can also describe these three works from the crucial standpoint of subject formation, whereby *ADD* and the first part of *TN* articulate an ideal subjective constitution of the human that inhabits the juridical and constitutional architecture of *AS*. Indeed, *AS*'s constitutional architecture depends on the generalized form of particular subjectivity that inhabits it; which is another way of saying that this very type of subjectivity is presupposed by the text's constitutional mapping.

ADD is therefore a socio-political, psycho-political, and constitutional treatise, all at once. It offers a sociology of politics, a sociology of religious formation, and a sociology of subjective constitution. Yet, we must resist viewing the treatise in the same way we view written works in our modernity, works that reflect individualistic and atomized authorial sites. Like many works written and structured *within* the various Islamic disciplines, *ADD* deploys two significant features that combine to make it not only an authoritative work but also an expression of a powerful culmination of a discursive tradition that brings under its wings a wide range of disciplines, cumulative practices, and authoritative voices. There lies in this work at least three centuries worth of a discursive tradition, and as such one can confidently claim it to be a representative work of mainstream vision and practices of Islam.

Māwardī did not invent the considerable body of materials contained in his work but rather compiled them systematically in order to produce a narrative that captures much of the average thinking about the matters with which the treatise is concerned. The systematization is precisely what makes the tradition speak coherently, giving future generations of scholars and political thinkers and practitioners a handle on the relevant themes in it. By all indications, *AS* was of the same type, and precisely because of their ability to "capture" the discursive tradition and living habitus, the two works remained relevant and foundational for many centuries to come.

ADD also builds the foundations for the further exploration of the relationship between politics and ethics that is undertaken in *TN*, and for Māwardī's account of the public constitution of politics in *AS*. Thus, taken together, the three works navigate the entire spectrum of constitutional construction; they start from the subjective psycho-epistemic formation of the individual and end by mapping out the institutional and conceptual terrains of the political constitution. The civic order, the sets of networks that sustained life in the social domain, occupies the spectral space between these two spheres. As we will see in due course, this coherent but markedly macroscopic and horizontal conception of the human world-order is given its vertical equivalent in Ibn ʿArabī's *al-Tadbīrat al-Ilāhiyya*. The total sum of this discourse is a cosmological, even macrocosmic, narrative in which political management and governance are situated.

Yet, the phrase "political management and governance" does not imply carving out an autonomous and qualitatively segregated space for the political in the constitution of the human. Management and governance are integral to human life from start to finish; they begin with the individual and then expand to social groupings and political life. Governance is as much about government of the self, any self, as it is about rule and political administration. Māwardī's concern is precisely this: the proper cultivation of subjectivity that aims to perfect, to the farthest extent possible, the quality of life in both this world and in the hereafter, the *dīn* and *dunyā*. He leaves out nothing crucial for attaining this quality. The point of departure is an investigation of the individual – their faculty of reasoning, their self-cultivation, and their education. Next, he moves on to the larger scope of political management, only to return once more to the microscopic qualities of the individual, understood as the most particular unit of the whole. For Māwardī, the body politic is a conglomerate of distinct individuals who participate in the government of the self, and by way of this practice, also participate in the government of others.

The point of departure is also exquisitely microscopic and epistemological, centering the gaze on the individual's acquisition of *ʿilm* ("knowledge") through *ʿaql* ("reason"), the latter being the quality that is thought to distinguish humans from all other animals, but one that is predicated on the ability to differentiate between good and evil. His inquiry into knowledge and learning begins with an investigation of reason, the means of attaining knowledge. Reason, therefore, is not only important for understanding the world at large and our place in it, but also specifically foundational for ethical cultivation and all political thought and action. *ʿAql*, properly defined, is always ethical reason.

II

Unlike the curtailed modern conception of reason,[8] Māwardī's notion of reason is complex, betraying the detailed dissections and elaborations that were standard fare in Islamic writings, including those of the Ṣūfī masters.[9] Every virtue, Māwardī insists, must have a foundation (*uss*), and every *adab* must have a source or a spring from which it flows. This foundation or spring of practical ethics – since practical ethics constitutes *adab* – is nothing but reason itself (*ʿaql*). Reason is the wellspring (*yunbūʿ*) and starting point of religion, as well as its pillar and mainstay.[10] This is why when a Muslim attains majority, it is assumed that their reason has reached maturity, or at least has become complete (*bāligh*). At this point, the individual becomes compos mentis, fully competent in the eyes of the law, and likewise responsible and accountable for their actions. Reason is likewise the means by which the affairs of the world are managed and run, despite the differences and potential disagreements and conflicts that may ensue among people.[11] The empire of reason, in other words, is what makes *dīn*, indeed human life on Earth, possible. It is no wonder then that this understanding of the essential role of *ʿaql* and its central importance makes for the first substantive paragraph to open *ADD*, the preceding page or so being introductory.

If "reason is the mainstay of proper living and the measure of worship and faith,"[12] then it is through reason and reason alone that phenomena and the truth of reality (*ḥaqāʾiq al-umūr*) can be apprehended. Reason's monumental accomplishment is that it is the only faculty that distinguishes between good and evil, a quality exclusively belonging to humans.[13] Non-human animals, one suspects, could not be charged with the burden of this distinction between good and evil.

According to Māwardī, reason (*ʿaql*) operates at two distinct yet interconnected levels. The first level is the instinctual (*gharīzī*), the basis of all thinking.

8 I discuss the instrumental and instrumentalizing nature of modern rationality in *Restating orientalism*. A foundational text in this regard is Max Horkheimer and Theodor Adorno, *Dialectic of Enlightenment*.

9 See, for example, Muḥāsibī, *Kitāb Māʾiyyat al-ʿAql*; Tirmidhī, *Bayān al-Farq Bayna al-Ṣadr wal-Qalb wal-Fuʾād wal-Lubb*.

10 *ADD*, 41: "*Al-ladhī jaʿalahu Allāhu subḥānahu lil-dīni aṣlan wa-lil-dunyā ʿimādan.*"

11 *ADD*, 41: "*Wa-jaʿala [Allāhu] al-dunyā mudabbaratan bi-aḥkāmihi [i.e., bi-aḥkāmi al-ʿaqli] wa-allafa bi-hi bayna khalqihi maʿ ikhtilāfi himamihim wa-maʾāribihim, wa-tabāyuni aghrāḍihim wa-maqāṣidihim.*"

12 As a Prophetic report has it. See *ADD*, 41.

13 *ADD*, 42.

Reason, when fully developed, is the faculty that endows humans with the capacity of legal obligation, the one that makes them the bearers of responsibility, accountability, duty, and right. Before Māwardī, various thinkers and groups had defined reason in many ways, but Māwardī rejects all these definitions either entirely or partially. He prefers to define reason as the capacity to apprehend knowable things necessarily (*al-ʿilm bil-mudrakāt al-ḍarūriyya*), and this occurs in two possible ways. The first is through sense perception (*ḥawās*), such as seeing, hearing, smelling, etc. The second occurs by means of *a priori* knowledge (*mubtadaʾ fil-nufūs*),[14] such as innate knowledge of the Law of Noncontradiction, the Law of the Excluded Middle, or numerical axioms, such as "the number one is smaller than the number two."[15] Together, the capacities of sensory perception and *a priori* knowledge combine in the innate and natural faculty of thinking, which enables the bearer of reason to seek benefit and avert harm – another way of saying that reason is the intellectual capacity to distinguish between good and evil.

The second level is reason that is acquired (*muktasab*). It *normally* rides on the back of the first, instinctual layer. It is, in Māwardī's terms, the result or the effect (*natīja*) of instinctual reasoning. It occurs in the individual in two ways, the first being direct experience of worldly affairs; the more reason is used and developed, the sharper it becomes. In this sense, acquired reason is akin to a muscle in the body that all individuals possess. The more it is used, and used in a certain manner, the stronger it becomes, in that manner. Yet, Māwardī's qualification that this reason "normally" develops out of instinctual reason does not mean that it invariably does. Some people, he argues, never attain this so-called normality of acquired reason, in which case they would be deprived of virtue (*maslūb al-faḍāʾil*), because they are deemed imbeciles or dense.[16]

The second venue through which acquired knowledge occurs, seemingly at once entwined with and superadded to the first, is a natural endowment of keen intelligence and strong intuition. Māwardī acknowledges that some people are naturally endowed with stronger perceptual and intellectual faculties than others.[17] They are thus able to derive greater insight from lived experience. Continuing with our biological analogy, while all humans have biceps and triceps, some are *naturally* more endowed with strength than others, and

14 The passive form *mubtadaʾ* is of course intended to mean that *a priori* knowledge is involuntary and by definition innate.

15 *ADD*, 42-44.

16 *ADD*, 55.

17 *ADD*, 46-47.

the *result* (Māwardī's *natīja*) of training such superior muscles in naturally gifted individuals would be a physical strength that is distinctly superior to the strength of others.

Here we note that there is no confusion between *a priori* knowledge and the second type of acquired reason that Māwardī classifies as a natural endowment. All humans without infirmities possess *a priori* knowledge, but not all of them enjoy this knowledge or even knowledge acquired via sense perception equally. Māwardī means that an extraordinary or exceptional endowment with respect to sensory and/or *a priori* knowledge can lead to a greater capacity for rational thinking. This makes some people more talented or more qualified than others to perform certain tasks.

Māwardī observes that Muslim scholars disagree about whether acquired reason necessarily leads to virtue. Some argue that an individual's acquired reason does not necessarily increase or even correlate to their virtue. Indeed, many believe that acquired reason increases an individual's propensity toward "contrivance and wiliness" (*makr wa-dahā'*) – qualities deemed antithetical to rectitude and virtue. Their reasoning takes seriously the implications of the Platonic-Aristotelian Happy Middle, namely, that virtue is the moderated middle ground between two extreme attributes. With too much courage, for instance, an individual is at risk of acting rashly, stupidly, or even committing serious self-harm; too little courage amounts to cowardice and incompetence. The same goes for acquired intelligence: exceptional and therefore excessive rational abilities were likewise thought by some Muslim scholars to lead to contrivance and wiliness. But Māwardī disagrees with this logic of the mean, because he believes that setting a limit on rational acquisition reduces our competence to judge what the Happy Middle is in the first place. If we insist that a "moderate" acquired intelligence determines the measure of virtue, then we cannot be sure that our best judgment has been exercised. A robust rational faculty, on the other hand, can be more certain of the validity and soundness of that Middle.[18]

At first blush, there seems to be a contradiction in Māwardī's position on rational competence: in his view, all attributes except reason conform to the Principle of the Happy Middle. But we must resist the urge to view this as a contradiction. Indeed, Māwardī was not alone in this view, which was backed by both precedent and sound argument.[19]

18 *ADD*, 51-52.

19 See main text above, at n. 9.

In the Arabic language, the technical lingua franca of Māwardī's period – and long before and after – *ʿaql* was the technical term for reason. Etymologically, the term referred to the rope or bond used to fix a camel to an anchor to keep it from straying.[20] By definition, *ʿaql* is the faculty that restrains or curbs the self from drifting toward the passions and to base desires and interests (*hawā*, of which *shahwa* [desire] is a major drive).[21] *ʿAql*, therefore, is not of the same species as the faculty whose virtue is governed by the logic of the Happy Middle but the commander who decides how different attributes interact with each other and what forms and results they yield.[22] It is the engine, so to speak, that moves and propels an attribute on the spectrum between its two extremes, the faculty challenged with locating that Happy Middle. Yet, it is important to realize that the Happy Middle is neither a mathematical nor a mechanical measure, the quantitative fixed middle point on a finite line. Rather, the Happy Middle is relative and changes according to changes in circumstance. The Happy Middle between cowardice and perilous rashness takes one form on a battlefield and quite another in an aggressive encounter with a frail drunkard on the street.

ʿAql is thus an endowment, and a composite one at that. Humans are born with innate qualities of rationality and intelligence whose strength and power vary among individuals. This variety means that some people are more competent than others when it comes to acting rationally. This feature of social life is not only epistemologically relevant, but it also has an important political dimension. Yet, the epistemological story of reason does not end here. Its sequel – likewise bearing political implications – entails the presence of an antonym to reason, which I insist is a logical entailment. Just as the proposition "I encountered a mother on the street" logically entails children, reason entails an ontological other, namely, the passions. The *raison d'être* of *ʿaql*, a quintessentially restrained reason, is precisely to combat the passions and the base desires (*hawā*). There would be no *ʿaql* without the passions. Here the ethical component of *ʿaql* cannot be missed.

Māwardī sums up the matter by approvingly citing authoritative scholars who insisted that they would not be willing to describe someone as having

20 *ADD*, 44.

21 *ADD*, 66.

22 In *TN*, Māwardī seems to subscribe to the very theory of the opponents he rejects here, namely, that reason is no different from all other virtues and is the result of the Happy Middle. Here, he says: "*ʿAql* is the middle between cunning and stupidity" (*Al-ʿaql wāsiṭatun bayna al-dahāʾi wal-ghabāʾ*); *TN*, 17.

ʿaql unless that person possesses the qualities of being "good and an adherent to *dīn*" (*khayyiran dayyinan*), because these qualities constitute indubitable entailments and necessary effects of *ʿaql*.[23] This is why, as we will see later, the Islamic concept of *ʿilm* ("knowledge") was seen as the consequence of the operations of *ʿaql*. Properly speaking, *ʿilm* is *the knowledge of divine command in all the acts of goodness that it embodies and entails*.[24]

Hawā thus contrasts with and impedes *ʿaql*.[25] It brings out the worst attributes in individuals and leads them to commit harmful and blameworthy acts. It is said by some to be a demigod, worshiped by those people who let it rule over their lives.[26] In a sense, it is the gate via which base desires manifest themselves, precisely because it has the power to allow them to come to the fore. *Hawā* relates to opinions and beliefs, a theoretical grip on reality, but *shahwa*, desire, is sensory and is defined by the acquisitive drive toward bodily pleasure. *Shahwa* is the product and result (*natīja*) of *hawā*, not the other way around; it is *shahwa*'s root and source (*aṣl*).[27] *Hawā* is thus a type of *fitna*, a strife destructive of the soul, just as political *fitna* is a civil strife that is destructive of the social and political fabrics. It is a pathology (*dā'*) whose remedy (*dawā'*) is disobedience (*ʿiṣyān*).[28] Whether at the level of the self, or with respect to caliphal and sultanic rule, disobedience against the passions is disobedience against injustice, since injustice is the essence of the passions. In this worldview and discourse, disobedience does not start and end with politics and political life, but rather is grounded in deeper dimensions of the human psyche – in the constitution of individual subjectivity itself.

In this system, *hawā* is likewise a *sulṭān*, a power that grips and overwhelms the self (*nafs*).[29] *ʿAql* comes to the fore to restrain the rebellious self, to make it realize (*yushʿiruhā*) the dire consequences of its predilections. In good Ṣūfī/*zuhd* manner, Māwardī locates the site of passions in the self, the pliable agency that must be brought under the command of *ʿaql*.[30] Because the self is torn in

23 *ADD*, 54.
24 *ADD*, 71-76.
25 *ADD*, 59: "*Fa'ammā al-hawā, fa-huwa ʿan al-khyri ṣāddun wal-lil-ʿaqli muḍādd.*"
26 A widely circulating statement attributed to the Companion and exegete ʿAbd Allāh Ibn ʿAbbās. *ADD*, 59.
27 *ADD*, 66.
28 Stated as a Prophetic report. *ADD*, 59.
29 *ADD*, 61: "*Kāna al-hawā ghāliban.*"
30 *ADD*, 61, 62: "*Fa-idhā inqādat al-nafsu lil-ʿaqli bi-mā qad ushʿirat min ʿawāqibi al-hawā lam yalbath al-hawā an yaṣīra bil-ʿaqli mazjūran.*"

different directions, the challenge for humans is to control it by making *ʿaql* the guardian and overseer (*raqīb*) of the passions, a bulwark against them. In this context, the nascent Ṣūfī concept of *mujāhada* appears,[31] a concept with etymological and conceptual connections to the juristic *jihād*. Māwardī's *ADD* is peppered from beginning to end with references to the psychological states and technologies of the self that emerge in the early Ṣūfī writings by authors such as Sarrāj and Hujwīrī.[32] The archetypal master of Ṣūfism, al-Ḥasan al-Baṣrī (d. 110/728), appears here to authorize the Islamic universal maxim that the best *jihād* is the one deployed against *hawā*, in contradistinction with, and in preference to, the much less significant military *jihād* (often termed minor *jihād*).[33] But it must not escape us that *ADD* is so saturated with Ṣūfī and mystical (*zuhd*) notions and discursive strategies that it might even be considered the forerunner of the celebrated *Iḥyā' ʿUlūm al-Dīn*, a text that shares its repeated emphasis on *askesis*.[34]

If *ʿaql* is by definition the faculty that instructs against and averts *hawā*, then rationality means habituation in virtue, with virtue being the knowledge and practice of *dīn*, the normative values of so-called religion. This is precisely *ʿilm*, but *ʿilm* is not just any kind of knowledge. Knowledge is of sorts, some more beneficial than others, "although all of them are meritorious."[35] Yet, no single individual is able to attain every kind of knowledge, a proposition that Māwardī takes for granted. A philosopher was once asked, "Who can know all knowledges," to which he replied "All people," the implication being that it takes many to know all fields of knowledge. No one individual, however, can master them all, just as not all people are endowed with the same skill or talent. Māwardī's social theory of cooperation thus extends to knowledge, not only to crafts and trades. The most important of these "knowledges" is the "science of religion" (*ʿilm al-dīn*),[36] because it instructs individuals in the good and virtuous ways of living. *ʿIlm al-dīn* is practical ethics and sound conduct, two in one. *ʿAmal* (practice/praxis) without *ʿilm* is not only unremarkable, it is useless. This is why the Prophet is said to have declared that the virtues of

31 *ADD*, 61.

32 Sarrāj, *Kitāb al-Lumaʿ*; Hujwīrī, *Kashf al-Maḥjūb*. See also *ADD*, 164 and 168.

33 *ADD*, 62: Baṣrī said: "*Afḍalu al-jihādi jihādu al-hawā*". For various Prophetic Ḥadīths speaking of religious works and technologies of the self as acts superior to military *jihād*, see Tirmidhī, *al-Jāmiʿ al-Ṣaḥīḥ*, III, 564-87.

34 Ghazālī, *Iḥyā' ʿUlūm al-Dīn*, 876-994, 1101-33. On *askesis*, see McGushin, *Foucault's Askesis*; Foucault, *Hermeneutics of the Subject*; see also Hadot, *Philosophy as a Way of Life*.

35 *ADD*, 73.

36 On translating *dīn* as religion, see Introduction, n. 2.

ʿilm are superior to the virtues of worship, because as a knowledge, worship might have a limited or even stunted understanding of its own foundations, implications, or teleology. Worship as a technique, in other words, can have a narrow epistemological range because we can do things without understanding their full implications.

ʿIlm, on the other hand, encompasses both knowledge of reasons for worship and of the acts of worship themselves. The deeper this knowledge is, the more profoundly cosmological, metaphysical, and worldly one's understanding of the reasons for worship becomes. Which is to say that the more complete a knowledge is, the more cosmologically and metaphysically grounded it becomes. To know and understand phenomena well is to know how humans are situated in the world and to understand their place in it.

The total effects of this dialectic between knowledge and praxis amount to care of the self, which Māwardī properly labels *ṣiyānat al-nafs* (an exact translation of the concept). This care, in turn, is tantamount to subjecting oneself to the technologies of the self, a deliberate and self-conscious operation of the self on the self, a technique of producing the ethical subject. Care of the self, Māwardī asserts, is the root and "source of all virtues" (*aṣl al-faḍāʾil*).[37] *ʿIlm*, the only means to cultivate this care, is therefore considered an ethical asset across the board for everyone. Indeed, care of the self transects the diverse spectra of individual, collective, psychological, social, and political life. This idea is encapsulated in the adage that "If God wants to be good to people, he plants *ʿilm* in their kings, and regal power in their men of learning."[38] Likewise, "*ʿilm* guarantees the virtue of kings, because it checks them from committing injustice; shepherds them to wisdom; prevents them from doing harm; and renders them compassionate toward their subjects."[39] It is not without good reason that the Prophet stipulated that "the quest after *ʿilm* is a duty upon every Muslim."[40]

If *ʿilm* is the means to the care of the self, then it is the very function of religion: a set of instructions, obligations, and rights that lead to the

37 *ADD*, 77, 78.

38 *ADD*, 79: "*Qāla baʿḍu ʿulamāʾi al-salafi: 'Idhā arāda Allāhu taʿālā bil-nāsi khayran jaʿala al-ʿilma fī mulūkihim wal-mulku fī ʿulamāʾihim'.*"

39 *ADD*, 79: "*Al-ʿilmu ʿiṣmatu al-mulūki, liʾannahu yamnaʿuhum mina al-ẓulmi wa-yarrudduhum ilā al-ḥikmati, wa-yaṣudduhum ʿan al-adhiyyati, wa-yuʿaṭṭifuhum ʿalā al-raʿiyya.*"

40 *ADD*, 75: "*Ṭalabu al-ʿilmi farīḍatun ʿalā kulli muslim.*" This is to be coupled with the other pseudo but immensely popular tradition which stipulates that "*ʿIlm* is to be sought after even in China" (*uṭlubū al-ʿilma wa-law fil-Ṣīn*).

good life. God sent prophets with religious missions not out of his own need, but rather as an act of grace toward humans to protect and support their countless interests.[41] These interests are not limited to the affairs of this world, but also extend to their future well-being in the hereafter. The protection of these interests therefore entails a matrix of vertical and horizontal relations, a structured view of life in the widest sense of the term, in its worldly, spiritual, and cosmological dimensions. These are at once epistemological and ontological structures of interests, engulfing all aspects of human and non-human interests. *Dīn* ("religion") is therefore a structured and disciplined way of living the good life, and *ʿilm* is the only path to its discovery. This is why the language of substantive law was called *fiqh*, namely, understanding (*fahm*) divine speech and developing, from evidence (*dalīl*), modes of reasoning in order to cultivate knowledge of practice optimally (*ijtihād*).[42]

As we have seen, *ʿaql*, with its layered operations, is the endowed rational capacity to understand things in the world. Since man cannot be God by definition, and is only derivative of the Omniscient, a further means to attain the true path of *dīn* is necessary. This means is revelation, both Qur'ānic and prophetic. Reason must be followed wherever revelation does not hinder it, whereas revelation must be followed in whatever reason does not rule out. Revelation will never dictate a matter which reason precludes, a principle equally applicable to reason *vs.* revelation.[43] This is why religious obligation, the task of individuals, does not apply except to those who are of sound and fully developed mind: madmen, imbeciles, and minors are exempted from religious obligation on the basis of this criterion.

Within this understanding of religion, the prophets came to convey and explain the divine message. In Islam, meanwhile, the ulama came to explicate and elaborate both God's Message as well as the Prophetic investment.[44] The ulama are given their name precisely because they are the custodians of *ʿilm*, deriving their title from what they do best. And what they do best begins

41 *ADD*, 147: "*Sharraʿa [Allāhu] lahum dīnahu li-ghayri ḥājatin daʿathu ilā taklīfihim... wa-innamā qaṣada nafʿahum tafaḍḍulan min-hu ʿalayhim, ka-mā tafaḍḍala bi-mā lā yuḥṣā ʿadadan min niʿamihi.*"

42 Mārdīnī, *al-Anjum al-Zāhirāt*, 80.

43 *ADD*, 147: "*Li'anna al-sharʿa lā yaridu bi-mā yamnaʿu min-hu al-ʿaqlu, wal-ʿaqlu lā yuttabaʿu fī-mā yamnaʿu min-hu al-sharʿ.*" A *locus classicus* of this doctrine may be found in Taqiyy al-Dīn Ibn Taymiyya's *Dar' Taʿāruḍ al-ʿAql wal-Naql*. See also El-Tobgui, *Ibn Taymiyya on Reason and Revelation*.

44 *ADD*, 148.

with enshrining the technologies of the self, which are the means to instill discipline and care of the self, themselves in turn the means to achieve the benefits intended by religion. The connection between the ulama, the cultivators of divine *ʿilm* (i.e., the law), and technologies of ethical self-formation is constantly made in the Islamic sources, acquiring its paradigmatic force even at the Qur'ānic level. As we will see in detail in chapter 4, the Qur'ānic command to cultivate the *ʿilm* of the law was specifically addressed to those who qualify as *rabbāniyyūn*, the educators (*rabbā, yurabbī*) responsible for cultivating *ʿilm*ic values "in the young before the old."[45]

The technologies of the self constitute complementary techniques that stand in a mutually dialectical relationship, each enhancing and propping the other. Prayer, for instance, establishes the worshipper's bonds of authority with and toward the Creator, since authority is the covenantal and quintessential foundation of their relationship. Fasting, on the other hand, is a practice for regulating, training, and disciplining the self, but it also serves as a socializing mechanism, helping to cultivate relationships of civility and empathy within communal existence. Furthermore, fasting not only actively precipitates the knowledge that man is ephemeral, needy, and contingent, one who can easily perish from lack of sustenance; it is also a bodily technique that generates awareness of the suffering of other humans who are hungry. Fasting therefore fosters social cohesion, solidarity, and thus community. Indeed, fasting is not just a spiritual practice; *it is no less than a socially and politically organizing principle*. It generates compassion, not only in the self of the performer, but also in the social body, since fasting yields a cumulative compassion in the communal fabric.

Now, alms taxes come to complete this process, with the well-to-do obliged to attend to the needs of the have-nots. Combined, the practices of fasting and alms taxes generate assistance, consolation, compassion, solidarity, and hope – all of which are intended to counter disconnection, envy, and hatred in the community. When hope is lacking and need is increasing, envy and hatred ensue, only to destroy the social fabric.[46] Fasting and alms taxes are, at once,

45 Bukhārī, *Ṣaḥīḥ*, I, 50.

46 *ADD*, 151: "*Fa-kāna fī ījābihā [i.e., al-zakāt] muwāsātun lil-fuqarā'i wa-maʿūnatun li-dhawī al-ḥājāti takuffuhum ʿan al-baghḍā'i wa-tamnaʿuhum ʿan al-taqāṭuʿi, wa-tabʿathuhum ʿalā al-tawāṣuli, li'anna al-āmila wāṣulun wal-rājiya hā'ibun, wa-idha zāla al-amalu, wa-inqataʿa al-rajā'u wa-ishtaddat al-ḥājatu, waqaʿat al-baghḍā'u wa-ishtadda al-ḥasadu wa-waqaʿat al-ʿadāwa*." Māwardī of course does not articulate the matter in terms of "class struggle" but he is aware of conflicts that result from economic inequality, as well as of the political implications of these conflicts.

cardinal obligations of religion and sustainers of political life, for there can be no politics without the Community, the differentiated equivalent of what we now call society.[47] No wonder then that the history of Islam from the start and down to the eighteenth century has been defined by considerable institutions and extensive practices of alms-giving and charitable endowments, all of which are entwined, as the five Pillars of Religion readily show, with praxis of dietary regulation and religious works.

It is worth noting briefly here that these complementary techniques of cultivating the self are standard fare, plainly but lucidly elaborated by Māwardī within the context of what makes for "public welfare." Yet, any discerning reader of this sage cannot fail to realize that these techniques are enshrined in a discourse that we have come to identify with Ṣūfī doctrine. If a major accomplishment of Ghazālī's *Iḥyā' 'Ulūm al-Dīn* was the entwining of Sharīʿa and Ṣūfism in a single mold, then *ADD* has preceded the *Iḥyā'* in this respect, though admittedly on a smaller scale. *ADD* and the entirety of Māwardī's philosophy of politics and sociality rest on these foundations, whether we call them Ṣūfī or not. But to say that Māwardī elaborated a "*juristic* doctrine" of governance and constitutional politics is not only to fail to see the import of *adab* as politics and Sharīʿa as ethics; it is also to entirely miss the pietistic and Ṣūfī-like foundations of his intellectual and political discourse. The so-called "juristic doctrine" of politics was never just juristic in the sense Orientalists made it to be, since its first articulator and systematizer, Māwardī, was knee-deep in the ethically and ascetically (*zuhd*) saturated discursive tradition.[48] This is evident in a section of his work that treats the subject of *riyāḍat al-nafs*, what Foucault called technologies of the self, a section that finds a parallel in an identically titled chapter in Ghazālī's *Iḥyā'*.[49]

The general theme of this section is the cultivation of a worldview as well as techniques of ethical self-formation that are grounded and cast in a *praxis* of ascetic modes of existence. The sum total of this care of the self is nothing

47 See chapter 12 for a "state-in-society" argument. I maintain that just as there were no states before modernity, there were no societies either. What we now know as "society" is almost entirely the product of the modern state. Strictly speaking, therefore, it is anachronistic to apply these terms to the period prior to the sixteenth century, whether in Europe or anywhere else.

48 Bringing in *zuhd* is intended to enhance the notion that "asceticism" in Islam possessed different genealogies and forms, extending over a wide spectrum of movements and personalities. Ṣūfism was the chief form of asceticism but by no means the only one. For these varied voices, see Reid's useful *Law and Piety*.

49 *ADD*, 178-207, but also on many pages preceding this section. Cf. Ghazālī, *Iḥyā'*, 929-63.

short of an ambitious quest to attain freedom, a kind of freedom that has become a stranger in modern conceptions, a freedom that heavily depends on the deliberate and structured behavioral modalities of detachment from worldly things and worldly attractions.[50] For after all, these are the techniques that permit the *ʿaql*, the mobilizing power and mechanizer of *ʿilm*, to win the war over the passions and the base desires of the self (*hawā/shahwa*), with the ultimate aim of *freeing* it, the self, from their command and tyranny. Reason and freedom are integral to each other.[51]

III

We recall that in Māwardī's theory of reason, the endowment of *ʿaql* varies among individuals, whether at the level of sensory perception, *a priori*, or acquired knowledge. People are never identical, and therefore never equal. This is the first cardinal theory that formed the basis of much Islamic (not to mention Greek) thinking, whether in the Sharʿī, Ṣūfī, or political domain.[52]

Māwardī begins his theorization of sociality with the postulate that, among all living creatures, humans are the neediest of each other. Many animal species are individually independent and can survive on their own. "Man is created in nature to need its own kind," an "essential quality inherent in his core being."[53] This distinctive quality stems from the fact that humans lack self-sufficiency, and since their inability to live autonomously is the greatest among living creatures, then their incapacity or incompetence is the greatest of all. This is

50 *ADD*, 178 ff., 185 ff., 192 ff.

51 Māwardī's discourse, being generally representative of mainstream Islamic discourse on reason and rationality, invites us to seriously reconsider the modern discourse on freedom as constrained and even lopsided, but mostly as a universalized and hegemonic notion that has largely succeeded in eliminating other concepts of freedom that were once themselves paradigmatic. For more on these two (schematically) competing concepts of freedom/liberty, as expressed by Isaiah Berlin, see Hallaq, *Reforming Modernity*, 168-69; and Berlin, "Two Concepts of Liberty."

52 The implications of this theory have yet to be addressed in scholarship, even at the most fundamental level. For one, this theory bars from Islam the idea of a "blindfolded lady of justice," which would be offensive to the Islamic sense of justice. On this, see my lecture "Philology and the New Human: Reflections on the Study of Muslims and Others," delivered at the University of Oxford (May 21, 2022).

53 *ADD*, 211: "*Al-insānu aktharu ḥājatan min jamīʿi al-ḥayawāni li'anna mina al-ḥayawāni mā yastaqillu bi-nafsihi ʿan jinsihi, wal-insānu maṭbūʿun ʿalā al-iftiqāri ilā jinsihi, wal-istiʿānatu bi-hi ṣifatun lāzimatun li-ṭabʿihi wa-khilqatun qā'imatun fī jawharihi.*" See also *TN*, 3-4.

the second cardinal theory of the original state of nature, constituting the first step of Māwardī's social and political thought, having been adopted later by Ibn Khaldūn (d. 808/1406),[54] and made a premier theory grounding Islamic political thought at large.

(It should be said here that Ibn Khaldūn's debt to Māwardī remains thus far largely unacknowledged in modern scholarship, not only in regards to this theory of sociality, but also much more. Arguably, nearly all central elements in Ibn Khaldūn's celebrated theses appear to be heavily indebted to Māwardī's writings,[55] irrespective of whether or not this latter is the sole or ultimate originator of these ideas [which, I wager, he is not]. For instance, we will see in due course that the building blocks of the concept of *ʿaṣabiyya*, central to Ibn Khaldūn's thought, are to be found in Māwardī as well. The implications of this evolving genealogy of concepts in Islam are quite serious, because much of the balance in Ibn Khaldūn's brilliant ideas may, after all, revert to

54 Articulated mainly in the first section of the first chapter of the *Muqaddima*, 122 ff.

55 Much of the Khaldūnian elements are found in Māwardī's *ADD*, with the single notable exception of the cyclical dynastic change and the stages of rise and decline within the *dawla*. But these latter are indeed found in a key paragraph in *TN*, 157. There Māwardī says: "Know that the *dawla* begins [in its first stages] with uncultivated instincts and extreme violence because this subdues people into obedience, then in its middle [stages] it becomes soft and virtuous, because rule had taken firm roots and tranquility reigned; thereafter, toward the end [of its life], oppression and weakness become widespread because of general collapse and lack of resolve/firmness.... Just as the *dawla* begins with power and ends with weakness, it also begins with loyalty and ends with treachery, because [with] loyalty [things] are raised, and with treachery dispersed": "*Wa- ʿlam anna al-dawlata tabtadi'u bi-khushūnati al-ṭibāʿi wa-shiddati al-baṭshi, li-tusriʿa al-nufūsu ilā badhli al-ṭāʿati, thumma tatawassaṭu bil-līni wal-istiqāmati li-istiqrāri al-mulki wa-ḥuṣūli al-diʿati, thumma tukhtamu bi-intishāri al-jūri wa-shiddati al-ḍaʿfi li-intiqāḍi al-amri wa-qillati al-ḥazmi.... wa-kamā tubtada'u al-dawlatu bil-quwwati wa-tukhtamu bil-ḍaʿfi ka-dhālika tubtada'u bil-wafā'i wa-tukhtamu bil-ghadri li-anna al-wafā'a mushayyidun wal-ghadra musharridun.*" All this, it must be said, gives credence to Cornel Fleischer's argument that the "Khaldūnian" theory is not unique to Ibn Khaldūn, and that the theory's general tenor permeated Islamic culture through and through (and I argue as early as the fourth/tenth or fifth/eleventh century). See Fleischer, "Royal Authority" (though a number of second-order assertions in this article are inaccurate). See also Hamid, "Al-Mawardi's Theory."

Yet, there is an even more convincing argument in favor of the embeddedness of the "Khaldūnian" ideas in Islamic political culture and social theory (as expounded, for instance, in Māwardī's *ADD*). Both works are effectively extended "annotations" of the modalities of the Circle of Justice (see Ibn Khaldūn, *Muqaddima*, 30; for Māwardī, see ch. 1, n. 102), as are almost all others dealing with the subject of governance (see, e.g., *TAJ*, 70; Ibn al-Mibrad, *Īḍāḥ*). In fact, one can comfortably say that Islamic political theory, constitutional thought, social theory, and social contract theory are all intertwined with, and implicitly "annotations" of the conception and logic of the Circle.

the common and mainstream Islamic traditions, not only in *ta'rīkh* [history], but also in *adab*, Sharīʿa, Ṣūfī ethics, and philosophy.)

Be that as it may, Māwardī continues to build his account of sociality and political association, stating that for humans to sustain themselves, they are bound by the natural need of cooperation, this also being a requisite to fulfill the requirements of *dīn*, for this "world is the abode of obligation and praxis."[56] He quickly averts a possible misunderstanding by remarking that there is no contradiction between this quest after worldly interests and the modalities of ascetic life he has prescribed as integral to the technologies of ethical self-cultivation. Ascetic modes of existence are still required, but to a limited extent; and the quest after worldly interests must be moderated. This is quite characteristic of his worldview in regard to almost all aspects of life, for his *ADD* and *TN* may be deemed together as an extensive engagement with the mainstream concept of moderation, what I have called the Happy Middle. Desire for the material world is blameworthy, as is indulgence in its bounties. Desire and indulgence entail the quest for that which is in excess of what one needs, a line of separation between the proper ascetic norms and their negative opposites. This is all summed up, as usual, in a piercing Prophetic report: "The most virtuous amongst you [Muslims] is not he who abandons worldly desires for the interests in the hereafter, nor he who does the opposite; rather it is he who takes [a bit of] this and [a bit of] that."[57]

Differences between and among individuals does not permit equal status, self-sufficiency, or happiness across the board. In all of these and in many other aspects of life, people differ from each other in both nature and circumstance, at times quite drastically. But it is these very differences that make their cooperation and group solidarity indispensable, even of the essence, to the nature of human cohabitation. Yet, this cohabitation is assumed to enjoy a particular quality, one that is taken for granted not only in Māwardī's thought but in the entire spectrum of Islamic juristic and Ṣūfist conception of sociality and communal existence. This quality is social equilibrium, where communal interaction yields a balance of give-and-take relations. Difference creates cooperation and mutual assistance, for the hand that is extended in need meets the extended hand that seeks to alleviate and relieve.[58] Socio-

56 *ADD*, 213: "*Al-dunyā jaʿalaha [Allahu] dāra taklīfin wa-ʿamal.*"

57 *ADD*, 213-14: "*Laysa khayrukum man taraka al-dunyā lil-ākhirati, wa-lā al-ākhirata lil-dunyā, lākinna khayrakum man akhadha min hādhihi wa-hādihi.*"

58 *ADD*, 215: "*Wa-idhā tabāyanū wa-ikhtalafū, ṣārū mu'talifīna bil-muʿāwanati mutawāṣilīna bil-ḥājati, li'anna dha al-ḥājati waṣūlun wal-muḥtāju ilayhi mawṣūlun.*"

economic interdependence and its consequence, cooperation, therefore constitute the original state of nature, not, for instance, freedom, as Locke, Rousseau, even Hobbes envisaged.

Having established his postulates about human exigencies of cooperation, Māwardī brings the charge of his ethical theory to bear upon the second prong of his concern, the affairs of this life, the *dunyā* (the first prong being *dīn*). This is where politics is situated, buffered, and contextualized. There are six pillars (*qawāʿid*) on which these affairs rest, the first of which is *al-dīn al-muttabaʿ*, applied religion, that which is put to practice, implemented, and followed as a set of techniques. The qualifier *muttabaʿ* appears to safeguard against, and exclude, religions that preach and instruct as a matter of ideal, without this entailing praxis. It is religion of *ʿilm* without *ʿamal*, without a unity or dialectic between the two spheres.

"Religion" in this encompassing meaning deters the self from following the passions, engendering conscientiousness and overseeing the self in an otherwise unchecked environment. There is nothing more powerful than religion in creating this fortified self,[59] what Pierre Hadot has called in a somewhat different context the "Inner Citadel." This is perhaps the very meaning and full implication of Māwardī's qualifier *al-muttabaʿ*, which is not just a matter of applying religion as a system of ritual and symbol, but rather as technologies of training and managing the self as a matter of daily living and systematic practice and praxis, the latter being the mechanism of maintenance dedicated to this "Citadel." Derivatively, "religion" is also the management of the others, for this competence is realized only after the proper management of the self is achieved. Applied religion therefore is the strongest pillar for achieving the good in this world, for creating the most efficient means for maintaining orderly life and safety.[60] Which is why God never left his human creation (*khalquhu*) without the endowment of Sharʿī obligation and religious belief, for these are the means by which humans are unified into communities that are not split asunder by the forces of the passions.[61]

The second pillar for achieving the best form of living is *sulṭān qāhir*, a ruler wielding coercive power. This is of course consistent with the Sunni political doctrine that the caliph is the deputy of the Prophet in the conduct of political matters, a doctrine that had already been enshrined as an integral part of Sunni political doctrine and practice by the middle of the second/eighth

59 *ADD*, 217: "*Wa-hādhihi umūrun lā yūṣalu bi-ghayri al-dīni ilayhā.*"

60 *ADD*, 217: "*Fa-kāna al-dīnu ajdā al-umūri nafʿan fī intiẓāmihā wa-salāmatihā.*"

61 Again, compare with Ibn Khaldūn, *Muqaddima*, 124-25.

century.[62] I said "consistent" in the sense that the Prophet's main mission was the installation and spread of religion, since he was the Messenger of God. If "applied religion" is the function of Prophethood, then political governance is the function of the caliph or his deputy, the sultan, whose coercive might has the effect of bringing people together under one banner. He protects the domains, suppresses oppressors, and curbs crime and nefarious activity, all of which are deemed forms of injustice (*ẓulm*).

The sultan's function and in fact *raison d'être* is to act as an all-encompassing deterrent (*rādiʿ maliyy*) against *ẓulm*. "The prevention of *ẓulm* is accomplished through four means that have no fifth to them: reprimanding reason, disciplining religion, a deterring sultan, or sheer disability."[63] The most effective among the four is sultanic power since reason and religion lack a coercive edge. This is the meaning of the rhymed Prophetic report that "God deters by means of the *sulṭān* more than he does by means of the Qur'ān."[64] The report comes to complement another: "The *sulṭān* is God's shadow on Earth; to him all the oppressed address themselves."[65] The metaphor of "God's shadow" stands for God's coercive power deployed to enforce God's just law.

Translated into earthly language, however, coercive power is a knife that cuts both ways, only one of which is admissible. In a crucial paragraph, Māwardī states that since the *raison d'être* of the sultan is to protect and defend religion, to repel those who aim to distort, manipulate, or corrupt it, he is regarded as the sanctified representative and defender of these interests. Which is to say that once he ceases to represent and defend these interests, the "hearts of the believers" would not "coalesce" in accepting him, in "obeying him." In such cases, "the sultan has no power of stay, peace recedes, and he would be

62 A doctrine articulately expressed as early as the middle of the second/eighth century by ʿUbayd Allāh b. Ḥasan al-ʿAnbarī. See Wakīʿ, *Akhbār*, II, 97 ff. See also Marsham, *Rituals*, 11, which makes the plausible argument that as a political model, the Prophet emerged only with the ʿAbbāsids, whereas the Umayyads resorted to "articulations of Arabian monotheism" instead. This thesis is consistent with the evolution of the Prophetic authority as formative of the law during the first half of the second/eighth century, reaching further heights by the end of it (with the likes of Ibn Idrīs al-Shāfiʿī, d. 204/820). On the evolution of meanings around the term *khalīfa*, see al-Qadi, "The Term Khalīfa;" and its sequel, Liew, "Caliphate of Adam." For an updated general survey, see Yücesoy, "Caliph and Caliphate."

63 *ADD*, 218: "*Wa-hādhihi al-ʿillatu al-mmāniʿatu mina al-ẓulmi lā takhlū min aḥadi arbaʿati ashyā'in: immā ʿaqlun zājirun, aw dīnun ḥājizun aw sulṭānun rādiʿun aw ʿajzun ṣāddun, lam tajid la-hā khāmisan yaqtarinu bi-hā*." I have opted here to translate the meaning rather than the literary form, since the adjectives in the four qualities have a basic common connotation.

64 *ADD*, 218-19: "*Inna Allāha la-yazaʿu bil-sulṭāni akthara mā yazaʿu bil-Qur'ān*."

65 *ADD*, 218-19: "*Inna al-sulṭāna ẓillu Allāhi fil-arḍi, ya'wī ilayhi kullu maẓlūm*."

deemed an agent of oppression and corruption."[66] The core and most essential functions of the sultan then amount to the promotion and defense of "*dīn*," the Islamic concept of so-called religion.

But what does "*dīn*" mean in the functional sultanic context? Or – put differently and without predetermining the boundaries of function – what is the positive range of the sultanic functions? Māwardī addresses this question in *AS* as well, giving there a more extensive list than he offered in *ADD*, although the latter contains elements not found in the former.

The first element of defining the sultanic functions is *ḥifẓ al-dīn* (preservation of religion). This requirement, apparently universal in its sway,[67] is found in both texts, with the same language. *AS* continues by saying that this preservation must proceed according to the way religion has been established and sanctioned by the predecessors.[68] Politically, this is intended to reassert the supremacy of the Sharīʿa over the interpretive and legislative impulses of the ruler, a constitutional act of the first order and one that Māwardī as well as every other Muslim writer insisted on. The choice of the term *dīn* appears deliberate, conveying the force of Sharīʿa as habitus and culture, as a fully lived experience. Rulership is always grounded and located in divine legal will, defined and bounded by it in every way. It is a foundational doctrine that seems to have been the subject of consensus from early times. Al-Qāsim b. Sallām (d. 224/838) had already noted the normative power of this doctrine in the early Community, having dominated without dissenting voices.[69]

The further implication of this doctrine is that the ruler is not to initiate any divergent interpretation of the Sharīʿa and must not let any other person or group engage in it either. Should there be such a heretical group that challenges this *dīn*, then the sultan must clarify, presumably with the help of his ulama's persuasive argumentative power, the tenets of Islam, explaining to the rebels the ways in which he deems them wrong.[70] Then, according to the established rules of the Sharīʿa, and if they do not repent, they must be tried according to the law. This way, the *umma* (Community), with its *dīn*, will be

---

66 *ADD*, 220: "*Kamā anna al-sulṭāna in lam yakun ʿan dīnin tajtamiʿu bi-hi al-qulūbu ḥattā yarā ahluhu al-ṭāʿata fīhi farḍan wal-tanāṣuru ʿalayhi ḥatman, lam yakun lil-sulṭāni labath wa-lā lil-ayyāmi ṣafw, wa-kāna sulṭāna qahrin wa-mufsida dahrin.*"

67 Ibn Khaldūn, *Muqaddima*, 151.

68 *AS*, 62.

69 Qāsim b. Sallām, *Kitāb al-Amwāl*, I, 31-39. See also Najib, "Common Wealth: Land Taxation in Early Islam," 260f.

70 Abou El Fadl, *Rebellion*, 167-68, 171-76.

kept intact.[71] The protection against heresy barely appears in *ADD*, and is mentioned briefly under the second condition, which primarily deals with internal security, including road safety and crimes against life and property.

However, under the first condition of *ADD* – i.e., "preservation of *dīn*" – there is a sub-requirement to the effect that the sultan's function includes the diligent "application" of *dīn* with a view to making it a praxis.[72] This requirement is consistent with Māwardī's first pillar in *ADD*, the pillar that sustains and props the public good (*ṣalāḥ al-dunyā*) and that makes the affairs of this world orderly, proper, and beneficial. Yet, this sub-requirement is not to be found in *AS*, an absence that is consistent with the fact that this work does not and was not intended to deal with the ethical formation of the social and political subject.

The second requirement in *ADD* relates to domestic and external security, the former including the protection from heretical groups that he mentions in *AS* under the first condition and securing life and property that he specifies under the third condition.

The third is "developing the regions" by propping and strengthening their businesses and building their roads and highways.[73] Curiously, this requirement is absent from *AS*, although it is generally found in many works dealing with this topic.[74]

The fourth is levying taxes according to the dictates of the law, while maintaining proper conduct in the process of collecting and redistributing them. This is nearly identical to the seventh and eighth conditions in *AS*.

The fifth is the duty to administer Sharīʿa and *maẓālim*[75] in a just and fair manner, while the sixth is to carry out the complementary ordinances of the weighty Qur'ānic punishments (*ḥudūd*). These have their parallel in the second and fourth requirements of *AS*, respectively. As we will see in Part II, it was within the scope of the fifth requirement or function that some of the most fundamental constitutional problems arose throughout the five centuries after Māwardī wrote.

71 *AS*, 10; *ADD*, 222.
72 *ADD*, 222. The full condition states: "*Ḥifẓu al-dīni min tabdīlin fīhi, wal-ḥaththu ʿalā al-ʿamali bi-hi, min ghayri ihmālin la-hu.*"
73 *ADD*, 222: "*ʿImāratu al-buldāni bi-iʿtimādi maṣāliḥihā wa-tahdhībi subulihā wa-masālikihā.*" Some others add to this the all-important "digging and maintaining irrigation canals" and "building and maintaining bridges," both of which are sultanic duties. See Qudāma Ibn Jaʿfar, *Kharāj*, 248; Niẓām al-Mulk, *Siyar al-Mulūk*, 50; Ibn Jamāʿa, *Taḥrīr*, 68. See also ch. 7, n. 49.
74 See previous note.
75 On *maẓālim*, see ch. 3.

Seventh, and finally, the sultan must select trustworthy and competent officials who will act as his deputies in running the affairs of the domains. This is equivalent to the ninth requirement in *AS*. The only requirement explicitly found in *AS* and only implied in *ADD* is launching *jihād* against the enemies of Islam.[76] *ADD*'s second requirement does not mention *jihād* by name but undoubtedly stipulates the duties falling under its jurisdiction.

With the fulfillment of these (time-honored)[77] duties, Māwardī writes, the sultan would be deemed to have met his obligations toward God, a language that suggests that the sultanic charge belongs to the rights of God (*ḥuqūqu Allāh*) as opposed to the rights of man (*ḥuqūqu al-ʿibād*). Yet, God's rights are themselves represented in the political interests of the Community, just as charity toward the poor is likewise a right of God.[78] It is only then that the sultan would be deserving of the Community's support, love, and obedience. Māwardī's language here is exquisitely refined: "*mustawjiban li-ṭāʿatihim wa-munāṣaḥatihim wa-khulūṣi niyyātihim, mustaḥiqqan li-ṣidqi maylihim wa-maḥabbatihim.*"[79] Other than the obvious "obedience" which comes first, the second denouement is *munāṣaḥa*, namely, sincere advice and faithful concern for the well-being of the ruler and success of his reign. Advice to the ruler had become an institution in Islam, so to speak.[80] Its significance is such

76 *AS*, 40.

77 The bulk of these duties were taken for granted by the middle of the second/eighth century. Around that time, the distinguished *qāḍī* ʿUbayd Allāh al-ʿAnbarī wrote to the caliph al-Mahdī a letter in which he summarized, among other things, the caliph's duties as consisting of four, all of which except one, are found in Māwardī's list. ʿAnbarī's list consists of the following tasks, and in this order: (1) *Thughūr*: defense of the borders and the establishment of garrison towns; (2) *Aḥkām*: enforcement of the Sharīʿa; (3) *Fay'*: land, taxation, etc.; and (4) *Ṣadaqa*: the distribution of taxes levied from Muslims and non-Muslims. The only missing item in ʿAnbarī's list, as compared to Māwardī's, is "developing the regions" (no. 3). See the letter in Wakīʿ, *Akhbār*, II, 97-107. See also Zaman, *Religion and Politics*, 85 ff.

78 On the rights of God and those of human beings, see Hallaq, " 'God Cannot be Harmed'."

79 *ADD*, 223.

80 A *locus classicus* of advice to the ruler appears in Niẓām al-Mulk's pragmatic treatise on governance, addressed to the Saljūq sultan Malik Shāh in 479/1086. Here, it is clear that Malik Shāh is seeking counsel from his senior aides, the most important of whom is Niẓām al-Mulk himself. Through a royal decree (*amrun malakiyyun*), the sultan asked his aids "to reflect" on matters of political management with a view to drawing the sultan's attention to any irregularity in the administration of justice and polity. "Have We missed anything that our predecessor-kings practiced correctly?" The aids are to "think carefully concerning any matter related to the foundations and rules of governance, as well as the [good] customs of previous kings of the Saljūqs" so as to "bring it to Our attention so that we look into it and thus decree that all religious and profane matters be applied according to proper principles ... commanding that the laws of God (*awāmiru Allāh*) be implemented." See Niẓām al-Mulk, *Siyar al-Mulūk*, 47.

that a Prophetic tradition came to express the importance of the purity of intent in offering the counsel, which is itself normatively mandated: "There are three things that the heart of the believer cannot/must not be hypocritical/deceptive about: faithfulness of acts dedicated to God, offering counsel to the ruler, and joining the Muslim body (i.e., *umma*, Community)."[81] Next is "*khulūṣu al-niyyati*", i.e., purity of intention, itself a political act of support. For all of the foregoing seems to culminate in the last phrase, "*mustaḥiqqan li-ṣidqi maylihim wa-maḥabbatihim*," being deserving of their "truthful inclination toward him, and love." This is not a dispassionate world in which political judgement is nothing more than a rational calculation of profit and loss, if not cynicism, but rather an affective relationship between ruler and ruled, a relationship whose basis and content cannot be separated from the psychological.

For the modern sensibility, this may strike the reader as frivolous emotivity or emotional idealism of a sort. But extreme caution is required when we inch toward the dismissal of a feature in human conduct that does not seem possible or plausible for us. This dismissal would be a classic example of ignoring the internal logic that we have spoken of at length in the Introduction. In a system that grounds itself in a personal connection with the Divine, one that is to be ethically emulated by humans as a prime desideratum, it is not surprising that relationships, at all levels of social and political interaction, are defined by emotive content as much they are constituted by contractual considerations and interest. If politics and political functions, as we have seen, are integral to ethics and ethical formation of the individual and the collectivity, then psychology should be expected to play a major role in defining relationships, much more than in a system of politics that has been segregated from ethics and one that is exclusively ruled by bureaucratic rationality and the logic of *raison d'état* to boot.

Now, should the ruler fall short of these responsibilities, he would be blameworthy and liable for punishment (*muʿāqaban*). His subjects would harbor resentment and conceal hate for him, awaiting any opportunity to rise

81 Ibn Manẓūr, *Lisān al-ʿArab*, XI, 597: "*Thalāthun lā yughillu ʿalayhinna qalbu mu'minin: ikhlāṣu al-ʿamali lil-Lāh wa-munāṣaḥatu dhawī al-amri, wa-luzūmu jamāʿat al-Muslimīn.*" See further Ḥaḍramī, *Kitāb al-Siyāsa*, 21-24; and Ṭurṭūshī, *Sirāj al-Mulūk*, 289-94. For an actual instance where a sultan requests counsel on a vast scale from his ministers, see Niẓām al-Mulk, *Siyar al-Mulūk*, 47, 51, 128-29. For counsel as a long-standing practice, taken for granted by the middle of the second/eighth century, see also Wakīʿ, *Akhbār*, II, 97. See also al-Qāsim b. Sallām (d. 224/838), *Kitāb al-Amwāl*, I, 32; Shaʿrānī, *Mukhtaṣar*, 159.

up in express disobedience (*ma'ṣiya*) to him.[82] The punishment, therefore, is not procedural since there was no specific course of action that would bring the ruler to account. But lack of technical procedure does not necessarily mean that the punishment is not institutional. We might want to consider that the bureaucratic procedures as we know them today, and by whose standard we tend to judge other systems, are uniquely modern and that there is no consensus on the value of value, where everyone knows that everyone knows what is accepted as normative and what is not. Concepts of legitimacy, justice, fairness, legality, and the like are no longer anchored in or defined by an agreed-upon ethical system but rather by the values of the realpolitik of *raison d'état*, which perpetually define and redefine social and political reality (as we will see in chapter 12).

In Māwardī's context, and for two centuries before him and several after, problems, large and small, were surely often solved by distinctly non-procedural and non-formal means, at variance with the Weberian sense I am referring to here. The solutions were fluid and contingent on circumstance, just as they were pliable and malleable. Yet, they were arrived at based on what is politically and ethically acceptable and what is not, let alone the obviously well-defined legal precepts and reigning socio-legal values. The dissatisfaction of the populace would therefore play an important role in motivating and pushing forward powerful contenders who relied on this popular support to depose the sitting sultan and take over his rule.

The third pillar for the good management of the political order is an "encompassing justice" (*'adlun shāmilun*) whose necessary effects are concord among people, obedience, and general prosperity in agrarian and mercantile economies. Encompassing justice also leads to a situation in which the sultan himself feels secure and assured of the loyalty of his subjects to him. "There is nothing that ensures the destruction of the Earth and corrupts people's conscience more than injustice (*jawr*). Injustice has neither limit nor end, each part of it contributing its share to malevolence until everything is corrupted."[83]

The indispensability of justice for the good management of the worldly order is such that one must attain it for oneself before he or she expects others to attain it for themselves. The battle is again with the self, the site of the unceasing antagonism between reason and the passions. The basic idea is to do good and abstain from evil. The desideratum is to attain the Happy

82 *ADD*, 223: "*Wa'in qaṣṣara... kāna bi-hā mu'ākhadhan wa-'alahyā mu'āqaban wa-huwa min al-ra'iyyati 'alā istibṭāni ma'ṣiyatin wa-maqtin yatarabbaṣūna al-furaṣata bi-iẓhārihimā.*"
83 *ADD*, 225. On *jawr* as it relates to *ẓulm*, see ch. 2, n. 44.

Middle, for the extremes invariably lead to injustice. The source of injustice, Māwardī explains, lies in the fact that the agent has failed to create this balance, this equilibrium, within himself first. "He who is unjust to his self is even more unjust to others."[84]

On the other hand, the category of justice toward others consists of three types, two of which are immediately relevant to our concerns: Justice toward superiors and justice toward inferiors.[85] The former requires obedience, support, and loyalty, while the latter demands the avoidance of imposing hardship and oppressive control, in addition to being fair and equitable.[86]

The fourth pillar is a condition of general security (*amnun ʿāmmun*) that allows for peaceful existence for the weak and disadvantaged and encourages hard work throughout; for fear deters people from embarking on business and taking initiative. This pillar is immediately relevant to the next, prosperity and abundance (*khiṣbun dārrun*), since without security they cannot be attained. Prosperity and abundance assure the reduction of envy, animosity, and hatred among people. They allow for wealth to trickle down, circulate, and create social cohesion. Even honesty, fair dealing, and generosity tend to increase under such favorable conditions. The notion that charity toward the poor is merely a "religious" obligation, confined to the spiritual and ethereal, is both incomplete and inaccurate, for the de-concentration and redistribution of wealth in Islam has a strictly defined political telos. Poverty is *also* a political problem since it is not only associated with decline of morals (which we in [late-]modernity realize to have likewise political significance) but also in increasing the likelihood of political discontent. "One of our Predecessors (*Salaf*) has said: the [highest] goods in the Here and Hereafter are [the qualities of] God-fearing and self-sufficiency, and the [highest] evils are depravity and poverty."[87]

The sixth pillar is abundant hope (*amalun fasīḥun*), defined as that which propels humans to acquire things which a whole life would not be enough to consume, even embarking on the construction of things that one has no assurance will be completed in one's own lifetime. Had it not been for this abundant hope, people would not build and plough, raise edifices and forge structures. God created hope for this particular purpose, namely, creating *ʿumrān* that

84 *ADD*, 226-27.

85 The third type is "justice between equals." *ADD*, 229.

86 *ADD*, 227.

87 *ADD*, 232-33: "*Khayru al-dunyā wal-ākhirati fil-taqwā wal-ghinā, wa-sharru al-dunyā wal-ākhirati fil-fujūri wal-faqr.*"

"endures from one century to the next"[88] through the persistent work of successive generations – a concept foundational for Māwardī's and Ibn Khaldūn's theories.[89] Without this ingrained quality of hope, humans would not work for more than their day's needs for survival, and Earth would be left barren and uninhabitable. The centrality of the concept of hope for Muslim understanding has been enshrined in a Prophetic report: "Hope is a divine bounty given to my Community. Had it not been for it, no trees would be planted and no mother would nurse her infant."[90]

When these six pillars coalesce, the affairs and well-being of life on Earth would reach their optimal and best form; but, Māwardī tells us, this is not a realistic and in fact a distant possibility. The reason he gives is not that the pillars are Utopic or in themselves unrealistic, but rather a sort of necessity. Coalescence and its attendant results never happen in their perfect form because life is made in such a way as to integrate, as an essential part of its mechanics of operation, the element of change, of generation and corruption. The lack of coalescence is not attributed to an artificial or superimposed quality on what the natural world is, a defect of some sort, but rather to the way things are, the way life, nature, and the world run.[91] It is the very imperfection of life that contains the key to the natural laws of generation and corruption.

With the elaboration of the six pillars, Māwardī has described the elements that make the good order of this life possible, in contradistinction with the sphere of works in preparation for the Hereafter. The focus was on the collective and communal as well as that which we call public, including government and human group psychology (e.g., hope in the socio-economic domain). Now he turns to a narrower focus, essentially addressing the well-being of individuals insofar as the concerns of worldly life, the here and now, are concerned. In the overall structure of his theory,

88 *ADD*, 234. *ʿUmrān,* a concept that will become important and more complex for Ibn Khaldūn, means urban material structures or material "civilization."

89 See also *TN*, 157. It is worth noting that an Islamic philosophy and politics of hope are subjects of research that have yet to be undertaken. It is essential to both projects that they be related to the concept of time in Islam. This latter field of inquiry is likewise severely neglected in research agenda. For a fruitful beginning, see Ben Hammed, "Contesting the Empty Time."

90 *ADD*, 235: "*Wa-ʿanhu ṣallā Allāhu ʿalayhi wa-sallam: al-amalu raḥmatun min Allāhi li-Ummatī, wa-lawlāhu mā ghurisa shajarun wa-lā arḍaʿat ummun waladahā.*"

91 *ADD*, 235: "*Wa-baʿīdun an yakūna amru al-dunyā tāmman kāmilan wa-an yakūna ṣalāḥuhā ʿāmman shāmilan li-annahā mawḍūʿatun ʿalā al-taghyīri/taghayyuri wal-fanāʾi wa-munshaʾatun ʿalā al-taṣarrumi wal-inqiḍāʾ.*"

the individual human is the most basic element of which the Community and polity are made, which also means that the formation of human subjectivity – or the processes of individual subjectivation – lies at the foundations of Māwardī's concerns.

He enumerates three foundations without which the good order of the individual will not be attained. These are an obedient self, social solidarity, and economic prosperity. The first, we have seen, has been largely covered by Māwardī, and it may be summed up in the need to sway the self from the passions through the rational thinking of *ʿaql*, while at the same time employing various techniques that operate on the self with a view to cultivating one's subjectivity through embodiment in an ethical manner. For our purposes, enough has also been said about economic prosperity as well, it being taken for granted as an important component of the good and orderly life, even of the ethical, as we have seen.

Since social solidarity has not been covered before, Māwardī gives it a lengthy treatment, and we shall do the same since what he has to say bears political significance not only for his own theory but also for what might be called the *grundnorm* of political thinking in the Islamic tradition. Social solidarity is necessary for all social groupings since it affords not only social cohesion and intimate relationships but also protection of the group against external threats, or against outlying elements of the social fabric. Social solidarity protects against encroachments on one's peace of mind, property, and well-being; and averts humiliation to boot. After this short introduction, Māwardī thinks through the causal means of intimate human association (*ulfa*)[92] that forges social solidarity; and here he provides the analytical grounds for Ibn Khaldūn's concept of *ʿaṣabiyya*, grounds that the latter appears to have taken for granted.[93]

Association through *ulfa* comes about through one of five routes, the first and most powerful of which is, again, *dīn* (what we now call "religion"). *Dīn* engenders mutual support and prevents animosity and fragmentation. The essential features of association in religion are stated in a report containing the Prophet's advice to his companions and Community: "Do not be hostile or inimical to each other;

92 *ADD*, 238. The radical *A.L.F.* connotes, among many things, the idea of "bringing together," connecting things together, or "in the company of" something or someone. Ibn Manẓūr, *Lisān al-ʿArab*, IX, 10 ff. For centuries, the term was also widely used for communal and inter-religious harmony and association, as powerfully attested in the nineteenth-century writings of Bustānī, *Nafīr Sūriyyah*, 35-37.

93 See also *TN*, 157; Ibn Khaldūn, *Muqaddima*, 102-3.

do not envy each other; and be brothers and sisters in the service of God."[94] Yet, while religion is a cause of unification and solidarity, it can be, with equal force, a cause for dispute, animosity, and fragmentation in intra-religious rivalry.

Second is familial association, for such social units are endowed with a sense of mutual protection and defense of kinsmen against external groups. This is why, Māwardī observes, the Arabic-speaking populations kept a record of their lineages, for this form of self-identification enabled them to unite against aggression and external threats so much so that they reached glorious heights.[95]

Association through kinship occurs either on the vertical line of grandparents-parents-children-grandchildren or by the relations immediately adjacent to these, such as aunts, uncles, nieces, nephews, etc. The former is more reliable and more solid, since there might be a certain degree of jealousy or competition between and among the latter's members, at least more so than that which may be found between and among members of the former class. Note here that Māwardī's classification does not resort to agnatic categories central to *fiqh*, since social ties that constitute social, socio-economic, and political solidarity could obtain equally from both the patrilineal and matrilineal lines. Association through familial relations also obtains through marriage (*muṣāhara*), which is known to perform political functions as well, such as creating royal and tribal alliances and even confederations.[96]

The fourth route to association is a bond of brotherly friendship (*mu'ākhāt*) which may either be agreed upon as a result of necessity or as a matter of free and deliberate choice, often out of personal liking. The first type, being the result of rational necessity, is said to be stronger because the compelling factors apparently strengthen the bond.[97]

Finally, the fifth route is *birr*, a category under which Māwardī elaborates what seems to be a subcategory of *dīn*, the first pillar and route in promoting the good life in the *dunyā*, the here and now. It seems that under the category of "religion" he meant to include those qualities in this cohesive force that deter and sculpt the self into an ethical agent, an intra-personal operation,

94 *ADD*, 239.

95 *ADD*, 241. The paragraph containing this language is crucial, since it is an essential idea in Ibn Khaldūn's *Muqaddima*: "*Wa-lidhālika ḥafiẓat al-ʿArabu ansābahā lammā imtanaʿat bi-hā ʿan sulṭānin yaqharuhā wa-yakuffu al-adhā ʿanhā, li-takūna bi-hi mutaẓāfiratun ʿalā man nāwa'ahā, mutanāṣiratun ʿalā man shāqqahā wa-ʿādāhā, ḥattā balaghat bi-ulfati al-ansābi wa-tanāṣurihā ʿizzata al-qawiyyi al-ayyid.*"

96 *ADD*, 241-49.

97 *ADD*, 261-67.

while *birr* is an externalized, proactive component that constructs interpersonal ties and bonds of association. *Birr* is truthfulness toward the other (*ṣidq*), loyalty, and, on the whole, *acting* with goodness (*khayr, ṣalāḥ*).[98] It is a complex and multilayered term whose meaning cannot be captured by any one synonym. Standing alone, and without context, it straddles a spectrum of meanings, ranging from "doing good of any kind," to being kind in deed and in word, compassionate, and seeking *riḍā* from people, that is, their state of mind being happy and contented with you. But this state in which people become contented with and happy to know you, is also a relationship, a forging of a social connection and even a bonding psychosocial tie with others. Thus, *birr* is one of those terms that combines in its very meaning both the cause and effect of an abstract noun: to have faith in God, to be truthful, to do good, and to establish bonds of loyalty and compassion with others as a result; it is to live "happily and contentedly" in social networks (*waṣl*).[99] But all of this is sourced from the act and practice of giving and from a deep sense of generosity, qualities essential to *birr* and its social consequences in creating strong bonds of association.[100]

IV

Māwardī's *ADD* is not just a work on *adab*, as the title may misleadingly suggest if viewed from a modernist linguistic viewpoint. In some ways, *adab* was about nearly everything, and as such, *ADD* is a *positive* account of life in its Islamic forms, life that is lived personally, spiritually, communally, economically, *and* politically. It is an account that encompasses even a philosophy of hope and a theory of econosociology.[101] As we will see throughout this book, the capacious purview of the account allows us to frame political and constitutional analysis,

98 Ibn Manẓūr, *Lisān al-ʿArab*, IV, 59 ff.

99 Ibn Manẓūr, *Lisān al-ʿArab*, IV, 59 ff.: "*Al-birru al-ṣidqu wal-ṭāʿatu,*" "*al-birru fiʿlu kulli khayrin min ayyi ḍarbin kān;*" "*al-birru* [*huwa*] *al-lutf,*" "*barartuhu birran waṣaltuhu.*" *ADD*, 294: "*Fil birri riḍā al nāsi wa man jamaʿa bayna riḍā Allāhi wa-riḍā al-nāsi faqad tammat saʿādatuhu wa-ʿammat niʿmatuhu.*"

100 *ADD*, 296-97, 322.

101 The reversal of "socio-economics" is intentional, as the qualifier here is the social order rather than its economics, the qualified. The focus here, in other words, is not on the social aspects of economics but rather on the economic aspects of what stands as paradigmatic, i.e., the social group or the community/Community.

analysis of sovereignty, as well as the set of relationships that substituted for Islam what Foucault called in the European context governmentality and biopower (however much these were conducted in that context to different effects).

The account furthermore is distinctly positive, not normative. Māwardī is not prescribing standards of value whose application is desirable or ethically deontological, but rather what schematically happens on the ground – or a theory of origins or epistemology – when facts as lived experiences cannot be always observed directly. Two respective cases in point here (already discussed above) are the origins of sociality and communal living and the theory of reason and rationality, taken along with its relations to the passions and desires. A third case is the role that *dīn* plays in the subjective constitution of the individual and the organization of political life as issuing from this mode of constitution.

On the whole, his discourse about the six pillars sustaining the management of life in this world is effectively a fleshed out socio-political account of the Circle of Justice, a prevailing and diffused perennial form of governance in West Asia.[102] The account is therefore not normative because Māwardī is not expressing or

102 On the Circle of Justice within the context of Sharīʿa, see Hallaq, *Sharīʿa*, 197-221. The origins of the concept of the "Circle of Justice" are variously attributed by Muslim authors to Greece and the pre-Islamic Persianate modalities of rule. Ḥaḍramī ascribes it to Aristotle: The world is a garden whose fence is the dynasty (*dawla*); the *dawla* is a power protected by the *sunna*; *sunna* is *siyāsa* (mode of governance) according to which the kings administer their realms; the king is a care-taker, supported by the army; the army are assistants and supporters who are maintained by money; money is wealth afforded by the subjects; the subjects are obedient denizens brought together [as a political community] by justice; justice is an established and commonly agreed upon [concept] by which the well-being of the world is maintained. Ḥaḍramī, like many others, does not let the reader rest without making it abundantly clear that justice is the lynchpin of the Circle. Ḥaḍramī, *Kitāb al-Siyāsa aw al-Ishāra fī Tadbīr al-Imāra*, 43. See also Ibn Khaldūn, *Muqaddima*, 30. For reflections on the purpose of the Circle, see London, "Circle of Justice." Linda Darling has convincingly argued that the Circle of Justice had been an integral part of West Asian political culture since ancient times, even before the Sassanids. In the abstract, she sums up her findings and sources as follows: "The stereotype sees the Circle as a Persian product; this article shows that the Circle of Justice emerged millennia before the Persians, that the Persians were actually slow to make it their own, that aspects of it were part of Arabic culture before Islam, and that many people other than Persian scribes quoted or used it in the early Islamic centuries. Examining ancient cuneiform royal inscriptions, Pahlavi documents, the poetry addressed to Umayyad and ʿAbbāsid rulers, and early works of history and political thought, the article traces the Circle's ideas down through the centuries until their encapsulation in the form we know today, the earliest version of which is found in the work of the historian and *adab* writer Ibn Qutayba." Darling, "Vicegerent of God,'" 407. For a comprehensive and masterly coverage of the life and function of the Circle of Justice, see Darling, *History of Social Justice*.

even insinuating "what is good" or "what should be" but rather "what happens" if certain conditions, all possible and tenable, obtain. It is an empirical account of the ordinary and average working of things social and political. Like Māwardī, Ibn Khaldūn was later to capture the positive power of the account when, after giving three different renditions of the Circle (two Sassanid and one Greek), he asserts that "if you contemplate what we have written in the chapters on *dawla*s and rule ... you will find it to consist of annotations of these words [i.e., the formula stating what the Circle is] and of detailed explanations that are demonstratively persuasive. This we have learned from neither the Persian king nor from Aristotle but have discovered for ourselves with the help of God."[103]

For worldly life to exist optimally, Māwardī enumerated six necessary conditions, which, from experience, are judged to be a sufficient condition when they come into reality. But he also told us that the optimal conditions rarely ever come about in their totality, a view that is navigating the positive and factual, rather than the normative and deontological.

Looking at it from the twenty-first century, it is clear that the world Māwardī was describing is an Islamic world operating within longstanding West Asian traditions of governance, especially the political component of it. Yet, the subjective modalities and techniques that enabled this world to maintain itself throughout the second half of the first millennium were Islamic in significance and in detail. It was so unique, as we will see, that no non-Muslim writer outside of the Dār al-Islām could have conceived of it in that particular way.

ADD frames the psychological, sociological, economic, and political in ways that a factual account cannot. A positive account does not describe the actual, quantitative, and exact facts on the ground, not only because the facts are also a matter of symbolic importance and can be organized, prioritized, and interpreted in any number of ways, but also because any factual account must necessarily belong to what we call microhistory. It is necessarily so because – as I have discussed in the Introduction – it is impossible, if not illusory, to arrive at a complete picture of the history of, say, governance and constitutionality in Islamic history from beginning to end. Even a history of the Mamlūk Empire – as relatively and comparatively short as it was – is nearly impossible because effectively every sultan's reign must command its own micro-history, with at least half of a shelf of books dedicated just to it. That is if we assume that authors and accounts are generally in agreement with each other, and that major debates have not in the meantime erupted about the central facts

103 Ibn Khaldūn, *Muqaddima*, 30.

of the account, making it controversial in the first place. A positive account, by contrast, allows for a narrative that captures the structure of relationships in a particular phenomenon, small or large. It does not sink into irresolvable debates about purported, presumed, or actual facts, and their endless array of interpretations, which are integral to the constitution of these "facts." A positive account is one that effectively supersedes and ultimately transcends the factual account, since a positive account is the desideratum of its factual equivalent. What is meaningful in an account or a narrative is the structure of relationships that constitute the average forms, conceptions, and practices of governance, not "studies" of a specific reign or period, which may or may not be representative, as if we could ever know from such micro-histories what the general picture ever was.

If I want to know how Muslims governed themselves over the millennium before European colonialists set foot in Muslim lands; if I want to decipher their theories of subjectivity in terms of political governance; if I aim to map out the constitutional arrangements they fashioned for themselves to determine the limits and interactions of separation of powers; if I wish to explore the domains of political subjectification – what Foucault called in the European context governmentality and biopower – and its effects on the constitution of the Muslim self; and if I aim to understand the quality or equivalent of the modern notion of sovereignty, a positive account would be the most efficient, useful, and productive substrate for my purposes. Accordingly, I shall henceforth pull the various central strands in Māwardī's sociological and political account and annotate them with a view to answering the queries I have just posed. I begin with the ethical formation of the ruler and the ruled with a view to delineating what political "society," or rather the *Umma*, means in political terms. In order to properly understand the *constitution* of Islamic polity, it is essential to differentiate between two drastically different types of politics: the ethically grounded, on the one hand, and that which is wholly anchored in the reality of *raison d'état*. While the next chapter lays the ground for this particular argument, chapter 12 aims to complete it.

Chapter 2

The Politics of Practical Ethics

I

If it is true that the good life of the here-and-now is predicated upon the fulfillment of six conditions (expounded in the previous chapter), then it is also true that there are relationships of complementarity, a dialectic, between and among these conditions. With whichever condition one chooses to start a list of the six, each and every one of them relates in integral ways to the others: without "abundant hope" there is no enterprising economy and accumulation of wealth, much less *ʿumrān* and culture. The totality of these latter effects is what Māwardī called *khiṣbun dārrun*, the fifth prop of prosperity and abundance. Without general safety and security, the fourth prop, neither hope nor material abundance can be possible; and without a coercive sultan, no security, not even *dīn* ("religion"), would be possible either. Religion and a coercive sultan are in fact of the essence for everything else, because they are the two foundations that can make the good worldly life possible. It is not without good reason that Ardashīr b. Babak's adage, "religion and kingship are twins,"[1] managed to gain enormous popularity in Muslim political writings.[2]

In the same vein, coercive power without the third prop, justice, is both loathsome and illegitimate, exonerating the subjects from loyalty to, and support of, the ruler. And there is nothing more equipped to oversee the integrity, the just character, of coercive power than *dīn*. *Dīn* is the

1 *NT*, 148-49. See also next note and n. 3.

2 It may be of interest to note that an excellent study of Ottoman governance in Lebanon's Tripoli during the eleventh/seventeenth and twelfth/eighteenth centuries describes the relationship between the governor and the *qāḍī* in the same manner, and apparently outside of the context of this Sassanid/Greek maxim. See Ziyādah, *al-Ṣūra al-Taqlīdiyya*, 57.

meta-source of justice and its ultimate reference. True, fairness, equitability, and charitable social welfare, among other qualities, are all rational values but they are also liable to subjective interpretations that may either modify them out of proportion or even cancel them altogether. *Dīn* is the bedrock in which these values are anchored and enshrined beyond the subjective manipulation or caprice of worldly power, a domain that is most susceptible to house the passions and the base, capricious desires. Even experience and venerable precedent, the high wisdom of trial and error, would not be sufficient props for the ethical in the political, because they do not anchor themselves in a cosmology that gives them force and sustenance. Nor are they necessarily or structurally associated with praxis, the modalities of embodiment and technologies of self-cultivation that integrate ethics into real life situations in politics.

The association and mutual dependence between religion and politics was regarded as a universal creed, not exclusively Islamic. When Māwardī – along with Ibn ʿAbd Rabbih, Masʿūdī, Nuwayrī, al-Rāghib al-Aṣfahānī, Ibn Khaldūn, and countless others – wished to cite an authority in support of this proposition, he invoked the Sassanid king Ardashīr b. Bābak (d. 242 AD) who is purported to have advised his son, Crown Prince Shāpūr I: "Religion and kingship are twins. Neither can endure without the other, since religion is the foundation and the king is the guard. One direly needs the other, because that which has no guard will be lost, and that which has not foundation will collapse."[3] In this context, religion for Māwardī is obviously not exclusively Islamic, for the concern is not with religious affiliation or membership as such, but rather with a particular positive content of the self, a discursive practice, applied doctrine, and a habituating technology of ethical principles that command, train, and produce a certain kind of subjects. The concern is with subjective formation or formation of subjectivity. This, incidentally, is why *adab* was so central to politics because *adab*, through ethical technologies of the self, forms subjects, political and otherwise.

The perpetual citations from Iranian and Greek voices of wisdom, be they philosophers or sagacious rulers, were integral to this conceptual terrain of subjective formation, and in many ways constituted organic and thus integral extensions to *adab* and constructive "religious" discourse. This explains why

3 *NT*, 148-49, and editor's note no. 5, 149-50: "*Al-Dīnu wal-mulku taw'amān lā qiwāma li-aḥadihimā illā bi-ṣāḥibihi, li'anna al-dīna ussun wal-malika ḥārisun, wa-lā budda lil-maliki min ussin, wa-lā budda lil-ussi min ḥārisin li'anna mā lā ḥārisa la-hu ḍā'iʿun, wa-mā lā ussa la-hu munhadimun.*" *Malik* here can also be read as *mulk*.

the Persians, the Greeks, the Prophet Muhammad, the Rāshidūn caliphs, and many Islamic others were all found intermingling and taking turns of appearance on the same pages of Islamic political treatises, of whatever kind they were.[4]

II

The range of this spiritual-doctrinal and praxis-based field of political management was so inclusive that almost all sources dealing with political ethics were integrated. The range is demonstrated in Māwardī's *TN* and indirectly even in *ADD*. It is also found in Ghazālī's works, especially *al-Tibr al-Masbūk fī Naṣīḥat al-Mulūk* (*TM*). In this chapter, I want to flesh out the themes implicated in what I have called practical political ethics,[5] with a view to shedding light on

4 Here, I join Ovamir Anjum – though on different grounds – in objecting to such binary characterizations as voiced by Charles Butterworth who saw a clear split between the jurists, or what he called the legalists, and the Greco-Muslim philosophers. He argued that the jurists' project was to implement the law as it is "set forth in the Qur'an and the Sunna," but the philosophers "sought to understand politics as a craft and an art and how one skilled in it could rule well." As this book shows, the "juristic" tradition as a mainstream expression of the practical concept of politics and rule was deeply preoccupied with what Butterworth thought the exclusive domain of the philosophers. If anything, and to supplement my reservations I voiced in the Introduction about the role of Greco-Islamic political philosophy, the major commonality between this philosophy and the mainstream politico-theological tradition was precisely the conception of this "art of rule," which was as much West Asian as it was Hellenic. See Butterworth, "Prudence Versus Legitimacy," 84-85. (Incidentally, it is eminently arguable that Hellenic Greece was culturally an integral part of West Asia, having in common much more with the culture of the Fertile Crescent than anything west or north of it. On this see Hallaq, *Origins*, 25-28 and sources cited therein). Anjum, on the other hand, objects to Butterworth on the grounds that Ibn Taymiyya, his focus, belonged to neither camp. My argument, however (as well as that of Sherman Jackson), is that "how to rule well" as an ethic of politics permeated political discourse in all of its stripes. Anjum, *Politics, Law, and Community*, 29-30. For Jackson, see his *Islamic Law*, 71. On the importance of the philosophy of justice and good governance in the ancient world of West Asia and the East Mediterranean basin, see the important work of Darling, *History of Social Justice*.

5 The idea behind this choice and order of words is that politics in Islam – like "law," "economy," the exact sciences, and much else – was derivative of higher moral principles. To reverse the order by making ethics a qualifying adjective would conceptually and ontologically subordinate ethics to politics, a clearly misconceived move. Inasmuch as we cannot describe the relation in Islam as "legal politics" but rather political law (since it is the law that dictates political rationality-cum-normativity), we cannot by the same reason designate the relationship of ethics to politics as "ethical politics."

the structures of thought and praxis that undergirded the Islamic conception of the caliphate-cum-sultanate. I will begin with Māwardī's *TN* and then bring in Ghazālī's *TM*, for this latter constitutes, for my purposes here, an analytical annotation of this theme in Māwardī's writings.

The first parts of *TN* and *TM*[6] also veer off the path taken in Māwardī's *ADD*. While the latter – as we saw – was positive, these two parts were normative.[7] But normativity has a distinct role to play and a function to fulfill. Together, *TN* and *TM* erect and likewise constitute the bulwark guarding the foundations that were made possible by *ADD*, a bulwark that will ground our analysis of Māwardī's celebrated treatise *al-Aḥkām al-Sulṭāniyya* (*AS*); for this latter squarely rests on the presuppositions and narratives of the foregoing three works. This is also to say that none of these works tell the whole story, but all of them, and many more – as we will see in due course – are needed to flesh out the important dimensions of constitutional structure of Sunni polity.

Methodologically, in yet other words, these works exegete each other, one rendering the other more, but by no means entirely, complete and explicable. They all belong to what might be called a discursive habitus, which is also to say that these texts, irrespective of their different authors, exact timeline, or varied subject matter, spoke the same language, the same political lingua franca, shared the same assumptions, including a matrix of doxastic knowledge.[8] Whether abstract or concrete, realistic or "moralizing," legal or rhetorical, language was performative.[9]

This discursive habitus begins to emerge even in the opening paragraphs of *TN*, where Māwardī in fact begins with his state of nature theory, namely, that because people are created different from each other in their capacities and general dispositions, they by nature resort to cooperation, in the process lending help to each other (*yatasāʿadū ʿalā al-taʿāwun*) and showing empathy and mutual compassion (*yataʿāṭafū bil-īthār*).[10] In their interactions, however,

6 *TN*, 7-142; *TM*, 6-42.

7 On the differences between positive, normative, and factual accounts, see ch. 1, sec. IV.

8 Generally, *doxa* is that which is taken for granted or knowledge that "does not know itself." For a discussion of habitus and *doxa*, see Introduction, ch. 1 and especially ch. 10 (sec. V).

9 The lack of appreciation for the non-empirical, non-scientific, and the moral, ethical, and spiritual, remains a fundamental weakness of Orientalism and like disciplines. A notable advance in this direction can be seen in the commendable approach of Ali Anooshahr, *Ghazi Sultans* (see particularly the conclusion).

10 *TN*, 3: "*Jaʿala [Allāhu] al-nāsa aṣnāfan mukhtalifīna, wa-aṭwāran mutabāyinīna, li-yakūnū bil-ikhtilāfi muʾtalifīna wa-bil-tabāyuni muttafiqqīna* fa-yataʿāṭafū *bil-īthāri tābiʿan wa-matbūʿan wa-yatasāʿadū ʿalā al-taʿāwuni āmiran wa-maʾmūran.*" See similar language

they at times tend to be unfair to each other, claiming more than they rightly deserve and trespassing in all sorts of ways. This is why and where coercive power becomes indispensable, for it is a pillar and a central tool in the organization of human groups. The wielder of this power is thus extraordinarily distinguished by virtue of the very fact of imposing order, resolving disputes, and administering justice, which is why he is "most deserving of attention" (*awlā al-nāsi bil-ʿināya*). But what kind of attention and attention by whom?

As we have seen in the previous chapter, giving and receiving counsel was enshrined in Islamic political culture as an ethos, akin to a religious obligation sanctioned by a Prophetic report.[11] The counsel may be solicited but often it was not; yet it was still given. Why? Because, as we recall, it was felt to be a putative religious obligation due to the crucial importance of rulership to the *Umma* and its well-being.[12] The jurists, the ulama, the thinkers, writers, scholars, and anyone in a proper position to offer advice was under an obligation to do so. This was an integral part of the political habitus, thus accepted as part of what is normal and even agreeable by rulers and ruled alike.

Integral to politics and political life, advice and counsel were then an essential part of that habitus, and the language in which the advice was given constituted therefore doxa proper. This discourse, Māwardī makes clear, is historically enshrined, where the act of giving advice and its content have been quite fixed in the tradition, and furthermore set into well-structured principles.[13] Despite the differences in the ways each political community (*milla*) and each age (*zamān*) governed themselves, "there are established ways in which the law is administered and politics conducted, ways that this book cannot but address, so that it will be consistent with the *dīn* and [at once] corresponding

in *ADD*, 215, quoted in ch. 1, n. 58. It is worthwhile noticing the term "*yataʿāṭafū*" in the sentence, which is anything but Hobbesian: the necessity for cooperation engenders "compassionate transactions" and "merciful interactions." Ibn Manẓūr defines the basic notion of the root ʿ*.Ṭ.F.* in terms of empathy and, generally, being or doing good. In the form of *ʿaṭuf* and *ʿaṭṭāf*, both terms refer to a person who "protects the defeated" (*yaḥmī al munhazimīn*); *ʿaṭūf*, like *ʿāṭif* and *ʿaṭṭāf*, also means someone who consistently (or repeatedly) does good (*ʿā'idun bi-faḍlihi*) and who behaves ethically (*ḥasanu al-khulq*); *al-ʿāṭifa*, on the other hand, indicates a person who is merciful or humane (*raḥim*). In modern colloquial Arabic of the Levant, *ʿāṭifiyy* indicates someone who has a tender heart, so much so that they are "emotional." This form, however, is not found in Ibn Manẓūr, *Lisān al-ʿArab*, IX, 298 ff. On the theory of nature that underlies the fundamentally political conception of cooperation, see Conclusion, n. 10.

11 See ch. 1, n. 81.

12 For an excellent study of the concept of *Umma*, see Jomaa, *Ummah*.

13 *TN*, 4: "*Aḥkama al-mutaqaddimūna qawāʿidahu.*" See also ch. 1, n. 81.

to worldly reality."[14] The book, Māwardī reasserts, covers both *customary belief and action*, as well as correctives to both the active and passive agents of these beliefs *and practices.*[15]

Māwardī has already expounded a great deal on ethics in his *ADD*, much of which is also found in *TN*. A major distinction he makes in the opening pages of *TN* is that between innate and acquired virtues.[16] Some people are endowed with virtuous attributes naturally, and this, like everything else, is a capacity that differs in intensity from one person to the next. Yet, this does not mean that those who possess more virtues are on the whole more virtuous, since someone with a lower level of natural aptitude may cultivate better and more numerous positive virtues by training the self (*riyāḍat al-nafs, iṣlāḥ al-shiyam*).

The commoners (*ʿāmma*) tend to be better equipped than kings at the acquisition of virtues, while kings are better endowed with them by nature. This is so because kings tend to hail from noble pedigrees, while the commoners, on the other hand, can spare more time and muster more patience than kings can for ethical self-cultivation. Their own rationale for acquiring the virtues tend to be related either to their usefulness in their lives, or fear of harm if they lack them. But kings in general are affected by neither consideration. Only some of them allow themselves to be positively affected by them and this is due to their noble character and generosity of spirit. Those kings tend to be more experienced in rule and therefore more successful than others in the art of governing. The effort they expend on ethical self-cultivation tends to garner appreciation and gratitude from the populace. This usually is not the case with kings whose virtues are innate to them, possessing them without much effort at acquisition. But in all cases, and irrespective of how they are acquired, the virtues are always deserving of praise.[17]

Sultans and all those in command are therefore under obligation to care for their selves, to cultivate virtue in their character,[18] because an ethical character

14 TN, 4: "*Wa-qad awjaztu bi-hādhā al-kitābi min siyāsati al-mulki mā aḥkama al-mutaqaddimūna qawāʿidahu, fa'inna li-kulli millatin sīra wa-li-kulli zamānin sarīra, fa-lam yughnī mā salafa ʿan mu'talafin min al-Sharīʿati ʿuhūduhā wa-min al-siyāsati maʿhūduhā, li-yakūna lil-dīni muwāfiqan wa-lil-dunyā muṭābiqan.*"

15 *TN*, 4: "*Mushtamilan ʿalā muʿtaqadin wa-mafʿūlin, wa-muṣliḥan li-ʿāmilin wa-maʿmūl.*"

16 *TN*, 10: "*Gharīziyya ṭubiʿa ʿalayhā, wa-muktasaba taṭabbaʿa ʿalayhā.*"

17 *TN*, 10.

18 *TN*, 8: "*Fa-ḥaqqun ʿalā dhī al-amri wal-sulṭāni an yahtamma bi-murāʿāti akhlāqihi, wa-iṣlāḥi shiyamihi.*"

is the engine of their power and authority and the foundation of their command. No one can hope to have a sufficient capital of these virtues merely due to natural endowment and temperament. Training through rectification, edification, refinement, and discipline remains of the essence.[19] Ethical self-cultivation is in fact the first step a king must take in the business of rule, not only because this cultivation is the best guarantee for the implementation of justice but also because a king, on principle, must rule himself first before he rules others. He who cannot rule and command his self, king or not, can never deal with others properly.

But political technologies of the self are a specific set that equips the ruler with the necessary tools of governance. Fairmindedness, forbearance, patience, and rectitude are attributes as indispensable as being taciturn and a secret-keeper.[20] And so are honoring promises and agreements, consulting others, and suppressing envy. The business of ruling justly likewise requires the skill of navigating the Happy Middle between opposite qualities, such as generosity and thriftiness, harsh and gentle dealings, stringency and leniency. These are modes of behavior not just to be displayed in public but which should rather become internalized states to be developed as second nature. Inspecting the self and reviewing at night what the ruler has done during the day are techniques essential for a just, successful, and enduring rule.[21] This was not elitist advice and high-flying wisdom but rather a benchmark integral to habitus. Violations of the benchmark are violations of public reason, which eventually will work itself out, bringing about "punishment" (*muʿāqaba*)[22] in one way or another, whether the way is defined through clear procedural mechanisms or not.

Thus far, we have in Māwardī's account a coverage of what might be called the political legacy of West Asian and East Mediterranean cultures, which seems to have formed a more or less single weave, one providing the warp and the other the weft. The Persian and Hellenic traditions were the matrices into which the Islamic was integrated and on the foundations of which it was further articulated to reflect a distinct cosmology and political vision. Which is to say that cosmology and politics are integral to each other, for politics and political constitution would not be intelligible without this cosmology. This is why it is a grave error to think that the connections between politics and

19 *TN*, 8: "*An yartāḍa la-hā bil-taqwīmi wal-tahdhībi, riyāḍata tahdhībin, wa-tadrījin wa-taʾdīb.*"

20 *TN*, 46-47, 72-73, 81, 89.

21 *TN*, 99, 109, 116-18, 119, 124, 141.

22 See ch. 1, at n. 82.

ethics in Islam are merely instructive modalities, textual and rhetorical embellishments that presumably hide the anxiety that arises from likely tyranny or at least the heavy hand of politics. Politics was integral and structurally tied to cosmology, theology and metaphysics. Politics derived its ethics from these very ties, which is to say that there is no politics and constitutional principles without ethics. To put it in yet clearer terms: It is impossible to conceive of governance and the political management needed to make it possible without ethics and the grounding of ethics in cosmology and theology.

III

Ghazālī's *al-Tibr al-Masbūk* (*TM*) structurally builds on Māwardī's *TN* and focuses the narrative of habitus within a well-defined Muslim ethos (which explains the immense popularity and significance of the work throughout Islamic history, including the Ottoman period).[23] In both works, gratitude is central to just politics, just as just politics is the direct consequence of an ethical formation of the self.

Māwardī speaks in imperative terms, using the expression *ḥaqqun ʿalā* to indicate a sense of duty incumbent upon the sultan. This duty is to repay the favors and kindnesses God bestowed on the sultan for being chosen to lead the *Umma* in this most cardinal role. *Ḥaqqun ʿalā* effectively speaks of a right that God has against the sultan, a right to demand acknowledgement and gratitude. The sultan is under the burden of this right as much as anyone else is under other Sharʿī burdens, paying taxes and debts being just two cases in point. "It is a right against anyone whom God the Exalted has given to rule over his lands and regions, and entrusted over his creatures and believing subjects, that he should repay this munificent boon by cultivating a good inner self and conducting himself with the subjects in pleasing ways."[24] "Pleasing ways" is "*jamīl al-sīra*," the second word in the pair indicating and referencing "a path of one's life," a biography, even a biographical exemplarity. The intimated

23 For example, *TM* was "the most translated text [into Ottoman Turkish] in the sixteenth century" and "probably the most influential text on Ottoman political thinking," one with which "the Ottomans were infatuated." Yilmaz, *Caliphate Redefined*, 25, 28, 58.

24 *TN*, 143: "*Ḥaqqun ʿalā man makkanahu Allāhu taʿālā min arḍihi wa-bilādihi wa'tamanahu ʿalā khalqihi wa-ʿibādihi an yuqābila jazīla niʿmatihi bi-ḥusni al-sarīrati wa-yajrī min al-raʿiyyati bi-jamīli al-sīrati.*"

connections with the Prophetic *sīra* cannot be missed, which is why Māwardī follows this sentence with a canonical Qur'ānic quotation: "O David, We have made you a deputy [of ours] on Earth, so judge among people with justice and do not follow the passions."[25] To be chosen as God's custodian on Earth is a monumental privilege that cannot be recompensed except through the implementation of justice in His kingdom.

In *TM*, Ghazālī resorts to a similar mode of expression, but in this particular work he is addressing the Saljūq King of the East Sanjar (d. 552/1157) directly.[26] The voice is patently imperious, and the projected acceptance of his commanding language is taken for granted. Ghazālī's language is doxastic, wholly assuming – because it is subconscious – that the conceptual presuppositions on which his commands and instructions to the powerful sultan are based are valid and unquestionable.

Ghazālī here is operating within a habitus in which he and the sultan were subsumed, subordinated, and given a predetermined status. In a habitus, one's knowledge and understanding of the world are always constructed by the rules and modes of existence determined by that habitus, however many variations of understanding, and of comprehending the world, there may be. An agent cannot impose his or her ways on a habitus but rather expresses the ways of doing things and engaging others, in practice or argument, according to accepted and tacitly agreed-upon presuppositions, premises, and modalities of operation and being. Through habitus, individuals *become themselves*, because the structures of the habitus *themselves structure and organize* practices, ways of doing and seeing things, thereby making subjects. These subjects in turn develop particular attitudes and dispositions and engage in practices in ways that express culturally and historically constituted values relevant to the domain in which they operate. Because acts and dispositions within a habitus take for granted predetermined sets of value, they are often unconscious and show themselves as natural and unquestionable.[27]

The values and judgements of subjects in a habitus are not to be confused with those who claim to know the workings of the habitus but do not live in it, those who are not subjects or objects of it. Descriptively knowing how a habitus works has little to no relation with living in a habitus, much less *living it*.

25 Qur'ān, 38:26.
26 For a useful account on the political context in which Ghazālī wrote his *TM*, see Garden, *First Islamic Revivor*, 17-29. On Ghazālī's heavy involvement in the politics of his day, see Decosimo, "Umma of Accountability."
27 For a more detailed account of habitus and *doxa*, see Introduction, ch. 1 and 10 (sec. IV).

To live (in) a habitus is generally not to question the agreed-upon fundamental values by which the very habitus is constituted,[28] which is quite different from knowing a habitus descriptively or analytically. Living in a habitus is a psychoepistemic matter, where subjectivity represents a porous and interflowing sedimentation of cerebral and emotive layers of the self.

However, such an organically grown constitution of the self, or self-constitution, can never be attained by the outside observer who by definition knows the habitus as a distant epistemic, analytical and/or descriptive phenomenon, and who may *sharply disagree with the doxa and the entire presumptions that that habitus deploys*. To observe a habitus from the outside is to miss its spiritual and, in our scientific vocabulary, its psychological and emotive constitution and multilayered make-up. It is not to grasp how psychology and emotive structures *structure* thought, intellect, reason, cosmology, and conceptions of ontology.[29] To dismiss in a habitus an element that seems irrelevant or negligible to the outside observer is a fatal error of misunderstanding, and in philology, it is an act of blind scholarship. To put it more precisely and concretely, a secular philology or a "secular-scientific" philological apparatus is unequipped and therefore unfit to study the kind of habitus we are dealing with here. It is to miss and, at best, to underrate what is important, and exaggerate and overrate what is marginal and secondary. Empathetic philology[30] is not merely a kind and humane way of studying the cultural and spiritual Other; it is also, and primarily, an intentional epistemological stance of the first order.[31] Empathetic philology means that the external observer understands the full implications and maximal effects of such concepts as divine power, the power and majesty of creation, creativity, sustenance, ownership of the world, omniscience, and the Day of Judgement – all of which, including the latter, possess potent political effects and meanings for those who believe in them.

To understand the habitus behind this Māwardīan-Ghazālīan world of discourse is to leave aside and completely abandon the doxastic and value-laden hegemony of the secular and secular-scientific modern. Which is to say that such abandonment would require the secular philologist to convert his or her own doxastic knowledge into an unsettled and questionable set of propositions.

---

28 Which does not necessarily exclude the ability of the habitus to change. On this, see Introduction, sec. II.

29 Giddens, *Central Problems in Social Theory*, 30, 61.

30 As discussed in the Introduction.

31 See Introduction.

It should not be astounding nor even surprising that Ghazālī began the treatise he is addressing to the "Sultan of the World,[32] the King of the East and the West," with the imperative form "*iʿlam*": know! It is, after the *basmalla*, the first word in the treatise, followed by the magnificent regal titles the sultan bore, a reminder to the effect that with all his might and glory, he is nothing to measure against the real Lord of the World. "Know, Sultan of the World, the King of the East and the West, that God has bestowed upon you manifest and abundant bounties, for which you ought to be thankful and which you should widely acknowledge and publicly recognize.[33] He who does not express gratitude for God's bounties – may He be praised, and His Names sanctified – would risk losing these bounties and would be ashamed of himself on the Day of Judgement."[34]

This type of admonishing discourse may appear to us too ethereal to be real or effective, but it is not. In one of the most practical political treatises of advice ever crafted in the history of Islam, this discourse appears as real as the detailed technical advice about the minute matters of government, military organization, espionage, and the like. It appears in none other than Niẓām al-Mulk's *Siyar al-Mulūk* (*SM*), written for the Saljūq sultan Malik Shāh in 479/1086, in compliance with a request the latter had made to the powerful vizier (as well as to courtly others) to furnish him with advice and suggestions for improving the management of his empire, this with a view to ensuring that Saljūq governance be aligned with the commands of the Sharīʿa.[35] Niẓām al-Mulk seems to have been all too happy to oblige the sultan, recording in detail "everything that I know, have seen, experienced, or learned from my teachers throughout my life."[36] This treatise clearly stands as distant as any writing can get from theoretical or abstract elaborations. Indeed, every line and paragraph in it seems to have practical relevance.[37]

32 The official title of Alp Arslān. See Ibn Kathīr, *al-Bidāya wal-Nihāya*, XII, 107.

33 A complementary perspective on the conception of the ruler in Ghazālī's thought is Decosimo's "Umma of Accountability," especially at 280-83.

34 *TM*, 6. "*Iʿlam yā sulṭān al ʿālam, maliku al-sharqi wal-gharbi, inna li-Lāhi ʿalayka niʿaman ẓāhiratan wa-ālāʾan mutakāthiratan yajibu ʿalayka shukrahā wa-yataʿayyanu ʿalayka idhāʿatahā wa-nashrahā, wa-man lam yashkur Allāha, jalla thanāʾuhu wa-taqaddasat asmāʾuhu, fa-qad ʿarraḍa tilka al-niʿmata lil-zawāli wa-khajila min taqṣīrihi yawma al-qiyāma.*" Cf. Ṭurṭushī, *Sirāj al-Mulūk*, 237, who uses a similar language.

35 *SM*, 47: "*Wa-naʾmuru biʾan tuṭabbaqa al-umūra al-dīniyyata wal-dunyawiyyata... wa-naqḍiya bi-tanfīdhi awāmiri Allāhi taʿālā wa-taṭbīqiha.*" He then states that nothing that violates the Sharʿ should remain: "[*Lā*] *tasīru fī-hā bi-khilāfi al-sharʿi wa-awāmiri Allāh.*" On the religious character of the early Saljūq sultans, see Tor, "Sovereign and Pious."

36 *SM*, 47.

37 Despite her generally negative depiction of Niẓām al-Mulk, Hillenbrand, in the

Containing this advice, *SM* states that the sultan should be grateful for everything he has, whether it is God's blessings in giving him to rule a vast and powerful empire, or his good looks, sense of justice, chivalrousness, learning, mercy and empathy. This is nearly identical to Ghazālī's language. The price of gratitude for these bounties is the sultan's "good deeds toward the people and spreading justice among them."[38] In one section after another throughout the treatise, the sultan is reminded that his good deeds and administration of justice will enter the accounting on the Day of Judgment, and will bring him the rewards of this life and the hereafter.[39] It is not a coincidence that such reminders often appear at the end of sections, as if they are the real conclusions to the technical counsel that just preceded.

This was the kind of discourse that everyone understood, internalized, and believed. It was a discourse that constituted the benchmark of the political habitus. Ghazālī's discourse was no different. Our author boldly offers the sobering reminder that these bounties, however munificent, will not last forever for they will vanish upon the death of the sultan, irrespective of how long he may live. The only bounty that will survive death and remain the sultan's companion for eternity is belief and true faith (*īmān*), for this alone is the foundation of, and guarantee of salvation.

Notice here the tenuous nature of all earthly possessions, whether material, imperial, or otherwise. The mere act of ungratefulness could cause the loss of all privilege, since there is nothing that can permanently affirm a sultanic eternal grip over anything in this world. Death has a distinct proprietary function. God's instalment of death signals the human limitations on a real form of ownership. It is the proof that He is the only Real Owner in this world,

---

conclusion to her article, says the following of this pragmatic vizier: "Nizām al-Mulk was attempting an almost impossible task: to achieve balance and harmony between various perennially conflicting forces, including the Turcomans and the sultans, the sultans and their relatives, the Seljuqs and their emirs, the cities and the nomads, and the Persian bureaucrats and the populations they ruled, from Jerusalem to Samarqand. Above all, he aimed to maintain stability in an empire that he almost singlehandedly built up to cover the land mass ruled by the ancient Sasanian Empire. While he was alive, the unity of the Seljuq state remained intact. But once he was dead, nothing worked as well again." See Hillenbrand, "Nizām al-Mulk," 37. What is remarkable is that with all the political complexity that Niẓām al-Mulk had to deal with, his treatise remained faithful to what has been dubbed by Orientalism as a juristic work. Despite the parables populating the work, the essential discourse is Sharʿī-based, as evidenced in the institutions of governance that he elaborated in his work and that he considered essential for Saljūq rule.

38 *SM*, 50, 52, 71.

39 See, e.g., *SM*, 52, 53, 61, 70, 78.

al-Mālik, a world in which humans own things merely tentatively and purely metaphorically (*majāzan*). Death is an equalizer, as it has always been. But in this political tradition, death functions as a constitutional deterrence. It is a constant reminder that no matter how mighty and richly endowed the sultan is, no matter how powerful the "King of the East and the West" is, he eventually and ineluctably will die like everything and everyone else, taking with him absolutely nothing, not even the body in which he was born. He is stripped of all power and wealth and glory, even of flesh and bones, to stand before God dispossessed as he is, to account for what he had done in the prior life. In a habitus where this is unquestioned belief whose certainty is beyond certainty, the imagery and the reality of it are terrifying. But all of this is merely the "theoretical" and "credal" knowledge of the "foundations of belief." There is much more that comes to build on these foundations, to prop them and give them a structured force of motives and ethical direction.

As typical of Ghazālī, he resorts to the arboreal metaphor of a tree that becomes at once an ontological and cosmological figuration of belief and its structural constitution of praxis. To believe, to have faith, is not just to have the conviction of God's existence and engage in ritualistic worship but rather to cultivate much more in and through that complex structure, a structure whose roots are planted deep in the earth and whose upper branches touch the highest heavens.[40] Faith and belief are the seeds that give life to the tree. Yet, much more needs to be done in order to make the tree grow and flourish, to make it a cosmological manifestation of political reality. To fail to cultivate the tree is to let the wind and storm sweep the seeds away, and if not the seeds, then even the sapling. The tree must be sturdy, strong, and enduring before the sultan breathes his last breath. If he should die, "God forbid," before this happens, then the sultan "will meet his Lord without the benefit of any kindness." The horror of this threat is all too obvious, even for a relative stranger to the habitus. The language is powerful, commanding, and able to put the sultan in his proper cosmological and even earthly place.

The tree has ten roots and ten branches, the roots having to do with the heart's belief while the branches with praxis, for the latter is the consequence and practical manifestation of the former. The Sublime sultan, who "was agreeable to have these ten roots and ten branches explained (*sharḥ*) to him, must work hard to cultivate this tree." The first of your duties, Ghazālī tells the sultan, is to allocate one day a week, Friday, for worship and prayer, a day entirely

40 *TM*, 6: "*Aṣluhā fī qaʿri al-arḍi wa-farʿuhā fil-samāʾ*."

dedicated to the Lord of the World, your Lord. This is not too much to ask, for if you were to order your own slave to exclusively dedicate just one day of the week to your service, you would certainly not deem it overly demanding. Should your slave disobey you, what would his fate at your hands be, although you are not the creator of your slave? You are merely his master, and in that way, you own him merely metaphorically (*majāzan*). But God owns you in the very real sense of the word (*ḥaqīqatan*), a qualitatively different type of ownership. Unlike your own slave, you are a real and true slave of God who owns you in every way imaginable. So why would you accept from your self what you would not accept from your slave?[41]

I have chosen to use the same active voice Ghazālī adopted in order to convey the directness and commanding tone in which he addressed the sultan. Ghazālī then tells him to wake up early every Friday, and to dress himself humbly, to fast, pray, to practice being silent, and to repeat the *Shāhāda* a thousand times, and then have a Qāri' recite the Qur'ān to him the whole day. Last but not least, he should give to charity as much as he is capable of. Friday's works will atone for the other days of the week. But the more important function of all these directives and prescriptions is their power as technologies of self-cultivation. The sultan is not just a proactive agent, operating on this in the world that lay outside him; rather, he is the site and object of an *iterative* ethical labor (praying in the regular and prescribed manner, repeating the *Shahāda* a thousand times, listening to Qur'ānic recitation all day, wearing a certain clothing, every Friday, etc.). He does not only rule under the terms of the established Law; he cultivates himself under the prescriptions of its ethical technologies as well. The true worldly freedom and eternal salvation of the sultan lie in the carriage of *ʿadl*, the expression of the proper management of the affairs of *dīn* and *dunyā*, the Māwardīan duo.

After this short introduction, Ghazālī begins to elaborate on the ten roots, which have the air of theological postulates, but we would gravely err to limit their significance and implications to abstract theology or merely suppositional metaphysics. Perhaps the first lesson we must learn about studying Islamic traditions and cultures in history is that phenomena is nearly always multilayered and porous, where nearly everything is interconnected. It is impossible to segregate metaphysics and cosmology from theology, and these three from politics or law, or *adab* or history, not even from astronomy and anatomy. In due course, I will dissect these relations in their own relative contexts, but for

41 *TM*, 7.

now I wish to stress that Ghazālī's heavy-sounding metaphysics and theology are prime materials for constitutional and political analysis.

The first root is the fact of creation and createdness. "Know, O' sultan, that you are a created thing and that you have a creator; He is the creator of the world and all that is in the world. He is one and has no partner ... and while everyone needs him, he needs no one."[42] This theological and metaphysical postulate is followed by a series of others that emphasize the omnipotence and omniscience of God.

Yet, the theological language cannot mask the political potency of this discourse, nor the more obvious political power of God: "His Rule is the highest point of perfection... He is the Owner of Kingship, and his Rule is the only real rule."[43] Here, Ghazālī establishes the sovereignty of God against the relatively puny sultan as he does against the latter's provisional, ephemeral, and earthly power. Delimiting the derivativeness of sultanic power is a primary constitutional fact, a foundational doctrine of Islamic constitutionalism. The sultan owes God for all his bounties and even basic possessions: his own body and body parts, the fact of his fortunate election by God to play this crucial role, his success in ruling a vast empire, but also the very recognition that he has an intangible and all-powerful owner and master. In this discourse, sultanic power is cut down to size. Notice, other than the opening line where the sultan's regal titles are invoked, Ghazālī offers the sultan neither accolades nor encomium. The sultanic power here is marginal, derivative, and altogether not worthy, relatively speaking, of much focus.

Putting the sultan in his place has thus far been a doctrinal and theoretical matter, which Ghazālī already underscored. The roots have to do with knowledge, faith, and belief, altogether amounting to *ʿilm*, *maʿrifa*, *īmān*, and *iʿtiqād*. The branches of the tree offer the balance, where deed meets belief and where praxis meets knowledge and faith. A limp branch is a sign of weak roots, just as the work of the body is the signature of the heart's faith. The roots therefore are nothing but works, praxis, and ultimately a complex process of embodiment. It is a process of translation, from the language of the heart and mind to the language of practice and doing actual things in the world (*aʿmāl*).

Aʿmāl are grounded in faith, in the way the branches grow out of the trunk and its roots. These works demand the avoidance of things prohibited and performance of those things mandated. In the case of sultans, *aʿmāl* are of

42 *TM*, 9.
43 *TM*, 10: "*Wa-annahu taʿālā ʿalā kulli shay'in qadīr. Wa-mulkuhu fī nihāyati al-kamāli... huwa māliku al-mulki lā mulka illā mulkuhu.*"

two kinds, one relating to "that which is between you and your God," whereas the other is that "which is between you and the people." The latter category is entirely construed around the quality of being just (*'adl*) toward the subjects, as well as refraining from engaging in *ẓulm* against them. *Ẓulm* is the antonym of *'adl*, essentially meaning a deviation from what is customary, what is generally expected or normative. *Ẓulm* is simply "putting something in a place to which it does not belong" or "veering away from the original intention;" "the source of *ẓulm* is *jawr*" and "exceeding a limit;" "*jawr*" is "an antonym of intention," in the sense that it is the "abandoning of the path or direction one was originally supposed to follow." *Ẓulm* and *jawr* are not just infractions; they are mere neglect, failure to meet the standard or what is expected, and can be committed by humans against God himself.[44]

44 Ibn Manẓūr, *Lisān al-'Arab*, IV, 179ff; XI, 514ff; XII, 433 ff.: "*Al-ẓulmu waḍ'u al-shay'i fī ghayri mawḍi'ihi;*" "*wa-aṣlu al-ẓulmi al-jawru wa-mujāwazatu al-ḥaddi, wal-ẓulmu al-maylu 'an al-qaṣd*"; "*al-jawru ḍiddu al-qaṣdi... wa-tarku al-qaṣda fil-sayr.*" "*Jāra yajūru, idhā māla wa-ḍalla.*" "*Al-'adlu mā qāma fil-nufūsi annahu mustaqīmun wa-huwa ḍiddu al-jawri... wa-fī asmā'i Allāhi al-ḥusnā, al-'adlu huwa al-ladhī lā yamīlu bi-hi al-hawā fa-yajūru fil-ḥukmi... wal-'adlu huwa al-ḥukmu bil-ḥaqq.*" In defining *ẓulm*, Ibn Manẓūr invokes the Qur'ānic meaning in Q. 31:13: "*Inna al-shirka la-ẓulmin 'aẓīmin*" ("associating with God is a great *ẓulm*"), saying that *shirk* is "the greatest of *ẓulm*" because *shirk* amounts to "attributing the bounties of God to someone else." Note here that *ẓulm* may be directed at a higher authority and does not necessarily presuppose an act directed by a superior against an inferior. In addition to "beating people" and subjecting them to excessive taxation and unlawfully "jailing them," Sha'rānī includes in *ẓulm* drinking intoxicants, fornication, and sodomy. Interestingly, Sha'rānī advised that the Ṣūfīs who befriend the ruling elite must distance themselves from these latter if they receive from them gifts of food and clothing, for he deemed such presents a form of *ẓulm*. *Mukhtaṣar Irshād al-Mughaffalīn*, 48, 164. Abū al-Baqā' defines *'adl* as the antonym of *jawr*: "*Al-'adlu aṣluhu ḍiddu al-jawr.*" To be a *'adl* is to be "straight" (*istiqāma*). In Sharī'a, he writes, *'adl* is the "right path" (*ṭarīqu al-ḥaqq*) consisting of the choice to avoid that which has been legally prohibited "*maḥẓūrun dīnan.*" It is, he says, of two kinds, the first of which is that which has been established on the basis of the apparent meaning of the law: "*Hiya mā thabata bi-ẓāhiri al-'aqli wal-dīni li-annahumā yaḥmilānahu 'alā al-istiqāmati wa-yazjirānahu 'an ghayrihā ẓāhiran.*" The other is internal, hidden, and thus subjective and so it is measured by the yardstick of consequences, namely, that which does not lead to undue difficulty, hardship, or misapplication of Sharī'a's rules and punishments: "*Bāṭina, wa-hiya lā yudraku madāhā li-annahā tatafāwatu, fa'tubira fī dhālika mā lā yu'addī ilā al-ḥaraji wal-mashaqqati wa-taḍyī'i ḥudūdi al-shar'i.*" This is known by experiment and experience (*tajriba*), where practice and action make it clear that reason and religion are being followed and applied, rather than the passions and base desires. It is by avoiding grave sins (murder, etc.) and the consistent or repeated commission of minor ones: "*Wa-huwa mā ẓahara bil-tajribati rujḥāna jihati al-dīni wal-'aqli 'alā ṭarīqi al-hawā wal-shahwāti bil-ijtinābi 'an al-kabā'iri wa-tarki al-iṣrāri 'alā al-ṣaghā'iri.*" *'Adl* is the exact application of the law and its values, no more and no less. It is to give what one owes and take what one is entitled to. To make this clear, Abū al-Baqā' distinguishes

Jawr and *ẓulm*, the two most distinguished political terms we nowadays use to describe modern tyranny, oppression, and injustice, had, in the linguistic and conceptual repertoire of premodern Arabic, a low degree of tolerance for deviation from the "normative path," that which has been defined according to the norms and values of the Sharīʿa.[45] Which is to say that for a ruler to engage in *ẓulm* and *jawr*, or to be described as *ẓālim* or *jāʾir*, he does not need to veer too much from the established path or the generally accepted norm. We therefore must be wary of charging these terms with too much meaning in reading their modern usages and connotations onto Islamic political practice before the nineteenth century. Sultanic acts do not have to indulge in plain tyranny or oppression to be called *ẓulm* or *jawr*.

To violate the divine charge of *ʿadl* is to betray God's trust, a breach deserving of a punishment far more severe than infractions committed in the first category. What is "between you and your God" may be liable for pardon, for God can decide for himself how commodious or sparing his forgiveness will be; but God will not pass in silence over the violations you commit against "your fellow human beings." In fact, no king can escape God's wrath, except one who is equitable and just, for this exaction defines the very idea of justice and fairness applied by God to such a king on the Day of Judgment.[46]

Ghazālī deploys here one of the most expansive definitions of *ʿadl*. Having a low bar, *ʿadl* can all too easily be violated. It is sensitive and quite brittle. Yet,

---

this concept from *iḥsān*, where one gives more than what one owes, and one willingly and happily receives less than one is owed. *ʿAdl* belongs to what is strictly owed, to all parties concerned, and what they strictly owe each other. *Iḥsān*, on the other hand, is optional and voluntary, since it involves supererogatory acts: "*Wal-ʿadlu huwa an yuʿṭī mā ʿalayhi wa-yaʾkhudha mā lahu; wal-iḥsānu huwa an yuʿtya akthara mimmā ʿalayhi wa-yaʾkhudha aqalla mimmā la-hu, fal-iḥsānu zāʾidun ʿalayhi, fa-taḥarrī al-ʿdla wājibun wa-taḥarri al-iḥsāna nadbun wa-taṭawwuʿun.*" Abū al-Baqāʾ, *Kulliyyāt*, 639-40. See also Nuwayrī, *Nihāyat al-Arab*, VI, 33-39, where *ʿadl* is contrasted to *ẓulm*, 39-41. In *ADD*, 227, Māwardī writes that the violation of *ʿadl* is *jawr* and *ẓulm*, but he sees a difference between the two: excessive *ʿadl*, meaning when too much is done to accomplish a goal (say the ruler's harsh punishments for the purpose of imposing public order) is *jawr* (also described as *ṭāghūt*, from the verb *ṭaghā*, that is, to exceed a limit, to overflow, or to transgress. Ibn Manẓūr, *Lisān al-ʿArab*, XV, 8 ff. In modern Arabic, *ṭāghūt* becomes a synonym for "tyranny."). However, when less than what is due is given or done (such as when a plaintiff or a victim is not awarded the damages or full compensation he or she is due), this would then constitute *ẓulm*.

45 A point made explicitly clear by Abū al-Baqāʾ, *Kulliyyāt*, 639-40. See previous note.

46 *TM*, 14: "*Wa-ammā mā yataʿallaqu bi-maẓālimi al-nāsi fa-innahu lā yatajāwazu bi-hi ʿanka ʿalā kulli ḥālin yawma al-qiyamati wa-khaṭaruhu ʿaẓīmun, wa-lā yaslamu min hādhā al-khaṭari aḥadun min al-mulūki illā malikun ʿamila bil-ʿadli wal-inṣāfi li-yaʿlama kayfa yaṭlubu al-ʿadla wal-inṣāfa yawma al-qiyāma.*"

despite its delicate constitution, or perhaps because of it, *ʿadl* is conceived to be grounded in many principles and practices, each of which is a necessary condition that needs to coalesce with the others in order to create the sufficient condition that produces this desideratum. The first condition is a deep awareness of the gravity of the task of ruling, for it is a divine grace and bounty. He who performs it properly, will be a favorite of God in the Hereafter, whereas he who mishandles it will suffer torment whose severity is not exceeded except by that inflicted on those who deny God's munificence. This theme is abundantly attested by pointed Prophetic traditions.[47]

The second necessary condition is for the sultan to look forward to meeting and consulting with the ulama, those learned in the law and the principles of *dīn* to whose advice and counsel he should listen and listen carefully. As we have seen and will continue to see throughout, the culture of political counsel in Islam was robust and integral to the political habitus, which is to say that it was taken as a truism and thus integral to the doxa. Seeking and giving advice was not merely a commendable practice, sanctioned by Prophetic authority, but was effectively enshrined in royal decrees of appointment as an essential requirement to be properly fulfilled.[48] It was, in other words, one of the forms of political participation.

Third: "It is not enough that you yourself do not commit an injustice; you should not accept an injustice from any of your officers, deputies, or delegates, for you are accountable [to God] for their *ẓulm*."[49] The fourth is controlling your anger, the source of much evil and of the commission of excesses. "He who accustoms himself to controlling his anger walks in the path of the prophets and the friends of God; he who fails to do so walks in the path of beasts and wild animals."[50]

The fifth is constantly assuming yourself to be in the place of people who seek your justice and file grievances against mistreatment. "Whatever you would not accept for yourself, you should not accept for others. If you do, then you have betrayed your subjects and cheated the people whom you have been charged to govern (*ahla wilāyatika*)."[51]

---

47 *TM*, 14-15: "The justice of a sultan on one day is more beloved to God than seventy years of worship"; and "the most beloved and closest of people to God the Exalted is a just sultan (*al-sulṭān al-ʿādil*), whereas the most hated and least close is a sultan *jā'ir*." *Jā'ir* is the active form of *jawr*, on which see n. 44, above.

48 See discussion of Qalqashandī's *ʿuhūd* in ch. 5.

49 *TM*, 22.

50 *TM*, 22-23.

51 *TM*, 26.

Sixth, "do not underrate the urgent need of people who stand at your door for help," for this is more important to fulfill than voluntary worship. Seventh, "do not let yourself be accustomed to engaging in desires, such as wearing ostentatious clothes and eating delicious foods. You should court contentment in all aspects of life, for there is no justice without contentment."[52] The idea here is that lack of contentment amounts to greed, and greed is one of the motives for transgressing the rights of others to satisfy one's avarice. Eighth, "whenever it is possible for you to do things gently and with kindness, and avoid harshness and bruteness, you should do so."[53] Ninth, you should endeavor (*tajtahid*) to please your subjects by conforming to the Sharʿ. And finally, tenth, no one should be satisfied at the expense of violating the Sharīʿa, for should someone grieve out of the bounds of Sharīʿa, then his grievance should not matter.[54]

Ghazālī then returns to the metaphor of the tree, saying that both the roots, branches, and all, maintain life by virtue of the provision of water from two sources, two springs of life, so to speak, two fonts of knowledge. The first font is the full cognition that life on Earth is ephemeral and that humans are mere travelers, and the distance of travel is from the mother's womb to the grave. Every passing year is a mile, and every month is a stop on the way. Every week, day, and hour are stations and curbs on the highway of life, and every breath is a walking step. With every breath, we come closer to the hereafter, for every breath is a reminder that the final settlement is the permanence and eternality of the next world. No one will take with them to that world except what they have done and did not do, their failures and sins, their successes and good deeds. And it is in that permanent world that one stands to account for the balance of the good and the bad, and live through the consequences, good or bad, for eternity.

The second font is an intimate knowledge of the last breath, and specifically its imminence. The highest form of rationality is to be fully cognizant of the continuity and continuousness of the relationship between living in the Here-and-Now and in the Hereafter. It is an obligation of all people to keep

52 *TM*, 27: "*Wa-lākin tastaʿmilu al-qanāʿata fī jamīʿi al-ashyāʾi fa-lā ʿadla bi-lā qanāʿa.*"

53 *TM*, 28. The terms used here are *rifq* and *luṭf* for being kind and gentle; and *shidda* and *ʿunf* for harshness and unkindness/bruteness, respectively. Arabic lexicons define *ʿunf* as an antonym of *rifq*, and *rifq* is given as a synonym of *luṭf* (kindness). *Rifq* is the quality of being gentle. Note here that definitions are given either by negation or by synonymity. The modern definition of *ʿunf* as violence, often extreme violence, does not appear in these classical and highly authoritative lexicons. We recall that a similar approach to defining terms occurred in the case of *ẓulm* and *jawr*. See n. 44, above.

54 *TM*, 28-29.

this idea in mind, especially kings. Kings often disturb the hearts of the people and send to them agents who do ill and sow fear among them, but all of this is not far from the presence (*ḥaḍra*) of a fellow called ʿIzrāʾīl, the angel of death. Ghazālī brings the potential horrors ʿIzrāʾīl could inflict through vivid images and graphic stories, of arrogant kings who are snatched, at the peak of their strength and glory, from the back of their horses by the inevitability of ʿIzrāʾīl's swift grip. In a world that did not know atheism, cosmic accident, and the other theology of scientific doubt, this is a horrifying picture whose power of deterrence is formidable. This was the habitus, and Ghazālī's discursive onslaught is nothing short of a *doxa*. To deny this doxastic power is to engage, historiographically, in an irredeemable anachronism.

One of the roots of the tree Ghazālī recounted is the acknowledgement of the Prophet. The discourse here and elsewhere, by Ghazālī and others, tends to the theological, and as such it has been invariably interpreted in these terms. But theology, at least in its mainstays, is eminently political. The idea of the dispensability of the caliphate and the array of debates that surrounded this issue in the twentieth century[55] would be properly vitiated at the first serious analysis of theology as constitutionalism and politics.[56] This is because we, in modernity, have always assumed that religion is an intrusion on politics, two domains that should be kept separate while at the same time giving politics and the state the power and authority to decide on the place and limit of religion in society and polity. This profoundly secularist assumption has qualitatively distorted, even fractured, the very foundations of our scholarship since it has *ab initio* precluded from discussion and consideration – that is from our epistemology – the fact that the political offices in Islam are organically and structurally connected with everything else, that if we were to take the concept of Prophethood in Islam seriously, the very question of the dispensability of the caliphate would amount to an act of dismembering not only the Islamic body politic but also Islam's very ways of life, be they directly political or not at all.

Even a glimpse at Māwardī's *ADD* reveals the political significance of Prophetic ethics. When discussing the concurrence, or entailment, between virtuousness and acts, Māwardī readily deploys the example of the Prophet as

55 Such as the works of Alī ʿAbd al-Rāziq, *Al-Islām wa-Uṣūl al-Ḥukm*, and Rashīd Riḍā, *al-Khilāfa*. For a thoughtful history of the institution and its articulations in Muslim political and *dīn*ic imagination, see Hassan, *Longing for the Lost Caliphate*.

56 For a useful account about the necessity of caliphate in early Islamic political writings, see Yücesoy, "Justification of Political Authority."

the site of this concurrence, with Qur'ānic citational support.[57] The structural connections between virtue and act manifest themselves best in the figure of the Prophet, because "in the created world, Prophethood is the highest of stations." This is because prophecy "encompasses the good of this world and the Hereafter." It is an all-inclusive function that has relevance to all aspects of life, material and spiritual, social and political. To promote these worldly and eschatological goods and interests, God sent to the Arabians and others a Prophet, whose competence and range of qualities are the best fit for the task. The Prophethood is the most complete set of qualities ever to be found in a human being, for they must cover every dimension of human life, in the here and the hereafter. This is why the *raison d'être* of Muhammad's Prophethood is thought to be summed up precisely in one of the most famous and authenticated reports: "I have been sent to you to perfect the goodness of virtue."[58]

Ghazālī explains to the King the fundamentals of the idea of Prophethood, which modern scholarship has largely missed as well. God, he says, has determined (*qaddara*) that humans, in their complicated lives, do not know what truly leads to happiness and what leads to misery, and so he created the angels in order to explain (*li-yuwaḍḍiḥū*) to people the "ways leading to happiness and misery." One of these people is "our Prophet Muhammad," the Seal of the Prophets whose mission is the most complete and perfect.[59]

The general understanding of this "completeness" and "perfection" has invariably been theological and, in modernity, particularly polemical. But there is much more to this immensely important concept than these sloganeering adages suggest. The concept of completeness of religion, of the perfection of it, is a substantive matter bearing grave implications. While it is proper to regard the Prophet as a person and his status as a personal manifestation of belief and exemplary conduct, we must resist the temptation to restrict our view to this dimension. The Prophet as a person and his Prophethood as a concept must not and cannot be segregated from each other, for they both mesh into each other as at once concrete and abstract categories. To maintain the personal imaginary of the Prophet as an exclusive meaning is to restrict the range of the abstract concept of Prophethood; it is to always see things

57 *TN*, 44; Q. 68:5.

58 *TN*, 44, and n. 4 therein. The Ḥadīth has more than one version, one of which is "*Buʿithtu bi makārimi al akhlāq*" while another is "*Buʿithtu li'utammima ḥusna al-akhlāq.*" See also Māwardī, *Al-Amthāl wal-Ḥikam*, 53. This Ḥadīth is the first to appear in the book, which consists of ten chapters, each containing, in this order, Prophetic reports, proverbs of wisdom, and poetry.

59 *TM*, 13.

within an individual and embodied context and semiotics; it is to restrict the applicability of the substantive content of what it means to be a Prophet to the personal and non-institutional, and to the concrete and immediate rather than to the abstract, notional, and structural. Arguably, these restrictions and confinements are the functions of a secular or secularizing mind, one that is no longer able to see the sacred as the ruling domain of the public. Reducing Prophethood to the personal and, by implication, to the private is at the core of the Wittgensteinian fallacies we have noted in the Introduction.

IV

It is a universal tenet of Islam that God chose to perform his task of revelation or of creating *dīn*s for humans through sending prophets, and Muhammad was obviously just one of them, with the historicizing and ethicizing proviso that he was the last. True, this tenet possesses clear theological, metaphysical, and spiritual significance, but the sum of this significance pales in comparison with the functional causality of this choice. With his omnipotence, God could have accomplished the task of creating *dīn* in any number of other ways, but the way he decided finally to do things cannot escape the verdict that it was about a choice of the instrument that could accomplish this goal.

The function, however, is as expansive and comprehensive as life itself, but not just life as individual life or even collective, generationally successive life on this Earth; it is life in the here and there, now and forever. Nor is life in this context a biological or physical matter of generation and corruption; it is life in all of its demands and complexity, its effects across generations, and its interconnectedness across social, anthropological, and political ages. To understand the dimensionality of Islamic Prophethood, we must look at the entire tradition-based, intellectual, and political landscape of Islam. Prophethood was so encompassing and pervasive – biographically, theologically, legally, epistemologically, ontologically, aesthetically, affectively and otherwise – that a categorical or wholesale application of it to any given context would be meaningless, if not altogether impossible. It operated as a multilayered concept which was to be pulled out in strands and slices, as deemed relevant to the situation at hand or field of practice or inquiry. In other words, the use of the Prophetic model had context-specific functional relevance. You cannot invoke the model wholesale for the whole of life or the world. You invoke it, apply it, and use it for specific contexts or fixed, bounded fields. And in every context, the strand would be context-specific, lacking the capability of total generalization or universalization. For example, the Prophet in the sphere of the law, of Ṣūfīsm, and of politics were three different things, three different identities, however much they were interlinked, and however much they constituted three sides or faces of the same personality, the same concept, or the same conceptual configuration of what it means to have a Muslim Prophethood.

In Ṣūfīsm, in all of its varieties, different intellectual voices, and markedly dissimilar orders, there remained a single teleology that unified all Ṣūfī strands into a cohesive whole, namely, to reach as complete knowledge of the self as possible through the operation of the self on the self by means of technologies of ethical cultivation. The core purpose of these technologies is the so-called purification of the self from bodily and physical attachments of the here and now, which is another way of saying that the purpose is to attain an inner freedom that allows the self to absorb divine qualities. These qualities cannot, of course, be known directly from God, leaving the Messenger as the next best point of access to the Highest Model, the divine model. The Prophet here is not just a personality, but a range of attributes and qualities that flesh out the range of virtuosity, the full scale of the Ethical. Here, the Ethical is the Prime Organizer of all life, in all of its aspects. The Ethical here is the subject and predicate of life, its grammar and syntax. The teleology of Ṣūfīsm is the dissolving of subjectivity in the world of the Ethical, a world driven by the Prime Mover of love and intense passion. Prophethood therefore is the mediation (*safāra*)[60] of the embodiment of Extreme Divine Love as it gives manifestation to the Ethical constitution of the human, whose highest form is the Perfect Human, the Prophethood itself.[61] This was the microscopic dimension of the Prophethood, that which attends to the individual in his or her spirituality, psychology, inner being, and inner constitution. Ṣūfīsm as a holistic technique of self-formation – and that is what it was[62] – is the individuated side of Prophethood and, accordingly, the superintendent of the individual soul and the self.

60 Māwardī, *A'lām al-Nubuwwa*, 181.
61 See also Qasṭalānī, *Mawāhib*, I, 87.
62 This is not to neglect the socio-economic and political aspects of the Ṣūfī orders and social movements, but it is to argue that the techniques and telos I am describing constituted the foundation (even the springboard) for later manifestations of the social, economic, and political effects.

For many modern commentators on Ṣūfism, it is difficult to detect a salient narrative of political structure in what is seen as an almost exclusively spiritual sphere. Ṣūfism is often viewed by these commentators not only as "legendary" and lacking in rationality, but also as markedly inattentive to the practical aspects of life.[63] While such charges are grounded in judgments or presuppositions that possess a fixed, and perhaps an excessively limited, conception of reality, it remains true that the Ṣūfī discursive tradition, with its varied versions or sub-traditions, does not engage the political sphere in the ways that have become familiar to us. There is no Ṣūfī work, for instance, that would be attentive, say, to delimiting the constitutional spheres, or to the technical modalities of governance, such as land tenure, taxation, irrigation systems, penal law, and military organization. Taking these for granted,[64] Ṣūfism attends to the inner constitution of the subject that *undertakes* these functions, that internal entity and foundational structures of the self which are intended to *prop up and sustain* the reality of these pragmatic and practical spheres.

Yet, it is precisely because this internal reality of the self is both particular and universal, individual and cosmological, that Ṣūfism is preeminently political. For the world of Ṣūfism, especially in its Akbarian version, is interconnected and made of one cloth, where the particular and the general, the spiritual and the material, the anthropological and the transcendental fuse into each other. Most important for our concern is the fusion of the spiritual and subjective with the political and the world of politics. And it is here where Ibn ʿArabī in particular is most helpful in the way he articulates the connections between the various ontological domains on which other writers normally fall largely silent.

Ibn ʿArabī commands the distinction of an exquisitely refined mind that unfailingly manages to tease out meanings often hidden to those otherwise great political thinkers such as Māwardī and even Ghazālī. The refinement is not merely rhetorical, poetic, or even conceptual. Rather it is the endless excavation of reality so as to discover (or uncover) the unity of ontology, in both its ontic and phenomenological necessary connections, that had existed between and among all things in the world. It is through exploring the fabric of this unity that Ibn ʿArabī unravels the structures of Islamic political thought by bringing to the fore the political elements of what I have described as an ethically enshrined epistemic genealogy, which has formed the foundation of the Islamic conception of politics.

---

63 See, for instance, the prominent case of Muḥammad ʿĀbid al-Jābirī. For a critique, see Hallaq, *Reforming Modernity*, 18-25.

64 As evidenced in Abū Naṣr al-Sarrāj's powerful argument. See his *al-Lumaʿ*, 21-39.

We have said much so far to explicate the hold that the institution of the caliphate/imamate has had over Muslim political imagination, and the political meaning that this institution possessed in mapping out the Islamic constitutional configuration. Now we must see how Ibn ʿArabī charts the archeology of this institution within the structures of human experience, an archeology that is totalistic and indivisible. Ibn ʿArabī speaks where silence prevails, and sheds light, through his telescopic vision, on the metaphorically dark and hidden universe that lies beyond the visible planetary constellations. It is my argument that politically speaking, Ibn ʿArabī does not so much introduce a new political line of thought as he brings to the surface the potential depth that was not articulated by the Māwardīs, Ghazālīs and Juwaynīs of the mainstream political tradition. It is this explication and excavation that interests me here.

We have also been speaking of the caliphate and the imamate interchangeably, reflecting accurately the Muslim writers' indiscriminate use of the terms. Reading Ibn ʿArabī, however, showcases the inaccuracy of this interchangeability, because the ontological and epistemological genealogy he charts will reveal that what is ultimately at stake is the very paradigmatic concept of *khilāfa* – the imamate being a confined appellation, if not a false equivalent and a crude political interpretation of that paradigmatic concept. *Khilāfa* or caliphate is not merely a designation of a function or a concrete political institution but rather the mass of threads that constitute the warp and weft – the very cloth – of which the reality of political-existence-as-a-being is made.[65] Which is also to say that being-*qua*-being itself is political, however spiritual, "religious," Godly, ethereal, or material it is. In order to reflect this cosmological meaning of the term, it would be rather apposite to translate Ibn ʿArabī's concept of *khilāfa* as caliphism.

On the first page of his remarkable essay *al-Insān al-Kāmil* (*IK*), Ibn ʿArabī outlines his conception of the origins of creation. Perhaps articulating the idea that there would be *no conception of existence without a human mind to conceive it*, he posits that the aim of creating the world was the actualization of the Perfect Human. This Human, therefore, is the *very reason* of creation.

The essay begins with the citation of Q. 2: 30-33:

> And when your Lord said to the angels "Indeed, I will make upon the Earth a *khalīfa*," they said "Will you place upon it one who causes

65 This sense is supported by the overall effect of the narratives reported and analyzed in Hassan, *Longing for the Lost Caliphate*.

> corruption therein and sheds blood, while we declare Your praise and sanctify You?" He said: "Indeed, I know that which you do not know." And He taught Adam the names, all of them. Then He presented them to the angels and said: "Inform me of the names of these, if you are truthful." They said: "Exalted are You, we have no knowledge except what You have taught us. Indeed, it is You who is the Knowing and the Wise." He said: "O Adam, inform them of their names," and when he had informed of their names, He said: "Did I not tell you that I know the Unseen [reality] of the heavens and the Earth? And I know what you reveal and what you conceal."

Ibn ʿArabī then augments this verse with a Prophetic report which declares that "God created Adam in His own image."[66] These texts are not only key to political genealogy but also constitute the matrix of the narrative that is to come. Here, there are two kinds of humans who emerge in the act of creation, the Perfect Human (*al-insān al-kāmil*) and the Animal Human (*al-insān al-ḥayawān*). The latter resembles the former in shape and appearance, so much so that not everyone can tell them apart. But the Perfect Human is sharply distinguished from the Animal Human, for the Perfect Human is the Custodian of Truth, this latter being the aggregation of disparate truths which have been gathered together to make a whole, of whose fabric the Perfect Human was made. This is the effect of God's teaching of Adam "all the names," names that even the angels and archangels did not know.

It is a cardinal tenet in Ibn ʿArabī that the Perfect Human is superior to the angels in every way,[67] because he is the replica of God. This is why in the process of creation, all the world has come from nothing into something, from inexistence to existence, except the Human.[68] Being the only entity that "emerged from one existence into another," the Human, the depository of God's knowledge, "has no like in the world." "If it were not for the Perfect Human, none of the world would have been created," for there is no other reason for creating the world.[69] This narrative would seem to smack of anthropocentrism, but as we will see throughout, it is anything but that. The human, challenged by the attainment of Perfection, is the site of a privilege that is holistically defined by the heavy burden of ethical responsibility and accountability. To be a Perfect

66 *IK*, 7.
67 *IK*, 19-20, 26.
68 *IK*, 8.
69 *IK*, 8.

Human, as Farīd al-Dīn al-ʿAṭṭār would affirm,[70] is to endure endless travails which themselves are the securities for the attainment and maintenance of that sublime status, human perfection, a privileged status of ethical restraint, responsibility, and accountability.

The Perfect Human is the highest point of intelligent creation. All animals possess knowledge of things in their world and can perform tasks, but these skills are instinctual, having been built into their initial constitution as animals. They do not comprehend the means (or methods?) through which their very knowledge and acts come about, which is to say that lack of self-awareness is not only what differentiates them from humans, but also defines the difference in the form of the rationalities that the two groups possess. Humans, on the other hand, comprehend the very processes involved in their thinking, which lead them to achieve theoretical and practical ends. The Perfect Human no doubt shares this form of rationality with the Animal Human but he also enjoys a superadded quality: Knowledge of Divine Knowledge.

At this point we discover that the Perfect Human is not the highest form of humanity. The Perfect Human is only the *khalīfa* of the Universal Human (*al-insān al-kull al-kabīr*) who does not materialize, Ibn ʿArabī seems to say, in any human or physical world. The Perfect Human is an abridgement of the Universal Human, the latter representing the world itself (*ʿālam*), in its design and createdness as an entity of Truth.[71] In *al-Tadbīrāt al-Ilāhiyya*, Ibn ʿArabī casts the matter in terms of Major and Minor Worlds, the latter being a microcosm of the former. All that is found scattered and seemingly disconnected in the *Magnus Mundus* comes cogently together in the form of the microcosmic world, the world of the Human.[72] This Human, whose apex is the Perfect type, is the soul that is endowed by God in the realm of earthly creation as a *khalīfa*, for the soul defines the quiddity of that which is ensouled.[73]

The superiority of the Perfect Human is such that what exists only in potentiality (*bil-quwwa*) in the Animal Human exists in him in actuality (*bil-fiʿl*). Which is also to say that the Animal Human does have the potential to rise to the rank of the Perfect Human who is an actualized manifestation of the Universal Human, this latter being a throwback to Plato's Theory of Forms. The Perfect Human possesses not only the rational knowledge of the Animal Human but also the capacity to derive knowledge through *kashf* and *dhawq*,

70 Attar, *Conference of the Birds*.
71 *IK*, 10; Ibn ʿArabī, *al-Tadbīrāt al-Ilāhiyya*, 8.
72 Ibn ʿArabī, *al-Tadbīrāt al-Ilāhiyya*, 8-11. See also Tazi Hemida, "Ṣūfī Conception of Order."
73 Ibn ʿArabī, *al-Tadbīrāt al-Ilāhiyya*, 20.

the cognitive and discursive means to emulate divine qualities.[74] This Human is therefore the final cause and ultimate telos (*ghāya*), the reason for the world and for all human life.[75]

The Perfect Human's endowment of perfection does not seem to be entirely a predetermined divine gift to certain human beings over others. Human agency is undoubtedly both a prerequisite and integral to cultivating perfection, but the site and subject matter of cultivation must be blessed by unabridged and wholesome faculties that possess the potential to bring perfection to a consummate status. These faculties are indeed God's gift, one that affords the full potential to reach perfection but not without individual agency, an ethico-rational autonomy that propels the self-cultivation of the Animal Human into the image of divine perfection.

Therefore, at the lowest rung of human existence stands the Animal Human who shares the very same form of the Perfect Human, the latter being the "shadow of God" (*ẓillu Allāh*) and the mouthpiece of God's sense of Right and Truth; which is why he is the "Deputy of Truth" (*Nā'ibu al-Ḥaqq*).[76] These two extremes, the Animal Human and the Perfect Human, stand at the opposite ends of a spectrum, along which are strung a variety of other types of Humans. "In the age of Prophethood, the Perfect Human would be a Prophet, but when

74 Kāshānī, *Mu'jam Iṣṭilāḥāt al-Ṣūfiyya*, 346.
75 *IK*, 12.
76 *IK*, 9. Ignoring constitutional and political-legal analysis, Orientalists, including Orientalized Muslim scholars, have misinterpreted the notion, expressed in a Prophetic Ḥadīth, that the Muslim ruler claimed to be "the shadow of God on Earth." The Ḥadīth runs as follows: "The *sulṭān* is God's shadow on Earth; to him all the oppressed address themselves." Ibn Taymiyya, for instance, emphasized the second part of the Ḥadīth, arguing that since God is merciful and always aims to improve the lot of those who worship him, then he who does good in accordance with God's will will have fulfilled a divine command. The sultan is the shadow of God on earth because he is the most powerful agent capable of fulfilling this command. Being a shadow therefore is a duty not a privilege. See Ibn Taymiyya, *al-Khilāfa wal-Mulk*, 54. Orientalists not only misunderstood the meaning of the Ḥadīth, they also constructed interpretations that do not sit well within Islam's constitutional conception. Titular claims and legitimizing ideological discourses are not to be confused with actual rule and divisions between and among constitutional powers. A sultan who might have "claimed divinity" in Islam is not to be equated with a king or emperor who did the same in Europe. A fundamental distinction must be drawn between the two, if only because there was no equivalence to the Sharī'a in Europe, past or even present. The Sharī'a is the difference, and no matter how much the Ṣafavid Shī'ī Ismā'īl I (907-30/1501-24) and others like him "claimed divinity," they could not stand above the law in practice. On the "legitimizing ideology" of Ismā'īl and others, see the otherwise useful work of Anne Broadbridge, *Kingship and Ideology in the Islamic and Mongol Worlds*, 11; 'Abbās, *al-Islām wal-Siyāsa*, 33 ff., 41 ff. See also main text of ch. 1, at n. 65. For the doctrinal differences between the Sunnis and Shī'īs in terms of the Imam's executive powers, see ch. 4, sec. II.

Prophethood comes to an end, the Perfect Human becomes an Heir" (*Wārith*), that is, a legatee to the last Prophet. For an heir is by definition an heir "only after the death of the one to whom he is an heir."[77] And since the "Gate of Revelation" has been shut due to the completion of the process of revealing a Sharīʿa, then the function of the Legatee is to supervise the implementation of his Prophet's Sharīʿa, and to maintain and strengthen it.

"The desired perfection for which the Human Being was created is therefore the *khilāfa*," another way of saying that humankind was created on Earth to be a *khalīfa*.[78] By virtue of divine grace, Adam (the archetype of humanity) was the first *khalīfa*, but not because he was a messenger (*rasūl*). Rather, the *khalīfa*, being an endowment from God, is privileged in a particular way, being specifically under duty to implement the divine decree through "what God shows him distinctly (*khāṣatan*)." The *khalīfa*'s attributes mirror those of the *mustakhlif* (i.e., God's), for the final verdict and rule belong to Him. The *khalīfa* is then the hand of God on Earth, reflecting His justice and all that He stands for.[79] It is clear then that the implementation of the divine decree entails governance (*ḥukm*/*taḥakkum*/v. *ḥakama*) in all this concept entails, including reward and punishment, let live or make die, to harm or to benefit.[80] Obviously, these binaries represent the force of the law, of protecting rights and punishing transgressors. The *khilāfa* is thus a productive and generative entity, for it causes acts to come into existence, thereby constituting reality (*takwīn*). Put in modern parlance, Ibn ʿArabī seems to argue that *khilāfa* is creative and performative.[81] This is why (in the Qur'ān) God gave it the feminine name of *khilāfa* and *khalīfa* – not the masculine *nā'ib*, otherwise a perfect synonym – because these divinely ordained names were meant to indicate creativity and creative (re)production.[82]

It is within this cosmological framework that the Prophet Muhammad emerges as the Perfect Human, the carrier of God's message and decree of earthly rule.[83] But Muhammad's disappearance from the world does not render this lower world devoid of Human Perfection. The Perfect Human has existed and continues to exist through time, for no humanity can exist without this

77 *IK*, 9.
78 *IK*, 23.
79 *IK*, 24: "*Fa'inna al-khalīfata maʿlūmun annahu lā yaẓharu illā bi-ṣifati man istakhlafahu, fal-ḥukmu li-man istakhlafahu.*"
80 *IK*, 23. On the constitutional and political meaning of divine *ḥukm*, see ch. 4, sec. I.
81 Hallaq, *Restating Orientalism*, 61-63; Austin, "Performative Utterances."
82 *IK*, 23. See also, generally, Shaikh, *Ṣūfī Narratives of Intimacy*.
83 *IK*, 27.

Human.[84] Even the Prophet himself did not, in one strong sense, vanish from the world, for he effectively did not die but merely went to sleep. "Know that with the loss of Muhammad today – in spirit, body, form, and meaning – he is [merely] asleep but not dead."[85] The metaphorical sleep is no empty metaphysical or theological spinning of a fictional narrative. Ibn ʿArabī is insisting here that self-consciousness and supreme forms of knowledge have been imparted to humans, the most privileged site of epistemological divine investment, even superior to the epistemic capacities of the Angels. Humans are the *khulafā'* of God on Earth and as long as they inhabit the Earth, they continue to be endowed with the duty to bear that Knowledge. Standing at the head of humanity is the Perfect Human who is the *ever-present* vessel through which divinely ordained human knowledge continues to manifest itself in the world. Adam was the first ever to bear it, and Muhammad the first Muslim to do so.[86]

The privileged position accorded Muhammad is epistemic, because "among all human beings, he is the most knowledgeable of God"[87] by virtue of his proximity to Him. To say "epistemic" is to speak of ethical knowledge, for all true knowledge is knowledge of the divine, which is ethical through and through.[88] And to speak of all this is to speak of an *ethical rationality* that not only maps out and effectively produces the world in its entirety but also incessantly replicates itself through the *khilāfa* of the Perfect Human throughout history.

This world of ours, Ibn ʿArabī continues, represents a House whose foundation is the Perfect Human as represented in the Messenger and the Guardians who follow upon his heel. The foundation, by necessary implication, consists of the Message itself (*Risāla*) and the Belief (*Īmān*) that underlies it. This House, originally founded by the Prophet Muhammad, is none other than the *Dīn*, the Religion that sustains all human socialization and political association.[89]

If this seems to echo Māwardī's investment in *dīn* as the most important foundation upon which the good life and a well-ordered society rest, it is because there is much that is shared between Māwardī and Ibn ʿArabī about the origins of politics and political management. Man, Ibn ʿArabī avers, is prone to dispute and conflict because he is made of the very binary qualities that are inscribed in the Names of God (*al-asmā' al-ilāhiyya al-mutaqābila*),

84 *IK*, 24.
85 *IK*, 27: "*Wa-ʿlam anna al-ʿālama al-yawma bi-faqdi Muḥammadin, ṣallā Allāhu ʿalayhi wa-sallam, fī ẓuhūrihi rūḥan wa-jisman wa-ṣūratan wa-maʿnan, nā'imun lā mayyitun.*"
86 *IK*, 27.
87 *IK*, 28: "*Li-annahu aʿlamu al-khalqi bi-Lāh;*" "*Li-annahu akmalu al-ʿulamā'i bil-Lāh.*"
88 See our discussion of Māwardī's concept of *ʿaql*/*ʿilm* in ch. 1, sec. II.
89 Ibn ʿArabī, *al-Quṭb al-Ghawth*, 4-5, 7.

otherwise known as the Beautiful Names of God. These qualities stand on a wide spectrum whose relative Happy Middle produces the ethical subject and therefore the good life.[90] But since the Happy Middle cannot always be attained, the disputes that arise from this failing require adjudicators "to whom people refer when they are entangled in [such] disputes."[91] This is why God gave the people an imam, a single imam, to whom all have recourse with a view to upholding the rules of religion, the Sharīʿa. In the same vein, God also commanded that they should neither challenge him nor engage in disputes with him; indeed, should anyone attempt to do so, he must be resisted and fought. Ibn ʿArabī's reasoning is that challenging and resisting the ruler is detrimental to *dīn*.

The ruler is thus an inevitable necessity. He is a wielder of power (*ẓāhiran bil-sayf*), though he may or may not be the Pole (Quṭb), the Perfect Human of the age. If he is both, as in the case of Abu Bakr, then the two functions unite in one figure. But if not, then the real *khalīfa* – who remains hidden from view – is the Pole while the imam would be his deputy (*nā'ib*). The quintessential difference between the two is that the Pole, unlike the mere *khalīfa*, is inherently incapable of committing injustice.[92] The *khalīfa* par excellence, the Pole and Lord of the Community (*Sayyid al-Jamāʿa*), owns both the apparent and hidden caliphate (*al-khilāfa al-ẓāhira/al-khilāfa al-bāṭina*).[93] At this point Ibn ʿArabī gives a list of caliphs who had succeeded in rising to this unified rank: Abū Bakr, ʿUmar b. al-Khaṭṭāb, ʿUthmān b. ʿAffān, ʿAlī b. Abī Ṭālib, al-Ḥasan b. ʿAlī, Muʿāwiya b. Yazīd, ʿUmar b. ʿAbd al-ʿAzīz, and caliph al-Mutawakkil ʿAlā Allāh (r. 232-47/847-61), the terminator of al-Miḥna. Those who held the Inner caliphate (*al-khilāfa al-bāṭina*), but not the apparent one, included some of the famous Ṣūfī masters, such as Aḥmad al-Sabtī, the son of the caliph Hārūn al-Rashīd, and Abū Yazīd al-Bisṭāmī.[94]

In the Sharīʿa, the role of Prophethood was relatively less psychological and spiritual, and much more disciplinary and organizational. The Prophet here remains an exemplarity, as it is everywhere, but the narrative of the personal biography is segregated into discrete textual units that become subjected to a complex hermeneutics and semiotics. Love as a driving matrix does not obtain at the stage of the legal, for the Sharīʿa's province is not primarily the inner

90 Ibn ʿArabī, *al-Quṭb al-Ghawth*, 9.
91 Ibn ʿArabī, *al-Quṭb al-Ghawth*, 9.
92 Ibn ʿArabī, *al-Quṭb al-Ghawth*, 9-10.
93 Ibn ʿArabī, *Al-Tadbīrāt al-Ilāhiyya*, 11.
94 Ibn ʿArabī, *al-Quṭb al-Ghawth*, 10-11.

emotive constitution of the subject. Rather, this constitution is relevant and important only insofar as it can be enlisted for the main task and challenge of the Sharīʿa: to organize the social life as lived ethically in its varied complexities, in the economic, criminal, marital, philanthropic, and in nearly countless other spheres of human activity. The main driver and prop of this organizing force remains the ethical, and it is, for the Sharīʿa, the central domain of Prophethood. Whereas the final destination of Ṣūfism is the inner constitution of the individual, the final destination of the Sharīʿa is the collective constitution and organization of the social. The focus is ultimately or entirely never on the husband in a marriage contract, the plaintiff in a litigation, the victim in a homicide, or the founder in an endowment deed; rather it is about everyone who has a legal and moral tie to the sphere of action, the wife, the family, the community, the defendant, the murderer, and the *waqf* (charitable endowment) beneficiaries, and all those affected by the legal construction of social, economic, communal, and other aspects of reality.[95] In other words, the Prophethood is an arena of specialization, providing the highest exemplarity for all fields of life's activity.

V

If Ṣūfism was devised to create the coherent, structured, cultivated, and loving ethical subject, the Sharīʿa was designed to place ethical individuals in well-defined roles that make sociality and human association and cooperation possible, even peaceful when possible. This is precisely the effect of Māwardī's synthetic sketch of *dīn* in *ADD*, which for him was the Sharīʿa in its full swing and operation. The "pillars" that constitute the first five and, indeed, foundational institutions of the Sharīʿa operated with a view to fashioning the technological basis of self-cultivation, enough to do the legal work. The rest – the intense technical preoccupation with contracts, commerce, marriage, divorce, child custody, theft, murder, and countless other major and minor spheres – were deliberate and structured ways to manage social life, and what we now call the population.

Enter the caliphate and sultanate. Just as much as Ṣūfism and the Sharīʿa were structurally intertwined with the Prophethood, so was the political

95 Hallaq, *Sharīʿa*, 159-96, and sources cited therein.

sphere, the *siyāsa shar'iyya*. If Ṣūfism came to structure and cultivate the individual as the microscopic participant in the Sharī'a, Sharī'a came to structure sociality and cooperation as the constitutive categories of the political sphere, that which is necessarily regulated by coercive power. Paradigmatically and schematically, Sharī'a would be nothing more than an idea without the political substrate, and Ṣūfism in its general manifestations would be a chaotic and anchorless enterprise without the Sharī'a. As much as Ṣūfism rode on the back of the Sharī'a, the Sharī'a rode on the back of the caliphate, which is but a conglomerate of processes and methods of political management.

In order to appreciate the full political effects of the concept of Prophethood on the constitutional landscape, we must consult yet another of Māwardī's works, namely, *A'lām al-Nubuwwa*. The work, like many others, would appear unrelated to matters of politics, much less to the specific interest in constitutional analysis. But we must resist this way of seeing the work of Muslim authors. We should always remember that our methodological approach risks fragmentation not because we lack analytical competence; rather, we *systemically* stand at risk because we are generally governed by a fragmented view of the world, where the spheres making up our own lives as modern subjects often sit next to each other uneasily, disjointedly, and often conflictedly. By virtue of our "secular age" – and secular it is, even amid all religious fervor – we lack a cosmological view of ourselves, of the relatedness of every act and thought we bring about to everything else in the world. We individually replicate much of the political forms that govern us, especially the state and its secular dispositions, without being aware of our ideological complicity. And so we always assume that life is experienced autonomously, where we are the proactive agents deciding how our own lives can be lived. Our secular disconnection from the forces that surround and make us is ever-present, and so we tend to think that that is how all people, past and present, live in and think the world. Because a secular mind assumes that religion has no business interfering either with the public domain or with politics, it finds it odd that a book on the Prophethood should have any connection with government or, much less, constitutional construction or analysis.

A'lām al-Nubuwwa is a work that bears directly on the constitutional division of labor. In chapter 20, and after discussing at great length various issues related to the knowledge of God, proofs of prophethood, miracles, and other doctrines, Māwardī discusses the "noble and perfect attributes" of the Prophet (*sharafu akhlāqihi wa-kamālu faḍā'ilihi*), the heading of the chapter itself. These attributes are "foundations" (*uṣūl*) that lead to acts that are "consonant with them" and "distinguish them from those that are different with and disagree with them." This language aims to convey the meaning that these attributes not only affirm the good and the virtuous but also abnegate harm and evil, a linguistic act of simultaneous inclusion and exclusion.[96]

The "Prophethood is the highest station in the world," an "emissary between God and his subjects."[97] Its purpose is the promotion of the people's interests and well-being and the worship and obedience to God. It makes perfect sense therefore that the most noble of humans is the one who is entitled to occupy it.[98] Here we see the distinction between the office, so to speak, and its occupant, between the institution and the person. The office – or station or institution – was created first, to be filled with an agent later. This is not only a temporal or ontological order, or a diachronic structure of creation; it is also a logical one. But what are the qualities and attributes that constitute the office that must be reflected in the person who fills it?

Māwardī divides these qualities into four categories, the first two of which include the traits of being graceful, charming, patient, resilient, determined, humble, and ascetic, this last commanding a particularly lengthy treatment. He is also said to be highly dignified and possessing a special ability to keep promises. The third category seems to coalesce around qualities having to do with what we might call brainpower and immense perspicacity, shining through in his juridical wisdom. His legal reasoning is described as "impeccable" and his linguistic expression a testament of eloquence and lucidity.[99] His competence in argumentation is exceptional. That he is by nature particularly invested in doing good and helping the poor is something to be taken for granted.[100]

The fourth category – defined as the arena of his "acts," rather than his "utterances" (third) or "virtues" (second) – meshes the Prophet's above-mentioned virtuous attributes (*ḥusnu sīratihi*) with a "healthy disposition for political management" (*ṣiḥḥatu siyāsatihi*). This skill is said to have been instrumental in founding and developing the new religion, with a law of its own, a religion brought to stability (*ḥattā istaqarra*) by "a superior design of [political]

96 Māwardī, *A ʿlām al-Nubuwwa*, 181.

97 Māwardī, *A ʿlām al-Nubuwwa*, 181: "*Hiya safāratun bayna Allāhi ta ʿālā wa-ʿibādihi.*"

98 Māwardī, *A ʿlām al-Nubuwwa*, 181: "[*Al-Nubuwwatu*] *tab ʿathu ʿalā maṣāliḥi al- khalqi wa-ṭā ʿati al-khāliqi fa-kāna afḍalu al-khalqi bi-hā akhaṣṣa wa-akmaluhum bi-shurūṭihā aḥaqqa wa-amass.*"

99 Māwardī, *A ʿlām al-Nubuwwa*, 189: "*Iḥkāmihi li-mā sharra ʿa bi-aẓhari dalīl.*" See also 190: "*Afṣaḥu al-nāsi lisānan wa-awḍaḥuhum bayānan.*"

100 Māwardī, *A ʿlām al-Nubuwwa*, 189.

management" (*tadbīrun aḥsana waḍ ʿahu*).[101] This process "transformed the *Umma*" (*naqala bi-hi al-Ummata*) from the familiar to the unfamiliar. With the new religion people succumbed to obedience either willingly or coercively, but in either case the ability of the Prophet as a political and even a military leader, capable of garnering the support of the people, is rather salient. The strength of the new faith was such that its "foundations were perpetually but also increasingly affirmed" from one generation to the next. It has been regarded as a stabilizing system throughout upheavals, "a proof against those who cast doubt on it."[102]

Finally, establishing the Sharīʿa in its theoretical, doctrinal, and practical aspects was necessarily complemented with the Prophetic ability to defend it through *jihād*, a quality that certain authors of prophetic biography emphasized and elaborated.[103] The Prophet was a chivalrous fighter certainly, but this military skill was deployed by the imperative of guarding *sharʿ al-dīn*.[104] All in all, Māwardī concludes, the totality of the Prophet's refined qualities and virtues is such that there is no wonder why he "qualifies for the leadership of this world, and for being in charge of attending to the well-being of people."[105]

Note that the qualities we have enumerated capture the essential attributes that defined many of the institutions that were to arise later in Islam. *Aʿlam al-Nubuwwa*'s full elaboration of *zuhd* lays the ground for the rise and spread of Ṣūfī and other pietistic movements;[106] the personal characteristics gave *adab* much of its content; and juridical wisdom paved the basis for *ijtihād*, in turn the bedrock of the law; and skills in argument would become the foundation of the science and practice of *jadal* and *munāẓara*. The emphasis on the Prophetic achievement of constructing the law and the legal system as a living tradition, and the need to protect this structure through loving care but also sheer power gives rise to the particular conception and practice of Islamic political management, generally expressed by Māwardī in terms of *siyāsa* and *tadbīr*. This is the meaning of the expression that the imam is the

101 Māwardī, *Aʿlām al-Nubuwwa*, 193.

102 Māwardī, *Aʿlām al-Nubuwwa*, 193: "*Yarūnahu niẓāman li-aʿṣārin tanqalibu ṣurūfuhā wa-yakhtalifu ma'lūfuhā.*"

103 Qasṭalānī, *Mawāhib*, II, 125-59, 164-67.

104 Māwardī, *Aʿlām al-Nubuwwa*, 195.

105 Māwardī, *Aʿlām al-Nubuwwa*, 197: "*An yakūna li-zaʿāmati al-ʿālami mu'ahhalan wa-lil-qiyāmi bi-maṣāliḥi al-khalqi muwakkalan.*"

106 For insightful distinctions between and amongst various pietistic and ascetic practices, see Reid, *Law and Piety*.

caliph of the Prophet.[107] The caliphate, like the Prophethood, is many things but its most significant function is the sustenance of the law through coercive power when all else fails.

But was the caliphate, from this structural perspective, different from the sultanate? When Māwardī and Ghazālī spoke of the comprehensive nature of the Prophethood, as the final perfection of the divine administration of the good life, they had no difficulty in carving out of the universal comprehensiveness of the Prophethood a sphere for the sultanate and emirate, just as easily as they did for the caliphate. Māwardī states:

> Because the Prophethood is the most noble station among created beings, encompassing as it is the interests of both the *dīn* and the *dunyā*, God has mandated for it someone who has the most perfect of human virtues and the most honorable pedigree, which is why the Prophet – peace be upon him – said: "I have been sent with the good virtues." *The same applies to the imāra and imāma.* Since they follow on the heel of Prophethood, *they should have the same constitutive attributes.* The [offices] should be assigned to those who have been raised and cultivated on virtue, and who have mastered, by training, the [office's] requirements with [the goal] of governing the subjects and supervising their affairs through their devices and crafts, respectively. This is why the Rāshidūn caliphs – May God be pleased with them – were the most deserving of those in whom the virtues were perfected by means of natural disposition as well as by training and cultivation.[108]

The delegatory, deputizing chain here is clear. The quality of justice as integral to ethical formation must always accompany the "specialization," in this case the technique of governance. The function, any function, is always the sum total of a matrix of ethics plus the toolbox that accomplishes a task or a

107 *AS*, 39.

108 *TN*, 44-45: "*Li'anna al-nubuwwata lammā kānat ashrafa manāzili al-khalqi li-ishtimālihā ʿalā maṣāliḥi al-dīni wal-dunyā, nadaba Allāhu taʿālā la-hā man qad akmala faḍāʾila al-akhlāqi wa-ḥāza ashrafa al-aʿrāqi, wa-li-dhālika qāla al-nabiyyu ʿalayhi al-salām ʿbuʿithtu bi-makārimi al-akhlāqi,ʾ* ka-dhālika al-imāra wal-imāma lammā *kānat tāliyatan li-ḥālihā* wajaba an takūna mushākilatan li-khiṣālihā *fa-lazima an yuntadaba la-hā man qad anhaḍathu al-faḍāʾilu ḥattā tahadhdhaba wa-istaqalla bi-ḥuqūqihā ḥattā tadarraba li-yasūsa al-raʿāyā bi-ālatihi wa-yubāshira al-tadbīra bi-ṣināʿatihi, fa-lidhālika kāna l-khulafāʾu al-rāshidūn – raḍwānu Allāhi ʿalayhim – aḥaqqa man takāmalat fī-him faḍāʾila al-akhlāqi ṭabʿan wa-taṭabbuʿan*" (emphasis mine).

set of tasks. And as a *function* of the executive (= coercive power), the Imāra appears to stand in Māwardī as equal to the Imāma, the caliphate, even given precedent in order of appearance.[109] The implications of cleaving the sultanate or imamate from the body of the *Umma* is therefore not a mere political act of replacing one institution with another. To cleave the sultanate or the imamate (both functionally identical) is to excise a Prophetic function from the Islamic way of life. It is tantamount to excising the Sunna and Ḥadīth from the Sharīʿa, the colossal Prophetic contributions to the Sharʿ. To do so is effectively to automatically abolish the Sharīʿa in its entirety, for the *fiqh* and its operations have the Sunna as their foundation and mainstay. It would also amount, and be equivalent, to excising the Perfect Human from the Ṣūfī worldview, and with this, from the iterative technologies of ethical self-cultivation. In short, such excisions would amount to severing Islamic practice from its font and source, from its ethical exemplarity, from its lineage of political functionality. It is to eliminate, in each sphere, an integral part of Prophethood as it came to constitute Islam in its ideas, practices, history, culture, and socio-economic institutions.

With this background, with this holistic approach to the Prophethood, the imamate, the sultanate, and constitutional theology (that is, theology as interpreted constitutionally), we can better appreciate Māwardī's *AS* and *ADD*, along with others, as a unified, integral, functionalist, positive, and paradigmatic account of Islamic constitutionalism.[110] The account came on the heel of four centuries of formative developments, when Islam settled on its main legal and political features. Only then could a clear and mature picture of constitutionalism emerge. Māwardī's oeuvre captured this scene better than anyone else, thereby becoming foundational to what is to come.

109 *TN*, 44, l. 13.
110 On the differences between positive, normative, and factual accounts, see ch. 1, sec. IV.

Chapter 3

Framing the Sultanic Executive

I

The functionalist analysis of Prophethood I deployed in the foregoing chapter frames Māwardī's principal concerns in his *AS*. It is by no means fortuitous that Māwardī's first substantive paragraph in the treatise situates politics within a cosmological scheme, a self-conscious discourse in which the order of things in the world is always a prime concern. The first line states that God "mandated to the *Umma* a leader to follow on the heels of the Prophethood, one who is surrounded by the Muslim *Milla* and to whom political management has been delegated." The foundation of this management (*tadbīr*) is the *dīnun mashrūʿun*, the religious system of Islam as sanctioned by the Sharīʿa. The "imama has therefore become a foundation on which the *Milla* fully rests, and by which its interests are regulated so that the general affairs [of the *Milla*'s life] are instituted and the official [government] appointments issued."[1] And if this language is unclear or not strong enough, Māwardī, two pages later, asserts with an unqualified intonation that "the imama was created to take the place of the Prophethood in *guarding* religion and managing the world of the Here-and-now."[2]

1 *AS*, 13: "*Fa'inna Allāha jallat qudratuhu nadaba lil-Ummati zaʿīman khalafa bi-hi al-nubuwwata wa-ḥāṭa bi-hi al-millata, wa-fawwaḍa ilayhi al-siyāsata, li-yaṣdura al-tadbīru ʿan dīnin mashrūʿin wa-tajtamiʿu al-kalimatu ʿalā ra'yin matbūʿin fa-kānat al-imāmatu aṣlan ʿalayhi istaqarrat qawāʿidu al-millati wa-intaẓamat bi-hi maṣāliḥu al-ummati ḥattā istathbatat bi-hā al-umūru al-ʿāmmatu, wa-ṣadarat ʿanhā al-wilayātu al-khāṣatu.*" On appointment decrees, see our discussion of Qalqashandī in ch. 5.

2 *AS*, 15: "*Al-imāmatu mawḍūʿatun li-khilāfati al-nubuwwati fī ḥirāsati al-dīni wa-siyāsati al-dunyā*" (emphasis in translation mine).

Māwardī's concern for order is not a scholastic obsession, nor an expression of a merely formalist predilection. The order is immensely meaningful because it lays down in black-and-white the genealogy of politics, the way life is ordered systemically, for after all, "applied religion,"[3] *Milla*, and *Umma*, would all be impossible without "political management." This latter in turn is entirely predicated on the imama/*khilāfa*, precisely the foundation of Muslim life as a polity and therefore as a political community and social organization. This is why Māwardī feels compelled to state, in the very first lines of the treatise, that "it is therefore imperative to discuss the imama's rules before those of the sultanate," even "before other religious considerations" (*naẓar dīnī*).[4] This statement has the tone of an apology, as if to beg leave to discuss that which seems less immediate before that which is more so. The order of things thus dictates setting aside a discussion of the sultanate, indeed a derivative, until the imamate – by his time eviscerated of all effective power – is analytically explicated and given its proper place as a foundational institution. But "proper place" is not a matter of honorary title and symbolic significance; rather, it is a place determined by cosmological, theological, epistemological, legal, and political considerations. It is, after all, the foundation and source of the sultanate itself, however ineffective or hollow it may be. Doing so is placing things where they belong (*nasaq mutanāsib*).[5] No matter how militarily feeble the imamate is, it remains the embodiment of the political constitution of Islam. And no matter how constitutional goods are calculated, it is always the mother and father of the sultanate.[6]

In page after page, Māwardī presents a systematic Sharʿī account of the caliphate, the only realist account that was conceivable. As typical of Sharʿī discourse and its manner of argumentation, the question of whether the office is mandated by reason or by divine command is posed first, as the fact of its indispensability is taken for granted and constitutes a consensus. He gives the views of those who argued for its necessity on rational grounds, then of those who thought that the office is mandated by divine command. The former argued that it is in the nature of rational people to concede to a leader who curbs their injustices in their dealings and interactions and resolves disputes and conflicts among them when they arise, for without

3 On "applied religion," see ch. 1, sec. III.
4 *AS*, 13.
5 *AS*, 13.
6 On the link between prophethood, the Prophet's message, and the early formation of the Muslim polity, see Farahat, "Peace to Those of Faith."

a ruler anarchy would rule instead. The advocates of the divine-command origins of the imamate argued that the institution is unnecessary because reason dictates that every rational agent would autonomously behave in a just manner and would not transgress against others in any way. But the truth of the matter, Māwardī retorts, is that "we have been commanded" to obey our leaders, the first and foremost of whom is the Prophet himself. After all, God said: "O you who believe, obey God and obey the messenger and the leaders among you."[7]

Note here that the distinction between the two camps' justification of government and rule is of monumental importance. The rationalists seem to closely echo Hobbesian political philosophy and similar social theory contracts, although there is no presumption here that man is evil or that life is inherently brutish. It is merely the case that in social interaction and transaction disputes and unjust behavior necessarily arise and so they require an entity powerful enough to settle them. Here, government is earthly and instrumental, and it is up to the people involved in each situation to determine the substance, content, and form of their government.

On the other hand, the divine-command theory of government is not limited to social and political organization but rather stands as an integral part of the all-pervasive structure called *dīn*, with its cosmology, metaphysics, prophets, and, significantly, vigorous ethical content. In justification of government, the theory transcends the limited function of resolving disputes and curbing injustices, extending its sway to the replication of Prophetic qualities and functions in the realm of politics. This is another way of saying that the social contract model can sway in any direction, with the distinct feature that it is not bound by any considerations other than the telos of arbitration of disputes and organization of public life. The revelatory model, on the other hand, is entwined, in form and content and in origins and telos, with the concept of Prophethood as an ethically and politically fleshed out institution and concept. Which is still to say that political leadership and rule in this tradition of political thought are never far from the Prophetic model, where an ethical benchmark remains a persistent feature and a minimal expectation of rule.[8]

This in part explains why a particular set of attributes are expected to be possessed for the holder of the office. The very first of these is the condition

7 Q. 4:59.

8 For a definition of benchmark, see Introduction, n. 71.

of justice (*sharṭ al-ʿadāla*),[9] a quality that defines not only the most central caliphal ambition but also the Prophetic constitution and even God's logic in creating the world; for it is a foundational Qur'ānic tenet that God himself created the world with justice.[10] Next comes sufficient knowledge of hermeneutics and the law that would enable the caliph to engage in *ijtihād*, a quality and skill that the Prophet possessed. This intellectual equipment must accompany good judgment and common sense (*ra'y*) in the administration of political life, as well as initiative and courage in protecting the domains against foreign invaders. To do all this a caliph must be assumed to enjoy the necessary bodily and mental functions so as to be capable of running the polity and oversee its demands and complications, and so eyesight, hearing, and the rest of sensory faculties must be intact. Finally, the caliph must hail from Quraysh,[11] the tribe of the Prophet, especially its Banū Hāshim branch.[12] This last was as much a moral requirement as it was a matter of lineal descent, but as we will see in the following chapters of the book, it was not an essential requirement for holding executive power.

Notice here the nature of these attributes: they are related to the very person of the candidate, which is to say that they are not external or attached to his character or physical body. They do not transcend natural endowments and gifts, for he must be sound of body and mind, just, courageous, and hail from a privileged lineage. Curiously missing here are the external attributes, so to speak, such as being a ferocious soldier or a military man, for one would expect the function of caliphate to require not only military prowess as a potential but also effective military power.[13] How would a body politic be run otherwise?

Immediately thereafter, Māwardī discusses the various modalities of selecting, electing, or appointing caliphs, followed by succession[14] and an enumeration of the duties of the caliph, this latter having already been discussed in chapter 1. What is relevant for us in this context is the issue of deviation from the norm and from what is commonly, customarily, or legally expected. As

9 *AS*, 19.
10 See ch. 4.
11 *AS*, 19-20.
12 On the Qurayshī lineage as specifically one of Banū Hāshim who were known for their chivalry, eloquence, temperance, and a host of other virtues, see Qaṣṭalanī, *Mawahib*, I, 85-98, esp. at 90.
13 Compare, for instance, with the desirable qualities of the prince in medieval European political thought. See Born, "Perfect Prince."
14 *AS*, 21-38.

we saw, such deviations, however minor, are what go into the definition of just rule (*ʿadl*).

Deviation from the attributes and states that qualify one to be an imam represents the general political anxiety that any complex society would have to experience simply by virtue of the fact that it is complex. Loss of sight, uprightness, or any faculty crucial for the operation of the political and military machinery would be cause for removal, and if not removal then functional replacement and substitution. This comes out clearly in the case of loss of freedom, which may be caused by falling in captivity or by legal interdiction (*ḥajr*). If ransom or other means are unsuccessful, and freedom appears unlikely, then Muslims must appoint another caliph.[15]

Legal interdiction demands different considerations. It is defined as a situation in which "one of the caliph's aids overpowers and dominates him, taking control of the affairs [of the kingdom] without plainly showing disobedience and without openly dissenting."[16] (In the American context, for instance, this is akin to a situation where the "President's men" effectively run the government, such as when Antony Blinken and associates ran US foreign policy during the last year of Biden's tenure.) Under this circumstance, Māwardī states, the validity of the appointment remains intact, ushering in one of two possible situations. If the usurper's rule is just and is carried out according to the dictates of the Sharīʿa, that is, according to "the rules of the *dīn*," then he is allowed to retain his hold and continue his work. The idea is to maintain the interests of the *Umma*, allowing the running of its normal affairs to continue unimpeded. If his deeds are unjust and violate the law, he is not permitted to remain in his hold, and everything must be done to have someone remove him.[17]

Translated into constitutional terms, this realistic scenario is pregnant with implications. Note here an iteration of the caliphal mandate, captured briskly by Māwardī as the essential function of this office: "to conduct the affairs of the Community according to the rules of the *dīn* and what justice dictates... thereby carrying out the tasks of the office [of the caliphate] and executing its rules."[18] The proper application of the latter ensues from a

15 *AS*, 47.

16 *AS*, 47: "*Fa-ammā al-ḥajru fa-huwa an yastawliya ʿalayhi min aʿwānihi man yastabiddu bi-tanfīdhi al-umūri min ghayri taẓāhurin bi-maʿṣiyyatin wa-lā mujāharatin bi-mushāqqa.*"

17 *AS*, 47.

18 *AS*, 47: "*Fa'in kānat [afʿālu man istawlā ʿalā al-umūri] jāriyatan ʿalā aḥkāmi al-dīni wa-muqtaḍā al-ʿadli jāza iqrāruhu ʿalayhā [i.e., al-imāma] tanfīdhan la-hā wa-imḍā'an li-aḥkāmihā.*"

proper adherence to the former, a process of administering governance and justice that is not determined by the usurper or even by the caliph himself. The determination of the "rules of religion" or those of the Sharīʿa – both being one and the same thing – is not in the caliph's hands. All he needs to do is apply and execute them, and whoever does the job is the right one for it. This is clearly an act of effective substitution (or, in formal terms, one of delegation), where one player takes the place of another as his representative or deputy. But the game and its rules are still in operation no matter who plays. Which is to say that the concern was not about the very person "elected" to the office, but rather about the substance, tasks, qualifications, and demands of the office itself. It is about the execution of predetermined tasks irrespective of the identity of the executor. This constitutional fact, as specific and particular as it is, therefore demonstrates the institutional nature of the caliphate and reduces the role of the individual *qua* specific and unique individual to near nullity.

I shall continue to reinforce this point, but it does not take much to adduce an equivalent that historically occurred much earlier than the sultanic overpowering, an equivalent that partook in the definition of what Islam was and became since the second/eighth century, if not before. This is the requirement of *ijtihād*, nearly always deemed desirable, if not necessary, for the imam to possess because he must, *within his executive competence*, be a dexterous and quick-witted leader. Yet, factually we know that most caliphs did not possess much of this capacity. And constitutionally speaking, it was not an essential requirement. It was the jurists who stepped in, *from the very beginning*, to take charge of this task. In fact, Bāqillānī, an influential early theorist of the imamate, made it clear on principle that *ijtihād* is not required because the proper and *absolutely necessary* functions of the ruler are the very same functions we have seen Māwardī elaborate.[19] Rather, it was the jurists as leaders and *mujtahids* who represented the Community and acted on its behalf, this being a legal, judicial, and political cornerstone of the system. But the Community was also God's protectorate in which God's rights (*ḥuqūq*

19 Bāqillānī, *Tamhīd*, 477-78. Having definitively asserted that *ijtihād* is not required of the imam, Bāqillānī says this: "*Fa'in qālū: Fa-limādhā yuqāmu al-imāmu? Qīla la-hum: li'ajli mā dhakarnāhu min qablu min tadbīri al-juyūshi wa-saddi al-thughūri wa-radʿi al-ẓālimi wal-akhdhi lil-maẓlūmi wa-iqāmati al-ḥudūdi wa-qasmi al-fay'i bayna al muslimīna wal-dafʿi bi-him fī ḥajjihim wa-ghazwihim… fa'in ghaliṭa fī shay'in min-hu aw ʿadala bi-hi ʿan mawḍiʿihi kānat al-Ummatu min warā'ihi li-taqwīmihi wal-akhdhi lahu bi-wājibihi.*" Note here that Bāqillānī is equating the *Umma* with its *mujtahids*, or, in other words, speaking of the *Umma* as being represented to the imam by its *mujtahids*.

Allāh) reside. We can therefore state it as a self-evident proposition that inasmuch as the jurists took over "legislation" and judicial administration as *autonomous* functionaries of the caliphate, the sultans and military emirs took over (well-defined) executive powers as *delegated* deputies of the same. In fact, coercive executive power, unlike *ijtihād*, defined the essence of the caliphate and so its presence was indispensable, whether borne by the caliph or any other pretender. The common Orientalist claim that this amounted to a concession that the jurists had to make to political and military power – with the clear implication that this act compromised the integrity of both the caliphate "office" and the Sharīʿa – therefore does not hold water. The loss of the caliphal coercive capacity was merely to be lamented as a symbolic diminution in the general spiritual image of the Prophetic line. But no compromise or any accommodation whatsoever was to be made with regard to the requirement of coercive executive power.

II

I have highlighted a difference between autonomous functionality and delegated deputization, differentiating between two types of delegation. As we will see in the next chapter, the transmission of knowledge from God's mind, so to speak, to humans on Earth was a momentous act, one through which the "rope" of knowledge was hung down to touch the believers through the Qur'ān.

The acquisition of knowledge, being wholly ethical, was a communal duty, which is to say that even the Prophet had no monopoly over it. If the caliph was charged with the management of the Muslim Community in all aspects of its life, he was charged – as we have seen in detail – to implement the ordinances that have already been established by the ulama, the custodians of God's *ʿilm*. One could say that the ulama were the partners of the caliphs whereas the sultans were his deputies. Both partners and deputies work for the interests of a common project, but they do so from two different sources of authorization. A partner is authorized by the originating contract of partnership whereas the deputy is authorized by the partner through such instruments as agency and hire.

The dominance of the establishment of religion and its "rules" (i.e., Sharīʿa) speaks of a political culture that does not offer a wide spectrum of personal or individual choices, where value is placed on a particular individual. Imagine, in a liberal democracy like the United States, that someone, say the vice president, somehow takes hold of the presidency and becomes the real actor in American politics, issuing presidential executive orders and the like. Despite the impersonal bureaucratic nature of the modern state in general, and even modern society and economy, such an act of substitution would not be tolerated, for when the candidate is voted into the Presidency, he or she is voted for their own individual identity, having run in a party race that placed them in the final electoral seat. In the Islamic political tradition, prime value was placed on personal qualities no doubt, but what mattered at the end of the day was the apparent conduct, the act or set of acts that came into view, those that could be perceived, assessed, and therefore judged.

This conception of qualities or attributes of the ruler versus his specific identity (that is, putting a face to the name as representing personal qualities) explains the presence, earlier in *AS*, of a subheading with regard to whether or not the *Umma* should know "the incumbent caliph" in person before he assumes office. The agreement of the general majority of scholars (*jumhūr al-nās*), Māwardī reports, has been that the "people" need only know the "generalities" (*jumla*) and not the "particularities/details" (*tafṣīl*). "Not everyone needs to know him individually and know his name."[20]

The caliphal function, later to become largely sultanic, had a precise and relatively well-defined executive purview, where the fulfillment of its demands and requirements was its own *raison d'être*. As we will see later, because the province of the executive was so crucial for the sustenance of the *dīn* – as Māwardī has already made abundantly clear – what Muslims cared for was the fulfillment of its mandate, without much care for the purity of intentions behind the executive performance. It would seem that in the world of realpolitik, where the executive metal hits the hard stone of reality, the finesse of *adab* and the devotional aspects of the moral law were luxuries. *What mattered in this specific and specialized organ of governance was executive power, the coercive might without which there can be no body politic. And without this body politic there would be no Islam to begin with.*

Yet, these and other caliphal qualities were not only desirable but also enshrined within the normative, even complicating the executive function. Take for instance the office of the vizier.[21] Māwardī tells us that the caliph is

20 *AS*, 39.
21 For the biographies of many (famous) viziers serving until the early sixth/twelfth century, see Ibn al-Ṣayrafī, *Ishāra*.

responsible for making appointments to officers who would represent him or act in his stead (*khulafā'*) in various functions necessary for the management of the polity. The most encompassing of powers is the vizierate which could have general competence in the entire range of the provinces (*a'māl*), powers that are effectively equal to those of the caliph himself. There are also other officers who have general competence, but only in specific regions of the kingdom (such as governors), or those who have specific mandate in the kingdom at large (such as the Chief Justice or the tax collector). Finally, there are those whose mandate is confined to a limited region or locale, such as the presiding judge (in a village or town) or the local tax collector.[22]

Normatively, the ideal type of vizier is captured by the monumental account that the caliph al-Ma'mūn (198/813-218/833) had once enunciated:

"The man I look for is one who is honorable in his disposition, straight in his ways, having been refined by *ādāb* (pl. of *adab*) and wisely shaped by experience; he keeps secrets and [successfully] carries out missions with which he is entrusted; he is patient and learned; smart enough to understand from a glance as well as from the subtlest of gestures; his combative skills (*ṣawla*) properly belong to what makes a military commander; his caution, humility, and comprehension are what the philosophers, ulama, and jurists are made of; he is ever grateful for favors he receives, and patient when suffering ills; he will not make a gain today at the expense of deprivation tomorrow; he is able to secure the empathy of others with his charming tongue and good turn of phrase."[23]

Māwardī then tells us that when all these qualities are found in one person, the consequence is an optimal good for everyone, and when not, the affairs of the world decline in proportion to the diminution that these qualities suffer. "Surely," he continues, "these are not strict legal conditions that must be met, but they are rather the requirements of political management (*siyāsa*) that overlap with the religious stipulations, for both the interest of the *Umma* and proper ways of the *Milla* depend on them."[24] Māwardī then makes the factual remark that these qualifications obtain only infrequently (*qalla mā takmul*).[25]

The vizierate can take two forms, one of which holds categorical power while the other is limited to acting on behalf of the caliph and only with his

22 *AS*, 50.
23 *AS*, 51.
24 *AS*, 51.
25 *AS*, 51.

continuing approval in running the affairs of the kingdom. This latter, which he called "executive vizierate" (*wizārat tanfīdh*) is not unusual since the vizier, like so many other functions, merely executes the orders of the caliph.

The first form, however, is of a particular analytical interest to us. The first major difference between these two forms revolves around the questions of agency and decision. Under the second form, the caliph is the effective source of decision and ultimate authority; the vizier here executes caliphal will, on matters large and small, as instructed. By sharp contrast, the first form is entirely delegatory (*tafwīḍ*) in both decision and authority, in the totalistic sense that the caliphal powers and competences are wholly transferred to the vizier. It is akin to the general power of attorney in the domain of law, but it is also qualitatively and effectively analogous to the scenario of seizure we have just discussed. But it also comports with situations, not infrequent in occurrence, where a member of the palace – such as a mother or a senior uncle – comes to possess effective command of the affairs of the polity. This happened almost invariably when the ruler was a minor or a teenager.

Wizārat al-tafwīḍ's most distinct characteristic is that the vizier runs the affairs of the polity according to his own knowledge, opinion, and understanding, all of which amount for Māwardī to *ra'y* and *ijtihād*. Technically, these two concepts connote reasoned argument and independent, reasoned thinking in assessing and evaluating what needs to be done in running the kingdom's affairs. In other words, the appointing authority effectively abdicates political will and power for the duration of the tenure, while officially and symbolically retaining the chief seat of government. In theory, he can decide the affairs of the kingdom as does the vizier, but in reality this was not the case. One can get a sense of the exclusive power of the delegatory vizier from a discussion that Māwardī conducts later in his treatise, where he asserts that whereas the caliph can appoint two executive viziers concurrently, he cannot do so in the case of delegatory viziership. This, he says, is because their powers are totalistic (*li-ʿumūmi wilāyattihimā*), analogous to the probation on appointing two caliphs concurrently, which is effectively a universal doctrine.[26] The point here is that political practice as well as the constitutional structures and juristic discourse that came to envelop, regulate, and define these practices all point out and try to make sense of the fact that delegatory viziership is simply the legalized seizure of pure executive power, an extraction of an executive prerogative from a normatively defined executive office.

26 *AS*, 60.

In another work entirely devoted to the craft of the vizierate, Māwardī tellingly states that most of the viziers under Persian rule (by which he means the Sassanids) were of the executive kind, while under the kings of Islam the majority were viziers of delegation. He adds the remarkably insightful sentence that "The vizierate of delegation is surrender, while the executive vizierate is derivative."[27]

In justification of the vizierate, Māwardī cites Q. 20: 29-32 in which "God's Prophet, Moses," asks his Lord to enlist the aid of his brother Hārūn as a vizier. Vizier is an Anglicized version of "*wazīr*," a noun formed from the root *W.Z.R.*, which lends itself to derivations associated with notions of "help," "support," and "alleviation of burden."[28] If prophets are permitted to have a helper/vizier, Māwardī argues, then the imamate is *a fortiori* more deserving of this entitlement, not to mention the consideration that "a second opinion" and "a helping hand" in the complex business of managing a kingdom are much better than none.[29]

It should not be surprising by now to find Māwardī affirming that the qualifications of the vizier of delegation are identical to those of the imam, except for the requirement of descent from Quraysh. Obviously, securing a Qurayshī vizier for every king who ever ruled in Muslim lands would have been utterly unrealistic. But the vizier was still expected to have a quality not required of the imam, an added credential that is both significant and instructive. The vizier

> must meet a condition over and above the conditions an imam must meet, namely, to be competent in his charge in the matters of war and tax collection, with expert and detailed knowledge of both fields. For he must at times engage them firsthand and at others by proxy, but in either case he would not be able to choose the best qualified personnel unless he is one of them and would be unable to perform the tasks by himself should he be unable to secure their support. The vizierate is predicated upon this condition, around which political management revolves.[30]

---

27 Māwardī, *Adab al-Wazīr*, 43: "*Wa-qad kāna aktharu wuzarā'i al-Fursi wuzarā'a tanfīdhin wa-aktharu wuzarā'i mulūki al-Islāmi wuzarā'a tafwīḍin, wa-wizārat al-tafwīḍ istislāmun wa-wizārat al-tanfīdh istimdād.*"

28 Zabīdī, *Tāj al-ʿArūs*, VII, 589-90.

29 *AS*, 50: "*Fa-idhā jāza dhālika fil-nubuwwati kāna fil-imāmati ajwaz.*"

30 *AS*, 50: "*Wa-yaḥtāju [al-Wazīru] fī-hā ilā sharṭin zā'idin ʿalā shurūṭi al-imāmati, wa-huwa an yakūna min ahli al-kifāyati fī-mā wukkila ilayhi min amri al-ḥarbi wal-kharāji khibratun bi-himā wa-maʿrifatun bi-tafṣīlihimā fa'innahu mubāshirun la-humā tāratan wa-mustanībun fī-himā ukhrā fa-lā yaṣilu ilā istinābati al-kufāti illā an yakūna min-hum ka-mā lā yaqdiru

Note here that this is the differential *par excellence* between the imamate and the vizierate, for, on the one hand, it is not a condition in the appointment of a caliph while, on the other, it is an absolutely necessary condition for the vizierate of delegation. Note also that the penultimate sentence in Māwardī's above-quoted passage masks but in no way negates the military association, if not competence, of the viziers, who themselves often commanded armies (note the phrase "one of them").[31] Thus the condition and function of the vizierate was intended to appear as more than just necessary; they constitute the very *raison d'être* not only of this kind of vizierate but the executive function they are intended to serve.

We also see that the caliphal/imamic position is not a matter of appointing a person, a mere spiritual leader. In fact, the Quraysh requirement is quickly dropped in favor of what truly matters: coercive force. If the *raison d'être* of the caliphate/imamate is political management (*siyāsa*), which it is, then coercive power defines that institution, and whoever happened to agree to take it up and perform its essential duties under the dictates of the Sharīʿa will have it, as long as his executive-coercive might is the most supreme. The Sharīʿa, the *Umma*, and the entire House of Islam *require*, for their best collective interests, the most potent and coercive form of executive power. In other words, instead of seeing this legal doctrine as a forced compromise (which Orientalist writings long declared to be the case), it is distinctly more sensible and logical to view it as an auspicious legal solution to a situation in which the caliph no longer possessed military might. The solution, furthermore, demonstrates both Sharīʿa's fluidity and its ability to accommodate change.[32] If the caliph had already delegated his judicial power to the Chief

ʿalā al-mubāsharati idhā qaṣṣara ʿanhum, wa-ʿalā hādhā al-sharṭi madāru al-wizārati wa-bihi tantaẓimu al-siyāsatu." Later on in the treatise, Māwardī also stipulates that in terms of competence, there are three more differences between the caliph and the vizier: (1) The vizier cannot designate an heir to the throne but the imam can; (2) The imam can resign himself but the vizier cannot resign him; and (3) The imam can discharge an official the vizier has appointed but the vizier does not have the power of discharge in the case of a caliphal appointment. *AS*, 54.

31 In *AS*, 63, the masked reality of the vizierate of delegation comes through when Māwardī distinguishes between this type of vizierate and the executive kind by saying that this latter is "appointed" (*muʿayyan*) while the former is "commandeering" (*mustabidd*). Again, we need not stress too much that executive viziers, or those who fulfill such a function without the title, may be members of the royal house, such as a senior uncle who may be in command of the army.

32 On Sharīʿa's inner dynamics of change, see Hallaq, *Authority*, 121-241. Here, it must be noted that Orientalism's duplicity is flagrant: the Sharīʿa has been (falsely) accused of

Justice (*Qāḍī al-Quḍāt*), then it is no surprise that he should do so in the case of competent military commanders. What necessitated the former was the caliph's inability to deal with the workload of litigation, auditing, supervision and all those tasks the *qāḍī*s normally carried out throughout the provinces; what necessitated the latter was the decline of his executive power, another kind of inability.

The vizier of delegation was not the only contender for coercive power, and in fact did not represent the legal complexity that another office had brought to the fore. This is the emirate of seizure (*imārat al-istīlā'*), both a functional and genealogical extension of the caliphate. Whereas the vizierate is the caliphal and sultanic site of aid and assistance, the emirate is an extension of the caliphal province, which is to say that the vizier is the personal helper of the caliph or sultan, whereas the emir is the vessel, so to speak, through which part, or nearly all, of the caliphal functions are exercised. The legal difference between the two is not merely formal but has political implications. Because the vizier is the caliph's helper, he is the personal employee of the caliph and thus is hired, fired, and compensated by the caliph himself, as a private person and employee. By contrast, the emirate is an essential part of the administrative political institution: every king, emperor or caliph needs governors who manage the provinces. The emirate is then a necessary extension of the caliphate, for the caliph rules from the center by proxy while the emir rules locally and directly. This explains why the emir is a "public employee," like the caliph himself. Both appointments are "made on behalf of Muslims" (*niyābatan ʿan al-Muslimīn*), the offices representing the interests of the Muslim population of the polity (*al-Muslimūn*).[33] The vizier is paid from the caliph's personal funds, while the emir is paid from the Public Treasury (*Bayt al-Māl*). This is also why the emir's tenure does not terminate upon the death of the caliph who appointed him, whereas the vizier's does.[34] But if the vizier had appointed the emir, then the emir's tenure comes to an end upon the death of the vizier.[35]

---

rigidity and ossification because it was seen as a "religious" system incapable of legal change, but when it patently demonstrates change, as in this case, it is accused of compromising its values and making undue concessions.

33 *AS*, 64.

34 This is the same logic that governs in the case of *qāḍī*s, whose tenure continues after the caliph's death and until the time specified by the decree of appointment. Ibn Māza, *Sharḥ Adab al-Qāḍī*, III, 151.

35 *AS*, 64.

III

This background paves the way for the systematic elaboration of a theory of seizure, accommodating coercive power in the executive organ. By the time of Māwardī, and for the two centuries prior, a new reality had reshaped the military structure of the Islamic empire. The early ʿAbbāsid caliphs began to face serious difficulties in recruiting soldiers from the local Arabic populations,[36] the area from western Iran to Egypt being largely populated by sedentary societies whose inclination to war and martial ways was weak. Their solution to this dilemma was to rely on the importation of mercenaries and children who were raised in the martial ways to become trained and skilled soldiers. These groups hailed usually from non-Arabic regions and were often non-Muslims, at times sweeping the Islamic imperial center as tribal federations. The tribal groups, mostly of Turkic ethnicity, specialized in warfare, cultivating violence as a political skill. Just as the market businesses were family affairs, tribal groups invested in warfare and built their names around it. Just as a merchant sought to make his fortunes in distant lands, these tribal groups sought to cultivate their military business wherever they could find a need for it. And Muslim polities needed them desperately.

This pattern of enlisting tribal groups and federations as executive powers – who would, after conquest, administer kingdoms and empires – was well understood by Muslim thinkers. The premiere articulator and theoretician of this pattern was Ibn Khaldūn who saw in Bedouin and tribal existence an original state of nature (*ṭabīʿiyy*). Groups living in this state are destined, in a logic of determinism, to seek settlement in "urban" settings (*lā budda min-hu fil-ʿumrān*).[37] The central quality of these tribal groups is their ferocity (*tawaḥḥush*) and martial competence, which equips them to take over "cities" and built environments (*ʿumrān*). Once there, and having seized control of those environments, they administer the affairs of the polity firmly and decisively. The first generation or two continue to preserve their military and martial ways, thus asserting themselves as competent leaders. But "urban" existence, especially for a ruling dynasty, necessarily brings with it luxurious, if not decadent, ways of living (*taraf*), this having the effect of "softening" and

36 I deliberately use the form "Arabic" to indicate a linguistic and cultural group, rather than "Arab," a term loaded with nationalist connotations. I do so in analogy to such notions as Arabic logic (*manṭiq*) rather than Arab logic.

37 Ibn Khaldūn, *Muqaddima*, 96, 97, l. 20.

thus weakening the dynasty's younger princely cohorts.[38] By the time the third or fourth generation of these royal aspirants ascends to the helm, the kingdom or empire begins to lose grip over its domains, with corruption and bad management becoming the rule of the day. The end of such an entity, which Ibn Khaldūn consistently identifies as a *dawla*, would near. All it takes is for a contender to arise and take over the realm, a contender backed by another tribal group that likewise had just left Bedouin-tribal existence behind.[39]

Empirical evidence overwhelmingly backs up Ibn Khaldūn's theorization and suggests that the military business in the Muslim regions was coveted by these tribal groups, for their martial skills and investment seem to have tallied well with the established structures and needs of Muslim polities. In other words, they were an excellent fit for each other, somewhat similar to standing armies that are largely technical units serving and servicing an essential part of the juridico-political structure of the modern state. The legal and constitutional structures that sustained and made up the Muslim polity were in need of a coercive power as much as this power was in need of installing itself within a polity. The roles, especially in the case of Islam, were well-defined, with a political culture whose rules and principles not only came through clearly to the traders of coercive power, but they came through so clearly because they had become fixed structures of operation before any such military arrangements were made. In other words, the military newcomers had to fit themselves in a well-ordered structure of governance, whose limits and boundaries they tacitly, perhaps unconsciously, accepted. It is my argument that this situation was doxastic.

It is an eloquent and telling testimonial of Sharīʿa's malleability, as well as its ability to change, that the new military-executive arrangement was rehabilitated within the old structures of governance. This comes through clearly in Māwardī's brilliant adaptation, one that was juridically performative, in the sense that it created a reality out of discourse.[40] It was performative because it had the force of the law behind it, just as when I say "I do" before an officer of the state, I become married with all the duties and obligations that that institution brings with it. This is not only because a tradition-based habitus is always in operation, with its unconscious pressures and forces, but it is also because the habitus is backed up by a juridical system, a system of law, that

38 Ibn Khaldūn, *Muqaddima*, 132-35.

39 Ibn Khaldūn, *Muqaddima*, 96-148.

40 On this in some detail, see Hallaq, *Restating Orientalism*, 12-13, 61-63; Austin, "Performative Utterances."

stood head and shoulders above the competence of politics – a thesis that I shall insist on and pursue throughout this book.

Before we pursue these themes, let us return to Māwardī's *AS*, to see how this tribal military power was juridically habituated within the executive organ. Māwardī takes it for granted that the caliphs have for long lacked military prowess, and that dynastic clans provided for the executive power that they needed. The typical mode of recruitment looked something like this: A caliph or sultan enlists the services of a military group (often mercenaries) which over the course of time weakens, with the inevitable effect that this group is replaced by another group that subjects it to defeat; or, if not, this group, because weak, seeks to recruit the services of another subgroup. In time this subgroup grows in force and power and finally pushes aside or ousts the "mother" group, and the cycle continues. This is effectively the Khaldūnian cycle of dynastic rotation (significantly and precisely named *duwal*).[41] The major provinces usually constitute the foremost venue through which coercive power emerges, which is why it routinely created anxiety for the central authority. A paradigmatically illustrative example is the renowned Ṣalāḥ al-Dīn al-Ayyūbī (532/1137-589/1193), a Kurdish commanding general who was sent by his master Nūr al-Dīn Zanghī to Fāṭimid Egypt to fight off the Crusades. After establishing a foothold in Egypt, the Kurdish general, largely with the support of his military family, took over not only Egypt but also the entire territories ruled by the Zanghid dynasty.

In Māwardī's terminology, the later Ṣalāḥ al-Dīn would be an emir when he embarked on these ambitious takeovers. A key phrase in Māwardī's constitutional language is that with which he opens the discussion about the emirate of seizure. "It is contracted," he says, "out of need."[42] Note here that the language contains two elements. The first is that the entire set of relations in this sphere of activity and interaction is fundamentally contractual. When things happen in constitutional contexts, they automatically fall into predetermined structures of governance, structures that are preeminently established as legal. In the

41 The concept of *dawla* combines the theme of rotation with domination, so that in a contest over something a participant has at times the upper hand over another and at others not. It applies to war if vocalized as *dawla* (p. *duwal*), and to wealth and money when vocalized as *dūla* (pl. *diwal*). In reference to war, it is used in the meaning of "an army that defeats another and then the victor is defeated [and so on]." Ibn Manẓūr, *Lisān al-ʿArab*, XI, 301 ff.

42 *AS*, 66: "*Wa-amma imaratu al-istila'i al-lati tuʿqadu ʿan iḍṭirarin....*" Ibn Manẓur, *Lisan al-ʿArab*, IV, 558, defines "*iḍṭirār*" as "needing something," "*al-iḥtiyāju ilā al-shay'i.*" On the meaning of *istīlā'*, see ch. 6, n. 37.

case of Islam, as I will argue, this structure was not the result of an event, so to speak – as it is in the case (and sense) of the US Constitution[43] – but rather of a historical process in which, due to certain high principles in the Islamic faith, the structure fell into place over a long stretch of time, and as an effect and result of other conscious acts. A dynast does not come to rule in Islam and then, as an afterthought, attempt to create and finally does create a suitable legal arrangement to enshrine his place or service in the system. Rather, the system has an already standing structure into which political and military entities fell, and fell thus automatically. As we will see in chapter 5, the Sharīʿa and its *dīwān*ic institutions provided these essential structures. And so once a dynast engaged this role, it was taken for granted that something in the order of an implied-in-fact contract had been entered. This was an integral part of doxastic political knowledge.

The second element in Māwardī's phrase is the substantive connotation of *iḍṭirār*, which I have translated, after the classical Arabic lexicons, as "need."[44] The meaning of the term can perhaps be further clarified when we look at the language that Māwardī employs immediately thereafter: "The emirate of seizure ... [occurs] when an emir takes over by strength (*bil-quwwa*) a certain region whose administration and management he undertakes by a delegatory appointment (*yufawwiḍu*) of the caliph."[45] Note here the conflation of the act

43 By "event" I do not mean that things happen necessarily overnight but rather through a deliberate process of action that has a well-defined trajectory of beginning, middle, and end and that produces a concrete result, in this case the written constitution. A paradigmatic example is the history of constitution-making in the US. Being unwritten, by contrast, the Islamic constitutional structure developed over an extended period and without deliberate or even conscious attempts to create such a structure – in fact even less deliberately than the English constitutional experience since the Magna Carta. The Islamic constitutional structure was a by-product of the cultural and political projects of building a system of governance, of answering the question "How do we wish to live our lives spiritually, socially, politically?" As I argue here and elsewhere, it took Muslims some four centuries before they answered this question and dynamically evolved the necessary structures to make their vision come true.

44 Ibn Manẓūr, *Lisān al-ʿArab*, IV, 558. See also n. 42, above.

45 *AS*, 66: "*Fa-huwa an yastawliya al-amīru bil-quwwati ʿalā bilādin yuqalliduhu al-khalīfatu imāratahā, wa-yufawwiḍu ilayhi tadbīrahā wa-siyāsatahā.*" It should be emphasized that the term *quwwa* in premodern Arabic does not necessarily connote force as violence. The standard dictionaries, both lexical and technical, define the terms as follows: "*al-quwwatu naqīḍu al-daʿfi,*" citing at least two Qur'ānic verses whose contextual connotations indicate the meaning of the term as "strength" and "assuredness". Q. 19:12: "*Yā Yaḥyā khudh al-kitāba bi-quwwatin.*" See also Q. 2:63, 2:93, 7:145. Tahānawī, *Kashshāf*, III, 577, writes that "the widespread and established meaning of '*quwwa*' (*ʿinda al-jumhūr*) is the capability of the animal to do hard labor.... This meaning is the opposite of

of seizure ("takes over by strength") with its juridical corralling ("delegatory appointment"). The latter is almost the natural consequence and extension of the former, as if it is a single act in two parts. The contractual effect (*tuʿqadu*) is the consequence of need (*iḍṭirār*), just as the subject of the contract, whether it is one of sale or service, is the need-based desideratum of contracting. In this case, the contract is one of service, defined as "having exclusive control over political management and administration" (*siyāsa wa-tadbīr*). The fact that the "seizing power" is contingent and not integral to the caliphal office and person makes it a situation that only needs to be accommodated in law by virtue of the fact that it is not enshrined in tradition (*kharaja ʿan ʿurfi al-taqlīdi al-muṭlaq*). The very accommodation, strictly juridical and grounded in an implied-in-fact contract, is that which precisely transforms brute power into a legitimate one (*li-yakhruja min al-fasādi ilā al-ṣiḥḥa*). The "need" is thus the very rationale of the contract, and the service is "the preservation of Sharʿī principles and the rules of religion."[46] Need, in other words, is the differential between the possession of coercive force internally – that is, from within the caliphal office itself – and having to accept it from an external source, due to incapability.[47]

The chief *constitutional* concern regarding emiric power was not power as such, since this is the very *raison d'être* of the office or function to begin with; coercive power was an intrinsic and central feature. The relevant characteristic was rather its extrinsic quality of being emiric, of not being caliphal, which is to say that it was presumed to be denuded of ethical Prophetic-caliphal pedigree. This is precisely what makes for the main political anxiety in Islam's constitutional history. It is not the bare fact that emiric or sultanic power is potent or that it is not in principle regulated by law – it was – but rather it was the constant threat that this potency may not be sufficiently restrained by Islam's cultural values and ethical restraints as defined in the various Muslim regions.

The presumption of a potential disjunction between emiric power and ethical pedigree also explains the nature of the seven requirements or conditions Māwardī demands that both fulfill. They all relate to "*qawānīn al-sharʿ*," "the regulations of the law," but the emir is under a "thicker" obligation to be

weakness.... *Quwwa* is capability." ("*Al-quwwatu maʿnāhā al-mashhūru ʿindu al-jumhūri huwa tamakkunu al-ḥayawāni min al-afʿāli al-shāqqati... wa-hādhā al-maʿnā yuqābil al-ḍaʿf... fa-hiya al-qudra.*")

46 *AS*, 66.

47 *AS*, 66: "*Li-wuqūʿi al-farqi bayna shurūṭi al-muknati wal-ʿajz.*"

bound by them than the caliph.[48] The requirements range from maintaining religious unity and emiric obedience to the caliphate to fair taxation and a just administration of the law. But the requirement listed first in order is particularly telling and perhaps the most important, since it not only captures by implication the themes of the six others, it also puts the emirate in its proper constitutional place. It may even be said to constitute the most significant function of the emirate: "To maintain the office of the imamate in its roles as the caliphate of the Prophethood and the manager of the affairs of the *Milla* so as to preserve that which the Shar' has commanded in the way of upholding it [viz., the imamate], and guard that which derives from it in the way of rights and obligations."[49]

Māwardī's constitutional stance is held up against the totality of pressures that the imamate was subjected to, even when the caliphate as a personal office suffered humiliation at the hands of the Būyids. Yet, this insistence is not formalistic in the least, for it could not conceive of Sunni constitutional politics in any other way. It was the embodiment of the *Umma*'s constitutional foundations, without which Sunnism as a polity and body politic has no existence. The litmus test was to appear again in more acute terms about half a century later, when Ghazālī had to defend the 'Abbāsid caliphate against the existential threat of the Bāṭinīs. The defense exposed the bare minimum of the theory that reflected the existing constitutional structures. That existential moment perforce reduced the discursive priorities to what is essential, to what cannot be done away with.

IV

Ghazālī's *Faḍā'iḥ al-Bāṭiniyya* (*FB*) is not only a refutation of Bāṭinī creeds, attempting to show their heresy and what the author saw as overly zealous political claims. It was equally a constitutional document of the first order, for it was the authorization of the imamate and its essential structure that were at stake. As we saw, the Māwardīan defense of the caliphate against political claimants was a second-order concern, for the prime and first-order task was

48 *AS*, 66: "*Wa-wujūbuhā fī jihati al-mutawallā aghlaẓ.*"
49 *AS*, 66: "*Ḥifẓu manṣibi al-imāmati fī khilāfati al-nubuwwati wa-tadbīri umūri al-millati li-yakūna mā awjabahu al-shar'u min iqāmatihā maḥfūẓan wa-mā tafarra'a 'anhā min al-ḥuqūqi maḥrūsan.*"

to establish the juridical basis of the institution in the same manner any institution or practice was subjected to a detailed legal elaboration. It is precisely this detail, this systematic exposition of legal doctrine, that demonstrates the scale of concern, above and beyond the circumstantial and relatively limited context of sectarian challenges. In being subject to juridification, the imamate was treated like any other institution or phenomenon, whether it is marriage, divorce, or the practices of pilgrimage or prayer, with the difference that everyone knew that the imamate is the most crucial edifice of all.

Like Māwardī's elaborations, Ghazālī's was not about a justification of effective power while embarking on a desperate and pathetic project to save the caliphate, as Orientalism has insisted for almost a century. Rather, Ghazālī was interested in the caliphate as a constitutional cornerstone of Sunni polity.

Perhaps the constitutional truth of this office could not have been afforded a better litmus test than the indirect and unintentional testimonial of *FB*, which makes it a work quite different in nature from Māwardī's. "Indirect and unintentional" because Ghazālī was not writing, nor did he mean to write, a political work of the *AS* type or any similar other. *FB*'s constitutional narrative is both spontaneous and a byproduct of larger concerns. It is in the intentional rebuttal of Bāṭinīsm as a politico-theological doctrine that the essential constitutional structures of Sunnism fortuitously come into view. And it is here where the unintentionality involved is significant: whereas Māwardī's and Ghazālī's works are quite different from each other, they score the same constitutional points. We will see further in chapter 6 that even when Juwaynī goes against the grain of the Māwardīan-Ghazālīan thesis, he nonetheless proves the rule. While the caliphate originates as an umbrella institution that is assumed to head all branches of government, its functional divisions become distributed through delegation, with the "legal branch" being entirely surrendered to the juristic class. The only significant bulk that remains associated, by necessity, with this institution is political and military management, expressed in the concepts of *kifāya* (general competence) and *shawka* (military power). In Māwardī and Ghazālī, the challenge was to habituate these two domains within the caliphate through emiric and sultanic delegation. And when Juwaynī tried to leave the caliphate behind (chapter 6), he ended up effectively underscoring the executive nature of the caliphate, delegated or not. This is also the effect of *FB*, although Ghazālī's strategy differed greatly from that of Juwaynī.

One of the main lines of *FB*'s defense (constituting the bulk of its chapter 9) is his argument that the legitimate and true imam, the one who is owed obedience, is the ʿAbbāsid al-Mustaẓhir bil-Lāh (r. 487-512/1094-1118).[50] In typical Ghazālīan fashion, *FB* constructs the argument in the syllogistic form (*burhān*). The first (major) premise of the argument is that "an imam is necessary in every age," while the second (minor) premise is that "he [al-Mustaẓhir] is the only candidate" for the office; "therefore," the syllogism continues, "he is the legitimate imam."[51] No one, including the Bāṭinīs, ever disputed the first premise, for the nemesis wishes to install their own imam, after all the crux and cause of the challenge they pose. The second premise pertains to the identity of the candidate: Should he be the ʿAbbāsid caliph or the Bāṭinī imam? If the imamate is a necessity by the agreement of all, and if there are two candidates, then "proving that one of them is not entitled to the imamate will eliminate all doubt as to the right of the other to it."[52]

Arguments against the Bāṭinī claims and in favor of "our claims" are countless, but two, Ghazālī declares, are particularly demonstrative and "everyone is compelled to accept them." The first, put briefly, is that Bāṭinī beliefs and theological creeds are false. Yet, in the final analysis, it turns out that this argument is not as demonstrative as Ghazālī had claimed, for he himself partially retracts on this account. Suppose, Ghazālī states for the sake of argument, that these creeds are sound, it would still be the case that there remains the final argument whose validity is irrefutable, one that would resolve any doubt and would prove with certitude that the legitimate caliph is the ʿAbbāsid one. This is the final line of defense, but one that comes with the assurance of multi-layered, fact-based and potent props. "The imamate that we advocate has been subject to consensus by the leaders and the scholars of the age," that is, the political leadership as well as the scholars of all regions.

In the way of further confirmation, Ghazālī adds that the vast majority of people (*jamāhīr al-khalq*) have partaken in this consensus. The Bāṭinīs are a relatively tiny lot who, in their totality, represent "no more than one percent (*ʿushr al-ʿashīr*) of the number of supporters backing up the victorious ʿAbbāsid *dawla*."[53] Here, we get to the crux of the matter, where the legitimacy of the "true" caliph (*al-imām al-ḥaqq*) is established and vindicated. It is what makes him the caliph *par excellence*.

The mainstay of the imama, he avers, is *shawka*; and *shawka* is strengthened by popular support of great numbers (*al-kathra fil-ittibāʿ wal-ashyāʿ*).[54] All

50 *FB*, 6, 169, 170.
51 *FB*, 170.
52 *FB*, 172.
53 *FB*, 173.
54 *FB*, 173, 177.

that is needed is to have available a person who delivers an oath of allegiance (*bay ʿa*) but one who wields a *shawka* backed by popular support and people's approval (*muwāfaqat al-jamāhīr*).[55] The individual identity of the person is inconsequential, for what matters is that popular support is garnered by the wielder of power who would by the nature of things obtain such support.[56] When ʿUmar b. al-Khaṭṭāb swore allegiance (*bāya ʿa*) to Abū Bakr, the latter's imamate was instantly validated (*in ʿaqadat*) by virtue of this allegiance, and because of the seriatim individual support he received (*li-tatābu ʿ al-aydī*). Had people disagreed with ʿUmar and broken ranks with him, leaving him the only supporter of Abū Bakr, or had the supporters been equal in size or number to the objectors, Abū Bakr's imamate would never have materialized. After all, the entire purpose of the imamate is to bring people together under one banner, a forceful presence that is respected and obeyed (*hayba* and *ṭā ʿa*).

Popular support is generated through *shawka*, which is to say, tautologically, that "*shawka* perforce cannot come into existence without the consent of the majority of those who matter."[57] A single person, therefore, can be sufficient to conclude the *bay ʿa*, as long as he garners popular support. "We deem an imamate legitimate not because the swearer of allegiance possesses any particular personal attribute but rather because people follow him and lend him support due to the obedience he commands."[58] If *shawka* is strength and dominance, then amassing followers is an essential ingredient of it. "It is the wholehearted show of support and obedience to his decrees and commands that validates the contract of the imamate."[59] "In our [Sunni] doctrine, the imamate is contracted by *shawka*, and *shawka* is validated by *bay ʿa*; and *bay ʿa* [in turn] cannot obtain without God compelling the hearts [of the masses] for support and loyalty."[60]

55 *FB*, 177.

56 *FB*, 177: "*Wa-laysa al-maqṣūdu a ʿyāna al-mubāyi ʿīna, wa-innamā al-gharaḍu qiyāmu shawkati al-imami bil-ittibā ʿi wal-ashyā ʿi, wa-dhālika yaḥṣulu bi-kulli mustawlin muṭā ʿ.*"

57 *FB*, 177: "*Fa-inna al-maqṣūda al-ladhī ṭalabnā la-hu al-imāmata jam ʿu shatāti al-ārā'i fī muṣṭadami ta ʿaruḍi al-ahwā'i, wa-lā tattafiqu al-irādātu al mutanāqiḍatu wal-Shāhawātu al mutabāyinatu al-mutanāfiratu ʿalā mutāba ʿati ra'yin wāḥidin illā idhā ẓaharat shawkatuhu wa- ʿaẓumat najdatuhu wa-tarassakhat fī al-nufūsi rahbatahu wa-mahābatuhu,* wa-madāru jamī ʿi dhālika ʿala al-shawkati, *wa-lā taqūmu al-shawkatu illā bi-muwāfaqati al-aktharīna min mu ʿtabarī kulli zamān*" (emphasis mine).

58 *FB*, 178: "*Wa-ḥakamnā bi-in ʿiqādi al-imāmati ʿinda bay ʿatihi lā li-tafarrudihi fī ʿaynihi, wa-lākin li-kawni al-nufusi maḥmūlatun ʿalā mutāba ʿatihi wa mubāya ʿati man adh ʿana huwa li-ṭā ʿatihi.*"

59 *FB*, 178: "*Wa-innama al-muṣaḥḥiḥu li- ʿaqdi al-imāmati inṣirāfu qulūbi al khalqi li-ṭa ʿatihi wal-inqiyādu la-hu fī amrihi wa-nahyihi.*"

60 *FB*, 179.

Ghazālī then defines *shawka* as integral to *najda*, which consists of military supremacy, effective command of the regions (by raising the banners and the flags), garnering popular support, suppression of sedition, heresy and rebellion, even before they arise. "*Shawka* in this age of ours happened to belong to the Turks, who by the grace of God were made to lend support" to the caliph al-Mustaẓhir.[61] The Saljūqs deem such support as a way to "become closer to God," for they have eagerly embraced his imamate and surrendered to his obedience, as evidenced in their submission to the law and the commands of God (*yatadayyanūna bi-wujūbi awāmiri Allāh*).[62]

At this point, Ghazālī's Bāṭinī interlocutor strikes back with a compelling statement of historical truth, namely, the harsh treatment and humiliation the caliph has suffered at the hands of the "brutish"[63] Turks/Saljūqs. As I intimated above, the conventional understanding has been that Māwardī's political writings, especially his *AS*, represented a defense of the ʿAbbāsid caliphate against the Shīʿī Būyids, an understanding that does not hold water in either constitutional or legal terms, for Ghazālī's similar defense of al-Mustaẓhirī shows that the stakes lay elsewhere. In this specific context, in *this* part of the argument, Ghazālī is not advocating Sunni institutions against any other, Shīʿī or not, but he is rather trying to elucidate the constitutional structures in a situation where both the effective military power (i.e., the Saljūqs) and the ʿAbbāsid caliph are both Sunni. Religious chasm *as such* therefore is not the point, nor is it a significant constitutional fact. He even deems the Bāṭinī factual objection hollow (*su'ālun fī ghāyati al-rakāka*), for, despite its historical accuracy, it misses the point altogether.

Ghazālī's reply is highly instructive, for it sheds light on more than the constitutional issues concerned. It highlights the entire relationship between the *salṭana* and the imamate, a relationship that does not revolve around harmonious or disharmonious interaction between the two. The relationship is instead juridico-political, however much one scorned the other on the personal or political level. Obedience of the Saljūqs to the caliph – or should we say caliphate – is no different from the obedience a slave owes to his master, or the obedience of Muslims to God and his Prophet. The relationship between the members of any two pairs can only be one of either consent or dissent. There is no third. A slave either accepts the lordship of his master or does not; and the individual who is the site of religious obligation either surrenders to God

61 *FB*, 182.
62 *FB*, 182.
63 *FB*, 183.

or does not. Whether these obey the master or God every time is no proof of their obedience, for they may disobey in certain instances but without dissenting in principle or in categorical terms.

The benchmark here is the recognition that upon the commission of infraction (i.e., disobedience) in certain circumstances or on particular points of conduct there is the concomitant realization that an infraction, a break in the rule, has been effected. Therefore, notwithstanding the infractions of the Saljūqs against the person of the caliph, they nonetheless "are of the belief that obedience is incumbent [upon them], and that dissent is prohibited and repugnant."[64] Obedience obtains in principle when there is the recognition that the particular infraction they committed is a misdeed (*isā'a*), this being in turn necessarily integral to the belief that consent and obedience are good. This is why, Ghazālī states, the Saljūqs "would not change their creed of loyalty [to the caliph] even if they were to be shred into pieces." To them, the defense of the ʿAbbāsid caliphate against insurgencies and rebels is no less a vigorous obligation than a *jihād* against the infidels. "Which obedience in God's world can top this obedience?" Ghazālī rhetorically asks.[65]

Against the Bāṭinī objection that the ʿAbbāsid caliph does not personally perform all functions of rule, Ghazālī retorts with the rhetorical interrogation: And who has ever made this a requirement of the caliphate! Of course, he says, the caliph may choose to personally deal with matters of governance, but he is under no obligation to do so. He can delegate matters of war to his armies, and he may take decisions from the center, should the battlefield be in close proximity. Otherwise, if distance is great, he is fully entitled to delegate matters to his generals on site.[66]

As I indicated earlier, there was nothing unusual about delegating offices and tasks in the Islamic tradition, political or otherwise. Delegation, as Ibn ʿArabī showed, was integral to the ubiquitous notion of *khilāfa*, a notion that suffused Islam's chain of being in every way. In discussing the second most important quality that the imam must possess, the concept of delegation looms large as well. This quality is *kifāya*, what might be described as rational or intellectual competence in finding proper and ethical solutions to complex problems, and when these are urgent, finding solutions on time. The quality is made up of two layers, one instinctual and inborn (including

64 *FB*, 183.
65 *FB*, 183.
66 *FB*, 184.

penetrating intelligence and rational power) and another, sitting on top of the first, acquired, a matter of making the right effort in consulting those who are in the know. This is the important concept and practice of *mushāwara*, consultation of the experts as well as of the learned and the wise. Seeking counsel was so important that God specifically commanded the Prophet to consult those who know. "Deeming one's opinion the only one that matters is rather reprehensible and repugnant, even though one might be in possession of a penetrating intelligence."[67]

The first layer of the quality of *kifāya* is thus instinctual, sort of a natural endowment of intelligence and good judgment. And it is here where judiciousness is exhibited in selecting the right persons to consult. Al-Mustaẓhirī, Ghazālī tells us, has been blessed by the presence next to him of his capable vizier, a reference likely to the powerful ʿAmīd al-Dawla. The latter is said to have met all the Sharʿī and rational qualifications (*al-sharʿ wal-ʿaql*) required of a statesman and a counselor, and repeatedly proven himself as a capable and competent manager of political affairs. Ghazālī here merely replicates a description once given to Niẓām al-Mulk, another distinguished vizier who effectively ran the affairs of an entire empire for over two decades just a few years earlier. Niẓām al-Mulk was not even a caliphal vizier but rather served two consecutive Saljūq sultans, Alp Arslān and Malik Shāh.

In a like manner, the quality of *ʿilm* can also obtain by substitution. Just as the caliph enlists in his service a vizier who is competent to undertake the burdens of administering the empire, he also has jurists to bear the burden of *ʿilm*. The caliph is not required to possess this latter quality in person, nor for that matter any other, except, obviously, the descent from Quraysh.[68] "Just as the caliph is strengthened in *shawka* by the mightiest people of the age, and in *kifāya* by the shrewdest and most percipient ... he is likewise strengthened by a senior jurist who can pour forth upon him his knowledge on all matters of the law."[69] Other than the descent from Quraysh, all other attributes of the imam have a direct relation to the *Umma*'s benefit and interests, for the realization of which the institution has been installed in the first place. As long as these benefits and interests accrue, it does not matter if it is the caliph himself or a deputy of his who ensures their realization or implementation. But the caliph stays.

67 *FB*, 185-86. The reference is to Q. 3:153. See also ch. 1, n. 81.
68 *FB*, 191.
69 *FB*, 192.

V

It is clear by now that the caliphate is not a dispensable institution; and institution it is. In strict constitutional terms, it is integral to the very order of things that made Islam what it is. In other words, the caliphate defines the Islamic concept of politics, political management and organization. It defines them, that is, in qualitative terms, making them the unique reflection of the Islamic political experience. It is nothing less than the backbone on which stands the Islamic body politic, the necessary organizational structure that permits an optimal operation of the Sharīʿa, itself the ultimate desideratum of Muslim life.

The caliphate is not merely a political structure either, however crucial political structures are: it is also an indispensable link that connects the various parts of the Islamic conception of the world, a conception that starts from the act of creation and the "sending down" of the contents of the Preserved Tablet to the reception of the Qur'ān and the formation of the Community in its fullest living detail. To extricate the caliphate from this Chain of Being is to cut the rope that ties the Community and Communal life in its smallest and greatest detail with the Divine architecture of justice, mercy, and love.[70] This is why Māwardī, and almost every writer down to Ottoman times, could not dispose of the institution and its functions, despite the political and military weakness of the individual caliphs.

But political and military weakness of the caliphs as leaders is one thing, and constitutional collapse is entirely another. The caliphate could not disappear from the world as long as Islam maintained its constitutional structure, that which made it what it was across the centuries. The caliphate is the *sine qua non* of Islamic constitutionalism. Even in a physically eviscerated form, the caliphate remains the source of all political, military, and administrative authority. Put even more cuttingly, the caliphate would substantively continue to be alive even when it is dead. As long as there is a Muslim polity, the caliphate would continue to hold its functions even if it vanishes into a nominal existence. The sultanate, the emirate, and the vizierate may play their own respective roles, but they cannot escape the fact that they are all the offspring of the caliphate, performing one aspect or another of the game whose rules the caliphate instituted. Put conversely, the continuing functions of these offices, as well as that of the judiciary, are themselves the realization of the caliphate and its operation.

70 See ch. 4.

In the first fifth of his *AS*, Māwardī completed his constitutional treatment of the caliphate and its rules. He thereafter declared, in the passive voice, that since the "rules of the imamate (*aḥkām al-Imāma*) ... have been established," there issues therefrom four types of "his *khulafā'*" (i.e., the caliphs of the caliph).[71] Here it becomes patently clear that the system is delegatory, from top to bottom. Each part, each body, each function, and each personnel performs a function delegated from higher up. The lower replicates the work of the higher. Just as the caliph is the *khalīfa* of the Prophet, the sultan is the *khalīfa* of the caliph, and just as the Chief Justice or Chief Tax Collector is the *khalīfa* of the sultan, the presiding judge or the local tax collector is the *khalīfa* of his respective superior.

Also note that the passive voice Māwardī deploys here, as elsewhere, is instructive. It speaks of a hidden power that authorizes the constitutional structure. This is because logically and historically, the law precedes the constitutional structure, which it effectively makes and modifies. If (as we will see later) the very idea of constitutional jurisprudence is modern, arising from the history that gave rise to the nation-state and its liberal concept of popular will, then we know that logically and theoretically the constitution comes first, for it constitutes the bodies and organs that make the law. This is the meaning of "the will" in "popular will." In the Islamic tradition, law comes first because law, being an expression of God's will, becomes the determinant of how life is to be lived. If one knows how life is to be lived, then one also derivatively knows how one is to govern and be governed. The "basic law" that was willed in Islam is the Qur'ān, a law that – as I show in chapter 4 – determines what governance must look like in principle.

Thus, in speaking of the remaining governmental functions that derive from the caliphate, Māwardī is enunciating the voice of the law that defines the boundaries and limits of each function, and, quite importantly, how they relate to each other. In almost every constitutional arena or enclave, Māwardī deployed an analytically comparative list of similarities and differences, in an attempt at sorting out the various responsibilities for, and boundaries of, each function or office. Once he completed the discussion of the caliphate, he outlined his constitutional concerns in terms of the scope that each of the functions covers. As we have intimated earlier, there are four categories, the first of which is that which is represented in the vizierate, since this office

71 *AS*, 49: "*Wa-idhā tamahhada mā waṣafnāhu min aḥkāmi al-khilāfati... inqasama mā ṣadara ʿanhu* [i.e., caliph] *min wilāyāti khulafā'ihi arbaʿata aqsām.*"

almost entirely replicates the caliphate's mandate. Which is to say that this is a universal mandate over all regions of the caliphate. The second category is an office whose mandate is likewise unqualified but is restricted to a specific region of the kingdom (such as the Governor). The third is an office whose mandate is limited in terms of function but possesses competence and is operative in the kingdom at large (such as the Chief Justice or the Chief Tax Collector). Finally, the fourth is a limited or specialized function confined to a limited region or locale, such as an army officer, a presiding judge, or a city tax collector.[72]

For the remainder of his treatise, Māwardī allocates a detailed discussion to some nine functions, with delegatory sub-functions. The total number comes to about a dozen, including the caliphate, vizierate, and emirate. The remaining offices are the military commander, the *qāḍī*, the Officer of Complaints (*ṣāḥib al-maẓālim*), the Prayer Leaders, the Protector of the Noble Lineage, Officer of Pilgrimage, Tax Collector, Market Inspector, and agents of criminal jurisdiction.

Note here that these functions are regulated by the law and constitute the entire extension of the caliphal office. On strict principle and in theory, the caliph himself is responsible for each and every function, but he delegates these responsibilities because of the obvious unfeasibility of performing all these tasks and functions himself. This functional diversity originates in unity, one that Ibn ʿArabī would capitalize on in his *al-Tadbīrāt al-Ilāhiyya* (as we saw in chapter 2).

For the remainder of this chapter and in illustration of the constitutional boundaries placed on the discretionary powers arrogated to the caliph and his deputies within the dozen or so executive functions Māwardī carves out, I shall focus on the office of the *maẓālim* as a case study. As stressed above, this area of caliphal competence is regulated by the Sharīʿa, in the sense that the already existing legal corpus decides on the limits and boundaries of this jurisdiction. Which is to say that the very function of this office within a constitutional whole, and the jurisprudential and institutional boundaries in which it is set, are not determined by the caliph himself or any of his deputies (*khulafāʾ*). Nor are they determined by any political authority or power. The deputies operate, and possess a degree of discretion, *within* its boundaries, but they by no means determine these boundaries. This is the meaning of the precedence of the law over politics and political expedient. But this self-evident

72 *AS*, 49.

truth must be squared with the caliphal privilege of exercising *ijtihād*. As we recall, the second qualification required of the caliph is "knowledge that leads to *ijtihād* in new cases and judgments."[73] So, can we assume that the caliph can make law? The question, it must be said, has universal relevance and is not limited to *maẓālim* alone.

The brief answer to this question is in the negative if we mean by law a *systematic, holistic production* of a substantive legal doctrine. This is so because no one had this power in the Islamic tradition in the first place. A *mujtahid*, the highest agent in legal production, was never in charge of "legislation" across the board. As we will see in chapter 4, no one was. And the very language of the caliphal qualifications we have cited says this much. The ability to exercise *ijtihād* was always limited to individual cases, whether they are the *nawāzil* (new cases), *masā'il* (unsettled legal questions) or *aḥkām* (legal norms of particular cases). This was the norm for all jurists, without exception. From the beginning of Islamic history, the Rāshidūn caliphs did espouse their own individual legal opinions, based as it were on *ijtihād*, but they never arrogated to themselves any *ijtihād*ic privilege or competence that stood above or beyond that of any other highly competent jurist. They possessed *ijtihād* competence primarily because they were Companions of the Prophet who also happened to be individually endowed with juristic skills. There is a good reason why there isn't a single caliph (of the Rāshidūn or not) nor a sultan across Islamic history and until the nineteenth century who entertained the idea that he could make the law of the domains, in whole or even in substantial part.[74] *Ijtihād*ic competence was therefore limited to individual cases, and these in reality were relatively few and far between.

As I have shown elsewhere,[75] the law of the Sharīʿa derived from a Qur'ānic *grundnorm* elaborated into detail by a class of pious individuals who did not derive their authority from a political office or a political entity. Nor did they hail from the upper social strata that may have had connections with the ruling elite.[76] The authorship of the law was thus a private enterprise, pure

73 AS, 19: "*Al-ʿilmu al-mu'addī ilā al-ijtihādi fī al-nawāzili wal-aḥkām.*"

74 Of course, proving absence is impossible, but neither Muslim historians nor modern Orientalists (who have been studying Islam for almost two centuries) could document any such phenomenon or even an attempt of a caliph or sultan to command the field of law and legislation.

75 Hallaq, *Origins*, 40-56, 63-74, 102 ff.

76 Cohen, "Economic Background," 16-61, esp. 43-45: "With the exception of the judges and a small number of theologians and traditionists, all these scholars functioned in an entirely private capacity, unappointed either by the authorities or by any religious institution.

and simple. True, certain aspects of the law, especially in matters of land, taxation, war, and crime (whose management was traditionally mandated by the Sharīʿa to the caliphs and their deputies) cited as authority the practices of the early caliphs, who mostly were, I stress, the Companions of the Prophet, but it was the private specialists who were the final arbiters of what counted as authority and law and what did not, even in these domains (Abū Yūsuf's *Kitāb al-Kharāj* is a prominent example in point).[77] Law was a communal and cumulative project, corralled into the *madhhab*s, the legal schools, and as such was beyond the legislative reach of a supreme political office.

This fact bears significantly on the deputized caliphal functions I have enumerated above, including that of the *maẓālim*. It means that whereas it may have been possible for a caliph, emir, or a deputized officer to exercise juristic discretion in one case or another, *the entire body of the law that regulated any of the dozen functions enumerated above was constructed outside of these political offices*. Not only that, the constitutional "location," or proper place of each office, and the complex of relationships that delimited the boundaries and overlaps between one function and another were wholly determined by the Sharīʿa. For the Sharīʿa could hypothetically carve a free space for these functions, including the *maẓālim*, tax collection, etc., only determining their external boundaries and constitutional location vis-à-vis other domains, but that was only half the story; the Sharīʿa *also* vastly regulated the internal workings and internal structure of each and every such domain. There of course was a place for situational discretion, including (as we will see in detail) substantial discretionary spaces within *siyāsa sharʿiyya*, but this discretion was bounded by institutional limits that were legally predetermined. This boundedness is the meaning of constitutional restraint.

When Māwardī corralled substantial legal doctrine in his constructive project of constitutional mapping, he was not presenting a "juristic" version or a "juristic" rendition of constitutional theory, as if there were any others that could compete for this role. Māwardī's juristic construction – *qua* juristic construction – was the only way the task of constitutional articulation could be achieved. There simply was no other. This is why he reappears as the authoritative author par excellence as late as the ninth/fifteenth century, and in no lesser work than that of Qalqashandī, a multivolume oeuvre that

In other words, unlike Christian clergy, they received no emoluments and had to support themselves, which they did in a variety of ways."

77 Abū Yūsuf, *Kitāb al-Kharāj*. See also Abū Hilāl al-ʿAskarī, *Mā Iḥtakama bi-hi al-Khulafāʾ*; Najib, "Common Wealth: Land Taxation in Early Islam."

describes in detail the actual operations of the various executive offices in Muslim polity.[78]

The *maẓālim* – as well as any of the other dozen units of government he discusses – squarely fell into this juristic context. The purview of this function was to carry out justice by threat of force (*rahba, hayba,* the very same terms that were to be associated with the caliphate and all executive power – the modern, in effect, included).[79] Niẓām al-Mulk discerned a double function for the *maẓālim,* a form of justice that he, like everyone else, deemed crucial for good governance.[80] One function is obviously implementing justice and effectively punishing trespassers and criminals. But there is a deterring force simultaneously at work. When people see the king allocating as many as two days a week to hearing the *maẓālim* complaints, those who entertain any ideas about committing wrong would think twice, fearing the consequences.[81]

The officer in charge of this jurisdiction must ideally possess effective power and eminent status, and must be feared, pious, and free of greed. He must combine both "the coercive power of protective guardians and the steady hand of *qāḍī*s," the former components, Māwardī divulges later, being "*quwwat al-salṭana,*" the might of the ruler.[82] In fact, *maẓālim*'s modus operandi on the whole must combine the two, which is to say that it was designed to aggregate powers, prerogatives, credentials, procedures, and methods of both the executive and the judicial. The function of the *maẓālim* is integral to the caliphal office as well as to any governmental office holding general powers, and because it is so integral to these functions, no appointment decree (*tafwīḍ*/

78 On the constitutional significance of Qalqashandī's work, *Ṣubḥ al-Aʿshā*, see ch. 5. On actual chancery practices and empirical data regarding the operation of governmental offices (under the Ayyūbids), see Ibn al-Mamātī, *Qawānīn al-Dawāwīn.*

79 *Rahba* and *hayba,* like *saṭwa, qahr* and *qamʿ*, are the main terms used by Māwardī to describe executive sultanic power. See *ADD*, 218. The modern state, especially its executive organs, claim the same powers. Even if we accept the contemporary challenges that privatization and globalization of violence chip at the monopoly of the state over it, we still have to concede that states make that claim and try hard to enforce it. See Anter, "The Modern State." It must also be stressed here that caution must be exercised to avoid conflating the meaning of these terms in the premodern context with that which modern Arabic has made them acquire. The term *qamʿ*, for instance, has acquired a thoroughly negative meaning in modern Arabic, almost exclusively referring to political oppression. In its premodern connotation, the term referred to the act of "rebuffing," "stopping," "putting down," "defeating." See Ibn Manẓūr, *Lisān al-ʿArab*, VIII, 349 ff.

80 True, the Ottomans abolished the *maẓālim* as an independent jurisdiction, but they subsumed the functions of this office under the *qāḍī*'s function.

81 *SM*, 54.

82 AS, 130: "*Saṭwat al-ḥumāti wa-thabati al-quḍāti.*" See also 131 for "*quwwat al-salṭana.*"

taqlīd/ʿahd) was needed for these. But if the appointment is limited (types 3 and 4 of caliphal deputies), then such a decree is required, provided the appointee fulfills the office's credentials. The credentials and levels of *hayba* may however not be found in the case of minor officials who are appointed to this function to reinforce the carriage of justice determined by the *qāḍīs*, but the qualities of being fair and honest remain a requirement.[83]

At this point, and after discussing the above requirements in one lengthy paragraph, Māwardī quickly begins to proffer a historical account of the institution of *maẓālim*. Constitutionally speaking, this account is not only significant for institutional self-awareness but it also *partakes in the very construction of constitutional discourse*. History here, in other words, creates a constitutional habitat. When an officer is introduced to the executive structures of governance, he is automatically habituated not just to what his task requires but also to an environment that grounds itself in what we call today a culture. History was integral to constitutional culture because it was part and parcel of the discursive fabric that made that culture what it was. By "discursive fabric" I mean the ordinary practices of the various offices and the discourses that regulated both the modus operandi and perception of what is entailed in the duties and work of that office. As we will see in chapter 5, the very history of the practice of governance, including the history of chancery, became an essential part of the positive and substantive rules regulating these constitutional structures.

We learn from Māwardī that the office or at least the practice of *maẓālim* did not start with Islam. He reports that the Persian kings, which I take to be the Sassanids, regarded this practice as essential to governance and to justice, without which the general well-being of the polity cannot be attained.[84] Likewise, the Qurayshīs themselves, even in the age of Jāhiliyya, instituted the *maẓālim*. And the Prophet himself is reported to have held a *maẓālim* tribunal at least in one instance, making the institution a part of the Prophetic Sunna. However, due to the spread of what we might call ordinary justice driven by the newly established zeal and (Qur'ānic) moral deterrents during the Rāshidūn Era, none of these caliphs practiced this form of adjudication.[85]

83 *AS*, 130.
84 *AS*, 132: "*Wa-qad kāna mulūku al-fursi yarūna dhālika min qawāʿidi al-mulki wa-qawānīni al-ʿadli al-ladhī lā yaʿummu al-ṣalāḥu illā bi-murāʿātihi wa-lā yatimmu al-tanāṣufu illā bi-mubāsharatihi.*"
85 *AS*, 130-31, for Quraysh, 132-33.

At least two points may be extracted from the foregoing account. First, the legitimacy of the *maẓālim* derives from a suggestion of universal history, in which pre- and extra-Islamic actors found it essential for a proper carriage of justice, both on imperial and local scales. Combined with an Islamic precedent, this history in turn bestowed on this type of tribunal a sort of universal truth and thus legitimacy. Second, this legitimacy, as we already intimated, was enhanced by nothing less than the Prophet's Sunna, the second most authoritative source of the law. And third, the case of the Rāshidūn is instructive, for it tells us that in a situation or context in which moral zeal and ethical deterrence are alive and optimally operative, there is no need for *maẓālim*. But aside from such exceptional contexts, the hand of coercive power is normally needed to enhance ordinary justice. This, however, is by no means exceptional, and here the first point comes to bolster the third. The carriage of justice always needs coercive power. The Persians had done it, and even the Quraysh engaged in it. But it also is the defining narrative of the modern state, where coercive power (i.e., "violence and the threat of it") constitute the *sine qua non* of justice.

After the passing of the Rāshidūn Era, Māwardī continues, injustices by the strong and powerful proliferated and so "sultanic power amalgamated with the equity of [*shar'ī*] *qaḍā*'" was in order. It was 'Abd al-Malik b. Marwān, the fifth Umayyad caliph (r. 65-86/685-705), who was the first to reinstitute this system, dedicating one day a week for presiding, himself, over *maẓālim* cases. However, 'Abd al-Malik did not himself adjudicate the cases but merely reviewed them (*yataṣaffaḥ qiṣaṣ al-mutaẓallimīn*). Māwardī gives us to understand that this caliph – or likely a presiding *maẓālim* judge under his direct supervision – rendered verdicts in the routine cases but would typically redirect the hard and difficult ones to the distinguished *qāḍī* Ibn Idrīs al-Awdī whose decisions the caliph implemented.

The point of this story is that the first caliph in Islam to practice the *maẓālim* did not engage in the full process, having depended heavily on his *qāḍīs*.[86] It was 'Umar II (r. 99-101/717-20) who would be the first to undertake the tasks of the *maẓālim* in whole, and undertake them against governors and powerful men. What is telling about 'Umar's work under the rubric of *maẓālim* was that he severely punished (*shaddada wa-aghlaẓa*) injustices committed by members of the Umayyad dynasty and their officers (*maẓālim Banī Umayya*),[87] an early indication that *maẓālim* tribunals have as their main

86 *AS*, 131: "*Fa-kāna Abū Idrīs huwa al-mubāshiru wa-'Abdu al-Maliki huwa al-āmir.*"
87 *AS*, 131.

purpose the crackdown on governmental abuse. Later on, this function seems to have become a routine practice of "a number of ʿAbbāsid caliphs," including al-Mahdī (158/775-169/785), the first ʿAbbāsid caliph to do so, as well as al-Hādī (169/785-170-786), al-Rashīd (170/786-193/809), al-Maʾmūn, and down to al-Muhtadī (255-56/869-70). Māwardī ends his historical narrative here, perhaps implying that the rest, leading up to his time, is to be viewed in a similar lens.

At this point, Māwardī moves on to discuss the personnel or assistants needed, directly or indirectly, for the *maẓālim* officer to do his work – assistants without whom his task could hardly be deemed orderly or complete.[88] These are of five categories. First, and quite integral to the office itself, the *maẓālim* chief must surround himself with "assistants and bodyguards" to keep order. Second, and consistent with the "combined" nature of this function, he needs to secure the presence and cooperation of the Chief Justices (*qāḍī al-quḍāt*s) and *qāḍī*s of the bench (*ḥukkām*; later also "*nāʾib*s"). These are the sitting *qāḍī*s and those who administratively oversee their work, these latter being the ones who appoint them, although they may or may not preside over actual adjudication. Both ranks are indispensable because they inform the *maẓālim* officer of all relevant matters, including claims, disputes, and even quotidian judicial routines that were brought before them in the course of their work. Needless to say, this is highly suggestive not only of the symbiotic relationship and thus the intimate connections between the Sharīʿa court and the *maẓālim*, but also of the channels of communication, direct or not, between the community and the *maẓālim* courts.[89]

Third, in difficult or hard cases, he must consult with the *fuqahāʾ*, the experts in the Sharʿ. Fourth, he needs scribes whose function it is to record the proceedings, noting down the rights and obligations of the litigants, as well as the testimonials required. Fifth, and finally, there must be witnesses of the court who will attest to the proceedings and verdicts, thereby validating them.[90]

The *maẓālim* courts possess auditing jurisdiction and remedial power over ten areas that define and delimit their purview. First, transgressions and

88 *AS*, 134: "*Lā yastaghnī ʿanhum wa-lā yantaẓimu naẓaruhu illā bi-him.*"
89 This practice is confirmed by Qalqashandī for the middle of the fourth/tenth century, where a decree of appointment issued on behalf of al-Muṭīʿ lil-Lāh for the *maẓālim* officer Ḥusayn b. Mūsā al-ʿAlawī commands him to consult with both *qāḍī*s and jurists (*fuqahāʾ*). Qalqashandī provides this document as an example of how to draw appointment decrees for *maẓālim* officers in his time, late eighth/fourteenth and early ninth/fifteenth century. See *SAQ*, X, 255.
90 *AS*, 134.

arbitrary conduct (*taʿaddī*, *ʿasf*) of governors (*wulāt*) "in the way they treat the common people." "This," Māwardī states, "is an essential task of the *maẓālim* purview." The officer must carefully review the conduct of governors and rulers, to "reaffirm their conduct of justice and rebuff them when engaging in arbitrary actions. If they commit injustice, he is to replace them."[91]

Second, unfair collection of taxes. The tax collector's actual levies must be compared with the allotments and quotas recorded in the *Dīwān* of Taxation. If people refuse to pay taxes, he is "to push them" to do so (*ḥamala ʿalā*), but if taxes were overpaid, then the excess balance must be restored to their rightful owners, even if it has already reached the central treasury. The practical and realist Niẓām al-Mulk elaborates further on this, saying that the Collectors' approach should be "kind and polite" when asking for payment, and that this payment should never be made or accepted before crops have been produced. As a vizier who himself oversaw the operation of the system of taxation in the entire empire, he counseled that the land tax administrators should even lend money to farmers who fall on bad times so that they remain in business.[92] The vizier's concern, however, was judiciously more with the misconduct of the tax officials who, like all office holders in the empire, should be subject to constant supervision and surveillance. An official who "deviates" from the proper path should be removed and replaced by another, and if he usurps people's property, it should be restored to its rightful owners. The sultan, as a matter of deterrence, should also confiscate his property and dispatch it to the Royal Treasury.[93]

Third, the work of scribes in the matter of keeping the *dīwāns*. As we will see in chapter 5, the *dīwāns* were instrumental in the modalities of governance, for their keepers are "the trustees over the Muslims' properties."[94] The *maẓālim* officer should inspect the expenditure and income to ensure accuracy.

Fourth, military expenditure and soldiers' pay. If the commanders or military superiors skim the soldiers' salaries, or delay their payment, they are to correct the situation, again by consulting and comparing the stipulations entered in the central military *dīwān* registry.

Fifth, restoring usurped property. If the usurpation was committed by a sultanic deputy or officer, the process of restoration should take effect irrespective

91 *AS*, 135.
92 *SM*, 62.
93 *SM*, 62. On the necessity of directly supervising the work of government officials, both at the center but also in the provincial regions, see *SM*, 69.
94 *AS*, 135: "*Li-annahum umanāʾu al-muslimīna ʿalā thubūti amwālihim.*"

of whether or not anyone initiated a claim. In other words, the remedy should be instituted without the existence of a plaintiff, unless of course the *maẓālim* officer was not aware of the wrong, in which case a complaint must be filed by the victim or someone acting on his or her behalf. Again, the basis of restorative action is the sultanic *dīwān*. If the entry in the *dīwān* is not consistent with the amount of seizure or if it does not justify it at all, no further evidence is needed to make the remedy. In other words, the victim does not need to produce evidence in support of his or her case. However, if the wrongdoer is a civilian, then the *maẓālim* officer is not to hear the case unless and until one of four conditions obtains: (1) a confession by the usurper; (2) knowledge of the case by the officer; (3) documentary evidence proving that usurpation has in fact taken place; and (4) widespread knowledge, presumably in the community, that such an act has occurred.[95]

Sixth, inspection of the *waqf*s, public and private. *Waqf* operations are generally supervised by the Sharīʿa *qāḍī*s, but the *maẓālim* officer is under duty to inspect the large public endowments for irregularities, without anyone filing a complaint. The golden standard against which an irregularity is judged is the founder's deed. In the case of public *waqf*s, the Sharīʿa court's records as well as the sultanic *dīwān*s are inspected, or any relevant "old document" (*kutub qadīma*). In these matters, the scope of jurisdiction is wider than that which the *maẓālim* officer has over private *waqf*s, which require a plaintiff in order for him to initiate inspectorial action and prosecution. In private *waqf*s, sultanic records possess no force, the only relevant evidence being the founder's deed and the previous records of litigation in the Sharīʿa court.[96]

Seventh, enforcing the *qāḍīs*' judgements against powerful individuals, since the *qāḍī* does not normally possess sufficient coercive force to implement punishments or remedies against the mighty and the powerful, be they private individuals or government officers.

Eighth, enforcing the work of the market inspector, the *muḥtasib*, in roughly the same manner as required for the *qāḍī*s.

Ninth, ensuring the observance of public rituals, such as Friday prayers, pilgrimage, and holidays (including closure of businesses and shops). These are considered the Rights of God and so the *maẓālim* officer is under duty to inspect them for regularity.

95 *AS*, 136-37.
96 AS, 137.

Tenth, and finally, resolving disputes and adjudicating cases between and among litigants, exactly in the manner a Sharīʿa judge would do. In other words, a *maẓālim* court can act as a Sharīʿa court, strictly conforming to its procedures and modus operandi. Given the average training of *maẓālim* officers and what seems to be a heavy presence of *qāḍī*s and jurists in the *maẓālim* courts, this is not surprising. Yet, the extrajudicial nature of these courts, with the relatively pliable procedural latitude they enjoyed, inevitably led to malpractice. Here, Māwardī makes a factual statement about what appears to be judicial intemperance, saying that some *maẓālim* officers "confuse their functions and so they commit excesses."[97]

Note here that the greatest bulk of the *maẓālim* work and scope of jurisdiction relates to government affairs and abuses. Areas 1-4, and 8-9, pertain exclusively to acts of government officials and what we might call public matters (enforcement of group worship, holidays, pilgrimage). Areas 5-7 involve both private and civic infractions as well as public ones. Only area 10 involves strictly civic and private disputes or infractions. Yet, this last raises a few important questions (which I will attempt to address in chapters 8-11): If the *maẓālim* officer is expected to know the Sharīʿa law (either as a self-cultivated skill or by reliance on Sharīʿa experts "in his company"),[98] then what is the difference, when he adjudicates legal cases in area 10, between him and the regular Sharīʿa judge?

This question – which Māwardī will answer momentarily – becomes all the more potent due to the plain fact that a Sharīʿa judge himself is also bound to consult *muftī*s when faced with hard cases, and is even highly encouraged to have jurists sit in his court as "observers" and advisers.[99] Furthermore, if Sharīʿa cases can fall on the *maẓālim* tribunal for adjudication, then what is the meaning of this competence in terms of the hierarchy that deputizes this office? Does it mean that the deputizing agency and the agency that deputizes this later *ad seriatum* possess the same powers of adjudication? And if this is the case, then what is the relationship between judicial power and its executive counterpart?

---

97 *AS*, 138: "*Wa-rubbamā ishtabaha ḥukmu al-maẓālimi ʿalā al-nāẓirīna fī-hā fa-yajūrūna fī aḥkāmihā wa-yakhrujūna ilā al-ḥaddi al-ladhī lā yasūghu fī-hā.*" On the meaning of *jawr*, see ch. 2, n. 44.

98 *AS*, 134, where, as I have outlined, the *maẓālim* officer is expected to surround himself with *fuqahā'* who function as his guides and legal experts: "*Yastakmilu majlisa naẓarihi bi-ḥuḍūri al-fuqahā'i li-yarjiʿa ilayhim fī-mā ashkala wa-yas'aluhum ʿammā ishtabaha wa-aʿḍala.*"

99 Ibn Māza, *Sharḥ Adab al-Qāḍī*, I, 182; Surūjī, *Adab*, 125-26.

Māwardī takes a step toward answering some of the issues raised by these questions in a long section where he discusses the differences between the office of the *maẓālim* and that of the Sharīʿa court judge, the *qāḍī*.[100] In fact, this section is an extensive elaboration and an attempt at setting the boundaries of the procedural powers he briefly stated in area 10, the single area, as I have noted, where the *maẓālim* and the *qāḍī*'s jurisdictions overlap completely.

First, the *maẓālim* tribunal enjoys enforcement tools and coercive powers that the Sharīʿa court does not possess. Numerically and in absolute numbers the *qāḍī* adjudicates the greatest bulk of disputes and performs nearly countless other auditorial and social functions (e.g., marriage guardian, trusteeship over orphan's affairs and properties, *waqf* auditor, building inspector, etc.),[101] but he does not overall possess executive powers in terms of enforcement of court decisions.

Second, the *maẓālim* office possesses competence to inspect, audit, and prosecute infractions in jurisdictions wider than those the Sharīʿa judge is charged with. This is so because the *qāḍī*'s court is not the usual venue in cases of abuses and crimes committed by the sultanic officials, and, furthermore, does not have powers of free prosecution (that is, initiating a lawsuit without plaintiff).

Third, the *maẓālim* officer is authorized to wield wider coercive powers and broader procedural methods than the *qāḍī*, who is relatively restricted by the rigorous rules and procedures available to him. Fourth, the *maẓālim* officer has the powers to inflict punitive measures with a view to correcting behavior (*ta'dīb*), a competence the *qāḍī* does not possess (I take this to be applicable to such cases as those involving damages, where the Sharīʿa court, according to the vast majority of opinions, cannot impose punitive damages but only compensatory ones).[102] Fifth, the officer of the *maẓālim* can wait on a complex case until further evidence becomes available, whereas the *qāḍī* must decide on cases as presented to him without delay. Sixth, the *maẓālim* officer has the authority to compel the parties to reach an amicable settlement whereas the *qāḍī* cannot. In the Sharīʿa court, amicable settlement is highly desirable but ultimately remains optional. Once the parties affirm that they

100 *AS*, 138-39.

101 See, e.g., Ibn Abī al-Damm, *Adab al-Qaḍā'*, I, 334-45. Ibn al-Qāṣṣ, *Adab al-Qāḍī*, 453 ff. and passim for the *fiqh* that applies to such domains as those with which the *qāḍī* is involved.

102 Hallaq, *Sharīʿa*, 303.

cannot reach such settlement, the *qāḍī* is under duty to begin the process of adjudication.[103]

Seventh, the *maẓālim* officer possesses extraordinary powers and means in compelling litigants to confess wrongs and to be bound by legal instruments that the *qāḍī* cannot impose on them. Eighth, he can validate certain evidentiary testimonies of character that would not meet the standards of the Sharīʿa court. Ninth, he is not bound by the strict procedural requirements concerning testimony of fact nor by the *fiqh*-stipulated number of witnesses. Tenth, and finally, the *maẓālim* officer possesses powers of discretion to begin his proceedings with examining witnesses whereas the Sharīʿa judge normally starts the process of litigation by hearing the plaintiff's claims first and only then enters the evidence.[104]

The rest of the chapter on *maẓālim* is dedicated to dissecting in staggering detail procedural and evidentiary differences between the two offices,[105] mainly as relating to the eighth, ninth, and tenth differences. It is noteworthy here that Māwardī does not engage in normative prescriptions concerning the wide powers of the *maẓālim*, trying to limit their sway or confine their jurisdiction. The language betrays a realistic description of practices on the ground, at least in the way they are conducted in general or on average. For instance, he recognizes that there is a spectrum of practices on the same matter among the *maẓālim* officers, and distinguishes between the experts in the business and those who are less so.[106] It is also noteworthy that the *maẓālim*'s range of procedures and doctrine is wider than those of the *fiqh*, which itself is varied and highly pluralist by any standard, especially the modern.[107] This is partly so because the *maẓālim* officer has a free hand to opt for any *fiqh* doctrine he sees fit, at times shifting authorities in the same case. "The *maẓālim* office is entitled to adopt that which is possible or permissible and is not confined to that which is obligatory."[108] Nonetheless, the *fiqh* doctrine is crucially the standard against which the *maẓālim* jurisdiction and its scope of authority are adjudged. The language of this habitus is never in the form that the *qāḍī*'s jurisdiction or power are less, more, or weaker than

103 Hallaq, *Sharīʿa*, 160-64.

104 *AS*, 139.

105 *AS*, 139-54.

106 *AS*, 142-43.

107 I am referring to the multiplicity of opinions on one and the same set of legal facts, on one and the same "case." Unlike the modern state's positive law, the *fiqh* does not adopt "one law."

108 *AS*, 141.

the *maẓālim*, but rather that the *maẓālim* are exceptions to the standard; and the standard is always Sharʿī.

This is also why the decrees of appointment for *qāḍī*s never mention the *maẓālim* and any need that the *qāḍī*s might have for them (much less the specific need for *maẓālim* officers to sit in a *qāḍī*'s court). But the presence of sitting *qāḍī*s and expert Sharʿī jurists seems to have been a requirement for holding *maẓālim* tribunals.[109] Put differently, while the *maẓālim* tribunals were equipped with extrajudicial-cum-coercive powers by the executive, it was the legislative – i.e., the law and culture of the Sharīʿa – that determined the legitimacy of these tribunals. As we will see in Part II, it was within this province of discretionary justice that the constitutional grind in the Islamic tradition occurred.

It is also striking that with all the differences Māwardī enumerates, and despite the wide range of choices available to the *maẓālim* officer, one comes out of reading the chapter on this subject with the distinct impression that the *maẓālim* are not arbitrary but are rather governed by an established doctrine and a long-standing way of doing things. In other words, the officer of the *maẓālim* does not reinvent the wheel at every turn but appears to locate himself in a well-bounded institution that has a long-established tradition, and, according to Māwardī, historical roots that go back to the ancient Persians. This much, I think, should be taken for granted, since abundant evidence from various quarters – e.g., the *dīwān*ic culture – confirms the same conception of a longstanding tradition.

VI

Now, we might want to compare Māwardī's positive account with Qalqashandī's factual citation[110] of a *maẓālim* appointment decree, issued by the caliph al-Muṭīʿ lil-Lāh (r. 334-63/946-74) for al-Ḥusayn b. Mūsā al-ʿAlawī.[111] The latter, a veteran government officer, was appointed to the *maẓālim* of Baghdad, the imperial capital, and its environs. The career history of ʿAlawī was so well-known that – deviating from general practice – no specific credentials of his were listed, other than the fact that he is a seasoned official and that his

109 *AS*, 134.
110 On the differences between positive, normative, and factual accounts, see ch. 1, sec. IV.
111 *SAQ*, X, 252-56.

record of service itself makes for an abundant attestation of his qualifications. As we will see in the case of *qāḍīs*' appointment decrees (chapter 5), after the opening of the decree – which speaks to the official's qualifications and reasons for appointment – the decree enumerates the tasks and duties assigned to the official appointed. These appear in the form of commands or orders (*amr*; pl. *awāmir*; v. *amara*).

It is noteworthy that much of the orders' substance is shared by those found in the *qāḍī*'s appointment decrees, beginning with the first two orders, which seem standard requirements for such appointments. These are heeding God (*taqwā*) and reciting the Qur'ān regularly, making it his guide and exemplar.[112] The third command is to make his *majlis* (assembly) accessible to one and all, where complainants' cases are heard patiently and carefully. The language of the decree's command is quite explicit (more so than Māwardī's discourse) regarding the *maẓālim* official's duty to respect venue. The official must scrutinize the complaint carefully and must redirect to the *qāḍī* of the Sharī'a court all those cases that belong to that jurisdiction. This seems to diverge from Māwardī's tenth specification, where he states that *maẓālim* courts can hear cases that otherwise belong to the *qāḍī*'s jurisdiction. Cases of usurpation that require investigation and the heavy hand of judicial exploration of evidence squarely belong to the *maẓālim*, either because these tribunals seem to involve powerful officials of government or because the evidence needed to establish the facts require evidential procedure not available to the *qāḍī*. But in carrying out these functions, 'Alawī is to conform to the Command of God (*Amru Allāh*) across the board, doing everything he can to advance the cause of justice. Interestingly, the *locus classicus* laying the foundations of this justice is Q. 38:26, the same paradigmatic text cited for both caliphs and *qāḍīs* in the carriage of their duties.[113]

The fourth command relates to the duty of care in deciphering the claims brought before 'Alawī. He should be patient with complainants who are weak and incapable of representing themselves properly, while on the other hand he is to exercise special caution in detecting the schemes of shrewd litigants and their cunning ways.

The fifth command comes to enhance the third, insisting that 'Alawī may not review or annul a *qāḍī*'s verdict unless there is clear and convincing evidence of injustice or wrongdoing. Otherwise, he is expected to sanction and

112 For a detailed discussion of such commands, see main text of ch. 5, at n. 90.
113 *SAQ*, X, 254.

endorse the work and decisions of the Sharīʿa court, for "truth is one although the ways to it are many."[114] This is to say that the *maẓālim* officer must respect the Sharīʿa venue, Sharʿī court decisions, as well as juristic disagreement, a sanctified principle that is endorsed by nothing less than the consensus of the Community and its juristic representatives.[115]

The sixth command goes further in clinching the *maẓālim* court within Sharīʿa structures. ʿAlawī must consult with the *qāḍī*s and jurists and must educate himself in *fiqh* through holding discussion sessions with them. This is especially imperative when he faces hard cases or "confusing situations."[116] Such a requirement was typical, for presiding Sharʿī *qāḍī*s themselves were also under the obligation to consult the expert jurists when faced with difficult cases.[117]

Finally, the seventh command pertains to what seems to be a deliberate caliphal act of subordinating the powers of Kūfa's governor to those of ʿAlawī, whose decisions he must carry out since they are binding upon him.[118]

Clearly, Māwardī's positive (in contradistinction with normative) account is more detailed, identifying specific duties of the *maẓālim* officer that the appointment decree of al-Muṭīʿ does not clearly stipulate, although it is not difficult to see the implication of various functions in the decree's general language. Constitutionally speaking, the decree is an eloquent testimony not only to the division of labor between the *maẓālim* office and the Sharīʿa court but also to the total jurisdictional subordination of the former to the latter. Here, the Sharīʿa reigns supreme, even when an expedient exception is to be made to it. It is precisely the exception that anchors the rule as paradigmatic and supreme. What ultimately matters in constitutional terms is the fact that the *maẓālim* system was regulated by the Sharīʿa, even where certain discretionary powers were concerned. Whether actual abuses occurred within the *maẓālim* or not is not a constitutional question (infractions are innate to all systems, without exception); what matters is that the constitutional *boundaries* of the system were clearly delineated by the law (and Māwardī's *fiqh* work, *AS*, is itself evidence of it) and their *substance* authorized by the same law. If the law

114 *SAQ*, X, 255: "*Wa-amarahu bi-an lā yarudda lil-quḍāti ḥukman yumḍūnahu wa-lā sijillan yunaffidhūnahu wa-lā yuʿqibu dhālika bi-faskhin…bal-yakūnu la-hum muwāfiqan muʾāziran wa-li-aḥkāmihim ʿāḍidan nāṣiran, idh kāna al-ḥaqqu wāḥidan wa-in ikhtalafat al-madhāhibu ilayhi.*"

115 For more on this crucial feature of the system, see below, ch. 4, 5 and 10, sec. II.

116 *SAQ*, X, 255.

117 Ibn Abī al-Damm, *Adab al-Qaḍā'*, I, 327; Ibn Māza, *Sharḥ Adab al-Qāḍī*, I, 193, 356-71.

118 *SAQ*, X, 255.

of the land designates a particular space for unspecified modes of operations, then that space is an integral part of the larger constitutional structure. Again, the delineation and authorization of the constitutional boundaries do not eliminate infractions and abuses, but they are of the essence in making claims and resolving problems through an appeal to an agreed standard. Everyone knew that everyone agreed to that standard, because the standard was the politico-juridical habitus of Islam.

Chapter 4

The Legislative: From Qur'ānic Constitutionalization to the *Madhhab*

We have so far outlined the caliphal constitutional boundaries in terms of governance, as well as the functional subordination of the *qāḍī*ship to caliphal and sultanic rule. I use "functional subordination" to delineate the fact that *qāḍī*ship as an office and function fell under the sway of the caliph/sultan, giving these rulers the exclusive power of appointment and dismissal. But no one other than the jurists could exercise control over the *substance* of the law applied in the courts. Until the end of the Mamlūk period – and, I hypothesize, everywhere else in the Muslim world until the very end of the fifteenth century – there seems to have been no caliphal or sultanic legislation, however thin, that entered into the sphere of the judiciary. The Mamlūk *ʿuhūd* and all political writings – not to mention modern scholarly writings – plainly attest to this much.[1] That the Ottomans engaged in legislation and created a competing legislative thrust is an argument that we will interrogate in chapter 11, only to conclude that, notwithstanding the *qānūn*ic legislation, this argument does not, constitutionally speaking, hold water.

Yet, it is not enough to say that the courts of the lands of Islam (until the end of the fifteenth century) were juridically independent, and that the law they applied was made neither by them nor by the executive power of the caliphate or sultanate. My argument is that while this independence was remarkable in itself, and probably unique in world history at the time, there is much for us to tease out about the nature and role that the Sharīʿa had played in the pre-nineteenth-century Islamic

1 On the absence of the Mongol *yasā/yasaq* from Mamlūk practice and dominion, as well as on related issues, see ch. 11, below.

world. I will discuss the far-reaching cultural implications of Islam's law-making[2] in later chapters, especially in the contexts of analyzing sovereignty and biopower (chapter 12). In the present chapter, I wish to trace the evolution of law-making in Islam from the very beginning, with a view to explaining the *constitutional effects* of this law on political management and organization.

It will be my argument that the substantive content of the law and the very mechanisms of law-making were themselves not only general and governing constitutional structures but that they also *constructed* the political constitutional structures as a matter of course. Equally important, this chapter will attempt to demonstrate that the so-called legislative power in Islam was both historically and ontologically separate from the executive, which is to say that the separation originated as fundamental to what Islam as a legal and constitutional system was. As a first step, I will discuss the Qur'ānic foundations of law-making and constitutional construction, and then move forward to show how *uṣūl al-fiqh* (legal theory), the *madhhab* (the legal "school"), as well as the various authoritative legal doctrines of the latter, created political constitutional structures and the necessary scaffoldings to maintain them for over a millennium.

I

I have argued elsewhere that the Qur'ānic conception of legislation is quite developed, which is also to say that both the Message and the Messenger were self-conscious of their legislative mission.[3] This argument was a rebuttal of the standard Orientalist doctrine to the effect that Muslims did not come to possess a law of their own for decades after the Prophet's *hijra*, and that both the Qur'ān and the Prophet, aiming to provide moral guidance and religious doctrine, were not cognizant of law as such, thus having no intention of creating a legal system.[4] It was only after most conquests were completed that

2 Strictly speaking, no human can make law in Islam; therefore "law-making" is a cultural translation at best. Law in the Sharīʿa is always preexistent in God's mind, and it is the jurist's *ijtihād* that brings it out into the open as the best attempt of the individual jurist at discovering the "legal solution." See Introduction, n. 107.

3 This section draws on my "Qur'ānic Constitutionalism and Moral Governmentality" which is a sequel to "Groundwork of the Moral Law." In the latter article, I argue that the Qur'ān was self-conscious about introducing a new law and even judiciary.

4 See cited references in the articles listed in the previous note. See also Black's representative statement in his *History of Islamic Political Thought*, 14: "Although the Qur'an is mostly

Muslims realized the need for law and so they borrowed it from the conquered populations.[5] The Qur'ān and "fabricated" Ḥadīth thus came to provide the Islamic "veneer" for the "borrowed" law, starting at about 100H.[6] The following account, pertinent to the Qur'ānic constitutional vision, runs diametrically opposite to this Orientalist narrative.

The foundational language with which we are concerned is found in Q. 5: 42-51, language relevant for the analysis of what I call organizational and structural conceptions, such as derivatives of *Ḥ.K.M.*, *A.M.R.*, *ʿ.L.M.*, and *Ḥ.Q.Q.*[7] Permeating the Text, such terms effectively organize and structure the Qur'ānic message, and as such they reign throughout all phases of revelation. They in fact do even more work than map out the architecture of Islamic legal cosmology; they provide conceptual anchorage for both law and politics, in this order.

Augmenting the power of their ubiquitous presence was also a set of semantically and conceptually supporting terms that synonymously bolster the structures of meaning that these four concepts comprised. The discrete conceptual-semantic units of these verses are as follows: (1) Whatever judgment you, Muhammad, pass must be just;[8] (2) Any judgment (rendered by anyone) must be in accordance with that which God has revealed;[9] (3) All prophets and religious leaders were given holy books according to which they had to judge;[10] (4) You, Muhammad, were given the Book that was revealed with the Truth and that confirms earlier scriptures (*muṣaddiqan*); and (5) God has chosen not to unite all human kind in a single religious community, but has given each its own "laws" and ways of conduct (*minhāj*).[11]

---

concerned with religion and ethics and has little to say about law and even less about government, it expresses a mood from which inferences can be taken. In particular, certain ideas cluster around its concept of community (umma)."

5 For an idea about the debate concerning "borrowings," "debts," and "foreign influences," see Hallaq, "Use and Abuse of Evidence."

6 The authoritative statement in Orientalism about this process and dating is of course that of Joseph Schacht, *Origins*, esp. 224-27.

7 *Ḥaqq* was a subject of discussion in "Groundwork of the Moral Law," 260. In this chapter, it will be shown to constitute a paradigmatic conceptual framework foregrounding the three other concepts. For a definition of paradigm, see Hallaq, *Impossible State*, 6-12.

8 Q. 5:42: "*Fa-ḥkum baynahum bil-qisṭ.*" Also Q. 10:47.

9 Q. 5:48: "*Fa-ḥkum baynahum bi-mā anzala Allāh.*" Also Q. 2:213, 4:58, 4:105, 5:44-45.

10 Q. 5:44-46: "*Innā anzalnā al-Tawrāta [fī hā ḥukmu Allāh]... yaḥkumu bi-hā al-nabiyyūna ... wal-rabbāniyyūna wal-aḥbāru bi-mā istaḥfaẓū min kitābi Allāhi ... wa-qaffaynā ʿalā atharihim bi-ʿĪsā ....*"

11 Q. 5:48: "*Li-kullin jaʿalnā minkum shirʿatan wa-minhājan wa-law shāʾa Allāhu la-jaʿalakum ummatan wāḥidatan.*"

Now, all five themes recounted above are stated repeatedly, often verbatim, throughout the Text. First, judging on the basis of justice is a notion that permeates the Qur'ān from beginning to end (after all, the world itself was created with justice; if the concrete matter of the world is the warp, then justice is the weft).[12] Q. 10:47 categorically states that every *umma* should have a messenger (*rasūl*), and when that messenger comes, he will rule and judge among his followers with justice (*qisṭ*, *ḥaqq*). To this theme, specifically and generally, pertain Q. 5:42, 7:29, 10:47, 57:25, 16:89-90, and 42:15, among others.

Second, every value assigned to a human affair, political or otherwise, must derive from, and be directed by, God's order (*ḥukm*, *amr*). God is the only and ultimate source of all knowledge, be it legal, moral, political, or otherwise. In modern parlance, He is the only sovereign. Q. 3:154 explicitly declares that all commands, or perhaps even *the Command* as a species, belong to Him and Him alone.[13] This theme of divine omnipotence is a foundational one, and concomitant with the Qur'ānic message as a whole.

Third, the theme that every *umma* has a messenger who possesses a Book containing "laws" of justice and moral and political guidance is attested throughout the Text, beginning with the earliest Meccan verses. Consider, for instance, the wording and language of Q. 2:129, 2:151, 2:213, 4:54, 4:113, 5:40, 10:47, 16:36, 21:73-79, 28:14-15, 38:26, 42:51, 45:16-18, 45:28, and 46:12, among many others.

Fourth, the Qur'ān as ratification of earlier scriptures is a theme of widest occurrence in the Text, one that is also acknowledged to have defined Islam as a monotheistic religion.

Fifth, God did not, in the final analysis, wish to create a single *umma* out of all human groupings, although at one point He did, and could have maintained that condition had He willed it. Q. 2:213, revealed four or five years before Q. 42:51, explicitly states that "people" (*nās*) were originally constituted as a single *umma* (*umma wāḥida*) but God sent the prophets with the Books so they might judge between and amongst people with justice (*ḥaqq*). Furthermore, the Meccan verse 11:118 states: "*wa-law shā'a Rabbuka la-ja'ala al-nāsa ummatan wāḥidatan*" ("If God had willed, He would have made all people a single community"), a language nearly identical to the corresponding part of Q. 5:48.

12 See Hallaq, "Groundwork of the Moral Law," 260.

13 "*In-il-ḥukmu illā li-Lāh;*" Q. 6:57, 6:62, 12:40, 12:67, 18:26, 28:88, 40:12; "*Alā la-hu al-ḥukm;*" 6:62; "*Man aḥsanu min al-Lāhi ḥukman,*" Q. 5:50. We will see in due course that Q. 30:4 belongs to this group of verses.

Finally, the late Meccan Q. 42:8-15 asserts all the above-mentioned elements but one, namely, that the Prophethood of Muhammad came to confirm earlier *dīns* (a theme abundantly attested elsewhere in the Text). The specific and novel meaning and significance of these verses relate to the relationship of the Prophet to *Ahl al-Kitāb*, especially the Jews. In effect, the message here is: Settle your own affairs and disputes in accordance with your own Books and systems of guidance and leave me out of it![14] In light of the repeated occurrence throughout the Qur'ān of the themes found in 5:42-51, one can hardly conclude that the Prophet suddenly realized that Muslims were entitled to their own "law." To Muhammad, that was a long-foregone conclusion, one that was inextricably enmeshed with the origins and inner structures of his message. As we will see, the Qur'ān gives birth not only to the moral law and a governing psychological system (i.e., articulation of internal states and technologies of the self), but also to fundamental epistemological and constitutional structures.

One of the most central concepts in the Qur'ān is *ḥukm*. The nominal form and other derivatives of *Ḥ.K.M.* appear dozens of times. *Ḥukm* is often semantically associated with the word *kitāb* (Book, Writing, Revelation),[15] a word that undergirds *ḥukm* and delimits the range of its conceptual sway as a divine source. In Q. 45:16, the Children of Israel were given "the Book, the *ḥukm*, and the Prophethood" (*nubuwwa*). More tellingly and emphatically, Q. 6:114 questions how there could be a *ḥakam*, the author of *ḥukm*, other than God who has revealed "unto you a lucid and specific Book" (*kitāb mufaṣṣal*).[16] To almost identical effect, Q. 3:79 questions human authority when "the *kitāb*, the *ḥukm* and Prophethood" have been sent down. More specifically, and in what we identify in modernity as a "strictly legal matter," Q. 2:231 urges the application of God's law in the context of divorce, i.e., "the *kitāb* and the *ḥikma* that were revealed unto you."[17] Finally, and among many others to this effect,

14 For the background to these verses, see Ṭabarī, *Tafsīr*, IV, 582-83.

15 Also referred to, among other designations, as *dhikr*. See, e.g., Q. 21:50 and 36:69.

16 M. M. Pickthall, influenced by the modern meaning of the term, erroneously translates *mufaṣṣal* as "fully explained" (*Meanings of the Glorious Koran*, Q. 6:115, p. 117). Khalidi, *Qur'ān*, 111, translates *mufaṣṣal* "as a specific Book tailored to the Peninsular Arabs' habits and customs," a more plausible translation in light of Nicolai Sinai's argument in "Qur'ānic Self-Referentiality," 120-22.

17 Reflecting modern understanding, both Pickthall (*Meanings*, 54) and Khalidi (*Qur'ān*, 31) erroneously translate *ḥikma* as "wisdom." In due course, we shall see why this translation of the term is inaccurate, although this verse alone demonstrates beyond doubt that "wisdom" is not the most relevant concept here and that the *ḥikma* of the *kitāb* denotes a more particular value relating to regulation of affairs and conduct. See further below for a discussion of the meaning of *ḥikma*/*ḥakīm*.

Q. 76:23-24 render *ḥukm* directly contingent upon the revelation of the Book: "It is We who have verily sent down the Qur'ān to you, so wait for the *ḥukm* of your Lord...."[18] The sum total of *ḥukm*'s meanings is thus God's exclusive legislative will that is supreme, binding, and unchallengeable.

A transcendental derivative, *ḥukm*'s venue is then revelation (*kitāb*), although *ḥukm* is also regarded as the Qur'ān itself, as Q. 13:37 suggests.[19] A number of prophets, once having attained middle age maturity,[20] are given *ḥukm* which, as we will see, is often associated with the concept of *ʿilm* ("knowledge"). On the authority of early Qur'ān scholars,[21] Ṭabarī defines

18 Khalidi (*Qur'ān*, 491) translates the verse as: "It is We Who revealed the Qur'ān to you – a revelation in very truth! So bear your Lord's verdict with Patience." This translation, especially the word "verdict," is belied by the next line, which Khalidi himself translates as "And obey not the blaspheming or sinful among them." Ṭabarī, *Tafsīr*, XII:373, explains that this last verse means the following: Muhammad is commanded not to obey the polytheists and the sinful among his people, those who commit wrong (*maʿṣiyya*). The reference to a specific act or set of acts, as denoted by "*li-ḥukmi rabbika*," is apparent in Ṭabarī's understanding of the term, which first includes the rules and commands revealed by God, to which he refers as *farā'iḍ*. In Ṭabarī's mind, this latter term is therefore equivalent to *ḥukm*.

19 Samarqandī, *Baḥr al-ʿUlūm*, II, 196 (l. 6). This is also the understanding of later legal theory, *uṣūl al-fiqh*. See Ramlī, *Ghāyat al-Ma'mūl*, 75.

20 The common expression here is "*wa-lammā balagha ashuddahu*" (see, e.g., Q. 12:22 and 28:14-15). Generally, the Qur'ān exegetes assign this level of maturity to the forties – or late thirties – of one's life. See Ṭabarī, *Tafsīr*, X, 41.

21 Skeptics may argue that citing Qur'ān commentary – early or late – to illuminate the text is a historiographically untenable venture. I beg to differ (especially insofar as the issues we are concerned with here), for a variety of reasons: It is important for us to know how the Qur'ān was understood during the first century or two by Muslims themselves, which, for our purposes, is an epistemic advantage rather than disadvantage. After all, our interest here is to enquire into the *effect* of the Qur'ān on the formation of early Sharīʿa and its conception of political governance, which is also to say that what matters is how first-century Muslims understood the text, not only what the text meant during the lifetime of the Prophet. Besides, no one can plausibly maintain that the text has a meaning outside of a subjective human audience, as if it were bestowed with objective meanings outside of a sociology of knowledge. There is no credible support for the position that the Qur'ān meant to convey meanings, and intended to accomplish certain ends, that escaped the early and/or later Muslims. Such ambiguities are standard, and represent the lot of every project of hermeneutics, which both the Qur'ān and the Sharīʿa were/are. Yet, even if we were to allow for the possibility that Muslims misunderstood certain terms or did not know their meanings, such a skeptical approach cannot, and thus does not, apply to the deep structures that our four terms convey. Furthermore, enquiring into "lost meanings" in the Qur'ān is not only a misguided historiography (asking the wrong questions in the first place) but also represents an unjustifiable self-creation of epistemic sovereign will. Finding its roots in the Enlightenment penchant for domination, this epistemic sovereignty lies at the core of the Orientalist project. On these associated themes, see Hallaq, "On Orientalism, Self-Consciousness and History." On sovereign knowledge as characteristic of Enlightenment thinking, see Hallaq, *Restating Orientalism*.

ḥukm as "penetrating knowledge of religion." The archetypal exegete Mujāhid (d. 103/722),[22] for instance, is said to have understood this Qur'ānic term to consist of "*fiqh*, *ʿaql*, and *ʿamal*." The first two combine to indicate the highest level of comprehension, including attainment of sound legal reasoning – a theme to which we shall return in due course. *ʿAmal*, on the other hand, expresses the application of this understanding and reasoning in practice. Likewise, Ibn Isḥāq regarded *ḥukm* as penetrating understanding of one's *dīn* and that of one's forefathers, which includes knowledge (*ʿilm*) of legislation and of the principled restraints and stipulations in one's religion (*sharāʾiʿ wa-ḥudūd*).[23]

In another context, Ṭabarī elaborates further on the meaning of *ḥukm*, emphasizing all the aforementioned elements and furthermore including the proactive effort to propagate the knowledge of religious commandments, legislation, and other religious requirements (*sharāʾiʿ dīnihi*).[24] *Ḥukm* is not only "the knowledge of God," but also of instructing people, the potential followers, in God's commandments and legislation. The prophets are the best bearers of *ḥukm* because they not only teach people but are also the best students of revealed scriptures.[25] *Ḥukm* then turns out to be not only His eschatological verdict[26] (as modern scholarship assumes) but also God's management of human affairs and dispensation of these affairs in accordance with his commands.[27] It is also, specifically, the theoretical and applied knowledge of God's substantive injunctions and prohibitions, His moral and universal laws, in the here and now.[28]

Illustrative of the judicial nature of *ḥukm* and its relationship to God's decree is Q. 21:73-79. Titled *The Prophets*, the Sūra's chief concern lies in the prophets, from Noah to Muhammad. These prophets, particularly in this context Lot, Abraham, Solomon, David, Isaac and Jacob, are said to have been given "the

22 Mujāhid is said to have consulted and interrogated Ibn ʿAbbās on every detail of the latter's entire body of *tafsīr*. See Ibn Taymiyya, *Dar' Taʿāruḍ al-ʿAql wal-Naql*, I, 120.

23 Ṭabarī, *Tafsīr*, X, 42.

24 Ṭabarī, *Tafsīr*, III, 322, commenting on Q. 3:79.

25 Ṭabarī, *Tafsīr*, III, 322: "W*a-an yakūnū ruʾasāʾan fil-maʿrifati bi-amri Allāhi wa-nahyihi ... bi-kawnihim muʿallimī al-nāsi al-Kitāba wa-bi-kawnihim dārisīh*."

26 Indicated by such verses as Q. 27:78.

27 Ṭabarī, *Tafsīr*, VIII:212, commenting on Q. 18:26.

28 Ibn Manẓur, *Lisan al-ʿArab*, XII, 163, gives the standard definition of *ḥukm* as "*ʿilm*, *fiqh* and judging with justice" (*wal-hukmu [huwa] al-ʿilmu wal-fiqhu wal-qaḍāʾu bil-ʿadl*). In Q. 34:6, *ʿilm* is made a corollary of *ḥaqq*: those who possess *ʿilm* recognize *ḥaqq*, and conversely, those who comprehend *ḥaqq* possess the *ʿilm*. Thus, if God is the *ʿAlīm*, it is because He is the *Ḥaqq*.

mantle of leadership," guiding people in accordance with God's commands and instructing them in good works and prayer, payment of alms and, on the whole, to obey God.[29] (Note here that God's commands, his law, and his *ḥukm* predate the prophethood.) Like the Prophet Lot, David and Solomon were "given *ḥukm* and *ʿilm*," evidenced by their involvement in what is clearly a case of damages.[30]

What matters in this context is the clarity with which the Qur'ān – despite the terseness of its language here – views the relationship between *ḥukm* and adjudication/litigation in what is most clearly a "legal" matter par excellence.[31] We may therefore conclude, keeping in mind all Qur'ānic contexts in which the term *ḥukm* appears, that the semantic and conceptual range of *ḥukm* extends from divine punishment and reward respecting the world and large groups (e.g., ʿĀd and Thamūd) to asymmetrical judgment in the social realm of individuals in the name of God's guidance. *Ḥukm* thus represents the widest spectrum of action, extending from transcendental power to individual human capacity to render judicial decisions. And this by now should not surprise, for it is consistent with the overarching Qur'ānic concept that morality is undistinguishably

29 *"Jaʿalnāhum a'immatan yahdūna bi-amrinā wa-awḥaynā ilayhim fiʿla al-khayrāti wa-iqāma al-ṣalāti wa-ītā'a al-zakāti wa-kānū lanā ʿābidīn."*

30 On the reported understanding of Ibn Masʿūd, David is said to have rendered a judgment in respect of agricultural crops (indicated by the Qur'ānic words *yaḥkumāni fil-ḥarth*). A flock of sheep or goats is supposed to have invaded the vineyard of a neighbor during the night, consuming and destroying the vines. Although both David and Solomon had by that time been granted the prophethood, it was for some reason only Solomon who was divinely inspired in this particular case (*"fa-fahhamnāhā Sulaymān"*). David ruled that as compensation to the victim (i.e., the owner of the vineyard), ownership of the invading animals ought to be transferred to him. Solomon, however, interfered, arguing against David that the vineyard be transferred to the care of the animals' original owner who should restore it to its former condition. Until such time as the restoration had been completed, the animals would remain in the custody of the vineyard's owner, apparently as a guarantee. Ibn ʿAbbās, on the other hand, proffered another solution, according to which Solomon thought that the victim was not entitled to the ownership of the flock itself but rather to its usufruct. As damages can be assessed and allotted a pecuniary value, Solomon reasoned, the victim ought to retain the flock and be entitled to *own* its usufruct – including offspring – while, in the meantime, the flock's owner was obliged to restore the vineyard to its former condition. Only upon complete restoration would the flock be returned to its owner. It is unclear from the texts whether the flock was to be returned only upon the satisfaction of the value of damages or upon the restoration of the vineyard, but all that is irrelevant to our concern. In fact, the Qur'ān exegetes provide other narratives of the solution, all of which are, for us, recognizably judicial. Ṭabarī, *Tafsīr*, IX, 50, 51-52.

31 It is noteworthy that in the index of Samʿānī's *Tafsīr*, the editor classifies this case under the heading of damages (*Kitāb al-Ḍamān*). See Samʿānī, *Tafsīr al-Qur'ān*, VI, 320 and, for the *tafsīr* of the verse, III, 394-96.

meshed with earthly law, as it is with cosmology and eschatology. We may say that the concept of *ḥukm* permeates the world in its two parts – the physical and the metaphysical – and connects them together as a single whole, the One Realm of Justice (*ḥaqq*, *ʿadl*, *qisṭ*).[32]

It is instructive that *ḥukm* stands closely tied to good works,[33] beginning with prayer, fasting, and payment of alms, and ending with other actions, be they related to inheritance, divorce, or compensatory damages. To exercise *ḥukm* is clearly to exercise *ḥaqq* and *ʿadl*, but these latter attributes or categories of action also translate into good works, the essence of the divine plan for humans.[34] When Abraham, in Q. 26:83, implored God to make him a good-doer, and to conscript him in the company of good-doers, he asked God to bestow on him the *ḥukm* (*Rabbī hab lī ḥukman wa-ilḥaqnī bil-ṣāliḥīn*). But Q. 12:22 reverses the order of relationship between *ḥukm* and good works. When Joseph attained middle age maturity, he was given *ḥukm* and *ʿilm* as a reward for his good deeds.[35] The relationship is thus dialectical, one causing or justifying the other. The attainment of *ḥukm* connotes the conscription of one's actions into the world of good works; and an all-encompassing technology of good works in turn justifies, if not generates, the capacity to exercise *ḥukm*. We may now therefore expand the purview of the concept of *ḥukm* and its semantic range: it is not only the justice of God's works in the universe and on Earth, nor is it just the moral and legal actions of humans; it is also all actions and feelings in their entirety, down to the manner in which one acts before and *feels* about the poor, the beggar, and all creation.[36]

A derivative of *Ḥ.K.M.*, and a conceptual cognate, is the term *ḥakīm*, often taken simplistically to mean "wise."[37] While it is not entirely incorrect, "wise" as a translation of *ḥakīm* possesses far wider and more abstract connotations than its semantic usage in the Qur'ān allows. Both the specific Qur'ānic contexts and the manner in which early Qur'ān exegetes understood the term

32 Thus, the "*ḥaqq*" in Q. 46:3 (as well as 64:3 and 45:22, among others) is identical to the "*ḥaqq*" in Q. 2:213, undoubtedly a worldly form of justice. The same is clearly indicated by Q. 2:42 and 2:109.

33 Hallaq, "Groundwork of the Moral Law," 266-77.

34 Hallaq, "Groundwork of the Moral Law," 266-77.

35 It is then unsurprising that the prophets, who are bestowed with *ḥukm* as a matter of course, are always present in the company of *ṣāliḥūn*. See, e.g., Q. 6:84-85, 21:72.

36 It also appears in the Qur'ān as mere common-sense judgment, lacking in the context of "*aṣḥāb al-janna*" in Q. 68:36. On the *asbāb al-nuzūl* narrative of this parable, see Ṭabarī, *Tafsīr*, XII, 189-96.

37 See, e.g., *The Qur'ān: Arabic Text with Corresponding English Meanings*, 561 (translation of Q. 30:27); Khalidi, *Qur'ān*, 328.

do not permit such a sweeping meaning. A typical context in which the term appears is that of God sending the prophets with the Books, with *ḥukm*, or with legislative inspiration (e.g., *awḥaynā*),[38] as we have seen to be the case in Q. 21:73 (see also Q. 42:51 and 3:79; note again here that God's commands and law precede the prophethood). On the authority of the earliest exegetes, Ṭabarī and Qurṭubī regarded *ḥakīm* as a synonym of *ḥākim*,[39] an active participle that connotes the possession of omnipotence and management, that is, a perfected and most consummate ability to regulate the affairs of created beings (*tadbīru khalqihi*), including meting out punishment and reward. Integral to this omnipotent regulation is the attribute of obedience, without which perfect management of human and other affairs would be rendered meaningless. This is precisely the effect of Q. 30:26-27, in which it is explicitly declared that all creatures are obedient (*qānitūn*), since God – and this appears as a causal link – is the *ʿAzīz* (Omnipotent) and the *Ḥakīm*.[40] It is also instructive that Māwardī, in elaborating the semantic connotations of *ḥakīm*, invokes the *qāḍī*, also well known by the title of *ḥakīm*, because his function, consisting in the pursuit of *ḥaqq*, is to resolve disputes, the very quality of the *ḥakīm* as a manager of affairs.[41]

Ḥikma is the attribute of the *ḥakīm*, and as such it is the knowledge of how to manage creatures' affairs, a competence for which legislation and regulation are indispensable.[42] When exercised in respect to one's own affairs, or when ordering or judging the affairs of others (i.e., when law and politics are involved), it also means conformity to the ethico-legal standards set by the Legislator's will. Ṭabarī and Ibn Kathīr, along with several earlier commentators, took *ḥikma* to mean *sunna*, by which they do not seem to have been referring specifically to the Prophetic exemplar but rather to the proper

38 See Q. 2:151, 2:231, 3:48, 3:81, and 17:39.

39 Ṭabarī, *Tafsīr*, I, 258; Qurṭubī, *Tafsīr*, I, 198. See also Ibn Kathīr, *Tafsīr al-Qur'ān al-ʿAẓīm*, I, 275. Ibn Manẓūr, *Lisān al-ʿArab*, XII, 163, states that *ḥakam*, *ḥakīm*, and *ḥākim* possess the same meaning (*al-ḥakamu wal-ḥakīm wa-humā bi-maʿnā al-ḥākim, wa-huwa al-qāḍī*). If *ḥākim* means *qāḍī*, then *ḥakam* and *ḥakīm*'s semantic and conceptual meanings are associated with adjudication, be it divine judgment, a court's decision, or settlement by tribal custom.

40 Ṭabarī, *Tafsīr*, X, 143-44, 178-79, 181. For a similar context, see Q. 43:63.

41 Māwardī, *al-Nukat wal-ʿUyūn*, I, 100.

42 See, e.g., Q. 2:129 and 2:151. In his *Tafsīr* (II, 132), Qurṭubī observes that "*ḥikma* is knowledge of religion and expert knowledge of interpretation (*fiqh fil-ta'wīl*). Mālik as well as Ibn Zayd held this view. Qatāda said that *ḥikma* is *sunna* and the interpretive determination of rulings (or divinely legislated norms [*sharāʾiʿ*]). It was also held that *ḥikma* is specifically *ḥukm* and *qaḍā'*, and the meaning is nearly the same."

conception and practice of religious values,[43] which by necessity encompass all human actions. "Some people argued that *ḥikma* is *sunna*" as well as a "penetrating understanding of religion's commandments (*fiqh fil-dīn*) as well as their application." All of this, however, leads to the same end, and "none entails a contradiction."[44] Like Ibn ʿAbbās,[45] Ṭabarī argues that *ḥikma* is "the knowledge of God's commandments,"[46] for what else could it be when "*ḥikma* is derived from *ḥukm*."[47] And Zamakhsharī sums up the matter well when he categorically states that "*ḥikma* is the *sharīʿa*[48] and the interpretive determination of behavioral rules."[49] In all cases, *ḥikma* is operative within a matrix of justice.[50]

Nor should it be surprising that the *ḥakam*, the possessor of *ḥukm*, is God himself. Q. 6:114 is clearly situated in the context of a God who is the sole possessor of *ʿilm* and the designer of *ḥaqq* (6:115-17). Here, *ḥakam* denotes the supreme Judge and Magistrate, whereas in Q. 4:35 and 2:188, he is a human arbitrator, magistrate and judge, little more than a metaphor of God's reality. In the latter two verses, it is equally important to note, the reference is to both tribal arbitrators and to judges in the "civil" sense, exemplified in Q. 2:188 which exclusively deals with "civil" damages.[51] Thus, like all structural terms we have indicated thus far, "*ḥakam*" possesses a cosmological conceptual and semantic range, one that begins with God and ends with individuals in their dealings with the large and small issues of life and living. *Ḥukm* is a just management of life, be it social, economic, legal, or political.

---

43 Ṭabarī, *Tafsīr*, I, 607; II, 273; Ibn Kathīr, *Tafsīr*, I, 275. On *sunna* as the proper ideal guiding the discovery and application of commands and prohibitions, see Ibn Taymiyya, *Darʾ Taʿāruḍ al-ʿAql wal-Naql*, I, 119-20. On the concept of *sunna* as exemplary conduct and its relationship to Prophetic Sunna, see Hallaq, *Origins*, 46-54.

44 Ibn Kathīr, *Tafsīr*, I, 275.

45 Bukhārī, *Kashf al-Asrār*, I, 24-25 (Bazdawī's original text). Bazdawī adds that the Qurʾānic concept of *ḥikma* encompasses both *ʿilm* and *ʿamal*, i.e., theoretical knowledge of right and wrong and practical ethics.

46 Ṭabarī, *Tafsīr*, I, 608: "*Wal-ṣawābu min al-qawli ʿindanā fil-ḥikmati annahā al-ʿilmu bi-aḥkāmi Allāh.*"

47 Ṭabarī, *Tafsīr*, I, 608.

48 It would be instructive here to recall that the term "*sharīʿa*" may have been the actual designation for "the legal-moral path to follow," and thus attested twice, in Q. 45:18 and, especially, 5:48, and altered to "*shirʿa*," in all likelihood by al-Ḥajjāj (see n. 100, below). Also relevant here is the verbal form (*sharʿa*), which occurs in Q. 42:13.

49 Zamakhsharī, *Tafsīr al-Kashshāf*, I, 188: "*Wal-ḥikmu [hiya] al-sharīʿa wa-bayān al aḥkām.*" See also Samarqandī, *Tafsīr*, I, 158.

50 In fact, Ibn Manẓūr gives it as a standard definition ("*wal-ḥikma [hiya] al-ʿadl*"). *Lisān al-ʿArab*, XII, 166.

51 And Q. 2:231, referring to *ḥikma* instead of *ḥukm*, directly relates to *ṭalāq*.

Clearly, the political implications of the term can hardly be missed. *Ḥ.K.M.* encompasses a wide spectrum of meanings that range from general judicious conduct and sound judgment to a just and equitable legal adjudication and political management. To lead with *ḥukm* and *ḥikma* is to bring the justice of God on Earth, socially, legally, and politically. Yet, throughout the entire spectrum of meanings, the ethical rules.

A cognate of *Ḥ.K.M.* and one that further delimits the divine source of *ḥukm* is the structural term *amr* (command, order). As in the case with *ḥukm* and *ḥaqq*, *amr* is applied to a wide spectrum of meanings, ranging from an order to create the world *ex nihilo* to the most specific of commands about a narrowly defined behavioral or "legal" matter. Here as always, there is neither terminological nor conceptual distinction between and among the cosmological, metaphysical, physical, moral, or legal domains. They are one mesh. It was by God's *amr* that the world was created, just as it was by the same command that there came to be the Books, the Guidance, the *ḥukm*, legal and political management, and all else. If the prophets receive guidance, inspiration, and the mantle of leadership (being *a'imma* in the first place), this was all by virtue of God's *amr*, as Q. 21:73 makes clear. Q. 42:15 sums up the matter well when it enjoins Muhammad to call people to the worship of God, to follow with uprightness God's legislated religion, and to desist from the ways of those who went astray. Muhammad is commanded to say that he believes in God's revealed books and that he is ordered to implement justice among people (*umirtu li-aʿdila baynakum*).[52] However, justice here is no abstract notion but one that clearly refers to, and ties in with, what we call legal and political actions. God's *amr* to the Messenger is directly related to the entire range of human conduct (*aʿmāl*), there being no separation whatsoever between one category of acts and another. It is unmistakable here that the *amr* addressed to Muhammad to do justice on Earth follows the same logic that God employed in his creation of the world. In this way, the logics of *amr* and *ḥukm* are identical.

Yet, we need to recognize another significant constitutional point in this context, namely, that the concepts of *amr* and *ḥukm* bolster each other and together give effective force to the meaning of what we call today divine sovereignty, better labelled as omnipotence. Like *ḥukm*, "all *amr* belongs to God" (*inna al-amra kulluhu li-Lāh*),[53] from the beginning of time to the end (*lil-Lāhi al-amru min qablu wa-min baʿd*).[54] The idea of divine omnipotence is one of

52 See also Q. 11:48 and Ṭabarī, *Tafsīr*, XI, 137.

53 Q. 30:154.

54 Q. 30:4.

the major structural concepts in the Qur'ān.[55] We may now add that it is a paradigmatic idea, meaning that it is not only the central idea of the Qur'ān, but also an idea that dictates, shapes, and colors nearly all other surrounding ideas.[56] If God is One (*aḥad*), it is to bolster and enhance the notion of omnipotence, to dispense with any ambiguity that may distract from the absoluteness of His ability alone to order and command, to legislate and decide. Decisively put, His omnipotence entails everything else: His mercy, love, wrath, generosity, and even oneness, but none of these and many others is a prerequisite for His omnipotence. He is the Will, in both potentiality and actuality.[57]

A pervasive and equally structural and structuring concept is *ʿilm*. Intimately connected with the term *ḥukm*, *ʿ.L.M.*'s derivatives appear no fewer than 590 times in the Qur'ān. While the couplet *ḥukm/ʿilm* appears on at least a few occasions,[58] *ḥakīm/ʿalīm* as a verse-ending couplet occurs no fewer than three dozen times.[59] Almost in every instance, *ʿilm* and its cognates appear in connection with revelation, Scriptures, and, most importantly, the understanding of God's plan in creating and *regulating* the world with justice. "We have given them a Book which We have elaborated with *ʿilm*,"[60] for "you should know that it was revealed through God's knowledge."[61] It is obvious enough that there is no *ʿilm* other than that of God, human *ʿilm* being a derivative and a metaphor of the original.[62]

Nor is it a coincidence that *ʿalīm*, the knowledgeable, is often associated with *ḥakīm*.[63] *ʿIlm* is not only the Qur'ān and substantive will as revealed in the scriptures,[64] but also the vessel through which *ḥukm*, *ḥikma*, *amr* and much of what God wills for humans is conveyed. It would seem that, had God created

55 In addition to *ḥukm* and *amr*, the semantic and conceptual range of creativity (*khalq*) and thus ownership (*milk*) partake in constituting the quality of sovereignty.

56 On the theory of paradigms and central domains, see Hallaq, *Impossible State*, 6-12.

57 On the concept of sovereignty, see Kahn, *Political Theology*; Schmitt, *Concept of the Political*; Schmitt, *Political Theology*. In the context of Islamic modernity, see Hallaq, *Impossible State*, 89-97, 99-110. In the context of this book, see ch. 12.

58 Q. 2: 32, 12: 22, 21: 74, 21: 79, and 28: 14.

59 E.g., Q. 4: 26, 6: 83, 8: 71, 9: 15, 9: 60, 12: 6, 15: 25, 22: 52, 24: 18, 27: 6, 43: 84, 49: 8, 51: 30, 60: 10, 66: 2, and 76: 30.

60 Q. 7:52.

61 Q. 11:14. See also Q. 13:43 and 27:40.

62 Q. 2:32: "We possess no knowledge other than that which you have taught us (*ʿallamtanā*). You are the *ʿAlīm* and the *Ḥakīm*." See also Q. 2:255, 5:109, 46:23, and 96:5.

63 Had *ḥakīm*'s meaning been indeed "Wise," as almost all Qur'ān translations present the term, then the use of *ʿalīm* in such couplets would be inexplicable and would, furthermore, make for an obvious redundancy.

64 As clearly indicated in Q. 10:93 and 11:14.

everything except *ʿilm*, there would be no way to convey his *ḥukm* and *amr* to humans. The will would remain hidden in the realm of potentiality. Q. 11:14 (*inna-mā unzila bi-ʿilmi Allāh*) and 27:40 clearly articulate the notion that the Qur'ān was revealed with or through *ʿilm*, although other instances represent the Qur'ān as itself being the *ʿilm*. Be that as it may, the interconnectedness and interdependence between and among *ʿilm*, *ḥukm*, *ḥikma*, and *amr* are clear. If *ḥukm* and *ḥikma* are *sharʿ*, *fiqh*, and divinely regulated legislation that run the affairs of this world, then *ʿilm* is the agglomeration of all these together as articulated in the mind, be it that of God, the prophets or any other human. It is the only venue through which human beings can be held responsible for their actions and ignorance (*jahl*). It would hardly be an exaggeration to say that the challenge, or at least the immediate task, before the Qur'ānic God was to expound and propound *ʿilm* through the prophets, particularly Muhammad. In Q. 2:129, as is the case in many other verses, a prophet is indispensable for "teaching" people (*yuʿallimuhum*) the *kitāb* and the *ḥikma*, both of which precede the deployment of the prophets.[65] Law as *ʿilm* is channeled through the latter.

The recipients of *ʿilm* are those who are blessed with knowledge of *ḥukm*, *kitāb*, and *ḥikma*, for true knowledge consists precisely of these epistemic spheres. "God revealed unto you the *kitāb* and the *ḥikma*, and taught you (*ʿallamakum*) that which you did not know."[66] Thus, possession of *ʿilm* raises the recipient to a higher state, having attained a true form of belief. Those who are "firmly grounded in *ʿilm* (*al-rāsikhūna fil-ʿilm*) announce that they believe in God, for everything comes from Him."[67] The *rāsikhūna fil-ʿilm* fully endorse and indeed internalize that which God has sent down,[68] by virtue of which they are "elevated" by degrees on the divine scale of rewards.[69] The ennoblement of their status is such that God – despite his omnipotence and ownership of the world – is "awed" by those who became *ʿālims*, i.e., those who attained true *ʿilm* (*yakhshā Allāhu min ʿibādihi al-ʿulamā'*).[70] Q. 35:28 is

65 See also Q. 2:151, 2:251, and 3:48.
66 Q. 4:113. See also Q. 2:129, 2:151, and 4:113.
67 Q. 3:7.
68 Q. 4:162.
69 Q. 58:11.
70 Q. 35:28. This is the "reading" of the distinguished caliph and Companion, ʿUmar b. ʿAbd al-ʿAzīz, as well as of the eponym of the Ḥanafī school, Abū Ḥanīfa. These are joined by the Successor Ibn Sīrīn. The reading assigns to the term ulama the accusative case. In the nominative, the term would become a subject rather than an object, making the ulama fear God. See Qurṭubī, *Tafsīr*, VII, 220 and Zamakhsharī, *Tafsīr*, III, 593, both of whom interpret the verb "*yakhshā*" as a sort of respect, but not actual fear. The problem for them,

profoundly instructive, as it implies (according to one reading) a metaphoric equalization – however partial – between God and "knowledgeable" human beings insofar as *ʿilm* is concerned, this perhaps being the only instance in the Qur'ān where God reveals himself as deeply respectful of created beings.[71] As we will see in due course, Q. 35:28 (and the entire semantic range supporting it in multiple other verses) has not only great ramifications in and of itself, but it also captures and sums up, in the most axiomatic fashion, the entire conceptual spectrum of Qur'ānic *ʿilm*.[72]

ʿIlm, therefore, is not only the knowledge of revelation as an earthly occurrence or a worldly text, but also, and indeed fundamentally, an unending process of engaging the human mind in pondering and reflecting on God's plan and intention in the Universe. The human engagement with *ʿilm* is, in every way, an engagement with the divine, with what it means for God to create the world, and for the world to be created, in accordance with what plan, and to what end. If real and true,[73] *ʿilm* is an exclusive property of God. When applied to humans, it is rendered as a metaphor of the original, which means that accessing the deeper and deeper dimensions of this original is a never-ending quest – what later came to be known as *ijtihād* in Sharīʿa, and *jihād* and *mujāhada* in the Sharʿī-Ṣūfī *askesis*.[74] The paradigmatic concept of *ijtihād* thus made the law and with it the *madhhab* (as we will momentarily see); and it was *ʿilm*, that divine source of all knowledge, that generated the Sharīʿa as a whole. *ʿIlm* therefore is a constitutional phenomenon.

---

as well as for other *mufassirūn* who did not accept this interpretation, is, of course, that God the Omnipotent cannot fear His own creation, and thus this sort of language should be understood as *istiʿāra* (metaphoric, metonymic or figurative expression). See also Nasafī, *Tafsīr al-Qur'ān*, III, 123; Rāzī, *al-Tafsīr al-Kabīr*, XVI, 21; Nīsābūrī, *Tafsīr al-Gharā'ib*, V, 515-516; Alūsī, *Rūḥ al-Maʿānī*, XXII,191-92. However, other instances in the Qur'ān decisively show the inversion of attributes, where God, for instance, feels grateful or thankful to his creatures (Q. 2:158; 4:147; 35:30; 76:22). In any case, even if we were not to take this interpretation into account, our argument continues to stand, since the theme of *ʿilm*'s prior importance and of the morally privileged status of those who are associated with it is beyond any doubt, it being not only pervasive but also paradigmatic within the Qur'ān's semantic and conceptual structures.

71 Just as He acknowledges himself to be grateful (*shakūr*) to certain human groups. See previous note.

72 Which is to say that even if its "accusative-case" rendering is rejected, the general meaning and signification of that construction can neither be dismissed nor minimized. In other words, while our argument is strengthened by the validity of this "reading," it cannot be weakened by its dismissal.

73 I.e., *ʿilm ḥaqīqī*, not *ʿilm majāzī*.

74 Farahat, "Generality and Exception."

If God found *ʿilm* indispensable for the conveyance of *ḥukm*, *amr*, *kitāb*, and *ḥikma*, then *ʿilm*, the work of the *ʿĀlim* (the Knower, the Omniscient) would be meaningless without a concept of transmission. And if God is the Ultimate Teacher (since he taught [*ʿallama*][75] the prophets), then anyone who comes to possess *ʿilm* can teach it (*yuʿallimu*) to others whose level of knowledge (*daraja*)[76] is lower. Like *ḥukm* and *amr*, *ʿilm* is thus both gradational and cosmic: it moves within a spectrum that ranges from the creation of the world by God (and thus it is His property alone) to the micro-knowledge of minute worldly matters,[77] knowledge shared by God with certainty and by humans with probability.

Accordingly, just as God is clearly portrayed in the Qur'ān as the Teacher or Conveyor of *ʿilm*, those who are "firmly grounded in knowledge" *ipso facto* qualify for that status within their respective communities (*umam*). *The individual is thus the exclusive site of ʿilm*, another significant constitutional fact. But unlike God, who need not exert Himself to cultivate *ʿilm*, human beings as individual scholars must work hard toward that end, with *dhikr* and especially *dars* being two important methods of instruction. While *dhikr* is the recitational technology[78] that cultivates *īmān* and, through it, knowledge of the *aḥkām*,[79] *dars* is, strictly speaking, the pedagogical process of learning the substance and implications of *ḥukm*, *ḥikma*, and *amr*. Q. 34:44 and 68:37 explicitly state the connection between revelation and the act of studying (*wa-mā ātaynāhum min kutubin yadrusūnahā*; *am lakum kitābun fī-hi tadrusūn*). Q. 3:79 contains even wider implications of "instruction" and "study," implications that are so profoundly relevant to our forthcoming constitutional argument that we must devote to it careful analysis. But for now it should not escape us that *"law-making" in the Qur'ān and what later emerged as Sharīʿa is an individualistic enterprise, the result of study and learning. It is not even collective, and certainly belongs to no political institution.*

Reflecting a paradigmatic Qur'ānic structure,[80] Q. 3:79-80 reads as follows: "*mā kāna li-basharin an yu'tiyahu Allāhu al-kitāba wal-ḥukma*

75 See Q. 2:129, 2:252, 96:5, 34:6, 5:110, 2:32, 4:113, 2:251 (in this order).

76 As in Q. 35:28.

77 To be later formulated under the philosophical question "Does God know particulars?" See, e.g., Marmura, "Some Aspects of Avicenna's Theory," 299-312.

78 On so-called "ritualistic" performances as technologies of the self, see Hallaq, *Impossible State*, 110-35. See also the aggregate meanings of Q. 3:58, 7:63, 15:9, on the one hand, and 6:80, 40:58, 32:4 and 33:41, on the other.

79 For a commentary on *dhikr* as occurring in Q. 41:41, see Qurṭubī, *Tafsīr*, XV: 239.

80 "Paradigmatic" is here advisedly used with reference to our theory of paradigms. See Hallaq, *Impossible State*, 6-12.

—wal-nubuwwata thumma yaqūla lil-nāsi kūnū ʿibādan liya min dūni Allāhi wa-lākin kūnū rabbāniyyīna bi-mā kuntum tuʿallimūna al-kitāba wa-bi-mā kuntum tadrusūn, wa-lā ya'murakum an tattakhidhū al-malā'ikata wal-nabiyyīna arbāban – aya'murukumu bil-kufri baʿda idh antum muslimūn." ("No human being who is the recipient of God's Book, *Ḥukm* and Prophethood may be allowed to tell people 'Be my subjects apart from God.' Instead [he should say]: 'Be instructional leaders on the basis of the Book you have been teaching and which you study.' God will not command you to take either the prophets or the angels as your lords – would He command you to apostatize after you have become Muslim".)[81]

This verse is said to have been revealed subsequent to a meeting between the Prophet and the religious leaders of the Christian and Jewish communities of Najrān. In this meeting, the Prophet called them to convert to the new religion. In what seems to have been a demurring question, a Jewish chieftain asked the Prophet: "Do you want us to worship you as the Christians worship Jesus the son of Mary?" This was immediately followed by an identical question, this time by a Christian leader in the group. While the Jewish interrogator objected to the Christian practice of Jesus being a son of God, the Christian's question was about the difference between this practice and what Muhammad's call entailed. Why would the Christians, he wondered, worship Muhammad when they already had their Christ to adore? The Prophet is reported to have replied, not without a sense of indignation: "God forbid! We worship none other than God, nor do we command others to worship another God; He did not send me, nor command me, to do such a thing?"[82]

The first issue to be raised here is the illegitimacy of empty excuses: those who are given the Divine Message cannot respond with anything other than genuine obedience to the dictates of the message. Knowledge creates obligation, and therefore responsibility and accountability, as Q. 40:66 strongly attests as well.

Second, *no human agency can mediate between God and other human beings.* This message – paradigmatic and abundantly attested in the Qur'ān[83] – has often been recognized as significant by students of Islam, but its significance has been confined to the "religious," whatever that means. It has been seen as a

81 Nīsābūrī, *Asbāb al-Nuzūl*, 64

82 Ṭabarī, *Tafsīr*, III, 315-27, esp. at 322-23.

83 See, e.g., Q. 3:64, 5:76, 5:116, 9:31, 10:104, 18:26, 19:81, 21:29, 21:66-67, 22:71, 25:18, 40:66, 42:31, 43:45, among many others.

"ritualistic" or at best institutional (or even anti-institutional) commandment, meaning that the individual Muslim is ordered to connect with, and pray to God directly, without the mediation of a synod, council, or church. But this message – especially as it came to be construed in formative Islamic civilization and culture, and continuously until the collapse of the system under the weight of Western colonialism[84] – *is to be understood in equally constitutional and political terms.*

What God is commanding in Q. 3:79 is that once revelation in general and *ḥukm* in particular have been revealed to any community, *human agency (including political agency) as an autonomous lawgiving power must be forgone entirely.*[85] The "law" and the prescriptions of its enforcement, whether worldly or otherwise, is the exclusive business of God, even when He does not tell us what He has decided in each and every case. This constitutional reading of the verse is made possible by virtue of the semantic and conceptual archeology of the term *ḥukm*. If *ḥukm* comprises the semantic-conceptual fields we have explicated, then we are compelled to conclude that the verse is no less than a constitutional article of the first order, especially because, as I have already emphasized, it captures a Qur'ānic paradigm.[86]

A third fundamental idea in this verse creates an intimate connection between knowledge and the epistemic fields of human action, on the one hand, and constitutional structures, on the other. The verse in effect stresses that the impermissible human mediation of *ḥukm* must be replaced by intellectual

---

84 Abū al-ʿAlā Mawdūdī and Sayyid Quṭb of course vehemently argued for divine sovereignty, but their writings are regarded by the great majority of scholars as reformist and apologetic, not describing or analyzing historical developments during Islam's formative period. It is telling that Quṭb passes over Q. 3:79 in near silence, devoting to it only a dozen lines and altogether missing its profound constitutional thrust. See his *Fī Ẓilāl al-Qur'ān*, I, 419-20. On Mawdūdī's concept of sovereignty, see Iqtidar and Scharbrodt, "Sovereignty, Morality and the State." On the collapse of the system during the nineteenth century and its devastating consequences, see Hallaq, *Sharīʿa*, part III.

85 In other words, this is not to say that human reason and hermeneutics are to be jettisoned. On the contrary, being integral to *ʿilm*, they constitute the very tools that are required to decipher the law, the expression of God's will. Obviously, this sentence (in the main text) rests on the underlying assumption that the modern *sovereign* state *creates the law as an autonomous, lawgiving, self-authorizing power*. On the distinctness of the modern concept of sovereignty, see Kahn, *Political Theology*; Schmitt, *Concept of the Political*; Schmitt, *Political Theology*. In the context of Islamic modernity, see Hallaq, *Impossible State*, 89-97, 99-110.

86 Needless to say, the force of this paradigm has shaped the very nature of *uṣūl al-fiqh*, a theory of law that articulated, maintained, and reflected the rule of law and thus constitutional organization. See, e.g., Ramlī, *Ghāyat al-Ma'mūl*, 75; Ibn Qudāma, *Rawḍat al-Nāẓir*, 60; Tilmisānī, *Sharḥ al-Maʿālim fī Uṣūl al-Fiqh*, 137.

guidance which, in the real world, translates into the governance of justice. Instead of a mediation that arrogates to some humans the right to be obeyed by many others, the Qur'ān here is commanding the adoption of *rabbāniyya*, the state of being a *rabbānī*. Somewhat close to its Hebraic equivalent, the term "*rabbāniyyūn*" in the verse is understood by a near consensus of scholars, including the earliest exegetes, to mean *'ulamā'* or *fuqahā'*,[87] a learned group of people whose knowledge of *ḥukm* and scriptures permits them to be educators of the general public.[88] As educators and thus guides, they are understood to be the leaders of the *umma* (*wulāt al-amr*) who occupy the highest epistemic position, for they know the law as life's guide.)

Their *'ilm*, we must emphasize, is not merely confined to what we ordinarily mean by the word "knowledge," for their *'ilm*, being a reflection of *ḥukm*, encompasses a consummate ability to manage the affairs of the public and oversee people's worldly and religious affairs. *'Ilm* is not only practice but praxis as well, technologies of an ethical embodiment that is indistinguishably "legal."[89] Ṭabarī sums it up on behalf of the majority of Qur'ān commentators when he defines *rabbāniyyūn* as "the sustainers of the people in *fiqh*, *'ilm* and the affairs of religion and the world. This is why Mujāhid said: 'They are of a higher stature than the *aḥbār*,' because the *aḥbār* are [merely] the *'ulamā'* but the *rabbānī* is the one who augments *'ilm* and *fiqh* with discernment for management and order (*al-siyāsa wal-tadbīr*), as well as superintending the affairs of subjects (*al-qiyām bi-umūr al-ra'iyya*), caring for what is in the latter's interests in religious and worldly affairs."[90] Knowledge here is a practical, not merely a theoretical, matter. Knowledge meshes with works, practice, as well as praxis.

Finally, the fourth component of this verse, and the culmination of its potent field of meanings, is the idea that the urging or command to be *rabbāniyyūn* rests squarely on the practice of learning and teaching (*dars*).[91] The guiding letter and spirit of the *rabbāniyyūn*'s leadership is nothing other than the *ḥukm*

---

87 See Ṭabarī, *Tafsīr*, III, 323-24, on the authorities of al-Ḥasan, Mujāhid, Qatāda, Ibn 'Abbās and Abū Razīn, among others.

88 Ṭabarī, *Tafsīr*, III, 325; Bukhārī, *Kashf al-Asrār*, I, 28-29; Suyūṭī, *al-Durr al-Manthūr*, II, 250-51.

89 On praxis, see *Reforming Modernity*, 38 ff. and passim.

90 Ṭabarī, *Tafsīr*, III, 322, 325.

91 The derivatives of *D.R.S.*, overwhelmingly referring to learning and instruction, may be found in Q. 6:105, 6:156, 7:169, and 34.44. See also Ṭabarī, *Tafsīr*, V, 300-301 and VI, 107. These derivatives are to be combined with the second verb form, *'allama/yu'allimū(kum)*, as found in Q. 2:129, 2:151, 3:164 and 62:2.

and the scripture enveloping it (i.e., the *kitāb*), *ʿilm* being the process by which the art and know-how of religious and worldly governance is accomplished. It is the study (and therefore knowledge)[92] of the Book that allows teaching, and it is both the acquired knowledge and the competence to teach it that constitute the necessary and sufficient conditions to lead and guide people to good practices. This is instruction neither in theory nor in a knowledge detached from the world, but rather in an all-encompassing knowledge, especially practical ethics (one that insists on the inseparability of rational inquiry and moral values). For *ʿilm* and *ḥukm* are primarily about knowledge of ethical practice, and only secondarily about speculative and theoretical knowledge. If the latter becomes necessary, it is because theoretical knowledge is an instrument and a means to achieving good works.[93] Theoretical knowledge can never be an end unto itself.

It is little wonder then that the ulama, the bearers of this knowledge, are said by the famous dictum to be the heirs of the prophets themselves,[94] particularly Muhammad; which is to say that they are not the Prophet's deputies nor, certainly, the deputies of the caliphs. Rather, they "inherit" the Prophet's knowledge,[95] this latter becoming as much theirs as it was the Prophet's. This is why the upper ranks of the ulama, the *muftī*s, were widely considered "those who sign on behalf of God,"[96] not the prophets, and certainly not the caliphs. Conversely, Muhammad himself is no source of legislation either. As we have repeatedly seen, he is the recipient of a predetermined *ḥukm*, and his pronouncements on matters of law are as credible as those of any *ʿālim* steeped in *ʿilm*. Most importantly, he can err like any other such *ʿālims*, as attested by more than one famous Ḥadīth.[97] *Therefore, the dictum that "the ulama are the*

92 Ṭabarī reports (*Tafsīr*, III, 326) that the majority of Qur'ān "readers" in the Ḥijāz and some of Baṣra's commentators read the word "*tu ʿallimūn*" (teach) as "*ta ʿlamūn*" (knowledge of). None of the variants, it must be stressed, can change the constitutional and epistemic effect and power of the verse in any way.

93 A point insightfully captured and vehemently asserted by Ibn Taymiyya. See Saleh, "Ibn Taymiyya and the Rise of Radical Hermeneutics," 129.

94 Bukhārī, *Ṣaḥīḥ*, I, 49.

95 Rāzī, *Maḥṣūl*, II, 491.

96 Nawawī, *Majmūʿ*, I, 72: "*Iʿlam anna al-iftāʾa ʿaẓīmu al-khaṭari kabīru al-mawqiʿi kathīru al-faḍli, li-ʾanna al-muftī wārithu al-anbiyāʾi, ṣalawātu al-Lāhi wa-salāmuhu ʿalayhim, wa-qāʾimun b-farḍi al-kifāyati, wa-lākinnahu muʿarraḍun lil-khaṭaʾi, wa-li-hādhā qālū ʿal-muftī muwaqqiʿun ʿan Allahi.*" See also Ibn Qayyim al-Jawziyya, *Iʿlām al-Muwaqqiʿīn*, esp. vol. 1.

97 Muslim, *Ṣaḥīḥ*, IV, 138. The Prophet in these Ḥadīths appears like any *mujtahid* scholar. His pronouncements are merely opinions subject to the test of probability, *ẓann*, and he errs like any other human: "*Faʾinni inna-mā ẓanantu ẓannan, fa-lā tuʾākhidhūnī bil-ẓanni, wa-lākin idhā ḥaddathukum ʿani Allāhi shayʾan fa-khudhū bi-hi;*" "*Inna-mā anā basharun.*"

heirs of the prophets" is a constitutional principle of the first order for it underlines the autonomy of the law-making competence, connecting it directly with the prophetic-divine line rather than with the caliphal strain.[98]

All this is consistent with Katrin Jomaa's research into the concept of *Umma* in the Qur'ān, especially, for our concerns, her findings with regard to the conceptual relationship between "*Umma*," on the one hand, and "imam" and "legal understanding" (=juristic knowledge), on the other. In the Qur'ānic conception, people or human groups are identified with their leader whereas the *Umma* is identified with a book, one that serves to both unify the *Umma* and provide the ethical font of guidance;[99] for the *Umma* is constituted ontologically by virtue of the Book, whose vessel of conveyance is the Messenger. Yet because this font is the source, it can by no means constitute the full range of the instructions of how to live life in its fullness. The book is assumed to be the subject of the *Umma*'s range of investigations and study by those who are "firmly grounded in knowledge." There is therefore no knowledge of the Book of ethics without the various subjective "voices" of the learned Muslim believers, those who represent the *Umma* in understanding the language of the revealed Book.

This conception circles back to the famous Prophetic adage that "the ulama are the heirs of the prophets." What must raise our curiosity is the use of the plural form, "prophets." Why is it not in the singular, referring to the ulama of Islam as the heirs of Prophet Muhammad, which would have been a most logical proposition? The answer harks back to our earlier discussion of Q. 5:48,[100]

98 See ch. 5, n. 3. It is neither unremarkable nor fortuitous that later ulama were not too keen on strengthening or supporting the caliphs. Writing on the caliphate under the Mamlūks, Mustafa Banister accurately observed: "[t]he caliphate's position in Mamluk society appeared to satisfy all parties. The caliphs themselves, with few exceptions, did little to seek a greater role than what they had. If ever they forayed into active politics, voluntarily or not, the sultans or ruling magnates ultimately made them regret it. For its part, the religious establishment also tended to withhold support for any increase of the caliph's political power. A few ulama were highly sympathetic to this trend and revered both the person of the caliph and his office, but many others maintained a suspicious indifference, perhaps fretful that the caliphate might threaten their own role as 'guardians of Islam.' Overall, both the amirs and the religious scholars tended to support the status quo." Banister, "'Naught Remains to the Caliph'," 244.

99 Jomaa, *Ummah*, 40.

100 "*Li kullin ja'alnā minkum shir'atan wa minhājan wa-law shā'a Allāhu la-ja'alakum ummatan wāḥidatan.*" Khalidi translates this sentence thus: "For every community We decreed a law and a way of life" (Khalidi, Qur'*ān*, 89). The term *shir'a* may have been al-Hajjāj's alteration from "*sharī'a*." Al-Azami, *History of the Qur'ānic Text*, 107. It is noteworthy that the term "*sharī'a*" does occur in another verse, i.e., Q. 45:18.

where God asserts that he has revealed a "Law and a way of conduct" for every community, every umma (anachronistically, "every nation"), including Muslims and Jews. This "Law" and "way of conduct" is revealed to these communities through a prophet, whose main responsibility is to convey the message and enforce its requirements and demands. This explains the multiplicity of so-called Biblical Prophets in Islam. But the fleshing out of the Law's details is not limited to these mortal prophets, whose death will inevitably put an end to their earthly involvements.

It is therefore the ulama "class" in each community/"society"/"nation" who are charged with taking up the task of cultivating the law; and it is them, as the communities' representatives, who will, one generation after another, elaborate the law as a technique for ethical self-formation.[101] Law is primarily a matter of knowledge (*ʿilm*) and praxis (*ʿamal*),[102] and only by extension a matter of politics and political leadership. It is the ulama (*ʿilm*'s possessors) of all communities who are entrusted with this unending task of "legislation," of uncovering, to the best of their knowledge, God's intentions and plan for humans.[103] This is the Sunna of God, his custom and habit in running the world (*ʿādat Allāh*).[104] It is also integral to this divine custom to regulate the world according to the law of generation and corruption, a law commanding that in the end of times the ulama, as a "species," shall be taken away from human existence. It is notable that in this doctrine the disappearance of the ulama necessarily entails the disappearance of *ʿilm*. The ulama and *ʿilm* stand in an extensive relationship of concomitance.[105]

Having discussed our four terms, we may now categorize them, proceeding thereafter to tease out their substantive, epistemic, and constitutional implications. First, we may note the near identity of *ḥukm* (including *ḥakam*, *ḥikma*, and *ḥakīm*) and *amr*, this including the significant overlap in their conceptual, cosmological-worldly range. Second, we have seen how the concept of *ʿilm*

101 Bukhārī, *Ṣaḥīḥ*, I, 50.

102 For a detailed discussion of praxis as distinguished from practice or action, see Hallaq, *Reforming Modernity*.

103 See Introduction, n. 107, and ch. 4, n. 2.

104 On *ʿādat Allāh*, see Wolfson, *Philosophy of the Kalam*, 544-551. For an elaborate treatment in the Arabic tradition, see ʿAbd al-Jabbār, *Mughnī*, XV, 335-82.

105 Bukhārī, *Ṣaḥīḥ*, I, 59: "*Samiʿtu Rasūla Allāhi yaqūlu: 'inna Allāha lā yaqbiḍu al-ʿilma intizāʿan yantaziʿuhu min al-ʿibādi, wa-lākin yaqbiḍu al-ʿilma bi-qabḍi al-ʿulamāʾi, ḥattā idhā lam yubqi ʿāliman ittakhadha al-nāsu ruʾūsan juhhālan.*'" "I heard the Messenger of God say: 'God will not expunge knowledge from people themselves, but will seize knowledge by taking away the ulama, so that when no ulama remain, people will take ignoramuses for their leaders.'"

operates to make sense of the latter conceptual range. By virtue of the divine act of delegation, *ʿilm* is the means by which human beings are given to discover the entire range of *ḥukm*. *ʿIlm, amr,* and *ḥukm* are therefore interconnected fields of action. Third, supported by *ʿadl* and *qisṭ*, both *ʿilm* and *ḥukm* are grounded in *ḥaqq*,[106] the idea that most powerfully dominated (if it did not structurally constitute) God's mind when he created the world. *Ḥukm* and *ʿilm* are thus infused with *ḥaqq*: if they are the warp and weft of the prescriptive code of ideal human conduct, then *ḥaqq* is the very fabric out of which the weave was made. Thus, if *ḥukm* and *ʿilm* make up the sum of the divine Code and its manifestation in the human world, then we ought to ask: What was the nature of this manifestation in the formative years of Islam? Which is also to ask: What actual role did they play in the origination and early evolution of Sharīʿa?

We can now identify at least three central features that the *ḥukm*/*ʿilm* complex generated in what would become the Sharīʿa. The first feature, which has been the focus of Western scholarship and to which this scholarship has found itself sorely confined, is "substantive law." When Orientalism spoke about the Qur'ān and its role in shaping the Sharīʿa, it always thought of the matter as belonging to the realm of legal rules and juristic principles, Eurocentrically so defined;[107] hence the powerful but mistaken thesis that the Qur'ān appeared on the legal scene as an afterthought, a century or so after the Hijra.[108] An earlier dating of a "turning point" around 5 H. commits the same qualitative error, looking for Islam's awareness of the need to have "our own law," like the Jews and others.[109]

However, the evidence derived from our four concepts speaks to a different effect. The Qur'ānic concept of *ḥukm* – running deep in the structures of the

106 For the cosmic range of *qisṭ*, see Q. 21:47, 3:18, 4:135 (dealing with *qisṭ* as a higher order), to Q. 3:21, 4:127, 5:8, 5:42, 6:152, and 11:85, among others.

107 Of course, the Qur'ān has always been associated with engendering "spirituality" throughout Islamic societies, and with a sense of awe in the divine, but all these never amounted to more than "religious" impulses and were never analytically taken to the level of governmentality or what might be called juridical embodiment. In other words, the function of this "spirituality" and even so-called "ritual" was never construed in legal terms. On the significance of these, see Hallaq, *Impossible State*, 98-138.

108 Hallaq, "Groundwork of the Moral Law," 240-43.

109 The implication here, confirmed by the "incident" between the Prophet and the Jews, is that if it were not for the Jews (who have the Torah), Muhammad would not have thought it necessary for Islam to have its own Law. Hence the importance of the "incident" as a catalyst. For a detailed critique of this thesis (advocated by Goitein, "Birth-Hour of Muslim Law"), see Hallaq, "Groundwork of the Moral Law," 246 f., 271-78.

Text – represented an acute awareness of the need for a comprehensive and categorical code of conduct from the first moments of revelation. Any claim to the contrary, or any claim in favor of a delayed awareness, must contend with solving a major problem, if not a paradox. In other words, it must bear the onus of disproving the presence of *ḥukm* as a pervasive, structural, and paradigmatic concept in the Qur'ān. It must show, in yet other words, that *ḥukm* either (1) does not possess the connotations we have assigned to it, or (2) that these connotations became structural at a later point in the Qur'ān's career. It has been our argument that neither is tenable because (a) the language of the Qur'ān itself and the manner in which this language was understood by the earliest and later commentators overwhelmingly and consistently drives at the single end we have identified, and (b) the many dozens of Qur'ānic contexts in which *ḥukm* and its derivatives occur are to be found spread over the entire period of revelation.

Nor should the meager supply of Qur'ānic substantive law deceive us into minimizing the Text's role in this sphere. It is striking that the Qur'ān was acutely cognizant of its sparce legislation, but it was concurrently aware that, given enough time, all, or at least many more, particular *ḥukm*s would be revealed. On many occasions, the Prophet is asked to be patient, for a *ḥukm* will be "sent down" in good time. "Wait with patience for your Lord's *ḥukm*," Q. 52:48 announces. Q. 68:48 repeats the same language to the letter. Q. 10:109 asks the Prophet to be patient until God passes his ruling or judgment (*wa-ṣbur ḥattā yaḥkuma Allāh*). Q. 21:37 indirectly urges patience in a similar context, and Q. 76:23-24 reminds the Prophet that the Qur'ān is revealed in installments and that he should be patient, for God's *ḥukm* will eventually be revealed (*innā naḥnu nazzalnā ʿalayka al-Qur'āna tanzīlan/fa-ṣbur li-ḥukmi Rabbika wa-lā tuṭiʿ min-hum āthiman aw kafūran*). The theme employing the imperative forms "be patient" (*uṣburū*) and "do not rush" (*lā tastaʿjilū*) controls other verses as well, including 2:109, 6:59, 7:87, and 16:1.

To conclude, within the conceptual range of *ḥukm*, *amr*, and "patience," the Qur'ān can be confidently said to have understood itself to be a legislator of *all* human affairs, effectively as time allowed, and potentially in absolute and unrestricted terms. It could not have been otherwise because it viewed itself (and was viewed by its intended readers/reciters) as the truest expression of an exclusive legislative will in the world. The stoppage of revelation with the death of the Prophet ushered in the next phase of extracting and deducing *ʿilm* from the extant revelation, and this process of inference, as we have seen, was the exclusive reserve of those *individuals* who bore this *ʿilm*, that is, the *rabbāniyyūn* and the *ʿulamāʾ*. (It might be worthwhile noting in this context that the conception of legislation in both the Qur'ān and Sharīʿa is not an event. With its multiplicity of *ijtihād*ic voices,[110] both synchronic and diachronic, the Sharīʿa places the act of "legislating" on a perpetual continuum where the discovery of God's intended "rule" or "judgment" in a particular case is a never-ending epistemic challenge, capable of revision and supersession. This was precisely the function of not just *ijtihād*, but also *takhrīj*, *tarjīḥ*, and *taṣḥīḥ*, among others.)[111]

The conceptual range of *ʿilm* and its inextricable and structural connections with *ḥukm* and *amr* must be regarded as the hermeneutical and epistemological backbone and blood supply of the Sharʿī system that evolved over the next two or three centuries; namely, *ijtihād*. Backbone, because without *ijtihād* the system would not have taken the structural shape it did in fact take; and blood supply, because without it the juristic, philosophical, and intellectual make-up of the system would not have operated or even existed in the way we have come to recognize. *Ijtihād*, therefore, is not just a jurisprudential method but a particular way of seeing the world, a *Weltanschauung* of the first order. It permeates the entire range of the Sharīʿa, which is also to say it suffuses every sphere of human life. *Ijtihād* is the matrix, substrate, and ethos of the Sharīʿa, and therefore of Islam itself.

Qur'ānic *ʿilm* and its associated *dars* are together an embryo of the later *ijtihād*, since it essentially gave rise to the socio-epistemic stratum called the *ʿulamāʾ*. This is another way of saying that the very term "*ʿulamāʾ*" *is* epistemically *entailed* by the range of meanings and intellectual operations embodied in the concept of *ijtihād*. As we have seen, Q. 34:44 and 68:37 explicitly state the organic connection between revelation and the act of studying (*wa-mā ātaynāhum min kutubin yadrusūnahā*; *am lakum kitābun fī-hi tadrusūn*). Studying and teaching are the pedagogical manifestations of the religio-moral obligation to at least attempt to disclose God's intentions for human beings in particular and for the world at large.[112] Human *ʿilm* is ever tantalizing, precisely because it is the lowest end of the divine rope, which can never be entirely pulled down to the human sphere. Nonetheless,

110 Unlike modern law, the substantive rules of the *fiqh* are pluralistic. On one and the same set of legal facts there exists a multiplicity of opinion, divided not only between and among four legal schools but each school (*madhhab*) may offer several legal opinions on the same set. See Hallaq, *Introduction*, 27, 165.

111 On these terms/modalities of legal reasoning, see Hallaq, *Authority*, 43-65, 127-32, 185-88. On other, associated terms, see 136, 146, 185.

112 See, e.g., the introductory sections of Ibn ʿAbd al-Barr, *Jāmiʿ Bayān al-ʿIlm wa-Faḍlihi*.

the more it is pulled down, the more respect God shows toward the *ijtihād*ic mind, for there is nothing more powerful and weighty in human existence than this accomplishment; it is the roadmap to understanding divine justice and ways of conduct, and to translating these ways into human terms and actionable praxis. This is why, as I have argued in detail elsewhere,[113] the bedrock of juristic accomplishment in Islam was epistemic, or, strictly speaking "epistemoral," since, as we have seen in several contexts, the moral and epistemic cannot be disentangled. This was so because the assumption – birthed by the Qur'ānic concept of *ʿilm* – has always been that true erudition and epistemic accomplishment must logically and ontologically entail the recognition of God's greater and smaller plans for justice (*ʿadl, ḥaqq, qisṭ*), which embody the conception of what is good and what is harmful. To be a true *ʿālim*, a seeker of *ʿilm*, is to apprehend the rationale and substance of *ḥukm* within the divine architecture of *ḥaqq*, *ʿadl*, and *qisṭ*, all of which, at the end of the day, are profoundly moral.

Historically, the Qur'ānic conceptual repertoire of *ḥukm*/*ʿilm* gave rise to two powerful and interrelated phenomena that defined both Sharīʿa and Islam, and in fact made them what they were for twelve centuries, namely, the phenomenon of jurists' law and a particular form of separation of powers. We now turn to a discussion of these two features.

It is often argued, and more often tacitly assumed, that the Sharīʿa's feature of jurists' law represents a Roman influence. However, this perception is largely untenable for at least four reasons. First, the concept of "jurists' law" is merely homonymous, indicating in each of the two legal systems a different conception and practice. The Roman jurists were neither an exclusive formal "source" of the law, nor did they play this role throughout the legal life of the Empire.[114] Second, as a body of legal experts, Roman jurists defined neither the

113 Hallaq, *Authority*.

114 Although they considerably contributed to the development of "private law," they remained, even in their heyday, subservient to an "authoritarian government" which had the highest authority of making law. See Wolff, *Roman Law*, 110. But even this constitutionally confined role was to largely disappear after the middle of the third century A.D. "After Modestinus," Wolff tells us, "there apparently was no other Roman jurisconsult who continued the classical tradition of giving *responsa* and who maintained the professional and personal prestige accorded to the classical jurists .... It is likely that there was no one reason, but rather a combination of reasons, to account for the decline of classical jurisprudence. Some of these may perhaps be found in the conditions and inherent character of classical jurisprudence itself. The final fixation of the praetorian Edict had ended the development of the *ius honorarium*.... It is certainly true that imperial legislative and judicial activities were widely determined by the great jurists in the imperial service. But the jurisconsults acted

form and content of the Roman legal system as a whole, nor the constitutional (and thus political) structures of that Empire.[115] By contrast, Muslim jurists played precisely both of these roles in their own system and legal culture. Third, as we shall see, the notion of jurists' law in Islam can be directly and causally linked to a paradigmatic and powerful idea in the Qur'ān, an idea whose origins are clearly located in the religious conditions of the Hijaz and Arabia, not in Rome or Roman Syria.[116]

It was the organic history of the first Islamic century that gave rise to a culture of law squarely grounded in jurists' law. We have come to call these jurists of the first century the "legal specialists,"[117] a class, so to speak, of private scholars who made the study of "law" (including the rules governing religious works) a matter of piety. They did not hail from a privileged political class (as the Roman jurists during the Republic generally did), nor did they receive financial remuneration for their efforts. Studying the "law" (i.e., studying and trying to "understand" what ought properly to be done in each eventuality) was an act of worship, compensated neither by governmental nor sultanic salary.

Furthermore, these jurists, who grew up mostly in the increasingly expanding garrison towns, assigned themselves the study of "law" at a time when the political and military enterprise of Islam was most powerful, and when the leaders of this enterprise were themselves concerned with the "law" as much as these legal specialists were. Yet, for all their tools of coercion and the political power they wielded, these leaders *never* attempted to legislate

---

here in their official capacity; there was no room for a *responsum* where an imperial rescript decided the issue" (127). Thus claiming continuity between Roman and Islamic jurists' law legal traditions must contend with at least two issues: (1) the significant qualitative difference between the two systems insofar as the Roman "state" made law and was the highest authority, in both theory and practice, as the lawgiver, whereas its Islamic counterpart never arrogated to itself, neither in theory nor in practice, such a role; and (2) the fact that the Roman tradition of jurists' law (even if we were to assume it to have been structurally similar to its Islamic counterpart) had been dead for at least four centuries when Muslims embarked on building their own law and legal system.

115 On Roman jurists and their middle location between the *ius civile* and the courts, see Frier, *Rise of the Roman Jurists*, 185-96.

116 This is not to preclude several features roughly common to the two systems, since both shared and depended upon a larger Near Eastern culture, the Syrian province (Ar. Bilad al-Sham) having been particularly influential in affecting both the Romans in the West and the Arabians in the South. On some Roman features similar to those in the Sharīʿa, see Frier, *Rise of the Roman Jurists*, 186-91. On the larger West Asian background and the "Genealogical Test" in determining borrowings, see Hallaq, *Origins*, 1-28.

117 On these specialists, see Hallaq, *Origins*, 63-74.

on behalf of what has quickly become an Islamic Empire.[118] Strikingly, and despite their interest in the study of "law," they left "law-finding" to the private scholars who clearly did not belong to the executive branch.[119] Even when the caliphs were legal experts of the first order, as many of them indeed were during the first half of the first century and beyond, they never once considered creating a "law" for the Empire, in the manner that the Roman, the Byzantine, or the Chinese emperors did. It is even striking that this was the case during the first few decades after the Prophet's death, when politico-legal power could potentially have taken any shape. For, as one historian rightly noted, one of the hallmarks of this early period was the "absence of a consensus on legitimate authority," where all power-groups, including the ruling one, "were equally legitimate."[120] The caliphs, in other words, were no legislators, in any of the ordinary (or modernist) senses of the term. They may have had absolute control in the military and narrowly defined political spheres,[121] but not in the central domain of governance, a domain that juristically determined the operation and modus vivendi of other spheres, including the "political."

None of this, however, explains why the mighty caliphs did not co-opt or even attempt to co-opt the legal specialists and jurists. They might well have allowed these specialists to do what they did so well, and precisely in the manner they saw fit, and still claim the "law" the specialists produced as an

118 Crone and Hinds's argument (*God's Caliph*, esp. 43-57) that the early caliphs legislated what amounted to decrees is a non-starter, and certainly has no effect on considerations of constitutional structures that operated in Islam from the beginning. There is nothing in what the Umayyad caliphs have legislated that was not done throughout the history of Islam. In fact, the Ottomans surpassed any other period in Islamic history in terms of "state legislative interference." And yet, as I will argue in detail in later chapters of this book, the history of the Ottoman Empire as well as that of any other Islamic society or empire is one that is squarely Sharʿī-based. No dynastic or caliphal power could conceivably legislate in any way that intruded on Sharīʿa's sovereignty. That was the golden rule, from the start. Furthermore, by comparison to the massive modern administrative state structures, the Islamic administrative legislation, especially that of the early caliphs, pales into insignificance. For the constitutional problems raised by the modern "administrative state," see Lawson, "Rise and Rise of the Administrative State."

119 For a fuller appreciation of this point, see Hallaq, *Impossible State*, 48-70.

120 Ahmed, *Religious Elite*, 21.

121 "Narrowly-defined political sphere" is intended to avoid the anachronism of assigning to these historical periods and contexts the same meaning of politics we have come to recognize in modernity and its nation-state. For a glimpse into what is meant by politics in modernity, see ch. 12 below as well as Carl Schmitt, *Concept of the Political*; Schmitt, *Political Theology*; Kahn, *Political Theology*. In the context of Islamic modernity, see Hallaq, *Impossible State*, 89-97, 99-110.

expression of caliphal will, this will constituting the location and terminus of authority. But they did not, and this can be explained by at least two reasons.

First, the knowledge of *aḥkām* (and we can now pluralize the term *ḥukm*) was a matter of direct engagement with the Qur'ān (along with the supportive edifice of the Sunna). As the product of pious knowledge, the *aḥkām* were a matter of personal, if not private, reflection, however methodologically rigorous this reflection was. Study circles and debates with colleagues were of course routine, but the process of "legal" reasoning and the conclusions reached were highly personal and intellectually individualistic. This phenomenon explains the rise of the *mujtahid*, always a Sharʿī intellectual voicing his own personal Sharʿī opinion (motivated and directed by piety and sincerity of belief and armed with methods of interpretation and reasoning that presuppose such psychological states).

But the phenomenon simultaneously explains the rise of the structurally associated feature of legal pluralism, where every *mujtahid* has an equally legitimate right to reach "legal" opinions or what he thinks to be God's *ḥukm* in any particular instance.[122] And these intellectuals were, without exception, organic to the social order from which they hailed. Constraining them as carriers of the Sharīʿa would have amounted to oppressing communal and social will, one which they were uniquely equipped to represent.[123] In other words, no one, including the caliphs, could control either their private activities or their numbers. If they were all equal as judges of divine intention and reasoners of its *aḥkām*, then which of them could hope for preference over others by having his jurisprudence adopted as "caliphal Law"? Juristic pluralism, egalitarian to the core,[124] simply precluded this hierarchical possibility, and if the caliph could not enforce his will to change the nature of this pluralism (assuming that he ever wished to do so), there was little reason for him to have dared to legislate. This, our second consideration, points to the *ethos* and Weltanschauung that the Qur'ān had engendered: No master but the Great Master, and no sovereign but the One Sovereign. Inserting any authority between believers and God would have been tantamount to militating against and subverting the very core of the Qur'ānic message and indeed Islam as a whole. It would have, in the same vein, amounted to betraying the sacred mission that the Prophet himself saw as the reason for his deployment by God in the first place. "*Lā ilāha illā Allah*," the invocation by which Muslims live

122 Expressed in the famous maxim "*Kullu mujtahid muṣīb*" ("Every *mujtahid* is correct").
123 On this representation, see Hallaq, *Impossible State*, 48-73.
124 See n. 122, above.

and die, and which defines Islam like no other, amounts to nothing less than a constitutional philosophy of the first order.

The Qur'ānic insistence on the elimination of any mediating authority (*sulṭān*, a readily recognizable Qur'ānic term)[125] is one of its greatest messages, a paradigmatic *tour de force*. No caliph or any other human being, not even Christ – the Prophet ʿĪsā b. Maryam – could play such a role.[126] Thus, while the insistent Qur'ānic elimination of mediating authority might have originally been a theological matter (having to do, among other things, with the Christian concept of Trinity and the three Jāhilī Daughters of God), its effects were constitutional and political in the most fundamental of ways.[127] We might want to extend this political theology even to the core of the Qur'ānic message. The denial of Christ as the son of God is grounded in the central, fundamental, and all-pervasive Qur'ānic message of the oneness of God (*Allāhu aḥad*), who has neither partners nor a divinely human mediation. The oneness of God is indeed the root of the political conception that He and He alone is the Ruler, King, and Emperor. Theology has never been far from politics.

Within the context of our general argument in this chapter, the constitutional effect of this theological doctrine also amounted to the founding principle that the political-military power in the body-politic – i.e., the executive – cannot and must not legislate, reflecting the Qur'ānic paradigm that the discovery of *aḥkām* is the prerogative and province of the learned, the only ones qualified and thus allowed to unravel God's intentions. If the learned happened to be caliphs, then the legitimacy of their contribution to the law stemmed from this erudition, not from their political office.

It is by now abundantly clear that the Qur'ān – and as an annotation of it, the Sunna – has prescribed study (that is, individual study) as the basis of *ʿilm*, the knowledge that leads to praxis. This *ʿilm*, we also saw, evolved into what came to be known as *ijtihād*: the juristic effort of reasoning and hermeneutics in developing legal norms for life's guidance. As we have seen, the Qur'ān itself

125 The term "*sulṭān*" appears some three dozen times in the Qur'ān. See the aggregate effect of Q. 7:71, 10:68, 12:40, 14:22, 15:42. 23:45, 40:56, and especially 4:144, 14:11, 17:65, 22:71, 53:23.

126 See in this connection Q. 3:79, discussed above, main text at nn. 80 and 93, above, which seems to have been revealed as a stern negation of the authority of Jesus Christ and Muhammad himself. Nīsābūrī, *Asbāb al-Nuzūl*, 64. On the prohibition of mediating human authority, see Q. 2:107, 2:165, 3:64, 4:173, 5:76, 5:116, 6:56, 9:31, 9:116, 10:104, 16:73, 17:2, 22:71, 51:51, among many others.

127 The pervasive understanding in modern scholarship that the Qur'ān did not specify the form of rule in Islam is therefore plainly and categorically wrong. For an articulate expression of this long-standing fallacy, see Bilqzīz, *al-Nubuwwa wal-Siyāsa*, 46 but also passim.

insists on the production of *ʿilm* through *dars*, and so the idea of an institution or a political office decreeing legal norms for the Muslim Community was *ab initio* precluded from consideration.

II

There was much that happened in the evolution of Sharīʿa during the first two and a half centuries of Islam. By the middle of the third/ninth century, all the essential features of substantive law and the judiciary – that is, what was immediately necessary to regulate social, political, and economic life on an empire-wide scale – reached a high level of maturity.[128] But one constitutive feature was still in the making, having taken another long century to attain final definition.[129] This was *uṣūl al-fiqh*, a hermeneutical methodology and a theory of reasoning methods intended to lay down the general precepts of legal sources and ways of extracting rules therefrom. It formally consisted of four sources: the Qur'ān, Sunna, consensus, and *qiyās*, the latter comprising a range of methods of legal reasoning that involved the use of analogical, inductive, syllogistic, relational, and other arguments.[130] One of the reasons for delay in the development of *uṣūl al-fiqh* lies in the very function of this methodology, namely, to draw on past legal practices, systematize them, and turn them into a prescriptive theory.[131] In other words, substantive law – as it stood in a dialectical relationship to practice on the ground – had to reach a level of maturity before legal theorists could tell which methods of interpretation worked and how these methods were finally structured, or to be structured.

But this theoretical-methodological evolution and its relative maturity were not just a matter of legal development in a harmonious environment. Rather, the development occurred in the midst of not only vigorous arguments and debates between and among discordant juristic groups but also within a context of serious political antagonisms. The chief opponents were those

128 For an account of the legal history of the first three centuries, see Hallaq, *Origins*. For a detailed and useful account of the formation of Islamic orthodoxy, see Khan, *Heresy and the Formation of Islamic Orthodoxy*.

129 See Hallaq, "Was al-Shāfiʿī the Master Architect of Islamic Jurisprudence?" and Hallaq, "*Uṣūl al-Fiqh* and Shāfiʿī's *Risāla*."

130 On the constitution of *qiyās*, see Hallaq, "Non-Analogical Arguments."

131 On the dialectic between description and prescription of *uṣūl al-fiqh*, see Hallaq, "Considerations on the Function and Character..."

camps that rallied around an imamic juridical-political authority collectively represented in the House of ʿAlī, on the one hand, and those that insisted on the Community and its power of consensus as the source of legal and political authority, on the other. The Sunni concept of consensus required all the *mujtahids*, as representatives of the Community, to agree, *ex post facto*, on a point of law. In Shīʿī doctrine, consensus acquires validity only if the infallible imam partakes in it; without him, simply put, the consensus of the jurists is (at least theoretically) worth nothing. The core distinction between these two groups was therefore a choice between legal-political authority devolving through the line of the individual imams of the ʿAlid House – the Shīʿīs – or through what has become known as the Middle Community, *Ahl al-Sunna wal-Jamāʿa, and its power of consensus.*

Consensus of the Community, the foundation of juristic consensus, was not just a legal "source" but one that also carried with it a central political founding thrust. For Sunni jurists to be able to identify its operations, this consensus had to be technically measurable and amenable to determination. As it were, the master jurists, the *mujtahids*, became the mouthpiece of the Community (*Umma*). When they happened to agree on a point of law, their agreement, always determined *ex post facto*, was considered irrevocable.[132] It is on the grounds of this theory that Juwaynī was later to argue that the caliphate was *ab initio* mandated by the law on the basis of consensus, *despite* the fact that the later jurists have no certain knowledge of the textual basis of that consensus. The assumption was that the early Muslims, with their widespread geographical distribution (i.e., they had no way of meeting at any point) and over generational difference, could not have conspired to reach consensus on the necessity of appointing an imam. Juwaynī argued that they must have had available to them a body of textual evidence that made such a consensus possible, for a consensus must by definition rest on such evidence.[133] This logic was categorically rejected by the Shīʿīs. The same consensus that validated the law and *uṣūl al-fiqh* itself also validated the Sunni concept and institution of the caliphate.

Furthermore, it is generally little known that the points of law subject to consensus were relatively few in number,[134] in totality a small fraction of all cases making up the whole corpus of substantive law subject to juristic

132 On consensus, see Hallaq, *History of Islamic Legal Theories*, 75-81.

133 *GU*, 36-42.

134 Compare, e.g., Ibn Ḥazm, *Marātib al-Ijmāʿ* and Ibn Taymiyya, *Naqd Marātib al-Ijmāʿ* with any average *fiqh* work, much less longer ones like Māwardī's *al-Ḥāwī al-Kabīr*.

disagreement. Being the third source/foundation of the law, consensus could not have acquired this high-ranking foundational status only by dint of this small body of agreed-upon cases. For the most significant role of consensus lay indeed elsewhere, that is, in the determination of the three other sources/foundations of the law, and how they stand together as one bounded whole (yet another consequential role will be shortly discussed in the context of the *madhhab*). The determination involved decisions over what sources of the law should be accepted and how they are to be utilized. The Qur'ān's and Sunna's validity as the primary material sources was not in question, but validity was not all that had to be decided and agreed upon. The questions that nagged Muslim legal theorists were, among others, these: What linguistic and hermeneutical methods were to operate on the Qur'ān and the Sunna subject matter? How is God's language to be understood, and what transmission methods of Prophetic Ḥadīth are deemed acceptable? No less significant was the determination by consensus to include *qiyās* as a founding source of the law, this source bearing the burden of establishing the inferential-logical methods needed to elaborate the law, and hence the definition of the structure and boundaries of the legal and political life of the Community.

The final settlement of the sources of the law together with the arguments and sub-arguments in justification of the contents and structure of these sources *was the moment when Sunnism emerged as a wholly delimited entity*, with a distinct legal and political identity, and standing in contrast to the Shīʿī vision of law and political governance (whatever changes or developments Shīʿism underwent in its later life have no effect on what had already become a *fait accompli* by the fifth/eleventh century).

Although the vast majority of substantive legal rules (*fiqh*) were common to the Sunnīs and Shīʿīs, the laws of inheritance were markedly different in their logic and gendered devolution. Whereas Sunni law of inheritance was patrilineal, the Shīʿī, by sharp contrast, was matrilineal, this latter in line with the political ambition to derive political authority through the line of Fāṭima, the daughter of the Prophet and the wife of ʿAlī, Muhammad's cousin. Likewise, the sources of the law of the two camps differed on the whole considerably. For the Shīʿīs in general,[135] the legal and political constitution of polity is determined ultimately by the infallible imam,[136] politically speaking

135 The Zaydīs were an exception, both in terms of their imamic theory and practice and their actual *fiqhī* rules, especially, for the latter, after the fifth/eleventh century. See Haider, "How to Make a Zaydi Imam."

136 *GU*, 70-74.

and in theory the rule of a single holder of power over all and everything else. Sunnism, by contrast, could never reduce either legal or political decision to any individual, nor even to a group that could congregate and confer with a view to making law or taking a decision. Sunnism operated by an entirely different logic, where no single jurist or even a council of jurists can command the law, change or amend it, or, much less, suspend it.

More importantly for our concerns is the fact that it is the collective operation of the Qur'ān, Sunna, and *qiyās*, with the *ijtihād*ic hermeneutical apparatus of *uṣūl al-fiqh* that had the exclusive competence to decide on matters of law and politics – indeed on all aspects of human conduct, political, personal, private, intimate, social, and all else. Which is to say that the development and final articulation of *uṣūl al-fiqh* was the construction of not just a legal foundation for the *Umma*, but also, and equally, deciding the constitutional structure of the system of political governance. Whereas Sunnism moved from law to politics, the Shīʿīs moved from politics to law, a radical difference indeed.

Once integrated into a complete whole, *Uṣūl al-fiqh represented a constitutional act of the first order*, one that reflected a universal decision within Sunnism to reject two fundamental features that often characterize other types of rule (including the modern): First, the power of an individual to decide on the law of the nation/Community or the law of the land; and for that matter any human prerogative – in principle or as a matter of actual practice – over legal change that goes beyond a case-by-case *ijtihād*ic basis. And the second was the total rejection of the possible dominance of the political over the legal. In other words, *uṣūl al-fiqh* created (but also reflected) a cultural environment or a habitus in which it was the legal and jurisprudential that determined the political and constitutional, never the other way around. The definition of Sunnism through its four foundational *legal* sources was thus a constitutional marker of the first order, one that *systemically* registered these two objections over and against other systems of law and governance. Put in still another way, *uṣūl al-fiqh* was, after the Qur'ān, the second systemic force that precluded, even preempted, not only autocratic rule but the very possibility of a Paradox of Sovereignty.

III

The third systemic constitutional force was the *madhhab*.

The story of how the work of early individual legal specialists culminated in what is known as the *madhhab* (legal school) is a long and detailed one, involving complex and complicated processes.[137] Yet, the very history of the *madhhab*'s evolution permits a view of the meaning and definition of the concept, since that history produced this concept in a theoretically evolving complexity. The *madhhab* defined the inner and outer boundaries of the law, and so we can confidently say that it was the *madhhab* in its final and most developed stage that provided the guarantee for constitutional protections. This is the argument that this section will make.

The term *madhhab* is associated with four conceptions, the first of which was simply the opinion – or idea – that one chooses to adopt. Within the domain of "law," it is the particular opinion of a legist or the opinion that a jurist "goes for" (this "going for" [*dhahaba ilā*] is in fact the basic and the most literal meaning of the term). This phenomenon is associated with what is known as "jurists' law," meaning that the law is produced – irrespective of the modalities of production – by individual jurists, in contradistinction with collective, institutional, or parliamentarian production. The doctrine is that which an individual person, a single jurist, goes for, never more. It is never associated with institutions or collective or corporate entities. In the Sharīʿa system, this also meant that law was an expression of pluralism, where there are many jurists each holding a different opinion on one and the same set of legal facts, on the same "case," so to speak. Whether the jurist holding the opinion was the one who originally formulated it through his own legal reasoning or not, what he opined or held was his *madhhab*.

The second conception was the doctrine of a major jurist who had a local or regional following. This was the so-called personal doctrine of distinguished jurists, a compendium of the opinions that made for a general way of doing "law."

The third was the technical meaning of the term as a principle underlying a set of cases subsumed under such a principle. For example, an assumption of the Ḥanafīs is that misappropriation, in order to obtain, must involve the unlawful removal of property from its original place, where it had been in the possession of the owner. The Ḥanbalīs, on the other hand, define misappropriation as mere seizure of property, even if it is not removed from its original place of ownership. Thus, taking possession of a rug by sitting on it (without

137 For an account of these processes, see Hallaq, *Origins*, 150-77; Hallaq, "From Geographical to Personal Schools?"

removing it) is considered misappropriation by the Ḥanbalīs, but not by the Ḥanafīs. In terms of recovery of damages, this basic difference in definition contributed to generating significant differences between the two schools. Whereas the Ḥanbalīs make the wrongdoer liable to the original owner for all growth of, and proceeds from, the misappropriated object, the Ḥanafīs place severe restrictions on the ability of the owner to recover his accruing rights. The reasoning being that the growth or proceeds of the misappropriated property were not yet in existence when the property was "removed" from the hands of the rightful owner, and since they were not in existence, no liability on the part of the wrongdoer is deemed to arise. This example illustrates a central meaning of the term *madhhab* as a legal doctrine concerning a group of cases – in this instance cases pertaining to the recovery of damages – which are subsumed under a larger principle. And it is in this sense that it can be said that one school's doctrine differs, sometimes significantly, from another's.

The fourth meaning of *madhhab* refers to a group of jurists who are loyal to a distinct, integral and, most importantly, *collective* legal doctrine attributed to a Master-Jurist, from whose doctrine and general methodology the school is known to have acquired distinctive characteristics, doctrine, and legitimacy.[138] The loyalty to a cumulative body of doctrine that was constructed and refined by generations of leading jurists is not to be confused with the individual doctrine of a single Master-Jurist. In the *madhhab*, the Master-Jurist, the eponym of the school, is a *primus inter pares*, often critiqued and corrected by his own followers.[139] Which is to say that the *madhhab* is not just a body of shared and common legal doctrine but also a colossus of interpretive disagreements (*ikhtilāf*) between and among the very members of each school, despite the generally unified principles that reign within the school.[140] By the same logic, it is also to be taken for granted that disagreements (that is differing and different interpretations of the law) were multitudinous between and among the *madhhab*s themselves. Yet, disagreements were all deemed legitimate, which is to say that all opinions within and without the *madhhab*s – rated as strong or not so strong – were considered "correct." Not only were they correct and thus having practical value (that is, applicable in a court of law), the disagreeing members were individually protected by the *madhhab* to which they belong. The protections, unqualified, were both inter- and intra-*madhhab*ic.[141]

138 On the construction of the Master-Jurist's authority, see Hallaq, *Authority*, 24-56.

139 See Hallaq, "From Geographical to Personal Schools?" 24 ff.

140 Nawawī, *Majmū'*, I, 18.

141 For a detailed and useful discussion of these *madhhab*ic processes, see Al-Azem,

As it came to pass, the standard reference of the technical term "*madhhab*" was to the doctrinal school that possessed several characteristics lacking in its personal counterpart. First, the personal school comprised the substantive legal doctrine of a single leading jurist, and at times, his doctrine as transmitted by one of his students. The doctrinal school, on the other hand, possessed a cumulative doctrine of substantive law in which the legal opinions of the leading jurist, now the assumed "founder,"[142] were the first among equals; that is, equal to the rest of the opinions and doctrines held by various other jurists, also considered leaders *within* the school. In other words, the doctrinal school was a collective and authoritative entity, whereas the personal school remained limited to the individual doctrine of a single jurist.

The second characteristic was that the doctrinal school constituted as much a methodological entity as a substantive, doctrinal one. In other words, what distinguished a particular doctrinal school from another was largely its legal methodology and the substantive principles it adopted in dealing with its own "law." Methodological awareness on this level had not yet existed in the personal schools, although it was on the increase beginning in the middle of the second/eighth century.

Third, a doctrinal school was defined by its substantive boundaries, namely, by a certain body of law and methodological principles that clearly identified the outer limits of the school as a collective entity. The personal schools, on the other hand, had no such well-defined boundaries, and departure from these boundaries in favor of other legal doctrines and principles was not uncommon.

The fourth characteristic, issuing from the third, was loyalty, for departure from legal doctrine and methodological principles amounted to abandoning the school, a major event in the life of a jurist. Doctrinal loyalty, in other words, was barely present in the personal schools, whereas in the later doctrinal schools, it was a defining feature of both the school itself and the careers of its members.

A central feature of the doctrinal school – yet a fifth characteristic distinguishing it from the personal school – was the creation of an axis of authority around which an entire methodology of law was constructed. This axis was the figure of the so-called founder, the leading Master-Jurist, in whose name the cumulative, collective principles of the school were propounded. What

Rule-Formulation.

142 Hallaq, *Authority*, 24-56.

made a *madhhab* (as a doctrinal school) a *madhhab* is therefore this feature of authoritative doctrine whose ultimate font is presumed to have been the absolute Master-Jurist, the founder, not the mere congregation of jurists under the name of a titular eponym. This congregation would have been meaningless without the centripetal effect of an authoritative, substantive, and methodological doctrine constructed in the name of a founder. Of all the leaders of the personal schools – and they were many – only four were raised to the level of "founder" of a doctrinal school (i.e., the Ḥanafī, Mālikī, Shāfiʿī, and Ḥanbalī). While the process of this transformation was long, it seems that the *madhhab*s finally came to full maturity sometime during the second half of the fourth/tenth century[143] ("full maturity" meaning here the disappearance of the feature of jurists moving between and among major juristic axes, thus firmly establishing the four schools as the only legitimate doctrinal formations).

Finally, we might well ask: Why did the doctrinal schools come into being in the first place? Wholly native to Islamic soil and without precedent in other legal cultures, the *madhhab*s and their early evolution were entirely occasioned by internal needs. We have noted that the embryonic formation of the schools started sometime during the last decade or so of the first/seventh century, simply taking the form of *scholarly circles* in which pious scholars debated religious issues and taught interested students. The knowledge and production of legal doctrine began in these circles – nowhere else. It did not begin and was never part of a royal court or any political office. Legal authority, therefore, was epistemic from the beginning, rather than political.

That epistemic authority is *the* defining feature of the Sharīʿa need not be doubted, which is to say (and this must by now be clear) that this authority was also indistinguishably moral. A masterly knowledge of the law was the sole criterion in deciding where legal authority resided; and it resided with the scholars.[144] This was as much true of the last decades of the first/seventh century as it was of the eighth century and thereafter. As we have seen, if a caliph actively participated in legal life, it was by virtue of his recognized personal knowledge of the law, not so much by virtue of his political office or military power. And if he was proficient enough in legal reasoning as to come up with his own legal opinion, then he would be counted as merely one of the mujtahids on this case, on which no one had a monopoly of final decision. Thus, legal authority in Islam was personal and private, however much that

143 See Hallaq, *Origins*; and especially Hallaq, "*Uṣūl al-Fiqh* and Shāfiʿī's *Risāla*."
144 On the scholars' *ijtihād* and *taqlīd* in the context of the *madhhab*'s constitutional protection, see Jackson, *Islamic Law*, 73-112.

authority became a school's standard authoritative doctrine;[145] it was in the persons of the individual jurists (be they laymen or, on relatively rare occasions, early caliphs) that authority resided, and it was this competence in ethical legal knowledge that was later to be known as *ijtihād* – the lifeblood of the Sharīʿa and its *fiqh*.

Because legal authority did not reside in the government or the ruler, nor in any of his offices, the *madhhab* arose as a substitute for what we call today the state's legal authority – however different these two are from each other. Whereas law, as a legislated system, was often "state"-based in other imperial and complex civilizations, in Islam – as we will see[146] – the ruling powers had, until the dawn of modernity, very little to do with the production and promulgation of substantive legal knowledge or law. Therefore, the need arose in Islamic culture to anchor law in a system of authority that was not political precisely because there was no way to give political leadership the competence to discover the law of God for the Muslim Community while skipping the divinely mandated individual pietistic voices of the Muslim Community. Legal creativity presumed a subjectivity of piety, with all that this meant in terms of ethical technologies of the self. And epistemic piety could not have been attained in the person of a ruler *as a ruler*, for knowledge of God's "ethico-legal mind" (a prerequisite for *ijtihād*) was not a political but an "epistemoral" matter. On this account alone, and without the other arguments adduced in the previous section and those we will proffer in chapter 12, it is a fundamental constitutional fact in Islam that the Paradox of Sovereignty could not have arisen in the first place.

The protected status of the *madhhab*s and their inter- and intra-disagreements raises the question of what gave them such a protection.[147] The answer is *ijmāʿ*, the consensus of the Community as represented by its jurists. But when "consensus" is invoked, there is implied in this invocation historical and cultural components that give consensus its finalistic force. First, consensus emerged as an integral part of how the law and legal system evolved, which is to say that it operated on the legal and political scenes from the very beginning. The political tradition grew from the time of the Rāshidūn with the structural and structuring idea that consensus is a final authority and a sacred institution. Put starkly, going against consensus was both a legal and political suicide.

145 Hallaq, *Authority*, 121-65.
146 See ch. 11.
147 On the legal aspects of this question, see Al-Azem, *Rule-Formulation*.

Nor could the jurists themselves change the law, not even collectively, *for no one jurist, or even a generation of jurists, possessed the law.* A jurist could claim ownership of his opinions only, but none of the rest of the law, because of the sacrosanct principle that "every *mujtahid* is correct," no one *mujtahid* and no ruler or even a great monarch could repeal, change, or suspend the law (i.e., there was no such a thing as "state of exception). The Sharīʿa as a legal system was autonomous, and the *madhhab* was at the core of this autonomy.

Part of the complexity of consensus I intimated earlier is that it emerges organically, and only in hindsight. Identifying consensus is always a posterior, *post eventum*, act. Which means that later jurists could not change consensus-based law, nor can they change the law itself except piecemeal, and on a case-by-case basis. This constrained even the jurists themselves, rendering them incapable of effecting any large-scale change in the law, as would happen in the modern codes, especially the founding ones, such as the Napoleonic code. The body of the law was guaranteed from interference both diachronically and synchronically, with the minor exception of change on a case-by-case basis – the exception having been vital for effecting legal change.[148]

Violating consensus was so grave because culture – the second component – was encrusted with this history and stood intermeshed with it. By culture I mean all values, beliefs, and practices that are taken for granted in a community, small or large. Culture here is the Foucauldian "Islamic episteme," the anthropological discursive formation (as seen to operate in tradition), and the Bourdieusian habitus, all at once. Just as it is an unquestioned national value in some modern liberal states not to allow the military to engage political questions or, much less, take political decisions, questioning or running against consensus was anathema, if not heresy and even monstrosity. This guarantee of the *madhhab*ic right to difference, and of the final doctrinal say of what law is,[149] was one of the two most important functions of consensus.[150] Therefore, to speak of consensus as guaranteeing the law is to speak of general culture, low and high, as well as of habitus and episteme as operating on the Islamic political scene. For it is because of this consensus-protected status that no ruler in Islam could venture to reject the law or, much less, to displace or

148 Hallaq, *Authority*.

149 See Jackson, *Islamic Law*, 106-12.

150 The second being the defining of the boundaries of Sunnism itself, as it came to maturity, through the final maturation of *uṣūl al-fiqh*, during the second half of the fourth/tenth century. See Hallaq, "Was Al-Shāfiʿī the Master Architect of Islamic Jurisprudence?" and especially Hallaq, "*Uṣūl al-Fiqh* and Shāfiʿī's *Risāla*."

replace it by a code of his own. In fact, the very idea that a ruler may co-opt a *madhhab* in order to suppress the others was thought to be tyranny, despite the fact that the *madhhab* is not of his making nor is it even a single juristic voice.[151] To the Muslim jurists flourishing during the first twelve centuries of Islam, the modern state would have appeared as the highest form of tyranny, if for no other reason than the fact that it espouses, at any given time, a single law for the same set of legal facts.

Finally, when we say that the Sharīʿa was culture we must also include the phenomenon of institutional proliferation. The Sharīʿa created and operated institutions and practices that defined the social order, and whenever a non-Sharʿī practice or institution was incorporated into Muslim communal life (e.g., customary law or "popular practices"), it was by virtue of Sharīʿa's authorization. The Sharīʿa created and validated the major projects of mercantile, agrarian, and maritime "economy"; it established and managed the operation of the all-important philanthropic and charitable institutions, primarily the *zakat* and *waqf*; the *waqf* institutions housed and regulated much of education, family property, welfare and civic services, public works, and much else. There was no communal aspect of Muslim life that did not lie within the gaze of Sharʿī management and organization. Even architecture was heavily regulated by Sharīʿa rules and principles.[152] As we will see in chapter 12, this Sharʿī culture was the Muslim substitute for what Foucault called biopower, a "culture" of a qualitatively different kind.

We can therefore confidently conclude that the Sharīʿa, *as both legal system and culture*, defined a way of life that no agent or institution, political or legal, could manipulate or change, much less override, suspend, or overthrow. It was a habitus and a discursive tradition all at once.[153] The *madhhab* and its

151 Jackson, *Islamic Law*, 185.

152 Ibn al-Rāmī al-Bannā', *al-Iʿlān bi-Aḥkām al-Bunyān*; Al-Hadhlūl, *al-Madīna al-ʿArabiyya al-Islāmiyya*, 83-139.

153 See Introduction, sec. II. In the context of her study of Juwaynī, Siddiqui (*Law and Politics*, 280), proffers an excellent definition of the Sharīʿa, one that comes close to the definition of both habitus and discursive tradition: "The Sharīʿa ... is not contingent on government, institutions, or even the juristic class; rather, it relies on a communal commitment to narrative and practice, which for al-Juwaynī are intimately intertwined. This communal element is precisely why the Sharīʿa remains a recognizable structuring force in society after the collapse of the imamate and even in the absence of *muftī-mujtahids*. Al Juwaynī declares the Sharīʿa completely extinguished only when no ostensible practice or memory of it can be identified in society. In [Robert] Cover's terminology, the *nomos* dies when its narrative does. From this perspective, the Sharīʿa is not merely constituted by the legal norms that prevail in society but also represents the centrifugal force of a narrative that connects

structural dominance decided the contours of politics and the system in which it operated, although it could no more decide the content of the operations of politics *within* the politico-military system than the caliph or sultan could decide what law the *qāḍī* was to apply in his court. Yet, just as the caliph or sultan had the authority to decide the outer administrative boundaries of the judiciary – deciding on hiring, firing, venue, etc. – so did the Sharīʿa decide the boundaries within which the executive could operate. The autonomy of both spheres – sultanic and *qaḍā'*ic – was guaranteed by the Sharīʿa-as-*madhhab*. We have seen this much appositely elaborated by Māwardī in the first two chapters above, especially in his account regarding the necessity of *sulṭān qāhir* for what John Rawls would in a different context call a "well-ordered society."

individuals. Therefore, knowledge and practice of the Sharīʿa along with its narrative are the key elements for evaluating its vitality. If knowledge of the Sharīʿa is ubiquitous, if the community is committed to its narrative, and if it is providing meaning for its followers, then the Sharīʿa is functioning optimally as a *nomos*. If, on the other hand, knowledge of the Sharīʿa remains present in society but its narrative and ability to provide meaning are weakening, the Sharīʿa as a governing force is in danger of enervation. Defining the Sharīʿa in this manner emphasizes the roles of the individual and the community that are neglected by other definitions."

Chapter 5

Locating the Judiciary

I

The cumulative effect of the previous chapters has made it abundantly clear that the office of Prophethood is an institution of aggregated leadership. Every aspect of leadership came to combine in the character of the Prophet. True, he was the vessel through which God spoke to humans, but he also acted as a legal, political, military, and exemplary leader, as he was in every other sphere of life. In Ṣūfism, *adab*, and other traditions of *askesis*, he constituted a model for ethical self-formation and an ideal for praxis.[1] In the political domain he was a shrewd statesman and a military commander. In the law itself he was a premier reasoner, an ethical thinker, as well as an adept judge.

The Rāshidūn, being the caliphs (or deputies) of the Prophet, had fulfilled all Prophetic functions, from end to end, with the obvious exception of being recipients of revelation. Yet, there is another class of functionaries who were, and continued to be, caliphs of the Rāshidūn,[2] even of the Prophet himself, caliphs who were seen by some jurists as deputized by that office, even skipping the Rāshidūn. In fact, there seems to have been a meaningful discussion among early scholars as to whether *qāḍīs* can be regarded as "caliphs of God," where the delegative powers bypass both the Prophet(s) and the Rāshidūn; but the majority eventually jettisoned this view in favor of the relative demotion to deputies (*khulafāʾ*) or heirs of the prophets (note, again, the plural form here).[3]

1 See ch. 2, above. On praxis, see Hallaq, *Reforming Modernity*, 39-40, 43, 45-46, 48, 152-53, 163-65, 174-75.
2 Ibn Māza, *Sharḥ Adab al-Qāḍī*, I, 133.
3 Ibn Māza, *Sharḥ Adab al-Qāḍī*, I, 163: "*Thumma takallama al-ʿulamāʾu fī annahu hall*

Ibn Abī al-Damm (d. 642/1244), a major author-jurist[4] on the law court (*adab al-qaḍā'*), declares that "judgeship (*qaḍā'*) is the sequel (*tilw*) to prophethood," a universalizing statement that transcends Islam. It asserts a universal "religious" truth to the effect that "God created humans and obligated them to follow the (divine) Laws, and for that he sent his prophets to act as judges so they adjudicate between and among them."[5] Once the prophets pass away, the *qāḍī*s inherit from them the function of adjudicating disputes. The universalism of this conception embodies in fact a categorical Qur'ānic proposition: "Mankind had been one community, and God sent unto them prophets as bearers of good tidings and as warners, and revealed therewith the Scripture with the truth that it might adjudicate between them in regards to that on which they disagreed."[6] "Adjudicating according to what God has revealed"[7] is thus a Qur'ānic desideratum, this revelation being always defined as "right" and "just" (*ḥaqq*). The Qur'ānic David was not only a Prophet but also God's caliph on Earth, one who was commanded to judge according to that which is right and just, the very opposite of the passions (*hawā*).[8] Judging therefore is one of the most important of the prophets' responsibilities and so it makes perfect sense that *qaḍā'* (judgeship) is truly the sequel of prophethood.

Notice here that there are two elements at play, and their combination is what makes the entire discourse about prophets and judgeship a juridical theology. The first is the hidden presupposition that judging and judgeship are integral to communal human existence. There is no social grouping possible without this function, as Māwardī has theorized in one of his first

---

yajūzu iṭlāqu ismi 'Khalīfatu Allāhi' ta'ālā 'alayhi [i.e., *'alā al-qāḍī*], *wa-aktharuhum 'alā annahu yuqālu khalīfatu rasūli al-Lāhi wa-wārithuhu, wa-lā yajūzu an yuqāla 'Khalīfatu Allāhi' ta'ālā li-anna hādhā al-isma khāṣṣun bil-anbiyā'i.*" Needless to say, the entire doctrine of *qāḍī*s as deputies and heirs of the prophets is integral to the larger discursive tradition in which the ulama are said to be the heirs of the prophets: "*al-ulamā'u warathatu al-anbiyā'i.*" See Bukhārī, *Ṣaḥīḥ*, I, 49; 'Umarī, *Ta'rīf*, 154; Qasṭalānī, *Mawāhib*, II, 701, and main text of ch. 4, at n. 98. It is noteworthy that the concept of ulama was, for good reason, distilled in later periods to include the jurisprudential elite of *muftī*s, who were, with the jurist-authors, responsible for the development of the law. See Nawawī, *al-Majmū'*, I, 72. On the author-jurist and the mufti as creative legal scholars, see Hallaq, *Authority*, 166-235.

4 On the centrality of the function of *taṣnīf*/author-jurist, see Hallaq, *Authority*, 167-71 and passim.

5 Ibn Abī al-Damm, *Adab al-Qaḍā'*, I, 252: "*Al-qaḍā'u tilwu al-nubuwwati, wa-khalaqa Allāhu ta'ālā al-khalqa wa-kallafahum al-akhdha bil-sharā'i'i, wa-ibta'atha rusulahu – ṣalawātu Allāhi wa-salāmuhu 'alayhim – quḍātan li-yaḥkumū baynahum.*"

6 Q. 2:213.

7 Q. 5:48-49.

8 Q. 38:26. See Ibn Māza, *Sharḥ Adab al-Qāḍī*, I, 128.

"genealogical" discourses.[9] But it is quite possible for judging and judgeship to stand on their own, associated, as we have it in modernity, with nothing more than the secular state, operating within a worldly and earthly context. Which is what makes the Islamic theory of judgeship quite remarkable, since it is given a theological genealogy associated with a cosmological law whose application in the social realm has been a task consigned to no less than the prophets. Why the prophets? Because they are the custodians of the Divine decree, the bearers of the Law, and the executors of divine wisdom but mostly divine justice – that logic of justice whose higher form was used by God to create the world.[10] Judging, therefore, is, in this tradition, necessarily a lower (i.e., human) application of the Divine administration of the law, a human yet divinity-based application of a just Law.

Judging according to what is right and just naturally entails competence in legal inference and ethics-based forms of reasoning. This is why *ijtihād*, the knowledge required to perform complex modes of reasoning, is one of the credentials required of caliphs.[11] In the case of *qāḍī*s, the requirement was likewise insisted upon by the majority of scholars, even as late as the fifth/eleventh century.[12] Whether the *qāḍī*s derived their judicial powers from the caliphs or directly from the Prophet or God himself,[13] it is clear that their province of jurisprudence was bounded by the scope of revelation, however this latter came to be defined. Thus, in this sense and like the caliphs, they were both "discoverers of the law" and adjudicators, always with the understanding that their "legislative" competence was atomistic and ungeneralizable beyond their court.[14]

For a scholar to be considered qualified as a *qāḍī*, he must meet a number of requirements, including being a Muslim, a free person, of age, in possession of sound vision, hearing, and speech, as well as possessing rectitude (*ʿadl*) – this latter deemed by some as the "premiere quality required."[15] He

---

9 See ch. 1, above.

10 On this, see next chapter, sec. I.

11 *AS*, 19

12 Ibn Māza, *Sharḥ Adab a-Qāḍī*, I, 126. On the evolution of this requirement in juristic thinking, see Hallaq, "*Iftā'* and *Ijtihād* in Sunni Legal Theory."

13 Ibn Māza, *Sharḥ Adab al-Qāḍī*, I, 163.

14 There was no "law reporter" in the Islamic legal system, nor a doctrine of *stare decisis*. The courts' decisions on hard cases were only generally taken into account by the *muftī* and/or the author-jurist. See Hallaq, *Authority*, 166-235.

15 Ibn Maza, *Sharḥ Adab a-Qāḍī*, 129: "*Wa-jaʿala al Khaṣṣafu raḥimahu Allāhu al-ʿadālata sharṭa al-awlawiyyati, fa-inna al-awlā an yakūna al-qāḍī ʿadlan.*" The qualities required of the *qāḍī* were many, some essential, some merely desirable. In addition to being just and

must also be proficient in Islamic jurisprudence (*al-aḥkām al-shar ʿiyya*), a requirement on which there is a consensus.[16] This proficiency was defined variably by different jurists. Some, such as Ibn Idrīs al-Shāfiʿī, required judges to attain the rank of absolute *ijtihād*, a rank achieved through the acquisition of proficient knowledge of the Qur'ān, the Sunna of the Prophet, consensus, and *qiyās*, an aggregate method of legal reasoning.[17] Shāfiʿī adds that the *qāḍī* must know "the language of the Arabs" and "*aqāwl al-nās*," which I take to be the legal opinions of the scholars, in their agreements and disagreements (*ijmāʿ* and *ikhtilāf*). Representing a wide segment of early scholars, Khaṣṣāf and Ibn Māza thought that no appointment for *qaḍā'* is to be made to someone who has not mastered the Qur'ān and the Sunna and who was incapable of *ijtihād*.[18] The knowledge of the Qur'ān and the Sunna must include mastery of their abrogating and abrogated passages, the general and specific language in every category of ambiguity, univocality, particularity, universality, and absolute clarity. He must also possess adequate knowledge of the modalities of Sunna narration, authenticating the transmitters and channels of transmission, and of the various types of transmitted reports, be they multiply transmitted, solitary, interrupted, or otherwise.[19] The entire sphere of consensus and the equally important juristic genre of disagreements (*ikhtilāf*) must also be under his belt, along with the various methods of legal reasoning.

These conditions clearly set a high bar, which Shāfiʿī had meant to be met by what came later to be called absolute *mujtahids*. These were the *mujtahids* who at times managed to attract followers who would form legal schools around their work. The *qāḍīs*, who could still perform their judicial functions most appropriately, did not master all these fields, and so in later

erudite in matters of law, the qualities included, but were not limited to: (1) self-knowledge, an attribute cognate with the Greco-Roman "knowing the self"; (2) acute intelligence; (3) trustworthiness; (4) eloquence; (5) patience; (6) alertness and cleverness; (7) "can neither be taken by surprise nor deceived;" (8) chasteness; (9) honesty and absence of greed; (10) personal maturity; (11) disinclination to rancor and aggressive demeanor; (12) disinclination to oppressive behavior and fanaticism; (13) competence in counsel and giving advice; (14) possession of a gentle approach and demeanor; (15) having a charismatic personality; (16) ability to make his interlocutors feel equal to him; (17) seriousness; and (18) having a dignified and respected presence. Ibn al-Qāṣṣ, *Adab al-Qāḍī*, 98.

16 Ibn Abī al-Damm, *Adab al-Qaḍā'*, I, 277.

17 For the array of interpretive methods in *qiyās*, see Hallaq, "Non-Analogical Reasoning."

18 Ibn Māza, *Sharḥ Adab al-Qāḍī*, I, 126, 128; Ibn al-Qāṣṣ, *Adab al-Qāḍī*, 101.

19 Ibn Abī al-Damm, *Adab al-Qaḍā'*, I, 277-78. On the various types of reports and their epistemic value, see Weiss, "Knowledge of the Past;" Hallaq, "On Inductive Corroboration."

centuries the criteria of *ijtihād* for judges became more modest,[20] even allowing judges to consult *muftīs* when they encountered hard cases.[21] By the fourth/tenth century, it has become clear that the legal schools took root as defining features of the legal system, which meant that the *qāḍīs* had henceforth to render judgments according to dominant doctrines within each of these schools.[22]

Writing probably in the first quarter of the seventh/thirteenth century, Ibn Abī al-Damm was quite confident in the assertion that no one in his age could rise to the rank of absolute *ijtihād* and that "it is valid to appoint *qāḍīs* who follow the doctrine of a school's imam," that is, an eponym and founder of a legal school.[23] A judge only needs to know the greater bulk of the school's doctrines (*ʿārifan bi-ghālibi madhhabibi*), its substantive law and legal formularies,[24] including the authoritative opinions of its masters. He should also possess a good intellect and sound predisposition to complex legal reasoning, so much so that he is expected to derive new meanings from settled language and doctrine and to weigh between and among various textual indicants with a view to preponderating the stronger ones (*tarjīḥ*).[25] "He who possesses these attributes, and nothing less, is the one who is legitimately appointed to *qāḍī*ship in these times of ours."[26]

What the early seventh/thirteenth-century jurist Ibn Abī al-Damm was describing is nothing short of the coming to maturity and enduring stability of the Islamic legal system, despite his nostalgic desire to encounter the revealed texts hermeneutically afresh, an engagement that was integral to *taʿabbud*, a complex of acts of worship of, and dedication to, the Creator. This is to say that with the passage of time, the exclusive authority of the Sharīʿa and its *fiqh* were increasingly established, defining the habitus of the social, political, and legal domains – which is also not to suggest that these domains were segregated in any important way. Notice here that in all the discussions with regard to the qualifications of the *qāḍī*, there is not the slightest hint that the *qāḍī* must know, much less yield, to any legal norms other than those of the Sharīʿa. The *qāḍī*'s education was Sharʿī through and through, as was his apprenticeship,

20 Ibn Abī al-Damm, *Adab al-Qaḍāʾ*, I, 279, 285.
21 Ibn Abī al-Damm, *Adab al-Qaḍāʾ*, I, 327; Ibn Māza, *Sharḥ Adab al-Qāḍī*, I, 193, 356-71.
22 Ibn Abī al-Damm, *Adab al-Qaḍāʾ*, I, 285; on the formation of the legal schools (*madhhabs*), see Hallaq, *Authority*; Melchert, *Formation*.
23 On authority construction of the "founders," see Hallaq, *Authority*, 24-120.
24 On legal formularies, see Hallaq, "Model *Shurūṭ* Works."
25 Al-Azem, *Rule-Formulation*, 102 ff., 126 ff. and passim.
26 Ibn Abī al-Damm, *Adab al-Qaḍāʾ*, I, 286-87.

which is spent under the guidance and direction of another *qāḍī*, trained in the same exact fields of legal knowledge as every other.

The *qāḍī* was not merely a skilled technician of the law, an expert in managing disputes and settling conflicts. The *qāḍī* was also the site of subjective formation. He is formed into a *ʿālim* first and only then into a *qāḍī*. His subjective genealogy is embedded in psychological, cultural, spiritual, and intellectual training, all of which are clothed and permeated by what we call legal technique, but a technique that acquired a psychosocial depth anchored in spiritual, ethical, and even ascetic technologies of self-cultivation.[27]

The *qāḍī* was supposed to be steeped in *adab*, which we have seen in chapter 1 to be a complex of behavioral training that crosses over and brings together various life techniques. The spectrum of such training is wide, and so he must, by necessity, condition himself to some extent, leaving the balance as optional (or, in the language of the learned, "recommended").[28] Nonetheless, the expectations in terms of *askesis* were substantial. "The *qāḍī* is among those who stand most under duty to acquire the *ādāb* (pl. of *adab*) of God, and to demand of his self to heed His judgments."[29] Fear of God and conscientious engagement in adjudication are indispensable for training the self,[30] as is the constant admonishment of it. "When the litigants stand before him in his court, he should keenly remember that on the Day of Judgment, he will stand next to them before God, the Most Magnificent Judge of all, who will judge amongst them. On that Day, no excuse can save the oppressors (*ẓālimūn*), who will be damned and assigned the worst of abodes."[31]

From the first stages of Qur'ānic and general education, to the cultivation of higher learning and jurisprudential training, to the acquisition of ascetic values through embodiment and habituation, the *qāḍī*'s pervasively acculturating environment is nothing short of a habitus. It is where theory, high learning, ethics, *askesis*, and engagement with the messy realia of life come together. The

27 On the ethical technologies of the self as integral to the credentials for holding office, see *SAQ*, X, 273-76, 286-89, 295-97.

28 Ibn Abī al-Damm, *Adab al-Qaḍā'*, I, 317: "*Wa-yanbaghī lil-qāḍī an yata'addaba fī qaḍā'ihi bi-ādābin sharʿiyyatin yastaḥiqqu ʿalayhi baʿḍuhā wa-baʿḍuhā yustaḥabbu la-hu al-ta'adduba bi-hā.*"

29 Ibn Abī al-Damm, *Adab al-Qaḍā'*, I, 317: "*Min aḥaqqi al-nāsi bil-ta'addubi bi-ādābi Allāhi, wa-muṭālabati al-nafsi bi-aḥkāmihi.*" No wonder then that a genre of *adab al-qāḍī* had emerged early on, stipulating the norms which regulate this judicial office.

30 *SAQ*, X, 288, 297.

31 Ibn Abī al-Damm, *Adab al-Qaḍā'*, I, 317. See also Ghuzzī, *Adab al-Qaḍā'*, 93-94.

qāḍī, in sum, was the child of the Sharīʿa, in its divine and worldly pedigree. Nothing in his education and apprenticeship was "secular" and nothing to do with his training and substantive legal knowledge originated in the sultanic executive.

Now, once a scholar attains these qualifications and credentials, he is eligible to be appointed as a *qāḍī*. Māwardī writes that there are only two possible appointing agencies, the first of which is obviously the caliph himself, because the office and function of *qāḍī*ship is "integral to his mandate" (*li-dukhūlihā fī ʿumūmi wilāyatihi*). As the head of Islamic polity, he is the ultimate source of appointment, which explains that "he cannot wait to make the appointment until he is requested to do so, but must make it instantaneously."[32] This statement is intended to draw a distinction between two types of duty that must be fulfilled by the functionary or officer in charge: one type must be carried out irrespective of whether someone requested the performance of a duty or an appointment to an office, while the other would be set in motion only after a request was made, as in the case of rendering a legal opinion (*fatwā*). The general Islamic ethos demands that a *muftī* not rush to solve problems or address questions that no one asked.[33] The performance of the duty of *iftā'* therefore hinges on an initiator, one who is indispensable for setting it in motion. But not so the caliphal appointment. Whenever a judge's tenure expires, the caliph must appoint a replacement immediately, whether the population of the locale in which the vacancy happened requested it or not.

The appointing agent, whether a caliph, sultan or a higher *qāḍī*, must have firsthand knowledge of the appointee's credentials. If he does not, then he must find a way to gain this knowledge. He must inquire about the matter among those who know the candidate, such as his colleagues or the community of jurists that know his credentials and work. If a good number of colleagues and associates recommend him, then the imam should accept their attestation and need not examine him directly. But if only two trustworthy people attest to his credentials, then he must interrogate and test him with regard to every essential requirement, beginning with the quality of just character.[34] As for his legal knowledge, the appointing agent must convene an assembly

32 Māwardī, *Adab al-Qāḍī*, I, 137; Shīrāzī, *Muhadhdhab*, V, 473.

33 Hallaq, *Authority*, 179. The partial exception to this generalization is a senior and distinguished *muftī* who, often independently of any request, issues a *fatwā* or writes a *risāla* regarding matters or problems that have wide public interest or significance, usually described as "*mā taʿummu bi-hi al-balwā*."

34 For an actual case of "testing," see *SAQ*, X, 273 and n. 88, above.

of senior Sharīʿa scholars who will, in his presence, debate difficult points of law with the candidate. Should he prove himself as a fully credentialed *qāḍī*, and provided that his faculties of hearing and vision are sound, the candidate is expected to assume office as decreed.[35]

The duty of the imam to appoint judges to the polity's various regions is both sweeping and categorical, to such an extent that if a town or village's population appointed its own *qāḍī* out of need, the appointment would be deemed null and void.[36] While the caliphal duty to appoint is mandatory, it is not an individual duty (*farḍ ʿayn*) upon legal scholars to serve in that function.[37] In this respect, the Islamic tradition divides duty and obligation into two types, insofar as the subject possesses full legal capacity. The first is one whose performance is incumbent upon every individual, such as prayer and payment of alms-tax. The second is a collective or general duty whose discharge by an individual or individuals will absolve the others of the obligation. Examples of this are helping the poor and the oppressed in addition to the rights delineated by operation of the law, as well as fulfilling the mandate of *qāḍī*ship. If a number of *qāḍī*s discharge this mandate, then the burden of obligation is waived for the others, who are otherwise qualified to serve in that capacity.[38] However, if only one qualified jurist is available in a locale, then the duty becomes individual (*ʿayn*), namely, it becomes incumbent upon him to serve if he is called upon. Otherwise, if there is more than one candidate, the jurists disagree on whether an imam can compel a jurist to serve as *qāḍī*.[39] Yet, he is not under the obligation to seek the office since the duty falls upon the appointing power (*muwallī*) to search for a candidate who will fill the vacancy. In fact, many if not most jurists found the quest for the office for oneself to be ethically dubious.[40]

The imam must be specific in his decree of appointment. The jurisdictional district, city, or locale to which an appointment is made must be closely defined, and so too competence to adjudicate in certain neighborhoods rather than others.[41] The outskirts of a town or city must be explicitly excluded or included. The decree would be deemed null and void should it not be so specific, unless it is customary in certain regions to include outskirts and environs under the

35 Ibn Abī al-Damm, *Adab al-Qaḍāʾ*, I, 297-98.
36 Māwardī, *Adab al-Qāḍī*, I, 140.
37 Ibn Abī al-Damm, *Adab al-Qaḍāʾ*, I, 290.
38 Māwardī, *Adab al-Qāḍī*, I, 142.
39 Māwardī, *Adab al-Qāḍī*, I, 145.
40 Māwardī, *Adab al-Qāḍī*, I, 145.
41 Shīrāzī, *Muhadhdhab*,V, 474.

name of the city.[42] The decree must also stipulate jurisdictional competence in regard to legal subjects, such as Sunnis, a particular group, or an ethnic neighborhood, and must specify the days of the week on which the *qāḍī* can hold court. An imam can, however, appoint more than one *qāḍī*, with general powers, to one and the same locale, although a few jurists deemed this impermissible. In avoiding confusion or conflict in identifying jurisdictional boundaries between courts, the leading principle here is that the plaintiff decides the venue.[43]

A general caliphal appointment that is predicated on a condition is deemed null and void, or at the least the condition would be quashed as invalid.[44] A decree of general appointment must include all aspects and locales of jurisdiction and cannot and must not be predicated on any conditions. A *qāḍī* cannot, for example, be appointed *in toto* with the added condition that he "adjudicate cases filed in mosque such-and-such," for "the caliph does not possess powers to restrict the *qāḍī* to sit in certain places."[45] The principle applying here is one that applies to the entire range of relationships between caliph and *qāḍī*: namely, that within the wider, even widest, limits of caliphal appointment, the *qāḍī* has full autonomy, and any discretionary caliphal intrusion is regarded as invalid. If, say, the appointment to a city is general, then the *qāḍī* has full powers to administer justice within that city, without further specifications or restrictions. If the appointment made is to adjudicate only cases of personal status in a neighborhood, then all other areas of the law are excluded, while everything that lies within the personal status sphere becomes the jurisdictional dominion of the *qāḍī*.

A *qāḍī* may also be appointed by another, superior *qāḍī*. The polity's Chief Justice (*Qāḍī al-Quḍāt*) – usually headquartered in the capital – may appoint a provincial or regional *qāḍī* who in turn appoints a presiding judge, often called *nā'ib*. The logic of this hierarchy is a matter of practicality and feasibility of administering justice, partly because *qāḍī*s may be appointed to adjudicate cases only in certain areas of the law to the exclusion of others, such as personal status or penal law. The duty of a provincial *qāḍī* to immediately appoint a *nā'ib* is entirely his own responsibility if the province is geographically distant from the caliphal capital. If it is not, then this duty devolves simultaneously upon both the provincial *qāḍī* and the caliph, and whoever makes the appointment

42 Māwardī, *Adab al-Qāḍī*, I, 154-55.
43 Māwardī, *Adab al-Qāḍī*, I, 158.
44 *Al-Mawsūʿa al-Fiqhiyya*, XXXIII, 300 ff.
45 Māwardī, *Adab al-Qāḍī*, I, 159.

first is said to discharge this burden on his own behalf and absolve the other of it as well.[46]

Although the act of appointment would endow the appointee with the same rights, duties, and jurisdictional powers – irrespective of the appointment's source – the dismissal of the *qāḍī* hinges on who appointed him. The imam has the power to dismiss any *qāḍī*, whether he appointed him or not, since his office constitutes the ultimate authority and power over appointment. And that which possesses the power to appoint also possesses the power to dismiss. However, neither the Chief *Qāḍī* nor any provincial judge can dismiss his own *nā'ib* if it was the imam who appointed him. The Chief *Qāḍī* may do so only if he himself was the appointing power.[47]

The power of dismissal seems to have been absolute.[48] A caliph or sultan could discharge a *qāḍī* from office at will, even if the dismissal was unjustified – although a few jurists appear to have objected to this.[49] The general position of jurists in this regard was that the power of dismissal stemmed from the nature of the contract of appointment between the caliph and *qāḍī*. In the Sharīʿa, contracts are divisible, inter alia, into binding (*lāzim*) and non-binding (*jā'iz*). In binding contracts, a party possesses no right to rescind the contract without the approval of the other party or parties, requiring *iqāla*, a mutual agreement to void the contract. Neither the death of the parties nor their *post eventum* insanity can be cause for annulment. Contracts of sale and hire belong to this type. Partnership, loan, and agency (*wakāla*) belong to the *jā'iz* type, a contract that can be annulled unilaterally.[50] As a legal category and type, agency is generally the contractual model for the juridico-political relationship between caliph and *qāḍī*.[51] Which is to say that both the *qāḍī* and the sultan can withdraw from the contract at will, the sultan dismissing the Qāḍī or the *qāḍī* resigning.

The caliph's powers to dismiss are in no way matched by his legal power. There is a consensus (*ijmāʿ*) that the caliph and the *qāḍī* need not belong to

46 Māwardī, *Adab al-Qāḍī*, I, 138.

47 On dismissing judges, see Māwardī, *Adab al-Qāḍī*, I, 138-42.

48 Ibn Abī al-Damm reports (*Adab al-Qaḍā'*, I, 303) that al-Qaffāl al-Shāshī (d. 365/976) held an opinion that imposed limits on the caliph's powers of dismissal, but the majority of jurists seems to have been reluctant to place such constraints upon the ruler.

49 Ibn Abī al-Damm, *Adab al-Qaḍā'*, I, 302-3. See also previous note.

50 See Hallaq, *Sharīʿa*, 245.

51 Ibn Abī al-Damm, *Adab al-Qaḍā'*, I, 301. See also the extensive argument on the basis of *wakāla* made by Ibn Taymiyya in *ITSS*, 15: "*Fa'inna al-khalqa ʿibādu Allāhi wal-wulātu nuwwābu Allāhi ʿalā ʿibādihi, wa-hum wukalā'u al-ʿibādi ʿalā nufūsihim, bi-manzilatī aḥadi al-sharīkayni maʿa al-ākhari, fa-fīhim maʿnā al-wilāyati wal-wakālati.*"

the same *madhhab*, each holding the legal doctrine he chooses. Even if the imam has attained the rank of absolute *ijtihād, he has no power whatever to impose his view on others*, including the *qāḍīs*.[52] This is a cardinal doctrine of monumental constitutional importance, one that was subject to consensus.[53] A caliph's *madhhab* has no impact whatever on what specific legal doctrine a *qāḍī* chooses to apply in his court, as long as he remains within the terms of appointment.

An imam may validly appoint a *qāḍī* from any *madhhab* other than his and has no right or legitimate power to dictate to the appointed *qāḍī* the doctrine on the basis of which he is to decide cases. Ibn Abī al-Damm writes that if a Shāfiʿī imam orders a Ḥanafī *qāḍī* to adjudicate on the basis of Shāfiʿī's *madhhab*, the *qāḍī* may rule according to what the Shāfiʿīs and Ḥanafīs agree on, but he is entitled to suspend judgment if they disagree on the case at hand. This is justified on the grounds (1) that his *madhhab* is not Shāfiʿī, and so he is under no obligation to adhere to other schools' doctrines, and (2) that he is not, in the first place, mandated by the caliph to rule according to his own (Ḥanafī) *madhhab*.[54] But, as Māwardī argued, if the *qāḍī*'s own *ijtihād* had led him to a judgment that happened to be identical to the doctrine of a school other than his own, then he was entitled to adjudicate the case in accordance with it.[55]

Some jurists begged to differ, however, arguing that such autonomy risks being suspicious, since deviating from the *madhhab* could expose the judge to the charge of manipulating the legal doctrine to accomplish ulterior interests or goals (*li-taṭarruqi al-tuhmati ilayhi*).[56] But the point of arrogating total autonomy to the *qāḍī* over the law is clear. It is brought to a climax in a *locus classicus*, where the powerful Companion ʿUmar I, the second caliph of Islam, used to consult the distinguished *qāḍī* Abū Mūsā al-Ashʿarī (d. ca. 44/665) on various matters of law in the business

52 Shīrāzī, *Muhadhdhab*, V, 474; Ibn Abī al-Damm, *Adab al-Qaḍā'*, I, 304: "*Ajmaʿa al-ʿulamāʾu ʿalā annahu lā yushtaraṭu tawāfuquhumā fil-madhhabi bal in kānā mujtahidayni ʿalā al-iṭlāqi fal-qāḍī yaḥkumu bi-ijtihādihi fil-mujtahadāti sawāʾu wāfaqa ijtihāduhu ijtihādi al-imāmi aw lā.*" It should be emphasized that later works ceased to discuss the question of whether the caliph can force a *qāḍī* to apply a *madhhab*-doctrine of the caliph's choosing (including one of a *mujtahid* belonging to a school other than the *qāḍī*'s), for it was taken for granted – probably by the fifth/eleventh century – that the caliph enjoys no such powers. See, e.g., Shaʿrānī, *al-Mīzān al-Kubrā*, II, 258–59.

53 See previous note: "*Ajmaʿa al-ulamāʾu....*"

54 Ibn Abī al-Damm, *Adab al-Qaḍā'*, I, 304.

55 Cited in Ibn Abī al-Damm, *Adab al-Qaḍā'*, I, 305.

56 Ibn Abī al-Damm, *Adab al-Qaḍā'*, I, 305.

of running the budding empire. But Abū Mūsā did the same, consulting at times with the caliph. "When ʿUmar's legal opinion agreed with Abū Mūsā's, he [Abū Mūsā] would apply it [in his court of law]. When it differed, he would adjudicate [the case] according to his own legal opinion, for he deems his own opinion correct, whereas he does not deem the opinion of the other(s) so correct. He adjudicates according to his own sense, not according to that of another."[57]

While the caliph can specify the legal school as the applicable doctrine in a *qāḍī*'s court, he cannot predicate his appointment on conditions of the *qāḍī*'s compliance to specific laws or rules that the caliph dictates. The jurists tended to institute the doctrine of non-interference through legal jargon but the effect of all their discourse goes to the protection of judicial autonomy. Any condition (*sharṭ*) of compliance to a specific law or rule or principle that may be attached to the decree of appointment would be rendered null and void, while leaving the appointment decree intact all the same.[58]

Yet, to say that the imam can always dismiss a *qāḍī* is not to suggest that dismissal is an arbitrary practice. The imam *must* in fact dismiss the *qāḍī*s he appoints after a short term, usually ranging from one to three years. Abū Ḥanīfa, for instance, railed against appointing a *qāḍī* for more than one year at a time, his reasoning being that a lengthy preoccupation with administering justice may cause the jurist to neglect the cultivation of his Sharʿī learning.[59] This is by now unsurprising, showing the epistemoral and pedagogical loyalties of the judiciary to the Sharīʿa. The caliph must dismiss a *qāḍī* not only when he detects a deterioration in the latter's intellectual capacities. He must dismiss all judges out of caution. "The sultan must tell the judge: 'I did not dismiss you for any fault you have, but I worry that you may forget your *ʿilm*. Go cultivate *ʿilm* and then return to us so that we appoint you again.'"[60] Another, more pragmatic, rationale that seems to have emerged later in the Muslim tradition is that such relatively short appointments make it more

57 Ibn Māza, *Sharḥ Adab al-Qāḍī*, I, 195. It is worth noting that this judicial independence was also prophetically endorsed. One of the most popular narratives in this regard (one that became normative irrespective of whether it was or was not "authentic") speaks of the Prophet asking Muʿādh b. Jabal about the modalities of reasoning he would employ as the judge of Yemen. When Muʿādh replied that he would exercise his own *ijtihād* if he found the Qur'ān and the Prophetic Sunna to be silent, the Prophet is said to have expressed his utmost pleasure. See Ibn Abī al-Damm, *Adab al-Qaḍā'*, I, 255-56.

58 Ibn Abī al-Damm, *Adab al-Qaḍā'*, I, 304-6. This was not entirely the case with the Ḥanafī school.

59 Surūjī, *Adab al-Qaḍā'*, 102.

60 Surūjī, *Adab al-Qaḍā'*, 102.

difficult for *qāḍī*s to establish local personal networks and continuous connections of interest and loyalty, all of which have the potential to contribute to corruption.[61]

As I have argued over the decades, the Sharīʿa as well as its courts were in tune with the social realia in which they operated. This is evidenced in the general policy of allocating short tenures for judges, as the foregoing paragraphs explained. But it is also evidenced in the juristic recognition that reality is not idealism and that a just and good ruler is not to be always had.[62] At one point or another, *qāḍī*s will inevitably be appointed by oppressive and unjust sultans and so it is no surprise that the question of the legality of such an appointment was raised by political theory.

Ibn Māza states that "it is permissible [for the *qāḍī*] to be appointed by either a just or unjust sultan (*jā'ir*)."[63] The justification he gives for this position is historical precedent. Appointments of unjust rulers were valid, as happened in the case of the first Umayyad caliph Muʿāwiya who appointed a number of no lesser than the Prophet's Companions to the judiciary. In the Muslim political imagination, Muʿāwiya is the quintessentially wicked ruler, having victimized ʿAlī, a distinguished Companion and the fourth of the Rāshidūn caliphs, among others. Yet, the permissibility of accepting is predicated on a crucially important condition, one that is central for the Muslim political tradition at large. "It is permissible [for a *qāḍī*] to accept appointment from an unjust sultan provided that he judges by the True Law," that is, the law of the Sharīʿa. "If the *qāḍī* cannot do so, then he is not permitted to accept." This rejection has its own precedent as well. When the judge al-Ḥakam b. ʿAmr al-Ghafārī was asked by Muʿāwiya to serve as a judge, he wrote back saying that "The Book of God precedes the Commander of the Faithful Muʿāwiya."[64]

The very assumption of an unjust caliph or sultan appointing a *qāḍī* was not only a matter of addressing and regulating such situations in reality. The relevant facts in such situations were, for the political thinkers, legal facts that determined how political management is to be conducted. The question here concerns the relationship between law and politics, between political expediency and ethical-judicial considerations. It is also about division of political and juridical labor and functional specialization. Each task has its own purview

61 Hallaq, *Sharīʿa*, 216-221.

62 This being a fully recognized reality by Muslim jurists. See, e.g., *ADD*, 215-16.

63 Ibn Māza, *Sharḥ Adab al-Qāḍī*, I, 129 ff. *Jā'ir* is the active participle of *J.W.R.* On *jawr*, see ch. 2, n. 44.

64 Ibn Māza, *Sharḥ Adab al-Qāḍī*, I, 130-31.

which determines its functional duties, which is to say that these duties delimit its desiderata and goals and thus establish the criteria necessary for accomplishing them. This logic is brought to bear on the "question" of whether a caliph or a *qāḍī* who has committed a sin (usually sexual in nature) or an immoral act should be discharged from their duties. The answer given by jurists is that the *qāḍī* should, but not the emir, the reason for this being that *qāḍī*ship is "founded on justice" whereas the office of the ruler is "founded on coercion and power."[65] This is a decisive constitutional distinction; for the rights, duties, and consequences of violating the rules of the office ultimately depend on the *raison d'être* of the office, that purpose or set of purposes for which it came into existence. The core and kernel of the imamate is coercive power, the reason for its existence in the first place. The core and kernel of judgeship is the execution of justice. These two offices could lose all other functions but not their core. It then behooves us to remember this fundamental principle of functional separation, since it underlies much of political and constitutional practice and political and juristic thought.

II

The account I have given thus far derives from the genre of *adab al-qāḍī* or *adab al-qaḍā'*. The writings in this genre are strictly juristic, which is another way of saying that they are systematized accounts of the historical and contemporary practices in the *qāḍī*'s court and of the context of relations between the court and the institutions that surround it. These include, among other things, the vertical relationships between the court and the higher political offices, as well as horizontal relationships with various social and economic activities and constellations. But the genre also betrays an authoritative discourse that continually transforms factual and positive phenomena into normative ones, creating thereby a prescriptive narrative out of a descriptive one. I have called this perpetual process the "dialectical wheel."[66]

65 Surūjī, *Adab al-Qaḍā'*, 112: "*Li'anna mabnā al-qaḍā'i 'alā al-'adli, wal-imārati 'alā al-qahri wal-ghalaba.*"

66 On the prescriptive/descriptive nature of Islamic legal works, see Hallaq, "Model *Shurūṭ* Works;" Hallaq, "Considerations on the Function and Character of Sunnī Legal Theory." On the systematization of actual legal practice, see Hallaq, "From *Fatwā*s to *Furu*"; and Hallaq, *Authority*, 121-65.

The advantage of this genre lies in the fact that it conveys a representation of the average practice that passed the authorization of the juridical lens. For example, in the discussion of whether a caliph or a *qāḍī* who has committed morally repugnant acts should be discharged from their duties, there lies the assumption that bad and unjust rulers are a real possibility, no less than the possibility of bad and unjust *qāḍīs*. There is no idealization here. The genre takes those possibilities for granted and can thereby be said to confront reality head-on. Yet, what *adab al-qāḍī* discourse attempts to accomplish here is to bring forth the principles on which this reality should be addressed. Juridical reality here becomes a set of political and legal facts that become integral to associated political and legal principles that constitute the basis for further thinking and action.

The disadvantage, on the other hand, is that the *adab al-qāḍī* genre does not tell us enough about concrete actual practice, since practice in the discursive elaborations of this genre is, by the nature of it, rendered schematized. "Actual practice" means at least two things here: It could mean a micro-account of concrete events, such as particular occurrences and disputes in a court of law, the misconduct of a judge or his scribe, the interference of a governor in a court litigation, and the like. Assuming that we have confidence in the sufficiency and strength of evidence with regard to a micro case-study, we would remain unsure how typical the case is and thus how representative. Orientalism has tended to focus on the exception, often making it the spokesman of the rule. The problem that persists in the field of micro-history is this: If we knew what the macro-history of a phenomenon is, we would not need micro-history, and since we by definition do not know what that macro-history looks like, it is impossible to give an adequate account of that macro-history without sufficient case-studies of micro-history – sufficient, that is, to exclude the possibility that the series of micro-historical accounts that have been obtained is cohesive enough as to make a valid generalization. Equally important, such a series cannot gain credibility unless it also shows that the cases under its purview do not present exceptions that in fact prove the rule.

This last proviso makes for a colossal difficulty for historians in light of the fact that the Muslim sources focused on the exception and the unusual. When things ran the average and ordinary course, there was no language to note and describe the quotidian routine and the "business-as-usual." In fact, that is exactly what the historical sources never cared to do, for *ta'rīkh* (history) consists of *ḥawādith* (occurrences, happenings). The historians of general *ta'rīkh* works (universal, century-type, or city-type) noted the exceptions of the lows and the highs, of the unusually bad and the unusually good. There was very little else that could tell about how things were ordinarily because the ordinary was taken for granted. Reporting on the ordinary would consume countless volumes for every day of Islamic history. Yet, the ordinary was the habitus, those structured ways of living life that were taken for granted – they were doxastic and often unremarkable. Often unconscious and themselves being natural and unquestionable, those ways of life were by definition commonplace and thus escaped description and conscious elaboration.[67]

Whereas the *adab al-qāḍī* works were systematizing and legally prescriptive, the *ʿuhūd/taqālīd/tafāwīḍ*[68] were factual and positive all at once. These are decrees of appointment that issue from a high office. Normally, the standard and archetypal *ʿahd* or *tafwīḍ* was composed and issued by the caliph's or sultan's *Dīwān al-Inshā'*, the Royal Office of Writing Appointments.[69] The scribes in this Office were highly trained secretaries in the art of composition (*inshā'*) with rounded knowledge of many subjects, including literature, writing and eloquence, calligraphy, geography, country and regional names, titles and forms of address, calendar and timekeeping, history in general and caliphal history in particular, and political theory and literature treating of *siyāsa sharʿiyya*.[70] It is said to be the first *dīwān* created in Islam, the Prophet having himself employed scribes who composed letters addressed to various chiefs, rulers, and emperors.[71] As such, it became a Sharʿī institution before any other *dīwān*, and had a continuously active life in West Asia until the Ottomans.[72]

---

67 On habitus, see Introduction, sec. II, ch. 1, 2, and 10 (sec. IV).

68 ʿUmarī (*Taʿrīf*, 119) asserts that most appointments for ordinary *qāḍī*s are termed *tafwīḍ*, but in the case of some *qāḍī al-quḍāt*s the appointment decree is called *taqlīd*. Qalqashandī uses the term "*ʿahd/ʿuhūd*" for the decrees of appointment he lists for *qāḍī al-quḍāt*s. See *SAQ*, X, 273.

69 See n. 72, below, and, generally, Heck, *Construction*.

70 *SAQ*, I, 7-13; III, 6.

71 SAQ, I, 125.

72 In the context of the importance of high Arabic to the practices of this *dīwān*, Qalqashandī (*SAQ*, 127-28) observes that the Mongols and their khanates changed the *dīwān*'s language into their native tongue and/or Persian. For a history of this *dīwān* in Syro-Egypt, see *SAQ*, 124-38. It is worth noting that *dīwān al-inshā'* stood above other *dīwān*s in rank, as it was charged with all the communiqués, account registration, and documentation related to the rest of the *dīwān*s. *SAQ*, I, 165-74, gives a "personnel history" of the institution, including the detailed tasks each official in this *dīwān* was responsible for. In the "old days," the *dīwān* was run by seven employees, the first of whom was the head of the *dīwān* and the confidante of the ruler. He was tasked with supervising the most important and sensitive

One of the most monumental works in this genre is Qalqashandī's *Ṣubḥ al-A ʿshā*, a colossal work consisting of prescriptions and instructions concerning the writing of royal proclamations, regal communiqués, and decrees of administrative appointments, among much else. Insofar as we are concerned in this work, its value stems from the fact that it not only contains model formularies for the reference and use of scribes of the royal court but *also describes the effective operationalization of the politico-legal discursive tradition*, as manifested in the *fiqh* works and the treatises we have been discussing (including Māwardī's).[73] More importantly, the jurisdictional boundaries

epistles, decrees of appointment, and letters. The second is his assistant who does much of the labor for his superior, the head of the *dīwān*, to approve. The next two scribes were responsible for the less important decrees and letters. The fifth employee was the copyist who had to be skilled in calligraphy and elegant writing. The sixth, whose credentials were demanding, was the editor who reviewed the documents and made suggestions for corrections. Interestingly, the seventh was the librarian who classified all incoming and (copies of) outgoing documents in their proper places and, furthermore, created catalogues which enabled the employees to locate them quickly when needed in the future (*fa-yakūnu istikhrājuhā min hādhihi al-tadhākiri aysara min al-tanqībi ʿanhā wal-tanqīri ʿanhā min al-aḍābīr*).This official was also responsible for creating registers of the various administrative ranks in the sultanate and of rulers of other domains, including the customary languages with which they are addressed. He is also charged with compiling a separate register of incoming communications in other languages. In addition to these seven functions/officials, there are two others not related to writing and documentation. These are (1) the "librarian" who registers the name of borrowers when they need older documents and who ensures the order and safety of the documents; and (2) the chamberlain (*ḥājib*) who guards the *dīwān*. Later on, under the Mamlūks, when administration became more complex, many more employees were retained to accomplish these tasks, but the functions *qua* functions appear to have remained the same.

73 In "Centrality of Sharīʿah," 39, Khaled Abou El Fadl argues the following:
"Although the idea of government limited by law is well-supported in the Islamic tradition, this does not necessarily amount to a principle of limited government or the rule of law. In a system where law is supreme or there is rule by law, the government is expected to be bound by particular substantive laws. However, in a system where there is rule of law, the government is not only bound by particular positive rules but by the process and institution of law. Arguably, this distinction could be valid because classical [Muslim] jurists did not advocate the notion of the supremacy of the rule of law, but did advocate the supremacy of legal rules. One could argue that the Islamic tradition did affirm the notion of rule by law or government limited by laws but it did not affirm the concept of rule of law. In other words, in their discourses, Muslim jurists were not articulating the idea that there is a process that guards core legal values and that this process is binding upon the government. Rather, they were arguing that the positive commandments of Sharīʿah, such as the punishment for adultery or the drinking of alcohol, ought to be respected and enforced by the government."

While I find the distinction between rule of law and rule by law useful, rule by law does not capture all that Islamic governance was. It is my argument, at least in this chapter, that the politico-legal *discursive tradition* in Islam encompassed the rule of law as well.

defined by these decrees in fact describe *the actual constitutional divisions between and among offices, rendering this genre central for constitutional studies.*[74] The texts of the decrees range from the highest appointments of caliphs and sultans to those of offices in the main locales of the empire's regions, usually cities. They are addressed to military generals of all major ranks, governors, chief *qāḍīs*, chief *muḥtasibs*, chief public finance secretaries, chief *madrasa* professors, chiefs of main professional guilds (especially general physicians, ophthalmologists, and surgeons) and religious leaders of the main denominations, such as Jacobite and Melkite patriarchs and Jewish rabbinic leaders.

Three further points must be noted about this work. The first is the specific and notable reference to Māwardī's work, especially to his *al-Aḥkām al-Sulṭāniyya.*[75] For Qalqashandī and for the entire genre of *dīwān al-inshā'*

Abou El Fadl is right to say that Islamic government was bound by "particular positive rules" as well as "by the process and institution of law." The analysis of Qalqashandī's work, entirely neglected in modern scholarship as a constitutional index, is intended precisely to show this bindingness. However, expecting "classical [Muslim] jurists" to "advocate the notion of the supremacy of the rule of law" – which Abou El Fadl denies they did – is a Eurocentric position that demands of the Other to conform not only to the substance of one's way of doing things but also to the linguistic form that expresses it. To say that the Islamic system did not possess a system of rule of law because Muslim jurists did not advocate it (i.e., in a language that we moderns can understand, and understand on our own terms) is, to say the least, to navigate at the surface of phenomena. And it is entirely unwarranted to claim that Muslim jurists did not "articulate" the "idea that there is a process that guards core legal values and that this process is binding upon the government." If anything, the present work demonstrates that the juridico-political habitus of Islam was committed to "core legal values" as well as to the "processes" that guard them. Māwardī's constitutional delimitations and carving of boundaries between and among various offices and powers, and Qalqashandī's institutional and practical-administrative mirroring of these divisions are alone persuasive arguments against such claims. But as we will see in the later chapters of the book, the practice on the ground until the later Ottomans was in step with these descriptive-prescriptive textual traditions. On what I have characterized elsewhere as the "dialectical wheel" – i.e., a method of interpreting the relationship between legal practice and its textual expression, see Hallaq, "Model *Shurūṭ* Works."

74 The genre of *rusūm* and *'uhūd* was, like the works of *fiqh* in law, indicative of a normatively operational system of political organization, and connoted a discursive tradition in this domain. See Ṣābī, *Rusūm Dār al-Khilāfa*, 111 ff., especially 113-21. See also 'Umarī, *al-Ta'rīf bil-Muṣṭalaḥ al-Sharīf.*

75 *SAQ*, II, 3, 5 ff.; III, 6. See the discussion of Māwardī's works in ch. 1 and 2. An index of the importance of Māwardī's work in later periods, see Qarāfī (d. 684/1285), al-*Dhakhīra*, vol. 10; and Ibn Farḥūn's *Tabṣirat al-Ḥukkām*, although he runs against Māwardī on multiple issues (still telling of Māwārdī's remarkable influence).

(and the later sub-genre *al-siyāsa al-sharʿiyya*),[76] Māwardī's work is both foundational and indispensable.[77]

The second point is that the model formularies were often real historical decrees of appointment, conveyed verbatim, with names of appointees and officials appointed.[78] And even when they were not, they more often were abstracted and edited versions of real decrees, a common practice in the administrative and legal fields.[79] As we will see, these decrees do not appoint in general terms but rather contain explicit and specific assignments and services to be rendered by the official appointed. In the manner they are cast, they lend themselves to a structural analysis of historical content, but also of what they include and, by implication, exclude. In other words, they do not only tell us about the nature and functions of the assigned office, but also delineate the lines of separation between the various offices. In this sense, they tacitly represent themselves as constitutional documents. Yet, they are also constitutional documents in a subjective sense, as we will see.

The third is that these works and the "model" documentary evidence they include represent a continuing and continuous tradition of political administration and management, dating back to the second/eighth century,[80] if not earlier, and consistently maintained as a stable repository of such representation. While adaptable and extraordinarily sensitive to regional and diachronic variations, these repositories can readily be said to have functioned as stabilizers of political rule and management. Just as the multiple dynasties across the centuries and regions took the Sharīʿa to be the law of the land, they also assumed the *Dīwān al-Inshā'* and its functioning to be the gold standard of governmental

76 The entire chapter on *siyāsa sharʿiyya* in Ṭūghān Shaykh al-Muḥammadī's *al-Muqaddima al-Sulṭāniyya* (fols. 150B-166A) is a verbatim citation of chapter 19 of Māwardī's *AS* (*Fī Aḥkām al-Jarā'im*, 322-37).

77 Qalqashandī in fact makes knowledge of the Sharīʿa one of the conditions for qualified *dīwān* scribes who should know which rules and precepts apply to which governmental office. In his *AS*, he says, Māwardī has offered "copious materials regarding these rules" (*mā fī-hi maqnaʿun min dhalik*). "In this book," Qalqashandī continues, "I will give a summary of each of [Māwardī's] chapters so that the scribe does not need to refer to any other book." This last statement, I infer, means that there were other, likely less authoritative, works resembling Māwardī's *AS* available to these scribes. *SAQ*, II, 5.

78 On the relationship between legal model formularies (and *fatwā*s) and social and economic realities, see Hallaq, "Model *Shurūṭ* Works;" Hallaq, "From *Fatwā*s to *Furū*ʿ;" Hallaq, *Authority*, 121-65.

79 For a similar "editorial" approach to *fatwā*s abstracted through *tajrīd*, *tanqīḥ*, and *talkīṣ*, see Hallaq, "From *Fatwā*s to *Furū*ʿ," 44-48.

80 See, for instance, caliph al-Manṣūr's appointment of the famous *qāḍī*, ʿUbayd Allāh b. al-Ḥasan al-ʿAnbarī in 156/773 in Wakīʿ, *Akhbār al-Quḍāt*, II, 91.

administration and royal documentation.[81] It is neither a coincidence nor an insignificant fact that the operations of the *dīwāns* and the conduct of their employees were supervised and audited by the *maẓālim* court.[82]

This feature of institutional continuity through the secretarial-administrative *dīwān* complex seems to be behind Niccolò Machiavelli's curious[83] remark that the "state of the Soldan" did not resemble European Princedoms in that "it can neither be classed as new, nor as hereditary. For the sons of a Soldan who die do not succeed to the kingdom as his heirs, but he who is elected to the post by those who have authority to make such elections. And this being the ancient and established order of things, the Princedom cannot be accounted new.... For although the Prince is new, the *institutions of the State are old* and are so contrived that the elected Prince is accepted as though he were an hereditary Sovereign."[84]

This is also borne out in Ibn Khaldūn's *Muqaddima*, where he speaks of the differences and similarities between any two succeeding *dawlas*. Each incoming *dawla*, he says, is somewhat different and somewhat similar to the *dawla* it had supplanted,[85] "somewhat" because the former adopts some of the practices and "customs" (*ʿawāʾid*) of the latter and yet it brings forth new ways of its own. Obviously, Ibn Khaldūn cannot mean that the incoming dynasty would borrow the tribal customs that are peculiar to each tribal federation seeking executive power, since these were obviously deep traditions entrenched in each tribal formation across generations. These represented the differences between one *dawla* and another. The similarities, on the other hand, were the administrative practices and ways of rule that were institutionally installed across dynasties, even from the time of the early caliphate. It was these practices that provided a qualitative institutional continuity of political administration.

The royal decrees appointing Chief Judges provide us with detailed information about the constitution of the judiciary and its place in the overall system

81 SAQ, I, 135 ff.
82 *AS*, 137.
83 On being a curious remark, see next note.
84 Machiavelli, *Prince*, 70-71 (emphasis mine). This particular passage in the work seems out of place in, and irrelevant to the theme of chapter XIX, titled "That a Prince Should Seek to Escape Contempt and Hatred" (62). It must have struck Machiavelli so much that he seems to have felt that it should be mentioned somewhere in his work.
85 Ibn Khaldūn, *Muqaddima*, 22-23: "*Wa-ahlu al-mulki wal-sulṭāni idhā istawlū ʿalā al-dawlati wal-amri, fa-lā budda wa-an yafzaʿū ilā ʿawāʾidi man qablihim, wa-yaʾkhudhū al-kathīra min-hā wa-lā yaghfalū ʿawāʾida jīlihim maʿ dhālika.... Faʾidhā jāʾat dawlatun ukhrā min baʿdihim wa-mazajat min ʿawāʾidim wa-ʿawāʾidihā khālafat ayḍan baʿḍa al-shayʾi.*" On the Saljūq dynasty's customary ways as a recognized category, see *SM*, 47.

of governance as well as about the communal and other functions of the *qāḍī*. They supply not only positive (in contradistinction to normative) data but also factual information,[86] especially about delineating the constitutional boundaries of the judiciary vs. sultanic and caliphal power.

The structure and content of the documents, if not the form as well, recall the claim that the *Dīwān al-Inshā'* and its conventional productions tell of an institutional continuity across the Islamic centuries. I will discuss one such *ʿahd* document in detail and compare it with others to illustrate similarities, but more often variations and differences. A comparison with the *Adab al-Qāḍī* "positive" narrative is also in order, with a view to probing the consistency of this narrative with the factual realities of the historical decrees.

The *ʿahd* document in question comes from the reign of the ʿAbbāsid caliph al-Mustarshid bil-Lāh (r. 512-29/1118-35). Its purpose is to appoint the distinguished jurist Abū al-Qāsim ʿAlī b. Ḥasan al-Zaynabī (d. 543/1148) to the rank of Chief Justice of the capital city, Baghdad, its environs and "all the regions [of the Empire], close or far, in the East and the West". This is the most significant appointment to the judiciary in the entire empire. The introduction to the main text of the document, including its style, was known as *barāʿat al-istihlāl*, in which the scribe detailed in an eloquent language the general characteristics of the appointee, including his credentials.[87] The *istihlāl* also offered the reasons behind the choice, which, in this case, included Zaynabī's "good ways," "sophistication of his creed," "popular commendation," and "praiseworthy work/accomplishments." What is remarkable in this instance is that when the candidate was highly accomplished and widely known to be so – as Zaynabī was – the appointing authority usually does not vet or examine him. But in this case, al-Mustarshid seems to have "tested" Zaynabī (*wajadahu ʿinda al-ikhtibār*), finding him to possess a solid intellect, strong religious foundations, trustworthiness, longstanding record of incorruptibility, fearfulness of God, lack of greed, and profuse erudition.[88]

This far-reaching and major appointment follows a longstanding tradition that is said to have been initiated by the Rāshidūn caliphs, in their practices of delegating (*tafwīḍ*) tasks, work, and functions to those who possess experience and especially those "servants of the reign" (*dawla*) who are eminently qualified

86 On the distinctions between positive, normative, and factual accounts, see ch. 1, sec. IV.
87 *SAQ*, IX, 276.
88 *SAQ*, X, 273: "*Wa-wajadahu ʿinda al-ikhtibāri wa-fī miḍmāri al-iʿtibāri rājiʿan ilā ʿaqlin raṣīnin, wa-dīnin matīnin, wa-ʿilmin tawwafara min-hu qismuhu....*"

to perform them.[89] With the invocation that "God may give the Commander of the Faithful success in his choice," the document proceeds to enumerate and outline, through discrete sections, the main tasks and functions of the appointment. The sections, twenty-one in number, are invariably opened with the expression *amarahu* ("He [the caliph] ordered him").

First, he ordered Zaynabī to "heed God." The term used here is *taqwā*,[90] deriving from the radical *W.Q.Y.*, which lends itself through derivation to the notion of "averting harm," that is, doing the right thing with the intention of avoiding God's punishment.[91] *Taqwā* brings happiness and well-being, and lack of it leads to misery. It is a "fortified citadel" against engaging in evil and injustice. What is taken for granted in this section are the technologies of the self that cultivate *taqwā*, but the absence speaks loudly for those who were involved in this communication, that is, the caliph, Zaynabī, the scribe who authored the text, as well as those who heard the text being read. The public reading of the text to the "people of the locales" to which the appointment was made was routine, and everyone understood what was involved in the cultivation of *taqwā*. The second section comes to reinforce the first, calling on Zaynabī to cultivate "God-fearing" attitudes (*khashyat Allāh*) as well.[92] It is curious that this "command" is not found in most other decrees of appointment,[93] but it is difficult to interpret the emphasis on *khashya* in the case of this particular appointee.

The third command is that Zaynabī should repeatedly and consistently recite the Qur'ān to himself, making it his guide, instructor, and final resort when passing judgments.[94] He will contemplate it to uncover its secrets, wisdom, and deterrents (*zawājir*). As we have seen in the previous chapters, the injunction to recite the Qur'ān repeatedly was integral to the formation of subjectivity, a technology of the self on its own. In this instance, the command comes from a superior to an inferior, in an attempt to create what we might call a Qur'ānic embodiment, but in the case of Ghazālī (as we saw in the previous chapter), the

89 *SAQ*, X, 274: "*Tafwīḍi al-umūri ilā akkifā'ihā wa-ahlihā, lā siyyamā awliyā'u dawlatihim.*"

90 *Taqwā* was deemed necessary for all "public" officers, beginning with the caliph and ending with junior judges and tax collectors. As Juwaynī put it incisively, if the testimony of a witness who is a *fāsiq* is deemed inadmissible in the most minor financial matters, how could we appoint a caliph who does not possess this quality? *Fāsiq*, an active form of *F.S.Q.*, is effectively the antonym of *taqwā*, as Juwaynī's language shows. See *GU*, 68.

91 Ibn Manẓūr, *Lisān al-'Arab*, XV, 469 ff.

92 *SAQ*, X, 274.

93 See, for example, *SAQ*, X, 288-89, 296.

94 *SAQ*, X, 275. See also p. 289, 296, where the same command is made, and roughly as the second or third in order.

same imperative was voiced by a jurist to a sultan. The force of the command does not therefore issue from rank, for the caliph is no more empowered to give it than a jurist. The force rather issues from the subject of the command itself, for the proposition of the Qur'ān's centrality and authoritativeness was integral to, if not creative of the habitus and its *doxa*. In other words, the force issues from the doxastic power of "commanding good and forbidding evil" (*al-amru bil-ma'rūfi wal-nahyi 'an al-munkar*).

The same imperative constitutes the theme of the fourth section: "to study the Prophetic Sunna" with a view to modeling himself according to the Prophet's example, in all his virtuous qualities (*makārim al-akhlāq*).[95] This self-cultivation, a form of piety and subject-formation, is inseparable from the practice of Ḥadīth-criticism which he should assiduously exercise. The activities of emulation and "academic" study of the Sunna thus make for one and the same practice, namely, *ta'abbud* (worship). The immediate practical goal here is of course the application of the spirit, if not letter, of the Sunna to his work as a *qāḍī*. Consistent with the theory of the law (*uṣūl al-fiqh*), the Qur'ān and Sunna constitute the two most important sources of understanding, including understanding what and how legal norms should be applied in a court of law.

In terms of the technologies of self-formation, the fourth command is a stone's throw from the next, namely, to hold the five daily prayers.[96] Again, this is neither a veritable nor an exclusive caliphal command but one that the habitus imposes as a normative practice. It comes to cap the preceding four commands whose telos is forming the pious, ethical subject. Yet, much of these religious works are not only forms of worship (*ta'abbud*) but also conducive to the cultivation of systematic legal learning that is presupposed in the business of adjudication.

The sixth command continues to reinforce this learning and legal erudition by making it a duty upon a judge to consult the senior jurists, especially on difficult and hard cases. The command to seek counsel (*mashūra*) sits well in this tradition, having had a long discursive history (that is, as an applied praxis which enshrines itself in articulated ideas derived from authoritative texts) that begins with the Prophet himself. The text of the *'ahd* explicitly speaks of God commanding the Prophet to seek counsel, "despite his noble and grand status."[97]

95 *SAQ*, X, 275-76, but also 297. This requirement is not found in some other decrees. See, e.g., X, 289.

96 *SAQ*, X, 276.

97 *SAQ*, X, 276-77.

The seventh command is for Zaynabī to choose a "wide space" to hold his court, to be just and accommodating, making the court welcoming and accessible to all litigants.[98] The language of the command bespeaks of the openness of the court, irrespective of the litigants' class, wealth, gender, or considerations of the like.

The eighth command goes to the central issue of which law to apply in the Chief Justice's courts: The sources of the law are the usual ones: the Qur'ān, the Sunna, "that which the predecessors have chosen," and the consensus of the *mujtahids*, the master-jurists.[99] If none is to be found, then he must reason his way through the case and reach a solution, either on his own (if he is a *mujtahid*) or through the help of the *mujtahid*-jurists. This help is not only integral to the requirement of seeking counsel (*mashūra*) stipulated in the sixth command but was also a common and widespread practice. Judges routinely consulted *muftīs*, who were the experts in legal reasoning, to help them decide on hard cases.[100]

The next two commands have to do with the mental state of the *qāḍī* when presiding over cases. He must be reasonably patient, focused, and alert to the devious ways of some litigants. He must not be distracted, sad, or upset when attending court.[101] These requirements or recommendations, integral to judicial culture, replicate the discourse of *fiqh* literature and the *adab al-qāḍī* works.[102] They are, in other words, constitutive of what *adab* was within the Sharʿī culture.[103]

The eleventh command focuses on *ḥudūd*, demanding the *qāḍī* exercise caution and adopt a steady pace, without undue rush or delay. He must examine witnesses and all evidence with great care and must not apply the penalties unless the evidence is overwhelming. The special care required here is due to the fact that the penalties of *ḥudūd* are severe, involving amputation of the limbs, lashing, and death.[104]

The twelfth command relates to character witnesses whose role in Sharīʿa litigation is central. Upon taking office he should vet them one by one, keeping

98 *SAQ*, X, 277: "*Fa-yūṣalu ilayhi kāffat al-khuṣūm.*" For the same command in other decrees, see X, 290, 297-98.
99 *SAQ*, X, 277-78. For the same command in other decrees, see X, 294-95.
100 Ibn Abī al-Damm, *Adab al-Qaḍā'*, I, 327; Ibn Māza, *Sharḥ Adab al-Qāḍī*, I, 193, 356-71; Hallaq, "From Fatwās to Furūʿ;" Heyd, "Some Aspects of the Ottoman Fetva."
101 *SAQ*, X, 278-79.
102 See, e.g., Ibn al-Qāṣṣ, *Adab al-Qāḍī*, 157 ff.
103 See the opening paragraphs of ch. 1.
104 Hallaq, *Sharīʿa*, 311-20.

those who meet the necessary qualifications and dismissing the rest. The qualifications include good conduct, respectable social background, piousness, intimate knowledge of the Qur'ān, Sharīʿa abidance, chastity, honesty, trustworthiness, and alertness, among other things.

The next sentence in the text reveals the realism and pragmatism of the *ʿahd*, as well as the judicial reality on the ground. At this point, the text states that if these conditions are not to be met by anyone available, then a religious and pious person who is scrupulous and incorruptible will do.[105] Obviously, the justice and fair-dealing of the court seriously depended on the proper work of these witnesses, to such a degree that exercising the utmost effort in selecting them was tantamount to the rewards the *mujtahid* would reap in the Hereafter. The suggestion was that corrupt witnesses are so calamitous for the justice system that the *qāḍī* appointing them, as well as the witnesses themselves, will burn in Hell till eternity. The crucial importance of these witnesses is such that the twelfth section is one of the longest, if not the longest, in the *ʿahd*.[106]

The next three commands pertain to (1) supervising the affairs of the orphans whose well-being the *qaḍı* is entrusted to preserve and whose interests (including property and financial affairs) he must defend and protect until they reach the age of majority and intellectual and experiential maturity; (2) marrying women who do not have a marriage guardian, and acting in their overall interests in the process of concluding the marriage; and (3) supervising and auditing the *waqf*s.[107]

The sixteenth command goes to the heart of Zaynabī's function as Chief Justice, responsible as he was for appointing qualified *qāḍī*s to all provinces and districts of the empire. The *ʿahd* does not detail the hierarchy of this function since much of it was so obvious that it was taken for granted. Zaynabī was at once a *qāḍī* and *qāḍī al-quḍāt*, that is a judge of Baghdad and its environs as well as the Chief Justice of the entire empire. It was often the case that the provincial *qāḍī* was also given the title of Chief Justice (*qāḍī al-quḍāt*) since he also, and on behalf of the empire's Chief Justice, appointed bench *qāḍī*s or *nā'ib*s, that is, judges who adjudicated cases in a regular fashion. The appointment of the *nā'ib*s can then take place at the behest of either the empire's or the province's Chief Justice. This act was called, unsurprisingly by now, *istikhlāf*, the act of appointing a *khalīfa*. This, Zaynabī's *ʿahd* states, "is just like (*bi-mithli*; analagous) the *ʿahd* with which the Commander of the Faithful has charged him [i.e., Zaynabī]."[108]

105 *SAQ*, X, 280.
106 *SAQ*, X, 279-80.
107 *SAQ*, X, 280-81.
108 *SAQ*, X, 282.

The seventeenth command requires Zaynabī not to review or overturn past court decisions, but instead affirm them irrespective of how differently they were reasoned by the preceding *qāḍī*s or *muftī*s (on the basis of whose *fatwā* the court decision was reached). The only exception that allows for judicial appeal is a situation in which the verdict contravenes consensus, which is to say previously established law that never was subject to juristic disagreement, or clear textual evidence on whose meaning no disagreement had ever arisen.[109] Notice here that no other law or legal source is mentioned, neither imperial nor customary law, nor any other. The Sharīʿa as commonly interpreted by the jural community is the only authoritative, paradigmatic and default law, the law of the land, as it were.

The next two commands are to appoint (1) a scribe of the court, who is adept at legal formularies (*shurūṭ wa-sijillāt*) and seasoned in the world of documentation and the art of keeping records; and (2) a chamberlain (*ḥājib*) of the court, whose function, in order of importance, comes after the *qāḍī* himself, the character witnesses, and the scribe. In keeping order in the court and controlling queues, the chamberlain must nonetheless be kind and friendly to people, maintaining a cheerful and modest attitude, among other charitable qualities.[110] Again, it bears repeating that this was not necessarily the actual reality at all times but rather the standard and the benchmark[111] against which conduct was judged, or supposed to be judged.

The twentieth command is to receive the records of the previous *qāḍī*, whose *dīwān al-qaḍāʾ*, *maḥāḍir*, and *sijillāt*[112] were crucial for maintaining continuity of judicial life. The transfer of this body of documentation must be attested by qualified witnesses, and thereafter they must be entrusted to the custody of a trustworthy keeper of the records.[113]

The twenty-first and final command is to attend to the supremely important and publicly beneficial office[114] of the *ḥisba* (market inspection), including the retention by Zaynabī of an honest and competent official to occupy this function.

109 *SAQ*, X, 283.
110 *SAQ*, X, 283: "*Mudarraʿan jilbāb al-ḥayāʾi, ṭaliqa al-wajhi... sahila al-jānibi... ghayra mutajahhimin lil-nāsi... wa-lā yuʿāmiluhum bi-ghayri al-bashāshati wal-īnāsi....*"
111 For more on benchmarks, see Introduction, n. 71.
112 On these court records and types of documentation, see Hallaq, "The Qāḍī's *Dīwān* (*Sijill*) before the Ottomans."
113 *SAQ*, X, 284. For the same command in other decrees, see X, 293-94, 300.
114 *SAQ, X, 284: "Faʾinnahā akbaru al-maṣāliḥi wa-ahammuhā, wa-ajmaʿuhā li-nafʿi al-nāsi wa-aʿammuhā."*

The *ʿahd* concludes with the warning, embodied in a proverb, that "every brilliant scholar errs, and every fit horse trips" and so Zaynabī should take special care not to succumb to the "ambitions of the passions" (*maṭāmiḥ al-hawā*) or to worldly temptations. If he were to encounter any excessive difficulty in dealing with the cases appearing before his court, he is advised to consult the Commander of the Faithful, the assumption being that this would happen after seeking the help of *muftī*s (commanded in the sixth section). But transcendental punishment for failing to maintain ethical standards, justice, fair dealing, or resisting the passions remains the sole effective deterrent. Dismissal from office or even worldly punishment (financial or corporal) seems to be such a secondary deterrent that it is not mentioned at all. In fact "social censure"[115] seems to play a more significant role as a deterrent.

Furthermore, I have noted in my discussion of the first command that the text of the *ʿahd* was normally read in the public square of the locale to which the appointment was made, as evidenced in the third-person language used throughout the *ʿahd*. "*Amarahu*" ("he commanded him") represents the caliph's address to the populace, towards whom the caliph has obligations and duties of performance, for he, like the *qāḍī*,[116] is effectively the agent of Muslims, the one who attends to their interests (*maṣāliḥ*) and manages their affairs (*tadbīr/siyāsa*). The *qāḍī* himself, often with others, delivered the document of the *ʿahd* to the locals, and he himself was the object of the very caliphal communication he transmitted. The functions specified in the *ʿahd* were the business of the Chief Justice Zaynabī, but the contractual or covenantal dealings articulated in the *ʿahd* were between the caliph and the populace. This is why the language is cast in the third person, not second.

III

Finally, and by way of concluding this chapter, a brief analytical comparison between *adab al-qāḍī* prescriptions and Zaynabī's *ʿahd* seems warranted.

115 *SAQ*, X, 285: "*Wa khshā mawqifan tashkhaṣu fī-hi al-abṣār*." Social censure was an integral part of the duty of "commanding good and forbidding evil" (*al-amru bil-maʿrūfi wal-nahyu ʿan al-munkar*). See Ghazalı, *Iḥya'*, 781 ff.

116 On the *qāḍī* being the "agent" (or "servant") "of Muslims" (*ʿāmilun min ʿummāli al-Muslimīn*), see Ibn al-Qāṣṣ, *Adab al-Qāḍī*, 109.

(One cannot overemphasize that the latter was typical and quite representative of the genre across many centuries.) The idea of the comparison is to stress the fundamental constitutional relations, and thus boundaries, between the judiciary and the caliphal office.

First, note the thorough emphasis on the technologies of the self and the detailed repertoire of *askesis*. Ethical formation of the *qāḍī* (as of any other "public" officer), underlies the foremost foundational premises on which the discourse of *adab al-qāḍī* genre is based. This was not a merely "theoretical" or idealized requirement, but rather one treated as a highly realizable praxis (because it was deployed purposively and apprehended solemnly) within the habitus. To be just is to mean to be just, to be faithful to a higher intention that wills justice, above and beyond one's comprehension, definition, and reasoning. The intention (*niyya*) here is a crucial ingredient in the technologies of the self, one in which it is crucial and most indispensable to exercise the operation of the self on the self. There is no *askesis* without this self-operation.[117] The technology's essence is to cultivate on a practical and rational level a connection between the concept of justice being deployed and consciousness or knowledge of a higher power of what the *qāḍī* is *intending*. Intention may not be a sufficient condition for justice, but it is certainly a necessary one.

This ethical component is the legacy of the legislative, one that entwined law with ethics, and politics and administrative power with law. Which is to say that the legislative (the Sharīʿa as both a legal apparatus *and* a culture) did not only bind the executive by Sharīʿa's "law" but also deployed together with this law a system of ethical self-formation that enveloped and delimited the values of the habitus from which no one could markedly escape.[118] Like law, ethics and ethical subjectivation were further constraints placed on everyone, including the judicial and executive officials.

Second, the *adab al-qāḍī* works seem so realistic and in tune with the realia of judicial practice that they at times appear less demanding than that practice, at least as it appears in the caliphal and sultanic decrees of appointment. The *adab al-qāḍī* writings appear to suggest that the caliph or sultan does not need to "examine" or "test" the jurist's knowledge, skills, or other characteristics if the jurist has a high standing in the scholarly and jural community. But in the case of Zaynabī, the caliph knew about Zaynabī's distinguished standing

117 Hujwīrī, *Kashf al-Maḥjūb*, 193.
118 For a context to this claim, see Introduction, sec. II.

among his peers and colleagues, and yet he seems to have still subjected him to interrogation and examination (*ikhtibār*).[119]

Finally, and most remarkably for our concerns, is the striking fact that both genres (the *adab al-qāḍī* and *'ahd/'uhūd*) as well as every source or authority we have cited since the opening of the first chapter affirm (1) that the Sharī'a – as wholly based on the Qur'ān, the Sunna, consensus, and juristic inference – is the standard, indisputable, authoritative, and reigning law of the land; (2) that this law is the law of the courts, to be applied across the board: peasants, merchants, women, men, religious minorities, civil servants, or employees of the sultanic or caliphal power; (3) that no other law shares any space with the Sharī'a as the default and enduring law of the land. Put differently, the applied law of the land is defined not just by its sources of authority (here God, not the state), but also by its special universality and temporal unboundedness (also oppositional to state law); and (4) that the caliph or sultan himself is subject to the same law which he is commanding the *qāḍī* to follow, but a law that stands outside and above both of them, and their offices.

119 See n. 88, above.

Chapter 6

The Exception that Proves the Rule: Juwaynī on Executive Power

I

In the foregoing chapters, I have argued that the Sharīʿa structures the political landscape by delineating the external boundaries of this landscape and partly regulating its internal fields of operation; that a central and crucial field in the configuration of the political is the caliphate, responsible as it was for the political management of the *Umma*; that the caliphate is the functional and deputized continuation of Prophethood; that the caliphal functions, by the same logic, are delegatory by way of deputization; that deputization included judicial and executive powers *but excluded law-making*; that law-making and law in general were communal products, manifested in the *madhhab*s as the sum total of individualistic and autonomous *ijtihād*; that caliphal judicial powers were administrative and not substantive; that the substantive part belonged to the Sharīʿa domain; and, finally, that the main residual caliphal powers were executive in nature. Chapter 12 will elaborate in some detail on the meaning and significance of the descriptor "residual," as well as on the meaning of communal law, but for now I wish to further underscore the constitutional boundaries of the caliphate as a largely executive function, one whose *raison d'être* was coercive power.[1]

In line with the firmly established traditions that preceded and followed them, Māwardī and Ghazālī advocated the caliphate as the site of general oversight, capable of deputizing what in effect belongs to it but not, in the end,

1 This was in evidence by the juristic and political distinction between *qaḍā'* and *salṭana*, the former's foundations or *raison d'être* being justice (*ʿadl*) while the latter's is sheer might and coercive strength. See Surūjī, *Adab al-Qaḍā'*, 112: "*Li'anna mabnā al-qaḍā'i ʿalā al-ʿadli, wal-imārati ʿalā al-qahri wal-ghalaba.*"

capable of continuing to muster, namely, executive power. Hence, the stakes were not about the caliphal loss of "law-making" since the autonomy of this sphere was never in question. It had always been in the hands of the jurist-scholars.[2] Nor was it about judicial competence, for appointing and dismissing judges throughout the domains was both expected and an indispensable mode of constitutional labor division. What generated the discursive mapping of constitutional caliphal boundaries was the act of deputizing executive power and the form that it should take. The possibility of extricating the executive functions from the caliphate was entertained[3] but the fact of this attempt's failure, in the long stretch of Islamic history, speaks for the enduring conception of the caliphate as a genealogical *Islamic* institution. It was genealogical in the sense that it connected all parts of the political domain together under the rubric of an *ontologically foundationalist* moral and political epistemology,[4] and this it did irrespective of whether it could or could not dominate, or assert itself, in military terms.

II

The attempt to extricate executive powers from the caliphate was made by Imām al-Ḥaramayn al-Juwaynī, a Saljūq loyalist but also an unconventional constitutional theorist.[5] His brilliant but failed attempt underscores what was at stake in the debate over the caliphate, and the long-held limits that were constitutionally imposed on it, by giving it its form and content, before his time.

I must first stress that Juwaynī's philosophical foundations of politics are not qualitatively different from that of the mainstream, especially as expounded by the paradigmatic theories of Māwardī and Ghazālī. In all societies and cultures, the *sharā'i'* (laws) were mandated – to all societies, Juwaynī seems to say – in

2 See previous chapter, sec. I in general, and especially main text in ch. 5, at n. 57.

3 See sec. II, below.

4 Ontologically foundationalist epistemology in the Islamic context is the study of how prescriptions and categorizations of human acts are to be interpretively derived (i.e., epistemology) from foundationalist texts that have their origins in the First Existent as Preexistent (i.e., ontology). The study of existence or being constituted the first inquiry of what might be called metaphysics or philosophical theology.

5 For a comprehensive treatment of Juwaynī's life and intellectual career, see Siddiqui, *Law and Politics*.

order to provide a hold over religion and piety.[6] This hold's desideratum is to combat the passions and harmful ways of living, for people often tend to follow their desires and seek that which undermines the good life. *Sharā'i'* are systems of regulation that differentiate between good and bad, corralling social life into the way that becomes the site of "legal" discipline (*niẓām*) and the enforcement of the "aims of the law" (*maqāṣid al-sharā'i'*), that is, the double-pronged promotion of virtues and deterrence against breaching them. The "laws" are thus installed to curb people's passions and ambitions and resolve disputes arising from them, and so God created political rulers (*salāṭīn*) to enforce these laws and create order in the affairs of the world (*fa-tantaẓimu umūru al-dunyā*). Beginning with the king-prophets – David, Solomon, et al. – and ending with Prophet Muhammad, Abū Bakr and the rest, God had sent these leaders the competence, capabilities, and might (*'idda* and *najda*) to enforce the laws for the purpose of promoting those interests (*maṣāliḥ*).[7]

Once this brief exposé of the foundations of politics was completed, Juwaynī hastens to add that "our aim in providing this introduction is to make clear what the rules governing the imamate involve. The universal premise here is this: The ultimate purpose is to maintain the foundations of Islam, by hook or crook."[8]

It is safe to say that the treatise is programmatic in its discursive tone, that is, there is almost nothing in it that does not bear, directly or indirectly, realistically or hypothetically, on Juwaynī's ultimate purpose: extricating the caliphate from the nominally ruling 'Abbāsids and bestowing it on the Saljūqs. It is likewise quite safe to say that the extrication of coercive might would apply all the same to the Saljūqs themselves once they fall into disrepair: the strongest man is "the choice of the age," no matter who he is.

In 445/1053, the Mu'tazilī-Ḥanafī 'Amīd al-Mulk al-Kundurī was acting as the vizier of Ṭughrul Beg, the powerful sultan of the Saljūqs. Kundurī had Ash'arīs and Rāfiḍīs denounced from the pulpits, forcing the Ash'arī Juwaynī to seek refuge first in Baghdad and then in Mecca and Medina, where he spent

6 *GU*, 133: "*Li-ya'lama ṭālibu al-ḥaqqi wa-bāghī al-ṣidqi anna maṭlūba al-sharā'i'i min al-khalā'iqi 'alā tafannuni al-milali wal-ṭarā'iqi al-istimsāku bil-dīni wal-taqwā.*" Note here the plural form of Sharī'a, intended to allow for multiplicity and variety among "nations"/parties/denominations (*milal wa-ṭarā'iq*) but nonetheless possessing the same function of constructing and maintaining the regulative force of *dīn*.

7 *GU*, 134-35.

8 *GU*, 135: "*Wa-gharaḍunā min taqdīmi hādhihi al-muqaddimati tawṭi'atu ṭuruqi al-afhāmi ilā mā yata'allaqu min al-aḥkāmi bil-imāmi; fal-qawlu al-kulliyyu inna al-gharaḍa istibqā'u qawā'ida al-Islāmi ṭaw'an aw kurhan.*"

about four years. In 455/1063, Juwaynī returned to Nishāpūr, most probably at the invitation of Niẓām al-Mulk, the vizier of the new sultan Alp Arslān, the nephew of Ṭughrul.[9] One of the shrewdest politicians of his day, this vizier realized – like many before and after him – the importance of the ulama as leaders and representatives of the Community, and thus endeavored to acquire their support. This was always a necessary step in shoring up legitimacy for executive power. One method by which he achieved such support was the founding of the now famous Shāfiʿī *madrasa*s in the major towns of the central and eastern lands of the caliphate. He built one in Nishāpūr, called al-Madrasa al-Maymūna al-Niẓāmiyya, in which Juwaynī was to teach from the time of its inauguration until his death in 478/1085.[10]

Niẓām al-Mulk's choice of Juwaynī to head the Niẓāmiyya of Nīshāpūr was not fortuitous. The vizier was acutely aware of the influence of these men of learning on their followers in each city, and by playing the role of patron he secured the popular support of the Shāfiʿīs in several localities. Juwaynī was a most useful agent in promoting Saljūq rule in Khurasān. As part of his pro-Saljūq activity in al-Madrasa al-Maymūna, Juwaynī composed two treatises at the instigation of Niẓām al-Mulk. The first, titled *al-ʿAqīda al-Niẓāmiyya,* was concerned with Ashʿarī theology[11] and the second, *Ghiyāth al-Umam (GU),* with government.

But we must be careful in defining, first, what it means for a major jurist, as Juwaynī was, to be "a useful agent," for it is essential to understand that this Jurist's loyalties were ultimately not to the Saljūqs as such but to the Sharīʿa, its habitus, culture, and the Community for which it was created in the first place.[12] Juwaynī happened to be a "useful agent" because his and the Saljūqs' interests aligned with each other: he sought to enlist the most potent executive power and they happened to possess it.

9 Ibn Kathīr, *al-Bidāya wal-Nihāya,* XII, 107.

10 Subkī, *Ṭabaqāt al-Shāfʿiyya al-Kubrā,* V, 171; Ibn al-Wardī, *Tarīkh,* I, 533.

11 *Al-ʿAqīda al-Niẓāmiyya fil-Arkān al-Islāmiyya* was translated into German by H. Klopfer, *Das Dogma des imam al-Haramain al-Djuwainī.*

12 It is in this context of association of the jurists with the ruling elite that we should interpret Suyūṭī's treatise *Mā Rawāhu al-Asāṭīn,* which condemns those ulama who frequent the courts of the rulers. Suyūṭī was not condemning a situation in which the ruler sought the advice of the ulama and their leading jurists, for as we have seen, offering *naṣīḥa* to the ruler is a *sunna,* that is, a highly recommended act. What is deplorable for Suyūṭī, however, was a situation in which the ulama are seen as sycophants. This is not an issue of mere corruption and unseemly behavior – although it is – but rather one of insistence that the Sharʿī legislative power must in no way associate with the executive on the latter's terms. See Suyūṭī, *Mā Rawāhu al-Asāṭīn.*

GU was written sometime between 470/1078 and 478/1085,[13] a period in which the main political actors were the ʿAbbāsid caliph al-Muqtadī, the teenage Saljūq sultan Malik Shāh, and his all-too-powerful and seasoned vizier Niẓām al-Mulk. The period was characterized by the domination of the Saljūqs over the vast lands of the declining caliphate as well as by their aspiration to acquire fuller legitimacy than that which was granted to their predecessors, the Būyids, by the caliph. Although they were the wielders of executive power, they nonetheless needed the endorsement of the caliph who, despite his weakness, possessed the final constitutional authority to declare – usually with the support of the jurists – what was legitimate and what was not. Resting in the hands of the ʿAbbāsids, this authority constituted for the Saljūqs the link between their status as sultans and their ambition to become the fully legitimate rulers of the Muslim empire.

Ṭughrul Beg, the first Saljūq majordomo to set foot in Baghdad, realized that such titles as "The King of the East and the West," bestowed on him by the caliph, did little but to circumscribe his powers and prerogatives as a sultan, for he was still subject to a higher authority. In a bid to arrogate to himself more prestige and power, he declared himself the "Exalted Emperor of Emperors," "The Reviver of Islam," and even "The Commander of the Faithful.[14] From the outset he was determined to unite his own dynasty's power with the authority vested in the caliphate. To carry out this policy, Ṭughrul Beg resorted to diplomacy, which seemed the only useful and realistic expedient. A military takeover of the caliphate was out of the question, for it would most likely have backfired, and disastrously so. This is so because they already had *de facto* power to rule, but seizing the rest of the constitutional powers of the caliph would have meant an institutional and cultural disruption in the moral, epistemic, and constitutional genealogy that appealed upward to the Prophetic station. Such an act, in other words, would have profoundly shaken the most sensitive core of the Muslim polity as a Prophetic legacy.

In good tradition, Ṭughrul Beg viewed the marriage between the ʿAbbāsid and the Saljūq Houses as a way to achieve his goal and thus went on to marry the daughter of the caliph, notwithstanding the latter's fierce opposition. He had in mind bringing into the world an heir-apparent who – being now of the ʿAbbāsid House – would unite in himself the effective power of the Saljūqs and the moral and constitutional authority of the ʿAbbāsids.[15] However,

---

13 On dating the work, see Hallaq, "Caliphs, Jurists, and the Saljūqs," 28, n. 12.

14 Ibn al-Jawzī, *al-Muntaẓam*, VIII, 223.

15 To secure his marriage with the caliph's daughter, Ṭughrul Beg seems to have been willing to sacrifice his good relations with the caliph himself, who first opposed the marriage. A few

this plan was thwarted due to the death of Ṭughrul Beg immediately after the marriage.

Another opportunity for uniting the lineages of the ʿAbbāsid and Saljūq Houses presented itself in 480/1087 when a son was born to the caliph al-Muqtadī and his wife, the daughter of the Saljūq sultan Malik Shāh. In 481/1088 the elder son and heir apparent of Malik Shāh, Aḥmad, was killed. Immediately thereafter, Malik Shāh requested that the caliphal palace allow his wife and their son Jaʿfar to leave Baghdad for Isfahān.[16] Jaʿfar became the favorite of his grandfather, who granted him exclusively the ʿAbbāsid title "Little Commander of the Faithful."[17] Hoping that little Jaʿfar would take the seat of the caliphate in Baghdad, Malik Shāh, together with his vizier Niẓām al-Mulk, set out to pave the grounds by making Baghdad their winter capital. For this purpose, many buildings were constructed.[18] In 485/1092, the caliph al-Muqtadī was asked to abdicate and was given a few days to leave Baghdad.[19] But before he did so, Malik Shāh died and with him died his plan to make Jaʿfar the Commander of the Faithful.

Malik Shah's policy, which aimed at blending the authority of the ʿAbbāsids with the dynastic power of the Saljūqs, was doubtless the brainchild of Niẓām al-Mulk. It is no secret that the real ruler of the Saljūq empire between 465/1072 and 485/1092 was Niẓām al-Mulk himself, not the young Malik Shāh. Since the beginning of his reign, the latter conferred on the former the title "Father-Lord" and charged him with all the affairs of the empire,[20] a function that Māwardī termed *wizārat tafwīḍ*.[21] Therefore, to speak of the policies of Niẓām al-Mulk and of Malik Shāh is to speak of one and the same policy.

Under these political circumstances, Juwaynī composed his treatise. Our author, for reasons to be discussed momentarily, found the claims of the Saljūqs

---

months after the engagement, Ṭughrul Beg came to Baghdad and demanded that the caliph's daughter accompany him to Iṣfahān, his capital. When the caliph objected on the grounds that Ṭughrul had no right to consummate the marriage ("*al-maqṣūdu bi-hādhihi al-waṣlati al-sharafu lā al-ijtimāʿ*"), Ṭughrul exercised pressure to obtain what he desired. His intention to create a blood relationship with the ʿAbbāsids was most evident in his oration on the occasion of the caliph's approval of the marriage. See excerpts of the speech in Ibn al-Athīr, *al-Kāmil*, I, 514.

16 Ibn al-Athīr, *al-Kāmil*, X, 70-71, 162, 169, 175.

17 Houtsma, "Malik Shāh," *Encyclopaedia of Islam*, III, pt. 1, 212.

18 Ibn al-Athīr, *al-Kāmil*, X, 199-200.

19 Houtsma, "Malik Shāh," III, pt. 1, 212.

20 Ibn al-Wardī, *Tārīkh*, I, 523; Ibn al-Athīr, *al-Kāmil*, X, 80; Makdisi, *Ibn ʿAqīl et la resurgence de l'Islam traditionaliste*, 129, 131-32. On the role of Niẓām al-Mulk in building the Saljūq empire, see Bosworth, "Political and Dynastic History," 68-83.

21 Māwardī, *Adab al-Wazīr*, 43.

to power legitimate. But he knew well that the juridico-political theory and consensus of his time, especially as represented in the authoritative work of Māwardī, could not justify the high ambitions of the Saljūqs. Māwardī's positivist account, which in many respects was an extension of the accounts of Ash'arī, Bāqillānī, and Baghdādī, and an expression of the accepted political practice of the time, aimed at maintaining the unity of the Community through the institution of the caliphate (and as a deputized manifestation of the *institution* of prophethood). This is why Māwardī, like the vast majority of political theorists and jurists, insisted on the caliphal institution as against Būyid and other claims. Juwaynī, on the other hand, seems to have lost hope in the revival of the 'Abbāsid House as an effective military power and thus attempted, with his sophisticated theoretical deployment, to ease the transition of executive power into a new dynastic locus.

Here lies the difference between Juwaynī and Māwardī. While the latter upheld the caliphate as the supreme office from which all subsidiary functions derive their authority and thus attempted to reduce the military rulers to constitutional subordinates, the former held as fully legitimate the rule of whoever was capable and willing to maintain peace and unity. The question for Juwaynī then was in which dynasty is executive power to be deposited.

Yet, Juwaynī did not differ in the least from Māwardī or any other political theorist with regard to the necessity (*wujūb*) of the imamate as such, a principle on which the "vast majority of leading figures (*a'imma*)" agreed.[22] The principle, furthermore, is said to have been sanctioned by revelatory decree rather than by pure reason,[23] perhaps due to the foundational premise, stated, after the exordium, in the first sentence of the book: "The imamate is a totalistic leadership and a universal command, pertaining to the elite and commoners in running the affairs of the religious and profane (*dīn* and *dunyā*), including the preservation of the domains and the protection of the populace, upholding the Call [of Islam] by means of intellectual defense as well as by sword, curbing deviations and injustice, to protect victims from their victimizers, and restore rights against violators to those entitled to them."[24] Nothing here is different from Māwardī's, and other jurists', requirements.

22 *GU*, 17.

23 *GU*, 17.

24 *GU*, 15: "*Al-imāmatu ri'āsatun tāmmatun wa-za'āmatun 'āmmatun tata'allaqu bil-khāṣati wal-'āmmati fī muhimmāti al-dīni wal-dunyā mutaḍammanuhā ḥifẓu al-ḥawzati wa-ri'āyatu al-ra'iyyati, wa-iqāmatu al-da'wati bil-ḥujjati wal-sayfi, wa-kaffu al-janafi wal-ḥayfi wal-intiṣāfu lil-maẓlūmīna min al-ẓālimīna wa-istīfā'u al-ḥuqūqi min al-mumtani'īna wa-īfā'uhā 'alā al-mustaḥiqqīn.*"

The moral epistemic link between the caliphate and the Prophethood – namely, what we have labelled foundationalist political epistemology – did not escape Juwaynī, for he was, as a jurist and political theorist, born into it, but this seemed to matter less to him than resolving the problematics of effective power that a weakened caliphate generated.

Juwaynī leaves the readers of his *GU* with little doubt that he is ready to dispose of the ʿAbbāsid House altogether in favor of a powerful sultan who will efficiently manage the affairs of the Community and fulfill the *institutional duties* of the caliphate, with or without a Qurayshī royal pedigree. In order to legitimize the rule of such a sultan within the domain of political theory, Juwaynī must have felt compelled to attack Māwardī's *AS*, which seems to have gained sufficient grounds in the juristic and probably political communities as to constitute a challenge that needs to be addressed. He therefore did not spare any opportunity to critique Māwardī's reasoning, even descending to quasi-personal attacks on his juristic competence.[25]

Yet, the main line of offence was juristic in nature, underscoring the fact that political reasoning is performed through legal categories. Throughout *GU*, Juwaynī repeatedly draws a distinction between final and revocable rulings *(aḥkām)* governing political institutions.[26] The distinction of course finds its origins in *uṣūl al-fiqh* and is based on a typology of textual evidence *(dalīl)*. A ruling derived from a univocal Qur'ānic verse, or a multiply transmitted and unequivocal prophetic *Ḥadīth*, is determined to be certain (*qaṭʿī*) and therefore final. On the other hand, a ruling derived from an equivocal verse or a solitary Ḥadīth is not accepted as final and thus remains subject to *ijtihād*, the interpretation and legal reasoning of jurists. Such a ruling is described as *ẓannī* or *maẓnūn*.

Juwaynī forcefully argues that little about the character of the caliphate is conclusively established in law because not much has come down in the Qur'ān and the Sunna about the details of this institution. Irrevocable rulings are relatively few and far in between, and are primarily based on consensus.[27] By so arguing, Juwaynī makes it clear that most legal questions related to the imamate (*masā'il al-imāma)* are open to fresh reasoning. He stresses this conclusion in reaction to the general discourse of Sunni political thought as

25 See, for example, *GU*, 152–53.
26 In his *Irshād*, 231, 240, he also draws a distinction between *al-qawāṭiʿ* (irrevocable rulings) and *al-mujtahadāt* (cases subject to the jurist's interpretation), which are ultimately *maẓnūnāt* (uncertain).
27 *GU*, 42, 48, 52, 59, 93, 99, 102, 103, 105 and passim.

expounded by Māwardī and his predecessors. Māwardī formulated his theory by appeal to the established and mainstream legal doctrines that pertained to the political domain, without distinguishing – or rather without alerting the reader to the distinction – between revocable and irrevocable rulings. He wrote as any jurist would write under normal circumstances, pointing out juristic disagreement when necessary, but he was under no obligation to articulate or highlight the juristically obvious *uṣūlist* distinction between certitude and weak probability, and all those degrees of knowledge that lay in between.

On these polemical grounds, Juwaynī rejects the arguments of *AS*[28] (a rejection that in the long run proved to be unpersuasive to Muslim theorists, and even to the critical modern reader). Yet, the distinction between revocable and irrevocable rulings allowed Juwaynī to evade those parts of the prevailing political thought that hindered his task and enabled him to reconstruct a theory that represented his concerns.

Juwaynī's method is clearly expressed in the arrangement of his treatise's subject matter, *which is* divided into three parts, each of which contains a set of precepts that govern a particular situation.[29] These situations, he admits, may or may not be real. The idea is to begin with a real or realistic scenario about politics and law, and then hypothesize (*taqdīr*) the gradual absence of elements (that is, deterioration) in each scenario, until the point that the Sharīʿa, the last major ingredient and the bastion of Islam, becomes itself extinct.[30] Which is to say that he posited that the last of the defining components of Islam to vanish was the Sharīʿa, since the Sharīʿa's end is the end of Islam as well. The implications of this seemingly universal conception seem clear enough: Political governance and politics in general are derivative and can disappear without the concomitant disappearance of Islam, especially its legal order. Every defining feature of Islam will vanish but Islam will remain in place if Sharīʿa can be maintained. Once again, constitutionally speaking, Juwaynī's hypothetical resolutely dissolves what has been called, in Western political thought, the Paradox of Sovereignty. If politics presupposes the law and can vanish without the law vanishing, then the Paradox cannot arise.

Note also the novel and unique nature of this work, one never attempted before or after Juwaynī. This calls for the speculation that the treatise was structured in this particular way as a ruse, as a camouflage for the audacious

---

28 *GU*, 104-105.

29 For a different, yet interesting, analysis of Juwaynī's hypothesis, see Abdel Meguid, "Reversing Schmitt."

30 *GU*, 13.

message that Juwaynī was trying to convey. He did not want to come out in plain view to declare the dispensability of the ʿAbbāsid House outright, for this would clash against the heavy weight of the longstanding Islamic political tradition that ran in the opposite direction. Dispensing with the ʿAbbāsid House in favor of a "foreign" dynasty which had barely entered the Muslim habitus was unthinkable because the ʿAbbāsid House maintained an ethical genealogy that the entrants sorely lacked. Juwaynī's way of avoiding what might have been considered outrageous deviation, and its aftermath, was to hypothesize the gradual decline and final collapse of the entire system and phenomenon called Islam, and thus hide the message of abdicating in favor of the Saljūqs behind it all. For after all, the idea of the end of Religion and the rise of the Day of Judgement was a pervasive theme in many Islamic genres.[31] But Juwaynī harnessed the eschatological narrative to a different end.

The hypothetical nature of *GU* prompted Juwaynī to characterize the work as *qalīlu al-jadwā ʿaẓīmu al-khaṭar*,[32] that is, "of little use but of grave consequence." In the classic Arabic dictionaries, to be in a state of "*khaṭar*" is to "approach death" or "to be close to perishing" (*al-ishrāfu ʿalā al-halāk*).[33] "*Jadwā*," on the other hand, means benefit or receiving a gift of some sort (*ʿaṭiyya*). The meaning of the phrase then is that the book in question does not yield a practical profit, as would for example a law manual or a treatise on *adab* or ethical cultivation. It is entirely "theoretical," having little to do with practical reality. Yet, it conveys a "grave message" about an imminent "grave situation," namely, of the impending collapse of Islamic polity and Community, and the need to "save them" (hence the title of the book). The savior is no other than the distinguished Saljūq vizier to whom an invitation to take over the caliphate was extended, an invitation that was couched in an exquisitely delicate and sinuous language of political realism, but ultimately one that did not escape the central domain of the law.

The first part of the *GU* (pp. 14-223) sets forth the theory of the imamate and the requirements that government personnel, including the imam and his electors, should meet. The second (pp. 224-283) deals with a situation in which the imam cannot meet some of these requirements. Here, Juwaynī also deals with the hypothetical of the imamate's extinction, in which case the military leaders and the ulama are to take affairs into their own hands. The third part

31 Hallaq, "On the Controversy of the Existence of Mujtahids," 137-38, and sources cited therein.

32 *GU*, 47.

33 Ibn Manẓūr, *Lisān al-ʿArab*, IV, 290 ff.

(pp. 284-380) assumes the extinction of the guardians of Sharīʿa and attempts to find a solution for holding the Community together. Since the third part does not deal with government proper, we will restrict our analysis to the first two.

Although Juwaynī has seen the almost total decline of the ʿAbbāsid caliphate and although he repeatedly asserts that his concern does not lie primarily with the ideal or consummate imamate,[34] he still devotes about sixty percent of his treatise to the first part alone. His justification for emphasizing the first part is that in order for one to identify a deficient imamate one must know what a perfect imamate looks like.[35] By emphasizing the conditions and qualifications that the consummate imam should possess, he is attempting to demonstrate how incompetent the ʿAbbāsid caliph in Baghdad was,[36] and thus to prepare the ground for a new theory in which military leaders and qualified scholars take the place of the imam.

Juwaynī's attitude towards the caliph of Baghdad must not be misinterpreted. Juwaynī held no grudge against him, personal, political, or otherwise. His language in reference to the caliph was in fact couched in terms of relative reverence, but he severely objected to his military incompetence and an irremediable inability to preserve the solidarity of the Community, which he viewed not only as the ultimate function and goal of government but also an end which justified almost every means. His willingness to serve the Saljūqs and to legitimize their rule stemmed from this very fact, namely, that they possessed considerable effective power to protect and manage the affairs of the Muslim polity. Unlike Māwardī who habituated the "emirate of seizure" *(imārat al-istīlāʾ)*[37] *within the conventional structures of governance*

34 *GU*, 13, 96, 223.

35 *GU*, 223.

36 This will be shown and documented in its proper context below. However, see *GU*, 89-90, 103.

37 Orientalism invariably defined the term *istīlāʾ* as "usurpation" and "taking sth by force." The term acquires these meaning in almost all modern dictionaries, including Dozy's *Supplément aux Dictionnaires arabes* and Mukhtār ʿUmar's *Muʿjam*. The latter, for instance, retains the premodern meanings, including "seizure of property not claimed by another owner with the intent to bring it under one's ownership." Yet, the greater part of the definition introduces new meanings to the term. He defines it as the taking over of rule "by seizure, force, weapons, and vanquishing strength" (*istawlā ʿalā al-ḥukmi ightaṣabahu wa-akhadhahu bil-quwwati wal-silāḥi wal-ghalaba*). In the most authoritative premodern dictionaries, however, these connotations either do not exist or else are given mostly non- or quasi-political meaning. The most common meaning of the term is located in the context of horse racing: *istīla'* is "reaching the finish line" (*ghāya/amad*) before the other competitor: "*Fa-istawlā aḥaduhumā ʿalā al-ghāyati idhā sabaqa al-ākhar.*" This is why Ibn Manẓūr reports that "departing from this meaning, one can say that so-and-so ʿ*istawlā*

in general and the imamate in particular, Juwaynī wished to dispose of this mediation and instead to create an identity between military, political, and administrative power, on the one hand, and this venerable and longstanding institution, on the other. For after all, like Māwardī, Ghazālī, and almost any other constitutional writer, Juwaynī's desideratum was ultimately the preservation of *dīn,* which can be practiced only when there is a well-ordered and well-governed community.

To this end, Juwaynī maintains, the appointment of the imam is obligatory. The practice of the Community, as evident from its history, has been to appoint a new imam as soon as the position becomes vacant. In support of this argument, Juwaynī introduces a historical anecdote about the failure of the Companions to bury the Prophet immediately after his death because they were preoccupied with the more urgent question of electing a successor.[38] On the basis of the Companions' consensus and the revealed texts,[39] therefore, the imamate is demanded by the Sharīʿa and not by pure human reason.[40]

Yet, unlike Māwardī and Ghazālī who emphasize the necessity of the imamate, Juwaynī states that the institution is obligatory only as long as it is possible to appoint an imam.[41] An explanation for this contention may be found later in *GU* where Juwaynī determines that if the designation of an imam induces rebellion or unrest he should not be installed, especially if it is thought that his appointment would generate more acrimony and destruction than a situation in which the Community remains imamless.[42] It is Juwaynī's assumption that there would still be influential people at the helm who can run the body politic, and so an immediate appointment can be postponed if a civil war or serious unrest might break out.

Juwaynī goes on to discuss the electors and then the candidates. The electors, chosen from amongst those who "can bind and unbind" (*ahl al-ḥall wal-ʿaqd*), must possess experience in matters of law, government, and administration. Unlike the imam himself, the electors are not required to be

ʿ*alā mālī,*' meaning he beat me to it": "*Wa-min hādhā yuqāl: istawlā fulānun ʿalā mālī ay ghalabanī ʿalayhi*". Zabīdī gives the same definitions and adds that "*istawlā ʿalā al-shay*'" means that the object (*shay*') fell into his possession: "*idhā ṣāra fī yadihi.*" See Ibn Manẓūr, *Lisān al-ʿArab*, XV, 482; Zabīdī, *Tāj al-ʿArūs*, XX, 313-14.

38 *GU*, 15-16.

39 Unlike Mawardī who cites Q. 4:62 in justification of the necessity of the imamate, Juwaynī (*GU*, 17) refers generally to the "revealed law" (*al-sharʿ al-manqūl).*

40 *GU*, 17-18.

41 *GU*, 15.

42 *GU*, 83.

mujtahids.[43] When discussing the number of those who can bind and unbind, Juwaynī accepts the election by a single elector.[44] The elector who is competent to designate an imam must be a wielder of *shawka*, that is, a possessor of effective military and political power, for it is only through *shawka* that peace is established and unity maintained. After all, Juwaynī relentlessly stresses, the purpose of the imamate is the attainment of obedience which power alone can procure.[45] The consensus of all scholars in the Islamic domain is determined to be unnecessary for confirming the *bay'a* (investiture). Juwaynī recalls the *bay'a* of Abū Bakr who, immediately after his election, proceeded to manage the affairs of the Community without awaiting the approval of those outside Medina. Entailing matters of grave importance, the affairs of political management require immediate attention and by the time a consensus on the new imam is reached, considerable damage might be already wrought on Islam.[46] Contrary to Bāqillānī who, drawing upon the need for witnesses in marriage, required witnesses in investiture, Juwaynī finds them unnecessary for the imam's designation. "If we assume that an elector of great importance and stature had secretively invested the imamate in a qualified candidate, thereby confirming the imamate by his *shawka*, then it is my opinion that such an imamate cannot be invalidated." But Juwaynī hastens to admit that this issue has not been settled (*maẓnūn*), having been subject to different interpretations.[47]

It cannot escape us here that Juwaynī's acute realism, even when he runs against the mainstream thinking about the imamate and the sultanate, underscores the essential requirement of what everyone agreed on, namely, the absolute necessity of coercive power. As long as this power was secured within the constitutional boundaries outlined by the jurists (e.g., as stated in Māwardī's *ADD* and *AS*), it did not matter who secured it. Like the discursive tradition that produced him (and in sharp contrast to the Weberian "formal-rational" procedures of modern bureaucracy),[48] Juwaynī was not obsessed with following procedures for their own sake. If the goal is securing an extremely powerful executive that can promote the goals of the *dīn*, then who cares what authority or entity accomplishes this goal, as long as there is nothing harmful or unlawful about the appointing power?

43 *GU*, 49-51, 57. For the various Islamic views about *ahl al-ḥall wal-'aqd*, see Afsaruddin, "Obedience to Political Authority," 37-42.

44 *GU*, 53-55.

45 *GU*, 56-57.

46 *GU*, 52-53; see also *Irshād*, 239.

47 *GU*, 59.

48 For a critique of procedure in the American context, see Bagley, "Procedure Fetish."

Juwaynī next takes up the ideal qualifications required of the imam. The first and basic requirement is that the imam must be physically fit, possessing the physical characteristics and bodily senses needed in the day-to-day administration of the domains. Second, and addressing the requirement of descent from Quraysh, he argues that the Ḥadīth "the imams are from Quraysh" is weak.[49] He argues that the sacrosanct nature of the office and the historical fact that it has always devolved upon a Qurayshī candidate as a matter of tradition has discouraged non-Qurayshīs from pursuing it. The requirement, he says, was merely intended to honor the Prophet's lineage and in effect has no bearing whatever on the institution and the performance of duties entrusted to the imam.[50] It is at best an *honoris causa*, a revered tradition, but hardly a binding one.

In addition to piety, freedom, majority, and maleness, the imam must possess *ʿilm* (knowledge) which leads to *ijtihād*, a quality indispensable in decision-making.[51] To be incapable of *ijtihād* would mean that the imam would have to depend on scholars who would undoubtedly express a variety of opinions on a single matter, a situation that is likely to lead him to confusion. But requiring *ijtihād* does not necessarily mean that the imam must handle decision-making single-handedly. Although he must eventually formulate his own opinion, the imam is under obligation to take into serious consideration the views of the scholars. His *ijtihād*, unsurprisingly, is no substitute for that of the ulama but rather a culmination of the collective effort that is his and theirs.[52]

The last but most important of the requirements is *istiqlāl* and *kifāya*, by which Juwaynī means the intellectual autonomy, personal skills, and effective power needed to maintain the orderly life and unity of the Community, to organize the armies, defend the frontiers, enforce the Sharīʿa, and command loyalties.[53] For our author, "the meaning of *kifāya* is *istiqlāl*,"[54] the ability for a leader to rise, on his own, to make things work, things that are geared toward the unity of the *Umma* and the promotion of its interests and well-being (*maṣlaḥa*). Lacking *ijtihād* would adversely affect *istiqlāl* and *kifāya*, because it takes away from the integrity and autonomy of the leader's otherwise essential decision-making competence.

---

49 *GU*, 60-63.

50 *GU*, 10-12, 225: "*Fa-inna al-nasaba thabata ishtirāṭuhu tashrīfan li-shajarati Rasūli al-Lāhi ṣallā Allāhu ʿalayhi wa sallam, idh lā yatawaqqafu shay'un min maqāṣidi al-imāmati ʿalā al-iʿtizā'i ilā nasabin wal intimā'i ilā ḥasab.*"

51 *GU*, 66, 112-113.

52 *GU*, 67.

53 *GU*, 68-69.

54 *GU*, 66-67.

But should the imam lose his freedom, renounce Islam, or be afflicted by a physical or mental ailment, he must be deposed by *ahl al-ḥall wa-ʿaqd* whenever they see fit and without obtaining the consensus of the Community.[55] Committing acts contrary to the rules of the Sharīʿa does not constitute grounds for deposition if they are not regular or heinous, or if the imam recants.[56] While Juwaynī is discussing these requirements and their conditions, he at one point starts a new section (*faṣl*) concerned with the imprisonment of the imam. What happens, he asks, if the imam falls prisoner to the enemy?

The reader of the treatise would at first glance expect Juwaynī to cover that subject in the way it has been traditionally treated. But Juwaynī gives it a significant twist. Three lines into that section, the discourse suddenly shifts back to the requirements of *kifāya* and *shawka*. After a meandering paragraph whose gist is that if the imam loses his effective power and is rendered incompetent due to the fact that he lost all backing and all supporters, then "there is an unbridgeable separation between Muslims and the one who is in charge."[57] By "unbridgeable separation," Juwaynī intends to draw an analogy with "falling into bondage." "In this case, appointing another imam who commands obedience becomes a duty," because this would be tantamount to a situation in which the imam has fallen prisoner into enemy hands where "Muslims have no way of reaching him." This is an allusion, as clear as it could be made, to the well-acknowledged fact that the ʿAbbāsid caliph under the Saljūqs was relegated to a nominal entity, literally a prisoner in his own palace in Baghdad. At this point, Juwaynī directly address himself to "Kahf al-Islām,"[58] Niẓām al-Mulk himself, by saying that he "has no doubt" that this powerful vizier must have thought of these matters, "the allusion to which renders it unnecessary to state the ultimate ends explicitly."[59] Insofar as I can tell, no one before or after Juwaynī reasoned his way juridically to converting the conventional chapter (or section) of "The imam Falling Prisoner to the Enemy" into a strategy of removal without him factually and formally falling into bondage.

In no case is it lawful to install two imams simultaneously. Since the aim of the imamate is to preserve the integrity of the *polity*, it stands to reason that one imam is better than two, for that would preempt potential disunity

55 *GU*, 75, 89-90.
56 *GU*, 79-98.
57 *GU*, 90: "*Fa-qad ḥīla bayna al-muslimīna wa-bayna wizrin yastaqqilu bil-amr.*"
58 Literally "The Cave of Islam," another way of saying "The Protector of Islam," since people seek shelter and thus protection in caves.
59 *GU*, 90.

and divisions in the ranks of the *Umma*. Two imams would tend to compete for influence and power, and this, Juwaynī contends, would lead to disaster.[60] For this reason, Juwaynī rejects the arguments of Ashʿarī (d. 324/936) and Abū Isḥāq al-Isfarāʾīnī (d. 417/1027) who permit two imams when one lacks sufficient power to control the remote provinces of the empire.[61] If control should be lost in these provinces, Juwaynī accepts only the rule of a powerful emir who, though in times of crises may act independently, must recognize the superiority of the incumbent imam and submit to his authority and orders, including when he is dismissed from office.[62] Given a situation in which there are two leaders who both claim the imamate in two different regions, Juwaynī recognizes one of them as the lawful imam and the other as emir. Should two acts of investiture designating two imams take place at the same time, one of them must be voided.[63] The rightful imam is he who has the allegiance of all Muslims.[64] This position runs against other dominant views that the time of appointment is of the essence, where the office goes to him who was appointed chronologically first.

In determining the functions of the imam, Juwaynī divides them according to the symbiotic categories of *dīn* and *dunyā*, already expounded by Māwardī. The functions in the former domain include the promotion of pious attitudes, the prevention of negative innovation (*bidʿa*), and the fighting of apostacy. Though one of the imam's duties is to pull together the divergent elements within Sunnism and Sunni polity, he must by no means attempt to unify the legal schools, but should support each one of them, each leading jurist and his followers, and all ulama. In other words, he has no business interfering in their *madhhab*ic arrangements, debates, and juristic disagreements, which is yet another way of indirectly saying – as everything else in the book – that the integrity of the *madhhab* structure cannot but be maintained, a reminder perhaps that it is the legal system and its *madhhab*ic edifice that constitute and determine the foundations of the political system and its executive power, not the other way around. He emphatically admonishes the imam and all political leaders to consult the ulama and seek their advice. The latter are to be charged even with political decision-making, and the ruler is under obligation of

60 *GU*, 126-127.

61 In *al-Irshād*, 239, which was most likely written before *Ghiyāth al-Umam*, Juwaynī accepts the possibility of two imams reigning simultaneously provided they are geographically distant from each other.

62 *GU*, 128-129.

63 *GU*, 131.

64 *GU*, 130-131.

enforcing their pronouncements by means of his *shawka*. The ulama, Juwaynī maintains, are the heirs of the prophets and the guardians of the Sharīʿa. It is the duty of the sultan and the imam, particularly if they exercise no *ijtihād*, to follow the lead of the *mujtahid*s just as kings had followed the lead of the Arab Prophet.[65]

As to theological differences, Juwaynī does not take the same neutral attitude. While he does not explicitly advise the imam to uphold a particular school of theology, he refers him to his book on Ashʿarī *kalām*, *al-ʿAqīda al-Niẓāmiyya,* which contains what he describes as the core of knowledge.[66] Note here that delineating the imamate's or (effectively) "sultanic" duties is not merely a formalistic matter, one of following the convention of writing within this political genre. Rather, it is to underscore in no uncertain terms the limitations on executive power, irrespective of the specific identity of the holder of this power. To invite the Saljūqs to take the reign of the imamate is not to grant them anything more or less than what the imamate as an executive power is entitled to. The substituting agency continues to be bound by the same constitutional structure and constitutional rules and limitations that have always been in place.

The most important among temporal functions is the duty of launching the holy war *(jihād)* against the infidels. Because military campaigns require a strong internal structure to sustain the expenses of wars, the imam must strengthen the administrative system and appoint officials and judges to attend to social, economic, and legal matters. Juwaynī particularly emphasizes the imam's duty to fight the enemy and to apply the religious law.[67] With this emphasis he aimed to show that these important functions were not, as a matter of fact, performed by the incompetent caliph but by the Saljūqs. (The continuous campaigns of Alp Arslān and Malik Shāh against the Byzantines and others, and the enthusiasm which the Saljūqs displayed in promoting the Sharīʿa are facts too well known to be discussed here.)[68]

To rule successfully, the imam must thus maintain a strong army. This would require vast revenues to be levied from several sources. Juwaynī enumerates the sources prescribed by the law, including war booty and various types of taxes,

65 *GU*, 227, 275, 283.
66 *GU*, 140.
67 *GU*, 153-177.
68 On these campaigns see Cahen, "The Turkish Invasion," I, 147-50. On the efforts of the Saljūqs to promote education and religious learning, see Bosworth, "Political and Dynastic History," 70 ff.

such as the *kharāj* and *zakāt*.[69] But what if, Juwaynī asks, the imam's budget still falls short of meeting the needs of the military? For solving this problem our author suggests that the imam should distribute estates to the officers of the army, who, by cultivating and managing these estates, will derive profit for themselves as well as maintain military units destined to fight in his army. Though Juwaynī makes this suggestion appear as if it were a long-standing Sharīʿa requirement, it is in fact a *post eventum* justification of the Būyid *iqṭāʿ* system which was adopted and fully developed by Niẓām al-Mulk.[70]

We recall that in the last two parts of *GU*, Juwaynī outlined a juridico-political doctrine to serve as a guide of conduct for Muslims when the extinction of their religious and political leadership becomes an accomplished fact.[71] This clearly explains the title that he gives to his book: "The Savior of [Political] Communities" – a pun-reference to the book as well as to the great vizier. Here, he deals with the possibility of the extinction of the imamate by assuming the decline or disappearance of the requirements generally and traditionally expected of the imam to meet. Again and again, Juwaynī reminds us that the imamate was created in the first place for the purpose of maintaining the political unity of Muslims by means of enforcing Sharīʿa's regulations pertaining to law and order,[72] and laments the fact – now in crystal clear language – that the contemporary imam of Baghdad, who is a Qurayshī, had failed to perform his duties and rise to the occasion. He practically describes the ʿAbbāsid imam of Baghdad as incompetent: "We see a Qurayshī [imam] reigning while the flock are fighting each other in the provinces and falling prey to death .... Therefore," he explains, "should a qualified candidate from a tribe other than Quraysh be available, it would not be unlawful to appoint him [in lieu of the ʿAbbāsid nominal entity]."[73]

Military and political power in Juwaynī's view take precedence over any other consideration,[74] for power constitutes the only means by which the ruler can properly run the affairs of the polity. A powerless ruler must, therefore, be replaced by a powerful one. Applying this argument to the political reality

69 *GU*, 178-189.

70 Cahen, "The Turkish Invasion," I, 158; Ashtor, *Social and Economic History*, 213-14.

71 *GU*, 13, 82, 223.

72 Juwaynī had already mentioned this in the very beginning of *GU*, 15.

73 *GU*, 226.

74 Nagel, *Staat und Glaubensgemeinschaft*, II, 80, has inaccurately observed that Juwaynī was the first Sunni jurist in whose theory power was a central theme. It is my argument, by contrast, that power, in Nagel's sense, was deemed the most essential feature of the sultanic executive by every Muslim political writer.

of Juwaynī's time amounted to demanding the ʿAbbāsid caliph abdicate in favor of the Saljūqs. In fact, Juwaynī argues in favor of this position: "If the imam loses his power and the flock disavow him for no obvious reason ... and if his supporters abandon him," he must be deposed and "the imamate should be entrusted to an imam whom people obey."[75] "The disobedience that we are witnessing now," he observes, "is due to the failure to appoint an imam who can, by virtue of his own power, resolve conflicts and quell revolts."[76] Therefore, should the imam fail to control the Community and should there be available another man whom Muslims will obey, it would be in the interest of everyone to depose the former and appoint the latter in his stead.[77] "The imam's failure to manage the affairs of the Community, to expand his control over the lands of Islam, and to suppress sedition" drives Juwaynī to call upon Niẓām al-Mulk, "who has reflected on the principles of this matter" with a view to ameliorating this situation.[78] This is a thinly veiled invitation to Niẓām-Mulk, as a representative of the Saljūqs, to assume caliphal power.

It is of little surprise then that throughout the book Juwaynī repeatedly attempts to present Niẓām al-Mulk as the savior of Islam, he who alone could serve so well the Community and polity and bring peace and prosperity back to the lands. Juwaynī conferred on him several honorary titles – such as "The Lord of the *Umma*," "The Refuge of People," "The Refuge of the *Dīn* and *Dunyā*," and "The Saviour of the *Dawla*" – all of which and others reflect the author's view of the Saljūq vizier as an effective and legitimate leader.[79]

At this point, Juwaynī enters into a polemic with a (hypothetical?) interlocutor who underestimates the achievements of the Saljūqs and claims against Juwaynī that they brought very little to improve the general state of affairs. Juwaynī uses this provocation to further elaborate in great detail on the great accomplishments of the Saljūqs, the services that they rendered to Sunni Islam, their victorious wars against the infidel Byzantines and others, the successful functioning of their administration, and more.[80] He asserts that "if the situation at this time of ours is compared with that in the past, it becomes clear how secure and prosperous our age is."[81] With all this Juwaynī wished to drive

75 *GU*, 89-90, 235 (ll. 2-3).
76 *GU*, 235 (ll. 4-6).
77 *GU*, 235 (ll. 10-13).
78 *GU*, 90 (ll. 9-10).
79 *GU*, 8-9, 13, 243, 260, 263, and passim.
80 *GU*, 246-55.
81 *GU*, 248 (ll. 7-8).

home the message that Niẓām al-Mulk in particular and the Saljūqs in general are eligible to take over the leadership of the Muslim *Umma*.

Juwaynī declares legitimate even the rule of a powerful group of people who have usurped power from a qualified imam, for it seems that the very fact of this usurpation is proof that no matter how competent the "seized" imam is, he would render himself and his rule superfluous in the presence of such a commanding power. Also valid are the appointments by this group of judges and officials serving in the provinces under their control. Consequently, legal decisions and decrees issued by these officials have equal legitimacy to those of the imam's appointed officials and may in fact supersede them. In justifying this claim he maintains that the nullification of the acts and decisions of those officials responsible to a body other than the imam would be detrimental to the well-being of the Community,[82] the highest desideratum and singularly supreme goal.

III

Juwaynī's radical hypotheticals about the total collapse of the imamate, the withering of its deputized offices, and the complete destruction of the Sharīʿa itself, inadvertently tells a constitutional story that is powerful precisely because it is hypothetical. In such scenarios as Juwaynī depicted, we can tell what matters and what does not, what comes as a first priority and what comes last. The scenarios present a picture in which all constitutional elements fit aggregately and symbiotically, but also separately, telling us how the entire political and legal systems of Islam, which are integral to each other, not only operated but also how the essential parts making the whole related to each other.

The profane military powers (mostly Turkic tribal federations taking over the business of rule in the Muslim world) were to be rehabilitated in the ethos of Muslim governance that, as we have seen, insisted on an unbreachable dialectic between the political and the ethical. The imamate was the embodiment of the institution of Prophethood, minus the original Prophetic function of delivering to humans a divine message. This latter, as we have seen, was deputized to the ulama as the interpreters of juridico-moral intent.

Māwardī, Ghazālī, and nearly every other political writer endeavored to maintain the caliphate within its epistemoral prophetic lineage, what I have

82 *GU*, 271-72.

coined as epistemoral genealogy. The insistence on this genealogical link was a stubborn refusal to abandon what I have elsewhere called the ethical benchmark,[83] one that would be comprehensively, even cosmologically, expounded by Ibn ʿArabī. Juwaynī, on the other hand, does not seem to have thought that the benchmark could be breached by his audacious proposal, for the foundations of the entire system, as well as its edifice and scaffoldings, were strong enough to maintain its ethos, one on the nature of which he as well as every other Sunni jurist agreed, even during the rule of the gunpowder empires. The safeguards that the system afforded seem to have assured him that, profane or not, the executive functions of the Saljūqs – as well as any other tribal power for that matter – would sit comfortably in the midst of communal life on the terms that that enduring system dictated, not on theirs. This is why he blatantly accused the ʿAbbāsid caliph of political and military incompetence and invited the Saljūqs, headed by their effective ruler, Niẓām al-Mulk, to take over the office.

Yet, at the very same time Juwaynī is glorifying Saljūq power and competence, he effectively insists, without a qualification, that nothing in the long-standing constitutional arrangements will change. Their caliph, like all other caliphs, is not entitled to make law and cannot even interfere in the least in the business of the law, be it the *madhhab* or the substantive enforcement of the legal system at large. Sharīʿa's determination of the division of legal labor gave the sultan what is to the sultan and to the jurists what is to the jurists, and the two were not to be confused or intermingled.

Juwaynī's radical scenarios further underscored this constitutional division of labor, one that was determined by no other than the Empire of Law. Not only is it that no matter who sits in the caliphal office will remain constantly obliged to fit within the dictates of this constitutional configuration; it is also that this very configuration had no genealogy other than what Hans Kelsen called, in a different context, the *Grundnorm*. In the strong implication of Juwaynī's unwitting hypothetical revelation, there is no recognized constitutional *Grundnorm* outside of the law. There is no polity or political culture that can, as a matter of law and politics, either legislate or determine the constitutional boundaries of the executive and the political. The law was the point of beginning and, as Juwaynī affirmed, end. The third part of the book depicts an Islamic world in which all political institutions have collapsed as an integral part of the Decline of History (*fasād al-zamān*), but the longest

83 See Introduction, n. 71.

surviving of all phenomena was the Sharīʿa, that which came first and that which disappeared last. This, as we will see in due course,[84] had decisively but *ab initio* resolved the so-called Paradox of Sovereignty. The Sharīʿa as culture, structure,[85] habitus, and discursive tradition could sustain governance in the absence of any props.[86]

Finally, we might ask whether or not Juwaynī's *GU* represents an exception to the general tenor of Islamic political writings which, we must insist, delineated the constitutional boundaries of the various organs of government. The specific invitation this illustrious jurist extended to the Saljūqs to claim the very office of the caliphate, and the political marriages that were initiated to substantiate this ambition, were highly exceptional indeed. The attempt to take over – not merely control – the ʿAbbāsid lineage in substantive and formal terms was unique, for to my knowledge no other sultanic entity had ever attempted such a venture. Yet this seeming exception must be read as a project of constitutional validation of the system that was not only in place but was rather entrenched in the juridico-political whole.

For Juwaynī to allow a tribal entity that had only recently entered the cultural dominion of Islam to take over a traditionally Qurayshī institution can be plausibly read as risking a derivative danger in favor of averting a foundationalist one. To avert the latter, it was a small price to pay to allow a tribalist protector to command the constitutional foundations of executive power. The safeguards of the juridical system were sufficiently solid and secure as to allow such a daring venture. The law was the decider, for it not only undergirded the political structures themselves but also outlasted them. Had the Saljūq "colonization" of the caliphate threatened the Sharʿī foundations of polity, Juwaynī would not have gone as far as he did. It was only a limitless trust in the solidity of the sustaining juridical structure that allowed Juwaynī to dare as he did. Juwaynī's seeming exceptionalism only affirms the basic assumptions which every other constitutional theorist knew all too well.

What generated this confidence is something that we will take up in the later chapters of this book. For now, we continue our narrative of constitutional mapping by looking into the rise of perhaps the most fundamental constitutional challenge in the history of premodern Islam, namely, the problem whose solution lay in the rise of *siyāsa sharʿiyya*.

84 See ch. 12, below.
85 As defined in the Introduction, sec. II.
86 See ch. 5, n. 153 and Siddiqui, "Power Vs. Authority," 198-99, 210 ff.

Part II

ADJUSTMENT AND CHANGE IN LATER EMPIRES

Chapter 7

Reaffirming the Boundaries of Executive Power: The Mamlūk Shāfiʿī Discursive Tradition

If by the early fifth/eleventh century the constitutional map of Islam was drawn to the last detail, the executive power and privilege was to remain, as it has always been everywhere,[1] a perennial concern. The general American anxiety about the so-called "twilight zone"[2] of presidential powers was almost always due to the fear of kingly excesses and monarchical abuses. I shall argue that this was not the most immediate concern of our Muslim constitutionalist thinkers, for their anxiety was rather about the insufficiency of coercive might within those constitutional boundaries that ought to belong to the executive domain.

The general *structure* of Islamic governance did not change much from the fourth/tenth century down to the Mamlūks, who ruled the greater parts of Syria, Egypt, and the Hijaz, roughly between 648/1250 and 923/1516. The salient features of this rule were military tribal powers invading the Eastern parts of Muslim domains and asserting dominance over the classical caliphate. The Mamlūks made every effort to transpose the remnants of the ʿAbbāsid House into Cairo, their capital, with the full recognition of the necessity of a caliph for the legitimacy of their rule. While the incumbent caliph possessed no effective powers whatever, legitimacy through the genealogy of the institution – what I have called the caliphal vessel – remained indispensable for governance.

1 See, for instance, Ackerman, *Decline and Fall of the American Republic*; Reinstein, "Limits of Executive Power."

2 Justice Jackson's expression in his celebrated opinion in *Youngstown Sheet & Tube Co. vs. Sawyer* (1952), which was adopted more than once by the US Supreme Court. See Reinstein, "Limits of Executive Power," 260, 262.

No administrative or political appointment would be deemed legitimate without the presumption of an authoritative issuance from caliphal will. As noted earlier, caliphal authorization of sultanic coercive power represented the Prophetic continuity, the Prophetic stamp, that gave Islamic executive power its distinctive religious and ethical form, and that differentiated it from the profane power of the Persian Kisrās, Byzantine Emperors, and their likes.

I

Our first constitutionalist thinker is Badr al-Dīn Ibn Jamā'a (639-733/1242-1333), a distinguished Shāfi'ī jurist and Ṣūfī who also acted as a Ḥadīth and law professor as well as Chief Justice of Egypt and Syria. His relevant work is titled *Taḥrīr al-Aḥkām fī Tadbīr Ahl al-Islām* (henceforth, *TAJ*), suggesting an attempt at articulating the rules and doctrines pertaining to the governance or management (*tadbīr*) of the Islamic domains. The first few lines of the treatise already establish a lineage with Māwardī's influential work, using virtually identical language. Ibn Jamā'a specifically states that his work is intended to engage in "*al-aḥkām al-sulṭāniyya*," the very words defining the celebrated title of Māwardī's tome.[3] The formal contents of the two works are likewise similar, but the referentiality to the different temporal locations and political experiences – separated by nearly three centuries – is unmistakably distinct in each work. It is not an overstretch to argue that Ibn Jamā'a's work – as well as those of the other constitutional thinkers to be discussed in the remaining parts of this chapter – represents a constitutional update for a different time and place. Such "textual" updates, reflecting the changing circumstances and the norms that govern them, were characteristic to the Islamic tradition, as massively evidenced in the development of the law.[4]

Consistent with Māwardī's foundational political philosophy, *TAJ* posits the indispensability of the ruler to adjudicate disputes between and among people "with justice." The ruling authority here is Qur'ān 38:26, where God commands David to act as his own deputy in dispensing justice on Earth.[5]

3 *TAJ*, 45. Also compare the language at *AS*, 15 and *TAJ*, 48 (par. 5).

4 On "generational updates" and legal change in the Sharī'a, see Hallaq, *Authority*.

5 "O David, We have made you a deputy [of ours] on Earth, so judge among people with justice and do not follow the passions." See *TAJ*, 48, and discussion of the verse in main text in ch. 2, at n. 25.

The essence of the function of the imam is to protect the weak, restore rights, rebuff aggression, and prevent corruption. These duties and tasks cannot be accomplished without a *sulṭān*, a term introduced interchangeably in the same passage in which the imam is declared indispensable. This is why, "as the wisemen (*ḥukamā'*) have pronounced, a sultan who rules unjustly for forty years is better than leaving the subjects (*ra'iyya*) to their own devices for one hour."[6] Even the arch-moralist Ibn Ḥanbal, the eponym of the Ḥanbalī legal school, is quoted by the Shāfi'ī author as saying: "If I were to be allowed only a single supplication that would be answered, it would be in favor of the sultan, because his justice brings forth justice in [his] lands and among people, but his corruption brings corruption to them both."[7]

All this is standard fare, having run throughout the centuries-long course of Islamic political wisdom. And so is, in substance, the distinction between the two types of imama, the voluntary and the involuntary (*ikhtiyāriyya/qahriyya*).[8] Ibn Jamā'a here enumerates the conditions of the classical, voluntary type and its modes of election, and then quickly moves to the involuntary type, the practice of his age and of the four centuries prior. When no imam of the first type can fulfill said requirements (already elaborated by Māwardī),[9] then obedience is due to the one who musters coercive force and dominant "popular" support,[10] with a view to enabling him to rule effectively, with or without recourse to the procedures of appointment which the classical imamate requires. In good Juwaynian fashion, the final arbiter in determining incumbency is sufficient, effective, coercive power and popular dominance to enforce law and order and to implement the necessary forms of governance (*tadbīr*). "If the imamate is contracted to someone, but then another has risen to defeat the former with his effective might and military power, then the former is deposed and the latter becomes the imam."[11]

---

6 *TAJ*, 49.
7 *TAJ*, 51.
8 *TAJ*, 51-56.
9 See ch. 2, above, and *AS*, 40; *ADD*, 222.
10 *TAJ*, 55. The expressions used by Ibn Jamā'a here are the familiar *shawka* and *ghalaba*, the latter more general and encompassing than the former in that it may include the support of the powerful dynastic members, the ulama, Ṣūfīs, and the masses; this last generally referring to the urban population of the main cities of the polity (this is what is usually meant when our authors speak of *atbā' wa-ashyā'*).
11 *TAJ*, 55: "*Wa-idhā in 'aqadat al-imāmatu bil-shawkati wal-ghalabati li-wāḥidin thumma qāma ākharun fa-qahara al-awwala bi-shawkatihi wa-junūdihi, in'azala al-awwalu wa-ṣāra al-thāni imāman.*"

Yet, the condition of effective power was not deemed fixed in its constitution but could be inflected according to need and circumstance. If the polity, for instance, is threatened by an external enemy when transition of power is taking place, then the candidate who possesses most military force should be installed. But if external borders are secure while internal sectarian dissention is rife, then military force would be insufficient, for knowledge (*ʿilm*) of the systems of belief and of the intellectual life of the Community would be an equally important, if not more crucial, requirement under the circumstances.[12]

Yet, there seems to be an inconsistency entailed in this vision of the transition in rule, where a powerful leader asserting his dominance over another would logically preclude any allowance for choosing and picking, by anyone. The possessor of *shawka* and *ghalaba* (ability to vanquish) will dominate irrespective of his qualities as a ruler. But this would be a warped reading of Ibn Jamāʿa, if we consider the political background and Mamlūk context of his theory. First, one should never assume that sultans and kings rose to power and rule without complex alliances and a heavy reliance on family, communal, and dynastic ties. Such leaders were surrounded by immediate and often powerful family members, including mothers, brothers, sisters, and uncles. They were as often surrounded by generals who might even be as powerful, if not more powerful than they are, especially under the Mamlūks. When an emir seized power, it was true that he was a dominating force, but not the only one. His rise to power could be after a take-over, such as an assassination or an ousting (usually involving the banishment of the deposed sultan) with the aid of other emirs. This explains why some sultans ruled more than one reign, often separated by years. Needless to say, individual political and personal interests were at stake, but the well-being of the Mamlūk House was considered more important. Threatening the very existence of this House was avoided at almost any cost, for loyalty to it was self-evidently paramount.

Second, Ibn Jamāʿa's assumption of ever-changing imminent threats (both external invasions and internal dissention) would not be plausible if we were to assume long-term rule of monarchs, but this was not the case under the Mamlūks. During his adult life, he witnessed eleven turns in rule, with no fewer than nine different sultans ruling,[13] and eight more after he

12 *TAJ*, 56.

13 The nine sultans are: al-Malik al-Ẓāhir, al-Malik al-Saʿīd, al-Malik al-ʿĀdil (Badr al-Dīn Salāmish), al-Malik al-Manṣūr (Qalāwūn), al-Malik Ashraf, al-Malik al-Nāṣir (three

was born,[14] including four Ayyubid monarchs. The average reign of sultans was less than six years, consistent with the entire history of Mamlūk rule. A reading of the Mamlūk annals clearly shows the quick turn of events and rapid changes in both internal and external threats, the menace of the Crusades being only one. Third, in the midst of all this fluid context, there were other significant pressure-groups that played a role in governance and thus in the dynamics of power-change, not least of which were the jurists and the Ṣūfīs. Thus, Ibn Jamāʿa's theorization comports well with the reality on the ground, allowing for seizure by force that is the *result* of a complex power dynamic that transcends the narrow limits and simplicity of mere military ascendancy.

The question that remains however is why would Ibn Jamāʿa still incorporate the classical theory of the imamate in the brief section opening his work, a terse yet pithy text of no more than eighty lines? As we have seen throughout our chapters thus far, the theory of the imamate is neither idealistic nor utopian. Rather, its statement and restatement by political writers captures the constitutional genealogy of Islamic governance, which always seeks to connect the boundaries and definition of executive power with their originalist caliphal conception. Whoever is charged with political rule must fulfill specific and well-defined functions, whether he is a caliph, sultan, or imam, this last being the more general and encompassing of the former two.

Oftentimes, Ibn Jamāʿa's language does not distinguish between one title and another, an indication not of confusion or weak theoretical thinking but rather of a clear understanding that no matter what the title may be, the functions remain within the outlined constitutional boundaries of the political *practice* of governance. This is clearly attested to in the first chapter, consisting of some eighty lines. The title of the chapter is "On the Necessity of the Imamate and the Conditions and Rules Governing the Imam."[15] The opening line cites the celebrated Qur'ānic verse of David, in which the key term is "*khalīfa*." This latter is thus quickly elided into the term and concept of the "imamate," only to segue, after two lines, into "*mulūk*," the plural form of the term *malik* (king). All these are again made to mutate within four more lines into the term "*sulṭān*," who is here equated with "imam." The second

reigns), al-Malik al-ʿĀdil (Zayn al-Dīn Kutbugha), al-Malik al-Manṣūr (Lājīn), and al-Malik al-Muẓaffar (Baybārs al-Jāshnakīr).

14 The first three Mamlūk sultans are: al-Malik al-Muʿizz, al-Malik al-Manṣūr (Nūr al-Dīn ʿAlī), and al-Muẓaffar (Quṭuz).

15 *TAJ*, 48: "*Fī wujūbi al-Imāmati wa-Shurūṭi al-Imāmi wa-Aḥkāmih.*"

paragraph of the book begins by the declaration that "It is necessary (*yajibu*) to appoint an imam ... because people's well-being cannot be achieved without a sultan...."[16] In the same vein, the next two short paragraphs alternate between "*sulṭān*" and "*malik*" and between "*malik*" and "*imām*." Ibn Jamāʿa even quotes an anonymous statement to the effect that no one ranks higher than a just sultan except a prophet or a beloved king.[17] In the remaining pages of this chapter, the imam is equated with "*sulṭān*," in that they both can hold power voluntarily or involuntarily. It is also clear beyond a shadow of doubt that "*imām*" and "*sulṭān*" are perfectly interchangeable.[18] This is particularly evident in the section dealing with the *bayʿa* to an involuntary imam, namely a sultan who takes over power by force.[19] "He to whom the *bayʿa* is contracted can be called *khalīfa*," that is, "*khalīfa* of God's Messenger, because he is his deputy (*khalīfa*) over his Community (*Ummatihi*). The more correct opinion (*aṣaḥḥ*)[20] is not to call him God's caliph."[21]

At a minimum, we can conclude with certainty that for Ibn Jamāʿa the terms "imam" and "sultan" are effectively one and the same. But to say, as some recent writers have done, that Ibn Jamāʿa disposed of the caliphate altogether is plainly wrong.[22] The caliphate was the constitutional font without which no further political office could have been legitimate.[23] The idea here is that whether nominal or effective, even existent or non-existent in political terms, the caliphate and its genealogical political structure remain necessary for Islamic governance to qualify as Islamic. The caliphate was not only an institution but also a discursive tradition and political and legal culture. And the reason is that it is the only institution and political form that could maintain, enforce, and promote the Sharīʿa, its institutions, and culture. The sultanate was simply the distilled form of the caliphate.

Now, with these constitutional postulates restated and reconfirmed, Ibn Jamāʿa is ready to move to the next stage of the argument, which captures the specific purpose of his work. While the imamate theory stands intact,

---

16 *TAJ*, 48.

17 *TAJ*, 50: "*Wa-qīla laysa fawqa rutbati al-sulṭāni al-ʿādili rutbatun illā nabiyyan mursalan aw malikan muqarraban.*"

18 See *TAJ*, 55-56, especially on the latter page, at section 3.

19 *TAJ*, 55, regarding "*al-bayʿa al-qahriyya.*"

20 On this concept, as standing in contradistinction with "correct," see Hallaq, *Authority*, 133-48, esp. at 136-39.

21 *TAJ*, 57.

22 El-Merheb, *Political Thought*, 67 and subtitle of book: "The Unnecessary Caliphate."

23 See for instance *TAJ*, 48, 55-57, 58, 79. See also n. 66, below, and ch. 2.

the changing political circumstances require the updating of the statement of constitutional boundaries and limits. This penchant for updating doctrine and discursive practice was standard fare in the juridical and political landscapes of Islam, and, I hypothesize, in all other major genres. Just as the jurists constantly updated substantive law itself,[24] they did the same in the case of governance and constitutional doctrine. (As I will argue in later chapters, the sphere of political doctrine experienced no less remarkable change than that of substantive law,[25] this later for long held by Orientalists to have been unchangeable and thus doomed to ossification.)

Ibn Jamāʿa's constitutional assumption is that the caliph is the one who makes all appointments, these being necessary on the grounds of practical need. The caliph cannot by himself administer the entirety of his far-flung domains.[26] In a clear reassertion of Māwardī's constitutional understanding, taken for granted as a habitus,[27] no delegated official of the caliph is allowed to exceed his functional jurisdiction. For instance, a military appointment cannot extend to financial administration unless his caliphal appointment decree stipulates so. The governing "custom in our times" has been for the caliphs to appoint kings and sultans to govern without functional or jurisdictional limitation. Their delegation is totalistic (*tafwīḍan ʿāmman*),[28] involving the range of responsibilities and duties that Māwardī and others have specified. This is why, Ibn Jamāʿa seems to argue, all credentials and conditions required of the caliph to qualify for the business of governing must obtain in the case of the sultans, except the condition of hailing from Quraysh.[29]

The symbiotic relationship between caliph and sultan assumed in this seemingly abstract and theoretical discourse cannot be simplistically reduced to an attempt at the legitimation of coercive might and physical power of compulsion. An invading army that aims to replace Islamic values and law by the invader's heretical or "loathsome" ways of living and governance would

24 See Hallaq, *Authority*, 208-35 and passim.
25 Hallaq, *Authority*.
26 *TAJ*, 58: "*Li'anna al-ḥājata tadʿū ilā dhālika, lā siyyamā fil-bilādi al-baʿīda.*"
27 On habitus, see Introduction, sec. I and II; ch. 1, 2, and 10 (sec. III). Māwardī's writings in *ADD*, *AS*, and *TN* (among others) represent the average, mainstream conception of not only the Sharʿī norms and institutional functioning, but also what we might call social contract theory and existing political norms-cum-imagination. Read properly, they are "cultural texts" as much as they are political, ethical, or constitutional.
28 *TAJ*, 60: "*Tafwīḍan ʿāmman, kaʿurfi al-mulūki wal-salāṭīna fī zamāninā.*"
29 *TAJ*, 60.

obviously not have received the endorsement of the constitutional theorists, for such a scenario would negate not only the very ideas and values they held dear but also the entire structure of Islamdom they stood for, served, and advocated. If the fundamental and governing assumption in caliphal rule is to govern efficiently and execute the law with justice and order, then the caliph – as well as any other functionary – must surrender this office and function to whomever can perform it better than he does.

The question that arises at this juncture is why would an incompetent power not be removed from the scene, and removed in its entirety? Why retain the caliphate if it is incompetent, and if it is clearly replaceable and substitutable? This crux is then about the persistence of what might mistakenly appear as the useless caliphate. And the answer – which ought to be almost self-evident by now – is that the caliphal genealogy of power effectively amounts to a definition of substantive content as well as the boundaries of the executive, that is, boundaries that marked a radical separation between the legislative and the executive.

It is not surprising then that Ibn Jamāʿa has no qualms in asserting that a caliph is in fact under duty to delegate all his executive powers and privileges to a mighty sultan who ascends to power by virtue of military strength. Should the pretender to power not meet the caliphal qualifications – which capture the range of duties incumbent upon the holder of executive power – the caliph should in this case appoint another official who will fulfill and supplement those duties that the pretender is unable to meet.[30] It thus remains true that as long as the duties of the imam are dispensed, it matters little who does the dispensing.

In an interesting presentation of the duties and rights of the "sultan and caliph," treated here interchangeably, Ibn Jamāʿa waxes rhetorical in a seeming attempt to equate between these rights and duties, on the one hand, and those belonging to the populace, on the other. Each of these consists of ten parts, but the math must not mask the substantive difference. There is much in Ibn Jamāʿa's theory that is revealed by a close examination of these mutual duties and rights, especially in comparison to Māwardī's foundational discourse. I will first deal with the duties the populace owes the rulers, be they sultans or caliphs.

In *AS*, Māwardī captures the duties of the subjects toward the sultan and caliph in no more than two lines, in effect saying that if these leaders fulfill their

30 *TAJ*, 61.

end of the bargain – namely, that they perform their duties as prescribed by the law[31] – then the subjects (for which Māwardī here uses the term "*Umma*") owe them obedience (*ṭāʿa*) and support (*nuṣra*). Our theorist offers no explication as to what these two concepts exactly mean. Be that as it may, obedience and support are furthermore predicated on the condition that the ruler continue to maintain the qualities and attributes he was elected for, such as sound sensory perception, freedom, etc.[32] For instance, should he be afflicted with loss of vision or fall into captivity, the people/*Umma*/subjects owe him no obedience or support, for he would be dismissed from office at any rate.

Ibn Jamāʿa, by contrast, elaborates these duties in ten points, expanding on and detailing Māwardī's terse account. It would seem that our Mamlūk author wishes to create a balanced contract or covenant between ruler and subject, one that bestows on both sides equivalence in duty and right. Yet, there is something artificial about this expansion, recursivity, and rhetorical flourish. The ten points he presents in fact boil down to hardly four substantive categories, the first of which is the familiar requirement of obedience, including the duty of the populace to abide "by his commands and prohibitions." Obedience should furthermore operate at the inner and external levels, meaning that it should be exhibited in public and believed by the heart, all the same. Yet, this is entirely predicated on the assumption that what the ruler commands and prohibits is consistent with the Sharīʿa, for "there is no obedience to a created being who disobeys the Creator."[33]

The second point is the duty of offering counsel, a venerable tradition that permeated the various facets of Islamic life and genres over centuries. Counsel should be offered both confidentially and publicly, which explains the proliferation of political advice literature, among others. To this category belong the fifth, sixth, and seventh points, which include alerting the ruler regarding possible errors of judgment and misconduct of his deputized officials, let alone warning him against impending dangers, betrayals, and the like.[34]

Third is the duty of support, again, both publicly and privately. The support should be maximal, to the best effort one can exert, for the ultimate beneficiary of this help (as of giving advice) are the Muslims and their polity, whose

---

31 Articulated in ten points in *AS*, 40-41, and in seven in *ADD*, 222.

32 *AS*, 42-47.

33 *TAJ*, 61-62. This is originally a Ḥadīth and a universally accepted legal and political maxim: "*Lā ṭāʿāta li-makhlūqin fī maʿṣiyati al-khāliq.*"

34 *TAJ*, 63-64.

protection against aggression and disruption is a priority. To this category of support belongs assistance and aid to the ruler (points eight and ten), as well as persuading people to empathize with him in word and deed (points nine and ten). Finally, the fourth point demands respect and appreciation for the ruler's status, a somewhat surprising requirement. Ibn Jamāʿa remarks that "the leading ulama of Islam," who are widely known for their piety and faith, have traditionally appreciated and respected the rulers, and obliged their requests. The last sentence in the relevant passage reveals why Ibn Jamāʿa has introduced this "duty" to his list. He complains that "what some of the followers of asceticism do in terms of treating the rulers with disrespect is not acceptable and does not comport with sunna/Sunna."[35] In light of the concluding synthetic remark to the "ten duties" he enumerated, it is not difficult to see why Ibn Jamāʿa offers such a mild criticism of "some ascetics." "If these ten duties are performed properly and carefully," then people will live with each other peacefully, and unity will be accomplished.[36]

Whereas the people's duties to the ruler are summed up under the categories of obedience, counsel, support, and respect, the ten duties of the ruler toward the people are extensive, detailed, and proliferating. It is worth stressing here that the term Ibn Jamāʿa chooses to use to present the two lists of duties is "*ḥaqq*," which literally means "a right," that which a party to a contract or covenant owes to another party by virtue of rights that arise from such an agreement. It should be understood therefore that when Ibn Jamāʿa speaks of duties that the populace and the imam owe each other, he is speaking of rights owed in both directions.

II

Now, comparing Ibn Jamāʿa's repertoire of duties to Māwardī's list is instructive. Ibn Jamāʿa begins with the duty to protect the borders (which is to say, the right of the populace to have the borders defended by the ruler), as well as the duty to rebuff external aggression, build and maintain the army and

35 He is likely referring to the Ṣūfī *shaykhs*. See *TAJ*, 63: "*Wa-mā yafʿaluhu baʿḍu al-muntasibīna ilā al-zuhdi min qillati al-adabi maʿhum fa-laysa min al-sunnati.*" The meaning of "*sunna*" here may refer to the Prophetic Sunna but could also mean "the normative, established, customary, or/and accepted practice."

36 *TAJ*, 64.

military fortresses. This requirement occupied third place in Māwardī's list, but Ibn Jamāʿa is fully justified in giving it first rank.[37] During his lifetime, he was witness to the repeated but existentially threatening Mongol and Crusading assaults on the Ayyūbid and Mamlūk domains. The survival of the Mamlūks against these enemies, who would upend Islamdom altogether should they defeat the slaves' dynasty, had an existential purpose no less crucial than the very survival of Islamdom itself.

The second of the ruler's duties is to "preserve religion" (*ḥifẓ al-dīn*) by way of fighting against heresy and the promotion of Islam's "religious" -institutions. This is also Māwardī's requirement (being the first in his list), but Ibn Jamāʿa supplements this requirement with the advice that the ruler should heed the ulama's counsel, including seeking advice about legal rulings and the lines of reasoning sustaining them (*mawārid al-aḥkām*). Again, the language of this requirement, especially the provision that appealing or upending an earlier court decision (*al-naqḍ wal-ibrām*)[38] should be avoided, rings true in light of the Mamlūk sultans' and emirs' incursions against the Sharīʿa and its judicial operation.[39]

The third requirement, entirely absent from Māwardī's *AS* and only hinted at in his *ADD*,[40] is the duty to uphold the "pillars" of Islam (*shaʿāʾr al-dīn*), such as public call for prayer, public sermons, fasting, holidays' public celebrations, and securing roads and logistics for pilgrimage.[41] This requirement is entirely absent from Māwardī, although it is faintly implied in the first item on his lists in *ADD* and *AS*.

The fourth duty is the appointment of qualified and trustworthy judges and governors to administer justice and resolve disputes. This is also weakly implied in Māwardī's second requirement, but its phraseology seems to overly stress the care the ruler should exercise in appointing upright and credentialed personnel.[42]

---

37 This continued to be one of the decisive elements, if not the most crucial, in the list of the ruler's duties, even as late as the dawn of early modernity. It is the duty that separated the sultanic class of officials (*ahl al-sayf*; Ottoman: *askeri*) from the juristic and learned class that represented the civic population. See the illustrative exchange between a *Yeniçeri* commander and the leading Ottoman jurists in Abou-El-Haj, "Power and Social Order," 82.

38 *TAJ*, 65.

39 See ch. 10, below, where I offer a detailed discussion of the unique circumstances that led to what one might describe as anarchy.

40 *AS*, 10–11; *ADD*, 222.

41 *TAJ*, 66.

42 *TAJ*, 67: "*Wa-lā yuwallī dhālika illā man yuthaqu bi-diyānatihi wa-amānatihi wa-ṣiyānatihi mina al-ʿulamāʾi wal-ṣulaḥāʾi wal-kufāti al-nuṣaḥāʾ*."

The fifth is the duty to perform *jihād*, beginning with the person of the caliph and sultan and extending to his armies. This should be performed at least once a year if the Muslim military is able to do so. This requirement is absent in Māwardī's *ADD*, but commands a little over a line in *AS*. The relative detail given to it by Ibn Jamāʿa again reflects the imminent existential threat that both the powerful Mongols and Crusades had posed to the Mamlūk dominions.

The sixth is the enforcement of "Qur'ānic punishments according to the dictated rules," this being "applicable to both the weak and the strong, the lowly and the noble."[43] This latter qualification in regard to the need to treat all transgressors, irrespective of their social status, equally does not appear in Māwardī's fourth point on *ḥudūd*.[44] The stress Ibn Jamāʿa brings to the fore might be a reflection of the Mamlūk tendency to overlook some of the emirs' abuses of power, which often went unpunished.[45]

The seventh – nearly identical in order and substance to its cognate in Māwardī's *AS* – is the collection and redistribution of taxes (*zakāt*, *jizya*, *fay'*, *kharāj*) according to Sharʿī rules, a charge that also requires mandating trustworthy officers to undertake these tasks.[46]

Eighth, supervision of the operation of charitable endowments (*waqf*s) and construction and repair of roads and irrigation canals. This bundle of requirements does not make an explicit appearance in Māwardī's *AS* but *ADD* lists it in a similar yet general language under the third duty.[47] In *TN*, however, Māwardī gives an elaborate account of these duties under the category of "construction projects."[48] In Cairo as well as in all towns located on the banks of the Nile, irrigation canals were crucial for the economic life of the country (and relevant to optimizing tax revenue from land and on agricultural production). And it was the Mamlūk sultan and senior emirs who were held responsible for their maintenance and proper

43 *TAJ*, 67: "*Iqāmatu al-ḥudūdi al-sharʿiyyati ʿalā al-shurūṭi al-marʿiyya*," the latter qualification being in reference to the elaborate rules of procedure surrounding Qur'ānic punishments (*ḥudūd*).

44 *AS*, 40. In *ADD*, 222, this duty appears sixth in order; here, Māwardī says that the Qur'ānic punishments should be implemented with neither excess nor undue restraint. For an explanation of the *ḥudūd* and their procedures, see ch. 8, n. 75.

45 For a detailed treatment of these infractions and for the exceptional circumstances that gave rise to them, see ch. 10, below.

46 *TAJ*, 68; AS, 40; In *ADD*, it briefly appears fourth in order.

47 *TAJ*, 68; *ADD*, 222.

48 TN, 163-64.

operation.[49] As we will see, the Mamlūk irrigation system was, within the context of the Nile floods and the Black Death, directly related to the collapse of the legal and, later, political system of the empire.[50]

Ninth, supervision of the division of booty, an important duty to the details of which Ibn Jamāʿa will dedicate a sizable chapter toward the end of his work.[51]

Tenth and last is the duty of the ruler to act justly in all aspects of governance. The duty amounts in effect to an essential right of the governed against those who govern them. Ibn Jamāʿa dedicates two full pages to this item, constituting almost half of the entire text allocated to the exposition of the ruler's duties. The discourse here ranges from the philosophers' political pronouncements about the symbiosis of the ruling elite and the ruled populace to the Ghazālīan remonstrance pertaining to the ruler's duty to act with justice as a loaded token of gratitude for the bounty that God has bestowed upon him in granting him the opportunity to rule. "Since there is no bounty weightier than that which God bestows on the sultan, the sultan's gratitude must be the greatest of all [forms of] gratitude."[52]

The expression and outer manifestation of this gratitude is justice, for there is no repayment for the boundless bounty the sultan receives for being who he became than the implementation of justice among God's own creatures. This is why, Ibn Jamāʿa explains, it was said in a Ḥadīth that "a single day of justice by the imam is better than him worshiping God for sixty years."[53] Yet, without considering divine reward, mere reason dictates that justice is good for worldly gains. Despite their heresy and disbelief in the rewards of the Hereafter, many of the Persian kings were just because they well knew that justice brings forth prosperity and thus the political longevity of their rule. "This is why the men of wisdom proclaimed: kingship is an edifice whose foundation is the military; the military is an army constituted by wealth; wealth is the fruit of constructive projects; and constructive projects are made possible through the implementation of justice."[54] In contrast, injustice and oppression lead

49 Canals and means of irrigation were standard obligations of the executive. See Qudāma Ibn Jaʿfar, *Kharāj*, 248; *SM*, 50; *TAJ*, 68; Black, *History of Islamic Political Thought*, 115. See also ch. 1, n. 73.

50 See ch. 10, especially at n. 118.

51 *TAJ*, 188-230.

52 *TAJ*, 69.

53 *TAJ* 69.

54 This is known as the Circle of Justice. *TAJ*, 70: "*Qāla al-ḥukamāʾu: al-mulku bināʾun asāsuhu al-jundu, wal-jundu jayshun yajmaʿuhum al-mālu, wal-mālu rizqun tajlibuhu al-*

to ruin, for everyone. This is not just a matter of revealed truth, within and without Islam, but also one universally dictated by reason.[55]

Two significant points arise from these rights and duties, which Ibn Jamāʿa conveys to his readers through the single expression of "*ḥaqq*." The term simultaneously functions in an oppositional manner. A *ḥaqq* to which someone is entitled (*ḥaqq lahu*) automatically gives rise to a corresponding duty on behalf of another (*ḥaqq ʿalayhi*). This is not to be confused with the autonomous use of the term, which connotes "the Truth," and usually prefaced with a definite article, as in "*wa-huwa al-ḥaqq*" ("this is the Truth"). In the domain of politics and legal obligation, *ḥaqq* engenders a duty or a counter-obligation, and vice versa; which is to say that *ḥaqq* operates within a relation. If someone is entitled to a *ḥaqq*, then another is under the obligation to meet that demand.[56] It is therefore essential to ask: By what authority is the distribution of *ḥaqq* as right and duty legitimated?

In the liberal tradition, as a major example, rights and duties are determined by the state, and often have no necessary trading worth in relation to each other. A right might arise and be sanctioned without a duty attached to it, this being grounded in a political conception that harks back to the venerated concept of natural rights, regarded, by definition, as intrinsic. The grounding here presupposes a non-integrated view of the world, where things are not inherently connected and tied with each other in an organically structured whole. In the liberal conception, even in as "religious" a country as the United States, the world as conceived by law and politics is not a system that is endowed with a mover, an agent who consciously and designedly manages the world in which we live. This is a crucial point of difference in comparison with a conception of a closely knitted universe, where everything ultimately connects with everything else, and that a necessary relation must exist, even by logical and ontological entailment, between and among things that encounter each other. Encounters, therefore, whether they are human or inanimate, are integral to a divine ecology from which arises a set of rights that are intrinsically and "naturally" accompanied by duties. Thus, when we state that Islam is a system of duties, we would be quite right to say so if and only if we mean that these duties always give rise to rights.

ʿimāratu, wal-ʿimāratu ʿamalun yanmū bil-ʿadl." On this Circle, see Darling, *History of Social Justice*; Hallaq, *Sharīʿa*, 197-221; and ch. 1, n. 102.

55 *TAJ*, 70: "*Wa-qad ittafaqat sharāʾiʿu al-anbiyāʾi wa-ārāʾu al-ḥukamāʾi wal-ʿuqalāʾi....*"

56 Zabīdī, *Tāj al-ʿArūs*, XIII, 80-81.

The second point concerns the crux of the relationship between these duties-as-rights and a legally defined sphere of politics. Having expounded the duties that the sultan owes his subjects, and those that the subjects owe their ruler, Ibn Jamāʿa stresses that in all other matters and spheres of life, the sultan is no different from anyone else. He is deemed to be of the same stock as all other Muslim individuals in rights and obligations as well as in matters of obedience or disobedience to the law. He must also see himself, vis-à-vis God, as standing in the shoes of his delegated officials and lieutenants because he is, like them, directly responsible for God's property, which is nothing other than the kingdom he rules. And he rules it by God's grace and order, and according to His Law (Sharīʿa), which obviously is not of his making or conception.[57] The law is thus categorically above him and above his dynasty, and thus, also categorically speaking, he is not to legislate. This becomes abundantly clear from a thorough examination of the list of the sultan's duties Ibn Jamāʿa has just articulated, a list that, in terms of rule of law, is nearly identical to all the writings of other constitutional thinkers that we have examined thus far. The landmark of this rule of law is the *radical* separation between the executive and the legislative, the latter being – as we saw – a systemic, communal, cultural, and generational product. It ought to be clear here that by "radical" I do not mean to indicate the state of being extreme (as in "radical political position") but rather that the separation occurred *at the root* (Lat., *radicalis*) of the very system we call Islam. The separation, that is to say, was foundational.[58]

III

It is precisely this radical separation that enabled the persistence of the legal against the political, sustaining the power of the legal norm to regulate and adjudicate politics and political practice. This power also created and maintained a political habitus, the conscious and unconscious norms (*doxa*), the

57 *TAJ*, 71: "*Wa-mā siwā dhālika* [i.e., what he expounded in terms of the subjects' and sultan's duties and rights toward and against each other] *fal-sulṭānu fīhi wāḥidun mina al-muslimīna, la-hu mā lahum wa-ʿalayhi mā ʿalayhim min farḍin wa sunnatin wa-ṭāʿatin wa-maʿṣiyatin wa-ḥalālin wa-harāmin wa-ghayri dhālika min al-aḥkāmi.... Yajibu ʿalā al-sulṭāni an yunzila nafsahu min Allāhi taʿala bi-manzilati wulātihi wa-nuwwābihi, li annahu fī milki il-lāhi al-ladhī aqāmahu fīhi yataṣarrafu, wa-bi-sharīʿatihi al-latī amarahu bi-hā yaʿmalu.*"

58 Hence the title of the present book.

benchmark within which governance was exercised and found cultural and political expression. The dominating discourse that propped this habitus and gave it its own expression was legal, largely expressed by the very treatises and the world of discourse they inhabited, treatises we have been exploring throughout this book. They naturally stood concomitant with the sociology that produced them and that was represented by the "legislative" population of scholars, otherwise known as the interpreters of the law.

The rest of Ibn Jamāʿa's book represents an extensive elaboration of the duties of the ruler, an elaboration that draws the lines of separation between the military and judicial administration, on the one hand, and the "legislative" and its institutional and cultural spheres, on the other (without this implying in any way that an extensive interaction between the two spheres did not happen). The executive category is intimately tied to military expenditure and the collection and distribution of booty, including the all-important land and its resources and revenues. The ten duties assigned to the ruler in effect represent the limits of his constitutional competence, the rights that the subjects are owed. Examined analytically, however, they are reducible to two main functions (with a derivative third).[59] The first is the protection of the domains. Duties 1, 5, 7, and 9 all stand in the service of this goal. The second is the upholding of the Sharīʿa and its institutions and practices,[60] which commands the focus of duties 2, 3, 4, 6, and 8. (It must be said, however, that the distinction between the two general functions must admittedly remain analytical for, after all, a good bulk of the first set of duties [e.g., taxation, land, conquered populations, prisoners of war, peace treaties, etc.] is dictated by the very *fiqh* laws of the Sharīʿa.)

The derivative and implied duty, occupying an initial part of the treatise, is the appointment of the various functions and personnel to carry out all the above tasks, these being both schematized and detailed, as we saw, in the voluminous administrative manual of Qalqashandī.[61] Duty 10, regarding justice, is synthetic. Justice is achieved when the nine duties are properly fulfilled. Justice (*ʿadl*) is done when the ruler does not diverge (*yaʿdil*) from the imperatives of these duties.[62]

---

59 Māwardī does include this duty as a discrete one, being the last in his list in *ADD*, 222, and the ninth in his *AS*, 40.

60 Which, by implication, includes Ṣūfī institutions. See Little, "Nature of the *Khānqāhs*, *Ribāṭs*, and *Zāwiyas*."

61 See ch. 5, above.

62 See ch. 2, n. 44.

The derivative duty is hierarchically structured. It begins with the responsibility to appoint a vizier, one of the most central and important offices in Islamic governance since earliest times.[63] Like Māwardī,[64] and reflecting the general practice over centuries of rule, the imam or the sultan may appoint a commanding vizier (*wazīr al-tafwīḍ*) who oversees the administration of the entire affairs of the kingdom.[65] He may also opt for the appointment of an executive vizier (*wazīr al-tanfīdh*) who is to carry out specific tasks or command specific domains, such as the military or taxation. (The same type of stratified appointment is applicable to *imāra*, i.e., the military command.)[66] The difference between the two types of vizier is not just a matter of scope of jurisdiction. The former, because he oversees the administration of the realm according to his own vision and considered opinion (*bi-ra'yihi wa-ijtihādihi*), effectively gains autonomy vis-à-vis the appointing power. Just as the sultan can manage the affairs of the domain without approval of or consultation with the caliph, this vizier is endowed with the same autonomy and competence. He in fact must fulfill all the conditions required of the other two, except for the Qurayshī descent.[67]

Furthermore, this vizier's appointments are delegatory, which is to say that his authority to appoint a deputy genealogically ran from caliph to sultan, and from the sultan down to him and then to the lowest office. Because such appointments were thought to stand within the "public" domain of service – that is, the appointed official, high or low, was deemed to be in the service of the Community of Muslims (*al-Muslimūn*), which was the *raison d'être* of governance and rule in the first place – their appointment was considered permanent. The death of the appointing agent did not bring their tenure in

63 The vizierial art of governance was already the subject of descriptive and prescriptive manuals toward the end of the third/ninth and early fourth/tenth centuries. See, for instance, Jahshayārī, *Kitāb al-Wuzarā' wal-Kuttāb*, whose history of secretaries/chancery (*kuttāb*) and ministers (viziers) goes back to Sassanid rule. See also Māwardī, *Adab al-Wazīr* and n. 65, below.

64 See ch. 3, above.

65 On the early history of the vizierate, see Goitein, "Origins of the Term Vizier," and writings cited therein (esp. by D. Sourdel and H.R. Gibb).

66 *TAJ*, 79-80, where Ibn Jamāʿa offers a classification of *imāra*. General *imāra* (*imāra ʿāmma*) is the *khilafa* itself, whose chief is the caliph himself, also known as the Commander of the Faithful (*Amīr al-Mu'minīn*). The "specific *imāra*" (*imāra khāṣṣā*) is either sultanic, "as it is the custom of our times now," or belongs to those who are in charge of specific duty, such as the command of the army in a given region or garrison. Note here the place of sultans in the hierarchy. They do not replace or displace the caliph but rather stand in a hierarchy in which the caliphate remains supreme.

67 *TAJ*, 77.

office to an end. By contrast, any appointments made privately – that is, as personal or private assistants to the hiring power – would be dismissed upon the death of the appointing authority. Since, in the case of the executive vizier, all appointments are made on behalf of the sultan and with his approval, these too remain in tenure, unlike the personnel that the executive vizier appoints as his personal assistants.[68]

The distilling of the ten duties into two substantive categories is readily shown in the concerns of Ibn Jamāʿa once his preliminary discussions about deputization and the various lines of its authority are completed. First, he disposes of the judicial duties of the ruler and quickly turns to the military and financial aspects of executive power. Between these two, the entire parameters of sultanic power, the executive, are set.

When I remark that at this juncture in his work Ibn Jamāʿa first disposes of the judicial functions of executive power, it is not to suggest that he pays to these functions no more than a lip service. In fact, the arrangement of the book would be nothing less than curious, if not odd, if we were to assume that he hastened to dispose of the treatment of the judiciary because it was not important to him. If this were the case, he would likely have left it to the end, to be dealt with as a mere supplement or addendum. The somewhat unexpected appearance of the chapter on the judiciary where Ibn Jamāʿa had in fact placed it seems to have two rationales behind it. The first is that it logically flows from chapter 3 that deals with the vizierate, since the delegatory vizier (*tanfīdh*) would be appointing all personnel in the judiciary. The function of chapter 3 then is to draw the constitutional lines of separation between the two types of vizierate and define their respective powers.

But Ibn Jamāʿa chose to dedicate chapter 4 to the military generals and the terms of their appointment, thereafter allocating chapter 5 to the judiciary, only to come back to military matters (including peace treaties, art of war, military *diwāns*, booty, taxation, occupied populations, *dhimmī* contracts, etc.) in chapters 6-17. Since the treatise reflects how Ibn Jamāʿa conceived of the range and limits of the various functions of governance, we can readily see that the military function was for him the most defining feature of the executive. He allocates to it about 180 pages as opposed to some 85 pages for the rest of subjects. But then no one would have argued that the judicial function, largely represented in Māwardī's potent expression "*ḥifẓ al-dīn*" (protection of religion), would lag far behind. And so, I suspect, that Ibn Jamāʿa worried

68 *TAJ*, 78.

that leaving the discussion of the judiciary to the end might give the wrong impression that it is not of central importance as well.

Yet, there is also the question of why he would allocate only one short chapter (of seven pages) to the judiciary, even though it stands as second to matters related to the broad category of the "protection of the domains." The answer resides in two main but interrelated considerations: First, and as intimated earlier, almost all the functions under the category of the "protection of the domains" are doctrinally prescribed by the Sharīʿa. What is not strictly Sharʿī are some details related to weapons and their types, military training and chivalry, horses and pedigrees, horsemanship, and the like.[69] But to say "doctrinally" is also to make the qualification that the vast bulk of these military matters was not under the *substantive* supervision or control of the jurists. Jurisprudence and law merely regulated them, the rest having been under the direct and exclusive control of the sultans and their emirs. But the judiciary – our second consideration – was indeed wholly made and run by the jurists, whether pedagogically, professionally, or even culturally. Put differently, Ibn Jamāʿa could not have worried much about the judiciary and its substantive operation, since it was safely contained within the abode of the Sharīʿa and protected by its personnel and culture. This explains the immense detail that our writer dedicated to the ruler's military duties and related matters, partly an expression of the universal anxiety about executive overreach in areas of action that the Sharīʿa has not regulated to a detail and where practice was not standardized due to the rotating nature of culturally varied dynastic powers (*duwal*; sing. *dawla*).

I said "partly" because Ibn Jamāʿa, like every other constitutional scholar, also asserted the rights and prerogatives of the ruler, those rights being integral to the duties entrusted to him. It is not therefore surprising that our author embarks on outlining the rules and principles pertaining to military power by positing – while invoking the Circle of Justice[70] – the necessity for rulers to have armies and to spend on them. It emerges that military spending makes for a considerable focus of *TAJ*, because "it is one of the most important public goods that money can buy."[71]

69 E.g., *TAJ*, 129-37, 170-87.

70 *TAJ*, 96-97.

71 *TAJ*, 98: "*Min ahammi al-maṣāliḥi al-latī tuṣrafu fī-hā al amwāl.*" See also *AS*, 305, where Māwardī states that the rationale for military stipends is to enable the military to dedicate all its energies and time to the defense of the realm (*bayḍa*) and not be distracted by the search for means of livelihood: "*Ḥattā yustaghnā bi-hā ʿan iltimāsi māddatin taqṭaʿuhu ʿan ḥimāyāti al-bayḍa.*"

Before addressing distribution of booty and military stipends (in chapter 8), Ibn Jamāʿa outlines the sources of income to be spent on this domain. Military salaries and stipend allocations are covered by incomes from *ʿaṭā'* and *iqṭāʿ*. The former is of four types, while the latter consists of three subcategories. *Fay'*, the first type of *ʿaṭā'*, represents wealth that "came to Muslims from non-Muslims without fighting," whether it is by terms of a treaty of conquest or property they left behind. The leading jurists traditionally held the average opinion (with many variations) that the sultan is entitled to spend the cash *fay'*, or most of it, on his armies and the construction and maintenance of garrisons.[72] However, if the *fay'* consists of real property, then it must be dedicated as *waqf* for the promotion of public good. The beneficiaries of this sphere are mosques and colleges as well as Qur'ān teachers, prayer leaders, *qāḍīs*, *muftīs*, and ulama in general, groups deemed to serve the public at large.[73]

The second type is *kharāj*, income (1) accruing from tax on land taken by a treaty after peaceful surrender; (2) levied as tax from a *waqf* originating in property taken from the enemy by force, and (3) from a *waqf* land originating as land abandoned by the enemy.[74] The third type is one-fifth of booty, while the fourth is the Public Treasury itself. There are six sources from which funds for the Public Treasury are collected: (1) The "Prophet's share," which is a fifth of one-fifth of both booty and *fay'*; (2) *Kharāj* revenues; (3) property of heirless persons; (4) property whose owner remains unknown; (5) *jizya* revenues; and (6) one-tenth tax on profits made by non-Muslim merchants.[75]

The sultan may also allocate *iqṭāʿ*s to his military, this allocation consisting of various categories, including, among other things, agricultural lands and mining areas. While the latter category of land has a definite duration for utilization,[76] the former does not. The cultivation and development of an *iqṭāʿ* that had consisted of dead-land (that is, *mawāt*, a land that has never been tilled or used before) will bestow on the recipient a perpetual right of unqualified ownership. In fact, anyone who cultivates such a land, without it being bestowed on a recipient by an act of *iqṭāʿ*, acquires this right, even

72 *TAJ*, 99-100.
73 *TAJ*, 100-1.
74 *TAJ*, 102-3.
75 *TAJ*, 107. For more on Public Treasury, see ʿAdlān, "Mu'assasat Bayt al-Māl fil-Niẓām al-Islāmī;" Jāsim, "Ṣalāḥiyyāt Waliy al-Amr."
76 *TAJ*, 115-16.

without the permission of the sultan. This is the majority juridical doctrine, the minority being Abū Ḥanīfa's opinion that makes the approval of the sultan or imam a prerequisite for the acquisition of such perpetual rights.[77] Ibn Jamāʿa is also careful to make clear that certain revenues and lands, such as the *jizya* and real property acquired by peace treaty, are not subject to allotment by the act of *iqṭāʿ*.[78]

The remaining parts of the book, substantial as they are,[79] deal with the rules of *jihād* warfare, techniques of fighting, division of spoils, truces and peace treaties, and the status of occupied populations, especially the *dhimmī*s and the rules that pertain to them. What is remarkable about all of this is that the business of warfare, conquest, taxation, and treatment of spoils and conquered populations are all regulated by the Sharīʿa, despite the might of the executive and its ability to physically quash any opposition. To say that the details of the law were closely and consistently applied in these domains may be to stretch the point (everyone knows what happens on the battlefields, in the modern and non-modern), but the general parameters of the law did represent the benchmark[80] when executive actions were set in motion.

IV

But it is a mistake to think that the parameters of the law were maintained out of what we moderns call "religious impulse," translated as intrinsic piety or devotion to a deity. While this certainly was the case at times, at others these did not constitute the real or only motives. The conformity, one might say, was *also* institutional. Which is to say that the institutions that were put in place corralled the executive powers into particular modalities of conduct. Ibn Jamāʿa's treatise is auspicious in documenting one type of such institutions, which we have grown to think of as non-Sharʿī, but in fact it was wholly so. This is the institution of the *dīwān*, acknowledged by our authors to be ancient, pre-Islamic, and Islamic all at once. Māwardī had already made a big deal of it, and so did Ibn Jamāʿa, allocating to it a

77 *TAJ*, 108.
78 *TAJ*, 114 f.
79 They occupy *TAJ*, 152-263, roughly half of the treatise.
80 For benchmarks, see Introduction, n. 71.

substantial chapter. The institution of the *dīwān* was not only the foundation of administration but constituted the normative and practical structures with which the business of rule conformed. Sultans and dynasties came and went, in a staggering row, but the Sharīʿa and its physical *dīwāns* remained and sustained.[81]

It is no exaggeration to say that the *dīwān* was constructive, in the sense that it not only constituted the structures of the executive institutions but provided constitutional continuity to boot. It may even be argued that it is one of the oldest Sharīʿa institutions, if not the oldest, since it was created as early as ʿUmar I's reign,[82] sometime between the year 10 and 20 of the Hijra.[83] The founding event was not the initiative of Umar I alone, but reportedly had the unqualified backing of ʿUthmān b. ʿAffān, later to become the third caliph, as well as powerful generals like Khālid b. al-Walīd.[84] At least the military *dīwān*, among the chief *dīwān*s that every Muslim ruler employed and the first to be instituted,[85] was said to hail from a Prophetic edict. Ibn Jamāʿa argues that the authority of this *dīwān*, and the others by implication, is anchored in Prophetic authority, the consensus of the Companions, and further justified by the Sharʿī principle of need (*ḥāja*).[86] Māwardī considers the founding of the military *dīwān* to be "in accordance with the Sharʿ."[87]

It is also remarkable in the first degree that the main structural features of the *dīwān*s remained constant throughout the centuries, at least from the early Fāṭimids, and very possibly from the end of the first century, down to the Mamlūks, as attested not only by the evident consistency between Māwardī's exposition and that of Ibn Jamāʿa, but by the massive evidence that Qalqashandī provides in his colossal manual for his intended readers, mainly practitioners of chancery. Indeed, Ibn Jamāʿa's discourse in the sphere of chancery practice is effectively a close recasting of Māwardī's classic.

It is an obligation (*yanbaghī*) upon the sultan to establish a military register (*dīwān al-jaysh*/*dīwān al-jund*), whose function is to stipulate

81 On the secretarial class running the *dīwāns*, see Ziyāda, *Kātib al-Sulṭān*.

82 *SAQ*, I, 91; Ṭabarī, *Tārīkh*, V, 64 ff.; Nuwayrī, *Nihāyat al-Arab*, VIII, 196 ff.

83 In *TAJ*, 139, Ibn Jamāʿa offers two possible temporal origins, one at 10 H., while the other at 20 H. Māwardī proffers a detailed account of the rise of the *dīwān*, placing it variably between these dates, although the latter is mentioned specifically. *AS*, 297-301, at 299.

84 *TAJ*, 138-39; AS, 298.

85 *AS*, 300. See also ch. 5, sec. II.

86 *TAJ*, 140: "*Fa-yaṣluḥu dhālika dalīlan ʿalā annahu min al-sunnati, wa-li-ittifāqi al-Ṣaḥābati ʿalayhi wa-li'anna al-ḥājata tadʿū ilayhi.*"

87 *TAJ*, 300: "*ʿAlā al-tartībi ... al-sharʿī.*"

stipends to soldiers, ranging from the commanding generals to the ordinary fighters. These must meet certain requirements, such as being of the age of majority, free, Muslim and physically capable of combat. *Dhimmīs*, women, madmen, or those of feeble physique are barred from military service, and thus must not be listed in the *dīwān*.[88] This is not to say that members of the latter category, or *dhimmīs*, were never listed in reality; the point being that if such a listing occurred and the circumstance was such that the act was disputed, the law was clear on the matter and a judgment had to be entered in accordance with it.

The *dīwān* entries demanded much detail, ranging from the forms of personal identification, affiliation to a tribe, clan or certain ethnic group (*jins*, e.g., Arabs, Turks, Circassians, etc.) to the amounts and types of stipends (cash, *iqṭāʿ*, etc.).[89] They also recognized military hierarchy and chain of command, including divisions headed by emirs, *naqīb*s, and *ʿarīf*s[90] (roughly equal to captain, lieutenant, and sergeant, respectively, although the rank of emir could also approximate that of field marshal or major general). It was also legally preferred (*mustaḥabb*) that the *dīwān* be structured hierarchically, whereby the groups closest to the Prophet and his family are listed first, then the rest of the Arab tribes, followed by non-Arabs. As these matters belong to the *mustaḥabb* category in the law, the sultan would not be deemed to have violated the law should he follow a different arrangement.[91] In fact, Qalqashandī reports that the configuration of military command, among other forms of military conduct and organization, changed with time, from the Ikhshīds (323-58/935-69) down to the Mamlūks (648-923/1250-1517) of his times.[92]

The second *dīwān* the sultan had to keep was that of the provincial exchequer (*rusūm al-amwāl*). This *dīwān* kept detailed records of revenues and expenditure,[93] as well as of every region and province, attending to their

88 *TAJ*, 140-41.
89 *TAJ*, 141-43.
90 On the various ranks of the Mamlūk military, see *SAQ*, IV, 14-16.
91 *TAJ*, 143, 144. See also AS, 303-4. In *Kharāj*, 21-32, Qudāma Ibn Jaʿfar (d. 329/941) observes that the military *dīwān* (apparently under the Būyids) were divided into sub-*dīwāns*, each specializing in a different unit of the army, such as the Palace Guard and the infantry.
92 *SAQ*, IV, 14-16, but also passim in vols. II and III.
93 It seems that this *dīwān* was known in early fourth/tenth-century Irāq as *dīwān al-nafaqāt*, which tracked, among many other things, the Royal Household's expenses. See Qudāma Ibn Jaʿfar, *Kharāj*, 33-35.

peculiarities and distinctive fiscal constitution.[94] The record must state the legal status of the various lands in each province and district, identifying those taken by force or by treaty, since this distinction was crucial in determining taxation, forms of revenue, and even the legal status of persons.[95] Cadastral and census surveys are under the jurisdiction of this *dīwān*, both necessary to determine what *dhimmī*s and the population at large owe in annual taxes, including who died and who reached majority. Taxes, Ibn Jamāʿa insists, must be according to the Sharʿ, "no more and no less, since more is an act of injustice toward the population, and less is an act of injustice toward the Public Treasury."[96] Levying taxes on Muslim trade and exchange of goods is utterly prohibited, it being a patent form of oppression and mistreatment. Ibn Jamāʿa's language of disapprobation here almost certainly represents a reaction to, and condemnation of, the Mamlūk practice of over-taxation, which the Sharīʿa and its jurists habitually condemned.

The third *dīwān*'s jurisdiction relates to official appointments (*al-ʿummāl*), including the credentials of the appointing and appointed officers, tenure duration, the language of the designation decree, as well as its terms of reference. Appointments by officers other than the imam, the sultan, *wazīr al-tanfīdh* or their likes are invalid, rendering the actions of the appointed official null and void. The appointed official must be qualified for the job assigned to him. A *dhimmī*, for instance, cannot be validly appointed to administer the affairs of Muslims, but may be charged with collecting taxes from *dhimmī* populations and non-Muslim merchants.[97] The scope and jurisdiction of the appointment personnel must be stipulated in detail, with specifications as to the particular charge and responsibilities of the office.[98] This *dīwān* is also responsible for determining the amount and form of pay, monitoring the duration of the appointment, and keeping track of the time when it comes to an end, unless the appointment is for life (as is the case, at times, with the *ḥisba* and *shurṭa*).[99]

94 *TAJ*, 144: "*An yumayyiza [al-dīwān] kulla ʿamalin bi-mā yatamayyazu bi-hi* [*ʿan*] *ghayrihi.*"
95 On this, see the valuable work of Najib, "Common Wealth: Land Taxation in Early Islam."
96 *TAJ*, 144-45: "*Li'anna al-ziyādata ḥayfun ʿalā al-raʿiyyati, wal-nuqṣāna ḥayfun ʿalā bayti al-māl.*"
97 See Introduction, n. 60.
98 *TAJ*, 147. The thrust of this prescription manifests itself in the detailed appointments decrees we have earlier encountered in Qalqashandī's *Ṣubḥ al-ʿAshā*. See ch. 5, above.
99 *TAJ*, 148-49.

The fourth *dīwān*'s jurisdiction is the Public Treasury (*Bayt al-Māl*), mainly attending to its sources of income and venues of expenditure. Ibn Jamāʿa is careful to dissociate illegitimate sources of income from this Treasury, saying that the taxes levied by the ruler from Muslim merchants or any other unlawful source must not belong to it, for these taxes are an expression of injustice and oppression in the first place.[100] Should this Treasury fall short of paying out its dues, it must borrow funds to dispense with those payments that are urgent, such as in the case of military pay. The debts accumulating against the Treasury are not extinguished with the death of the borrowing sultan but remain the obligation of his successors.[101]

Finally, and in the same manner of maintaining an army for external defense and internal security, and managing land and its revenue, the sultan's charge consists of what Māwardī called *ḥifẓ al-dīn*, the preservation and upkeep of "religion." Ibn Jamāʿa calls it "*ḥifz al-awḍāʿ al-sharʿiyya*"[102] (preservation of Sharʿī state of affairs), a cognate of the former. Sultans, kings, and emirs are all responsible for the protection (*ḥimāya*) of Sharīʿa's institutions, practices, and personnel. Some of the latter function as judges, while others as *muftīs*, professors, *ḥisba* inspectors, *waqf* auditors, or caretakers of legally incapacitated individuals. These are the five Sharʿī categories[103] of officials who are appointed, directly or indirectly, by executive power. Ibn Jamāʿa dwells on the qualifications that must be met for each office, this being less of a discursive formality than a conscious delimitation of their constitutional purview. The specification that the personnel serving in all these functions must be Muslim (where the last two categories are derivative of the *qaḍā'* office) amounts to saying that non-Muslims cannot be enlisted to perform these functions[104] – in the same manner, for instance, as a green-card holder (otherwise known as a Lawful Permanent Resident) cannot, unless certain conditions obtain, become a justice of the court in

100 *TAJ*, 150: "*Mā yu'khadhu min amwāl al-muslimīna fī tijārātihim wa-maʿāyishihim min al-mukūsi wal-ḍarā'ibi, fa'inna dhālika kullahu ẓulmun bayyinun wa-ḥayfun mutaʿayyanun, wa-laysa min bayti al-māli fī shay'.*"

101 *TAJ*, 151. For actual cases of sultanic borrowing from merchants and the Public Treasury (including Orphans' Funds) and repayments of said debts, see Maqrīzī, *Sulūk*, I, 235, 235, 403.

102 The language of chapter 5's title. *TAJ*, 87.

103 Ibn Jamāʿa includes the category of teachers and professors in his introductory remarks to the chapter (*TAJ*, 88), but these educators do not make a show when he discusses the five categories individually (88-93).

104 *TAJ*, 88, 90, 91, 93.

the US.[105] All of them, however, must enjoy two essential conditions: skills and competence relevant for the proper performance of the tasks of the particular office (*kifāya*) and the quality of justice (*ʿadāla*, consisting, *inter alia*, of rectitude and trustworthiness).[106] Again, the combination of these two qualities signals the inseparability of the "technical" and the moral, that is, the functional competence and the technological-subjective formation of the ethical.

Insofar as *kifāya* is concerned, the *qāḍī* would have been vetted as a prerequisite for the appointment. This is why Ibn Jamāʿa does not introduce language relevant to the issue of competence, since the technical qualifications of the candidate would have been established. The main concern is rather about honesty, rectitude, and good social standing (*sīra mashkūra*), safeguards against judicial bias and corruption. The *muftī*, on the other hand, is not subject to such scrutiny, because *muftīs*, generally speaking, were not subject to appointment. They must fulfill all those conditions that the *qāḍī* must meet, in addition to being in possession of adept knowledge of the law (including competence in *uṣūl al-fiqh*, *furūʿ*, as well as in cases on which the jurists disagree [*khilāf*] and those on which they reached consensus [*ijmāʿ*]). Should he prove himself to be less than competent in these spheres of expertise, then the *muftī* should be barred from issuing *fatwās* (*lā yumakkanu min al-fatwā*). The passive form of the verb here should not mask Ibn Jamāʿa's reference to the ruler as the agent responsible for placing this interdiction on pretenders.[107] "Leading people astray"[108] is a public offense, the very opposite of public good, a sphere of action for which the imam or the sultan is responsible. Yet, the verdict on fraudulent *iftā'* does not issue from the executive office itself, for the sultan is unqualified to judge a matter of this nature. Nor can a judgment of what constitutes a juristic infraction be sourced in the opinion or decision of a single jurist. Rather, such a matter can be resolved only by reference to the doctrine of the *madhhab*, the final determinant of the parameters within which the spectrum of legal opinions operates. What the *madhhab* says and does not say, or allows or forbids, are all matters decided upon by the qualified

---

105 With the exception that the Permanent Resident be eligible to apply within six months for (and thus obtain) citizenship status. See https://www.uscourts.gov/careers/search-judiciary-jobs/citizenship-requirements-employment-judiciary. See Introduction, n. 60.
106 *TAJ*, 88-89.
107 *TAJ*, 90.
108 *TAJ*, 90: "*Kay lā yaghtarra al-nāsu bi-hi wa-yaqaʿū fil-khaṭa'i bi-sababihi.*"

jurists whose credentials and status as major legal figures are established by the inner workings of their schools.[109]

The third sphere of judicial appointments is that of the *muḥtasib*, often rendered into English as the "market inspector." The office of *ḥisba*, however, is the fulfillment of just a part of the wide-ranging duty of "commanding good and forbidding evil,"[110] a duty incumbent upon every Muslim individual. Māwardī allocates a fairly detailed discussion about the difference between the duty of the commoner and that of the appointed officer, the former deemed a volunteer (*mutaṭawwiʿ*) whereas the latter was a mandated appointee. As such, he is under the obligation to address complaints addressed to him, and to pursue and prosecute violators, whereas the volunteer is forbidden from doing so.[111] Due to the public nature of the function, the *muḥtasib* normally recruits assistants and deputies to help him in dispensing his tasks, and to inflict punishments on those found guilty, but the volunteer must not engage in such activities. Finally, the official, being an employee of the executive on behalf of the *Umma*, receives a salary from the Public Treasury, whereas the volunteer does not.[112]

Ibn Jamāʿa states that *ḥisba* "used to be at times a branch of *qaḍāʾ*, while at others a sultanic appointment."[113] Māwardī, speaking in the present tense,

---

109 The credentialization of the chief jurists occurred as a result of a series of intellectual-juristic achievements, such as *taṣnīf* and debate. On *taṣnīf*, see Hallaq, *Authority*, 167-74 and passim; on debate, see Makdisi, *Rise of Colleges*, 150-52, 249-56, 284-89; Young, *Dialectical Forge*; Hallaq, "Tenth-Eleventh Century Treatise on Juridical Dialectic."

110 For the authoritativeness (*ḥujjiyya*) of "commanding good and forbidding evil" (*al-amru bil-maʿrūfi wal-nahyi ʿan al-munkar*), see Ghazālī, *Iḥyāʾ*, 782-87. Ghazālī observes that *ḥisba* is the "general representation" (*ʿibāra shāmila*) of this pervasive command.

111 *AS*, 349-50.

112 *AS*, 350.

113 *TAJ*, 91: "*Wa-kānat fī al-azmāni al-sālifati farʿan min furūʿi al-qaḍāʾi tāratan, wa-min jihati al-sulṭāni tāratan ukhrā.*" James Baldwin notes against Haim Gerber that in eighteenth-century Cairo, the *muḥtasib*'s jurisdiction "was alive and well." Gerber "has claimed," Baldwin says, "that under Ottoman rule the muḥtasib's jurisdiction was subsumed under that of the qāḍī." Baldwin objected, and rightly so, that Gerber generalized about the Ottoman Empire. But this "disagreement" would be readily resolved and the history of the institution better understood if we were to view the matter from a constitutional point of view, as Ibn Jamāʿa and Māwardī, among many others, have long done. Baldwin seems to think it a discovery that the function of the *muḥtasib* was shared by three authorities, the *qāḍī*, the police chief, and the Janissary Āghā (Baldwin, *Islamic Law*, 41-2). While such a finding may be valuable for the social and legal micro-history of eighteenth-century Cairo, the true significance lies in the way these functions operated in a constitutional manner. Once we understand the deeper rationale behind the constitutional divisions, then we might stop squabbling over regional differences, and instead see their larger significance *as structural modalities of governance.*

confirms that the office corresponds to the functions of Sharʿī *qaḍā'* in two ways, while diverging from *qaḍā'* in four other ways, two of which are additional powers given to the *ḥisba* office while two others are "subtractions" from jurisdiction. Like the *qāḍī*, the *muḥtasib* can hear cases brought to him by plaintiffs against defendants, but such cases are limited to infractions related to measures and weights used in the marketplace, fraudulent commercial transactions, and non-payment of due debts. The *muḥtasib*'s duties also include the enforcement of closures of businesses during communal prayers, sale of intoxicants, the proper functioning of sewage systems, and the like.[114] Otherwise, the *muḥtasib* must not entertain – and is unqualified to hear – cases in the general areas of the law, unless he was specifically mandated by the sultan to do so. In fact, unlike the *qāḍī* and the *maẓālim* official, he is not to hear cases that require decisions on the basis of legal reasoning.[115] But even in those cases in which the legal norms are not clearly applicable, and which require resolving issues involving denials of claims, the *muḥtasib* must not engage in the evaluation of evidence and its truth-claims, matters regarding which only the *qāḍī* can pronounce.[116]

As for the two aspects of *ḥisba* that do not fall within the jurisdiction of the *qaḍā'*, the *muḥtasib* can prosecute infractions without these being brought to him by a plaintiff. The proactive nature of *iḥtisāb* is such that the *muḥtasib*, like the *maẓālim* functionary, pursues wrongs wherever he finds them, and uses methods of deterrence not available to the *qāḍī*. Yet, importantly, the *maẓālim* and *ḥisba* differ from each other vis-à-vis *qaḍā'* in that *maẓālim*, as we have seen, finds its *raison d'être* as a complement to *qaḍā'*, for the latter does not possess the coercive and "persuasive" power of the *maẓālim*, including expansive competence and disposition over adjectival law. *Ḥisba*, on the other hand, deals with the market aspects of the *qaḍā'* jurisdiction in order to leave the *qāḍī* and his court untarnished by base and unsavory disputes of

114 *TAJ*, 91-92. On the various crafts, professions, and practices subject to the *ḥisba* inspection, see Shayzarī, *Nihāyat al-Rutba fī Ṭalab al-Ḥisba*, 223-68.

115 *AS*, 354. Which is to say that his functions are generally restricted to checking "facts" rather than reasoning from legal facts to reach judicial verdicts, such as inspecting the accuracy of weights and measures in the marketplace, (over-)pricing, pursuing sellers of alcoholic beverages, and monitoring shop closure during communal prayer time, among similar duties. *TAJ*, 91-93. The identification of *munkar* objects or acts (those that are considered immoral) must also be known "without *ijtihād*." Ghazālī, *Iḥyā'*, 802.

116 *AS*, 353: "*Wal-wajhu al-thānī annahā maqṣūratun ʿalā al-ḥuqūqi al-muʿtarafu bi-hā, fa'ammā mā yatadākhaluhu al-tajāḥudu wal-tanākuru, fa-lā yajūzu lil-muḥtasibi an yasmaʿa bayyinatan ʿalā ithbāti al-ḥaqqi wa-lā an yuḥallifa yamīnan ʿalā nafyi al-ḥaqqi, wal-quḍātu wal-ḥukkāmu bi-samāʿi al-bayyinati wa-iḥlāfi al-khuṣūmi aḥaqq.*"

the marketplace, disputes and infractions that need a rough hand to handle (*ghilẓa*).[117] Māwardī underscores the relative competence of the three offices by offering a schematic ordering of their powers: The officer of the *maẓālim* has the competence to issue injunctions or rescripts (*yuwaqqi'*)[118] for both the *qāḍī* and the *muḥtasib*, but the *qāḍī*, while competent to issue injunctions for the *muḥtasib*, possesses no authority to do so for the *maẓālim* officer.[119]

The fourth judicial duty of the sultan is to ensure the proper functioning of the *waqf*s, both private and public.[120] The implementation of this duty normally devolves upon the *qāḍī* and his court, unless a special official is charged with a specific mandate in this regard. The *qāḍī*'s duty typically consists of an annual audit, with powers for correction and reorganization of *waqf* administration if wrongdoing or mishandling is proven. It is important to note that this power of oversight over *waqf*s does not, to my knowledge, appear in Māwardī, likely because *waqf*s had not yet acquired the prominent presence they had achieved by Mamlūk times.

Finally, the fifth duty, also normally mandated to the *qāḍī*, is supervision of the orphans, fools,[121] and mentally infirm persons (*aytām*, *sufahā'*, and *majānīn*, respectively). The supervision and auditing of their affairs obtains irrespective of whether or not they have been assigned guardians. In the event of mismanagement, the guardian is warned and/or replaced, and if unable to handle the obligation properly, would be assigned an assistant or a "backer."[122]

In conclusion, this chapter has aimed at outlining the limits and boundaries of constitutional powers in a Mamlūk-era treatise, authored by the distinguished and leading Shāfiʿī jurist Ibn Jamāʿa. The argument of this chapter is that this work is an "update" of the *aḥkām al-sulṭāniyya* genre, an update – a common practice in Sharīʿa's disciplines – that reflected the particular conditions of Islamic governance under the Mamlūk *dawla*, this latter term being understood as an executive power. Taking into consideration the realities of Mamlūk rule, the work accounted for the extreme pressures this dynasty

117 *AS*, 353: "*Wal-naẓaru fil-ḥisbati mawḍūʿun li-mā rafaha ʿanhu al-quḍāt*" (the text's editor has it as "*raffaha*," which seems inconsistent with proper usage. See Zabīdī, *Tāj al-ʿArūs*, XIX, 38-39.

118 For a detailed definition of "*waqqaʿa*/*tawqīʿ*" see Zabīdī, *Tāj al-ʿArūs*, XI, 522-27.

119 *AS*, 353-54.

120 *TAJ*, 93: "*Al-awqāfu al-khāṣṣatu wal-ʿāmmatu*." The private *waqfs* are included because, Ibn Jamāʿa states, they eventually revert to public welfare ("*li'anna al-khāṣṣāta ta'ūlu ilā al-ʿāmmati*").

121 On the *safīh* as a legal category, see *al-Mawsūʿa al-Fiqhiyya*, XXV, 47 ff.

122 *TAJ*, 93.

faced, from both outside and inside its borders. Yet Ibn Jamāʿa's update must be seen as a reaffirmation of the constitutional configuration that had become deeply rooted in Islamic West Asia by his time, a configuration that reflected the tenacity of the political tradition that had formed a century or two before his predecessor and constitutional articulator Māwardī. By all indications, including Qalqashandī's stupendous testimonials of administrative-executive practice on the ground,[123] we can speak of Ibn Jamāʿa's work as a fairly accurate constitutional mapping of Islamic West Asia around the 700s/1300s. In what follows, I shall trace the developments and adjustments that occurred within the established constitutional divisions and boundaries as outlined by both Māwardī and Ibn Jamāʿa, with the hope of showing that while these divisions and boundaries were solidly maintained within what I call an Islamic constitutional ecology, change and pliable adjustments effectively occurred within the next three or four centuries.

123 This is also applicable to vol. 8 of Nuwayrī's *Nihāyat al-Arab*. See VIII, 200 ff.

Chapter 8

Moral Distension of Judicial and Executive Oversight: A Mamlūk Ḥanbalī Posture

I

Ibn Jamāʿa's *Taḥrīr*, we have seen, generally falls within the genre of so-called *al-aḥkām al-sulṭāniyya*, not because it is, like its Māwardīan predecessor, a Shāfiʿī work but rather due to the kind of discourse it proffers. The Mamlūk-era work therefore reflected both an enduring political epistemology and a long-standing political discursive tradition, all at once. As we will see, the Ḥanbalī jurist Ibn al-Mibrad (d. 909/1504), also a Mamlūk-era jurist, writes his *Īḍāḥ Ṭuruq al-Istiqāma fī Aḥkām al-Wilāya wal-Imāma* within the same genre, but in this case, the progenitor of his work was an earlier Ḥanbalī treatise, Abū Yaʿlā al-Farrā's *al-Aḥkām al-Sulṭāniyya*, in title, contents, and often in phraseology a near mimesis of Māwardī's better known monograph.[1]

However, the later Ḥanbalīs, especially Taqiyy al-Dīn Ibn Taymiyya (d. 728/1328) and his disciple, Shams al-Dīn Ibn Qayyim al-Jawziyya (d. 751/1350), initiated another sub-genre that has gone under the designation *siyāsa sharʿiyya*, to be slightly differentiated from the master genre of *al-aḥkām al-sulṭāniyya*. This latter was wholly lodged within the boundaries of the juridically delimited domain of politics and constitutional divisions, as it was the chief terrain in which executive powers were discursively constructed within a genealogy of politics, where governance as tradition was historically defined,

1 A contemporary of Māwardī, Abū Yaʿlā al-Farrā' died in 458/1066. It is impossible for any careful reader to miss the fact that Abū Yaʿlā's treatise is nearly identical to Māwardī's work. In all likelihood, the composition of the latter preceded that of the former in point of time. For a comparison of the two works, see Hurvitz, *Competing Texts*. For a discussion of this phenomenon of transposition, see ch. 10, below.

redefined and negotiated. *Al-aḥkām al-sulṭāniyya* thus represented an exposition of the constitutive conceptual relationships that existed between law and politics, between the idea of political rule and the legal matrix that sustained it. *Siyāsa sharʿiyya*, on the other hand, was a specialized genre, focusing on suppositions already proven in *al-aḥkām al-sulṭāniyya*, and thus confining itself to the definition of executive power as well as the delineation of its outer limits and internal divisions.

Within these spheres of specialization, works on *siyāsa sharʿiyya* emphasized or deemphasized certain topics. Some treatises focused on financial administration of government, while others on the armies or procedural law. Yet, in all cases, *siyāsa sharʿiyya* was the constitutional space where executive power was accommodated, negotiated, expanded, but ultimately brought under constitutional control. The very rise of *siyāsa sharʿiyya* as a genre was therefore a discursive constitutional act representing the law's oversight over the practice of executive governance. It might be worth emphasizing that this oversight would in all likelihood have developed under any form of executive power – caliphal, sultanic, or even emiric. The constitutional grind was not about the titular and formal form of rule (which "office" decides what) but rather about the perennial (nay, universal) legal struggle to curb the executive through a heteronomous law. For the executive has, ever since the dawn of time, been the threat that hung over the head of all societies and peoples.

Later in the chapter, I will discuss the rise of *siyāsa sharʿiyya* and its Ḥanbalī disposition as represented in the thinking of Ibn ʿAqīl and Ibn Qayyim al-Jawziyya,[2] a disciple of Ibn Taymiyya and an original exponent of his doctrines. Ibn al-Qayyim took for granted, or at least assumed as valid, Ibn Taymiyya's foundational discourse, which was seminal within the Islamic tradition by its own right.[3]

2 Aziz al-Azmeh attributes "the formulation" of the genre of *siyāsa sharʿiyya* to Māwardī and Abū Yaʿlā al-Farrā'. It is one thing to say that *siyāsa sharʿiyya* is a subgenre of *al-aḥkām al-sulṭāniyya* and quite another to say that it originated concurrently with the latter. As we will see, the earliest use of the concept is found in Ibn ʿAqīl, who flourished about two generations after Māwardī. See Al-Azmeh, *Muslim Kingship*, 99. Before gaining ground and centuries before it developed into a specific field of discourse, the descriptor seems to have been "*siyāsa dīniyya*," used by Māwardī himself (*AS*, 322), but quite likely having been used somewhat earlier. A similar pattern in the development of names for genres occurred in *uṣūl al-fiqh*. See Hallaq, "*Uṣūl al-Fiqh* and Shāfiʿī's *Risāla* Revisited."

3 For an excellent background to Ibn Taymiyya's political thought, covering his theological positions, see Anjum, *Politics, Law, and Community*, 173-232.

II

In Ibn Taymiyya's work, we see that *siyāsa shar'iyya* attempts to accomplish a number of interconnected goals, but it is undeniable that it ultimately rests on the bedrock of the same political jurisprudence that framed *al-aḥkām al-sulṭāniyya*. In his work, we observe the workings of the bare conditions of politics and governance, where the formalities of these institutions are disposed of in favor of what might be called functional governance: it does not matter who and what performs a task of governance; it does not matter what they are titled or named; all that matters is that the constitutional functions be fulfilled, and tasks be performed in the business of good governance, in accordance with the demands specified within each of these functions. Everyone is responsible for a certain task, small or large, and all work in consort, according to capacity, for the single purpose of upholding the law and *dīn* of God.

It is wrong to think that Ibn Taymiyya departed significantly from the mainstream Sunni understanding of political constitution. As we will see, he does relax the rules of procedural law in criminal matters and does refine the juristic categories that govern political management, endowing them with sophisticated legal props, but the refinements remained imbedded in the generally accepted philosophy of governance, a habitus on its own.

Ibn Taymiyya's philosophy of political foundations shares with the mainstream tradition the presumption that cooperation and communal living constitute the rationale for governance.[4] Living together, and living well and justly, represent the desiderata of the Sharī'a, ultimately itself the guardian of *dīn*, the ideal form of belief and practice in the world. Governance is not just rulership and command. It is *wilāya*, a general guardianship over, and political management of, the affairs of Muslims.

Wilāya is among the greatest obligations of *dīn*, for without it neither the *dīn* itself nor the affairs of the world could be sustained.[5] Human beings cannot secure their beneficial interests except by coming together, by working and cooperating with one another in a bid to help and support each other (*ta'āwunan wa-tanāṣuran*). "They help each other to bring about benefit (*manfa'a*) and support each other to avert harm (*maḍarra*). For no single individual can, on his own, secure all his beneficial interests and avert all the harm that may come to him."[6] But when people come together in this manner,

4 On cooperation as the foundation of political association, see ch. 1, above.
5 Ibn Taymiyya, *al-Siyāsa al-Shar'iyya*, 232 (henceforth, *ITSS*).
6 *ITSS*, 232. See also Ibn Taymiyya, *Qā'ida fil-Ḥisba*, 39.

it is necessary for them to have a "head" (*ra's*). Even in simple matters, such as in group travel, a head, a leader, is necessary. The Prophet said – Ibn Taymiyya tells his reader – that even if only three people embark on travel, they should choose one of them as a leader; which means, *a fortiori*, that in more extensive and complex forms of communal association the need for *wilāya*, taking the form of *imāra*-cum-*quwwa* (i.e., effective leadership), is essential.[7]

To impose order necessary for implementing the maxim of "commanding good and forbidding evil," for bringing forth justice and fulfillment of duties necessary for communal existence (e.g., enforcing penal law, creating auspicious conditions for travel for pilgrims, supporting the oppressed, protecting the borders, etc.), effective leadership is an indispensable mandate. "This is why it has been said," Ibn Taymiyya asserts, that "'sixty years of rule by an unjust ruler is better than one night without him.'[8] Experience has proven this to be true. Whenever and wherever there is an absence of a sultan – due to rebellion, internal struggle, or insurrection – the degree of devastation is so great that only God knows its true extent." Political leadership is not only essential but also represents, when it is in compliance with the Sharīʿa, "the best form of closeness to God."[9] Politics and political management then are not only mandated by *dīn*; they are an integral part of religious obligation. But this, it must be stressed, is neither a new nor an innovative argument. Ibn Taymiyya merely captures an age-old conception in a characteristically incisive language.

Seeking positions of power and accumulation of wealth through these positions constitutes a corruption of this ideal. The very striving for positions of power is a form of injustice (*ẓulm*), Ibn Taymiyya stresses, since people are created as one kind (*jins wāḥid*), where no one naturally stands in a lowly or superior position. In other words, the very striving or the intention to dominate is itself the vice that suggests corruption and injustice. But it is in the nature of rule and political management that some people will inevitably have to lead others and thus stand above them in rank (*daraja*). The ultimate difference between the two types of position-holders is that the former seek self-benefit and abuse of power for self-interest while the latter find themselves installed in these positions to serve the Community and its law and *dīn*. Whenever rule (*sulṭān*) stands apart from the *dīn*, deterioration of the financial affairs of people will inevitably result. The *dīn* is a system that regulates government

7 A point also emphasized in *Qāʿida fil-Ḥisba*, 40.
8 *ITSS*, 233: "*Wa-yuqālu: 'sittūna sanatin min imāmin jā'irin aṣlaḥu min laylatin wāḥidatin bi-lā sulṭān...*"
9 *ITSS*, 235.

of the self and of others. And when rule and wealth are directed to promote the interests of *dīn*, then the life of the Community and its *dīn*ic affairs will benefit and flourish considerably.[10]

It seems that Ibn Taymiyya is here arguing against the stereotypical and seemingly widespread view that political rule is inherently unjust and corrupt, a perception that seems to have appeared to him as nihilistic. Rule is essential, and good and just rule is the highest desideratum. It is essential, even if unjust,[11] because without it there cannot be political organization, the foundation of the Community and its *dīn*.

A culmination of at least six centuries' worth of political experience and political thought, Ibn Taymiyya's theory articulated the state-of-the-art conclusion of this historical experience in the postulate that the functions of government are not a matter of personal power and prerogative but are instead institutional structures that specialize in the implementation of specific tasks. "Any office or function of government that abides by the dictates of God and his Messenger" would be said to have dispensed with its mandate and would thus be judged a "*sharʿī* function" (*wilaya sharʿiyya*).[12] While this appears as a tautology, Ibn Taymiyya is underscoring a powerful point by virtue of using the quantifier "any." The idea here is that it does not matter who performs which function. What matters is that the performance of the function be in accordance with the requirements of the Sharīʿa. And the *qāḍī*, Ibn Taymiyya asserts, is not the only one charged with carrying out the ordinances of the Law, "as many people have come to think." The generalization of the requirement to fulfill the various functions of government according to law by any means, and by anyone who is competent to perform the function, is consistent with the generalized duty, demanded of all legally capacitated Muslims, to "command

10 *ITSS*, 240.

11 It bears repeating and emphasizing the crucial argument that an unjust ruler in the Islamic system is more tolerable than, say, an unjust modern government, because the Muslim "ruler" represented the executive and a curbed one at that (in comparison with the American presidency, for example). As we will see in chapter 12, biopower (the formation and continual maintenance of social and communal structures) was not controlled by the executive but rather by the legislative, that is, the Sharīʿa as a cultural and institutional phenomenon. This is not to say that executive injustice had no adverse effects on the Islamic social and communal order, but it is to say that the effects are of an entirely different quality and quantity from those that may be observed in the totalistic and unitary modern states. To equate between them is not only anachronistic but also betrays a severe misunderstanding of the limited nature of sultanic sources of social power. For more on this, see ch. 10, sec. V, and ch. 12.

12 *ITSS*, 193: "*Wa'ayyu shay'in min al-wilāyāti ʿumila fī-hi bi-ṭāʿati Allāhi wa-rasūlihi kānat wilāyatan sharʿiyyatan.*"

good and avert evil."[13] The implementation of the law, of "the commands of God and his Prophet," is not just a legal charge but also a moral one, first and foremost. Enforcing the Sharīʿa is the ultimate telos, and it matters little who performs which function as long as the function is fulfilled on these terms. "God's law is binding on everyone."[14]

At this point, Ibn Taymiyya makes general but revealing observations of fact. There is no question with regard to the normative demands of observing the law along with the rules and principles that this law dictates. These are not only unquestionable but rather constitute an integral part of a cultural habitus. The question here is factual, pertaining to the extent to which the various offices and functions of government apply the Sharīʿa. "It is often the case," Ibn Taymiyya observes, "that the deputy-judge, the governor, and the *muḥtasib* abide by the Sharʿ. But it is also oftentimes the case that some judges violate it."[15]

It is instructive to note here the reasons for this "violation" (*mukhālafa*). It might be motivated by "evil purposes," clearly implying deliberate corruption. But this is only one among other reasons. Lack of legal knowledge, a subjective state for the ignoramus, may account for some of these improper practices. Ibn Taymiyya seems to say that this deficient knowledge of the law may be due to simple ignorance, or lack of qualification and credentials, but it may also be the result of following the doctrine of an authority that is either invalid or unsound, or that the doctrine itself was misunderstood by the follower (the *muqallid qāḍī*) in the first place. On the other hand, those non-*qāḍī*s who follow the Sharʿ may do so by virtue of different and quite divergent reasons. It may be the case that it is merely common sense that leads them to this concord with the Sharʿ; or it could be that they unconsciously follow the prevailing norms and customs which are widespread and unquestioned (implying here a habitus of a kind). But it could still also be because they do reason correctly on the basis of the Book and the Sunna, or validly follow the authority of a *mujtahid*. On balance, Ibn Taymiyya asserts, the domain of *qaḍā'* tends to be more in conformity with the Sharʿ than other domains.[16] Yet, our author immediately retracts, only to point the finger at the *qāḍī*s again for "having in fact" fallen short of the normative expectations insofar as conforming to the

13 *ITSS*, 96.
14 *ITSS*, 193: "*Al-sharʿu ismun li-mā baʿatha Allāhu taʿālā bi-hi rasūlahu Muḥammadan, ṣalʿam, mina al-kitābi wal-ḥikmati*, wa-ḥukmuhu lāzimun jamīʿa al-khalqi" (emphasis mine).
15 *ITSS*, 193.
16 *ITSS*, 193.

Sharī'a. "It has been observed (*wa-qad ru'iya*) that some government officials are more virtuous than most *qāḍīs*, and it has [in fact] also been observed that some *qāḍīs* are worse than corrupt government officials."[17]

Why does Ibn Taymiyya come across here as condemning, if not deprecating, the *qāḍīs*, despite his clear admission that they tend to be more in conformity with the Shar' than is the case with other domains of government administration? He sums up the general answer by saying that "the goal is to be faithful to the *dīn* in all things,"[18] in all spheres of life, irrespective of who performs which task. And if this faithfulness is the general presumption and foundational premise, then it matters little who performs which function. A *wālī* who implements the Sharī'a ordinances faithfully would be more meritorious and loyal to the Community than a corrupt *qāḍī*, despite the *Shar'ī* learning and code of ethics the latter is supposed to command. "The ultimate goal is loyalty to the *dīn* in all things, and this cannot be achieved except through communal living and political authority. If [such] an authority upholds the *dīn* in a law-abiding manner, then this is the goal of the office's mandate [whatever it may be]."[19]

Ibn Taymiyya effectively argues that any executive or government office or function that enforces the ordinances of the Sharī'a is a *qadā'* office, since a large community of jurists have held the view that the *wilāya* of *qaḍā'* is a general category that subsumes a variety of functions, which custom and the language of the appointment decree define. The *wilāya* over a minor is defined by the Shar', whereas the parameters of *wilāya* over commanding armies is defined by the customary (*'urf*) practices of rulership.[20] But since the Shar'ī *qāḍī* is the official who knows best how to administer the *qaḍā'* function – because he is supposed to have perfected both the legal training for this task

17 *ITSS*, 193: "*Wa-qad ru'iya min al-wulāti man huwa khayrun min akthari al-quḍāti, wa-ru'iya min al-quḍāti man huwa sharrun min fussāqi al-wulāt.*"

18 *ITSS*, 194: "*Wal-maqṣūdu huwa amānatu al-dīni fī jamī'i al-ashyā'i.*" This telos drives Ibn Taymiyya's thought in all matters social and political. In his *Qa'ida fil-Ḥisba*, he states this postulate in even clearer terms: "*Aṣlu dhālika an ta'lama anna jamī'a al-wilāyāti fil-Islāmi maqṣuduha an yakuna al-dinu kullahu li-Lah, wa'an takuna kalimatu Allahi hiya al-'ulya, fa'inna Allāha, subḥānahu wa-ta'ālā, innamā khalaqa al-khalqa li-dhālika*" ["You ought to know the founding principle, that the goal of all appointments/functions/offices in Islam is that the *dīn* be entirely for the sake of God, that the word of God be the most high, for He, praised and exalted may He be, has created the human kind for that purpose."]

19 *ITSS*, 194: "*Wal-maqṣūdu huwa amānatu al-dīni fī jamī'i al-ashyā'i, wa-lā yatimmu dhālika illā bil-ijtimā'i wal-sulṭāni, fa-idhā ju'ila sulṭānun yuqāmu bi-hi al-dīnu 'alā al-wajhi al-mashrū'i, kāna dhālika maqṣūda al-wilāyati.*" See also his *Qā'ida fil-Ḥisba*, 38.

20 *ITSS*, 194; *Qā'ida fil-Ḥisba*, 43.

as well as the required technologies of the self that are appropriate to it – then he is the one who is expected more than any other official to carry out this function in the most adequate manner. In other words, the *qāḍī*s are supposed to rise to the highest form of ethical judicial practice.

These ideas are foundational in Ibn Taymiyya's theory of government, since they explain why he bothers little with the formal procedures of caliphal appointment, caliphal qualifications, elections, and other issues of this kind. The commitment in his thought is not to a (Weberian) charismatic figure, a traditional authority, or any specific government agency traditionally so defined, but rather to the telos of all judicial and executive offices. It matters little if we call the ruler a caliph, a sultan, a *wālī*, or even a *qāḍī*. What matters is that when a specific government function is to be fulfilled, whatever its mandate may be, the enforcement of the ordinances of the Sharʿ – as regulated by the Sharʿ and as appropriate to the assigned tasks of that office – stand as the ultimate measure and goal. Understanding the goal (*maqṣūd*) is the desideratum that enables the fulfillment of the relevant function – always according to the Sharīʿa – in the most appropriate manner possible.[21]

Ibn Taymiyya's theory on this issue seems at odds with the mainstream doctrine – articulated, for instance, by Māwardī and Ibn Jamāʿa – regulating the jurisdictional boundaries between and among various offices of government. This may be explained in two interconnected ways. First, it is possible that his doctrine is formulated in response to the recent emergence of the Mamlūk practice of military commanders and emirs adjudicating cases otherwise belonging to the Sharīʿa court, such as matters of personal status.[22] As we will see in chapter 10, there was an expansion in this practice during the last decades of the Mamlūk dynasty, long after Ibn Taymiyya died. But the trend seems to have faintly started during his lifetime, which led him to craft a doctrinal solution bringing to the fore a fundamental issue in the conception of the separation of various governmental powers.

In modern systems, the separation of powers is predicated on the assumption that each branch serves its own interests and that the overtaking of a function by a branch other than that which is constitutionally assigned to administer it would be deemed a violation of the principle of separation. It would amount to vitiating the principle that the ambition and greed of one

21 *ITSS*, 28. On Ibn Taymiyya's conflation of the caliphate with the general term imamate, see Kūnākātā, *al-Naẓariyya al-Siyāsiyya*, 75-82, esp. at 79-80 (Ibn Taymiyya: "*Inna shawba al-khilāfati bil-mulki jā'iz*;" 80).

22 On this, see ch. 10, below.

branch countervails the ambition and greed of another. When the functions of two branches are united under the administration of one power, one office, it is said that this would constitute the road to tyranny. As we will see in chapter 12, judicial review – an act of the judiciary striking down laws enacted by the legislative – and the combining of the three powers in the hands of administrative agencies (in what has been called "the rise and rise of the administrative state") would be classical examples of the "road to tyranny," the sites that generated vehement debates among American and European constitutional scholars as to whether these phenomena have effectively depleted the doctrine of separation of powers of its real meaning.

But this is not what Ibn Taymiyya is legitimizing. What he is rather insisting on is that a governmental function is performed properly ("constitutionally") as long as two conditions are met, irrespective of who performs the task. The first condition, which he would have every right to assume to be tenable, is that every governmental function is defined by the law to the letter, which is to say that the very detailed regulations of the office and its functioning in themselves fully guarantee the "constitutionality" of its operation. This in fact is the constitutional effect and power of the *madhhab* whose bindingness, as a matter of legal and political culture, is itself a constitutional restraint.[23]

Second, Ibn Taymiyya is also taking for granted that each governmental office or function embodies a set of technologies of ethical comportment, which make for further insurance that no matter who fulfills these functions does so on terms of the office, not on those that represent a class, a group, or an economic or political interest. This is why the proliferated works of *adab al-qāḍī* (and the *adab* of every other sphere of life) detail the ethical and moral comportment of the *qāḍī* as much as they articulate his technical and strictly legal responsibilities. What Ibn Taymiyya seems to be saying is that it does not matter which players play the game as long as the game itself is maintained and its rules respected.

An independent thinker who possesses a sophisticated understanding of law and politics, Ibn Taymiyya charted a discursive model of governance that brought Māwardī's and Juwaynī's realistic systems of governance to a new height, effectively resolving the paradoxes that resulted from the disjunctions of authority and power in the caliphal office. In his theoretical deployment, Islamic governance is boiled down to its fundamentals. Whoever and whatever can maintain the rule of law is the true ruler or governor, for to conform to the

23 On the *madhhab* as a constitutional and constitutionalizing entity, see ch. 4, sec. III, above.

law and its imperatives is to fulfill the caliphal mandate, no matter what name an office is given. This is neither the bureaucratic formalism of the modern state, nor is it the semblance or façade of law's rule. This is rather a substantive take on a mode of governance that seeks to achieve the goals of constitutional division and the rule of law without being constrained by a rigid formalistic division of governmental functions. Ibn Taymiyya understood what only some in modernity began to understand, that formalism and procedural mechanisms are neither guarantees nor a sufficient cause for good governance. This also raises the fundamental point that it is the separation between functions and offices that matters, not the separation between the personnel that run these units. For what guarantees separation is the substantive contents and boundaries of the office, no matter who is managing it. And if, hypothetically, one office dispenses with the obligations of another, then Ibn Taymiyya, I understand, would have no objection. This is so simply because the dispensation is assumed to be carried out not only according to the Shar', but also because it is a fulfillment of a Shar'ī requirement.

True, Ibn Taymiyya's thought reflects a demanding and strict system of the rule of law but it is one that is simultaneously flexible and pragmatic. Or, put conversely, despite its adaptability and pragmatism, his thought reflects a stubborn commitment to the rule of law. The modalities of politics and political actors may change, but the principle that the Sharī'a dominates remained unshakeable.

While Māwardī, Ibn Jamā'a, and many other jurists represented a contingency that defined the limits of executive power through a quantitative enumeration of rights and duties, Ibn Taymiyya cuts across the empirical in order to derive the fundamental principles that anchor rule and governance. His theory is not about personnel, their credentials, or terms of appointment to political offices. Rather, it is concerned with the contractual ties between the ruler and his men, on the one hand, and the ruled populace, on the other, a relationship resting on the logical foundations of what one owes the other. His theory is logically the neatest that has been elaborated by his time, since it captures the structure of Islamic governance through an incisive and pithily coherent logical and legal analysis.

Al-Siyāsa al-Shar'iyya is clearly a *risāla*, a work written for a particular person, either at the invitation of the recipient or by initiative of the author. We have repeatedly seen thus far that in Islamic political culture, offering or seeking advice about good governance was a staple of the system. In all likelihood, the *risāla* was written to a Mamlūk sultan or a powerful Mamlūk emir.[24] It is based, Ibn Taymiyya clarifies, on what he calls Āyat al-Umarā', the Qur'ānic verse (4:58-59) pertaining to rule and rulers:

> God commands you to render trusts (*amānāt*) to whom they are due and when you judge between people to judge with justice (*'adl*). Excellent is that which God instructs you. Indeed, God is ever Hearing and Seeing [58]. O you who have believed, obey God and obey the Messenger and those in authority over you. And if you disagree among yourselves over anything then refer it back to God and the Messenger if you truly believe in God and the Last Day. That is a good (course), leading to the most excellent outcome [59].

From this verse, Ibn Taymiyya derives two first-order political principles, namely, that the rulers are, on the one hand, under a fiduciary duty toward their subjects, and, on the other hand, they are bound by the principles of justice. The treatise is mostly preoccupied with three main themes, the sum of which constitute a theory of executive power. The first theme, the most original of the treatise, deals with the duties and responsibilities of the ruler, especially in charting the administration of governance in the polity and the relative qualifications of each executive function. The second is the theme of the fisc, collection of taxes, and their distribution, etc. The third is the enforcement of what might be called public law, and the rights and punishments that arise from public interest, such as the *ḥudūd* and related spheres. In the previous chapters of this book, we had plenty of occasion to discuss the second and third themes, and Ibn Taymiyya here does not differ much from other jurists. The first theme, however, deserves special attention, as it contains a theory of law that frames the sultanic executive in terms of hire, agency, and their concomitant terms of fiduciary duty.

The first of the Qur'ānic verses cited above enjoins Muslims in general and their leaders in particular to conduct themselves as unwavering trustees of what has been entrusted to them. Among the key tasks assigned to the ruler is the appointment of competent and qualified officials, whose function is to assist him and act on his behalf in dispensing justice. "He who appoints someone over the affairs of Muslims when he could have found another who would be more beneficial to Muslims is one who has betrayed God, his Messenger,

24 *ITSS*, 4: "*Fa-hādhihi risālatun ... iqtaḍāhā man awjaba Allāhu nuṣḥahu min wulāti al-umūri.*" See also Bori, "Istanbul, Süleymaniye Kütüphanesi MS Sehid Ali Pasa 1553," 54.

and the Believers."[25] This Prophetic report is further endorsed by three other authoritative statements to the same effect, emphasizing the element of treason in the business of government appointments. The "best man" available should always be appointed, and anyone less qualified would not do.[26] An earnest search for the most qualified government official for the relevant vacant office is thus a trust whose breach constitutes an act of betrayal.

The ruler's burden of trusteeship genealogically stems from two presumed juridical facts, namely, that (1) he is a hiree (*ajīr*), an employee, of the Muslim Community;[27] and (2) he is its agent (*wakīl*).[28] The legal instrument that constructs the fact of hire is known as *ijāra*, essentially a contract of exchange, combining both the rent of objects and the hire of human labor and animals. This contract, of the binding type (*lāzim*),[29] may be concluded through language that directly or indirectly connotes the meaning of rent or hire, as long as such expressions are accompanied by stipulations to the effect that a usufruct is exchanged for consideration. But given the political context we are discussing, it is important to note that this contract may also be concluded through *muʿāṭāt* – a sort of silent transactional exchange, such as when a person, without any verbal pronouncement, pays a shopkeeper the price of an item and the latter accepts the sum.[30] The custom-based presumption of a mutual agreement among the parties makes the formal requirements of expressive language unnecessary. By the agreement of all four schools, the services rendered in hire contracts are therefore largely defined by customary usage, which constitutes the benchmark of the parties' expectations.[31]

Likewise, agency (*wakālah*) is a contract that may either arise by implication, such as in the context of partnerships (*sharikāt*), or be created as such by an independent contract. It represents a *jā'iz* contract between a principal (*muwakkil*) and an agent (*wakīl*), whereby the former endows the latter with a capacity to act on his behalf in undertaking lawful and reasonably defined acts. Furthermore, whether he is working for a fee or not, the agent has a fiduciary duty (*amāna*) toward the principal, and thus can be

25 *ITSS*, 7.
26 *ITSS*, 8-9, 229.
27 *ITSS*, 14.
28 *ITSS*, 15.
29 That is, it cannot be annulled unilaterally. See Nawawī, *Rawḍa*, III, 100.
30 Hallaq, *Sharīʿa*, 240-41.
31 Māwardī, *al-Ḥāwī al-Kabīr*, V, 14; VII, 393; Misri, *Reliance of the Traveler*, 439–45; Ibn Rushd, *Distinguished Jurist's Primer*, II, 264–81; Hallaq, *Sharīʿa*, 256-58.

held liable for damages caused by his negligence (*taqṣīr*) or transgression (*ʿudwān/taʿaddī*).[32]

These legal categories are situated within an originary state in which it is politically presupposed that Muslims, as worshipers of God, are His servants while the rulers are deputized by God (*nuwwāb Allāh*) to govern the Community as caretakers (sing. *rāʿī*). In its legal framing, this political doctrine is as old as Bāqillānī (d. 403/1013), who had already taken it for granted that the entire function of the imam – namely, to "enforce the established Sharīʿa" – is grounded in the principles of deputization and agency. The imam is both the *nā'ib* (deputy) and *wakīl* (legal agent) of the Muslim Community.[33]

In this capacity, the rulers function as agents, as *wakīls*, "standing in the same position as one of the two partners [in a contract] vis-à-vis the other." Their relationship, Ibn Taymiyya states, is one that "embodies the meanings of *wilāya* and *wakāla*," with all the fiduciary duty that this relationship entails.[34] If a person or an agent, who is in charge of performing a commercial transaction, deputizes someone to run his business on behalf of the main partner (the owner of the capital) or on behalf of the *muwakkil*, he, the agent, would be deemed in breach of fiduciary duty should there have been available for hire a person who is more qualified. In selecting his men to run the affairs of the kingdom on his behalf, the ruler would thus be regarded as a *khā'in*, a betrayer of trust, should he not select the best available officials for the job. Ibn Taymiyya makes it clear that these terms and conditions are not meant to be idealistic and unfeasible but rather represent the essential need to select "the best in what is available" (*aṣlaḥ al-mawjūd*). If the ruler exercises his best effort in choosing the "best man" for the job, then he would be deemed to have satisfactorily performed his fiduciary duty (*amāna*).[35]

Amāna continues to run through the vine, for every government office requires it. The other category of qualifications necessary as a concomitant is *quwwa*, namely, the capability to carry the substantive duties of the office.

32 Miṣrī, *Reliance*, 419–23; Ibn Rushd, *Distinguished Jurist's Primer*, II, 363–67; Shaʿrānī, *Mīzān*, II, 111; *Al-Mawsūʿa al-Fiqhiyya*, XLV, 5 ff.

33 Bāqillānī, *Tamhīd*, 476: "*Al-imām[u] yunṣabu li-iqāmati al-aḥkāmi [wal-]ḥudūdi wa-umūrin qad sharraʿahā al-Rasūlu... wa-qad taqaddama ʿilmu al-Ummati bi-hā wa-huwa fī jamīʿi mā yatawallāhu wakīlun lil-Ummati wa-nā'ibun ʿanhā.*" For a simplified account, see Jaʿfar, "Naẓariyyat al-Imāma ʿInda al-Bāqillānī."

34 *ITSS*, 15: "*Wa-hādhā ẓāhiru al-iʿtibāri, fa'inna al-khalqa ʿibādu Allāhi wal-wulātu nuwwābu Allāhi ʿalā ʿibādihi, wa-hum wukalā'u al-ʿibādi ʿalā nufūsihim, bi-manzilati aḥadi al-sharīkayni maʿa al-ākhari, fa-fīhim maʿnā al-wilāyati wal-wakālati.*"

35 *ITSS*, 16, 28.

Quwwa in military appointments, for instance, encompasses courage and expert knowledge in the art of war, including strategic military deception.[36] In matters of judgeship, *quwwa* requires knowledge of what justice (*ʿadl*) entails, the application and enforcement of the laws derived from the Book and the Sunna, etc.[37] The message that Ibn Taymiyya is driving home here is that while the components and attributes of *quwwa* vary with each government office, *amāna* is a constant, a common denominator that ultimately presupposes fear of God (*khishya*), not of humans. In some offices, such as appointments to the Public Treasury, considerations of *amāna* outweigh substantive qualifications, because fiduciary trust is the foundation of credentials for holding such a grave responsibility.[38]

Amāna stands as the cornerstone not only of governmental appointments but also of the collection and distribution of taxes, as well as in all transactions involving wealth and money (*amwāl*) and requiring fiduciary duty. In all these spheres,[39] the ruler and his men stand fully under the duty of trust in their capacity as custodians, agents of *wakāla*, and deputies, for most of the wealth collected as taxes and the like (such as the wealth of intestate or heirless persons) belongs to Muslims (= Public Treasury) and not to the ruling elite.[40] Here, Ibn Taymiyya devotes extensive space for discussing the allocation of taxes and other financial issues, connecting the latter with the penal sphere. He warns against waiving physical punishments in favor of monetary penalties[41] and discusses a variety of infringements that became common under the Mamlūks. It is not difficult to tally his abstract, juridical, and theoretical account with the annals that recorded Mamlūk societies and history. His juridico-political expositions seem not only to mirror these historical accounts but also to provide corrective reactions to them.

Finally, Ibn Taymiyya, like the majority of writers on the subject, addresses the limits of executive power in the sphere of penal law, an arena where much of the constitutional grind took place for the next four centuries. The Qur'ānic *ḥudūd* are delimited by law to a detail, allowing little, if any, discretion for

36 On strategic military deception, see van Vleet, "Tactical Military Deception."

37 *ITSS*, 17-18.

38 *ITSS*, 18, 25.

39 Which Ibn Taymiyya discusses at length (*ITSS*, 40-83, *inter alia*), but which constitute standard accounts in many other political treatises. See our discussion of such matters in ch. 7, above, as expounded in Ibn Jamāʿa's theory, as well as in the early third/ninth-century treatise of Al-Qāsim b. Sallām, *Kitāb al-Amwāl*, I, 34-36.

40 *ITSS*, 44, 57-60.

41 *ITSS*, 89-93.

subjective juristic interpretation. *Ta'zīr*, on the other hand, permitted somewhat free space for the ruler and his men to inflict punishments as they saw appropriate and proportional to the crime, as long as these punishments – according to the majority view – do not exceed the *ḥudūd*. Sexual behavior without penetration, defaming others in matters not related to adultery or fornication, stealing that does not involve break and entry, betrayal of fiduciary trusts in the management of *waqf*s and public moneys, cheating in weights and measures, or testifying falsely – all these and similar infractions are punishable by the ruler and his deputies in ways that they see fit. The "bigger the offense, the more severe the punishment."[42] By the consensus of the jurists, repeat offenders command a particularly stiff punishment. But none of the *ta'zīr* penalties should rise to the level of the *ḥudūd* penalties within each category: Non-adulterous sexual violations, for example, are not punishable to the extent that *zinā* is punished, although the penalty may exceed that which is assigned for defamation (*qadhf*).[43] As we will see later in this chapter, a few jurists permitted the infliction of capital punishment on enemy spies, inciters of heresy, and those who "spread corruption on Earth" (*fasād fil-arḍ*).[44]

III

Ibn Taymiyya, however, begins to chart a path that would constitute the foundations for a robust expansion at the hands of his student Ibn Qayyim al-Jawziyya. It seems to me beyond doubt that the master's intentions were both moral and sincere, but their constitutional ramifications were significant – perhaps beyond what our great thinker foresaw. In the sections dealing with punishments (*'uqūbāt*), he articulates the idea that the formal rules and dictates of the Sharī'a are not the only means to achieve the goals of the law

42 *ITSS*, 144-45.

43 *ITSS*, 145-47. *Qadhf* is the false accusation of *zinā* (adultery/fornication). It gives rise to the application of the *ḥadd* penalty, with or without the victim's willingness or ability to prosecute (since the offense can also be prosecuted on behalf of deceased individuals). It is thus the only strictly *ḥadd* offense that need not await prosecution by the victim or his kin but can be tried and punished on the instigation of the general public or government authorities. See Hallaq, *Sharī'a*, 315 and passim. On some of the *ta'zīr* punishments, see Lange, *Justice, Punishment*, 223-39.

44 *ITSS*, 148. On the important concept of *fasād fil-arḍ*, see Aykan, "A Legal Concept in Motion."

in the creation and maintenance of a moral order, where the imperatives of the *dīn* are the telos.

Punishments, he argues, are not the only means to force compliance with the law and to desist from wrongdoing. The Sharʿ has legislated subsidiary and supporting props that "help to achieve" these goals (*mā yuʿīnu ʿalā dhālik*).[45] A father, for instance, may create opportunities for business, education, or otherwise in order to reform his son who may be in violation of the moral law. His punishment, by the government or by himself, is not the only means to guide him to the right path. The goals of the law may be achieved by the means of the law, but Ibn Taymiyya is insisting that the means are countless and boundless. Therefore, "*any means possible*" to achieve the good and advance the cause of the law can and should be employed.[46]

When "any means possible" intrudes on the law of procedure, then the entirety of the law can be subjected to a qualitative revaluation, perhaps changing its nature, even ontology and teleology. If it is true that procedure is the thread by which the law hangs, then procedure can determine not only what the law is but also what its goals and priorities are. In advancing the cause of moral and legal compliance, Ibn Taymiyya decided to stand on the side of ethical caution, where doubt (*shubha*) ceases to be a cause for averting stiff penalties and instead becomes the grounds which justify a proactive enforcement of the law. In courses of legal action in which the purpose is to avert harm but not to punish for a wrong committed, all that is needed is an indication (*dalāla*) or a mere probability (*maẓanna*).[47] By virtue of being communal knowledge, widespread hearsay (*istifāḍa*) can constitute evidence, on its own, and without further verification of the truthfulness of the testimony.[48] Even "less than *istifāḍa* may do, for one can know a person's [character] from [the character of] those with whom he associates."[49] *Qāḍī*s, rulers, governors, and all their deputized officials must be experts in detecting the signs (*ʿalāmāt*) that portend evil and its forewarnings (*asbāb*). Criminal suspicion, even assuming the worst (*sūʾ al-ẓann*), is thus a necessary modus operandi "in order to avert harm," though "it is not permitted to punish a person on the grounds of it."[50]

45 *ITSS*, 181.

46 *ITSS*, 181: "*Wa-kamā anna al-ʿuqūbāta shurriʿat dāʿiyatan ilā fiʿli al-wājibāti wa-tarki al-muḥarramāti, fa-qad shurriʿa ayḍan kullu mā yuʿīnu ʿalā dhālika, fa-yanbaghī taysīra ṭarīqi al-khayri wal-ṭāʿati wal-iʿānati ʿalayhi wal-targhībi fī-hi* bikulli mumkinin" (emphasis mine).

47 *ITSS*, 186 (l. 7), 186 (l. 5).

48 *ITSS*, 186, 188. On *istifāḍa* as widespread hearsay, see *al-Mawsūʿa al-Fiqhiyya*, IV, 45-46.

49 *ITSS*, 188.

50 *ITSS*, 188.

"Knowledge and acumen are thus quintessential to governance, for *siyāsa* by good judgment and experience is superior to, and more beneficial than, *siyāsa* by courage and might."[51]

Ibn Taymiyya's expansion of executive prerogatives seems to me to revert to the forms of *siyāsa* practice that existed before the full rise of the Sharīʿa, in the so-called early formative period.[52] With the development of the Sharīʿa, its institutions, practices, and intellectual matrix, Sharʿī culture increasingly endowed political life with a new habitus, curbing the excesses of earlier *siyāsa* and pressuring it to conform to the more cautious procedures of the Sharīʿa. Ibn Taymiyya seems to have pursued a Ḥanbalī line of thinking which would effectively bring the Sharīʿa back to an early state of evolution, when it fought hard to resist and overcome exactly what Ibn Taymiyya wished to (re)introduce.

It is my argument that at least in terms of origins, the compound noun "*siyāsa sharʿiyya*" is Ḥanbalī in emphasis and tint. Yet, the earliest use of the expression I know of appears in Ibn ʿAqīl's *Kitāb al-Funūn*, another distinguished Ḥanbalī intellectual who died in 513/1119, some two centuries before Ibn Taymiyya flourished.[53] Relatively little survived from Ibn ʿAqīl's work,[54] and none, it seems, from his writings on politics and "constitutional" topics. What we possess is a selection of his statements recorded, among other sources, in Ibn al-Qayyim's work, *al-Ṭuruq al-Ḥukmiyya fil-Siyāsa al-Sharʿiyya*. The published remnants from his *Kitāb al-Funūn*[55] do not contain, insofar as I can

51 *ITSS*, 190: "*Wal-siyāsatu bil-ra'yi wal-khibrati aʿẓamu min al-siyāsati bil-shajāʿati wal-quwwa wa-anfaʿ*."

52 Yücesoy, *Disenchanting the Caliphate*.

53 Cf. Belhaj, "Law and Public Order," who argues that Ibn ʿArabī (d. 638/1240) was, to his knowledge, the first to employ the expression, and that Ibn Taymiyya borrowed it from his *Futūḥāt*, a work that Ibn Taymiyya detested. It makes much better sense that he simply followed his school associate, the distinguished Ḥanbalī thinker Ibn ʿAqīl, who not only used the term but also argued for a doctrine of *siyāsa sharʿiyya* that – though perhaps in a skeletal form – anticipated the thinking of both Ibn al-Qayyim and Ibn Taymiyya on the subject. On Ibn Taymiyya's critique of Ibn ʿArabī, see Hallaq, *Ibn Taymiyya Against the Greek Logicians*, xii–xiii, xxiv, xxvi. We have seen that Māwardī uses "*siyāsa dīniyya*," *AS*, 322, while a contemporary of Ibn ʿAqīl, the Andalusian Mālikī and Iraqī-trained Ṭurtūshī (d. 520/1126) knows only of *siyāsa*, *siyāsa ʿāmma* (general *siyāsa*), and *al-siyāsa al-iṣṭilāḥiyya* (generic *siyāsa* that is adopted by "nontheistic" Kings, Persian Shāhs, Muslim rulers, as well as others). See his *Sirāj al-Mulūk*, 64, 159, 197, 203–5. It is interesting to note that the eighth/fourteenth century Ibn Khaldūn, *Muqaddima*, 150, continues to use the expression "*siyāsa dīniyya*."

54 Ibn ʿAqīl was a prolific author, who claims to his name a number of large and small works in various fields. See George Makdisi's Introduction to the author's work *al-Waḍiḥ fil-Uṣūl* (p. 1m), which he edited and published in Beirut (Franz Steiner, 1996).

55 Published in fragments in Damanhūr, Egypt, in 1991.

tell, the sections from which Ibn al-Qayyim drew his materials, and which the latter clearly identified as hailing from that impressive work.

It is in Ibn ʿAqīl's work that we find, hitherto, the earliest use of the expression "*siyāsa sharʿiyya*." The expression seems to have emerged during the second half of the fifth/eleventh century, since Māwardī himself does not use it; instead, he employs the appellation of "*al-siyāsa al-dīniyya*,"[56] a clear antecedent and predecessor of the later designation. In fact, the late Mamlūk writer Ṭūghān Shaykh al-Muḥammadī, when quoting Māwardī at length, took Māwardī's expression to be "*siyāsa sharʿiyya*," disposing of the original expression.[57]

Standing alone, the term "*siyāsa*" was known from the first half of the second century of the Hijra – as attested in Ibn al-Muqaffaʿ's renowned tract *Risāla fil-Ṣaḥāba*[58] – if not earlier.[59] While Ibn al-Muqaffaʿ uses the term in passing, hardly defining what it precisely means,[60] Ibn ʿAqīl sheds much light on its connotations. *Siyāsa sharʿiyya*, he says, is a legitimate tool of *salṭana* (which I here take to mean the business of political administration) and integral to it as a matter of course. All master jurists (*imāms*) acknowledged it as such. In the exercise of rule, he adds, the expression indicates *ḥazm*, the ability to manage a matter with reason, experience, and prudence.[61] No ruler can dispense the affairs of governance without it.

56 *AS*, 322, l. 4. Prototypes that reference "*dīn*" as a general category and are typical in the development of disciplines and genres. Before "*uṣūl al-fiqh*" acquired its final technical designation, for instance, it was labelled by the founders as "*uṣūl al-dīn*." See Hallaq, "*Uṣūl al-Fiqh* and Shāfiʿī's *Risāla*," 166.

57 Ṭūghān Shaykhul-Muḥammadī, *Al-Muqaddima al-Sulṭāniyya*, fol. 150b. Ṭūghān, writing toward the end of the ninth/fifteenth century, dedicated the book to the sultan al-Ashraf Qaytbāy (r. 872-901/1468-96). See Fu'ād ʿAbd al-Munʿim's Introduction to Dāda Afandī, *al-Siyāsa al-Sharʿiyya* (*SSD*), 55. It is worth noting that while Ṭūghān recasts Māwardī's "*siyāsa dīniyya*" into "*siyāsa sharʿiyya*," he does use the latter expression ("*aḥkām siyāsiyya dīniyya*") in the opening folios of his treatise (fol. 5A).

58 Ibn al-Muqaffaʿ, *Risāla*, 319 (l. 11).

59 Yücesoy, *Disenchanting the Caliphate*, 82 ff., 106 ff.

60 Judging from the context, "*siyāsa*" for Ibn al-Muqaffaʿ carried a positive connotation. Referring to certain formerly government-appointed agents as corrupt, he says that the latter's acts soil healthy social associations (*ḥasab*), proper conduct (*adab*) and good governance (*siyāsa*). *Risāla*, 319.

61 Ibn al-Qayyim, *al-Ṭuruq al-Ḥukmiyya*, 12 (henceforth *TH*). Zabīdī defines *ḥazm* as prudence (*ʿaql, ḥinka*) and precaution (*ḥadhar*). See *Tāj al-ʿArūs*, XVI, 145. In his *Taʿrīfāt*, 91, Jurjānī defines the term as "managing affairs with consensual assent" (*akhdhu al-umūri bil-ittifāq*). Ibn Manẓūr writes that it is "controlling one's affairs with confidence" (*al-ḥazmu ḍabṭu al-insāni amrahu wal-akhdhu fīhi bil-thiqa*). He who exercises *ḥazm*, he continues, "is a rational, intellectually mature person who is seasoned" (*huwa al-ʿāqilu al-mumayyizu*

A Shāfiʿī interlocutor objected that *siyāsa* cannot or must not violate the Sharʿ, to which Ibn ʿAqīl replied that despite the fact that "neither the Prophet nor the Qur'ān legislated it, it is any action that promotes the welfare of people and draws them away from corruption/immorality." If, he added in response, "you mean that it is [an act] that does not contradict the Sharʿ, then that is correct." But if "you mean that no *siyāsa* is valid unless the Sharʿ declares it so, then that is not only an error (*ghalaṭ*) but [a declaration that] effectively charges the Rāshidūn caliphs with having committed an error (*taghlīṭ*). Any person who truly knows their *sunan* or the established and verified ways of their conduct would not be able to deny that they resorted to harsh penalties, including capital punishment."[62] Examples of their *siyāsa*-based conduct abound, ranging from ʿUthmān who burned the variant copies of the Qur'ān (with a view to creating a vulgate), to ʿAlī who burned certain heretics (*zindīq*s) at the stake. Even the Prophet himself is claimed by Ibn ʿAqīl to have implemented penalties that were not "statutory,"[63] such as smashing wine vessels (instead of washing them) and inflicting unusual punishments for those convicted of drinking alcoholic substances after the prohibition.[64]

IV

Ibn ʿAqīl's objections to his interlocutor draw a sharp line of difference between the textualism of the Shāfiʿīs and the moral supra-textualism of the Ḥanbalī school, or at least a branch of it.[65] The difference is amplified by Ibn al-Qayyim,

dhū al-ḥinka). *Lisān al-ʿArab*, XII, 152. It is to be noted that the modern connotation of the term as "firmness" or "resoluteness" was not its dominant meaning in premodern Arabic. See Wehr, *Dictionary of Modern Written Arabic*, 173.

62 *TH*, 12: "*Qāla Ibn ʿAqīl: Al-siyāsatu mā kāna fiʿlan yakūnu maʿhu al-nāsu aqrabu ilā al-ṣalāḥi, wa-abʿadu ʿani al-fasādi, wa'in lam yaḍaʿhu al-Rasūlu wa-lā nazila bi-hi waḥyun.*"

63 I mean by "statutory" penalties those punishments whose lower and upper limit are stipulated by the law, not just the *ḥudūd* punishments, including those within the sphere of *taʿzīr*.

64 *TH*, 12-15.

65 Arguably, the Ḥanbalī school was divided into two branches on matters of politics and constitutional matters, especially as pertains to executive powers. Ibn ʿAqīl and Abū Yaʿlā al-Farrā' represented this difference, establishing (or reaffirming) a tradition of intra school division that continued for centuries to come. The heirs of this difference in the later school were represented by Ibn Taymiyya and Ibn Qayyim al-Jawziyya, on the one hand, and Ibn al-Mibrad and Buhūtī, on the other. For a strong indication of the division of the school as represented by Ibn ʿAqīl and Abū Yaʿlā al-Farrā', see *ITSS*, 148.

who rightly argues that drawing the outer boundaries of *siyāsa shar'iyya* has been a confusing and perplexing matter, leading many people to error. He criticizes those who bestow both too wide and too narrow an interpretation on the meaning and scope of this domain, but the latter in particular receives his unrestrained wrath. The uneven criticism already foretells Ibn al-Qayyim's bias in favor of an expansive jurisdiction of the domain of *siyāsa shar'iyya*, because, he argues, the latter group's stance has led to much corruption, rendered the Sharī'a incapable of "taking care of people's interests" and thus in need of external, non-Shar'ī tools of governance.[66] He does not specify what these tools are but says that the rulers (*wulāt al-umūr*), when facing this narrow definition of juristic *siyāsa*, have had no choice but to make recourse to all sorts of measures and extra-measures that resulted in a wide range of evil and modes of corruption, to such an extent that "it has become extremely difficult for those who truly know the Shar' [i.e., the ulama] to extricate people from this situation."[67]

It is noteworthy that in Ibn al-Qayyim's evaluation, the rulers did not resort to such extraordinary and clearly outrageous methods of governance out of whim or mere capriciousness but rather because they did not find the proper tools of governance within the Sharī'a's domain, or because they were not properly advised about the legal course of action. The implication of his language is quite clear: that governance must be undertaken out of necessity, that it is impossible to govern with the existing Shar'ī tools, and that "added, extra-measures have become necessary for ordering the affairs [of the social world]."[68]

Ibn al-Qayyim does not tire of repeating that the ultimate goal of the law is bringing forth justice and that any method or way that can lead to justice, wherever it may be found, would be Sharī'a-sanctioned.[69] Yet, he also seems

---

66 *TH*, 13: "*Wa-ja'alū al-Sharī'ata qāṣiratan lā taqūmu bi-maṣāliḥi al-'ibādi, muḥtājatan ilā ghayrihā.*"

67 *TH*, 13: "*Fa-lammā ra'ā wulātu al-umūri dhālika,* wa'anna al-nāsa lā yastaqīmu amruhum illā bi'amrin warā'a mā fahimahu hā'ulā'u mina al-Sharī'ati [i.e., the jurists upholding the narrow interpretation], *aḥdathū min awḍā'i siyāsatihim sharran ṭawīlan wa-fasādan 'arīḍan, fa-tafāqama al-amru wa-ta'adhdhara istidrākahu wa-'azza 'alā al-'ālimīna bi-ḥaqā'iqi al-shar'i takhlīṣa al-nufūsi min dhalika*" (emphasis mine). (The editor vocalizes "*'ālimīna*" as "*'ālamīna,*" which is obviously an error.)

68 Hence the thrust of the emphasis in the previous quote. This understanding is consistent with Opwis's general conclusions regarding the punishment for consuming intoxicants. See her "Shifting Legal Authority," 89-92.

69 *TH*, 13: "*Fa-'idhā ẓaharat imāratu al-'adli wa-asfara wajhuhu bi'ayyi ṭarīqin kāna, fa-thumma shar'u Allāhi .... Fa'ayyu ṭarīqin istukhrija bi-hā al-'adlu wal-qisṭu fa-hiya min al-dīni wa-laysat mukhālifatan la-hu.*"

adamant at distinguishing a just *siyāsa* (*ʿādila*) from an unjust one (*ẓālima*), the latter being "forbidden by the Sharīʿa."[70] The former, obviously, never contradicts the Sharʿ, for it is consistent with the commands of the law and thus "an integral part of it." "We call it *siyāsa*," Ibn al-Qayyim adds, "merely to follow their customary labelling,"[71] but he does not specify who "they" are. It is my suspicion that the reference is mostly to the Shāfiʿīs who largely controlled the judiciary and judicial administration under the Mamlūks, and *who upheld a significantly Māwardīan boundary for executive oversight.* The fact of the matter, our jurist asserts, is that the practices of the Prophet and his Companions demonstrate that *siyāsa* is integral to the Sharīʿa. It is so because for him it is nonsensical to abide by the formal and restrictively interpreted procedural law of the Sharīʿa when it is obvious, through external evidence, that a particular person had committed a criminal act. The Prophet, he says, imprisoned and physically punished criminals when "signs (*amārāt*/ *ʿalāmāt*) appeared on the suspected wrongdoer. He who releases someone after making him take an oath – saying 'I cannot arrest him without the testimonies of two just witnesses' [the required evidentiary grounds for conviction] – would have violated the *siyāsa sharʿiyya*, because he knows that [the person of interest] is notorious for spreading corruption on Earth, having committed multiple thefts."[72]

Nor should the Sharīʿa, he argues, be contented with what he implies to be excessively cautious or formalistic procedures. The "interest of the *Umma* does not depend on [the modalities of] a plaintiff and defendant," for these procedural formalities "would ruin these interests and disrupt order." The government official (*mutawallī*) must transcend these procedural rules, deciding on matters through "apparent signs" and "clear circumstantial evidence."[73]

Ibn al-Qayyim's logic entails the necessary conclusion that abiding by the strict letter of the law yields unlawful results and defeats the intentions of the Sharīʿa. Yet, opening the floodgates of subjective procedure and adjectival

---

70 *TII*, 4.

71 *TH*, 14.

72 *TH*, 14: "*Fa-man aṭlaqa kullan min-hum wa-ḥallafahu wa-khallā sabīlahu, maʿ ʿilmihi bi-ishtihārihi bil-fusūdi fil-arḍi, wa-kathrati sariqātihi, wa-qāla lā ākhudhhu illā bi-shāhidayyi ʿadlin, fa-qawluhu mukhālifun lil-siyāsati al-sharʿiyyati.*"

73 *TH*, 222: "*Wal-maqṣūdu anna hadhihi aḥkāmun sharʿiyyatun, la-hā ṭuruqun sharʿiyyatun lā tatimmu maṣlaḥatu al-ummati illā bi-hā, wa-lā tatawaqqafu ʿalā muddaʿin wa-muddaʿā ʿalyhi, bal law tawaqqafat ʿalā dhālika fasadat maṣāliḥu al-Ummati wa-khtalla al-niẓāmu, bal yaḥkumu fī-hā mutawallī dhālika bil-amārāti wal-ʿalāmāti al-ẓāhirati wal-qarāʾini al-bayyinati.*"

law in such a manner risks running down a slippery slope to flagrant abuse and, indeed, "corruption on Earth," turning the intention to do good, as our author certainly entertained, on its head. The only caveat that would safeguard against such abuses and maltreatment would involve the assumption that the *wulāt*, the men in power, approach each case with a healthy dose of rectitude and ethical conduct, an assumption that the jurists at large could hardly grant the *dawla*'s administrative personnel. So what was Ibn al-Qayyim, along with his Shaykh before him, trying to accomplish?

The majority of Muslim jurists, including the dominant Shāfiʿīs and a weighty section of the Hanbalī school, espoused a dualistic penal system that gave the sultanic executive a right to punish its own officials in the way it saw fit, having reserved the Sharīʿa-based penal regulations for the vast bulk of what may be described as the civic population, the so-called *raʿāyā*. As we saw earlier in the sections treating *maẓālim*, the officials of the executive could adjudicate a spectrum of matters employing wider discretionary powers than those enjoyed by the *qāḍī*/*ḥākim*. But caution must be exercised not to equate the penal field in executive governance with *maẓālim*, since the latter possesses much wider competence than the former. For instance, the *maẓālim* office oversees the auditing of tax collection, the *dīwān*s, and management of major *awqāf*, and is furthermore competent to seize and restore property – in cases of usurpation – and to enforce the *qāḍī* and *muḥtasib*'s decisions.[74] But there is a section of the penal sphere that bifurcates into fixed Sharʿī penalties (known as *ḥudūd*) and discretionary ones (known as *taʿzīr*), and it is mainly within the latter sub-sphere that issues of under- or overreach of executive powers arise for the *maẓālim*, the *qāḍī*'s court, and all rulers, governors and their deputies, precisely because these penalties are discretionary and therefore controversial. Yet, executive power also possessed the right to hear cases of *ḥudūd*,[75] which,

74 See discussions above, ch. 3, and *AS*, 134-39.

75 The severe sanctions applied to the *ḥudūd* offenses were intended to deter (*zajr*) and were thus infrequently implemented in practice. This is exceedingly clear from the strict evidential procedures required to prove them. Yet, the harsh penalties inflicted on the *ḥudūd* transgressors represented only one element of their value as deterrence, the other being their enshrinement in a moral code that bestowed on them a prohibitory force far more effective than their judicial enforceability in the here and now. Their commission, when not punished in this world, was said to land the offender in eternal Hellfire, an eschatological notion that tended to engender moral compliance on a deep psychological level. The extreme economy with which the *ḥudūd* were invoked was motivated by the maxim, generated from a Prophetic Ḥadīth, that they had to be "averted at the existence of the slightest doubt." In fact, standard legal rules, otherwise invoked in all other branches of *fiqh*, were applied differently where the *ḥudūd* were concerned. For instance, in any

while fixed in terms of penalties, are equally subject to two modes of proof in the processes of adjudicating them. To sum up:

The *qāḍī*'s court is:

1. bound by a fixed procedure and fixed penalties in the case of the *ḥudūd*; and
2. bound by a fixed procedure and discretionary yet statutory penalties in the case of *ta'zīr*.

The executive, however, is:

1. bound by the statutory *ḥudūd* penalties but not by a particular procedure or evidentiary rules; and
2. bound by neither procedure nor (according to some jurists) statutory penalties in the case of *ta'zīr*.

The crux of the problem then is defining the minimal and maximal limits of all these spheres of action – procedural and punitive – except for the fixed penalties of *ḥudūd*.

Ibn al-Qayyim and his mentor were, in this regard, responding to a legal tradition that may be summed up and represented in Māwardī's (and perhaps Abū Ya'lā's) seminal work, though this treatise was, in the long run, far more influential than its Ḥanbalī counterpart. In his *al-Aḥkām al-Sulṭāniyya*, Māwardī dedicates chapter nine to what he calls *aḥkām al-jarā'im*, the procedural rules pertaining to crime. As mentioned earlier, here he distinguishes between the spheres of *siyāsa dīniyya* and *aḥkām shar'iyya*,[76] the former belonging to the ruler and his deputized executives (to the exclusion of the judiciary) while the latter to the *qāḍī*'s court.

A key term in the discussion is *tuhma*, i.e., suspicion of criminal conduct. In *ḥudūd*, Sharī'a's adjectival law does not permit the *qāḍī* to institute

other area of the law, confession (*iqrār*) was irrevocable, but not so in the *ḥudūd* (except in *qadhf*=defamation=slanderous accusation) where a *ḥadd* proven by confession was cancelled upon the withdrawal of that confession. In the same vein, the testimony of a secondary witness (*shahāda 'alā al-shahāda*), otherwise admissible in law in general, was inadmissible in *ḥudūd*, as was any written communication between judges (*kitāb al-qāḍī ilā al-qāḍī*). While each *ḥadd* was bounded by relevant evidentiary rules, these rules were highly constricting, exclusionary, and demanding. Cases of *zinā* (fornication/adultery) and theft, the only offenses that required, respectively, capital punishment or mutilation – aside from highway robbery – were, short of confession, nearly impossible to establish. See Māwardī, *Ḥāwī*, XIII, 210-41, 253-65; Nawawī, *Rawḍa*, VII, 305-7.

76 *AS*, 322.

procedural action or judicial injunction (such as imprisonment for purposes of investigation) on the basis of mere suspicion, nor to torture the suspect with a view to obtaining evidence or proof of criminal conduct.[77] There is a series of additional constraining procedural rules that likewise obtains in the case of the *qāḍī*, while the same cannot be said of the *emir* or his deputies, including the officer in charge of prosecuting crime (*wālī al-jarā'im*). Māwardī (and identically Abū Ya'lā) offers in several points a detailed description of executive procedural rights that the emir possesses, while the *qāḍī* does not:[78]

First, the emir can rely on the statements or findings of his deputies with regard to the reputation of the accused. If the latter has a record of misconduct bearing on the crime he is charged with, the inquiry should be intensified and he will be subjected to further investigative measures. Second, recourse to circumstantial evidence is made. If, for instance, it is a case of adultery or fornication, the accused will be subjected to more intense investigation if he is known to be a seducer of women or a philanderer. Third, the emir can imprison a person, without proof of guilt, for purposes of investigation and inquiry. Some jurists permitted a maximum of one month for this type of detention, while others did not impose any time-limit on the executive authority to complete its investigation. Fourth, the emir can use physical punishment equal to the measures of *ta'zīr*, but not to *ḥudūd*, in order to extract confession or evidence. Fifth, the emir can indefinitely imprison a repeat offender who has earlier been punished, that is, until he meets his natural death. During imprisonment, the Public Treasury would take care of his food and clothing. And sixth, the emir may, among other things, hear the testimonies of members of religious minorities against Muslim offenders, and may use threat of severe punishment to force a criminal to repent.

None of these procedures are allowed in the case of *qāḍīs*, since, Māwardī states, they belong to the sphere of *siyāsa*, the province of the emir and his deputies, but not to Shar'ī *aḥkām* (rules), the operative sphere of the *qāḍīs*. However, once the criminal is convicted and his crime proven to have taken

77 *AS*, 322: "*Fa'in kāna ḥākiman rufi'a ilayhi rajulun qad ittuhima bi-sariqatin aw zinan, lam yakun li-tuhmatin bi-hā ta'thīrun 'indahu, wa-lam yajūzu an yaḥbisahu li-kashfin wa-lā istibrā'in, wa-lā an ya'khudahu bi-asbābi al-iqrāri ijbāran.*" See identical language in Abū Ya'lā, *al-Aḥkām al-Sulṭāniyya*, 257.

78 *AS*, 322-24; Abu Ya'lā, *Aḥkām al-Sulṭāniyya*, 258-60. On *tuhma* in relation to Sharī'a's procedural law, see Johansen, "Signs as Evidence," 168–93. Johansen centered his attention on procedural law, leaving aside the important constitutional implications of Ibn al-Qayyim's doctrine.

place, both the *qāḍīs* and the emirs are bound by the fixed *ḥudūd* punishments.[79] In other words, it is only in the way cases of crime are tried that there were differences between the justice of the men of the sword and that of the men of the pen.[80]

As for *ta ʿzīr*, the punishment should be proportional to the offense committed and to the social standing and the criminal history of the convicted. A mild infraction committed by an honorable person of good social standing would not require more than a rebuke, for even such a light reprimand would be sufficient punishment in such a context. A repeat offender of plebeian social standing would demand a harsher and more flagrant punishment.

Verbal admonishment is the mildest form of punishment in *ta ʿzīr*, rising to imprisonment from one day to six months, again, depending on the crime in question and the criminal record of the offender. The next level of penalty is banishment (*nafy/ib ʿād*), which, according to the Shāfiʿī school, cannot exceed a year short of one day. The Mālikī school, known for its generally harsher penalties, allows for a longer period in the case of more serious offenses.[81] It must be remembered, however, that this school had relatively few followers in the Mamlūk domains, and did not have the judicial and jurisprudential sway that the dominant Shāfiʿīs enjoyed, and toward whom both Ibn Taymiyya and Ibn al-Qayyim seem to have been directing their criticism.[82]

The next level of *ta ʿzīr* penalty was lashing by the whip. The Shāfiʿīs permitted a maximum of thirty-nine lashes for free persons, and nineteen for slaves, one strike short of the minimal penalty for the consumption of alcoholic beverage. Abū Ḥanīfa allowed thirty-nine for both freemen and slaves, and Mālik did not set an upper limit. Although Abū Yaʿlā offers a different list of minimal and maximal penalties for *ta ʿzīr*, he roughly agrees with Māwardī, and explicitly states that these penalties cannot exceed the minimum of penalties in the *ḥudūd* counterparts, also excluding monetary penalties and the cutting of limbs.[83] Yet again, we see that the schools that popularly and politically ruled in the Mamlūk domains – the Shāfiʿīs and the Ḥanafīs – set statutory limits

79 *AS*, 324-25; Abū Yaʿlā, *al-Aḥkām al-Sulṭāniyya*, 260.
80 See also *TAB*, 124.
81 *AS*, 344.
82 The Mālikī school enjoyed almost exclusive juristic sway in North Africa, from Tunis to Muslim Spain, and its presence was quite partial in Cairo, Baghdad, and greater Syria. See Hallaq, *Introduction*, 2009, 37
83 Abū Yaʿlā, *al-Aḥkām al-Sulṭāniyya*, 280, 81: "*Li-yanquṣa ʿan adna al-ḥudūd*;" "*fa-lā yablughu fī ta ʿzīrihi adnā al-ḥudūd*." See also Buhūtī, *Kashshāf*, VI, 130 who adds to these stipulations the condemnation of judges and possibly rulers who do so.

on *ta ʿzīr* punishments, all dictated by the principle that these penalties must not exceed those stipulated for *ḥudūd* crimes.

Finally, Māwardī stipulates that while bodily harm in *ḥudūd* penalties is not compensable, any injury or destruction resulting from *ta ʿzīr* gives rise to damages. He cites as an authoritative basis for this position the case of a woman who suffered miscarriage when the caliph ʿUmar I somehow frightened her. Upon consulting with ʿAlī b. Abī Ṭālib, another Companion proficient in the law, he decreed what both appeared to have opined, namely, that the woman should be monetarily compensated for her loss. But the jurists of the legal schools at large, Māwardī reports, disagreed on who should make the payment, the personal coffer of the ruler or the Public Treasury.[84] On the Ḥanbalī side, and in an instance of disagreement with *AS*, Abū Yaʿlā did not allow for damages in any punitive form of *ta ʿzīr*.[85]

From the foregoing discussion, we can see that in the Ḥanbalī school prior to Ibn al-Qayyim and his Shaykh, Ibn ʿAqīl seems to be the only jurist who espoused unconstrained *ta ʿzīr* powers for the ruler. One might expect that the influential Ibn Taymiyya and his disciple would have left a dent in their school's doctrine on *ta ʿzīr*, but this does not appear to be the case. Writing three centuries after Ibn al-Qayyim, the Ḥanbalī jurist Manṣūr Ibn Idrīs al-Buhūtī (d. 1051/1642) headed his school in Egypt, now over a century under the dominion of the Ottomans. In his *Kashshāf al-Qināʿ*, he elaborates on the doctrine of *ta ʿzīr* while heavily drawing on former legal authorities that defined the authoritative law of his *madhhab*. He does list Ibn Taymiyya as one of his authorities, but Abū Yaʿlā and especially the Jerusalemite-Damascene jurist Muwaffaq al-Dīn Ibn Qudāma lead. Ibn al-Qayyim makes no show whatever.[86]

The default punishment in the spectrum of *ta ʿzīr* lashing "is no more than ten whips," Buhūtī states, apparently taking for granted the lesser penalties of verbal rebuke, admonishment, and statutory imprisonment.[87] "Default," because in matters of sexual misconduct and consumption of alcohol under circumstances that do not meet the exacting procedural requirement of the *ḥudūd*, the punishments exceed this limit but stand short of those imple-

84 *AS*, 347.

85 Abū Yaʿlā, *al-Aḥkām al-Sulṭāniyya*, 282.

86 Buhūtī, *Kashshāf*, I, 51. The work is a commentary on *al-Iqnāʿ* by Sharaf al-Dīn Mūsā b. Aḥmad b. Sālim al-Maqdisī al-Hajjāwī (d. 968/1560).

87 Buhūtī, *Kashshāf*, VI, 129. The lesser penalties are specified in his other work, *Sharḥ Muntahā al-Irādāt*, V, 1556-57.

mented for relevant *ḥudūd* offenses by one lashing – the standard authoritative doctrine in most schools, to the exception of Mālik and some Mālikīs. This is why Buhūtī says that the ten lashes requirement obtains "by general agreement except in those cases," i.e., sexual misdemeanor and consumption of intoxicants.[88] In his *Sharḥ Muntahā al-Irādāt*, he confirms the same doctrine even more explicitly.[89]

Being the maximal limit, the stipulation of ten lashes may be reduced by the imam or the *qāḍī*, or waived altogether – depending on the situation – for there is no statutory minimum.[90] In some cases of flagrant harm, capital punishment is allowed, however. If a criminal's destructive acts and corruption (*fasād*) cannot be stopped without putting him to death, after having applied to him without success all the relevant statutory *taʿzīr* penalties, then in this case the capital penalty is permitted.[91] The same penalty applies to heretical groups, according to Mālik and Ibn Ḥanbal. These are seen as constituting a threat not only to communities and the civilian population in general but also to public order and polity at large.[92] Tellingly, Buhūtī cites Ibn ʿAqīl who espoused the view that spies for the enemy should be killed. He immediately added that Abū Yaʿlā – a premier authority in his work – opined that such spies should be subjected only to *taʿzīr* penalties and harsh rebuke but not killed. Ibn ʿAqīl, he continues, upheld the opinion that "the sultan has the right to apply *siyāsa* that does not stop at what the Sharʿ dictates." With cutting and dismissive language, Buhūtī responds: "I say: nor does *siyāsa* exceed what the Sharʿ commands or prohibits!"[93]

It is clear that Ibn ʿAqīl charted a path that ran counter to the *madhhab*ic doctrine of the Ḥanbalī school. His position would probably have sunk into oblivion had it not been for Ibn Taymiyya's forceful resurrection and expansion of the meaning and scope of *siyāsa*. But we must be wary not to treat Ibn al-Qayyim's elaborations as mere commentary on his master's doctrine, for the former, in his further explications in *al-Ṭuruq al-Ḥukmiyya*, had advanced

88 Buhūtī, *Kashshāf*, VI, 129: "*Muttafaqun ʿalayhi fī ghayri hādhā al-mawḍiʿ*."
89 Buhūtī, *Sharh Muntahā al-Irādāt*, V, 1556.
90 Buhūtī, *Kashshāf*, VI, 130: "*Wa-yajūzu naqṣu al-taʿzīri ʿan ʿashari jaladātin idh laysa [li-]aqallihi miqdārun, fa-yarjiʿu ilā ijtihādi al-imāmi aw al-ḥākim*."
91 Buhūtī, *Kashshāf*, VI, 130.
92 Buhūtī, *Kashshāf*, VI, 131. See also *TII*, 223.
93 Buhūtī, *Kashshāf*, VI, 132: "*Wa-jawwaza Ibnu ʿAqīlin qatla muslimin jāsūsin lil-kuffāri.... Wa-fil-*Funūn, *lil-sulṭāni sulūku al-siyāsati, wa-huwa al-ḥazmu ʿindanā, wa-la taqifu al-siyāsatu ʿalā mā naṭaqa bi-hi al-sharʿu ... Qultu: wa-lā takhruju ʿammā amara bi-hi aw nahā ʿanhu*." For Ibn ʿAqīl's doctrine, see also *ITSS*, 148.

even more aggressively the cause of *siyāsa* and its prerogatives. The question before us then is: What did Ibn al-Qayyim try to accomplish?

A holistic examination of the work reveals that Ibn al-Qayyim had three concomitant missions in mind. The first, making for the greater bulk of the work, is a restatement of Sharīʿa's procedural law from a Ḥanbalī standpoint, particularly as it pertains to the law of crime and offenses, those spheres whose jurisdiction fell to both the *qāḍī* and the ruler and his deputies. While rules of personal status – i.e., marriage, divorce, custody, inheritance, etc. – partnerships, contracts and the like were often cited as evidence supporting his theses and arguments, they were not as such his direct concern. Rather, it was infractions within what may be termed the public order that were the focus of his gaze, infractions pertaining to sexual morality, crime, road security, and cognate spheres of social and market transactions (e.g., *ḥisba*, price fixing, etc.).[94] In nearly all these spheres, he attempted to expand, if not loosen, the normative stipulations of Sharīʿa's procedural law.

The second mission was likewise to expand the range of the judicial and executive competence on the matter of punitive measures, while the third was the unification of the various and disparate prerogatives of these two competences under one roof. In other words, he aimed to integrate *siyāsa* competence into the Sharīʿa by expanding and loosening the latter's established procedural methods and punitive tools. In constitutional parlance, his was an attempt at expanding executive power and anchoring the expansion in a legitimate Sharʿī foundation that had simultaneously been stretched to the limit. It is my argument that this represented a risky constitutional move, resembling in so many fundamental ways the controversial measures taken relatively recently by the US government.[95]

Ibn al-Qayyim deploys his treatise in the form of an answer to a question of "momentous importance," although it is difficult to tell if the questioner was a real or hypothetical person: Is it legitimate for a judge or a *wālī* (ruler, governor, or any overseer of an administrative function) to decide cases by *firāsa* or *qarā'in*, not limiting himself to the apparent meaning and signification of standard evidence (*bayyināt*, mainly consisting of witness[es]' testimony and an oath) or to confession? *Firāsa* is generally translated as physiognomy, but it has a thick meaning in the Arabic language. Briefly put, it is an intuitive

94 See Belhaj, "Law and Public Order," which rightly stresses this domain as Ibn Taymiyya's and Ibn al-Qayyim's main concern.

95 On the detrimental constitutional and legal effects of the Patriot Act of 2001, see Evans, "Hijacking Civil Liberties;" Saito, "Whose Liberty? Whose Security?"

and inferential knowledge which proceeds from an observation of apparent states to make judgments on motives and internal disposition.[96] The term *qarā'in* (sing. *qarīna*), generally speaking, connotes circumstantial evidence of sorts.[97] Thus, the question provides a prompt that launches the discourse sustaining the first mission.

The issue at stake here is whether a judge or a magistrate can move beyond the outer limits of the standard rules of procedure (*bayyina*) to engage in what many consider a subjective interpretation of evidence. Again, Ibn ʿAqīl appears here as an advocate of this distension.[98] Ibn al-Qayyim favorably quotes him to say that "if you think about the Sharʿ carefully, you will find it to have made recourse to such [ways]."[99] In other words, the rules of evidence Ibn al-Qayyim wishes to append to the Sharʿ are, *effectively*, already part of the Sharʿ. Which is to say that his proposed distension builds on what he seems to have thought to be an active potential in the Sharʿī repertoire of evidence that the jurists at large did not and do not appreciate. The Sharīʿa, he avers, is all-inclusive and any form of conduct or governance that promotes justice is an integral part of it. If it is an injurious *siyāsa*, the Sharīʿa obviously forbids it; if it is a just *siyāsa*, then it is already an integral part of the Sharīʿa. His argument, in effect, is that missing the opportunity to bring out and develop this potential in the Sharīʿa into a more complete system of procedure would result in grave injustice.[100]

The physiognomic knowledge that Ibn al-Qayyim is thinking of may best be illustrated by examples. ʿUmar I as well as other Companions ruled that a woman who was pregnant but who was neither married nor a concubine had committed fornication and was sentenced accordingly. The case in point here is that the signs of pregnancy combined with the absence of a lawful sexual partner had constituted proof of guilt. In Sharīʿa's standard procedure, the proof (*bayyina*) must consist either of a confession or of the testimony of four males who can attest to having seen the very act of penetration, their testimony being combined with a cross-examination with a view to establishing that no witness may contradict another about the details of the contextual circumstances in which the act took place.

96 See Zabīdī, *Tāj*, VIII, 395-96.
97 Hallaq, "Notes on the Term *Qarīna*," 475–80.
98 *TH*, 3.
99 *TH*, 3: "*Wa-idhā ta'ammaltumu al-sharʿa, wajadtumuhu yujawwizu al-taʿwīla ʿalā dhālika.*"
100 *TH*, 4.

Ibn al-Qayyim forcefully argued that ignoring physiognomic evidence will "waste much justice," for in this case it comes through clearly that an act of fornication has indeed taken place, yet the inability to meet the requirement of four male witnesses would have forfeited the case of justice (*ḥaqq*/ *ʿadl*). The idea here, Ibn al-Qayyim seems to say, is that circumstantial evidence (*qarāʾin*) can be cultivated in a manner that produces evidence which otherwise would not be deemed satisfactory or admissible by the law. "If we see a man not wearing a headgear when it is his habit to do so, and then we observe another man running in front of him while holding a headgear [in his hand], we judge with certainty that the headgear belongs to the [first] man, not [to the second] who has assuredly come to be in possession [of the headgear] through injustice and usurpation. [Here], the apparent circumstantial evidence (*qarīna ẓāhira*) is much stronger than a straightforward *bayyina* or confession," either of which "may or may not bear the truth."[101] *Bayyina*, then, is "any evidence through which the truth is revealed, and those who confine it to two witnesses, or four or one [the standard doctrine of proof], would do the concept no justice. By *bayyina*, the Qur'ān never meant to refer only to two witnesses but rather to reasoned proof (*ḥujja*), indication/indicant (*dalīl*), and demonstration (*burhān*), aggregately or severally."[102] Plenty of evidence in the Qur'ān and Ḥadīth attests to the evidentiary validity of contextual indications (*dalālāt al-aḥwāl*), signs/indicants (*amārāt*), and circumstantial evidence (*qarāʾin*).[103]

Again, in a bid to naturalize these evidentiary instruments within the law, Ibn al-Qayyim cites Ibn ʿAqīl who declared that "this is not *firāsa*," meaning that the entire range of these evidentiary methods cannot be reduced to physiognomy and that they are part of the Sharʿī methods of proof. Ibn al-Qayyim promptly adds: "there is nothing wrong in calling it *firāsa*, for it is in reality *firāsa*."[104] Name it what you want, he seems to say, any evidence leading to the truth – and thus to justice – should be, and indeed potentially is, encompassed by the Sharʿ.[105] As we will see in the following chapter, other distinguished jurists begged to differ.

---

101 *TH*, 6-7.

102 *TH*, 11: "*Wa-bil-jumlati fal-bayyinatu ismun li-kulli mā yubayyinu al-ḥaqqa wa-yuẓhiruhu, wa-man khaṣṣahā bil-shāhidayni aw al-arbaʿati aw al-shāhidi, lam yuwfi musammāhā ḥaqqahu wa-lam taʾti al-bayyinatu qaṭṭu fil-Qurʾāni murādan bi-hā al-shāhidān, wa-innamā atat murādan bi-hā al-ḥujjatu wal-dalīlu wal-burhānu, mufradatan majmūʿatan.*" See also 24.

103 Which *TH*, 12, lists in the form of verses and Prophetic Ḥadīth.

104 *TH*, 12.

105 *TH*, 24.

If justice is the telos, and the ways to attain it are expansive, then this expansiveness may entail loosely defined concepts that allow for much interpretive latitude and consequential evidentiary subjectivity. Ibn al-Qayyim goes as far as to argue that "clever judges and rulers" can arrive at the truth in a dispute through a variety of intuitive, physiognomic, and contextual inferences, thereby disposing of the need to abide by the fixed standards of proof in the Sharīʿa. "A judge is permitted – other than in [matters of] *ḥudūd* – to decide a case on the basis of the testimony of a single witness if he knows that the witness is truthful. God never commanded judges to rule on the basis of two witnesses; rather, he commanded the party seeking redress to produce either two witnesses or a male-witness plus two female-witnesses.[106] This [verse] does not prove that the judge cannot decide on the grounds of a lesser number. The Prophet had indeed decided [cases] on the basis of one [male] witness and an oath, and [at times] by a single witness."[107] Ibn al-Qayyim goes to great lengths to show that the standard number of witnesses [for each category of offenses] does not have to be met and that "even a single witness without an oath" can fulfill this requirement.[108]

For Ibn al-Qayyim to argue that a judge or a ruler is permitted to satisfy the burden of proof by a single witness – *provided he knows that the witness is truthful* – invites questions about the quality and source of evidentiary knowledge the *qāḍī* or ruler has acquired: Is it private or prior knowledge or is it acquired solely on the basis of the single witness's testimony? The fundamental epistemological question here is the rationale behind the dualism in the standard two male witnesses requirement – a question that is not addressed in the treatise. What is the reason for the second Sharʿ-stipulated testimony? Is it to reduce doubt presumed to inhere in the first testimony? Or does it stand as a confirmation of the first? Ibn al-Qayyim marshals multiple historical examples to show that earlier Muslim figures resorted to a lower bar of evidentiary proof, but to my knowledge he never addresses the epistemological foundations of the standard Sharʿī procedural requirements.

Be that as it may, both Ibn al-Qayyim and Ibn Taymiyya draw a straight line of connection between what they see as the desired expanded domain of procedure and an equally expanded rights of judges and particularly rulers and their deputies to inflict *taʿzīr* punishments on the grounds of "suspicion" (*tuhma*). The connection is made clear in the heavy citations made by Ibn

106 The reference is to the Qur'ān's II, 282. See *TH*, 64.

107 *TH*, 60.

108 *TH*, 68.

al-Qayyim from a *fatwā* that Ibn Taymiyya had issued. The question that opens the *fatwā* asks whether or not the beating and imprisonment by *taʿzīr* is Sharīʿa-based, who can implement such punishments, and what are the terms of imprisonment and maximal limit of beating?

Ibn Taymiyya initiates his answer with a general provision to the effect that those in charge of Muslims' affairs (*wulāt al-umūr*) are Sharīʿa judges, rulers, provincial governors, or their deputies, including the *maẓālim* officers. Whatever the customary title of any of these appointed officials may be, they are all responsible for the implementation of God's commands, with the ultimate and final goal of attaining justice (*ʿadl/qisṭ*). He then promptly delves into a discussion of *daʿāwī* – i.e., judicial claims brought to these officials – which he divides into two types. One type is *daʿāwī tuhma*, essentially penal claims, such as homicide, highway robbery, theft, etc. In these and similar cases, he importantly remarks, "it is often difficult to procure evidentiary proof."[109] The other type encompasses essentially civil claims that pertain to sales, loans, guaranty, and the like. The strictly penal types are deemed God's rights (*ḥuqūq Allāh*), while the others belong to people's rights (*ḥuqūq al-ʿibād*). Some offences, such as theft and highway robbery, belong to both, as they involve government-prosecutable public offenses as well as private wrongs (theft of property).[110]

The question that centers Ibn Taymiyya's proliferating discussions and citations is the set of evidentiary proofs required for each type of infraction. The most common and widely accepted maxim in procedural law is that "the burden of proof rests with the plaintiff while the defendant's burden is an oath."[111] The "proof" (*bayyina/ḥujja sharʿiyya*), however, variably consists of two male witnesses, one man and two women, four men, three men, one woman, etc., depending on the nature of the case. For example, three men are needed to satisfy the evidentiary requirement in cases of insolvency, while a single female witness would be sufficient for testifying in respect of medical examination of women's bodies (in cases of bodily harm and rape, among others). Ibn Taymiyya stresses that in certain situations it would be impossible to procure more than an oath, at times even a refusal to take it (*nukūl*). The range of testimonial requirements and evidentiary proof is wide, sometimes satisfied by signs and indications (*ʿalāmāt*), as in cases of parentage where a child is found to resemble a man so much that the man is judged to be his

109 *TH*, 82: "*Yataʿadhdharu iqāmatu al-bayyinati ʿalayhi fī ghālibi al-aḥwāl.*"
110 *TH*, 82.
111 *TH*, 83: "*Al-bayyinatu ʿalā man iddaʿā wal-yamīnu ʿalā man ankar.*"

father.[112] Signs would include the inference, relevant to cases of insolvency, with regard to a defendant who would be judged to be still in possession of large sums of money (in hiding) on the grounds that he could not have spent it in the short period of time he is known to have had it.[113]

Obviously, the emphasis that both Ibn al-Qayyim and Ibn Taymiyya laid on the indispensability of signs as proof has to do with the difficulty of procuring evidence in cases of highway brigandage, homicide, and theft, a difficulty they already noted. In such situations, Ibn al-Qayyim argues, the person charged would have to belong to one of three types: the accused may have a spotless record and be known, from his general circumstances, not to be the "type" of person who would engage in such unlawful activities. In this case, not only the *tuhma* against him must be dropped, but he is not to be punished and must be released at once. According to most jurists, his accuser is to be punished but Mālik and some of his school members permitted punishment if it could be shown that the plaintiff made his accusation maliciously, deliberately attempting to defame and harm the defendant.[114]

The second type is a person of neutral reputation, in the sense that he is known to be neither "good" nor "bad." In this case, if a trial cannot be held immediately, a temporary arrest is permitted, "until the judge sorts his situation out."[115] The arrest is held by some jurists to have the maximal limit of one month, whereas other jurists, such as Māwardī, held that the duration should not be predetermined, leaving it to the ruler to decide. Nor is this an imprisonment in the ordinary sense of the term. He makes it clear that it is a sort of house arrest, or a stay in the mosque. The accused may also continue to be free but the plaintiff has the right to follow him (*mulāzama*) in his comings and goings.[116]

The third type is a person who has a criminal record and is known for his "corruption." Ibn Taymiyya held that no authoritative scholar objected to imprisonment, and "whoever holds that [imprisonment is not mandated] by the Shar' ... would be committing a grave error and would be running against the Prophet's clear texts and the consensus of the *Umma*."[117] Ibn al-Qayyim adds that it is also permissible to beat him, citing a spectrum of juristic opinion

112 *TH*, 85.
113 *TH*, 87.
114 *TH*, 88.
115 *TH*, 89: "*Ḥattā yatabayyana lil-ḥākimi amruhu.*"
116 *TH*, 89-90.
117 *TH*, 91.

that ranges from harsh punishments to reprieve to release. Some jurists argued that he should only be imprisoned, while others espoused the opinion that he should also be whipped with his back disrobed. Others held that he should be imprisoned for as long as the *wālī* deems necessary but other jurists stipulated a term of life imprisonment.[118]

Taʿzīr's upper limit is subject to juristic disagreement. Some permitted the ruler or his deputies to decide according to circumstance and need. Others upheld the *taʿzīr* to have a maximum equal to the minimum of *ḥudūd* punishments, usually forty or eighty lashes. Yet others opined that it may not exceed ten lashes, which Buhūtī had told us to be an authoritative position within the Ḥanbalī school, although Ibn al-Qayyim claimed it to be "one of the opinions in Aḥmad's *madhhab* [i.e., the Ḥanbalī school]. Ibn al-Qayyim sides with another view, one that is the harshest of all statutory penalties. He says that "the best of all opinions is that *taʿzīr* should not exceed the relevant *ḥudūd* punishment." For instance in the matter of sexual infractions falling below the bar of *ḥudūd*, the penalty shall not be in excess of that stipulated by the *ḥudūd* stipulated for this category.[119] He also allowed punitive monetary penalties (i.e., in cases not involving damages), a precept banned by the majority of Muslim jurists.[120] As we saw above, recourse to capital punishment in *taʿzīr* is permitted only in cases of habitual criminal activity and "spreading corruption" on Earth, including sectarian political insurgency, with some jurists allowing this punishment of spies for the enemy.[121]

Ibn Taymiyya states that Ibn Ḥanbal and some Shāfiʿīs held the view that it is the *wālī*, to the exclusion of the *qāḍī*, who possesses the competence to inflict physical punishment on persons with a criminal record. The reasoning behind this position is grounded in the assumption that the *raison d'être* of *wālī*-ship is "to fight against corruption on Earth (*al-fasād fil-arḍ*) and to suppress evildoers and aggressors."[122] This mission cannot be accomplished without penalizing offenders and those who are notorious for their criminal record. The *qāḍī*-ship, on the other hand, has a different jurisdiction, namely, judging between people with fairness and justice and giving rights where rights are due. Ibn al-Qayyim agrees with Ibn Taymiyya that each office comes with

118 *TH*, 91-92.

119 *TH*, 94.

120 *TH*, 224-26, 232-33.

121 *TH*, 94.

122 *TH*, 92: "*Wal-ladhīna jaʿalū ʿuqūbatahu lil-wālī dūna al-qāḍī qālū: wilāyatu amīri al-ḥarbi muʿtamaduhā al-manʿu min al-fasādi fil-arḍi wa-qamʿu ahli al-sharri wal-ʿudwān.*"

and is defined by a different mandate, but all of these are nonetheless regulated by the Sharīʿa (*al-taqayyud bil-Sharīʿa*).[123]

This last qualification allows Ibn al-Qayyim to make the point that what matters in jurisdictional divisions is not a predetermined or natural segregation of offices and functions. Rather, the division of labor is purely customary and is relative to time and place. The *wālī* "in our Egyptian and Syrian domains nowadays" possesses the jurisdiction over the *ḥudūd* and physical punishment, including cases of *tuhma* where it is often the case that neither confession nor even witnesses can be procured. The judge, in these regions, oversees disputes in the law of personal status, testimony, acknowledgements and confessions, contracts, etc., and supervises *waqf*s, orphans, among others. By contrast, in the western regions of Islam – by which he means western North Africa and Andalusia – "the *wālī* does not decide on anything, but merely carries out what the *qāḍī* commands."[124] What matters, therefore, is not the formal boundary or the delimited functions of an office for its own sake, or who does what within a specific competence, but rather that whatever charge an office is assigned at a particular time or tenure or period, it is be carried out according to the Sharīʿa laws and procedures. All government offices are Sharʿī and all have the single telos of justice,[125] driven by the foundational injunction of commanding good and prohibiting evil.[126]

Yet, Ibn al-Qayyim's diachronic and synchronic relativism does not stop here. It is now banal to say that the Sharīʿa and its political imperatives reasonably changed from one place or time to another.[127] But it is quite a different matter to argue that the very law of procedure or the substantive contents of the law could be suspended at will, and for Ibn al-Qayyim, it is largely political will that is at stake. In the beginning of his work, he marshals page after page[128] of examples where the otherwise standard substantive provisions of the law are said to have been set aside in favor of an "internalist" reading of adjectival law, a reflection in his mind of the decisive power of "signs," of presumptions of correct practice or "silent contracts" (*muʿāṭāt*) according to customary law, and the like.[129]

123 *TH*, 92.
124 *TH*, 201.
125 *TH*, 201.
126 *TH*, 199.
127 Hallaq, "Was the Gate of Ijtihad Closed?"; Johansen, "Legal Literature;" Hallaq, "From *Fatwās* to *Furūʿ*;" Hallaq, *Authority*.
128 *TH*, 6-24.
129 For examples of customary practices and their effects on an "internalist" reading of

It is no coincidence that the vast majority of these "examples" hail from the Companions' period, obviously before the formation of the *madhhabs*, whose constitutional authority and legal grip over the political we have already discussed. But Ibn al-Qayyim realizes that the long list of cases or illustrative examples he presents to the reader are exceptions to the rule, representing *siyāsa* as applied to particular issues and problems, a phenomenon he calls "partial *siyāsa* in accordance with public interest."[130] This *siyāsa*, he adds, "changes with the changing of times, though some people think that it is a general law that binds the *Umma* until the Day of Judgment. However, each [advocate of either argument, i.e., changeability or fixity] has his rationale (*ʿudhr*) and recompense (*ajr*); for anyone who exercises *ijtihād* ... would be the recipient of either one reward or two."[131]

Again, we see here that Ibn al-Qayyim is harnessing to a maximum the relativism of *ijtihād* doctrine, to argue, it seems, that since the door of juristic reasoning is open, either camp would be legitimate in whatever it espouses. The doctrine, a high expression of juridico-academic freedom, might become problematic in such a context of debate as engineered by Ibn al-Qayyim. For the doctrine holds that any *mujtahid* will be granted a reward in the hereafter for at least his effort, and even if he errs, since engagement with *ijtihād* is a form of piety, a close second to such forms of worship as prayer and fasting.[132] If the *mujtahid* arrives at the truth, he would be rewarded twice, the second reward being a prize for his success. But the key element for Ibn al-Qayyim in this context is that no one knows, except God, who got it right and who got it wrong. And so with a sense of impunity, he continues to argue that "this *siyāsa*, by which the [Muslim rulers] governed the *Umma* ... is an interpretation of

---

law and its procedure, see *TH*, 20-21. On the *muʿāṭāt* contract, see *TH*, 21, and Hallaq, *Sharīʿa*, 241, 242, 250-51.

130 *TH*, 19: "*Wal-maqṣūdu anna hādhā wa-amthālahu siyāsatun juz'iyyatun bi-ḥasabi al-maṣlaḥati.*"

131 *TH*, 19. The meaning being here that if the *mujtahid* arrives at a correct conclusion, he is granted a double reward; but if he errs, then only one. The latter is bestowed in recognition of the effort (*jahd*/*ijtihād*/*badhlu al-wisʿi*) the *mujtahid* expends in working the case at hand. The rewards are of course divine, distributed in the Hereafter; which is to say that only God knows who erred and who got it right. Ibn Abī al-Damm, *Adab al-Qaḍā'*, I, 254.

132 "A close second" because, formally speaking, prayer and fasting are two of the Islamic pillars (*arkān*). Substantively, however, it is arguable that *ijtihād*, a paradigmatic form of knowledge production, is weightier than even these pillars because it fulfills a communal duty on which "public good" depends. Prayer and fasting, on the other hand, are activities or forms of devotion that do not, in and of themselves, directly benefit the *Umma* at large.

the Qur'ān and the Sunna."[133] Thus *siyāsa* becomes an agnate, if not a twin, of juristic *ijtihād*, with an output that is as legitimate as, if not more legitimate than, what is otherwise a paradigmatic *ijtihād*. The only question that remains unresolved, and Ibn al-Qayyim leaves it entirely unanswered, is this: Is *siyāsa* a universal law that does not change with the changes of time or is it a provisional *siyāsa* that is contingent on public interest, predicated on it in time and place?[134]

The crux of the dilemma that Ibn al-Qayyim is tackling is that strict adherence to what he seems to consider the formalism of the law has led to a distortion of the Sharīʿa, or at least, what it is capable of. "He who does not apply the [doctrine of] signs (*ʿalāmāt*) in the law would in effect render null and void countless rules/judgments (*aḥkām*) and would squander many of the [people's] rights (*ḥuqūq*)." Ibn Taymiyya is quoted quite approvingly as saying that "in these times of ours," the Sharīʿa has been misapplied and "many rulers have committed wrongs out of sheer ignorance, causing much harm to people."[135] In a significant passage, Ibn Taymiyya asserted that the term "Sharīʿa" has in his age come to carry three meanings. The first is the revealed Sharʿ (*al-Sharʿ al-munazzal*), as represented in the Book and the Sunna. Abiding by the dictates of this Sharʿ is not only mandatory but anyone who turns away from, or spurns, it (*kharaja ʿan*) must be fought. In this concept of Sharīʿa are included "the legal doctrine and its (theological-metaphysical) founding principles (*uṣūl al-dīn wa-furūʿihi*); the *siyāsa* of rulers, their fiscal agents, the rulings of judges, the teachings of the law professors, the *ḥisba* officials, etc. All these ought to govern according to the revealed Sharʿ and must not deviate from it."[136]

The second meaning is the interpretable Sharʿ, a domain in which *ijtihād* is exercised and the major jurists disagree. Here, no one is obliged to accept the product of any individual jurist's *ijtihād* unless it is supported by a compelling, clear proof lodged in the Qur'ān or the Sunna.

Third is the corrupted Sharʿ (*mubaddal*), where several malpractices prevail, ranging from the admission of false testimony and concocted acknowledgements (*iqrārs*),[137] to the intentional misuse and manipulation of the procedural rules in the law of inheritance, and the like. If the judge "knows within his

133 *TH*, 19: "*Wa-hādhihi al-siyāsatu allatī sāsū bi-hā al-umma, wa-aḍʿāfuhā hiya ta'wīlu al-Qur'ani wal-Sunna.*"

134 *TH*, 19: "*Wa-lākin hal hiya min al-sharā'iʿi al-kulliyyati al-latī lā tataghayyaru bi-taghayyuri al-azminati am min al-siyāsāti al-juzʾiyyati al-tabiʿati lil-maṣāliḥ fa-tataqayyadu bi-hā zamānan wa-makānan.*"

135 *TH*, 87.

136 *TH*, 88.

137 On *iqrārs*, see *Al-Mawsūʿa al-Fiqhiyya*, XI, 46-79.

conscience that the truth of the matter (*bāṭin al-amr*) does not correspond to what is true and right (*ḥaqq*), then he would be committing a grave injustice."[138]

It is precisely the idea of correspondence (*muṭābaqa/muṭābiq*)[139] between the realia of practice and the requirements of the Sharīʿa that stands at the center of Ibn al-Qayyim's gaze, and no less of his Shaykh's. The universal precept that Sharīʿa guides life and human conduct from beginning to end, in all the realities of existence and layers of action, had a universal power, but none more than for these two Ḥanbalīs. They saw the general misapplication of the Sharīʿa not only as a violation but also a generalized attack on the very concept of order and its desideratum, namely, public and communal welfare. These pervasive infractions against the law of the land were perceived by them as cause to create a certain dualism in the system of governance, one which gave rulers leeway to depart from the Sharīʿa (*mukhālafat al-Sharʿ*) and to "imagine it to have no capacity to sustain *siyāsa* generally, standing incapable of attending to the interests of the *Umma*." They have violated the stipulations of God's law and "caused, with their ignorance ... much oppression, injustice, and bad *siyāsa*." Some, Ibn al-Qayyim complained, regarded this "*siyāsa* as an integral part of the Sharʿ, while others viewed it as Sharīʿa's partner and [standing as] a parallel [to it]."[140]

V

The deep concern with procedural law, which occupies the bulk of *TH*, stemmed from Ibn al-Qayyim's and Ibn Taymiyya's correct understanding that procedure is the thread by which law and its proper implementation hang. Their attempt to expand the limits of the rules of evidence was thus an attempt to rein in, under an expansive definition of the Sharīʿa, all administrative and *siyāsa* affairs. But this was also an act of streamlining and consolidation, whereby the chaotic Mamlūk management within the hardly demarcated field of *siyāsa* could be given some order and, furthermore, corralled within

138 *TH*, 88.

139 *TH*, 87, 91.

140 *TH*, 91: "*Tajarraʾa al-wulātu ʿalā mukhālafati al-sharʿi wa-tawwahamū anna al-sharʿa lā yaqūmu bi-siyāsati al-ʿālami wa-maṣlaḥati al-ummati. Wa-taʿaddū ḥudūda Allāhi wa-tawallada min jahli al-farīqayni bi-ḥaqīqati al-sharʿi khurūjan ʿanhu ilā anwāʿin min al-ẓulmi wal-bidaʿi wal-siyāsati, jaʿalahā hāʾulāʾu min al-Sharʿi, wa-jaʿalahā hāʾulāʾu qasīmatan wa-muqābilatan la-hu, wa-zaʿamū anna al-sharʿa nāqiṣun lā yaqūmu bi-maṣāliḥi al-nāsi.*"

a controlled Sharʿī parameter. Ibn al-Qayyim's and Ibn Taymiyya's discourses will make good sense if we consider the general conditions that structured their interests, concerns, and anxieties.

The perils of social and political chaos under the Mamlūks, combined with the recent memory of the existential threats posed by the repeated waves of Mongol invasions from the East and the Crusaders from the West, the menacing Black Death (striking hard in 749/1347), drought, famine, and depopulation[141] – all contributed to a sense of doom that unmistakably colored the annals of Mamlūk history, especially during Ibn al-Qayyim's life. This existential threat, the result of multiple concurrent factors, called for drastic measures that involved loosening the standard procedural law of the Sharīʿa, a law that did not presume to interpret the hidden motives and inner thoughts of the law's subject, nor did it risk the arrogation to the *qāḍī* of subjective interpretation and judgment of motives. The logic of the Sharīʿa was to stand on the side of caution even if the price was to let an offender go.[142] But in times of crisis, when collapse of the system appears imminent, this caution becomes a luxury. Ibn Taymiyya and his dogged disciple wished to contain the damage and reverse the trend. Yet, the price for this reversal, that is, for injecting adjectival law with a thick layer of subjective interpretation, meant that executive power as well as the *qāḍī* himself would possess tools of coercion that border on the oppressive and the tyrannical. This is not to argue, however, that Ibn al-Qayyim, even with his elevation of *siyāsa* to the rank of paradigmatic juristic *ijtihād*, reached the limits of the Schmittian conception of deciding on the exception, but he certainly came close. There is no doubt that our two prominent jurists were bursting with good intentions, but we also know that the road to the perditions of tyranny is thickly paved with them.

141 See ch. 10, below, especially n. 118.

142 *TH*, 91, where Ibn Taymiyya implies that this practice is unacceptable, if not altogether unlawful.

Chapter 9

A Constitutional Synthesis: Mālikī Delimitation of Executive Power and the Triumph of the Judiciary

I

If Ibn Taymiyya, and more so Ibn Qayyim al-Jawziyya, stretched the limits of executive and judicial power to extremes, the Mālikī jurist Ibn Farḥūn (d. 799/1397) responded to virtually the same political and social circumstances while striking a balance, or a synthesis, between the standard political doctrine of the Sharīʿa and the forceful Ḥanbalī reaction to it. We should not therefore lump Ibn Farḥūn's doctrine under the same category to which Ibn al-Qayyim belonged, as some modern writers have done.[1]

Ibn Farḥūn is depicted by our sources as a monumental figure in the Mālikī school, and his book *Tabṣirat al-Ḥukkām* (*TAB*)[2] – our focus here – as "unprecedented."[3] As we will see, though the Mālikī *Tabṣira* builds on the Ḥanbalī tradition to expand and systematize the *siyāsa sharʿiyya* doctrine, it became in turn the basis for the later Mamlūk-Ḥanafī and Ottoman-Ḥanafī traditions in elaborating their own doctrines in this domain.

Significantly, Ibn Farḥūn is not the typical Mālikī jurist of western North Africa and Andalusia, but rather one whose life was wholly spent in the Mamlūk domains. He was born in Medina but seems to have lived for years in Egypt, visiting Palestine and Syria, the trio being the enduring holdings of the Mamlūk polity. As we will see, his intimate knowledge of the judicial and political practices of his day in the four important Mamlūk cities (Medina, Cairo, Jerusalem, and Damascus) bestowed on his work and expertise an aura of authority.

1 See Johansen, "Signs as Evidence," 168-193.

2 Henceforth quoted as *TAB*. The reference is always to vol. 2, unless otherwise stated.

3 Tinbaktī, *Nayl al-Dībāj*, 33-35, at 34. See also the editor's Introduction to Ibn Farḥūn's biographical work *al-Dībāj al-Mudhahhab*, 9-10.

Ibn Farḥūn's work is not only erudite and juristically sophisticated but also highly systematic, especially if compared with Ibn al-Qayyim's *TH*. The seventieth chapter of *TAB* deals with contextual circumstantial evidence (*qarā'in al-aḥwāl*), indicants (*amārāt*), and physiognomic knowledge (*firāsa*) as methods of proof.[4] Our author first enlists the authority of the Qur'ān in favor of the use of indicants and signs (*ʿalāmāt*), moving thereafter to excavate evidence from the Sunna and what he effectively describes as the general practice (*ʿamal*) of the four schools.[5]

The main Qur'ānic evidence consists of the story of Joseph which teaches, he argues, how God made a sign offset another in order to produce evidentiary proof. Joseph's brothers returned to their father, Jacob, claiming that a wolf devoured their little brother, and as (falsified) evidence they produced Joseph's bloodied shirt. Jacob nonetheless concluded that their story was concocted, for he immediately realized that the shirt was not torn. Jacob rhetorically asked, "since when is the wolf so smart as to devour Joseph while leaving his shirt entirely intact?"[6] The legal issue here is that no witness was available to attest to the fact that Joseph was thrown alive in the well, and that he was also taken alive to Egypt by the passing caravan. The Sharīʿa's standard procedure, as I have explained before, is that the *bayyina* (the witness's testimony) is the only acceptable means of proof. Yet, in this case, and by the authority of nothing less than the Qur'ān, a contextual sign was sufficient to disprove the brothers' lie. Circumstantial evidence (*qarā'in*) may therefore substitute for witnesses.[7]

In the same vein, the Sunna is replete with examples in support of this doctrine. Ibn al-Qayyim had already presented much of the Sunnaic evidence that Ibn Farḥūn deploys. Pregnancy, we have seen, is sufficient to convict a woman who has no lawful partner. Another example is when "we see a man who has been killed and whose blood is still seeping, and we know that there is no one in the house but another man whom we have witnessed to leave the house in a suspicious manner (*ḥāla munkara*), we then know that he is the killer."[8] Again, the case in point here is that there are no witnesses to attest to the very act of stabbing, but because the house is otherwise empty of people other than the

4 For these terms, see the previous chapter.
5 *TAB*, 101.
6 *TAB*, 101.
7 *TAB*, 102: "*Wa-ʿindī ... anna al-qarā'ina taqūmu maqāma al-shāhid.*" This sentence is a paraphrase of Māzirī's statement which Ibn Farḥūn quotes approvingly.
8 *TAB*, 107.

suspect who left the house in a clearly suspicious manner, and because the murder is fresh (blood continues to seep), it could not be the case that someone else had committed the murder. ʿUmar I and other Companions routinely resorted to signs as methods of evidentiary proof, a fact frequently recalled by our two jurists.

A general survey of the list of cases involving signs and contextual evidence reveals that a vast majority of them have a logical structure of entailment. Given a particular set of facts, other facts *necessarily* follow. To this extent, neither guesswork nor suspicion (*tuhma*) play a role. Thus, it would not be surprising that many jurists, though not all, subscribed to this adjectival doctrine. But *firāsa* ("physiognomic reading") is another matter altogether, one that Ibn al-Qayyim notoriously embraced while Ibn Farḥūn categorically rejected.

No doubt, *firāsa* is a highly regarded attribute. It is the result of an "excellent intellectual disposition" (*jawdat al-qarīḥa*), acute insightfulness (*ḥiddat al-naẓar*), and clarity of thinking (*ṣafāʾ al-fikr*).[9] Believers who enjoy this faculty, the Qurʾān declares, will see the signs of the divine everywhere.[10] It was even employed in some adjudicative cases as an exclusive evidentiary tool, by no lesser than ʿUmar I, ʿAlī, and other Companions.[11] Yet, Ibn Farḥūn insists, these cases are the exceptions rather than the rule, and they arose out of dire necessity.[12] He seems to suggest that it may be inevitable for judges endowed with the faculty of *firāsa* to think about a case they are adjudicating with the aid of this insight, but this can in no way be more than a supplementary and supporting means, for "no judicial decision can be rendered on the basis of it."[13] It is of tremendous significance that Ibn Farḥūn concludes his discussion with the explicit statement that rendering decisions on the basis of *firāsa* is a work of conjecture (*ẓann*), guesswork (*ḥazr*), and speculation (*takhmīn*). Recourse to it is a slippery slope, inevitably leading the *qāḍī* to injustice (*jawr*) and corruption (*fasād*).[14]

If *firāsa* is rejected while *ʿalāmāt* and *qarāʾin* are countenanced as logical methods of interpreting evidence, then what is the evidentiary purview of *siyāsa sharʿiyya*? Or, put differently, what are the maximal limits of its juridically adjectival boundaries? Ibn Farḥūn discusses *siyāsa sharʿiyya* in Part Three of the

9 *TAB*, 114.

10 *TAB*, 114.

11 *TAB*, 115.

12 *TAB*, 115: "*Wa-innamā ujīzat ... fī maḥallin makhṣūṣin lil-ḍarūra.*"

13 *TAB*, 115: "*Al-firāsatu lā yataratabu ʿalayhā ḥukm,*" favorably quoted from Abū Bakr Ibn al-ʿArabī (d. 543/1148).

14 *TAB*, 114.

book, opening with the statement that there are two approaches to, or types of, *siyāsa*: either unjust and injurious or just. The latter "extracts rights from the oppressors," "rebuffs acts of injury," "deters people given to corruption," and, in sum, "leads to the achievement of the Purposes of the Law" (*al-maqāṣid al-shar'iyya*). Yet, despite the central importance and absolute necessity of this tool of governance, *siyāsa* is a complex and confusing subject, Ibn Farḥūn promptly adds. Many jurists have gone astray, and so it is crucial to understand what this tool requires and what it rejects. He lists three approaches among jurists: First, a faulty understanding that *siyāsa* is effectively an intrusion upon the Sharī'a, with the result that its purview has been unduly restricted, thus leading to "blocking many rights." This is not to mention, moreover, that this approach contradicts the practices of the Companions and "belies" them to boot. Second are those jurists who bestowed excessive power on this domain, allowing for the perpetration of much injustice and oppression. Third, the middle-roaders, who "brought together *siyāsa* and Shar', succeeding in averting wrong-doing and rendering the Shar' victorious."[15]

In order to situate *siyāsa shar'iyya* in its proper context, Ibn Farḥūn argues on a grand scale that the Sharī'a as a whole was decreed to achieve five main goals, all of which are necessary for the good life. The first, central to the Islamic conception of the ethical individual/subject, are those practices that "curb the self" (*kasr al-nafs*) a reference to religious works (*'ibādāt*) as technologies of the self. Second, to promote the human good and the protections necessary to secure food, shelter, marriage, etc. Third, to regulate human relations, such as sales, contracts, agricultural leases, and the like. Fourth, to promote and cultivate kind human interactions and performance of good deeds, such as philanthropy, gifting, freeing slaves, consolation (*muwāsāt*) of acquaintances, and the like. Fifth, and finally, is the goal of political management (*siyāsa*) and deterrence (*zajr*), broad terms that encompass six derivative goals.

The first of these goals is the preservation of life by installing punishments for homicide and bodily injury. The main concern here is life itself, the highest value of existence. The relevant value structuring the six goals is not punishment as such but rather the protection of life, family, cohesive communal existence and, as a second order, wealth and the like. This is why the safeguarding of property comes fourth in rank, reflecting the general order of what is otherwise known as the Five Universals of the Law.

15 *TAB*, 115-16.

The second goal is the punishment of adultery and fornication, not only because they are morally repugnant, but also, and perhaps mainly, because the telos of the Shar' is "the preservation of lineage" (*ḥifẓ al-ansāb*).[16] The third goal comes to complement this, by insisting on the protection of honor, dignity, good reputation, and social standing. "Protecting honor is one of the greatest desiderata."[17] The fourth, as already mentioned, is the ordaining of penal laws that aim to protect property, such as the laws of theft and brigandage. The fifth is the "preservation of the mind" (*ḥifẓ al-'aql*), this being the rationale to legislate laws against such infractions as consuming intoxicants.

The sixth goal, however, has to do with confession and deterrence (*rad'*) in general, as well as with punishment of offences not stipulated by the Qur'ān. One of the main rationales for *siyāsa* is the fact that in the real world of crime and criminal law, the Sharī'a laws of procedure are insufficient to achieve a state of law and order. Essentially, the Sharī'a in its mainstream tradition does not allow for punishment until a conviction is entered. This is why torture, or any means of coercion intended to extract confession, are strictly prohibited within its purview. But not so in *siyāsa*. For instance, torturing someone thought to be a spy for the enemy would be a lawful act under *siyāsa*.[18] If such cases were to be left to be treated by the Sharī'a's law of procedure, many such criminals would walk. The Companions have also resorted to a variety of methods that they felt compelled to use due to necessity, these now becoming authorities for justifying exceptions. Caliph 'Umar I, for instance, burned down a wine bar. Caliph Uthman ordered the burning of the variants of the Qur'ān except for one, all in the interest of the Community. Various cases involving threats of punishment and beating – often before a judgement is rendered – were adduced as precedents for legitimate *siyāsa* conduct.[19] At times, *siyāsa* was the site of decision on irregular phenomena, having not been regulated by the law. Caliph Alī was asked about the inheritance of an infant born with two heads – does it inherit once or twice?[20] His answer – that both inherit if they are compos mentis – illustrates not a juristic skill as much as the necessity to deal with emergent cases with deftness and practical agility.

16 *TAB*, 116.

17 *TAB*, 116: "*Li'anna ṣiyānatahā min akbari al-aghrāḍi.*"

18 *TAB*, 119.

19 *TAB*, 119-21.

20 *TAB*, 121; see also *TH*, 48.

Yet, as investigative methods and procedural techniques, *siyāsa* is not precisely a substantive Sharʿī form, which is to say that it does not possess the consistency of law proper. It is a complement to the law, an addendum that strives to deal with the messiness of realia while maintaining, to the utmost extent possible, a legally grounded political order. This is why the Sharīʿa carved out for this field of operation a relatively discretionary space under the name of *siyāsa sharʿiyya*, to distinguish it from injurious and oppressive forms that go – and have gone – under the general name "*siyāsa*."

While rejecting *firāsa* and the tenor of subjectivity that is concomitant with it, Ibn Farḥūn does capitalize on both Mālikī and Ḥanbalī authorities to carve out for *siyāsa* an expanded space. Which is to say that his work represents a modification and expansion of the standard but dominant Shafiʿī (and possibly Ḥanafī) doctrine, on the one hand, and a moderation, even scaling down, of the Qaymiyyan drastic distension of it, on the other. This synthesis appears most clearly in a chapter that has the form of a *fatwā*. It opens with a series of interrelated questions. Given that rulers, governors, and other government officials possess jurisdiction over *siyāsa sharʿiyya*, the question that Ibn Farḥūn asks now is whether or not Sharīʿa judges (*ḥukkām*, *quḍāt*) can hear and adjudicate cases of *siyāsa*. "Are they competent to decide cases on the grounds of *siyāsa* that have to do with the indictment of thieves, evildoers, and transgressors? Can they investigate criminals? Can they adjudicate [cases] on the grounds of *qarā'in* that lead to truth, not stopping at mere confessions and witnesses, the longstanding Sharʿī procedural requirements? Can they threaten, beat, or interrogate a litigant if he appears to them to be an evildoer?"[21]

Having listed these questions, Ibn Farḥūn's answers begin by approvingly citing Ibn al-Qayyim's writings on the subject. It is interesting to note that when Ibn Farḥūn rejects *firāsa*, he, being anything but confrontational, does not cite any authorities who espoused its validity; he merely asserts *firāsa*'s untenability in deciding judicial cases. Which is to say that there is a clear tenor in the manner he writes in expounding his ideas, in that he names Ibn

21 *TAB*, 121: "*Fa-hall lil-quḍāti an yatʿāṭaw al-ḥukma bi-hā fīmā yurfaʿu ilayhim min ittihāmi al-luṣūṣi wa-ahli al-sharri wal-taʿaddī? Wa-hall la-hum al-kashfu ʿan aṣḥābi al jarā'imi? Wa-hall la-hum an yuhaddidū al-khaṣma idhā ẓahara annahu mubṭil? Aw ḍarbuhu aw su'āluhu ʿan ashyā'in tadullu ʿalā ṣūrat al-ḥāl*?" I have omitted from the translation the last words, "*tadullu ʿalā ṣūrat al-ḥāl*" because the English rendering of "witnesses" includes the meaning of attesting to the events or happenings in a case or situation. The Arabic qualification was intended to distinguish this type of witness from witnesses of character (*shuhūd ʿadl*).

al-Qayyim and extensively cites his positions only when he is in agreement with him but remains silent on naming him when he rejects certain of his doctrines.[22]

Be that as it may, Ibn al-Qayyim is cited in full thrust here to address these questions. Government appointments, whether having wide jurisdictions or specialized mandates, have no fixed boundaries, for the Sharīʿa has never made it its business to define any specific or formal boundaries for particular offices or functions. For example, judgeship may include certain functions in certain periods or epochs but may not encompass them in others.[23] The boundaries are rather determined by customary usage (*ʿurf*) or by the exigencies of particular situations (*aḥwāl*). A *qāḍī* may thus hold certain military functions at one time or place but may be entirely absolved of military duties at another. The same goes for military commanders who may or may not, during certain periods or regions, command the function of *qaḍāʾ*. The matter of jurisdictional purview has never been settled by the Sharʿ in the case of *qaḍāʾ* and *maẓālim*. This is not to say that the two functions are interchangeable or mixable, however, for they differ from each other in several respects.[24] What is being asserted here is merely that some of the *qāḍī*'s functions may be exercised by the *maẓālim* officer, and vice versa. But even when this "interjurisdictional" oversight occurs, no jurist has ever held the position that any office or function can be administered by the rules of another. Whoever presides over a Sharīʿa court, for instance, must apply the *fiqh*, irrespective of whether he is an ordinary *qāḍī*, an emir, or a sultan.

Yet, Ibn Farḥūn's specific concern is not as much with the *maẓālim* officer as it is *with the qāḍī's functions and the quest to expand them into the maẓālim field of operations*. He runs against Māwardī here, saying that this latter held the view – which by implication and quite tactfully he rejects – that the *qāḍī* has no competence to adjudicate *siyāsa* cases. He immediately retorts, again quite prudently and indirectly: "I will mention here what Qarāfī has argued [in regard to these matters], and I will follow this by briefly listing the doctrines of the [Mālikī] *madhhab*." The effect of all these citations is a totalistic

22 Ibn Farḥūn's indirect and non-confrontational approach may also account for the fact that he goes after Māwardī's restrictive views of the *siyāsa*-powers of the *qāḍī*, rather than those of his schoolmate Abū Yaʿlā al-Farrāʾ, whose doctrine is nearly identical to that of the Shāfiʿī Māwardī. For the near identity of the two texts, cf. *AS*, 322-24 and Abū Yaʿlā, *al-Aḥkām al-Sulṭāniyya*, 258-60.

23 *TAB*, 131. See, for instance, the mutations in the office's early history, in Hallaq, *Origins*, 57-68.

24 On the relationship between *maẓālim* and *qaḍāʾ*, including common grounds, similarities, and differences, see ch. 3, sec. V.

rejection of Māwardī's view. The *qāḍī*, it thus turns out, is as much entitled to adjudicate cases in accordance with *siyāsa* as the *maẓālim* officer or any other governmental deputy.[25]

Ibn Farḥūn promptly gives a faithful rendition of Māwardī's list of differences between the functions and prerogatives of the *qāḍī*'s office, on the one hand, and those of the *maẓālim*, on the other – a list we already discussed in chapter 3. However, unlike Māwardī's Shāfiʿīsm, the doctrine of the Mālikī *madhhab*, he asserts, "requires the *qāḍī* to fulfill most of these functions."[26] This was already noted even by the Ḥanbalī Ibn al-Qayyim, who unequivocally stated that in the Mālikī domains of North Africa and Andalusia the ruler "does not decide on anything, but merely carries out what the *qāḍī* commands."[27] Ibn Farḥūn asserted the *madhhab*'s doctrine, saying that the early preeminent Mālikī authority Saḥnūn (d. 240/855), for instance, held the view that "the *qāḍī* must be capable of severity, enough to be able to extract the truth."[28] Ibn Baṭṭāl (d. 449/1083), who transmitted Saḥnūn's doctrine, opined that the latter's position authoritatively endorses the *qāḍī*'s use of force (*quwwa*) and fear (*hayba*). Furthermore, the *qāḍī*, like the *maẓālim/siyāsa* officer, may adjudicate cases on the basis of *qarā'in* evidence and, by implication, *ʿalāmāt*.

It is quite instructive that Ibn Farḥūn's authority for this position is Mālik b. Anas, the eponym of his school, although Ibn Farḥūn's knowledge of it seems to come from the Ḥanbalī Ibn al-Qayyim, rather than from a Mālikī source. Mālik himself, Ibn Farḥūn observes while citing Ibn al-Qayyim, espoused the doctrine that the *qāḍī* may use any method of investigation that allows him to get to the truth. But this abstraction seems to be immediately restricted and delimited by what seems to be Ibn Farḥūn's own citation of the Qur'ānic verse 12:25, regarding the fact that because Joseph's shirt was torn from behind, Pharoah's wife was found to be the one who in fact assaulted him rather than the other way around.[29] This, being similar to

25 *TAB*, 121: "*Wa-ammā nuṣūṣu ahli al-madhhabi al-Andalusiyyīn fa-ṣarīha bi-'anna la-hum taʿāṭī dhālika ʿalā mā sa-nadhkuruhu.*"
26 *TAB*, 122: "*Wa-nuṣūṣu al-madhhabi taqtaḍī anna lil-qāḍī taʿāṭī akthara hādhihi al-umūri.*"
27 *TII*, 201. See previous chapter.
28 *TAB*, 122: "*Yanbaghī lil-qāḍī an yashtadda ḥattā yastanṭiqa al-ḥaqqa.*"
29 The background to this Qur'ānic story is that Pharoah's wife was infatuated by Joseph and, in a moment of seclusion, had attempted to have sexual intercourse with him. But virtuous Jospeh rushed to exit the room to avoid falling in sin, when Her Royal Highness gripped his shirt from behind and caused it to tear. This tear in the back of the shirt, rather than the front, was precisely the evidence in favor of Joseph's innocence.

Joseph's bloodied shirt when he was a child, pertains to the detective work of gathering evidence, this being logical thinking and minimally subjective, if at all. It does not give the *qāḍī* absolute powers to use any means whatever. In other words, it is a relative language that is pitted specifically against the otherwise commanding presence of the mainstream but unduly cautious doctrine of *bayyina=shahāda/iqrār*.

Ibn Farḥūn seems to be arguing that if the *qāḍī* sees fit to resort to *qarā'in*, *ʿalāmāt*, or *amārāt*, then he may do so.[30] In sum, therefore, there is nothing new in Ibn Farḥūn's doctrine other than the expansion of evidentiary tools to include *qarā'in* and *ʿalāmāt* (joining thus Ibn al-Qayyim in this specific matter, but effectively objecting vehemently to the inclusion of *firāsa*), and, significantly, giving the *qāḍī* jurisdictional power over *siyāsa*, almost equal to the powers the ruler and his deputized executives possess in this sphere.

This last is perhaps the most distinct novelty in the system of governance, one that the Mamlūk socio-legal system seems to have engineered and which Ibn Taymiyya, Ibn al-Qayyim, and Ibn Farḥūn henceforth integrated into, indeed naturalized within, their respective madhhabs. Yet, as we have seen in the case of Buhūtī, it is one thing to naturalize a doctrine within the *madhhab* and quite another to say that the doctrine is *the madhahb*ic doctrine. The latter is always superior, with the distinct power to win the day.

In what respects then does the *qāḍī* share such powers with the sultanic executives? Ibn Farḥūn is effectively militating against al-Qarāfī who has heavily relied on Māwardī's restricted vision of the *qāḍī*'s competence. Al-Qarāfī has extensively cited Māwardī in his *Dhakhīra*,[31] and it is against this background of citations that Ibn Farḥūn is responding both to his more cautious colleagues, like al-Qarāfī, and to the influential Shāfiʿīs as well. The latter, we must remember, not only possessed the largest and most influential legal school at the time, but they also had on their side the weight and prestige of Māwardī himself.

In the preceding chapters, we had occasion to discuss Māwardī's list of the powers and prerogatives that the *wālī al-jarā'im* (Officer of Criminal Matters) commanded, and that the *qāḍī* did not.[32] Ibn Farḥūn quotes Qarāfī's "summary quotation" from Māwardī and promptly follows it with the statement: "You ought to know that the *qāḍī*s have much wider jurisdiction over matters [than

30 *TAB*, 122.

31 Qarāfī, *Dhakhīra*, X: 38-42. See also corresponding texts of *AS*, 322-24 and Abū Yaʿlā, *al-Aḥkām al-Sulṭāniyya*, 258-60.

32 See previous chapter, especially main text at n. 77.

Māwardī and Qarāfī indicate].”[33] First, a *qāḍī* may resort to circumstantial evidence and evidence of signs as much as the ruler does, a point that Ibn Farḥūn had already covered in detail. For instance, in a case of suspected adultery or fornication, the accused will be subjected by the *qāḍī* to more intense investigation if the former is known through *qarā'in* and *'alāmāt* to have a history of pursuing women and seducing them. Otherwise, the Shar'ī rules of evidence as well as of punishment continue to obtain. If a man claims that he saw another “between the thighs of a woman,”[34] and if this witness has been unquestionably known to be of good character and without any criminal record (*'adlan lam yu'āqab*), while the accused was known to have a history of seducing women, then “he must be punished.” However, the punishment must not reach the maximal limit of *ta'zīr*, much less of *ḥudūd*;[35] rather, he may inflict a lighter penalty that aims to deter him and reform his character (*min bāb al-adab wal-zajr*).[36] Should the accused be a repeat offender despite suffering earlier punishments, then the *qāḍī* has the right to keep him in prison indefinitely (*istidāmat ḥabsihi*).[37]

Note here that notwithstanding the *qāḍī*'s and ruler's competence to inflict what may be called here investigative punishment, and despite the seeming distension in the *qāḍī*'s powers (*tawsi'a*),[38] the Shar'ī rules continue to prevail. To find a man “between the thighs of a woman” does not necessarily lead to a charge of fornication or adultery, because the four male witnesses requirement has not been satisfied. There might be every reason to think that full sexual intercourse has taken place, but the *bayyina* paradigm of four witnesses attesting to the smallest details of the very act of penetration dominates.

Second, we recall that in Māwardī's doctrine the emir, but not the *qāḍī*, can rely on the findings of his deputies as to the reputation of the accused. If they attest to the fact that he has a criminal record or a history of wrongdoing, the inquiry would be intensified, and he would be subjected to further investigation. Ibn Farḥūn begs to differ: he argues that the *qāḍī* does customarily retain an assistant, a *kāshif*, who secretly investigates the case with

33 *TAB*, 124: “*Wa-i'lam anna lil-quḍāti ta'āṭī kathīran min hādhihi al-umūr.*”

34 The meaning here is that while the couple may be engaged in an intimate activity, there is no allegation of full sexual intercourse. For an accusation of *zinā* to hold, there must be, among other things, a claim that is supported by four male witnesses.

35 For a detailed discussion of *ta'zīr* punishments, see *TAB*, 217-41.

36 *TAB*, 125.

37 *TAB*, 125.

38 For this term, see, e.g., *TAB*, 126, l. 17; 127, ll. 18-24.

a view to affirming or refuting the testimony of witnesses or the claims or reputation of the parties to the litigation. Whatever the *kāshif* reports to the *qāḍī* is generally accepted as truthful. The *qāḍī* is also entitled to secretly approach various other people, including prominent personalities and "men of rectitude" to inquire about the cases tried in his court as well as about the individuals involved in them. Even a single *kāshif* is sufficient to impeach the character of a witness or a party to a dispute, this running against the general rule of two witnesses.[39]

Third, like the emir, the *qāḍī* has the power to imprison or beat a person, without proof of guilt, for purposes of investigation and inquiry. Most jurists, it so appears, permitted a maximum of one month for this type of detention, while others did not impose a maximal time-limit. Ibn Farḥūn states that the Mālikī *madhhab* allows both types of punishment only if *tuhma* (suspicion) is strong and persistent, as long as the *ḥudūd* limits are not surpassed within each category of crime (e.g., theft, *zinā*, intoxication). This seems to have been a hard rule, which Ibn Farḥūn narrates on the authority of Mālik himself. When Mālik was asked whether sizzling oil or flesh-eating/foul-smelling insects (*khanāfis*) can be used in investigative torture, he firmly replied in the negative, saying "either the whip or the prison." When he was further pressed about the possibility of the accused dying under the whip, he said "what must be done must be done [i.e., law is the law], either the whip on the back or the jail."[40]

The exceptions that Ibn Farḥūn is making for increased powers of judicial investigation in criminal matters – and only in criminal matters – must thus not imply a universal relaxation of procedural law, not even in the case of the ruler, who is always assumed to possess more expansive powers than the *qāḍī* does. He reports that Mālik was once asked: Is it repugnant (*ayukrahu*) for the sultan, once he suspects a person of wrongdoing, to say: "I vouch for your safety if you tell me the truth [of what happened]?" Mālik said: "Yes, I find this repugnant (*akrahu dhālika*) for it is deceptive and much like cunning."[41] Ibn Rushd the Grandfather explained that this (confession) constitutes inadmissible evidence because it is akin to coercion in obtaining testimonial proof,

39 *TAB*, 124-25.

40 *TAB*, 125.

41 *TAB*, 122: "*Fa-qāla: Ay wa-Allāhi innī la-akrahu dhālika, an yaqūla la-hum wa-yaghurrahum wa-huwa min wajhi al-khadīʿa.*"

for the accused may be telling a lie in order to avoid punishment. However, if the judge or governor have good reason to suspect that the accused is a habitual wrongdoer or that he has likely committed a wrong, then he may resort to *ta'dīb*,[42] a form of relatively mild punishment intended to "correct" the malefactor's behavior – all this being a derivative of the familiar *ta'zīr*.[43]

Yet, when all things stand equal, and when, in the absence of *bayyina*, there is no clear sign to show that one side had a criminal record or a penchant for wrongdoing, then the *qāḍī* or ruler had to exercise caution and be duly patient (*ta'annī*). He must thoroughly interrogate the parties to the dispute, with due forbearance, in order to get to the bottom of things. This, Ibn Farḥūn says, is the doctrine of the *madhhab*.[44]

There are thus three possible scenarios in dealing with *tuhma*, to the elucidation of which Ibn Farḥūn dedicates an entire chapter.[45] A chief presumption in all the scenarios is social standing in the community, whose judgement and (e)valuation of the individual are most crucial. The community is obviously not a mere aggregation of individuals but rather a habitus-producing agency. The community is also an epistemic site, where judgment of moral value is not just an expression of individual opinion. The communal evaluation of the individual's moral worth rests on multiple and intricate relationships between that individual and the rest but also between and amongst the rest as enveloping the life of the individual. My argument here is that communal evaluation of the reputation, standing, and moral worth or depravity of an individual is an epistemic judgment that is grounded in a shared system of value, precisely that which produces the habitus and its doxa.[46] Within the habitus, none of these judgments is subjective or relative. The very idea of doxa runs diametrically opposite to such relativism.

The first scenario assumes the defendant not only to be "innocent" (*barī'an*) of ill-repute, any misdeed, or bad company, but also enjoying a high and honorable social standing. In this case, suspicion (*tuhma*) is not to be associated with him. Mere allegation of a plaintiff in no way leads to his punishment, for

42 *TAB*, 122. *Ta'dīb* derives from the well-known term *adab*, generally meaning "good, proper, or ethical behavior." It means to cultivate *adab* in someone. The punishment for *ta'dīb* may include rebuke, admonishment, imprisonment for a duration, or even parading the accused on the back of a donkey while facing backwards.

43 *TAB*, 123. See also previous note.

44 *TAB*, 123: "*Wa-ammā ta'annīhi fī tardīdi al-khusūmi 'inda al-labsi li-yum'ina fil-kashfi, fa-hādhā huwa al-madhhab.*"

45 *TAB*, 128-32.

46 See Hallaq, *Sharī'a*, 164-76, and sources cited therein.

the *tuhma* has no grounds for validation. But is the plaintiff to be punished? Ibn Farḥūn states that the "correct opinion" (*al-qawl al-ṣaḥīḥ*) is that he should be punished as a matter of deterrence to him as well as to others, in a bid to quash the tendency of easy slander of people of good character. Aṣbagh (d. 225/840) added that the punishment should be inflicted whether or not a malicious intent is proven. But another opinion, held by both Mālik and Ashhab (d. 204/820), does not demand punishment, especially if the plaintiff is thought to be genuinely seeking the restoration of his rights without intending slander or malice.[47]

In the second scenario, the opposite is assumed: the accused would be a scoundrel and of ill-repute, having a criminal record. The investigation and the means of extracting evidence would be proportionate to the severity of the record and involvement in crime. As we have seen before, the extraction of confession would be by means of beating or prison, with no other option. Here, Ibn Farḥūn extensively cites Ibn al-Qayyim's argument in favor of this doctrine. The latter had famously asserted that he "does not know any of the leading Muslim scholars who held the opinion that someone who has been charged with such crimes is made to swear an oath and then released, without imprisonment or otherwise." None of the "four eponymic imams, or any other jurists," held a doctrine requiring this. If "we release [a criminal] upon the taking of an oath," and "if he is known for his corruption on Earth and multiple acts of theft, and we insist not to convict him without two just witnesses – this act would be contrary to *siyāsa shar'iyya*." In fact, Ibn al-Qayyim continues, it would even more fundamentally contradict the clear Sunna (*nuṣūṣ Rasūl Allāh*) and the consensus of the Community (*ijmā' al-Umma*).[48]

It is because of this "grave misunderstanding that the rulers have dared to violate the Shar', imagining that *siyāsa shar'iyya* is insufficient to lead the people and protect the interests of the *Umma*." This "ignorance of the Sharī'a and its ways" led them to "transgress God's *ḥudūd* and deviate from the Shar'," thereby committing "all sorts of injustice and embarking on unlawful innovation in [the business of] *siyāsa*."[49] The central idea here is that

47 *TAB*, 128.

48 *TAB*, 129, 130.

49 *TAB*, 129: "*Qāla Ibnu Qayyimi al-Jawziyyati al-Ḥanbalī: Mā 'alimtu aḥadan min a'immati al-muslimīna yaqūlu inna hādhā al-mudda'ā 'alayhi bi-hādhihi al-da'wā wa-mā ashbahihā yuḥallafu wa-yursalu bi-lā ḥabsin wa-lā ghayrihi. Wa-laysa taḥlīfuhu wa-irsāluhu madhhaban li-aḥadin min al-a'immati al-arba'ati wa-lā ghayrihim. Wa-law ḥallafnā kulla wāḥidin min-hum wa-aṭlaqnāhu wa-khallaynā sabīlahu, ma' al-'ilmi bi-ishtihārihi bil-fasādi fil-arḍi wa-kathrati sariqātihi, wa-qulnā innā lā na'khudhhu illā bi-shāhidayyi 'adlin, kāna*

to strip *siyāsa* of its teeth opens the door for violations of the law, allowing rulers unconstrained powers of action. To delimit *siyāsa* and endow it with both a Sharʿī content and Sharʿī-defined boundaries is to give the executive as well as the judiciary the extra teeth needed to implement justice and instill order. Thus, to saturate *siyāsa* with Sharīʿa's substantive and procedural law would serve the cause of justice well. But to do so, the Sharīʿa must relax its law of evidence pertaining to crime, so as to contain and regulate a hitherto discretionary executive domain.

It is no trifle to ask, under this scenario, who is to implement the investigative punishment, the *qāḍī* (judiciary) or the ruler (executive)? The division of labor after the verdict is rendered has never been in question, but in the case of *tuhma* a form of punishment takes place *before* a judicial decision is given. Mālik, Ashhab, Ibn Ḥabīb (d. 238/853), and apparently other Mālikīs held the opinion that either the *qāḍī* or the *wālī* can beat or imprison the suspect. Ibn Ḥanbal, Ibn Farḥūn adds, also held this view. Other Ḥanbalīs as well as the Shāfiʿīs disallowed punishment by the *qāḍī*. They justified their position on the grounds that the only punitive competence of the *qāḍī* is confined to the *ḥudūd* and *taʿzīrāt*, which cannot be enforced until conviction is obtained. Furthermore, there is a distinctly different telos for the *qāḍī*'s office, on the one hand, and that of the ruler and his deputized executives, on the other: the former task is the adjudication of disputes and "giving back the rights to those who are entitled to them," while the ruler's mission is to prevent and eliminate "corruption of Earth, and the suppression of evil-doers and transgressors."[50] Ibn Farḥūn the Mālikī sides with the Ḥanbalīs, naming Ibn al-Qayyim in particular, and argues that his *madhhab* permits the *qāḍī* to implement pre-trial punishment.[51] Here, he again emphasizes Ibn al-Qayyim's contention that the boundaries of the *qāḍī*'s office in Islam have neither been defined nor fixed by the Sharīʿa, for they change according to customary usage and local convention.[52]

---

al-fiʿlu mukhālifan lil-siyasati al-sharʿiyyati.... Wa-li'ajli hādhā al ghalaṭi al-fāḥishi tajarra'a al-wulatu ʿala mukhālafati al-sharʿi wa-tawahhamū anna al-siyāsata al-sharʿiyyata qāṣiratun ʿalā siyāsati al-khalqi wa-maṣlaḥati al-ummati, fa-taʿaddū ḥudūda Allāhi taʿālā wa-kharajū ʿan al-sharʿi ilā anwāʿin min al-ẓulmi wal-bidʿati fī al-siyāsati ʿalā wajhin lā yajūzu, wa-sababu dhālika al-jahlu bil-Sharīʿa."

50 *TAB*, 131: "*Wa-mawḍiʿu wilāyati al-wālī al-manʿu min al-fasādi fil-arḍi, wa-qamʿu ahli al-sharri wal-ʿudwāni .... bi-khilāfi wilāyati al-ḥākimi, fa'inna mawḍūʿahā īṣālu al-huqūqi wa-ithbātuhā.*"

51 *TAB*, 131.

52 *TAB*, 131.

The third scenario assumes the suspect to be unknown (*majhūl al-ḥāl*) insofar as reputation, social company, or communal standing are concerned. Once a claim is lodged against him in a court of law, he is to be arrested by either the *wālī* or the *qāḍī* (according to the majority opinion) until the investigation is complete. Ibn Farḥūn here adds the qualification, on the authority of Ibn Ḥabīb, that the term of imprisonment "should not be long," the implication being that if the investigation does not yield results within a reasonable period of time, the accused should be released (*yukhallā sabīlahu*).[53] Abū al-Walīd al-Bājī narrated on the authority of Saḥnūn's *Mudawwana* that a mere allegation of the plaintiff constitutes insufficient grounds for arrest. The defendant who is not known for any criminal priors would be sworn that he did not commit the crime and then released. Other Mālikī jurists held the opinion that even an oath is not required, and that arrest is entirely unwarranted. Prison and beating are the lot of defendants who clearly possess a criminal record.[54]

At one point, Ibn Farḥūn stands at a remove from the massive details involved in his reformist narrative of procedural law and takes stock of the larger picture of his project, which is as much constitutional as it is legal. He cites Qarāfī quite approvingly, who argues that the expansion or "distension of the *qāḍī*'s judicial *siyāsa* prerogatives does not disagree with the Sharʿ"; if anything, he asserts, the vast body of evidence marshalled attests precisely to their congruity. There are thus six considerations that coalesce to produce a full justification for this distension:

First, viewed historically, corruption has become more extensive and intensive than ever, especially as compared to the early age of Islam. This, Ibn Farḥūn avers, has the consequence of changing legal rules, which continue, within the change, to be integral to the Sharīʿa. Change in law is necessary and thus cannot be set aside nor avoided, this being consistent with the maxim "No harm shall be inflicted nor reciprocated."[55] In other words, failing to implement necessary changes in the law amounts to causing harm in and to Islam.[56]

Second, the Mālikī school upholds the doctrine of *maṣāliḥ mursala*, to the effect that considerations of public interest are taken into account without

53 *TAB*, 131, 132.

54 *TAB*, 132.

55 *TAB*, 126: "*Inna al-fasāda qad kathura wa-intashara, bi-khilāfi al-ʿaṣri al-awwali, wa-muqtaḍā dhālika ikhtilāfu al-aḥkāmi bi-ḥaythu lā takhruju ʿan al-sharʿi bil-kulliyya, li-qawlihi ṣalʿam 'lā ḍarara wa-lā ḍarāra,' wa-tarku hādhihi al-qawānīni yu'addī ilā al-ḍarari.*"

56 On the mechanics of legal change, see Hallaq, *Authority*.

there being clear textual evidence in the revealed sources either in support or in rejection of these considerations. But we know that these considerations must be acted upon (*al-ʿamalu ʿalayhā*) because the leading Companions have done so, without there being any textual bases for them. Writing down a Qur'ānic vulgate, for instance, has neither a divine command to recommend it nor a precedent; nor was there any revelatory support for the way the caliphate had devolved upon Abū Bakr from the Prophet. The same goes for ʿUmar's establishment of the *dīwān*s of government, minting, and building prisons, among many other projects. "All of this, and much more, was done on the grounds of considerations of pure *maṣlaḥa*."[57]

Third, the principle that different and special circumstances and challenges require different and special solutions has been a venerable one, applicable across the Sharʿ from beginning to end. For example, the Sharʿ has been both strict and demanding regarding testimony, more so than it has been in respect of transmission reports (both these being fundamentally reliant on shared epistemological criteria of authentication). This is because in testimony there is good reason to suspect animosity and intention to transgress, both being presumed in the nature of disputes among litigating individuals (*tawahhum al-ʿadāwa*). Testimony can thus consist of one, two, three, or four witnesses, with added requirements such as freedom or gender (e.g., four male witnesses in *zinā*). In contracts, necessity and exigency required exceptions, such as the sale of non-existent objects (e.g., ordering a ship that has not been built yet). By contrast, in *zinā* cases, the demands of proof are made extremely strict, requiring four male witnesses to attest to the specific circumstances of the sexual act, including the specifics of place and time, and seeing the full details of the very act of penetration (as one sees "the pen immersed in the ink bottle"). On the other hand, in cases of homicide two witnesses are sufficient, although murder is a far weightier affair than *zinā*. "These divergences are many in the Sharʿ because the circumstances and contexts (*aḥwāl*) are likewise different. Differences in time and place must be given full consideration, this being a first-order principle, "even higher than *maṣāliḥ mursala*." This first-order principle thus demands the changes and developments in the rules of *siyāsa* (*al-qawānīn al-siyāsiyya*) and provides a robust and unassailable prop for them.[58]

57 *TAB*, 126.

58 *TAB*, 127: "*Wa-hādhihi al-mubāyanātu wal-ikhtilāfātu kathīratun fil-sharʿı li-ikhtilāfi al-aḥwāli fa-kadhālika yanbaghī an yurāʿā ikhtilāfu al-aḥwāli wal-azmāni, fa-takūnu al-munasabatu al-wāqiʿatu fī hādhihi al-qawānīni al-siyāsiyyati mimmā shahadat la-hu al-*

Fourth, and again related to legal change, is the consideration that different times and places require different approaches.[59] But unlike the previous consideration whereby the law itself, as a technique of reasoning, responds to various states of affairs according to requirement, need, and exigency, here the change is one of adjustment in the standards of legal application and compliance rather than a qualitative adaptation of substantive or procedural law to a new circumstance or exceptional situation. The law of procedure for instance requires witnesses across the board to have a just character (*ʿadl*), with rectitude as a chief attribute. Citing a string of Mālikī authorities to this effect, Ibn Farḥūn argues that in such locales where people of just character cannot be found, "we then admit for testimony the best and least corrupt of them.... The same applies to the appointment of *qāḍī*s and others," with the distinct implication that deputized government officials are subject to the same standard. The Mālikī jurists ground this general doctrine in the reasoning that failure to make such adjustments would cause harm to public interest, which is why "no one would disagree on this issue."[60] "Obligation has always been predicated on capability. If corruption pervades society, then it is lawful to appoint corrupt witnesses."[61] Qarāfī has even boldly argued that "had our contemporary *qāḍī*s, or their vetting witnesses, assistants, or secretaries been born in the early ages of Islam, they would not have been appointed and would not be of much use.... The best men of our age are the despicable ones of those [early] times. What used to be ugly/bad is now beautiful/good, what is now unconstrained (*ittasaʿa*) used to be restrained (*ḍayyiqan*), and so the rules have changed with the change of times."[62]

Fifth, despite the deterioration of general conditions, such a distension in rules, laws, and procedures remains enshrined in the logic of the law's general principles, for wherever one looks one would find the allowances for such a distension pervasive. Many examples can be cited but it suffices to illustrate the point with the case of dispensing with no lesser duty than prayer when, during

qawāʿidu bil-iʿtibāri, fa-lā takūnu min al-maṣāliḥi al-mursalati bal aʿlā rutbatan fa-talḥaqu bil-qawāʿidi al-aṣliyyati."

59 *TAB*, 127.

60 *TAB*, 127.

61 *TAB*, 127: "*Fa-inna al-taklīfa mashrūṭun bil-imkāni, wa-idhan jāza naṣbu al-shuhūdi fasaqatan li-ajli ʿumūmi al-fasādi; wa-jāza al-tawassuʿu fil-aḥkāmi al-siyāsiyyati li-ajli kathrati fasādi al-zamāni wa-ahlihi.*"

62 *TAB*, 127. It is perhaps important to note that in Qarāfī's *Dhakhīra*, the last three sentences have been excised and joined to the fifth consideration, a move that seems understandable given the connections between the arguments of the fourth and fifth considerations.

travel, the Muslim's security is threatened or when circumstances otherwise conducive to prayer become harsh.[63]

Finally, Qarāfī and Ibn Farḥūn take a long view of history, beginning from the start of creation down to their own times. During the Age of Adam, the human condition was simple and uncomplicated, where brothers married their own sisters, and other broad licenses were granted, but with the passage of time, things acquired complexity and underwent distension. When the Children of Israel became numerous and their lives increasingly complicated, such marriages were banned, and rules and regulations multiplied, including the Shabbat's injunctions, "the fifty prayers," dietary rules, and much else. In later ages of humanity, the rules – as in the Age of Adam – were again relaxed and the strictures of the law mitigated. "It is therefore obvious that legal systems and rules change with the changing of times, and this is one of the graces of God, may He be exalted. It is his Law that he enacted for his human creatures. It is thus clear that *siyāsa* rules do not diverge from the general [first-order] principles of the Law, nor are they innovations [violating] the decrees of the honorable Sharʿ."[64]

II

Now, what does this all mean? Why is it that Ibn Farḥūn's discussion has wound up focusing on the narrow issue of crime? How does crime relate to the constitutional division of labor or to the rule of law? How does Ibn Farḥūn's treatise fit into the genre of constitutional writings? And finally, in accommodating the much-recognized legal change and its inevitability, what has been gained and lost?

To answer the last question first, we observe that Ibn Farḥūn dealt with the same questions that challenged Ibn Qayyim al-Jawziyya, with the difference that the former emerged far more successful than the latter. Ibn Farḥūn prudently avoided the subjectivism that engulfed Ibn al-Qayyim's project, and his rejection of *firāsa* was particularly perspicacious, if not brilliant. *Firāsa*,

63 *TAB*, 127.

64 *TAB*, 127-28: "*Fa-qad ẓahara anna al-aḥkāma wal-sharāʾiʿa bi-ḥasabi ikhtilāfi al-azmāni, wa-dhālika min luṭfi Allāhi ʿazza wa-jalla bi ʿibādihi wa-sunnatihi al-jāriyati fī khalqihi, fa-ẓahara anna al-qawānīna lā takhruju ʿan uṣūli al-qawāʿidi, wa-laysat bidaʿan ʿammā jāʾa bi-hi al-sharʿu al-karīmu.*"

among other similar notions, seems to have emerged as the litmus test that finely separated the subjective from the non-subjective, and the potentially arbitrary from the objectively restraining and binding.

Ibn Farḥūn navigated a cautious path where he opened the door for *siyāsa* accommodation while remaining bound by the central doctrines of the law. Pretrial torture was given an entry into the Shar' but with a thick fence that delimited and confined this procedure to its localized and limited sphere. His colossal project represented a synthesis between the formalism of the Shar'ī mainstream and the excesses of Ibn al-Qayyim. Ibn Farḥūn, in other words, had his cake and ate it too: He preserved the greatest bulk of Sharī'a's procedural law, secured *siyāsa* within the fold of the Sharī'a, and, most importantly, ushered in the *qāḍī* as a full *siyāsa* functionary. In other words, his doctrine represented the success of the third stage in the life of *siyāsa* and its relationship to law: The first stage was its rise in Islam as an integral Near Eastern tradition of political management and rule; that was the time when the Sharī'a was being formed, still moving about in its embryonic form. *Siyāsa* had already been well-established, even strongly so in the Sassanid polity, and perhaps in some forms in the Byzantine. In this early phase, *siyāsa* was neither systematic nor well-defined, and was noticeably unconstrained by Shar'ī-mindedness.

When the Sharī'a came to maturity during the fourth/tenth century, *siyāsa* was brought along the side of Sharī'a to share and cooperate in the business of executive governance; which is to say that bringing the two together, the second stage, was a mutual act of concession: The *siyāsa* retained its effective powers as the coercive hand of the sultan but the Sharī'a came to envelop it – or surround it from the outside, so to speak – as a matter of constitutional corralling. The Sharī'a's constitutional sway could not reduce the effective powers of the *maẓālim* as an extra-judicial organ, but it brought it under a regime of law that defined its functions and jurisdictions. The *maẓālim*, on the other hand, retained these effective powers but lost its freedom of action outside of the limits set by the Sharī'a. Māwardī's *AS* is the most eloquent depiction of this symbiotic relationship.

The third stage, as the works of Ibn Taymiyya, Ibn al-Qayyim and Ibn Farḥūn have shown, was the gradual absorption of the *maẓālim* within the Sharī'a institution of *qaḍā'*. Now the *qāḍī* begins to adjudicate matters of *siyāsa* as much as the *maẓālim*-deputized official does. By the end of the Mamlūk period, this process was brought to full culmination, and when the Ottomans conquered the Mamlūk domains in 921-23/1515-17, they saw no need to retain the *maẓālim*, having incorporated this function in most regions within the office of the *qāḍī*, the defining judicial and administrative unit under the Ottomans prior to the nineteenth century. *Which is to say, importantly, that the elimination of the* maẓālim *was not an Ottoman initiative but rather a Sharʿī process of absorption that had already begun in the seventh/thirteenth century.* As recent scholarship has shown, some of the last Mamlūk sultans attempted to place a limit on the jurisdiction of *siyāsa* tribunals, in a bid to streamline the justice system within the parameters of the Sharīʿa.[65] *The Ottomans merely acted on a foregone conclusion, but the real work of the transformation was slow and institutional, a transformation that was corralled over the haul of two or three centuries by none other than the jurists.* It was their evolving *madhhab*ic claims that allowed the Sharīʿa to envelop and finally absorb the *maẓālim* and even define the limits of *siyāsa* powers through the installation of the office of Shaykh al-Islām in Istanbul. This was one of the most cardinal constitutional developments in the history of Islam.

The same developments can be viewed from a different perspective. For an observer looking at a global picture of Islamic political and constitutional writings it is readily apparent that there was a chronological discursive narrowing in the scope of these writings. Before the sixth/twelfth century, *Kitāb al-Imāma* was typically a chapter with which books on *kalām* and *uṣūl al-dīn* ended, these works having provided the philosophical foundations for theories of knowledge, existence, God and his attributes, revelation, miracles, prophethood, and political leadership (this last representing the imama chapter).[66] As we have seen, Māwardī appears to be the first to have brought together these theological and philosophical underpinnings under the wings of juristic-political elaborations that have accrued since the beginning of Islam. By Māwardī's time, the Sharīʿa, having developed its mature forms, not only had come into its own but also emerged as a central domain, a paradigmatic structure whose priorities and problems radiated over the peripheral domains and determined the latter's values in accord with these priorities.[67] In other words, when Māwardī was writing his *Adab al-Dīn wal-Dunyā*, *Tashīl al-Naẓar*, and *Al-Aḥkām al-Sulṭāniyya*, he was writing from a position of primacy and strength, where the Sharīʿa had established its dominion over the political, determining both the structures of governance and much of the political and ethical values that pervaded these structures. Specifically, Māwardī's oeuvre worked through a

65 See Rapoport, "Royal Justice," 98-99.
66 See, for instance, Bāqillānī, *Kitāb Tamhīd al-Awaʾil wa-Talkhīṣ al-Dalāʾil*, 467-558; Baghdādī, *Uṣūl al-Dīn*, 270-86.
67 For a more detailed discussion of central domains, see Hallaq, *Impossible State*, 6-12.

synthesis of the theological, philosophical, and legal productions to arrive at a general, but ultimately juristic, doctrine of good governance. When I say "juristic," I do not mean that there were at his time other, competing or autonomous genres spouting political ideas and political doctrines relevant to the experiences of Islamic polity. In fact, there were none. (The *falsafa* political doctrines of Fārābī and his likes, for instance, continued to stand at the margins, though the mainstream Sharʿī project did absorb from this generally Hellenic tradition certain ethical elements.) By juristic I therefore mean that the empire of law was the foundation of the empire of politics, not the other way around – an issue to be theorized in the later parts of this book. Politics, especially its institutional forms of governance, were defined and maintained by the force of the legal habitus.

Yet, the juridico-political landscape along with legal doctrine were fast changing, as Ibn Farḥūn's (and Qarāfī's) discourses about the necessity and inevitability of legal change acutely attest. True, more than three centuries after Māwardī, Ibn Jamāʿa and Ibn al-Mibrad produced variations on his constitutional themes, as he had elaborated them in his *al-Aḥkām al-Sulṭāniyya*. But by their time, much had changed, as Ibn Farḥūn's astute remarks about legal change demonstrate. The juridico-political change stemmed from the fact that by the eighth/fourteenth century, the phenomenon of "foreign" usurpers of power had been domesticated, whereby the sultan had long become the executive head and hands of the caliphal body. The caliphate became the institutional imagery in whose body flowed the various functions of society and government. The issue was no longer this domestication but rather the maintenance of law and order by the judiciary and executive under a particularly difficult set of circumstances. This was now the age of *siyāsa sharʿiyya*, the grounds on which certain constitutional components of *al-aḥkām al-sulṭāniyya* were being negotiated and transformed.

But the transformations were the product of grim realities. Prolonged periods of drought, famine, recurrent Black Death, frequent Crusading campaigns, and the Mongol invasions were among the factors that hammered the Mamlūk domains, often repeatedly and with merciless power. A survey of the annals of Muslim history from the Fāṭimids to the sixteenth-century rise of Ottoman imperial power reveals the general hardships and economic disarray that particularly afflicted the Mamlūk period, especially the second half of it.[68]

68 On the Black Death, depopulation, famine, and the collapse of the agricultural system and the effects of all these factors on the Mamlūk order and the legal system, see the next chapter.

Poverty and hunger were rife, and so was crime and corruption. Our Mamlūk authors were not voicing a theological formula or an eschatological reverberation when they complained that their times were particularly beset by low morals, crime, and corruption. Their challenge was therefore the cementing of the constitutional relationship between these emerging socio-economic and political challenges, on the one hand, and the prerogative of judicial and executive powers, on the other. The jurists, whose own engagement in the intellectual and political interests of the Community was a form of worship (*ʿibāda*), yet again rose to the occasion and yet again proved that they were, *as an institution*, the heirs of the prophets.

In the new accommodation of the emerging socio-economic realities into the constitutional framework, we see that Ibn Taymiyya drew on a long tradition of Ḥanbalī debate to inaugurate what appears to have been the first treatise in what soon would become the sub-genre of *siyāsa sharʿiyya*. His treatise takes for granted much of the Māwardian-Farrā'ian imamate discourse, and instead dwells on sultanic and emiric duties and prerogatives. While *al-aḥkām al-sulṭāniyya* constituted a global discourse about Islamic governance and the interrelationships between and among its constituent parts, *siyāsa sharʿiyya* focused on the executive as the subject of Sharʿī legal delimitations in matters of public order and security. *Siyāsa sharʿiyya* laid the foundation for the more specific interest in penal matters, an interest which Ibn al-Qayyim pursued with zeal, going considerably beyond the formulations of his teacher. His innovative *Al-Ṭuruq al-Ḥukmiyya* almost exclusively deals with procedural law in general, yet with an intense focus on punishment and crime, a set of concerns reflected in the very title of the treatise. Ibn Farḥūn's *Tabṣira* enjoys a somewhat larger scope, for it falls squarely within the *adab al-qāḍī* genre. Yet, it is quite remarkable and telling that over a quarter of the treatise is dedicated to what goes on in the *qāḍī*'s court under the rubric of *siyāsa sharʿiyya*.[69] The very fact that *siyāsa sharʿiyya* has now become an integral part of *adab al-qāḍī* work is of monumental significance, marking the absorption of *siyāsa* entirely within the Sharʿī framework. Arguably, Ibn Farḥūn's enterprise generally marks the completed transformation of enveloping and systematizing the *siyāsa* within the law of the land.

In the introduction to his work, Ibn Farḥūn lays out his plans and intentions for the book, saying that experience in the actual practice of *quḍā'* is one

69 *TAB*, 115-276, although, as we saw, other discussions pertaining to *siyāsa sharʿiyya* were conducted earlier in the treatise. See, e.g., 101-15.

thing while the knowledge of *fiqh* is quite another (reminiscent of modern-day recent law graduates who find themselves lost in clerking). Court litigation rests on judicial presuppositions (*muqaddimmāt*) "most of which have not been elaborated in the registers of *fiqh*; and the *faqīh* has no idea what these presuppositions are." "This is why some jurists in our *madhhab* have authored books on court documentation and have discussed the foundations of this science, however brief and [unduly] abridged these works remain."[70] Ibn Farḥūn's *Tabṣira* thus comes to remedy this situation, with a detailed statement on the "foundations of this science, and a thorough elucidation of the rules of evidence and *siyāsa sharʿiyya* principles that go into resolving judicial disputes."[71] The practical bent of the work and its acute awareness of and sensitivity to the realia of practice cannot escape the treatise's reader.

Considering the detailed and innovative expositions in, and overall size of the *Tabṣira* (as well as Ibn al-Qayyim's *al-Ṭuruq al-Ḥukmiyya*), we are confronted with the rise of a new sub-genre, one that is unprecedented in Islamic legal and political-constitutional history. These are not merely *adab al-qāḍī* works, in the manner that Māwardī himself authored some three centuries earlier, but rather a new generation of works that not only reigns in *siyāsa* within the imperatives of law's empire but also deploys the judiciary as an adjudicator and enforcer virtually equal to those men of the sword who had for centuries commanded *siyāsa* for themselves. If the ruler and his men can adjudicate in the law through *maẓālim* and *siyāsa*, then the jurists can decide the course of *siyāsa* through the paradigmatic law. As the Ottoman Dede Efendī would sum up the situation in the middle of the tenth/sixteenth century: If it is true that *siyāsa* is an integral part of the Sharīʿa, then the men of the Sharīʿa can dispense *siyāsa*.[72] The interflow is now complete.

---

70 *TAB*, I, 4.

71 *TAB*, I, 4: "*Li-anna al-gharaḍa bi-hādhā al-ta'līfi dhikru qawāʿidi hādhā al-ʿilmi, wa-bayānu mā tufṣalu bi-hi al-aqḍiyatu min al-ḥujaji wa-aḥkāmi al-siyāsati al-sharʿiyya.*"

72 *SSD*, 105.

Chapter 10

The Ḥanafī Tradition, Circassian Anarchy, and Pre-Colonial Ottoman Constitutionalization

From the end of the Fāṭimid Empire till the conquests of the Ottomans in the early 1500s, the regions extending from Egypt and the Hejaz in the south to Palestine, northern Syria, and Iraq was predominantly Shāfiʿī, both demographically and politically, the latter meaning that the Shāfiʿī school was both widespread and officially sponsored by both the Ayyūbid and the Mamlūk dynasties. With the rise of the Ottomans, these regions fell under a Ḥanafī modality of judicial administration, this school being the *madhhab*ic choice of this long-lasting empire. During the tenth/sixteenth century, especially under the leadership of Sultan Sulaymān the Magnificent, the Ottoman Empire underwent a process of administrative and judicial organization that was to constitute the governing structure of the empire until the thirteenth/nineteenth century, when the European colonial project of displacement, reorganization, and Westernization was set in motion.

The previous three chapters have covered the main constitutional doctrines of the Shāfiʿīs, Ḥanbalīs, and Mālikīs. Yet, the coverage was not motivated by the intention to be thorough or systematic, giving a "complete" account of the schools' constitutional involvement. Rather, it was necessitated by the nature of the constitutional questions that posed themselves in the course of our inquiry. For we have seen that the discourses emanating from these schools were not neatly divided and segregated from each other according to *madhhab*ic lines, as a study of *fiqh* doctrine usually entails. The *madhhab*ic intertextuality with regard to constitutional questions therefore means that the schools fed on each other and were heavily involved in the articulation of the constitutional domain in its various stages of development. The concern here was about the overall interests of the Community and polity, just as *uṣūl al-fiqh* (another inter-school intertextuality) was about the overall interests of the law's empire.

In this chapter, I trace the rise of a Ḥanafī-Ottoman constitutional arrangement that reflected a development which in effect began with the Mamlūk-era Ḥanbalīs and Mālikīs of the seventh/thirteenth and eighth/fourteenth centuries, and that culminated with the Ḥanafī-Ottoman political writings in the tenth/sixteenth century and beyond. It was on the basis of this arrangement that the Ottoman dynasty constructed its characteristic system of government.

I

Sometime during the middle third of the tenth/sixteenth century, an undistinguished Ottoman jurist by the name of Dede Jöngi Efendī (who died in 973/1566, and who is otherwise known to Arab readers as Dāda Afandī) wrote a book under the generic title of *al-Siyāsa al-Shar'iyya*.[1] Some modern writers, giving a short shrift to the work, characterized its author as lacking originality.[2] This is true, but it is in this very truth, as we will see, that the work is most valuable for our concerns.

I argue that the significance of Dede Efendī's work lies in the fact that it is a close reproduction of pre-Ottoman works, especially the Mamlūk-era Ḥanafī treatise *Mu'īn al-Ḥukkām*,[3] compiled by the jurist and judge 'Alā' al-Dīn al-Ṭarābulsī (d. 844/1440). It is crucial to observe that Ṭarābulsī's Ḥanafī work is heavily reliant and often verbatim duplication of the famous and "unprecedented" work of the Mālikī jurist and judge Ibn Farḥūn. As we saw in the previous chapter, Ibn Farḥūn's work possesses a doctrinal genealogy that integrates thick elements of Ḥanbalism, a genealogy that seems to begin with Ibn 'Aqīl and to have acquired extensive systematic elaboration at the hands of Ibn Taymiyya and especially Ibn al-Qayyim, whose authority, despite his Ḥanbalism, appears to have been accepted widely among Ottoman Ḥanafī

1 Henceforth cited as *SSD*.
2 See, for instance, Heyd, *Studies*, 198-99, 202 (last line).
3 'Alā' al-Dīn Abū al-Ḥasan 'Alī b. Khalīl al-Ṭarābulsī, *Mu'īn al-Ḥukkām fī-mā Yataraddadu bayna al-Khaṣmayni min Al-Aḥkām*. Henceforth cited as *TMH*.

writers till the middle of the nineteenth century.[4] Dede Efendī's work, on the other hand, was translated into Turkish at least twice and became a standard reference for Ottoman writers on *siyāsa sharʿiyya.*[5]

Dede Efendī begins by giving a succinct but pointed definition of *siyāsa*. Here the expression no longer appears as part of a necessary compound noun: The qualifying term "*sharʿiyya*" is dropped out while the subject noun, "*siyāsa*," standing alone, is defined as "*Sharīʿa mughallaẓa*."[6] It is as if to take it for granted that the concept is Sharʿī-based and that it does not differ from Sharīʿa except in the fact that it takes a "severe," "thick," or "hardened" form, a sort of "heavy-duty Sharīʿa."[7] But Sharīʿa-based nonetheless. What we have here is therefore the completion of the process to a full circle: in the early formative period, the term was used independently to signal the ruler's absolute prerogatives over this domain, without it being hampered by a law that has not yet fully developed. With Ibn Farḥūn and Dede Efendī, the term is back in use without the qualifier "*sharʿiyya*," but now to indicate that its Sharʿī circumscription is complete.

This definition of *siyāsa* as a "heavy-duty Sharīʿa" is taken straight out of Ṭarābulsī, who likewise begins the discussion of *siyāsa sharʿiyya* with the same exact language.[8] The Ḥanafī Akmal al-Dīn Bābartī (d. 786/1384) is also quoted here as saying that "*siyāsa* is the hardened punishment for a criminal offense that has a Sharʿī ruling [intended to] stem the capacity for corruption."[9]

Once the succinct definition is offered, Dede Efendī immediately continues to quote Ṭarābulsī, with the resumptive proposition "*thumma*." "And then he [Ṭarābulsī] said (*thumma qāla*) that *siyāsa* is of two kinds."[10] What follows is in fact not Ṭarābulsī's language but rather an extensive reproduction by our Ḥanafī author of Ibn Farḥūn's very language with regard to two types of *siyāsa*, one being in conformity with the Sharīʿa, and therefore just, while the other is contrary to the law of the land and thus deemed unjust and oppressive.[11]

---

4 See, for instance, Ibn ʿĀbidīn, *Ḥāshiya*, VI, 126.
5 Heyd, *Studies*, 198; see also Ibn ʿĀbidīn, *Ḥāshiya*, VI, 126.
6 *SSD*, 74.
7 See Ibn Manẓūr, *Lisān al-ʿArab*, VII, 507-8. *Al-ghilaẓ*, Ibn Manẓūr writes, is that which is the antonym of tenderness (*ḍiddu al-riqqati*), either in manners, ethical disposition, behavior, or in lifestyle.
8 *TMH*, 207.
9 *SSD*, 73-74: "*Al-siyāsatu taghlīzu jazāʾi jināyatin la-hā ḥukmun sharʿiyyun ḥasman li-māddati al-fasādi.*"
10 *SSD*, 74.
11 See previous chapter and *TAB*, 115-16; *TMH*, 207.

Thereafter, he replicates Ibn Farḥūn's language in the name of Ṭarābulsī, to the effect that there exist three juristic attitudes to the relationship between *siyāsa* and Sharīʿa: (1) that *siyāsa* is an intrusion upon the Sharīʿa and that it should not be regulated by the law of the land; (2) that *siyāsa* should be regulated and given extraordinary powers to boot; and (3) that the relationship between *siyāsa* and Sharīʿa should be balanced.[12] Obviously, this last is the proper path that leads not only to justice but also to the fulfillment of the Goals of the Law (*maqāṣid al-Sharīʿa*). Here, as Ibn Farḥūn does and Ṭarābulsī follows to the letter (meaning a wholesale replication of language), a long discussion is presented concerning the place and function of *siyāsa* in fulfilling these Goals.[13] This is followed by a section in which it is shown how the Qur'ān and Sunna authorize *siyāsa*. But Dede Efendī skips both these discussions and instead merely hints at them thus: "These are multifaceted arguments, covered in the *aṣl*."[14] The "*aṣl*," for Dede Efendī, is Ṭarābulsī's work, not Ibn Farḥūn's (a Mālikī work). In like manner, he also skips the "long" list of *siyāsa* acts carried out by the Prophet and his Companions, where severe punishments were inflicted on perpetrators of corruption (*fasād*). The penalties ranged from beating suspects and burning houses to torturing debtors suspected of hiding their wealth.[15]

At this juncture, and before we proceed, it is profoundly important to understand the processes of authorization that Dede Efendī established for his text, for the matter does not only go to the question of how authority is created and maintained but also to the long-standing debate over the extent to which the Ottoman Empire innovated over previous Muslim dynasties. It is my contention here (and elsewhere)[16] that the claims for Ottoman exceptionalism are largely unwarranted.

For modern academics, the heavy textual borrowings our "author" indulged in may appear as wholesale forgery, but this impression must be resisted at any cost. What we are dealing with here is not academic and scholarly research embedded in the *modern* epistemic structure we have come to know, where supposed "originality" is an expression of intellectual freedom in its best

12 *TMH*, 207; *TAB*, 115-16; *SSD*, 74-76. See also the corresponding discussion of Ibn Farḥūn in the previous chapter.

13 See the detailed account offered in the previous chapter. See also *TAB*, 116 ff.; *TMH*, 208 f.

14 *SSD*, 76.

15 *TAB*, 117-21; *TMH*, 208 ff.

16 See, for instance, Hallaq, "'Qāḍī's *Dīwān* (*Sijill*)' before the Ottomans."

Kantian form.[17] Apart from the problematics of our modern concept, Dede Efendī's "authorial" venture was not about originality but rather the affirmation of a practical legal and political discursive tradition as ontologically continuous with best historical practice. His project was about legal and juristically based political authorization, not research, intellectual theorization or the like. In fact, "originality" (whatever it means) would not only be the last thing on his mind but also a concept that would have militated against his project and telos. Yet, the question before us is why would he copy entire sections from other works, almost without any contribution of his own? It is certainly the case that thinking about this in terms of originality or lack of it would be misleading. He effectively acted as a compiler, the activity of compiling being a remarkably efficient means to engender authorization, for it is tantamount to a project of excavation for relevant, useful, supportive, and authenticating materials that altogether go into constructing the *madhhab*-doctrine – or at least an attempt to do so.

In this case, the *madhhab*-doctrine is not only fluid but also highly open to interpretation. We recall Juwaynī's percipient insistence that most issues related to the imamate and political governance are *maẓnūnāt*, namely, questions open to debate and recurrent legal reasoning.[18] And as Ibn Farḥūn eloquently and perspicaciously argued,[19] the constantly changing conditions in the world of political governance require a commensurately continuous activity of *ijtihād*. But *ijtihād* would obviously not be needed, nor even desired, if an area of knowledge in the law had been settled – that is, settled as the cornerstone of the discursive tradition. For the desideratum is not *ijtihād* in and by itself – *ijtihād* being no more than a means to an end – but rather the furnishing of a practical solution to a problem at hand. This is the mandate of the law.

It is my contention that the *siyāsa* jurisprudence in early Ottoman times – a jurisprudence that dictated the terms of political play for the three centuries after sultan Sulaymān the Magnificent completed his project of judicial reorganization – was continuous with its sister jurisprudence under the Mamlūks, the Ḥanafī jurists having already completed the project of jurisprudential

17 On the problematics of originality and for a typology of the "author," see my *Restating Orientalism*, 27-57, 171 ff. It is to be noted that I italicize "modern" to draw attention to the crucial fact that "the modern" is not as much a temporal space as it is a quality, a particular structure, and for my concerns, a unique epistemology.

18 *GU*, 48 and passim.

19 See previous chapter.

engineering more than half a century before the Ottomans conquered the Arab lands making up the Mamlūk sultanate. All Dede Efendī had to do was to reproduce Ṭarābulsī's writings – along with supporting Ḥanafī *fiqh* materials – as attestations to the already established Ḥanafī *madhhab*ic doctrine regarding political governance. This Ḥanafī development, I stress once more, occurred decades before the conquests of the Ottomans.[20]

Ṭarābulsī had already done the work of Ḥanafīzing the Mālikī doctrine, which itself found inspiration in Ḥanbalī jurisprudence. The Ḥanbalīs, from Ibn ʿAqīl to Ibn al-Qayyim, parted ways with the mainstream Sharʿī jurisprudence (including Māwardī and their own Abū Yaʿlā al-Farrāʾ), declaring for themselves what might be nowadays called a radical position. Ibn Farḥūn's work, more than any other Mālikī production, mitigated the Ḥanbalī stance, thereby creating a synthesis of a kind (see previous chapter). It was this synthesis that was to dominate in Sharīʿa's political jurisprudence until the effective fall of the Ottoman Empire under the weight of nineteenth century colonialism. The Ḥanafīs seem to have been more than happy to adopt the Mālikī synthesis which Ibn Farḥūn brilliantly forged. But how did they accomplish this project?

The answer to this question lies in the art of textualization, that is, the skill and aptitude of writing, revising, reviewing, manipulating, interpolating, and excising earlier, established texts. All Dede Efendī had to do was cleverly compile the relevant portions of Ṭarābulsī's *Muʿīn al-Ḥukkām*, itself a *textualized* work that had already accomplished the desideratum of Ḥanafīzing the doctrine of political governance. And Ṭarābulsī's ground of precedence was no other than Ibn Farḥūn's work. This, it is important to note, is precisely the textual relationship that stands between Māwardī's *al-Aḥkām al-Sulṭāniyya* and Abū Yaʿlā's work with the same title. (Based on a comparison of a fairly large number of instances of identity between the two texts, I am of the firm opinion that Māwardī's is the original treatise and that Abū Yaʿlā's work represented the Ḥanbalīzation of *al-Aḥkām al-Sulṭāniyya*.)

How, then, was the Ḥanafīzation of Ibn Farḥūn's Mālikī text accomplished at the hands of Ṭarābulsī? First, it is clear that reproducing Ibn Farḥūn's text verbatim did not represent for Ṭarābulsī an improper act in any way. That he or any of his contemporaries might have thought it to be an act of forgery was inconceivable. And thus there was nothing to conceal or camouflage, for he was merely reproducing a field of knowledge that was common property, namely, a property belonging to the general body of the Muslim Community.

20 Since, as noted above, Ṭarābulsī died in 844/1440.

Being a form of worship (*taʿabbud*), the production of knowledge was akin to prayer, fasting, and alms tax. As a scholar, you produce knowledge for your fellow Muslims just as you would help your neighbor in need or pay the *zakāt*. And since all wealth and property, material or otherwise, belong eventually to God, so does knowledge (*ʿilm*) by subsumption.[21] For in a strong sense, *ʿilm* was the road to God.

There was nothing to conceal or camouflage to the extent that the act of wholesale transcription begins immediately after the five-lined preamble is presented – when *ammā baʿd* appears. The text is reproduced almost wholly word-for-word, including chapter and section titles. For example, chapter 3, dealing with the scope of the *qāḍī*'s jurisdiction, has a title consisting of twenty-five words, identical in both works. Ibn Farḥūn naturally begins the chapter by citing his schoolmate al-Qarāfī, naming him without any further qualification. Ṭarābulsī here adds the title of Qarāfī's work, al-*Dhakhīra*, probably because the Ḥanafīs may not be readily familiar with the author and his works. Then Qarāfī's view of the *qāḍī*'s jurisdiction is stated: The *qāḍī* adjudicates disputes and has no business engaging *siyāsa*-at-large (*al-siyāsa al-ʿāmma*). Mostly, he has no power of execution but merely decides on, and issues decrees for punishment. It is up to the ruler to enforce them or not. Ṭarābulsī thus far adopts Ibn Farḥūn's exact language, and adds, like him, the qualification that "what Qarāfī said is open to discussion" (*fī-hi naẓar*). "The transmitted [authoritative] doctrine of the *madhhab* is that the *qāḍī* can indeed implement the *ḥudūd*."[22] Curiously, Ṭarābulsī adopts the same language here too. What is good for the Mālikī *madhhab* is good for his as well.

Yet, in this context Ibn Farḥūn gives a specific reference to a distinguished Mālikī authority, Ibn al-Ḥājib (d. 646/1249), supported by the authority of the even more distinguished Shāfiʿī jurist Ibn ʿAbd al-Salām (d. 660/1262). Ṭarābulsī omits these authorities altogether and jumps to the next phrase in which Ibn Farḥūn asserts that implementing the capital punishment is not the prerogative of any executive officer, not even of the provincial governor. (This doctrine – apparently dominating throughout Islamic history – is backed by the authority of Companion and caliph, ʿUmar I, who forbade carrying out this penalty without his explicit permission. The same appears to have been the case during the long haul of the Ottoman Empire.)[23] Yet, Ibn Farḥūn continues,

21 For the genealogy and cosmology of *ʿilm*, see Hallaq, "Qur'ānic Constitutionalism and Moral Governmentality," 21-25.

22 *TAB*, 15; *TMH*, 11: "*Wal-manqūlu fil-madhhabi anna la-hu iqāmatu al-ḥudūd.*"

23 Heyd, *Studies*, 192 but see also 227 ff.

the *qāḍīs* possess the power to sentence *ḥudūd*-convicts to death, which, by definition, makes the *qāḍīs* integral to the operation of at least some aspects of *siyāsa* administration.

Here, Ibn Farḥūn again invokes the authority of the Mālikī jurist Ibn Sahl (d. 486/1093),[24] whereas Ṭarābulsī replaces the Mālikī name and reference with the phrase: "some jurists said...."[25] This replacement, and often omission of Mālikī names, recurs throughout Ṭarābulsī's work. In the paragraph following this discussion, Qarāfī's name is again deleted from Ṭarābulsī's text and instead replaced by: "Some honorable jurists said..."[26] At times, however, the Mālikī authorities are not just deleted or replaced; Ṭarābulsī, while suppressing their identities, even declares the contents of their doctrine to be the *madhhab* dictum of his own school. This, for instance, occurs in the context of the discussion to the effect that a judge is under duty to find the least corrupt of witnesses, and to accept their testimonies as valid to boot – assuming, of course, that just witnesses cannot be found. This is the Mālikī doctrine narrated by Qarāfī from Ibn Abī Zayd al-Qayrawānī (d. 386/996). Ṭarābulsī simply replaces this authority-reference with: "Some scholars held the *madhhab*-opinion that ..." (*qāla ba'ḍu al-'ulamā'i, wa-huwa al-madhhabu, 'alā annahu...*).[27] At times, when Ibn Farḥūn lists the opinions of a series of Mālikī scholars regarding an issue, Ṭarābulsī omits the entire material and replaces it with similar content from his school's authorities.[28] Be that as it may, to the exception of the naturally distinctive Ḥanafī *fiqh*, Ṭarābulsī's work is, in my rough estimate, over ninety-five percent a duplication of Ibn Farḥūn's work. Insofar as the organization of the work is concerned, it is also an almost exact replica.

None of this, however, should be taken to mean that the identity of Ibn Farḥūn, Qarāfī, or other Mālikīs as sources of Ṭarābulsī's work is left without recognition. Dede Efendī is fully aware that the distension in the *qāḍīs*' *siyāsa* mandate comes from the Mālikīs, and acknowledges, furthermore, the

24 The editor of *TAB* has the name as Ibn Suhayl (p. 15), a name, to my knowledge, not associated with the Mālikī school. The reference must be to Abū Al-Aṣbagh Ibn Sahl al-Asdī, the author of *al-Aḥkām al-Kubrā*. On this jurist, see Marin, "Law and Piety."

25 *TMH*, 11; *TAB*, 15.

26 *TMH*, 12: "*Fa-qāla ba'ḍu al-fuḍalā'i.*" See also *TAB*, 127, l. 10; cf. *TMH*, 217, l. 7, where Ibn Abī Zayd's *Nawādir* is obviated in favor of "some scholars, and this is the *madhhab* dictum [of the Ḥanafīs]."

27 *TAB*, 127 (l. 10); *TMH*, 217 (l. 7). In the chapter on apostasy (*ridda*), Ṭarābulsī adopts Mālikī Ibn al-Ḥājib's dictum while omitting his name from what is otherwise an exact replication of Ibn Farḥūn's *Tabṣira*. Compare *TAB*, 210, with *TMH*, 228.

28 See, for instance, *TAB*, 125, ll. 8-15; cf. *TMH*, 215, ll. 17-22.

transmission of the material through the pen of Ṭarābulsī.[29] Here, he replicates the six considerations[30] that coalesce to produce a full justification for this distension, including the unprecedented spread of corruption, the operation of *maṣāliḥ mursala* to protect public interest, the need to change the law with the changes in circumstances and conditions over time, the inherent pliability of the legal system to respond to such changes, and the general principle that legal systems in history (since Prophet Adam) always undergo change.[31]

With this frame of mind as an underlying legal philosophy, it is no surprise that the extrajudicial penalties inflicted by the Prophet and his Companions are integrated within *siyāsa* administration, however much they may be exceptions to the standard Sharīʿa doctrine and practices. Dede Efendī resorts to the body of Ḥadīth in order to pluck reports in which the Prophet is said to have inflicted particularly severe punishments. In one such Ḥadīth, he is reported to have said: "He who drowns us we drown him, and he who burns us we burn him." "This," Dede Efendī added, "bears upon *siyāsa*,"[32] with the implication that the crime of corruption on Earth (*fasād*) necessarily elicits a punitive response in kind – again, however much of an exception to the Sharīʿa it may be. As is well known, burning humans at the stake is generally forbidden in Islam, since only God has the prerogative to inflict this punishment in the Hereafter. Dede Efendī even cites the Prophetic report to this effect: "The Prophet, may peace be upon him, said that only God can punish with fire." Yet, the incidence in which the Companion and caliph ʿAlī b. Abī Ṭālib is reported to have burned a group of heretics was taken to be a lawful act "in the way of [applying] *siyāsa*" (*lil-siyāsa*). "It is an intensified act of deterrence, and the imam has the right to do so if public interest requires it."[33] By the same logic, a man proven to have engaged with another man in full sexual intercourse (*lā'iṭ*) is to be put to death according to *siyāsa*, although in the Sharīʿa the act does not meet the bar of evidentiary proof. Likewise, a witness who retracts his testimony in a case of homicide, after the death penalty was implemented against the accused, will be liable in *siyāsa* to capital punishment.[34]

In line with Ibn al-Qayyim and Ibn Farḥūn, Dede Efendī endorses the view that defendants with criminal records must be subjected to a severe

29 See, e.g., *SSD*, 82.
30 See the previous chapter, main text at nn. 56-59.
31 *SSD*, 83-90.
32 *SSD*, 77.
33 *SSD*, 78: "*Lil-mubālaghati fil-zajri, wa-lil-imāmi dhālika idhā daʿati al-maṣlaḥa.*"
34 *SSD*, 79-81.

form of investigation. But his sources of authority, expectedly, are now Ḥanafī. He invokes Bukhārī's *Khulāṣat al-Fatāwā*[35] and Ibn Bazzāz's *al-Fatāwa al-Bazzāziyya*,[36] who in turn fall back on Shaybānī's doctrine in his *Aṣl*.[37] The "general view of the Ḥanafī masters is that if the defendant denies the charge, the imam may subject him to extrajudicial punishment [for purposes of procuring confession] if he finds him to be subject of *tuhma*, in that he knows him to walk with thieves or to keep company with habitual alcohol users, even though he himself may not consume alcohol."[38] Likewise, on the authority of Ibn Bazzāz and Ibn Māza,[39] it is reported that the early Ḥanafī master al-Ḥasan b. Ziyād (who was a disciple of Abū Yūsuf and Ẓufar) replied in the affirmative to the question of whether or not a *tuhma*-defendant can be beaten, and added the proviso "as long as the beating does not cause flesh wounds or bone exposure."[40] The earlier Ḥanafī jurist and Chief Justice al-Nāṣiḥī[41] held the view that it is lawful (*mashrūʿ*) to execute a defendant who has an extensive criminal record of "corruption on Earth" (*yasʿā fil-arḍi bil-fasād/fasād fil-arḍ*) and who has (repeatedly) visited evil upon people.[42] That these allowances, otherwise rejected by Sharʿī standards, represent a necessary evil is captured by an apparently Ḥanafī authority who said that "I have not seen an oppression [i.e., this form of *siyāsa*] closer to justice than this."[43]

With these allowances established, Dede Efendī opens his chapter 2 with the now classic question: Can *qāḍī*s adjudicate cases of criminal law according to *siyāsa*? In other words, are judges competent to investigate and decide, in accord with *siyāsa*, such cases as may involve habitual thieves, evildoers, and transgressors (always with the assumption that these miscreants have a criminal record)? Like Ibn Farḥūn, he answers the question by approvingly citing what is by now Ibn al-Qayyim's well-known language on the subject:

35 Ṭāhir b. Aḥmad b. ʿAbd al-Rashīd al-Bukhārī (d. 542/1148), *Khulāṣat al-Fatāwā*.

36 Muḥammad b. Muḥammad b. Shihāb Ibn al-Bazzāz al-Kurdarī (d. 827/1424), *al-Fatāwā al-Bazzāziyya*.

37 Muḥammad b. al-Ḥasan al-Shaybānī (d. 189/805) was one of the three major imams and "founders" of the Ḥanafī school.

38 *SSD*, 92.

39 Burhān al-Dīn Maḥmūd b. Tāj al-Dīn Ṣadr al-Sharīʿa al-Shahīd Ibn Māza (d. 616/1220), *al-Muḥīṭ al-Burhānī*.

40 *SSD*, 94.

41 ʿAbd Allāh b. al-Ḥusayn Abū ʿAlī al-Nāṣiḥī (d. 447/1056) authored *Tahdhīb Adab al-Qaḍā' lil-Khaṣṣāf* and served as *qāḍī al-quḍāt* under the Ghaznawid sultan Maḥmūd Ibn Sabaktakīn (Sebükteghīn) who ruled between 388/998 and 421/1030.

42 *SSD*, 96.

43 *SSD*, 93: "*Mā ra'aytu ẓulman ashbahu bil-ʿadli min-hu.*"

namely, that the mandate and purview of the *qāḍī*'s jurisdiction is relative to time and place.[44] Dede Efendī's conclusion: "The clear-cut *madhhab*-doctrine is that the *qāḍī* can do so, as we will explain, God willing!"[45]

Dede Efendī takes the discussion to the next stage. Yet again, the materials are wholly appropriated from Ibn Farḥūn via Ṭarābulsī's Ḥanafīzed work. The topic now is the extent of the difference between the scope of the *qāḍī*'s jurisdiction and that of *wālī al-jarā'im*, the lieutenant of crime or criminal police. Once Māwardī's list is recorded, he, like Ṭarābulsī and Ibn Farḥūn before him, remarks that "our clear-cut *madhhab*-doctrine requires the *qāḍī* to deal with most of these matters," "these matters" being the responsibilities and prerogatives of *wālī al-jarā'im*.[46]

Yet, Dede Efendī takes the view against the *qāḍī*'s prerogative to torture a defendant in order to procure confession. The works of the Ḥanafī school, he says, disallow coercion (*ikrāh*) in the *qāḍī*'s court. The authoritative *al-Fatāwā al-Khāniyya* declares that if a *qāḍī* coerces (*law akraha*) a person to confess to a crime of theft or homicide or bodily harm, and, having confessed, he is punished accordingly, then the *qāḍī* is personally liable for damages if the coerced confessor can be shown to have always enjoyed a good reputation in his community. If he is subject to *tuhma* (that is, having a reputation for engaging in crime or having a criminal record), then the *qāḍī* is liable to damages according to some jurists.[47] The general tenor of the *madhhab*, Dede Efendī qualifies, is that coercion in non-*tuhma* cases is not permitted, and the *qāḍī* is to be dismissed if he resorts to it. This position is likewise upheld in *al-Fatāwā al-Khāniyya*.[48]

---

44 *SSD*, 105; *TMH*, 212; *TAB*, 121.

45 *SSD*, 106. Almost a century after Dede Efendī died, the distinguished Ottoman jurist ʿAbd al-Raḥmān b. Muḥammad al-Kaylūbī Shaykhzādeh (d. 1078/1667) described the juristic scene thus: "If [a thief] confesses [to theft] under coercion, [the confession] is not valid. However, some of the more recent jurists have issued *fatwā*s to the effect that [such a confession] is valid and that beating is allowed. But this is not an authoritative opinion [*lā yuftā bi-hi*] because it is injustice. In the *Minaḥ* [probably *Minaḥ al Ghaffār* by Timurtāshī, d. 1003/1595]: "If [the accused] is known for immoral behavior that fits the accusation, then some jurists hold that the governor (*wālī*) or the *qāḍī* may beat him, whereas others maintain that only the governor may do so. But there are also jurists who hold that he [the accused] is not to be beaten. If the [accused's] circumstances are not known, he is to be imprisoned until the matter becomes clear. Some say that he must be imprisoned for a month and others that he may be imprisoned as long as the ruler (*walī al-amr*) thinks fit." Quoted, with all parentheses, from Peters, *Crime and Punishment in Islamic Law*, 83.

46 *SSD*, 114, 116. See the previous chapter for a detailed discussion.

47 *SSD*, 130-31; Qāḍīkhān, *Al-Fatāwā al-Khān*iyya, III, 486-87.

48 *SSD*, 130.

Finally, Dede Efendī deals with two issues toward the end of his treatise, both of which are significant for our concerns. The first is "*taʿzīr* by monetary penalty," as, for example, in the penalization of a man who refuses to attend Friday prayer. There is no mention here of the general Sharīʿa attitude against monetary *taʿzīr*, nor of the specific and weighty objections voiced by Abū Ḥanīfa, Shaybānī, and most leading Ḥanafī authorities.[49] The list of authorities he marshals stand in support of the doctrine that "if public interest requires it, then pecuniary penalties are permitted."[50]

Second, and finally, is the problem of venue and the overlapping jurisdictions of the sultan and the *qāḍī*. The question here is whether the sultan's venue overrides that of the *qāḍī*. Some jurists, Dede Efendī states, permitted claimants to approach the sultan's tribunal before or without addressing themselves to the *qāḍī*'s court. Other jurists, apparently a majority, objected to this doctrine, arguing that only when the *qāḍī* proves incapable (*ʿajiza*) of addressing the wrong that a person may approach the sultan's tribunal. This doctrine goes so far as to insist that if the sultan decides for the plaintiff a larger amount of compensation than would a *qāḍī*, then the difference must be returned to the defendant.[51] In other words, the standard doctrine – apparently for all the four schools – is that the default venue is always the Sharīʿa court except in cases involving *siyāsa*. Yet, even in such cases, the *qāḍī*'s involvement in one role or another was, as we will see, necessary.

II

In the early 1970s, Uriel Heyd – hitherto probably the most distinguished expert on early Ottoman criminal law – wrote that Dede Efendī's "treatise is the best-known Ottoman discussion of *siyāsa* penal law. His views may therefore be assumed to reflect or to have influenced the attitude of many Turkish *ʿulema* over a long period."[52] This seems to be an accurate assessment. The legal tradition that Dede Efendī inherited from the latter-day Ḥanbalīs and Ibn Farḥūn via Ṭarābulsī continued with the same genealogy and structure for at least three centuries.

49 See *RMI*, VI, 105-6.

50 *SSD*, 138-39: "*Al-taʿzīru bi-akhdhi al-māli anna al-maṣlaḥata fī-hi jāʾiza.*"

51 *SSD*, 134.

52 Heyd, *Studies*, 189-90.

In the first third of the thirteenth/nineteenth century, and just before the Ottoman Empire was to undergo major structural changes at the hands of colonialist Europe, Ibn ʿĀbidīn (d. 1252/1836) dedicated a section of his *Radd al-Muḥtār ʿalā al-Durr al-Mukhtār* to the subject of *siyāsa sharʿiyya*.[53] Dede Efendī's treatise looms large, although Ibn ʿĀbidīn knows of it through intermediary sources. These latter appear to have been Egyptian Ḥanafīs, with Aḥmad b. Muḥammad al-Ḥamawī (d. 1098/1687) being the final link, but one who clearly drew on Ṭarābulsī. In a key paragraph, and using what he considers Ṭarābulsī's language, he defines *siyāsa* as "*Sharʿ mughallaẓ*" (see above) to be distinguished into two types, just and unjust. He immediately continues to say, again using Ṭarābulsī's/Ibn Farḥūn's language, that "it is a big subject – he who wishes to delve into its details must review *Muʿīn al-Ḥukk*ām of al-Qāḍī ʿAlā' al-Dīn al-Aswad al-Ṭarābulsī al-Ḥanafī."[54] Of course, the language turns out to be almost exactly that which Ibn Farḥūn used.

Ibn ʿĀbidīn's discourse seems to echo a controversy in the Ḥanafī school as to the scope of *siyāsa*, for apparently some Ḥanafıs argued that it is confined to sexual crimes.[55] Other Ḥanafīs retorted that *siyāsa* has to do with all criminal violations and that this sphere of the law is up to the imam's discretion.[56] This includes putting to death subversive elements whose activities threaten to spread corruption in the community, though they may not be heretics. Ibn ʿĀbidīn briefly outlines the etymological denotations of the term *siyāsa* only to conclude that it is a policy of guiding and directing people to the paths of conduct that lead to the good life, in the Here and Hereafter. In some general sense, he says, this is true of the entire Sharīʿa, but technically "*siyāsa* has to do with deterrence and correction, even though this may require capital punishment" in the case of repeat offenders.[57] This is why some jurists defined it as "a hardened punishment (*mughallaẓa*) for a criminal offense that has a Sharʿī ruling

53 Henceforth cited as *RMI*.

54 *RMI*, VI, 20: "*Wa-hiya bābun wāsiʿun fa-man arāda tafṣīlahā fa-ʿalayhi bi-murājaʿati kitābi* Muʿīnu al-Ḥukkāmi *lil-qāḍī ʿAlā' al-Dīn al-Aswad al-Ṭarābulsī al-Ḥanafī*." See also *TAB*, 115.

55 This may become understandable if we consider that 28 per cent of all articles of the famous *qānūnnāmeh* of sultan Sulaymān the Magnificent treat sexual offenses. See Peters, *Crime*, 94.

56 *RMI*, VI, 20: "*Wal-ra'yu fī-hā ilā al-imām*."

57 *RMI*, VI, 20: "*Zajrun wa-ta'dībun, wa-law bil-qatli, kama qalu* [vis. the Ḥanafī jurists] *fī al-liwāṭiyyi wal-sāriqi wal-khannāqi idhā takarrara min-hum dhālika ḥalla qatluhum siyāsatan*."

[intended to] stem the capacity for corruption."[58] But to say that it "has a Sharʿī ruling" does not mean that there is specific textual evidence or a scriptural indicant to support it, but rather that its rationale is subsumed under the general principles and goals of the law (*qawāʿid al-sharʿ*), since stemming corruption on Earth is integral to the principles and goals of promoting human flourishing (*baqāʾ al-ʿālam*).

Continuing the effort to define the term, Ibn ʿĀbidīn conflates *siyāsa* with *taʿzīr*, saying that they are synonymous and are thus used with the same level of clarity either aggregately or interchangeably. Some jurists, he adds, use only the term *taʿzīr*, for the meaning of this term is akin to the desiderata of *siyāsa* in that the purpose of the latter is deterrence. It is not necessarily a response to an actual violation or a criminal offense, for it could well be ethically instructive and future oriented.[59]

Both criminal punishment and corrective behavior (*taʿzīr=siyāsa*) are the mandate of the ruler, usually expressed in juristic works with the phrase "*al-taʿzīr mawkūl/mufawwaḍ ilā raʾy al-imām*."[60] By the early thirteenth/nineteenth century, jurists no longer seem pressed to introduce the older language of whether or not, or the extent to which, the *qāḍī* shares the sphere of *siyāsa* with the executive authorities. Rather, Ibn ʿĀbidīn and his authorities, for instance, take it for granted, stating as a matter of course that the *qāḍī* shares this jurisdiction with the ruler: "the act of *siyāsa* is the mandate of the *qāḍī* as well, for the expression '*imām*' [as in "*al-taʿzīr mawkūl ilā raʾy al-imām*"] is not intended to exclude the *qāḍī* but rather to refer to the imam as the source (*aṣl*) [of authority]; for the *qāḍī* is his deputy in implementing the law."[61] Yet, the general rule remains that for the exception of major crime committed by habitual criminals (such as murderers), the *taʿzīr* punishment cannot exceed that of the *ḥudūd* within each category. The difference remains that the *ḥadd* is fixed while the *taʿzīr* is up to the *qāḍī*'s or the imam's discretion.

Another major difference is that the *ḥadd* punishment is mitigated upon the slightest doubt (*shubha*), while *taʿzīr* becomes obligatory precisely when doubt gains ground.[62] Furthermore, the *ḥadd* punishment cannot be suspended

58 *RMI*, VI, 20; *SSD*, 73-74.

59 *RMI*, VI, 20: "*Al-taʿẓīr[u] taʾdīb[un]... wa-lā yalzamu an yakūna bi-muqābalati maʿṣiya.*"

60 *RMI*, VI, 21, 103.

61 *RMI*, VI, 21, but especially 104.

62 *RMI*, VI, 103: "*Al-ḥaddu yudraʾu bil-shubuhāti wal-taʿzīru yajibu maʿhā.*" He likewise lists secondary differences, such as that the *ḥudūd* cannot be implemented for minors but *taʿzīr*, being an instructive and correctional measure, is in fact lawfully non-optional in

or mitigated, whereas the *ta'zīr* is proportional to the crime and relative to the social status of the perpetrator. The rebuke of a person hailing from a high social status – considered demeaning in the extreme and therefore punitive – would not be sufficient in the case of the miscreants or dregs of society.[63]

There seem to have been two *ta'zīr/siyāsa* punishments to which the Ottomans commonly made recourse, and which elicited substantial juristic discussion. The first is banishment (*taghrīb*), usually for one year, according to a stipulation of a Prophetic report. Ibn 'Ābidīn lists various juristic opinions and Companion reports and concludes therefrom that banishment is not a desirable penalty, because sending a convict away to a locale and social context in which he lacks supervision and societal guidance is not conducive to improving his behavior – the very telos of *ta'zīr/siyāsa*. Yet, if the imam (or *qāḍī*) sees it fit that a particular criminal be banished, "then he has the competence to do so."[64]

The second punishment, quite common, is *ta'zīr* by extracting wealth. Unlike Dede Efendī and other jurists,[65] Ibn 'Ābidīn vies against this practice of *siyāsa*, saying that in "our *madhhab* there is no taking of money" as a form of *ta'zīr*.[66] The Chief Justice and distinguished jurist Abū Yūsuf, he says, reportedly approved the practice as a matter of law, but Abū Ḥanīfa and Shaybānī, as well as "the rest of major jurists" in the Ḥanafī school did not.[67] Some jurists permitted temporary expropriation of wealth but required a complete refund upon repentance or when the violator demonstrates compliance with the law. The only situation in which expropriation of wealth is permitted (other than cases of common theft) is when someone seizes public funds illegally, in which case the wealth or money should be returned to the Public Treasury.[68]

Finally, Ibn 'Ābidīn deals with the fundamental issue of *tuhma*, the site of the crucial controversy which the latter-day Ḥanbalīs created and which Ibn Farḥūn, as we have seen, synthesized and integrated into mainstream jurisprudence. Ibn 'Ābidīn significantly begins his discussion with this

---

their case (*shar'un 'alayhi*). For the same reason, *ta'zīr* at large is also the responsibility of non-governmental individuals, such as teachers and parents.

63 *RMI*, VI, 106.

64 *RMI*, VI, 19-20: "*Fa-lahu an yaf'alahu.*"

65 *RMI*, VI, 106, ll. 11-12.

66 *RMI*, VI, 105: "*Lā bi-akhdhi mālin fil-madhhab.*"

67 *RMI*, VI, 105-106: "*Wa-'an Abī Yūsufa: yajūzu al-ta'zīru lil-sulṭāni bi-akhdhi al-māli, wa-'inda-humā* [i.e., Abū Ḥanīfa and Shaybānī] *wa-bāqī al-a'immati lā yajūz.*"

68 *RMI*, VI, 106.

language: "In the book of *kafāla*, they [*vis.* the jurists] stated that *tuhma* is proven by two *mastūr*[69] witnesses or a single *ʿadl* witness, which means that if one *mastūr* and one *fāsiq* witness testify before a *qāḍī* to the effect that a person/defendant is *fāsiq*, then the judge cannot imprison him [as a matter of *taʿzīr/siyāsa*]. But he can do so if both witnesses are *mastūr*."[70] It is quite significant that the issue of character-vetting is discussed in the chapter of *kafāla* (guaranty), rather than, for example, in criminal procedural law or the rules of evidence in the chapter of *bayyināt*. We will see in due course that communal cohesion and collective opinion and evaluation are crucial for criminal proceedings. But the point here is that the evidentiary bar for criminal conviction hinges on a single just witness (*ʿadl*) or two *mastūr* witnesses, namely, persons confirmed to be neither *ʿadl* in character nor corrupt (*fāsiq*).

Communal knowledge can result in lowering the bar of standard evidentiary requirements even further. If the accused is notorious for engaging in corruption (*mashhūr bil-fasād*), then the *qāḍī*'s knowledge is sufficient to convict him.[71] This, however, is not as subjective as it may appear at first blush, for what is involved here are multiple chains of attestation, since the knowledge derived is neither individual nor limited to a handful of witnesses. Rather, it is widespread communal knowledge, where error is most unlikely to take place.[72]

Drawing on Dede Efendī's treatise again, Ibn ʿĀbidīn cites no other than the Ḥanbalī Ibn al-Qayyim's by now well-known passage to the effect that not a single Muslim jurist ever upheld the opinion that a person whose character is associated with *tuhma* is to be left without arrest or imprisonment. It is interesting that Ibn ʿĀbidīn's source for Ibn al-Qayyim is not Ṭarābulsī but Dede Efendī. Equally interesting is the citation of the Ḥanafī al-Zaylaʿī (who must be ʿUthmān b. ʿAlī; d. 743/1342)[73] to the effect that a

69 "*Mastūr*" is a person who is known neither for tarnished nor untarnished reputation, which is to say that he or she has not been vetted as being of just or unjust character. On the technical meaning of *mastūr*, see Jurjānī, *Taʿrīfāt*, 210. A person who is *ʿadl*, by contrast, is one who has been vetted as trustworthy and of impeachable character.

70 *RMI*, VI, 126.

71 *RMI*, VI, 126.

72 The concept of the *mashhūr* is also an epistemic category of Ḥadīth-criticism and evaluation that goes to establishing the authenticity of Prophetic reports. On the analytics and logical structure of transmission/witnessing, see Hallaq, "On Inductive Corroboration," 3-31.

73 Zaylaʿī does not appear in Ibn ʿĀbidīn's list of sources which he acknowledges to be his authorities in writing the work. See his introduction to *RMI*, I, 69-74.

qāḍī, to extract confession, can lawfully beat an accused who is associated with *tuhma*.[74] But Ibn ʿĀbidīn asserts that this can be done only upon the availability of evidentiary proof, as he stated above. The *qāḍī*'s knowledge, in other words, cannot stand on its own but must be based on testimonial evidence that reflects either communal knowledge, confession, or the attestation of witnesses.[75]

III

Now that we have a fairly good sketch of jurisprudential and constitutional developments from pre- to late-Ottoman times, it would be auspicious to check the theory we have described thus far against practice, if only to examine the degree to which the latter conformed to the former; or, rather conversely, to check the extent to which the jurists' discourse reflected the realpolitik and actual modes of governance that dominated during Mamlūk and Ottoman times, the two periods – worth together at least six centuries – most heavily documented in Islamic history.

The Ottoman concept of governance rested on the assumption that the law of the land is the Sharīʿa, and that the sultanic executive is mandated by the Sharīʿa to manage the spheres assigned to it as a matter of constitutional specialization. As we saw in Māwardī, and later in all writings of other jurists dealing with the subject, the ruler is responsible for specific and well-defined tasks, all of which belong to executive competence, and none of which is strictly legislative. These tasks include (1) the securitization of the borders and internal network of roads; (2) the preservation of religious institutions, their personnel, and various practices of communal ritual; (3) developing the cities, irrigation canals, bridges, and other public works throughout the sultanic domains; and (4) collection of taxes and management of land – effectively the payoff for the foregoing services. But the most relevant of the tasks for our present concerns is (5) the sultanic executive's charge to implement the *ḥudūd* and to hold *maẓālim* tribunals, a charge that encompasses the duty to manage the sphere of *taʿzīr*. As Ibn ʿĀbidīn has just averred, *taʿzīr*, in its best form, is nothing but *siyāsa sharʿiyya*.

74 *RMI*, VI, 126.
75 *RMI*, VI, 126-27.

The overwhelming evidence from both Mamlūk and Ottoman periods points to the fact that this constitutional understanding was both unquestioned and unquestionable, notwithstanding the occasional violations of the law (on this point see the Introduction, above). The Ottomans promulgated *qānūnnāmes* that were intended to serve the ultimate goals of the Sharʿ,[76] and they did so within the constitutional framework that Māwardī and all later Muslim jurists tenaciously upheld.[77]

A survey of the Ottoman Criminal Code (*OCC*)[78] reveals that the vast bulk of its articles belong mostly to two or three of the duties of the ruler that Māwardī and Ibn Jamāʿa, among others, stipulated. Articles 1-9, 13, 22-35, 54-55, 57, 100, 113-14, and 124 (all relating to sexual offenses), and articles 36-53, 56, 58-82, 87-94, 98, 104-9, 112, 117-22 (relating to abduction, bodily harm, homicide, theft and alcohol consumption) belong to the second and fourth duties on Māwardī's list and to the fourth and sixth on Ibn Jamāʿa's list. Articles 83-88, dealing with safety of the caravanserai, are covered under the third and fourth duties in Māwardī and the first and sixth in Ibn Jamāʿa. The remaining dozen articles, dealing with taxation, *qāḍī*'s supervision, duty to pray, interest (*ribā*), disturbing the peace, etc. fall under duties 1, 2, 3, 8, 9, and 10 in Māwardī's list, and duties 1, 2, 3, 4, 6, and 7 in Ibn Jamāʿa's.[79] *None of the 126 articles making up the qānūnnāme's text concerns itself with a matter outside the purview of the duties on the two jurists' lists.* What is most remarkable is that the *qānūnnāme*, in its entirety and in all of its varied and diverse subject matter, fits comfortably within the overall scope of these duties. Even if we add the famous *Qānūnnāma Miṣr* (promulgated in 931/1525) to this comparison, the tally between the juristic demands and the *qānūnnāmes* fares even better, since the latter also deals with administrative and military organization.

As the preamble of the *Qānūnnāme Miṣr* declared, "the Ottoman sultans have, since olden times, laid down regulations (*qānūn*) in conformity with

76 This is not to say that the *qānūn* always conformed to the Sharīʿa and its *fiqh*. In fact, at times it did not, although, generally speaking, conformity far outweighed divergence. A notable such divergence in the *OCC*, for instance, is the monetization of fines, especially for *zinā* (fornication and adultery). Instead of the corporal punishments (which differed in the cases of married and unmarried convicts), a graded fine was imposed, depending on the economic status of the individual. See, for instance, *OCC*, art. 1-6.

77 See Heyd, *Studies*, 201-2, and my critique of Heyd's thesis below.

78 On Heyd's dating and methods of compilation of this code from various sources, see Halil İnalcik's critique in his review of the work, 696-98.

79 See analysis of Māwardī and Ibn Jamāʿa's list of the ruler's duties above, ch. 1, sec. II, and ch. 7.

the Sharīʿa and anyone who commits a crime is to be punished in accordance with them."[80] Modern scholars have also perceptively noticed that several other *qānūnnāmes* also speak of their own telos, namely, the protection of the population against the oppression of government officials, not to mention criminal conduct. Which is to say that the *qānūn* identifies itself as being integral to the framework and concept of the *maẓālim*.[81]

Indicative of the primacy of the Sharīʿa in the Ottoman *qānūn* system is the fact that the *qāḍī* and his court feature prominently across the board of *siyāsa* administration.[82] Inspection, auditing, reporting and much else are added (or have indeed been for long integral) to his adjudicative duties. He is involved with the governor and other government officials, almost on equal footing, in inspecting and auditing the Public Treasury, tax collection, and *waqf* foundations; supervising residential occupancy, land surveyorship, land distribution, implementing gun control, levying and reporting maritime custom duties, and much else.[83] Other than the provincial governor, the sultan and vizier, the *qāḍī* appears to have been involved in most government business, at least in the Ottoman Empire.

The *qāḍī*'s court (*majlis*) was central to the overall administration of the empire. We recall the foregoing juristic debate about venue. The debate seems open-ended and quite pliable, a picture contrasted sharply by the insistence of the *qānūn* (i.e., the will of the sultanic executive itself) on the *qāḍī*'s court as the default venue. Article 41 of *Qānūnnāme* of Egypt stipulates:

> When people engage in dispute and conflict, they seek the governor of the city (*vali-i şehir*/*wālī al-madīna*) in order to have him settle their disputes, and [they do so] before they go to the Sharʿī court. This practice is forbidden. The governor shall not settle any dispute without the [prior] knowledge of the *qāḍī*. He must send all litigants to the Sharʿī *qāḍī* before anything else, so that the *qāḍī* adjudicates in accordance with the rules of the Sharīʿa. The Chief of Police then executes [the *qāḍī*'s] decision. The governor shall not implement a matter without the knowledge of the *qāḍī*. If someone disobeys this

80 Heyd's translation. See his *Studies*, 3, and Atçil, *Scholars and Sultans*, 96

81 Heyd, *Studies*, 3; Atçil, *Scholars and Sultans*, 96 (and sources cited in n. 44). See also the *Qanunama Mısr*, art. 23.

82 Ziyādah, *al-Ṣūra al-Taqlīdiyya*, 46-48, 57.

83 *Qānūnnāma Miṣr*, articles 2, 27, 35, 44, 45, 46; Ziyādah, *al-Ṣūra al-Taqlīdiyya*, 61.

> after the present warning, he shall be dismissed from office and may be liable to punishment.

The centrality of the *qāḍī*'s office in the Ottoman imperial administration was such that copies of the *qānūnnāmes*, at least most of them, had to be delivered to all law courts under their purview – since *qānūnnāmes* were variably applicable to cities and their environs, districts, provinces, or to the empire as a whole. The typical practice was for *qānūnnāmes* to be bound and sent to all courts in their stipulated jurisdictions, with the instruction that the *qāḍīs* were to administer justice "in accordance with the noble *sharīʿa* and the *qānūnnāmes* deposited in the courts of law."[84] The *qāḍīs* were duty-bound to record the contents of the *qānūnnāme* in the court's register (*sijill, dīwān, maḥḍar*).[85] Yet, and as if to underscore the integral relevance of the *qānūn* to *siyāsa*, it was common practice for copies of criminal *qānūnnāmes* to be so deposited in the *qāḍī*'s courts, but not those that pertained to taxation and land. These latter, usually delivered only to provincial and district governors, were the exclusive business of the executive administration, the *qāḍīs* having played a marginal role in this sphere, and only when the governor needed them for the auxiliary tasks of auditing, supervision, or the like.[86]

The *qāḍīs* were thus heavily involved in the application of criminal law as it came down entwined with the *qānūn/siyāsa* and the Sharīʿa. Prosecution of criminals started in the Sharīʿa court, where it was standard procedure for the executive officials (*subaşis, ehl-i ʿörf*) to bring claims before the *qāḍīs* against individuals suspected of crime, asking them to investigate and issue a verdict in accordance with the *qānūn/siyāsa*.[87] The *qāḍī*'s court was likewise the venue for private individuals to bring such claims. The *qāḍī* would often issue decrees to the effect that certain individuals accused of committing a crime be dispatched to the executive officers with a view to being tortured.[88] In these cases, the *tuhma* association would be established.

But the *qāḍīs* also played an equally important function in maintaining a system of checks and balances vis-à-vis executive power. At least as early as

84 Heyd, *Studies*, 18, 151. Citation (at p. 151) is taken from a sultanic decree (*ʿadāletnāme*) in Mehmet III's reign (1595-1602).
85 Heyd, *Studies*, 151.
86 Peters, *Crime*, 93.
87 *OCC*, art. 88. (in Heyd, *Studies*, 132-47).
88 Heyd, *Studies*, 152.

the reign of sultan Sulaymān the Magnificent, the *qāḍī*s were endowed with sufficient powers as to constitute checks on the actions of executive officials. They were put in charge of monitoring the legality of these actions, deciding on whether or not these officials can remand into custody or torture individuals accused of committing a crime.[89]

With the turn of successive sultanic reigns after Sulaymān the Magnificent, *qānūnnāme*s were subjected to constant revision. Oftentimes, the corrections to the *qānūnnāme*s appear to be due to the jurists' objections, and so various articles and stipulations were struck down on the grounds that they contradict the Sharīʿa. The most common commentary on these *qānūnnāme*s ran something like this: "The injunction of the holy law is valid; there is no *qānūn* (in this matter)."[90] Some of the latest emendations and repeals, according to Heyd, were apparently made according to *fatwā*s as well as quotations from authoritative Ḥanafī *fiqh* works, all of which were to the effect of demonstrating the contradictions in the provisions of the *qānūnnāme*s.[91] Article 116 of the *OCC* stipulates that "The executive officers (ehl-i ʿörf) shall not imprison and hurt any person unless [he is convicted] by the cadi." Furthermore, if any fine "more than what is due" is imposed by these officers, "the cadi shall give judgment with respect to the excess of the fine and let [the offender] recover [it]."

It was not just the *qānūn*'s legality that was evaluated by the standards of Sharīʿa's substantive law, this being the hermeneutical object of the *fatwā*. The *fatwā*, throughout the well-nigh millennium of Islamic legal history before the Ottomans, was an integral part of the *qāḍī*'s court, where at times a *muftī* would be a constant member of the "court audience."[92] But when he was not, hard cases were often referred to him by the *qāḍī* himself, and more often by the litigants themselves, even if the case was routine. In other words, the *qāḍī* was always functioning under the rubric of Sharīʿa's supervision, on

89 Peters, *Crime*, 75, 76.

90 Heyd, *Studies*, 149-50.

91 Heyd, *Studies*, 150, 153-55. The virtue of Heyd's work lies in the fact that he reproduces extensive citations, often verbatim, from the Ottoman archives. His narrative throughout the book combines history in the traditional sense and descriptions of archival materials, making the latter, on the whole, the center of his interest. This is in addition to the fact that his work contains the texts of *qānūnnāme*s and translations into English (56 131, *OCC*; 132-47, Dulkadir Regulations).

92 See, e.g., Jennings, "Kadi, Court, and legal Procedure," 134-36, 142-48; Hallaq, "'Qāḍī's *Dīwān*' (*Sijill*) before the Ottomans," 415–436; Hallaq, *Authority*, 174-95, 66-75 and passim; Hallaq, *Introduction*, 9-13, 60-64; Imber, *Ebu's-Suʿud*, 7.

the one hand, and dispensing justice with the assistance of executive powers, on the other.[93]

Ottoman criminal law closely echoed the juristic discussions with regard to *tuhma* (suspicion), addressing legal situations accordingly. Executive officials were in principle entitled to torture suspected persons (*müttehem*) in order to extract confession, but only if the "suspicion" is proven as warranted. It was the exclusive prerogative of the *qāḍī* to establish whether or not there are sufficient grounds for such a suspicion to hold, grounds that required a judicial inquiry into the communal reputation of the individual concerned, the existence of a criminal record, or the presence of a motive, such as an enmity between him and the victim on whose behalf the matter has been litigated.[94] The executive officers, on the other hand, were not empowered to engage in any of these procedures.

Speaking of the administration of justice in eleventh/seventeenth-century Kayseri, Jennings has this to say:

> The people of Kayseri knew this legal system guaranteed them a number of divinely ordained inalienable rights which no official could take away. Every inhabitant of the province (except the imperial *kul*) was guaranteed rights of life, liberty, and the pursuit of happiness, as well as inalienable rights of property. Hence the Porte [viz. central government in Istanbul, WH] could order the Karaman beglerbegi to kill the Kayseri sancak begi as a brigand; but if the suspected brigand was a poor villager, even a zimmi, the Porte would only pass along the complaint it had received and order the kadi to look into the matter and to carry out the *şer*ʿ. Every inhabitant had an unequivocal right to a public hearing before an imperial judge [=*qāḍī*] and to the due process of law. He was considered innocent until proven guilty (or having become notorious). Even the fiat of the sultan did not alter these rights.[95]

Specifically, the *qāḍī*'s court also represented to the consumers of justice a venue in which they could seek protection against potential accusations of *tuhma*. An illustrative case may be found in a *qāḍī*'s court in Salonika, where,

93 See Ginio, "Administration of Criminal Justice," 185-209, esp. at 209; Jennings, "Kadi, Court, and Legal Procedure," 136. See also sources cited in the previous note.

94 Peters, *Crime*, 77; *OCC*, art. 43.

95 Jennings, "Kadi, Court, and Legal Procedure," 141-42.

in the twelfth/eighteenth century, a group of elders approached the court to make a deposition to the effect that a certain Niko had an irreproachable reputation (that is, he is not a subject of *tuhma*). This latter, anticipating the plans of an executive officer to arrest him on a charge of theft, had the elders preempt the charge, through the deposition, at the *qāḍī*'s court.[96] Thus, for *tuhma* to constitute the grounds of a lawful charge, it must be entered as a claim into the court's record. From this point onwards, and until the charge is proved or disproved – a process that may involve communal participation as part of the necessary evidentiary proof – it is the *qāḍī*, and only the *qāḍī*, who administers and conducts the whole process. The executive officers can bring a claim to the court – very much like public prosecutors nowadays – and they must execute the *qāḍī*'s judgment, but they do not have any powers to determine the process in between. Judicially speaking, the *qānūn* and the *siyāsa* conception that underlies it thus fell entirely under the *qāḍī*'s jurisdiction.[97] As we saw and will continue to see, this accommodation represented both sultanic political will and Sharī'a's response to socio-political exigencies.[98]

In an important work on Ottoman criminal law,[99] Heyd argued that the *qānūn* was gradually discarded after the tenth/sixteenth century. Taxation, land tenure, and crime – the three spheres that constituted the *qānūn*'s domain and fields of operation – were increasingly brought, by sultanic decrees, under the purview of the Sharī'a.[100] At times, as evident in a *qānūnnāme* issued by Mehmet IV in 1081/1670, these imperial decrees explicitly cited the practices of the Rāshidūn caliphs in these three spheres as an expression of Shar'ī will.[101] In 1107/1696, sultan Muṣṭafā II issued a *firmān* in which he asserted that all matters, whether private or public, were to be categorically regulated and adjudicated by the Qur'ān and the Sharī'a.[102] No penalties were to be implemented unless they were grounded in the holy law. "Interference by anyone else in the commands of the illustrious *Sharī'a* is null and is rejected." The *firmān* goes on to say that even associating the term "*qānūn*" with that of "Sharī'a" (as in the oft-used language in imperial orders "to implement

96 Ginio, "Administration of Criminal Justice," 185-209, at 204; also Peters, *Crime*, 77.
97 Jennings, "Kadi, Court, and Legal Procedure," 137-42.
98 The accommodation was also reflected in Ottoman political culture at large. See Darling, "Political Literature."
99 See n. 91, above.
100 Heyd, *Studies*, 152-57, at 153.
101 Heyd, *Studies*, 153.
102 Tezcan, *Second Ottoman Empire*, 27.

the decrees of the *qānūn* and Shar') was both "unbefitting" and a "massive sinning."[103] The *firmān* issues a grave warning "against coupling of the [terms?] noble *sharīʿa* and *kānūn*."[104]

By the 1100s/1700s, the word *qānūn* dropped out of usage in many *firmāns* and *ʿadāletnāmes*, though by no means in all. "But," Heyd asserted, "there can be little doubt that in the course of the seventeenth and eighteenth centuries the Ottoman Criminal Code was gradually discarded as a source of penal law, and finally completely forgotten."[105] But even more generally, it would not be an exaggeration at all to say that the very practice of *qānūn* promulgation in all spheres of Ottoman administration underwent a drastic diminution,[106] to the extent that "[n]o new comprehensive codes were issued during this period [1600-1800]."[107]

In a section titled "The Code Discarded," Heyd attempts to give an explanation as to why the *qānūn* largely fell out of use. One of the reasons he advances is that the taxes stipulated in these sultanic decrees did not change enough over more than two centuries, despite marked devaluations in currency. It is "no wonder" then that "those authorized to collect fines completely disregarded the prescriptions of the kanun."[108] This, however, does not so much explain the decline in the issuance of, or the will to propound, the *qānūns* – which is the case in point – as it explains the refusal to abide by the substance of the *qānūn* decrees – two different matters altogether.

Another reason he advances is that the "military authorities" – by which he means executive officials – were "anxious to get rid of these regulations, which limited their freedom of action, especially in regard to the imposition of excessive fines." This reason of course does not do any explanatory work, since it is trumped by the question of why the earlier executives, Ottoman or otherwise, could not prevent the rise of the *qānūn* in the first place, it being taken for granted that their will to free themselves of such constraints had always existed. This is in addition to the fact that being anxious to bring the *qānūn* down does not automatically translate into an actual power against the central sultanic authority. But Heyd promptly adds that "the decline of the Central

103 For the text of the *Qānūn* as conforming to the Sharīʿa, see Abou-El-Haj, "Power and Social Order," 99. It is noteworthy that Abou-El-Haj describes this Qānūn as "a radical 'constitutional' amendment" (p. 83).

104 Heyd, *Studies*, 154-55; see also İnalcik, "Kānūn," 560a.

105 Heyd, *Studies*, 155. See also Tezcan, *Second Ottoman Empire*, 27, 30.

106 Tezcan, *Second Ottoman Empire*, 24 ff.

107 Abou-El-Haj, "Power and Social Order," 91.

108 Heyd, 156-57, which cover all the reasons for the *qānūn*'s decline.

Government's power and its increasing inability to restrain its officials" is the overarching reason due to which all other factors were subsidiary. Yet, what is truly at stake here is the very concept of decline, an Orientalist trope that cannot be taken for granted.

The paradigm of decline in Heyd's mind seems to overshadow multiple considerations. In a note which he wrote on the margin of his manuscript, and which the editor, V. L. Ménage, posthumously incorporated in the published version, he noted that among other possible reasons for the *qānūn*'s decline is that "law, like other fields of inquiry, was affected by the general intellectual stagnation which prevailed in the later years of the Ottoman Empire." One wonders how this, assuming it is true, can explain anything about the central authority's will to enforce certain regulations, most, if not all, of which require nothing more than an elementary education.[109]

Finally, the most interesting reason Heyd proffered was this: that the "cadis and other *ʿulema*, whose political power and influence increased considerably during the seventeenth and eighteenth centuries, had never fully countenanced the criminal regulations of the *kānun*, particularly where they were contrary to the *sharīʿa*."[110] But full acceptance is not a condition of possibility for the decline and fizzling out of the *qānūn*. The jurists could and did object to some provisions of these regulations, hence the corrections that were made to it over the eleventh/seventeenth and twelfth/eighteenth centuries (see above). Opposition has no necessary logical correlation or entailment with the drastic weakening in the very production of the *qānūn*, at source or as a species. Put differently, like their executive counterparts in the provinces, the jurists and ulama at large could object to certain provisions of the *qānūn* endlessly, but that does not exactly translate into the loss of central power's interest in, or capability of, issuing them. Empire never rests on the total satisfaction of its own servants, much less its own subjects. As we will see in the next chapter,

109 For examples of the "intellectual level" of the *qānūnnāmes*, see *Qānūnnāme Miṣr* and the *OCC*.

110 Heyd, *Studies*, 156. This narrative of the *qānūn*'s decline is also consistent with Yilmaz, "Containing Sultanic Authority," 238: "Despite his designation as the head of the ulema in the code of Mehmed II, unlike the grand vizier, the şeyhülislam barely possessed any executive power until the early sixteenth century. He never had a regular seat in the imperial council, and his superiority to the grand vizier was only honorary. But during the sixteenth and seventeenth centuries, şeyhulıslams successfully exploited their honorary position to acquire political authority and began to exert a more orderly influence on government, especially after gaining control of educational institutions (*medreses*) and the judiciary. By the seventeenth century, şeyhülislams were frequently participating in the imperial council meetings or hosting major consultative gatherings (*meclis-i meşveret*) at their residences."

the jurists' stiff opposition to the *qānūn*, and the final ascendancy of the Sharīʿa over it, were related to the empire's extensive needs to depend on the latter for the administration of a far-flung empire. The *qānūn* was originally installed for the organized, uniform, and well-structured extraction of surplus production from the provinces, this being integral to establishing a consistent and, most importantly, centralized and overarching administrative system.[111] But once this system was installed and set in motion, the Sharīʿa increasingly took over the task of its day-to-day functioning, finally rendering it, by dint of further socio-economic transformations,[112] a nearly defunct intrusion.

Later in the book, and in a discussion of the "doctrine of *siyāsa sharʿiyya*," Heyd speaks rather accurately of the "close similarity" of the *qānūn* to "*siyāsa sharʿiyya* as elaborated by the Muslim legists," although his view of the similar pair as independent entities is highly problematic. The *qānūn*, he recognizes, is "a supplement to the *sharīʿa*," and "claims to help in achieving [its] fundamental objects [sic] by making it easier to bring the truth to light, to punish criminals adequately, and to deter potential offenders."[113]

Heyd then proceeds to make a most accurate observation, namely, that the objective of both domains was "to bridge the gulf between the two separate jurisdictions, the religious and the secular, by making the cadis too apply the criminal regulations outside the strict *sharīʿa* law."[114] In point of fact, Heyd could have made his argument stronger had he noticed that the elimination of the *maẓālim* courts under the Ottomans[115] bore directly on the Ottomans' "great" efforts to "eliminate the dichotomy in regard both to the two separate jurisdictions, the administrative and the judicial, and to the two different systems of law, the customary [i.e., *qānūn*, WH] and the religious."[116] The elimination of the *maẓālim* by subsuming their work under the *qāḍī*'s jurisdiction was the final act whereby the extrajudicial apparatus of governance (what scholars wrongly describe as secular justice) was not only subordinated to the Sharʿī judicial and administrative organs but was made to comport with their legal precepts in general, and rules of procedure, in particular.

111 Abou-El-Haj, "Power and Social Order," 78, 91.
112 To be discussed briefly in the next chapter.
113 Heyd, *Studies*, 201-2.
114 Heyd, *Studies*, 202.
115 See Jennings, "Kadi, Court, and Legal Procedure," 148 f.: "The Kayseri 'police' had no *maẓālim* court to which to turn and they were responsible to and responsive to the kadi in matters of law enforcement. They were subject to the šerʿ personally and officially in the performance of their duties." See also p. 136.
116 Heyd, *Studies*, 2.

It did not seem to occur to Heyd that this act of streamlining is precisely why the *qānūn* was waning after the eleventh/sixteenth century. Whatever the exact historical details that contributed to the integration of the *qāḍī*s into the criminal administration of *siyāsa shar'iyya*, it is clear – even from our mapping of the Mamlūk and early Ottoman jurists[117] – that long before the Ottomans attained the "status" of empire (i.e., prior to 800/1400), the process of integration had already begun.

With our current knowledge of the Mamlūk period, it is difficult to say whether the integration was due to political need or juristic dominance, that is, whether it was the sultanic administration of polity or the venture of the jurists as guardians of the Community that made the conjunction possible. My own sense is that it was both, with the latter having in fact the greater force. The increasing professionalization and social power of the ulama made them indispensable for political governance – they effectively filled all important administrative functions, and ran the administration of the empire, as they have done before, according to a *diwān*ic culture largely shaped by Shar'ī imperatives. This, in conjunction with their discursive and ideological power, paved the grounds for them to seize on the need of the executive to legitimize its rule and optimize its efficiency.

Getting the jurists on board meant not only that the executive's work and investment in the criminal field is reduced, but also that the unification of the criminal system under the Sharī'a and its men would render governance at once more efficient and wholly legitimate. This is the arrangement that was juristically prepared for and constructed by the end of the fourteenth century in the Mamlūk domains, and it is the same arrangement that was brought to full consummation by the Ottomans during the four centuries prior to Europe's colonialist ventures. Heyd would have offered a more convincing interpretation of the invaluable body of evidence he had gathered had he studied the jurisprudential developments that occurred during the Mamlūk and Ottoman eras.

IV

I have thus far deliberately left out an account of the investment that the legal and political capital of the Mamlūk period made in this development.

117 See the three foregoing chapters.

This is because, I argue, it was the second half of the Mamlūk rule that was in some significant ways the exception, rather than the rule, to the general contours of Islamic legal and constitutional history (an exception on which most legal Orientalists capitalized with a view to universalizing their findings to Islamic history in general). I thus also argue that modern scholarship in the West has not done well in generalizing from this relatively short period about much of Islamic legal and political history, especially in light of the fact that this period is often studied from a legal perspective without any regard to the specific worldly context that produced it – "worldly context" here meaning anything from economic and military conditions to natural disasters and plagues. As if law and the legal system are insulated from famine, collapse of the agricultural and industrial systems, natural disasters, and so much else of the like, modern scholarship goes on to write the legal history of the Mamlūks with no attention to these associated phenomena, despite the fact that scholarship on the Mamlūk infrastructures of agriculture, demography, economy, and social disintegration is fairly abundant.[118]

118 It seems that the most pronounced problem in the study of Egypt's history during the last century and a half of Mamlūk rule is the fact that historians remain largely insulated within their own field of expertise. Historians of epidemics appear detached from agricultural and demographic historians, and these in turn from political and legal historians – and the cycle of disciplinary segregation seems to largely perpetuate itself (exceptions may be found in such works as those of Janet Abu-Lughod's enduring work *Before European Hegemony*, 236-39; and Qāsim, *ʿAṣr Salāṭīn al-Mamālīk*, 159-190). Reading a variety of sources from all these historical specializations reveals a complex and complicated picture of intimate interconnections and interrelations between the onset of the Black Death, depopulation, the Nile flooding, famine, and the disintegration of the basic infrastructures that had enabled a reasonable order of governance and the maintenance of polity. No one who reads this literature – and I have by no means perused even most of it – will retain any doubt as to the astounding conditions that ruled Egypt as of 748-49/1347, when the first major plague assaulted the country mercilessly. Told in a rudimentary manner, the story of this devastation combined the following various elements:
(1) As of 749/1347, and probably before, Egypt and Syria were hit with a major wave of the Black Death, a disease originating in China or Mongolia and transmitted through the Silk Road. It appears that major environmental disturbances led to zoological changes that drove "rodents beyond their normally very restricted habitat into contact with domestic rodents and human settlements, carrying the epizootic with them." Dols, *Black Death in the Middle East*, 39; Ibn al-Wardī, *Tatimmat al-Mukhtaṣar*, II, 497-500. On average thereafter, Egypt and Syria suffered an assault about every seven years until the end of Mamlūk rule. For a chronology of plagues during the Mamlūk rule (occurring in 1347-49, 1360-64, 1373-75, 1379-81, 1388-89, 1397-98, 1403-07, 1410-11, 1415-19, 1429-30, 1438-39, 1444-49, 1455, 1459-60, 1468-69, 1476-77, 1492, 1498, 1504-05, and 1513-14), see Shoshan, "Notes sur les épidémies de peste en Egypte," 395–403. For a vividly detailed report on the 832-33/1429-

30 plague in the Eastern Mediterranean, see Ibn Ṭaghrībirdī, *Nujūm*, XIV, 237-45. On the general conditions of Egypt in the ninth/fifteenth century from a social point of view, see Elbendary, *Crowds and Sultans*, 19-69.
(2) As a consequence of the pandemic, Egypt was considerably depopulated. For example, as a result of just two major epidemics in 833/1430 and 864/1460 (and possibly 749/1347), it is estimated that a little less than half of Cairo's population vanished. Statistical estimates are to be found in Borsch and Sabraa, "Plague Mortality in Late Medieval Cairo;" see also Holt, *Age of the Crusades*, 194-95. In Alexandria alone, it is estimated that in the beginning of the first major plague of 749/1347, some 200 people died every day, and at its peak, the pestilence killed about 7,000 a day. See Borsch, "Plague Depopulation and Irrigation Decay," 125; Ibn Iyās, *Badāʾiʿ al-Zuhūr*, I, 528, gives a total number of 900,000 deaths in Cairo for the same wave.
(3) As a consequence of depopulation but also because of what appears to have been a natural increase in the Nile's body of water, lower Egypt, with much of its agricultural land, was constantly and ruinously flooded, partly due to the lack of maintenance of irrigation canals and dikes. One historian estimates that during the Mamlūk rule, the water level rose "almost twice as much as it had increased in the previous five centuries," with "90% of this increase occur[ing] in the 150 years following the arrival of the Black Death [in 749/1347] and the onset of repeated plague epidemics." See Borsch, "Nile Floods and the Irrigation," 134. Borsch sums up the consequences of the flooding, the Plague and decay in the irrigation system in these words: "Starting with the Black Death [of 1347-48], and continuing over the century and a half that followed, plague depopulation brought about the ruin of Egypt's irrigation system, the motor of its economy. For many generations, the Egyptians who survived the plague therefore faced a tragic new reality: a transformed landscape and way of life significantly worsened by plague, a situation very different from that of plague survivors in Europe" (156).
(4) With the massive collapse of the irrigation system, there emerged large swathes of wasteland suitable for grazing livestock. This effectively invited the Bedouins to invade these lands, which contributed to the growth in their numbers and power. The Bedouins were mostly immune to the plague because they lived away from the densely populated towns and cities, and because their modes of economic existence were more autarchic and primary. These factors "thus opened a large ecological niche which allowed the Bedouin to turn many areas of organized basin agriculture into pastoral land upon which they flourished." See Borsch, "Nile Floods," 139. If the Mamlūk regime had always faced the problem of Bedouin incursions and harassment of the urban population, after the Plague it had to reckon with the problem multiplied; and
(5) The plague and its associated consequences – depopulation, agricultural collapse, famine, etc. – wrought havoc with the Mamlūk army. Epidemics led to a severe disorganization of the Mamlūk military units, handicapping operations and security checks. As Ayalon noted, the "plague also brought about vast changes and considerable confusion in the ownership of feudal fiefs (*iqṭāʿāt*) and military property. In some outbreaks of plague one fief changed hands from three to nine times. Tailors and shoemakers took fiefs belonging to the *ḥalqa* [freeborn cavalrymen – who perished in the plague, WH] and donned military uniforms. In another outbreak the number of fiefs that became available was so large, and there was so much confusion and seizure of property, that even the *kuttābiyya*, studying in the military schools, took fiefs before their release and prior to obtaining their horses.... During epidemics the *julbān* used to take advantage of the prevailing disorder to seize fiefs belonging to weaker formations." Neustadt (Ayalon), "Plague and its Effects Upon the Mamlūk Army," 72-73 (including n. 2 on p. 73). See also Holt, *Age of the Crusades*, 192 f. In another famous study, Ayalon summed up the anarchic conditions caused by the Julbān

On the other hand, what I have been aiming to do here is not to provide a chronological narrative of this history (otherwise my presentation of the Mamlūk period would have had to come earlier) but rather to tease out a general structure of the constitutional modalities by which Muslims governed themselves in the central lands of Islam. Giving a structural account of the Ottoman juristic and constitutional experience will help situate the Mamlūk venture in its proper context. My argument is that the exceptionality and the constitutional disorder that took over the Mamlūk polity during the second part of its reign was the prime reason for the subsumption of *siyāsa* under the wings of Sharīʿa; or, put differently, it is precisely *that* disorder which stood behind the final push to lodge *siyāsa* entirely into Sharīʿa's direct supervision.

If it is true – and it is – that *siyāsa* was the discretionary sphere hitherto left by the Sharīʿa for the ruler to conduct the business of governance, the Mamlūk experience generated a reaction that tightened Sharīʿa's grip over that sphere. The Mamlūk-era jurists made the concession of relaxing Sharīʿa's formalistic rules of evidence only for the Ottomans, both government and jurists, to seize

(also known as *ajlāb*, *mushtarawāt*, or *al-mamālīk al-sulṭāniyya*), this time connecting their brutality and abuse with the legal system:
"From the middle of the 9th [15th] century onward, Mamlūk sources are permeated with the terror of the *ajlāb*, and a very great number of pages are devoted to its description. There are whole years [in the accounts of the annals, WH] in which little would remain if the description of these nefarious activities were removed. Hundreds of stories are told of the expulsion of high state officials (mostly those connected with payments to the army), the burning of their houses, the pillaging of the markets and shops of the capital, the burning down of the townspeople's houses, the abduction of women without any voice being raised in protest, the amirs' fear of the *ajlāb*, from whom they hide their treasures, etc. The sultan completely loses control of the *ajlāb*, who stone him and put him to shame in public. Whenever they wish to extort something from the sultan, they prohibit his going up to the citadel. They intervene in questions of appointments and depositions of sultans, and they have their way in the appointment of the king of Cyprus and that of the highest amirs of the kingdom. The situation had the effect of terrorizing the population, for it was known in advance that 'whatever they do will be permitted them, and the sultan will not protect those oppressed by them.' In such an anarchical state of affairs, the law courts lost all their value, and whoever desired anything addressed himself not to the tribunals, but to the *ajlāb*. One of the main reasons for the Circassian sultans' infrequent departures from the capital was the constant state of upheaval into which the city was thrown by the activities of the *Julbān*. When Qaytbay allowed himself to leave the city more frequently than his predecessors he came in for severe criticism. For all their misdeeds the *Julbān* were given surprisingly light penalties.... Some *ajlāb* who had killed a Mamlūk amir, were only beaten and imprisoned.... Moreover, even in cases where the sultan had intended firm punishment and condemned the offenders to death or to having their hands cut off, he commutes the penalty to lashing. The sultan's order to the *qāḍī*s forbidding them to marry the *ajlāb* without his permission was totally ignored by the latter." See Ayalon, "Studies on the Structure of the Mamlūk Army," 212-13.

on this accomplishment by integrating *siyāsa*, and even later the *qānūn*, under the central domain of the Sharīʿa. There is no doubt that juristically – that is, as a matter of legal doctrine and jurisprudential elaboration – the Ottoman period was a natural continuation of the Mamlūk discursive tradition (in its anthropological sense). But the Ottomans departed significantly from Mamlūk practice, *both judicially and administratively*, effectively restoring autonomous legal powers to the *qāḍī* (hence to the Sharīʿa as well) and even bolstering the judicial powers of this institution with administrative prerogatives and oversight.

In an article that draws on primary sources while synthesizing (and critiquing) earlier scholarship in the field, Y. Rapoport argued that Mamlūk legal history is divisible into three "distinct stages." The first is characterized by (1) the construction of a Dār al-ʿAdl, that is, the Palace of Justice; (2) the appointment of a chief *qāḍī* for each of the four *madhhab*s; and (3) a limited jurisdiction of the executive courts over penal law. The second stage, beginning around 750/1350, is marked by the expansion of the jurisdiction of the executive class, especially that of the chamberlains, whereby they begin to adjudicate matters related to family law and debts. In the third stage, formed during the reigns of Qaytbāy and Qānṣūh al-Ghawrī (906-922/1501-16), we "see a concentration of all jurisdictions in the hands of the sultans, who present themselves as champions of the sharīʿa and openly dispute the formalistic doctrines of the judiciary."[119]

Insofar as we are concerned in this chapter and book, the issue at stake here is executive overreach. To sum up the Mamlūk situation during the last century or so of its rule, I quote at length a modern historian of the period, on whose account Rapoport himself relies:

> Indeed, not only did the hajibs usurp judicial powers that were formerly exercised by the *qāḍīs*, but other military officers also did the same.... However, the military usurpation of judicial powers only seems to have become flagrant and pervasive in the opening decades of the fifteenth century [800s A.H.].... It is quite likely that there were other amirs and Mamlūks who tried to deliver justice according to the precepts of the sharīʿah, or at least according to a sense of equity, but evidently other Mamlūks were selling verdicts for money and receiving petitions in order to exercise patronage and develop local clienteles.... At first the

119 Rapoport, "Royal Justice and Religious Law," 76.

> *ḥājib*s, acting as delegates of the sultan, exercised a kind of administrative jurisdiction over matters relating to the army and the *dīwāns*. Then they took to hearing cases presented by merchants and other civilians and thereby encroached on the jurisdiction of the *qāḍīs*, at which point judicial and executive powers became utterly confounded. Then other quite junior officers, such as the deputy *dawādār*, arrogated the same jurisdiction to themselves. Then even purchased Mamlūks took to receiving petitions from all and sundry and using their muscles to enforce their ad hoc jurisdiction. However, the fragmentary and somewhat speculative nature of the evidence of abuses in *maẓālim* jurisdiction described above is obvious. Pious chroniclers complained repeatedly about the way that the provisions of the sharīʿah were being breached, but they did not actually dwell upon the matter, nor did they systematically record the way in which *maẓālim* justice was delegated and diffused to such an extent that justice shaded into racketeering and any Mamlūk with a sword could pose as an officer of the law. It was hardly a matter for celebration.[120]

Soon after assuming power, Baybārs built a new Dār al-ʿAdl in 660/1262, this time geographically closer to the civilian population of Cairo. Dār al-ʿAdl was not a Mamlūk innovation. It can be documented as early as the Ghaznawīd dynasty in the sixth/twelfth century as well as under the Zangīds in Damascus and Aleppo and under the Ayyūbids in Cairo around the same time.[121] It was usually the sultan in the capital or the governors in the provinces who presided over this institution, holding *maẓālim* sessions and adjudicating cases mostly related to abuses and violations of government officials against the civic population or to disputes among these officials themselves. Almost always present in the hearings were the chief justices, senior *muftī*s and at times other jurists, this being a legal tradition since early Islamic times.[122] High military and executive officers were a permanent fixture as well. The historian Maqrīzī reports that sessions of Dār al-ʿAdl were "held in full court, to which generally the ambassadors of rulers were summoned."[123] Rapoport argues that these

120 Irwin, "Privatization of 'Justice'," 65, 70.

121 Hallaq, *Sharīʿa*, 201; Rapoport, "Royal Justice and Religious Law," 81.

122 As Māwardī (*AS*, 134) and Qalqashandī (SAQ, 255) insisted, this was the practice. See main text of ch. 3, at nn. 89-90.

123 Cited in Holt, *Age of the Crusades*, 144. It is worth citing here the entire relevant paragraph from Maqrīzī, describing the constitution of sessions in Dār al-ʿAdl:
"It was the custom of the sultan to sit in this hall at daybreak on Mondays and Thursdays

tribunals reflected "a formalization of royal justice and a greater emphasis on the judicial functions of the sultan," this marking "a closer integration of the ruler in the administration of justice."[124]

The point at issue here is the kind of justice being administered in this "development" as well as its significance for determining constitutional boundaries. What does "formalization of royal justice" mean here? And what does "a greater emphasis on the judicial functions of the sultan" signify in terms of integrating the ruler in *a particular type* of judicial administration or a system of justice? The tenor of Rapoport's overall argument is that Dār al-ʿAdl signified a royal institutional paraphernalia, a material symbolization of sultanic prerogative that asserted the discretionary power of politics over the Sharīʿa. Which is to say that the material emphasis represented in the construction of Dār al-ʿAdl was, in Rapoport's view, the beginning of a predetermined trend that would

---

throughout the year, except for the month of Ramadan, when he would not hold these sittings. Such a session was solely for the [redress of] wrongs. It was held in full court, to which generally the ambassadors of rulers were summoned.... It was at first the usage for the chief judges of the four madhhabs to take their seats on his [the sultan's] right, the senior of them being the Shāfiʿī, who was next to the sultan, then beside the Shāfiʿī the Ḥanafī, then the Mālikī, then the Ḥanbalī. Beside the Ḥanbalī was the agent of the treasury, then the supervisor of the Ḥisba in Cairo. On the left of the sultan sat the secretary, in front of him the supervisor of the army, and the corps of writers (known as the clerks of the bench and the writers of the bench) completing the circle. If the wazir was one of the Men of the Pens, he was between the sultan and the secretary; if the wazir was one of the Men of the Swords, he would stand apart from the rest of the officials. If there was a vicegerent, he would stand with the officials. Behind the sultan to his right and left stood two ranks of the sword-bearers, the pages of the Wardrobe, and the pages of the Privy Chamber. At a distance of fifteen cubits to his right and left sat the elderly and venerable great amirs of a Hundred, who were called the amirs of the council. Next below them were the great amirs and the officials, who were standing, and the rest of the amirs, who were standing behind the amirs of the council. Standing behind this circle surrounding the sultan were the chamberlains and the dawādārs to offer the petitions of the people, and to summon the ambassadors, plaintiffs and those submitting their needs and wants. The secretary and the writers of the bench read the petitions to the sultan, and if necessary he would take the advice of the judges on what related to legal matters and religious jurisdiction. In matters relating to the army, if the petitions involved amirs holding assignments, the supervisor of the army would read them. If he needed to take advice concerning the army, he would confer with the chamberlain and the clerk of the army. Otherwise, the sultan would command as he thought fit" (Holt, *Age*, 144-45).

It is also worth noting that P. M. Holt, a non-legal historian, had already noticed the executive overreach in the early 1980s: "Perhaps it was as a result of the formality of this *maẓālim* procedure that another extra-canonical jurisdiction developed in the first half of the ninth/fifteenth century, when the chamberlain (Ḥājib), a military officer, extended his functions from the hearing of soldiers' disputes to those of ordinary subjects – to the detriment of the Shariʿa courts" (145).

124 Rapoport, "Royal Justice and Religious Law," 81.

bring "the state" (his term) into a closer management of justice, as much on its own terms as on those of the Sharīʿa, if not more so in fact. This is why he vehemently argues against some recent scholars whom he thought advocated a view of the Sharīʿa as pure, and furthermore innocent of realpolitik and political effects.[125] And this is why he concludes his article with the assertion that "the *siyāsah* of the state was not only an integral and legitimate element of the Sharīʿa, but also an increasingly central one," a conception, he argues, that "*fits with a much wider pattern in Muslim societies of the Middle Ages and the Early modern period*."[126]

Rapoport's overall argument and interpretation of facts, common in the field at large, suffer from three main problems. The first is a confusion between what belongs to the constitutional, strictly speaking, and to the legal. The Mamlūk sultans' adjudication of cases of commercial law and personal status by "common sense,"[127] and settling disputes among the jurists to boot, was not just a matter of law, but a constitutional act of the first order. It amounts to an executive overreach whereby the sultan makes, adjudicates, and executes the law all at once. This is a wholly different way of "doing law," because both the preceding and following periods of Islamic legal and constitutional history witnessed the total independence of the legislative and a remarkable judicial autonomy to boot.

Second, Rapoport's narrative is deeply embedded in a linear account of Islamic history, one that is steeped in a theology of progress.[128] As earlier studies have shown,[129] and as briefly presented earlier in this chapter, the Ottoman legal and constitutional experience until the early parts of the nineteenth century reversed and corrected the later Mamlūk experimentation with executive overreach, giving the *qāḍī* not only legal autonomy but also Sharʿī powers of administrative management. This is in addition to the virtual elimination of the *maẓālim* tribunals in favor of an enhancement of his discretionary powers within the relatively new and evolving legal conception of *taʿzīr* and *siyāsa* (discussed in this and the two preceding chapters).

The linear narrative typified in Rapoport's account is an ideologically programmatic discourse intended to show the civilizational march throughout

125 Rapoport, "Royal Justice," 74, 101.
126 Rapoport, "Royal Justice," 101-2 (emphasis mine).
127 Rapoport, "Royal Justice," 90. Irwin, "Privatization," 70, calls it "a sense of equity."
128 On the theology of progress and its malevolent effects, see ch. 12, n. 129 and Hallaq, *Impossible State*, 12-18; Hallaq, *Restating Orientalism*, 107-112, 150-54, 157-58, 194-95.
129 For these studies, see the account and sources drawn upon in Hallaq, *Sharīʿa*, 125-221, 357-550.

history, always defined by European standards and values, and one that exonerates the European colonialist venture and structural intervention in Muslim lands, including the introduction of the modern state into the world as historically predetermined and inevitable. The severity of the problem arises from the necessary implications of this narrative, namely, that there is a latent (i.e., assumed but not declared) organic or structural continuity between the colonial injection of the modern state (and capitalism) into Islamic societies in the second half of the nineteenth century and thereafter, on the one hand, and the Mamlūk constitutional overreach during the fifteenth century, on the other. What compounds this problematic understanding is the lack of appreciation for constitutional implications. The intervention of the "state" in Mamlūk times (with all its anarchic dealings) is thus seen as both analogous and a forerunner to the modern state's assertion of itself over the social, economic, or legal (see chapter 12).

Third, and on account of the foregoing consideration, Rapoport's narrative is factually incorrect, since no continuity existed between the Mamlūk and Ottoman experiences insofar as executive overreach is concerned. The later Mamlūk experience, stretching over well-nigh a century and a half, is *constitutionally not of a piece with* the Ottoman structure of governance. Rapoport himself acknowledges that "the kanun was accepted as an integral part of the legal culture required by the shariʿah," though nowhere does he mention the decline of this instrument after the eleventh/sixteenth century – thus giving the wrong impression that the *qānūn* continued to the end of the Ottoman Empire. He even goes further to state that the "whole administration of justice was based on the shariʿah, the authority to administer justice was given to the *qāḍī*, and the office of the grand *muftī*, Shaykh al-Islām, was responsible for assuring the observance of the sacred law in the state."[130] This depiction wholly contradicts Rapoport's – as well as other historians' – fairly accurate account of the Mamlūk overreach. Yet, in a remark buried in a footnote, Rapoport states, here quite inaccurately, that "in standard accounts of the history of Islamic law, the Ottoman legal system is invariably seen as an exception."[131]

It is remarkable that Rapoport himself thought the last century and a half of Mamlūk rule to be different from the first period of the same dynasty, by virtue of the "stages" of "development" and account of shifts he provided (see above). He also specifically segregates the last half century, which ended

130 Rapoport, "Royal Justice," 74.

131 Rapoport, "Royal Justice," 74, n. 18. All citations in this paragraph are from this page.

with the Ottoman conquest, as having "represent[ed] an unprecedented degree of royal intervention in the administration of justice."[132] The general tenor of the narrative therefore goes like this: The last fifty years (1468-1517) were unprecedented, but nonetheless had been the culmination of another unprecedented development (1350-1468) against a background of traditional governance between 1250 and 1350. And then comes the alleged Ottoman exception to the exception!

Be that as it may, and as I have stated earlier, Rapaport, and nearly all other commentators on the Mamlūk regime as a legal and constitutional order, never bother with the complex circumstances that culminated in this exception, studying the period without regard to histories of viral and bacterial epidemiology, ecological shifts, and the resultant dramatic demographic transformations, and even more dramatic economic and social changes. In fact, none of these major and traumatic events are taken into account as important historical factors. As we have seen,[133] Egypt and Greater Syria, the chief domains of the Mamlūks, underwent major and fairly sudden changes in all these spheres, especially after the crucial year of 748/1347, precisely the time that Rapoport identified as the beginning of the havoc that ruled the legal history of the Mamlūk sultanate.

Of utmost relevance for our concerns – in explaining the legal quasi-anarchy during the last century or so of Mamlūk rule – is the rise of the Julbān, the military units brought into the Mamlūk army during the reign of sultan Sayf al-Dīn Barqūq (ruling twice, in 784-91/1382-89 and 792-801/1390-99).[134] Due to the death of colossal numbers of Turkish Mamlūk soldiers over four major epidemics (1347-48, 1360-64, 1373-75, and 1379-81), and the decline in the Kipchak migration to Egypt (from where the Turkish Mamlūks were procured), Barqūq seized on the opportunity of enlisting the Julbān from the floods of migration from Circassia, his own homeland.[135] The acquisition of the Julbān, who were "confined to one age-group, namely, adolescents,"[136] had

132 Rapoport, "Royal Justice," 97.

133 See n. 118, above.

134 Ayalon, "Circassians in the Mamlūk Kingdom," 138: "Barqūq, as we have seen, was the sultan who effected the greatest and most far-reaching racial transformation in the entire history of the Mamlūk Kingdom. He was able to oust the *Turks* and replace them with his fellow-Circassians." See also Ṭarkhān, *Miṣr*, 36-38, 42-44.

135 Ibn Ṭaghrībirdī, *Nujūm*, XI, 225, reports on the "large groups" of Circassians arriving in Cairo between the reign of Barqūq and that of sultan Nāṣir al-Dīn Faraj, who ruled until 815/1412.

136 Ayalon, "Circassians in the Mamlūk Kingdom," 136.

a major effect on the sultanate, having changed its nature and modus operandi, if not modus vivendi. It is with excellent reason that the Mamlūk sultanate is invariably viewed as having two distinct phases, the first belonging to the *Atrāk* while the second to the *Jarkas*.

While it is true that many senior emirs were raised from childhood on Muslim soil and acculturated according to the values of Islam, the Julbān were Christian in upbringing and alien to Egyptian and Syrian Muslim cultures.[137] They not only spoke a different language and did not know Arabic – the sources speak of even the Turkish Mamlūks as failing to some extent on this account as well – but they were notorious in disrespecting the Egyptian population and its cultural values, and even their own emirs and the sultan himself.

The Mamlūk historians are unanimous, not only in the condemnation of this group but also in describing them as a gang of thugs who wrought havoc on nearly everyone and everything around them.[138] For example, in just one account of their transgressions during the year of 832/1428-29, which runs into several pages in Ibn Ṭaghrībirdī's *al-Nujum al-Zāhira*,[139] it is reported that when Sūdūn Min ʿAbd al-Raḥmān, the Governor of Greater Syria, arrived in Cairo, he met with the sultan al-Ashraf Sayf al-Dīn Barsbāy to update him on the general situation in Syria but also to file a complaint against the Julbān who had assaulted and mistreated "officers and others," including attacks on the senior officials of the sultanate as well as on the latter's residences and properties. They rebelled against Sayf al-Dīn Īnāl (1453-61) seven times during the eight years of his reign, and had given much trouble to Qaytbāy.[140] Barsbāy, desperately retorting with the admission that "I have failed to reform them," took off "his headgear [in anger] and started cursing them, repeatedly wishing them death."[141] Jār Quṭlū, a distinguished senior emir in audience, suggested to the sultan "to put them to the sword" (*ḍaʿ fī-him al-sayf*) and to buy another group to replace them, for they are so useless, he argued, that "a hundred of the Qarānīṣ are better than a thousand of them" (the Qarānīṣ being troops or brigades of earlier sultans, and named after them, e.g., Ẓāhiriyya, Naṣiriyya, and Mu'ayyadiyya).

137 Ṭarkhān, *Miṣr*, 12.
138 Ibn Shāhīn, *Nayl*, II, pt. viii, 43-44, 76, 78, 86, 89, 91, 156, 170, 215.
139 Ibn Ṭaghrībirdī, *Nujūm*, XIV, 326-33, wherefrom the account in the following paragraphs derives.
140 Ṭarkhān, *Miṣr*, 36, 38, 42-44.
141 This apparently happened quite often, expressing the sultan's frustration with them. See Ibn Ṭaghrībirdī, *Nujūm*, XIV, 356.

Upon hearing Jar Quṭlū's suggestion, the sultan began to entertain the idea of arresting some of the Julbān, exiling others, and dispersing the rest by assimilating them into the larger units of various senior emirs. He is reported to have said that they brought him nothing good and that he would write off the money he had spent on them as a loss. However, Baybughā al-Muẓaffarī, a senior emir in attendance, objected and warned the sultan of embarking on such a risky venture.

Despite the sultan's instruction that the discussions of this meeting remain confidential, it seems that Baybughā leaked Jār Quṭlū's proposal to the Julbān, who now set themselves the task of killing the emir, together with his *mamlūks* and supporters. A few days later, when the Julbān rode in search of Jār Quṭlū and his men, the people of Cairo, preparing for the worst, closed their shops, bought supplies and provisions, locked the gates to their houses and blocked their neighborhood streets. The sultan repeatedly sent several emissaries to ask the Julbān to return to their barracks, threatening them with punishment, but they "did not pay any attention" to him. When they arrived at Jār Quṭlū's residence, a battle erupted between them and his soldiers, where exchanges of arrows took place throughout the whole day. The Julbān, despite their greater number, could not subdue Jār Quṭlū's smaller units, for they "lacked the knowledge and practice of fighting." On the same day, and for some reason, they also assaulted one of their own unit commanders (*ustādh*) as well as others.

The sultan's anger is said to have skyrocketed, such that he raised the idea of eliminating them altogether with the help of his senior emirs. But the latter advised him against taking such a step for fear of the Julbān's retaliation. Two days later, a Thursday, the Julbān demanded that the sultan punish Jār Quṭlū's soldiers who fought against them. The sultan refused to do so for a while, but then grudgingly succumbed to their requests. He sent after Jār Quṭlū's men who were alleged to have "started the fight," punished them with a beating, and then sent them to prison. Ibn Ṭaghrībirdī reports that this episode left the senior emirs of the sultanate entirely resentful and insecure, for they said [to themselves?]: "If this could happen to such a senior emir, then it could happen to any of us."[142] Jār Quṭlū is reported to have resented the sultan for what he had done, leading him to conspire against him sometime later when the sultan led a campaign with Jār Quṭlū to subdue the city of Āmid in Diyārbakr.

Less than two months later, the Julbān demanded the sultan pay them their monthly salaries, but they refused to accept the payments, "insisting" on

142 Ibn Ṭaghrībirdī, *Nujūm*, XIV, 329.

an increase of 600 dirhams each. After an intense negotiation over four days, where emissaries were sent back and forth (between the Qalʿa, the sultan's headquarters, and the Julbāns' barracks), the sultan had to accede to their demands and pay them what they had asked for.[143]

As if all this was not enough, the Julbān, after receiving their salary increase, went down to the city and started a fight with another group, leading to loss of life apparently on both sides. We do not hear from the sources of any punitive action on the part of the intimidated sultan. Things seemed to die down until about a month later, when the Mamlūk armies, in both of its Egyptian and Syrian contingents, headed north to rebuff the Qara Qoynlū incursions into the city of al-Ruhā (today's Urfa) in Diyārbakr. Upon arrival, many skirmishes and battles erupted, but the city was soon taken. The fortress of the city, however, remained under siege, with what appears to have been a stiff resistance on the part of its defenders. But after about two days of being pounded with catapults and battering rams, the defenders sent a message with their emissary to declare their willingness to surrender, with the condition that if they did so, their lives would be spared and no harm would come to them from the Mamlūks. The emissary then had the senior emirs and governors, Sūdūn Min ʿAbd al-Raḥmān and Qaṣrūh, take an oath (*ḥallafū*) to that effect, which they duly did.

When all the senior emirs gathered and proceeded to the fortress to have it delivered to them, they found the Julbān waiting at the gate. The governors pleaded with them to stand aside and keep out, explaining that "we have guaranteed them an *amān*" (safe conduct). Upon their refusal, the governors gave orders for the Julbān to stand down, which they not only refused but responded to with abusive language.[144] When the governors further insisted that the Julbān refrain from entering the fortress (knowing what they would do if they were to get inside), the Julbān simply forced an entry "against the will of the governors and the senior emirs." It appears that they, in their great numbers and forces,[145] even prevented the latter from entering, and so the top brass of the army returned to their campground "with a heavy heart" (*shaqqa ʿalayhum*). Together with some Turkmen and tribesmen, the Julbān killed all combatants inside, and then pillaged and raped, crowning their savagery by burning "the entire city" of al-Ruhā, including the women and children who took to hiding inside the houses fearing for their lives.

143 Ibn Ṭaghrībirdī, *Nujūm*, XIV, 230.
144 Ibn Ṭaghrībirdī, *Nujūm*, XIV, 332: "*Fa-afḥashū fil-raddi ʿalā al-nuwwāb.*"
145 Ibn Tughrī Birdī, *Nujūm*, XIV, 332-33.

The atrocities they committed were said to be "worse than those perpetrated by the Mongols."[146] Ibn Ṭaghrībirdī lamented that the rulers of Egypt used to condemn all such acts when others committed them, but now "we ourselves commit the worst of the ugly and the forbidden." He then woefully added that what these "thugs" had done was not with the permission of the sultan, nor was it expressive of his will. "As we have seen, even the governors and the senior emirs [with all their forces] could not prevent them from entering the fortress."[147]

A modern historian of the sultanate remarked that the bulk of Mamlūk annals would be significantly reduced if it were not for the accounts describing the horrors perpetrated by these factions. They rioted routinely; expelled even high government officials from their jobs; beat them; burned the houses of the rich and powerful as much as those of the poor and downtrodden; pillaged markets and shops; and abducted women at will. With total impunity, they stoned the sultan himself, and shamed him in public. They would at times prevent him from leaving his citadel until he succumbed to their endless demands. They ignored his royal decrees altogether, including a ban he installed on the *qāḍī*s to preside over their marriages. They easily dared to intervene in government appointments, even in renewal of the tenure of vassal kings. "In such an anarchical state of affairs, the law courts lost all their value, and whoever desired anything addressed himself not to the [Sharīʿa] tribunals, but to the *ajlāb* [Julbān]."[148]

I have chosen to give a detailed and vivid account of the events of just one year to convey a sense of the level of terror the Julbān visited upon, and the breaches they committed against, both their own commanders and leaders as well as the population at large.[149] The account is also intended as a marker of institutional and structural violations. The fact that the Royal Mamlūks were Circassian-Christians, coming to Egypt at an unusually

146 Ibn Ṭaghrībirdī, *Nujūm*, XIV, 333: "*Fa-qad faʿalū bi-madīnat al-Ruhā fiʿla al-Tīmūrlankiyyīn wa-ziyādatan min al-qatli wal-asri wal-iḥrāqi wal-fujūri bil-nisā'.*"

147 Ibn Ṭaghrībirdī, *Nujūm*, XIV, 333-34.

148 Ayalon, "Studies," 212-13. See also, as samples, Ibn Ṭaghrībirdī, *Nujūm*, XIV, 356; XV, 50-51; Ibn Ṭaghrībirdī, *Ḥawādith al-Duhūr*, I, 69-70 (for the year of 846/1442-43). See also Ṭarkhān, *Miṣr*, 36, 38, 42-44.

149 It might be tempting for some historians to argue that the Julbān were much like the later Ottoman Janissaries in their ability to rebel against the sultans, but the differences between the groups are immense, if only because the latter consistently represented the interests of the populace and the social communities of which they were an integral part. On the Janissaries as popular political opposition, see Tezcan, *Second Ottoman Empire*, 6-7. For more on this, see chapter 11, below.

older age and under trying circumstances in the life of country, must be seen as crucial.

As we have noted before, the Circassian contingent, at all military ranks, were often accompanied by their relatives and servants. The extensive presence in Egypt of these kinsmen and familial relations was noted by historians, and their attitude to local Egyptian and Muslim culture appears to have been negative, if not condescending. Even sultan Barqūq's father was disgruntled and discontented, despite the fact that he, like many other Circassians, was appointed to high positions in the army without being qualified. He is reported to have been so unhappy that when he was approached by a senior Circassian emir asking him to respect local practices, "he refused, got angry, and demanded that he return to the Country of the Circassians."[150] As we have seen, the attitudes of the Julbān are described by the historians over the stretch of decades to be consistently supremacist and disrespectful of almost everything local, including toward the Circassian sultans themselves, who of course converted to Islam. The Circassians in general were also known to have stood aloof from the local population,[151] and largely from the Turkish contingent of the Mamlūk House.[152] But it is also of tremendous interest that the sources, mostly written by Turks and some Arabs, are notably silent about what the Julbān said or articulated as a matter of language, as if they were mute. I suspect that these historians and the population at large did not understand the Circassian language, and so it was only their deeds, acts, and mostly misdeeds, that were put down in the annals. If a picture is worth a thousand words, an act is worth far more.

V

The question that poses itself then is how do we interpret this intrusive Circassian phenomenon, or interlude, in constitutional terms? I meant to dwell on this phenomenon because I think it is of utmost importance in understanding how constitutional, legal, or political cultures are made and unmade. The relevance of this interlude is such that it bears not only on the explanation of the later Mamlūk "developments" but also on what it means, substantively and theoretically, to inject a habitus and its doxastic constituents

150 Ibn Ṭaghrībirdī, *Nujūm*, XI, 225.
151 Ṭarkhān, *Miṣr*, 12.
152 Ayalon, "Circassians in the Mamlūk Kingdom."

with subversive actors. Because my take on the issue is as theoretical as it is substantive and historical, I argue that the basic and fundamental principles of operation here are likewise applicable to the transformations that took over the Islamic constitutional system in the nineteenth and twentieth centuries.

To have an analytical grip over the phenomenon of the Circassian Mamlūks, it is worthwhile viewing it in terms of habitus, tradition, and doxa. I will argue that the latter two operate within the ambit of the first, the largest analytical unit that bestows structural meaning on this phenomenon.[153] Otherwise, the entire phenomenon, stretching over decades, will remain nothing more than a swathe of meaningless detail.

We had an occasion in the Introduction and chapter 2 to proffer the briefest description of habitus. The history of the evolution of the term is itself meaningful, shedding light on the concept's genealogy, variations, and different approaches to it by philosophers, anthropologists, and sociologists. In its Aristotelian-Thomist meaning, and in the way Max Weber employed it, the term "refers to a virtuous way of life based on deliberately adopted habits."[154] This Greco-Latin genealogy, incidentally, is not much different from its Islamic sister, articulated by an extensive and long string of writers, as exemplified by the discourses of Ghazālī and Ibn Khaldūn, among others.

In modernity, however, the Thomist concept has undergone transformations by way of secularization, wherein the ethical element that had constituted it in whole has now become only one among other elements of its analytic operation. But "habit" and its conceptual meanings remained the single constant and invariable, since habit, rules of conduct, and social dispositions make up some of the major constituent categories through which we are able to understand how a society or a community works, why people do and believe certain things in an apparent regenerative continuity, and why, for instance, a group within the social order accepts its inferior status and thinks it normal, etc. This last concern lies at the heart of Bourdieu's interest in the notion of habitus, which he saw as a system of dispositions that survives in individual and collective behavior in the present.[155] The survival of these dispositions is precisely what analysts saw as constituting "habit," but one that is structured within an internal logic of social behavior. For Husserl, for instance, habitus includes decisions taken in past generations but ones that are transformed in time into convictions and beliefs which constitute the individual's character as

153 On habitus, see also Introduction (sec. II), ch. 1 and 2.

154 Sapiro, "Habitus," 484-489.

155 Bourdieu, *Outline of a Theory of Practice*, 78-95.

a stable and conforming ego.[156] For Durkheim, it is a process of socialization that instills in the individual society's "system of ideas, feelings and habits… moral beliefs and practices, national or professional traditions, and collective opinions of all sorts."[157] Building on this, Marcel Mauss developed the concept further in his famous article "Techniques of the Body," where he argues – against earlier theories that emphasized the transmission of habitus through imitation – that education-as-training is the mechanism through which habitus maintains itself by internalizing in the body social representations as well as rules of conduct and a wide range of practices (what has come to be known in anthropology and sociology as embodiment).[158]

Building on a rich philosophical and sociological discourse on habitus, Bourdieu argued that it is the embodiment of cultural capital, including the deeply ingrained habits, skills, and dispositions that we possess due to our life experience. It also extends to our tastes for cultural objects, such as food, clothing, and art. Habitus is a "system of lasting transposable dispositions which, integrating past experiences, functions at every moment as a *matrix of perceptions, appreciations, and actions* and makes possible the achievement of infinitely diversified tasks, thanks to analogical transfers of schemes permitting the solution of similarly shaped problems."[159] Habitus is made of "fields" like art, religion, law, education, etc., each with their rules and knowledge forms. Bourdieu maintained that an individual's habitus consists of unconscious mechanisms of integrating new situations that do not require conscious mental processing but instead rely, by virtue of perpetual exposure to social conditioning, on instinctual understanding based on previous experiences. The individual thus stands unconsciously constrained by the givens imposed by the structures of thought and action surrounding him or her. Which is also to say that the context in which the individual stands when encountering the new circumstances are *structured structures* produced by, and making up, that context. Yet it is also *structuring structures* in that the presupposed context shapes the new experiences by adapting them to the new circumstance and giving them form and coherence.

Significantly, Bourdieu insists that despite the fact this latter force within the habitus allows for adaptation through stimuli, the habitus is extremely stable, always anchored in preexisting boundaries even when its telos is addressing

156 Sapiro, "Habitus," 485.
157 Ottaway, "Educational Sociology of Émile Durkheim," 216; Sapiro, "Habitus," 485.
158 Mauss, "Techniques of the Body."
159 Bourdieu, *Outline*, 83.

everchanging conditions of existence. As an effect of the relative fixedness and stability of habitus, the individual develops a common sense of what can and cannot be done, and, importantly, what is thinkable and unthinkable, with the consequence that these attitudes come to be perceived as self-evident and natural. The depth of these perceptions is such that they define the general contours and parameters of thought and action and often render them as unquestionable and taken for granted. This is the *doxa* that is foundational for the maintenance of orthodoxy.[160] All things that stand outside of this entrenched perception or contradict it become unorthodox and are perceived to constitute a threat to the rules and norms of habitus, if not to the habitus itself in its entirety.[161] Examples of these range from the religious and theological wars in Christendom to the Schmittian existential threat in the age of the political, although the same dynamic may exist in smaller groupings and communities (e.g., Jewish and Islamic denominations in Euro-America).

As I have shown in the Introduction (sec. II), a central point of debate in the prolific discourses on habitus over the past century or so has been about the extent to which the continuity of habitus across time is due to rational autonomy or to so-called imitation. The struggle between the two camps, with the many shades of variations between and among the various positions, reflected the divides between the Cartesian-Kantian notions of rationality, on the one hand, and the psychoanalytical and Durkheimian explorations of the unconscious, on the other, whereby the individual is partly the product of his or her social habitat, being affected and considerably formed by it more than standing as an active agent operating autonomously.

From the perspective of our concerns in this book, the debate about rational autonomy or collective decision is not the most productive question that the theory of habitus raises. My interest in habitus relates mainly to the other fundamental feature of the theory, namely, its power of continuity, a power that by definition reduces the weight of claims for rational autonomy, without it necessarily diminishing them into insignificance. The works of Edward Shils[162] and, especially, Alasdair MacIntyre[163] have amply demonstrated how traditions retain the power of transmission and continuity without there being a reduction in the scope and depth of rational inquiry. It is also worth noting here that Talal Asad's deliberations, quite in line with those of MacIntyre, focus

160 Bourdieu, *Outline*, 164-71.

161 Bourdieu, *Outline*, 72-95.

162 Shils, *Tradition*.

163 Explored thoroughly in his *After Virtue* and *Whose Justice? Which Rationality?*

on this dimension of the old debate as a rejoinder to the Orientalist negative and false depictions of an Islamic Orient that is mired by an irrational and unreflective traditionalism.[164]

Instead of this focus, I wish to emphasize the other aspect of the debate that is concerned with the factors and causes which enable a habitus to maintain continuity or fail to do so, eventually leading to its demise. And it is useful here, if not also necessary, to distinguish between the concepts of habitus and tradition, for as is well known, an entire tradition that stretched from Aristotle and Aquinas to Husserl, Durkheim, and Bourdieu, spoke of habitus as the proper category of analysis, while another string of writers, such as Shils, MacIntyre, and Asad, spoke of tradition as the site of transmitted and continuing sociality and embodiment.

In the way I employ it here, habitus is a more expansive category than tradition, which is to say that habitus includes elements of social and psychological existence that sit outside the domain of tradition as the site of rational inquiry and replicative socio-moral praxis. In a habitus, one can speak of habitual perceptions and practices that enable us to act, in certain situations, without having always to reflect on, and be fully aware, of what we are doing (switching off lights when we leave a room, heading in a particular direction, and not to another, when we walk to the kitchen in our home, etc.).[165] In the same vein, habitus may include what we might call "profane acts" in spheres of action that constitute part of our transmitted sociality and practice (think of our memories of childhood, of, say, picnicking with our family members, which we tend to replicate with our own children, something different from discursive tradition). These spheres may also include social and political behavior that is not regulated by tradition as defined by such thinkers as MacIntyre, if for no other reason than the fact that such behavior is not subject to the requirement of rational inquiry. Nor is it subject to the constituent feature of tradition that Asad characterized as consisting "essentially of discourses that seek to instruct practitioners regarding the correct form and purpose of a given practice that, precisely because it is established, has a history." This history harks back, Asad argues, to various sources that include and relate themselves, in a profound and comprehensive way, to "the founding texts of the Qur'an and the Ḥadīth."[166]

164 See, for instance, his "Idea of an Anthropology of Islam."
165 On the "motor dimension" of habitus, see Vakalopoulos, "Shedding Some (More) Light on Bourdieu's Habitus and Doxa," 257 f.
166 Asad, "Idea," 20.

My argument here is that while tradition as here defined pertains to what Māwardī and others called *dīn*, habitus encompasses both domains, *dīn* and *dunyā*, the latter being the domain of the "profane" (but a domain that is ultimately subject to the pervasive powers of *dīn*, the exact diametrical opposite of the standing modern relationship between the so-called "religious" and the secular, the private and the public).

To take a relevant example from within our field of concern, we by now know that the domain of *siyāsa sharʿiyya* carved a space for the rulers to conduct the affairs of government that pertain to the military in the ways they saw fit, a domain of activities which the jurists and the law at large did not even attempt to regulate. This domain was commonly known to belong to the *ʿurf*, the customary practices introduced by each dynasty as its own way of constituting itself militarily, ideologically, and generally as an executive power. The notion, as we saw, is most clearly apparent in the Ottoman nomenclature "*ehl-i ʿörf*," an expression that exclusively referred to the servants of the dynasty, be they governors, military commanders, policemen, soldiers, tax farmers, and similar others.

Integral to the secular field of *siyāsa sharʿiyya* was the ideological constitution of the army, where matters of morale, courage, and esprit de corps constituted the backbone of the executive power. Each dynasty appears to have introduced its own forms of ideological cohesion within its military, constituting an essential part of what we might call generally the habitus of the executive. This ideology was cultivated through structured forms of socialization, which was typically instilled in the individual *mamlūks* (slave-soldiers) – be they Mamlūk, Ayyūbid, early ʿAbbāsid or Ottoman – from a rather young age. The system of servitude in the Mamlūk sultanate inculcated in the *mamlūk* a feeling of profound loyalty not only toward his master and manumitter (*ustādh*) but also for his comrades and peers (*khushdāshiyya*). "This twofold loyalty was one of the principal axes around which revolved the entire military and social system of Mamlūk hierarchy." The sultan as well as every senior emir and his *mamlūk*s "formed a tightly knit association, whose members were united by strong bonds of solidarity" that were sustained by a dialectic of concomitance: "they were in power only so long as he ruled, and he ruled only so long as his power was based on them."[167]

In the expansive definition given to tradition by Edward Shils, this modality of military cohesion and bonding loyalty may qualify as integral to tradition, but

167 Ayalon, "Studies on the Structure," 206-7.

not so in the discourses of MacIntyre and Asad. There is obviously a rational element to this arrangement, one of basic, if not primeval, expediency. But this is not the sort of complex rational argument that sustains discursive traditions, that is, forms of knowledge *and argument* that are entwined with praxis as technologies of the self (the Maussian techniques of the body). Nor does the modality of cultivating loyalty rest on a cosmological view that anchors and sustains the forms of belief and action of the tradition's subject. Nor, still, does it rest, as tradition necessarily requires, on a necessary link with the past as a source of authority, one that gives power and meaning to present practice and future action. It is a technology of subject-formation only insofar as the *mamlūk*'s subjectivity vis-à-vis his master is concerned, but it can tell us little about the general constitution of his worldview, his modus vivendi and modus operandi in the social world at large, or the aspects of the social life that lies outside the parameters of military subjective formation and training. Loyalty, for example, does not tell us much about the *mamlūk*'s engagement in religious habituation and discursive praxis, for we know that some members of this military class invested heavily in legal, Qur'ānic, and Ḥadīthic studies.[168]

Yet, by contrast, all the above-mentioned thinkers on habitus would agree that this limited aspect of socialization-into-loyalty squarely belongs to habitus. My point in emphasizing the differences between the two concepts is to underscore the point that constitutional structures require more than tradition to keep them afloat, to endow them with maintenance and continuity, although tradition obviously remains essential for their survival. In other words, tradition, despite its profound importance to habitus, is a necessary but not a sufficient condition to constitute itself as habitus in its entirety.

Be that as it may, the question remains as to the factors that cause the decline and final collapse of a habitus, including its dominant tradition. And here I wish to register a strong objection to the major discourses that attempted to explain this collapse.

There is a good reason to think that one of the most effective explanations for the demise of traditions (which for us constitute a major bulk of habitus) is MacIntyre's, in both of his celebrated works, *After Virtue* and *Whose Justice? Which Rationality*? There is also good reason to think that MacIntyre took Thomas Kuhn's *Structure of Scientific Revolutions* seriously and adapted much of its central arguments about science to moral traditions (just as

168 See, e.g., Ibn al-Jazarī, *Ḥawādith*, I, 35, 348, 271-72, 446; II, 110; Ibn Shāhīn, *Nayl*, II, vii, 370, 389; viii, 117.

Asad adapted the latter's theory to elaborate a concept of Islamic discursive tradition).[169] For MacIntyre, the lifeblood of traditions is their ability to justify themselves rationally across time, to produce principles based on rational argument. After all, tradition, as he sees it, is "an argument extended through time."[170] But argument in his usage is a fairly complicated matter. To argue is to advance a reason or reasons.[171] And to establish or maintain a principle successfully – for after all principles stand at the core of traditions – depends on one's ability to advance reasons that recommend its acceptance within both the tradition itself and vis-à-vis the rival traditions. Reasoning in this fashion thus assumes a structure which derives from, and depends on, first principles that are integral to the tradition's general argument. But the first principles and the argument on the basis of which they give structure and meaning must be justified as superior to other attempts which aim to formulate the tradition through a different modality of reasons and even a varying set of first principles. These attempts at rearticulation, MacIntyre thinks, are advanced usually as a response to epistemological crisis. The attempts may fail or succeed, but they stand or fall on the power of their ability to advance rational solutions to the tradition and its problems as a historically embedded but evolving structure.

There is a thin thread in MacIntyre's theory which acknowledges the force of extra-rational historical circumstances in the decline of traditions. A reason or reasons cannot be a good reason or reasons for generating the required principles without understanding the various historical circumstances by which the tradition in question is historically conditioned. As I will argue, the rational superiority of an argument is not the only factor deciding the argument's value, effect, and staying power. As we know well, the fighter jet, the tank, the banks, and political power can destroy society with its traditions. MacIntyre is not interested in this aspect of the decline of tradition, leaving the matter largely and its philosophical implications unattended.[172] What he instead focuses on – as Kuhn does with scientific paradigm – is the intellectual coherence of the tradition's argument and general rational posture. Incoherence of beliefs and practices exposes the tradition to contradictions and weakens the power of its conceptual and argumentative resources.[173]

---

169 See, for instance, Angier, "Alasdair MacIntyre's Analysis of Tradition."
170 MacIntyre, *Whose Justice?* 12.
171 On reasons within this context, see Hallaq, *Impossible State*, 164 ff.
172 See, for instance, Annas, "MacIntyre on Traditions," 394.
173 Angier, "Alasdair MacIntyre," 545.

This of course is a crude summary of MacIntyre's complex theory of tradition, but the crux of it is clear. As with Kuhn and others, MacIntyre's empirical repertoire remains the European experience, which moved from the Hellenic to the modern through Aristotle, Aquinas, and Hume. Any normative power that his theory retains derives from the modern debates that shaped Euro-American thought since Hume wrote, with the long shadow of Kant cast on it through and through. Put plainly, the historical experience defining how a tradition flourishes and survives the ravages of time does not account for other histories, at least those histories that are not made with the same agency with which Europe forged its own destiny from the sixteenth and seventeenth centuries.[174] The Eurocentrism of the theory leaves out of account institutional and sociological factors of deterioration, decline, and final demise that by definition go well beyond intellectual coherence and successful rational defense of argument.

It is my argument that intellectual incoherence is a necessary but insufficient condition for explaining the decline and perishing of a tradition or even a habitus (which I have argued to be more encompassing than, but inclusive of, tradition). For a tradition or, properly speaking, a habitus to successfully survive challenges of rival traditions and historical vicissitudes, it must possess at least three additional features, however interrelated they may be. First, a habitus survives and flourishes only when all the major challenges it encounters are resolved in accordance with, and on terms of, the rules and norms constituting the habitus, even when the tradition within the habitus fails to lead to advancing a coherent argument (in the MacIntyrian sense). This feature in fact rests on a foundational assumption in MacIntyre's work, but it does not seem to have emerged as a notable consequence in his theory. For his project, as I understand it, runs against the Cartesian and Kantian ventures in that it refuses to ground virtue ethics in axiomatic abstract rules of logic, the so-called indubitable ideas, the *cogito ergo sum* that grounds Descartes' philosophy; nor does it admit the universalistic rule-based account of the Kantian concepts of duty and Categorical Imperative.

Sharing in this respect much with the general average of the Islamic moral experience, MacIntyre regards practice-based and moral education, learned from teachers and masters, as the cornerstone of virtue ethics. It is practice and praxis, sustained by an ongoing intellectual justification, that constitute ethics.[175]

---

174 On this theme, see Hallaq, *Restating Orientalism*, 65-137, and passim.

175 For a modern interpretation of traditional Islamic praxis as integral to knowledge and doctrine, see Hallaq, *Reforming Modernity*, 45-48, 151-75, 234-36, and passim.

Yet, what seems less emphasized in MacIntyre's work is that the world of praxis and habitus-defined moral instruction are social and cultural phenomena that both foreground and ground the rational argument. Which is to say, importantly, that moral practice, moral instruction, and virtue-ethics may exist in social spaces where the concern with intellectual coherence of argument and rational defense are not regarded as central. Yet, it is the support that these social spaces lend to the tradition that allows the latter, together with its habitus, to sustain the assault of either a rival tradition or, generally, the ravages of time. As we will see, the Sharīʿa-as-culture constituted the site of these social spaces.

Second, it is also my argument that the strength of tradition and habitus resides equally – that is, in addition to rational argument and coherence – in institutional strength. As I have emphasized throughout, institutions are not just material or organizational structures, but also conceptual edifices that are materially performative.[176] A prominent and relevant case in point is the very notion of *khilāfa*, the supreme office and institution in Islam, not by virtue of its material structures (in fact it did not possess much of such a structure after the third/ninth centuries) but rather because it was an archetypal, genealogical, and constitutive idea, defining the core and general body of the Islamic polity and its forms of governance. The same is the case with Sharʿī education, which at times took the physical form in the *madrasa*ic instruction, but the *madrasa* was never an essential requisite for its operation, much less for its reproduction.[177] Which brings us to a requisite concomitant with institutional strength, an integral part of their strength, which is that institutions are able to reproduce the habitus and its traditions, not only epistemologically and intellectually (MacIntyre), but also normatively, socially, and culturally.

Third, a habitus must have the support of political power, for without such a support, the very viability of the habitus is threatened. By political support, I mean the spectrum on which ranges anything from a positive acceptance of the central values of the habitus to outright advocacy of these values and of the institutions and personnel that promote them. This support is not to be confused with the Foucauldian theory of power/knowledge, nor with the modern political seizure of knowledge, nor still, with the organically symbiotic existence of knowledge and power (the latter, in this case, being defined expansively, since power for Foucault is not just political). Rather, political support manifests itself when the political elite shares the spaces of habitus

176 On this type of performative power, see Hallaq, *Restating Orientalism*, 12-13, 61-63.
177 On this point, see Hallaq, *Sharīʿa*, 124-46, esp. at 135 ff.

with social forces, social power,[178] and the dominant culture as the defining and organizing structure of the polity.

Rational argument and coherence are thus superstructures that sit on top of a sociology of knowledge[179] and a complex matrix of institutional structures that are both material and intangible, but ones that exercise tremendous power in sustaining rational argument and coherence (both of which are a function of this sociology and matrix). Put differently, the ideational superstructure entails, both logically and ontologically, a sociological and institutional infrastructure. Yet, infrastructures and superstructures are not concomitant, for, as we will see, the former may exist without the latter, whereas the reverse is neither true nor possible. There is obviously no superstructure that can come into being without a reproductive epistemic sociology and sustaining social institutions.

Now, how does all this bear upon the Circassian period and the anarchic climate brought about by epidemiological, environmental, and economic conditions that culminated in the introduction of Circassian rule and its problematic Julbān? It is my argument that this period constituted an ephemeral phase in the constitutional history of the central lands of Islam. But in order to understand why this is the case, it is analytically constructive to compare – within the theoretical framework outlined above – the Circassian period with the profoundly structural transformations that overtook the Ottoman Empire in the nineteenth century, transformations from which the empire and the entirety of West Asian and North African regions – if not the world at large – never recovered.

The Julbānic anarchy must not be seen as an aberration of the Circassian period, but rather as a phenomenon integral to, and symptomatic of, the general conditions plaguing the sultanate (pun intended). First, as we have seen, we can comfortably speak of economic collapse that affected all levels of society, including the Mamlūk military elite (the sultan and the senior

178 I am not using the expression "social power" in exactly the same sense and significance intended in Michael Mann's *Sources of Social Power*. Despite his garbled and highly Eurocentric four-page account of Islam (vol. 1, 344-48), he does have a good general sense of the loci of social power (note the emphasis on the "cultural"): "Thus the wider sense of community has possessed a technical infrastructure of language, literacy, education, law, and ritual in which the primary transmitters have been culture and the family. A diffuse and extensive sense of cultural community, a precise infrastructure centered on a monopoly of literacy, [and] a fairly high level of intensive penetration of everyday life" (347-48).

179 On sociology of knowledge as it bears on Islamic studies, and for a list of sources, see Hallaq, "On Orientalism, Self-Consciousness and History."

emirs) which was all too frequently left with empty coffers. Second, we must not underrate the effects of the economic and epidemiological conditions[180] that caused huge migrations and destabilization of traditional and settled societal configurations. Third, and particularly characteristic of this period, we see a general tendency among the Sharʿī administrators of justice to cultivate a culture of venality and purchase of judicial posts, among other forms of corruption,[181] a culture which the ruling elite promoted and nourished.[182] Fourth, there is a virtual collapse of military discipline and chain of command, where, as we have seen, the Royal Mamlūks regularly revolted against their sultan and his senior emirs, beating them and viciously violating the sanctity of the residential quarters of the civil population. For all this signaled the depletion of the bonding glue of loyalty that had characterized the Mamlūk armies during the first century of the sultanate. Fifth, and most significant for us, is the emergence of what might be called mob justice, first begun to some extent by the *dawādār*s but now taken over on a wider scale by the Julbān and their kangaroo courts.

Yet, it is crucial to understand that for all the corruption and breakdowns in the quotidian operation of justice, the habitus and its tradition suffered no *structural damage*.[183] Sharīʿa's culture at large, as well as its sociology of knowledge, remained intact. Its juristic doctrines, together with its system of interpretation and legal theory, did not suffer in the least. Its pedagogical institutions, be they the nonformal *ḥalqa*s or the *madrasa* forum, continued to operate unabated. So did the epistemic generational reproduction of

180 See n. 118, above.

181 This explains the appearance of relatively new forms of discourse that spoke of the corruption that ensues when the ulama "get too close" to the sultans, which in constitutional terms translates into a rich but unjustifiable porousness between the executive and the legislative. See, for instance, Suyūṭī, *Mā Rawāhu al-Asāṭīn*, 23-68, where he lists dozens of Ḥadīths – both spurious and authentic – warning of the ills and evils that ensue from the close proximity of the ulama to executive sultanism. This, for him, leads not only to corruption but also to the legislative's incapacity to speak truth to power. See p. 67. Suyūṭī (d. 911/1505) was a considerable jurist and intellectual who flourished under the last phase of Mamlūk rule and during the near anarchy the prevailed in Egypt then.

182 See, for instance, Morimoto, "What Ibn Khaldūn Saw." However, the article, impressionistic and theoretically inadequate, makes an exaggerated case. Methodologically, it is essential for historians to keep in mind that it was the business of the historians to record the exceptions, the anomalies, and the disorderly (generally known as *ḥawādith* = "*novelties*"), not what is ordinary and orderly. The latter was the vast, regular bulk that went unnoticed, for it was just that: mundane and ordinary.

183 This also includes the kind of social change that Elbendary alluded to throughout her *Crowds and Sultans*.

the ulama class. In fact, there is reason to think that elite contributions to the building of law colleges and associated academic endeavors may have increased. In other words, the *systemic reproduction* of legal knowledge continued unhampered. And even if we assume that all this did not take place in Egypt for a few Mamlūk decades, it remains true that it continued to happen everywhere else.

As important, Sharīʿa's values and telos remained indubitable, forming a thick substrate of doxastic knowledge, that which is not only *consciously unquestioned* but also tacitly taken for granted. The ultimate verdict on areas of conflict, dispute, and violations was rendered according to the Sharʿī benchmarks of value, even while breaches of the ordinary process of justice were being committed.[184] Moreover, it must be stressed, the Egyptian-Syrian juristic constellation constituted an integral part of a wider network of the Sharīʿa system (involving, among other things, robust mobility of senior jurists and general migration of ulama), stretching north to the rising Ottoman Empire, and east and west to the still mostly Ḥanafī Iran and Mālikī North Africa, respectively.[185] For all its anarchic events, the Egyptian-Syrian system during the long ninth/fifteenth century was cushioned, both diachronically and synchronically, by the tectonic constellations of the Sharīʿa surrounding the Mamlūk sultanate. In other words, these conditions, however severe they may have been, effected neither systemic nor systematic change.

Furthermore, and going to the argument of "diachronic cushioning," we have seen how the Ottomans, once they occupied the lands of the Mamlūk sultanate, resumed Islamic governance and even installed sharper administrative divisions between and among constitutional units, giving the Sharʿī *qāḍī* supreme administrative and judicial powers. In one strong sense, the Ottoman restoration of judicial order and their robust administrative apparatus had rendered the Circassian phase all the more ephemeral, as if it had never existed.[186]

184 On benchmarks and violations, see Introduction, n. 71.
185 For instance, almost every page in Ṭāshkuprīzādeh's *al-Shaqā'iq al-Nuʿmāniyya fī ʿUlamā' al-Dawla al-ʿUthmāniyya* attests to a scholar or more travelling or resettling in those regions (e.g., 6, 7, 8, 9, 10, 11, 13, and passim); Atçıl, *Scholars and Sultans*, 41 ff.; Abisaab, *Converting Persia*; Burak, *Second Formation*, 72 and passim; on scholars' mobility in Islamic societies in general, see El-Merheb et al., *Professional Mobility in Islamic Societies*.
186 On the cultural integration of the Arab provinces into the Ottoman system, see Pfeifer's excellent account, *Empire of Salons*, especially 166-24.

VI

In conclusion, and to place the Circassian period in its proper constitutional context, we will do well to compare it, as a matter of *qualitative* contrast, with the structural changes that overtook the Ottoman Empire in the nineteenth century. This comparison is not just heuristic but also leads to a substantive understanding of what went wrong, constitutionally speaking, in the wake of European colonization and the implementation of so-called reforms.

Elsewhere,[187] I have dealt with these structural changes in a detail that does not bear repeating here. But the fundamental features of these changes involved the restructuring of the entire system, judicial, legislative and political, all the while increasing the power of the executive manifold. And here we shall assume, again for the sake of illustrative contrast (but not quite accurately), that the Ottoman legal system – during the second half of the eighteenth century and throughout the nineteenth – functioned smoothly and without the presence of anarchic conditions similar to those plaguing the later Mamlūk legal system.

As of 1826, we see a massive overhaul of the *waqf* system, which led to imperial control from the center (Istanbul), an overhaul whose effect was the depletion of the budgets of the empire's large law colleges that had formerly been autonomous and richly self-sustaining. The impact of the "reforms" was so considerable that to many observers these colleges appeared to stand at the brink of total collapse.[188] This step alone would have weakened the ulama and the entire judicial personnel, for its substantive effect was to strike hard against the reproductive powers of the very class of professionals who managed the judicial affairs of the empire, let alone the support these institutions had given to the promotion of legal education and its generational perpetuation.

Furthermore, as of about the 1840s, new civil councils were established, with a structure that was intended to mark a departure from the traditional, *qāḍī*-centered law court and *qāḍī*-centered administration. Whereas the *qāḍī*, as we saw, was the leading judicial and administrative officer from the tenth/sixteenth century, he was now relegated to a secondary position, or at least as one among many others of equal importance. This shuffling of offices and powers, as one noted historian remarked, "was aimed at

187 Hallaq, *Sharīʿa*, 357-429, especially at 396-420.
188 Hallaq, *Sharīʿa*, 403.

bringing provincial administration under more stringent control by the central government by freeing it somewhat from the power of the local *ulemā* and notables."[189]

At around the same time, a New Order (*Niẓām-i Cedīd*) was gradually coming into being, producing with it new courts, new laws, a new judicial process, and consequently a new legal culture, all of which having a distinct European imprint.[190] For the first time in the history of the empire, if not of Islam from the beginning, the New Order placed the sultan and his centralized and fast expanding bureaucratic machine above the Sharīʿa, which was now no longer the law of the land but one that competed with, but finally lost to, the monopoly of the state as a law-making machine. The former sultanic executive, which possessed limited competence and had almost no effect on the Sharīʿa-defined legislative, had now become not only the conduit of legislation, but also commandeered this power exclusively for itself. From the perspective of Islamic history and its strong sense of constitutionalism, the rapacious state could have easily appeared to them to be much more than a mere leviathan or even "the coldest of all cold monsters."

Beginning in the 1850s, the new state introduced a Western code of commerce inspired by French codification. In the same year, a penal code was promulgated, defining in great detail the jurisdictional boundaries between the Sharīʿa courts and the new criminal courts that were being introduced on the European model. The introduction of further codes and laws continued unabated, until, in 1917, the last major transformative act was undertaken, when the law of personal status became subject to state engineering.[191] All in all, little of the Sharīʿa's substantive and procedural law survived, but more crucially, the autonomy of the legislative and judicial powers was severely compromised by the act of subsuming law-making under the centralized and autocratic power of the capital's ruling elite.

To speak of violations and rebellious behavior of inferiors against their superiors, or even of a mob that hijacked part of the justice system, is one thing – but to speak of a centralized political elite (the Kantian "band of devils")[192] that succeeded in restructuring the entire legal system and changing

189 İnalcik, "Application of the Tanzimat," 108.

190 For these developments, see Rubin, *Ottoman Nizamiye Courts*; Hallaq, *Sharīʿa*, 396-420; İnalcik, "Application of the Tanzimat."

191 On the general ill-effects of 1917 family law, see Tucker, "Revisiting Reform;" Cuno, "Reorganization of the Sharia Courts."

192 Schmitt, *Political Romanticism*, 111.

the ecology of its division of powers, is quite another. The Circassian period was a temporary swerve from twelve hundred years of a fairly consistent constitutional system. The modern state's emergence changed not only the players and rules of the game, but the very game itself. The millennial Muslim habitus had now ceased to exist.

Chapter 11

Ottoman "Dynastic Law" and Sharīʿa's Constitutionalism: Whose Law?

A year before the Glorious Revolution took place in England, in the early morning of Saturday, November 8, 1687, the leading jurists of the Ottoman Empire convened at the Mosque of Ayasofya (the former Cathedral of Hagia Sophia) to discuss for the last time the demands of the army to depose Mehmed IV. When the grand muftī, the chief jurisconsult of the empire, asked the dignitaries present whether the sultan should be deposed, Mehmed, the chief justice of the Asian and African provinces, was the first one to give an affirmative answer. The father of this Mehmed, Abdürrahim, had issued the legal opinion that legitimized the regicide of Mehmed IV's father Ibrahim in 1648, and had even overseen the execution personally. Mehmed's son, Yahya, was to be elected chief justice of the Asian and African provinces by the opposition forces in Istanbul in 1703, and to take part in the deposition of Mehmed IV's son Mustafa II. This Mustafa II came to be deposed, among others, by a jurist whose father had deposed his father and whose grandfather had deposed and executed his own grandfather.[1]

This account tells a story of law's power over political leadership, including the sultan himself, often misdescribed in modern scholarship as the sovereign. Yet, having a jurist depose a sultan who is a "sovereign" brings forth a great potential for contradiction, for this particular ruler, the Ottoman,

1 Tezcan, *Second Ottoman Empire*, 7.

post-Mongol dynastic majordomo – who is said to hail from tribal traditions strong in upholding rule by divine power – is "sovereign" despite the glaring fact that the Sharīʿa, even in its weakest form, remained largely outside of his control. The crucial and most fundamental constitutional question therefore is the relationship between these two forces, the force of the Sharīʿa and that of the "post-Mongol ruler," or more aptly put, of that particular form of executive rule.

I

The rise of the "post-Mongol" ruler represents in recent scholarship a new breed of monarch, one who brings with him a divine mandate to legislate. This kind of ruler is mostly associated with the gunpowder empires, though the Mamlūks, flourishing after the Chinggisid invasions, have now dropped out of the picture as a likely source to produce this variety of divinely-ordained rulers. It is now common knowledge in the field that the Mamlūks had no penchant to legislate beyond their administrative competence and that they were not, after all, in possession of the Mongol law of *yasā/yasaq/jasagh*. In fact, as we have seen throughout the preceding four chapters, the discretionary powers that were otherwise arrogated to the early Mamlūk sultans, as well as to their predecessors, had become absorbed toward the end of Mamlūk rule by Sharʿī regulative mechanisms, whereby the expanding executive powers were legislated and regimented for the sultan by the Sharīʿa itself. This later Mamlūk-era development, we have also seen, was carried over to Ottoman jurisprudence and judicial practice.[2] All in all, the emerging picture further complicates the modern scholarly narrative of a post-Mongol "sovereign" whose representation seems always concomitant with the notion of a divine right to legislate.

Yet, given Sharīʿa's penchant for autonomy, the case for sultanic legislation could not be easily made, leaving modern scholars to search for ways to affirm this dynastic power outside the possibility of an "absolute monarchy," that form of rule potently latent in the Western historiographical and political imagination.[3] The typical technique for claiming this "post-Mongol" legislative

2 See ch. 8-10.

3 In addition to the authors we will discuss below, we might note that earlier Orientalist writers have perpetuated a Eurocentric narrative that seems always to misunderstand. A

charge was to claim certain powers for the *qānūn* under the Ottomans, these latter being generally regarded as the most successful Islamic empire to have integrated dynastic law in a dominant position within what is considered the law of the land.

Insofar as I can tell, the most radical claim made in this direction comes from G. Burak who argued that it was through the legal-bureaucratic technique of the *qānūn* that the Ottomans, as a dynasty, managed to assert their legislative dominance.[4] Integral to this technique, at least as a bureaucratic function, was the unprecedented segregation of the Ḥanafī *madhhab* as the "official" school of the empire. It was thus the interplay between these two forces, and the ways in which the former allegedly shaped the latter, that "dynastic law" came to manage, manipulate, and even corral the Sharīʿa.

Burak's argument revolves around "four major, closely interlocking developments" that came to shape what he anachronistically calls a "state *madhhab*." The first is the rise of an imperial hierarchy, while the second is the emergence of the practice of "state-appointed" *muftī*s, another anachronism. The third is the dynasty/state's "regulation of the structure and doctrine of the school." Finally, the fourth development, on which the first three were predicated, is the rise of dynastic law in the post-Mongol eastern Islamic lands.[5] The first two "developments," as described by Burak, effectively constituted a single constellation of appointing "state" *muftī*s within a supposedly clearly defined and structured judicial hierarchy headed by Shaykh al-Islām, the empire's chief *muftī*.

Stated differently, Burak's overall argument consists of the following sub-arguments: (1) that the dynastic *qānūn* was of a different quality from the Sharīʿa, so much so that it constituted a tool by which the Sharīʿa underwent a certain transformation, although we are never told what the effects of this transformation ultimately were; (2) that it was through this *qānūn* that the Ḥanafī *madhhab* was segregated and made not only the official administrative tool of the empire but also a newly reconstituted and canonized legal entity different from its parent school, what might be called traditional Ḥanafīsm; (3) that an official hierarchy, headed by a chief *muftī*, produced the judicial and administrative officers of the empire; (4) that the elite of this hierarchy also generated, *in its capacity as an "official" entity*, a legal doctrine different

notable case in this context is Colin Imber, *Ebu's-suʿud*, reviewed and critiqued soundly by Engin Akarli.

4 James E. Baldwin makes a similar argument, however briefly. See his *Islamic Law*, 76 ff.

5 Burak, *Second Formation*, 10-11.

from that produced by traditional Ḥanafīsm; and (5) that all this created a new kind of Islamic law, one so different from what preceded it that it may be aptly described as having gone through a "second formation," the first having been the evolutionary process that brought that very system of the Sharīʿa and its classical Ḥanafī school into existence.

First, we note that the anachronistic terminology which structures Burak's narrative already foretells a bias in favor of a presumed "state" as well as a "sovereign" that act and function like a hegemonic modern state. We will see the effects of such mistaken presumptions as may emanate from a notion of "state *madhhab*,"[6] an oxymoron for anyone who correctly understands what a *madhhab* is. The narrative also exaggerates the effects of "state hierarchy" by reducing the significance of what lay outside of it, especially in the Arabic[7] lands where the *madhhab*s continued to reproduce themselves in the manner established well before the Ottomans appeared on the scene.

Focusing on imperial *fatwā*s and a particular juristic biographical genre of *ṭabaqāt* – whose scope happened to be the imperial hierarchy – is likewise seen as an implied displacement, if not a qualitative reduction, of the non-dynastic juristic structures that lay outside of the imperial judicial administration. For a historian of non-dynastic law, the picture would appear quite different, giving more credit to the continuation of the law in *largely* – though of course non-monolithically – the same way it had existed before. One reason behind Burak's diminution of the importance of "non-official" doctrine is the stark fact of confusing "official doctrine" with "authoritative doctrine" – for there is no *necessary concomitance* between the two. An "official doctrine," whatever that means, can never become authoritative in any school without following the standard criteria of *ijtihād*ic reasoning, those established by the *madhhab* for centuries.[8] Likewise, an authoritative doctrine will inevitably and by definition be authoritative irrespective of whether it is issued or adopted by a Shaykh al-Islām or any other major jurist. In other words, it was the *madhhab* and its epistemologically entrenched hermeneutics that determined authoritativeness, not the sultan. Even in those cases where the sultan endorsed a particular doctrine and sanctioned it for application in

6 Burak, *Second Formation*, 223 and passim.

7 I deliberately employ the term "Arabic," not "Arab," to avoid the association of the latter with a nationalist or ethnic understanding of juristic identity, which did not exist prior to the nineteenth century.

8 For the structure of doctrine within the *madhhab* as well as for the processes of constructing substantive juristic authority, see Hallaq, *Authority*, 86-165, but also passim.

courts of law, the doctrine or opinion would have to acquire its authority and force due to the fact that it rests within the *madhhab*ic system of hermeneutics and legal reasoning (as the oeuvre of the distinguished Abū al-Suʿūd attests).[9] Burak's study therefore sheds no meaningful light on "non-dynastic" legal development, one that, with its undeniably porous relationships with the "dynastic," constituted much of the field of legal doctrine and judicial and customary practice on the ground.

There is no doubt that the Ottomans were markedly driven toward centralization and tighter administrative control than had been the case before them, but the real question is the extent to which their centralizing apparatus amounted to the subordination of the Sharīʿa to "dynastic law." More precisely, the fundamental issue here is the degree to which the Ottoman juridico-political system transcended the limits already set by the Sharʿī delineations of *siyāsa sharʿiyya* and its boundaries. These are profoundly constitutional considerations that Burak does not address.

Burak also asserts that the Ottoman biographical works marginalized the jurists of the Arab provinces, which he takes to be an indication of the dominance of the empire-affiliated jurists, those who belonged to what he regarded as a clearly defined "state" judicial hierarchy. But this view of genres and of Islamic biographical literature at large is a distorted one. For it is a universal feature of Islamic intellectual culture to classify and categorize any phenomenon once it had increased in complexity, which I suspect is a function and modus operandi of all complex systems. The specialization of biography (i.e., with a focus on the Ottoman establishment) is analogous to many trends of historical writing, of recording, classifying, and authoritative structuring of systems (of which process of authorization the *ṭabaqāt* were a prime example).[10] It is not uncommon to find biographical works dedicated to regions.[11] By the sixth/twelfth century, and upon the effective (though not institutional)[12] demise of the ʿAbbāsid caliphate as a quasi-unifying power, historical (and historicizing)

9 See, e.g., Imber, *Ebu's-Suʿud*.

10 Ṭabaqāt works, especially those of the jurists, are often seen as biographical accounts, recounting the jurist's general educational background, teachers, students, and curriculum vitae. But there is much more to them than this ambition, for they partook in the authorization of the *madhhab*s as much as legal doctrine did. Insofar as I know, this aspect of the work has not been properly studied.

11 See, e.g., Ibn al-Ṭaḥḥān, *Tārīkh ʿUlamāʾ Ahl Miṣr*.

12 On the *institutional* legitimacy of the caliphate and its durability, see ch. 2, above. It cannot be stressed enough that this institutional legitimacy is to be sharply distinguished from military and effective power.

literature mushroomed into specializations, such as annals and biographies dedicated to dynasties, individual sultans, regions, early or later generations of scholars within a school, or even biographies dedicated to scholars, physicians, theologians, and notables who flourished within "centuries."[13] The histories of individual cities had already appeared two centuries earlier, Baghdādī's *Ta'rīkh Baghdād* being a prime example. Mistaking literary specialization for privileging, authorization, or marginalization is a profound substantive and methodological error.

But even if we assume that such marginalization had indeed been attempted, it does not necessarily follow from such a phenomenon that tribal or dynastic law had gained control over the Sharīʿa. The most radical conclusion that can be inferred from this alleged deemphasis on the Arab jurists is that the center of legal power has shifted to another location. In fact, the same pattern had already occurred three centuries earlier, when, after the Mongol invasions, the legal center of the Sharīʿa shifted from ʿAbbāsid Baghdad to Mamlūk Cairo and Damascus.

Attempting to show biographical marginalization was not Burak's final goal; rather, it was for him a means of arguing that the administrative hierarchy was systemically geared toward a manipulation of the law in favor of producing an authoritative and canonic dynastic reading, even by appealing to otherwise weak opinions.[14] The materials he chose to study were carefully selected *fatwā*s that hardly represent the general body of doctrine in the schools, the Ḥanafī included. A *fatwā* can have an effect in a particular case or group of cases, even throughout the empire (the cash *waqf* being a prominent example), but this hardly translates into the incorporation of the individual *fatwā* as the standard doctrine of the *madhhab*. This is to say, as I have shown in detail elsewhere,[15] that even if a *fatwā* proved successful in entering the canonized body of *furūʿ*, it does not necessarily mean that the *fatwā* becomes a *madhhab*-doctrine or, much less, that it reflects the general or only doctrine of the school.

Jurists and judges continued, as they had done for centuries earlier, to structure their *fiqh* irrespective of such "minority" *fatwā*s, this being a part of the maintenance of their *madhhab*ic structure that usually survived not only imperial intrusions but also judicial malpractice. We have seen a major

13 See, e.g., Shihāb al-Dīn Abū Shāma, *Tarājim Rijāl*; ʿAsqalānī, *Al-Durar al-Kāmina*; Udfawī, *al-Ṭāliʿ al-Saʿīd*; Suyūṭī, *Ḥusn al-Muḥāḍara*; Shawkānī, *al-Badr al-Ṭāliʿ*; ʿĀmirī, *Bahjat al-Nāẓirīn*.

14 Burak, *Second Formation*, 11.

15 Hallaq, *Authority*, 186-208; Hallaq, "Murder in Cordoba."

example of this in the foregoing chapter, where the Sharīʿa managed, in the most remarkable manner, to survive the devastations wrought upon it by a collapsing Mamlūk judicial system and by the violent disruptions brought about by plagues, wars, and the rogue Circassians. Yavuz Aykan is therefore right in noting that "Burak fails to answer whether the impact of the alleged tension between *rumi* [i.e., dynastic Istanbul-centered] and Greater Syrian [i.e., 'Arab'] jurists can be traced in the doctrinal preferences of these jurists in their jurisprudential works."[16] Burak likewise fails to see, because he has no rear-view mirror, that there is relatively little that is remarkable or exceptional about the Ottoman period he studied. As I noted earlier, the scholarly community that tends to advocate Ottoman exceptionalism is also, unsurprisingly, characterized by its weak, at times non-existent, knowledge of the pre-Ottoman periods.

Another part of Burak's larger argument is that the *fatwā*s of the Arabic jurists were less influential than those issued by members of the Ottoman legal hierarchy. But one is hard pressed to find a substantiation of this claim in either the doctrinal domains (i.e., in the *fiqh* doctrinal elaborations) or in the practices of the courts throughout. The superiority of these *fatwā*s, for him, is evidence of the monopoly or dominance of the "post-Mongol" dynastic law, just as *al-Fatāwā al-Hindiyya* represented, in his mind, though again erroneously, a parallel case of dynastic intrusion.[17]

Furthermore, the reader leaves the book with the impression that there were almost two separate and distinct systems of law operating side by side in the empire, one official and another not, one having a particular juristic membership and another having a different axis of association. The abundant detail he allocates to the career of Muḥyī al-Dīn Khayr al-Dīn al-Ramlī of Palestine[18] demonstrates not only that the "non-official" Ḥanafī *madhhab* flourished all the same, but that this part or "branch" of Ḥanafīsm was no less important than what he identified as "official," a term or category that Burak does not, in the first place, define or articulate in any meaningful way (a fatal weakness of his overall argument). Ramlī and the many other major jurists who flourished up to the end of Ḥanafīsm – when it was destroyed at the hands of colonialism in the nineteenth century – remained central to the Sharīʿa and its operation outside of the artificially constructed "officialism" of the school.

16 See Aykan's review of Burak's work, 794.

17 Burak, *Second Formation*, 212-13. For a detailed refutation of this and similar views of *al-Fatāwā al-Hindiyya*, see Hallaq, "Model *Shurūṭ* Works," 122-23.

18 Burak, *Second Formation*, 34 ff., 147-54, and passim.

Furthermore, Burak's narrative drives a sharp wedge between Ottoman and pre-Ottoman constructions of law and constitutional effect, practically making a case for Ottoman exceptionalism (if not Turkic ethnocentrism).[19] We can likewise clearly see how Burak's superimposed divisions and reified ruptures between Ottoman/post-Mongol, on the one hand, and Mamlūk, on the other, run diametrically counter to the continuities I have shown in the previous chapter in regard to *siyāsa sharʿiyya*.

Nor should we take Burak's word about the *qānūn*'s origins at face value. There are good grounds to think that the *qānūn* is not directly related to Mongol dynastic and tribal law, if for no reason other than the fact that this connection has never been established beyond sweeping Orientalist impressions and very likely the "invention of the Turkish nationalists," as the historian Colin Imber puts it in rejecting Burak's larger argument.[20] There is instead every reason to believe that the *qānūn* came to bolster the aims of the Sharīʿa,[21] and as we have seen in the preceding chapter, claiming for *qānūn* a non-subsidiary status was seen as repugnant by the Ottoman political elite, leading eventually to its radical decline. If the subject matter of the *qānūnnāme*s was predominantly the standardization of the management of land tenure, taxation, and the *tīmār* systems, with sporadic attention to crime and sexual infractions, then none of this, as we have seen, breaches the boundaries of the ruler's responsibilities as aptly delineated in the *siyāsa sharʿiyya* and *aḥkām al-sulṭāniyya* doctrines.

Furthermore, Burak takes the appointment of a chief *muftī* for the empire as an indication of the control that the political establishment exercised over the Sharīʿa. Given that Burak did not distinguish between "official" and authoritative law, it can hardly be shown that Shaykh al-Islām was creating imperial rather than *madhhab*ic law. And given, among much else, the powerful epigraph opening this chapter, recounting depositions and

19 See Burak, *Second Formation*, 55 – although he places the term "ethnic" in quotes and says that the case "should not be overstated." Yet, his invocation of this proto-nationalistic category in the context of admission that the Sharīʿa personnel could not have cared less about "ethnicity" is quite telling. It might also be pointed out here that in addition to his anachronistic uses of terms, Burak is also ideologically teleological in arguing for Ottoman "state" intervention as a natural process of development and progress, ignoring, like so many Orientalists, the basic and stark facts of nineteenth-century colonialism, which upended the structures of society and law in the Muslim world. See his "Between the Qānūn of Qaytbay...," 23. On the colonial destruction of Muslim legal institutions during the nineteenth century, see Hallaq, *Sharīʿa*, 371-442.

20 See Colin Imber's review in the *Journal of Islamic Studies*, 392-94.

21 Hallaq, *Sharīʿa*, 214-16 and passim; Peirce, *Morality Tales*, 119, 122, 327.

executions of sultans at the hands of Shaykh al-Islāms, it is doubtful that this control had any real meaning. The same facts on which Burak bases his interpretation can be harnessed to an entirely different, if not diametrically opposite effect. It is my argument that the Ottomans realized early on that the best way to administer their large empire was to use and enhance a law that was already paradigmatic and culturally pervasive, namely, that of the Sharīʿa. Every other dynasty had done the same. In fact, it would seem that going against the Sharīʿa, whether by Ottoman, Mamlūk, or any other dynastic initiative, would have amounted not only to a grave mistake and a lack of rational clarity, but also to a political suicide. The Sharīʿa was the law of the land by force of doxa. Appointing a Shaykh al-Islām was a recognition of this fundamental fact; it was an act even geared toward an enhancement of Sharīʿa's stature and power, where the rule of law commanded and directed imperial administrative practice, not the other way around. The power and influence of Shaykh al-Islām no doubt varied according to context and circumstance, as well as to charisma and a host of other considerations, but structurally this office restrained political rule and brought it largely in line with the legal imperatives of the Sharīʿa. A strong Shaykh al-Islām could bring a sultanic reign to an end, and a weak one was a major bone in its throat.

Finally, but most centrally, Burak's detailed description of the learned hierarchy of Ottoman administration masks the real issue that is declared to be the ultimate quest of his monograph: How is the presumed "dynastic Ḥanafī law" different in content from what would have evolved in its stead if there was no such dynastic "branch" of Ḥanafīsm? In other words, we do not see how this supposedly "state-created" law is different from the overall Ḥanafī *madhhab*, a school that continued to operate by the same hermeneutical *ijtihād*ic apparatus under the Ottomans as it did before, notwithstanding the restrictions imposed on the purview of its otherwise varied doctrines. No wonder then that a number of Ottomanists judged Burak's work as having failed in its declared mission, however valuable its detailed descriptions of the judicial hierarchy may be.[22] Other than the relatively few famous cases[23] where the Chief Muftīs

22 See bibliography for the reviews of Burak's work by Yavuz Aykan, Colin Imber and Amir Toft.

23 Of these cases, James Baldwin focuses on the statute of limitations of 957/1551, which set a time limit on litigation, ten years in respect of land and fifteen for "most [other] cases." The regulation is said to originate from non-*fiqhi* sources and represented a sultanic order par excellence, although no scholar could thus far identify these sources or even the circumstances and the debates that gave rise to the regulation itself. In other

of the empire seem to have overstretched the internal hermeneutics of the Ḥanafī school to arrive at expedient solutions, the law continued to operate, and dynamically at that, as it had for centuries. It continued to operate within the contours of the Ḥanafī school, according to the conventional constitutional boundaries, and thus from within the larger purview of the Sharīʿa; this despite the Ottoman insistence on dictating to their *qāḍīs* the application of a specific doctrine within that *madhhab*.[24]

To answer the questions that Burak's work poses and to prove its larger hypothesis, one must show that the dynastic impositions not only gave the empire a particular form of judicial hierarchy but also that this latter – or

---

words, we know virtually nothing about its origins and even less of the circumstances that led to Sulaymān the Magnificent's edict to make it a formal doctrine of the empire. The non-*fiqhī* origins of the rule seem assumed rather than proven. It is therefore baffling that Baldwin speaks with certainty about its imperial origins (not being sure if it were Ottoman, Mamlūk, or Dhulqādir). Yet, more striking is the conclusion he draws from this bundle of highly probabilistic evidence. The adoption of this rule during the centuries of the empire "illustrates that the codification project [of the modern period] drew on a longer tradition of intervention by the executive authorities into legal doctrine." If this astonishing statement, made in the most banal manner, betrays anything, it is the latent desperation to maintain the residue of the myth of undue sultanic intervention. Even if we assume that there indeed were thirty-two cases in which the Ottoman sultans, over five centuries, dictated what the applicable law was (see Tezcan, next paragraph), it is quite a stretch to reach the conclusion about the modern state "intervention" in light of the fact that the cases of the applicable and effectively applied *fiqh* were in the tens of thousands, if not more. See Baldwin, *Islamic Law*, 75-76 and n. 8 at p. 186.

The main cases in point, however, relate to the cash *waqf*, statute of limitations, and a few others. Tezcan, *Second Ottoman Empire*, 34, puts the matter in a proper perspective. He argues that "Suleyman's decree concerning cash *waqf*s was arguably his most significant intervention in the law. Ebussuʿud once noted that there were altogether thirty-two such cases in which the political authority expressed a preference among the competing opinions in the Ḥanafī School on a particular question to determine the preponderant opinion to be applied in the courts of law – unfortunately without identifying them. Yet none of the other cases was apparently deemed to as radically alter the spirit of the Ḥanafī School of jurists' law as the one on the cash *waqf* which continued to be the only exception mentioned in the appointment letters of Ottoman judges. These letters instructed the appointees to follow the soundest opinion in cases where there was a disagreement among the Ḥanafī jurists 'except for [the case of] the registration of trusts endowed with cash.' In that case the weak opinion was to be preferred – a truly substantial intervention in the law. Thus the most significant intervention of the political authority into the domain of jurists' law was one in which it acted to free up a process of economic change that had already been started by social dynamics. The dynastic authority was not the agent of change, but rather its client. Having become so enmeshed in jurists' law, the political authority could not then stop the jurists themselves from entering its own domain, where they would soon decide who would be the next emperor."

24 As argued by Peters in "What Does it Mean to be an Official Madhhab?"

anything else emanating from Istanbul – did effectively change the law, so much so that one can say that the law that applied to the Ottoman population represented the will of the sultan and the dynasty that stood behind him. One must also show that "biopower" was appropriated by the sultanic executive, "biopower" being perhaps the highest measure of sovereignty.[25] But none of this could be argued, either by Burak or anyone else thus far. In fact, Rudolph Peters' pioneering study, which appears to have influenced Burak's work considerably, and which is more judicious in formulating the phenomenon of Ḥanafīzing the empire, concluded that the "Ottomans could both uphold Ḥanafī supremacy and meet the practical demands of the local population." And he immediately and prudently added: "However, we must not exaggerate the practical importance of this system. It functioned only in a few large cities."[26] As importantly, Peters never argued that this system, having operated on such a limited scale, was endowed with anything like the sovereign power that Burak arrogated to it.

II

Radical as it is, Burak's argument met with opposition even from quarters that espouse the view of tilting the relationship between sultanic law and the Sharīʿa in favor of the former. Samy Ayoub argues for a middle position in contemporary scholarship, effectively rejecting Burak's sweeping generalizations as well as the stance, on the other side of the spectrum, that "legal authority in Islamic law is epistemically divorced from political authority, and legal knowledge is the exclusive domain of the jurists."[27]

Ayoub begins his argument with the assertion that "Ḥanafī legal commentaries (*shurūḥ*) and *fatwās* from the Mamlūk period authorize and acknowledge the discretionary powers of the political authority (*siyāsa*), without, however, authorizing legislation from, or a legislative role for, the political authority."[28] This situation, he states, had changed under the Ottomans during the seventeenth and eighteenth centuries, when the Ḥanafī school was "reconfigured

25 On biopower within the context of the arguments of this book, see ch. 12.
26 Peters, "What Does it Mean to be an Official Madhhab?" 157, 158.
27 Ayoub, "Sultan Says," 240. This last stance he accurately attributes to this writer, as extracted from my "Juristic Authority," 243.
28 Ayoub, "Sultan Says," 243-44.

to accept a legislative role for the Ottoman state and to assign authoritative value to its orders and edicts."[29] To demonstrate his thesis that the Ḥanafī school was "reconfigured to accept a *legislative role* for the Ottoman state,"[30] he marshals a number of legal cases hailing from the works of four Ḥanafī-Ottoman jurists.

In arguing his case, Ayoub embraces a questionable interpretation of evidence, giving undue constitutional weight to the Ottoman executive's involvement in legislation. It is striking that none of the cases he adduces are legislated by the Sublime Porte, and all of them find their roots and branches in the terrains of Ḥanafī doctrine.[31] This is a constitutional fact of the first order. The Ottoman "state" did not legislate *fiqh* cases (precisely because it was not a state). It unwaveringly left this sphere of judicial activity to the jurists. A proper analysis of the cases places them squarely either in the *fiqh* doctrine or, in rare cases, in the domain of *siyāsa shar'iyya,* although the lines of demarcation between these two domains was not always made clear. Almost in every instance, the Sublime Porte intervened to assert a weaker or a minority opinion in the school, and often to settle what we nowadays call legal indeterminacy, usually in cases of severe disagreements among the jurists about a certain matter (the most well-known case in Ayoub's list is the statute of limitations).[32] When not settling juristic disagreement, it was to intervene in cases pertaining to public interest, which we have seen to be one of the sultanic functions and duties stipulated by constitutional law.[33]

Ayoub argues that this was effectively an Ottoman innovation, or a Ḥanafī "turn" from a previous doctrine of the school aiming to accommodate Ottoman policies. But this argument is inaccurate as a matter of principle. Ayoub recognizes some elements of the principle's practice but does not think to explore it as a juristic principle *par excellence* (for a full acknowledgement of the principle would run diametrically opposite to his thesis). The principle, having endured for centuries in the life of the Ḥanafī school, takes it for granted that the caliph or, in his stead, the sultan has the power of judicial delegation

29 Ayoub, "Sultan Says," 248.

30 Ayoub, "Sultan Says," 248 (emphasis mine).

31 My findings are consistent with İnalcik's conclusions that the Ottoman *'urfī* (executive) officers lacked "any authority to give *legal* decisions" (his emphasis), and that this authority "was delegated only to the [Shar'ī] cadis." *Ahl al-'urf* could only execute the *qāḍī*'s decisions, he added. See his review of U. Heyd's *Studies*, 698.

32 See n. 23, above.

33 See relevant discussions in Māwardī and Ibn Jamā'a in ch. 1 (sec. III), 3 and 7, above.

or deputization (*ināba, niyāba*). Capturing the range of doctrines prevailing in his school for the four centuries prior, the pre-Ottoman Ḥanafī jurist Ibn Māza (d. 616/1219) offers a list of the ruler's prerogatives in judicial appointments, capturing the principle that gives rise to these executive powers. Within the constitutional limits of these powers as delineated by Māwardī, among many others,[34] the ruler, being in charge of appointing administrators for all government functions, is responsible for delegating (*istināba*) the function of adjudication (*qaḍāʾ*) to qualified legists. Accepting the constitutional fact that he cannot properly legislate, he is empowered by the Muslim Community to hire and dismiss judges.

But integral to this power of "hiring" is also the equally administrative competence to limit or particularize the appointed *qāḍī*'s jurisdiction. He who has the competence to delegate a defined scope of powers also has the competence to abridge them within that scope. The abridgement may relate to place or time, such as appointing a judge to a certain city, or even decide the specific place where he can preside, including, for example, in which mosque. He can delimit the duration of judicial delegation for a certain period, to a year, month, even just one day.[35] The sultan may also appoint a judge to a locale, with full jurisdictional sway, but forbid him from adjudicating a case brought to his court by a specific person or by a class of litigants.[36] This of course presumes that there is a reason for this exception, but we must also presume that this rule is only an atomized part of a larger and complex procedural arrangement. Such decrees containing clauses of exclusion (*istithnāʾ*) and particularization (*takhṣīṣ*) have been put into practice from early Islamic times,[37] and are legally valid, "because delegated appointments (*taqālīd*) are effectively [acts of] deputization (*ināba*), confirmed to the extent the deputizing power stipulates."[38] In Ḥanafī law itself, therefore, a ruler is legally competent to restrict the range of juristic doctrine to be applied by a judge or a group of judges.

This is not all, however. The fact that all the Ottoman cases cited by Ayoub – to the effect that a minority or weak opinion was imposed as the default doctrine of the court – were approved and reasoned by Shaykh al-Islām

34 As we have seen in the previous chapters and will continue to see throughout this book.
35 Ibn Māza, *Muḥīṭ*, VIII, 14-15.
36 Ibn Māza, *Muḥīṭ*, VIII, 16.
37 Hallaq, *Origins*, 80. See also Ibn al-Qāṣṣ, *Adab al-Qāḍī*, 133.
38 Ibn Māza, *Muḥīṭ*, VIII, 16: "*Wa-hādhā li'anna al-taqlīda inābatun, fa'innamā yathbutu bi-qadri mā anāba.*"

signifies much as well. The implication here is that as a preeminent jurist, Shaykh al-Islām exercised his juristic duty and right to rehabilitate an opinion within the school by appealing to the *madhhab*'s *own* methods of legal reasoning and techniques of "preponderance," activities that are in no way unusual, in the Ḥanafī as well as all three other schools.[39] This is a further indication of the constitutional limits by which executive sultanism understood itself to be bound. True, for the Sublime Porte, Shaykh al-Islām was instrumental in permitting it to streamline and hierarchize the judicial establishment, to optimize its effectiveness, predictability, and consistency, but this quintessentially Sharʿī office also effectively bound the dynastic executive by the very principle of the rule of law that gave it its legal prerogatives to rule and administer the empire.

While it is also true that Ottoman judicial activism was remarkable in comparison with that of previous dynastic executives, it did not violate the principles of the Sharīʿa, especially its discretionary domain of *siyāsa sharʿiyya*. Ayoub is right in noting this energetic judicial activism, but he misconstrues its constitutional nature and effect. His repeated references to the Sublime Porte as "a state" ("Ottoman state," "state decision," "state orders," etc.) betrays his lack of discrimination between the constitutional divisions that sharply separated the Ottoman and Islamic forms of rule, on the one hand, and those of the modern state, on the other. The proposition that the Ḥanafī school "embraced the indispensability of the state in the law-making process" is practically an oxymoron, evident to the naked eye when translated into a modern cognate: "The American legal system and juridical doctrine embraced the indispensability of the state, of which the legal system and its doctrine are integral parts, in the law-making process." This proposition is redundant and begs the fallacy of *petitio principii* to boot. By contrast, it is apt to say that "the American executive exercised a judicial overreach against the judiciary."

Furthermore, Ayoub's language, like Burak's, is anachronistic, if for no other reason than the fact that the Sublime Porte could not have constituted a "state," even if we assume that a modern state had existed prior to the sixteenth or seventeenth century. Obviously, the state is much more than an executive. But the terminology betrays a lack of realization that the modern state possesses features that Islamic governance never knew, including, among other things,

39 For various types of legal reasoning involved in the reassessment of the opinions already existing within a school, such as *tarjīḥ*, *takhrīj*, and *taṣḥīḥ*, see Hallaq, *Authority*, 43-56, 127-48, 185-88, and passim; Hallaq, "*Takhrīj* and the Construction of Juristic Authority."

a massive so-called "rational" bureaucracy, a historically unique concept of *raison d'état*, and a distinctly political concept of sovereignty and biopower (discussed in chapter 12).[40]

Burak's and Ayoub's writings are useful because they confirm the opposite of what they set out to prove, especially the former, whose claims are more ambitious than the latter. The hypothesis of a dynastic law intruding on the substance and methodology of the Sharīʿa has been proven unsuccessful. What is at stake in the constitutional question of who or what ultimately makes the law is the fact of who or what decides how people live or should live. This question is directly related to the will, that is, the will to power, the will to rule and govern. This latter is of remarkable importance because governing entails a particular kind of sovereign power to form and shape the lives of the subjects, as individuals, familial groups, communal and political subjects, and even as psycho-epistemic subjectivities. Therefore, the central question in this constitutional matter is not just who commands the making of the law but also what the content of the law itself is. The *substance, quality, and telos* of the law are as important as the principle of the rule of law itself. After all, many authoritarian and genocidal regimes, not least Nazi Germany, are states that possess a robust concept of the rule of law.

What is more, the dynastic intervention in the *madhhab* in favor of minority and otherwise weak opinions does not seem to have been in favor of bolstering or defending dynastic power. Every case mentioned by Ayoub, for instance, as well as the two most notorious executive interventions regarding cash *waqf*s and statute of limitations, betrayed governmental concerns for public interest. In other words, the intervention was a matter of public policy rather than a narrow interest in augmenting sultanic power (or, as we will see in the next chapter, the perpetual definition and redefinition of the human).

It is therefore of crucial importance to understand the preset boundaries that surround and confine the significance of this intervention. Ordering judges to apply a minority or weak opinion does not go much in the way of asserting executive power in the substantive, socially significant, sense, *for it remains the case that the minority opinion is an integral part of Sharīʿa's substantive law*. In fact, asserting the superiority of an otherwise minority opinion is methodologically conceivable, that is, conceivably possible within,

40 On traditional and modern forms of authority, see Şentürk, "Between Traditional and New Forms of Authority." See also Hallaq, *Impossible State*.

and in accordance with, the *madhhabs*' own principles of legal reasoning. Anyone who knows the *fiqh*'s world of reasoning will know this much. The competition in the hierarchy of opinions within a single school is not only stiff but also dynamic. In relative terms, it is not so often the case that one can find a *madhhab*-opinion – that is, the opinion that reigns as the *madhhab*'s authoritative, strongest, or most favored opinion – that maintains its status unchanged across the centuries or for all time. Theoretically, and given time, any ordinary school opinion can become, under favorable circumstances, the *madhhab*-opinion and vice versa. The crux of the matter, therefore, is this: that insofar as the questions of who decides the law and who decides the range of its substantive possibilities and thus of the widest limits of its content, the answer is one and only one: the *madhhab*, the most powerful edifice of the Sharīʿa, and politically unassailable by any executive until the colonization of Muslim lands in the nineteenth century.

This colonization has much to do with the emergence of a new discourse that would normalize the *qānūn* as a problematic. Had it not been Europe who wrote Islam's legal, social, and political history, we probably would not be discussing this "historiographic" problematic in the first place. The appearance of the *qānūn* as a central issue is a reflection of Europe's own struggles with its despotic demons, be they the Church's merciless oppression or the harsh monarchical tyrannies. They are the projections of Europe on its premier enemy, the single cultural entity that threatened it from every strategic direction. Yet, the emergence of the Sharīʿa in recent scholarship as a supreme power to whom caliphs and sultans bowed in obedience has diminished the ability of Orientalist-colonialist discourse to claim for the *qānūn* any monarchic or despotic power. Burak's and Ayoub's seem to be some of the last attempts to manufacture a genealogical link between the *qānūn* and the modern state.

In fact, the *qānūn* has little in common with the modalities of modern codifications and much of it was consistent with the Sharīʿa. True, substantive *qānūn* encroachments upon the Sharīʿa did at times occur,[41] but the *qāḍīs* and *muftīs* ignored them whenever they could.[42] And as we have seen in the previous chapter, they nearly vanished from Ottoman practice of rule after the eleventh/seventeenth century.[43] If there was a genetic link between the *qānūn* and the modern state legislation, the former would not have suffered such a dismal fate.

---

41 Heyd, *Studies*, 180–83.

42 Gerber, *State, Society*, 64–65; Heyd, *Studies*, 191–92.

43 See ch. 10, sec. III.

Decisively more remarkable, however, were the similarities between the two. As Leslie Peirce has perceptively noted,[44] both the *qānūn* and Ḥanafī law recognized, each in its own sphere but also mutually, a cumulative tradition: the later texts of the Ḥanafī school never abrogated the earlier ones, and the founding fathers' doctrines continued to be enmeshed in the much later *fatwā* literature and author-jurist compilations.[45] The *qānūn* too was a cumulative discourse, each sultan propounding his own decrees while largely maintaining the sultanic laws of his predecessors. To be sustainable, it was in the nature of these cumulative legal traditions to integrate into their structure the viability and necessity of juridical difference. The concept of individual *ijtihād* in the legal schools constituted an analogue to the individual sultanic will that produced different *qānūn*s at different times and places. The internal differences exhibited by the two traditions were clearly intended to accommodate the local and regional differences throughout the empire. Just as the Sharīʿa insisted on local custom as a guiding principle of the *fiqh*'s application,[46] the *qānūn*, in its various compilations, catered to the needs of particular towns, districts, and provinces. *Qānūnnāme*s were issued at each of these levels, as well as at the universal level of the empire. And like Sharīʿa's *fiqh*, the *qānūn* developed structural mechanisms to accommodate change and to respond to diachronic and synchronic geographical variations. Finally, and no less importantly, both systems viewed their own laws as a "statement of the limits of the tolerable rather than a set of inflexible rules to be imposed regardless of circumstances."[47]

What is striking about the *qānūn*, and consistent with the Ottoman policy of allowing the widest scope for Sharīʿa justice, is the fact that the *qāḍī* stood as the exclusive agent of the *qānūn*'s enforcement, consistent with our conclusions regarding *siyāsa shqrʿiyya*.[48] On the ground, he was the ultimate administrator and final interpreter of the *qānūn*, which was unwavering in reiterating the decree that no punishment could be meted out without a trial by a *qāḍī*; and indeed, evidence from court records overwhelmingly shows that the decision to punish was exclusively the *qāḍī*'s, and that the meting out of penalties was normally the province of executive authority. The *qānūn*'s decree, frequently restated in the *qānūnnāme*s of several

44 Peirce, *Morality Tales*, 122 ff.

45 Hallaq, *Authority*, 57-120.

46 On custom's role in the judicial system, see Hanna, "Administration of Courts," 51-52.

47 Peirce, *Morality Tales*, 122.

48 See ch. 8-10.

succeeding sultans, in effect constituted a direct prohibition against conduct by government servants that might lead to injustice being inflicted upon the civilian population.[49] The *qānūn* of Sulaymān the Magnificent, for example, states that the "executive officials shall not imprison nor injure any person without the cognizance of the [Sharīʿa] judge. And they shall collect a fine according to [the nature of] a person's offense and they shall take no more [than is due]. If they do, the judge shall rule on the amount of the excess and restore it [to the victim]."[50]

The *qānūn* therefore upheld the Sharīʿa by enhancing and supplementing its position and provisions, while the Sharīʿa, on the other hand, required the intervention of sultanic justice. This complementary duality, characteristic of the sixteenth and seventeenth centuries, was endlessly expressed in various decrees and letters in the judicial discourse of the Ottoman authorities, be they sultans, Shaykh al-Islams, viziers, or *qāḍī*s: justice had always to be carried out "according to the Sharʿ and *qānūn*."[51] Until, of course, the *qānūn* gradually dropped out of reference.

III

Taking account of socio-economic changes that swept the empire in its middle period, Baki Tezcan's *The Second Ottoman Empire: Political and Social Transformations in the Early Modern World*[52] offers a more balanced assessment than did our two previous historians. He argues that the Ottoman Empire underwent such profound socio-economic changes that it is apt to recognize it as having become a "second empire" within its larger historical whole, something akin to the transformation of the Roman polity from a republic to

49 Heyd, *Studies*, 177: In combating the abuses of executive officials, the *qānānnāme*s "had to be brought to the knowledge of the people, so that every citizen would be aware of his rights or, more correctly, of the limits to the rights of the authorities. For this reason the cadis or governors to whom they were sent were often explicitly ordered to have them read out to the public." In the *ʿadāletnāme*, a new sultan confirmed his "wish to see justice done to all his subjects, particularly the poor and the helpless, and strictly forbidding all sorts of oppression by government officials" (Heyd, *Studies*, 150, n. 4). See also İnalcık, "Suleiman the Lawgiver," 105.

50 Peirce, *Morality Tales*, 119, 327; İnalcık, "Suleiman the Lawgiver," 111–26.

51 Jennings, "Limitations," 166, 168; Peirce, *Morality Tales*, 119.

52 See also his "Ottoman 'Mevali'."

an empire. The duration of this second empire stretched from 1580 to 1826, when the Janissary corps were abolished.[53]

In brief, the said socio-economic transformations centered around the crucial fact that the Janissaries became increasingly constituted of commoners (artisans, craftsmen, merchants, and tax collectors without military skills) who, now as Janissaries themselves, held socio-economic privileges that translated into political power. Somewhat anachronistically, though without major jeopardy, Tezcan represents the increasingly powerful Janissaries as "constitutionalists," checking the power of the sultanic "absolutists."[54] Membership in the army gave these commoners certain kinds of immunities and military privileges, including availability of credit, but the point of identifying this development is that this emerging group is said to have manifested itself as a popular and socially embedded movement.

By the eighteenth century, the Ottoman government had come to "represent a much larger spectrum of social interests than ever before ... [including] the merchant elite in the cities."[55] Their power was such that they could buck sultanic actions and policies, even cause the Sharīʿa establishment, represented by Shaykh al-Islām, to depose and even execute sultans.[56] Yet, Tezcan also demonstrates that the dynasty also worked hard to cultivate the support of the *mevali*, whom he calls "the lords of the law." The sultanic alignment with the jurists of the Sharīʿa was also concomitant with the decline of the *qānūn* we have described in the previous chapter, and with the reassertion of the Sharīʿa as the unrivaled law of the land.

Tezcan also argues that the Ottoman creation of Ḥanafī legal-administrative hierarchy was not only a matter of centralization and an effective

53 See, to the same point, Yilmaz's argument in "Containing Sultanic Authority," 260: "this study argues that the gradual transformation of the classical Ottoman system of the sixteenth century brought about new social formations, administrative structures, legal arrangements, and political principles of constitutional import. As a result, throughout the early modern period, the sultan's political power gradually declined and countered by the power of newly arising groups that became part of the decision making process."

54 I say "anachronistically" because it is impossible to conceive sultanic power in Islam without the Sharīʿa always partaking in the business of governance, even framing it. Put logically, to say "sultanic power" in the Islamic context is like uttering the word "mother," which by entailments requires the existence of children. To conjecture that sultanism in Islam, without the existence of Sharīʿa at all, would have ruled (even roughly) as European kings and emperors had done prior to the French Revolution – which seems to be Tezcan's presupposition – is to assume Europe as *the* model.

55 Tezcan, "Second Empire," 568.

56 Tezcan, *Second Ottoman Empire*, 7.

way to administer the imperial domains but also aimed at garnering an undisputed and universal Sunni legitimacy. This argument clearly runs diametrically opposite to Burak's conjecture. The "second empire," for Tezcan, continues with the adoption of the same Ḥanafī tradition that muzzled the *qānūn*, despite his full recognition of the innovative efficacy of the legal administrative hierarchy. It would seem that the same pool of facts accepted by Burak have led to an entirely different and more convincing conclusion at Tezcan's hands:

> A more significant dynamic that led the Ottoman administrative military apparatus to consolidate the legal structures that support the application of Islamic jurists' law was the systematization of the law to create an empire-wide system of rule, arguably in order to respond to the needs of an empire-wide economic market. The jurists' law, with its openness to local traditions and administrative practices in many spheres of law, presented an opportunity for the Ottoman administration to offer an umbrella institution to cover the many administrative, financial, and criminal law practices that co-existed in the Ottoman realms and gradually mold them together.... [T]hese legal developments were led by a socio-economic transformation towards a more market-oriented society in the Ottoman Empire of the sixteenth century. In short, the two needs of developing an empire-wide administrative-judicial apparatus governed by systematized legal structures and rising to the challenge of an ideological rival in the east [i.e., the Safavids], moved the Ottomans towards a more centralized system of jurists' law and a more orthodox interpretation of Islam, *both of which made their political leaders indebted to their jurists, who had the legitimacy to articulate the jurists' law and define Sunni Islam.*[57] Moving toward a more centralized system of jurists' law ... made the Ottoman dynasty indebted to the jurists, who were the *only legitimate interpreters and practitioners of the law.*[58]

Yet, the jurists were not just the legitimate interpreters and practitioners of the law, the *fiqh* of the Sharīʿa; they also were the interpreters of what the *qānūn* meant for them and for their sacrosanct law. There is almost a

57 Tezcan, "Ottoman 'Mevali'," 387 (emphasis mine). See also Tezcan, *Second Ottoman Empire*, 19, 24-25.

58 Tezcan, *Second Ottoman Empire*, 36 (emphasis mine).

universal agreement among scholars that the Ottomans at large, whether executive officials or Sharʿī personnel, viewed the *qānūn* as subordinate and a complement to the Sharīʿa, provisionally expanding and strengthening its ordinances and regulations. As such, the *qānūn* on the whole could hardly contradict the Sharīʿa's provisions. Which is another way of saying that the *qānūn*, to be applied, had to undergo a scrutiny of the Sharīʿa court on the basis of its procedural law. "These," James E. Baldwin concludes, "were legal procedures that served to evaluate claims and to establish what was legally true," but procedures wholly drawn from "the chapters of *fiqh* texts, and which defined the practice of courts across the Ottoman Empire and in the premodern Muslim world in general. The epistemology of the sharīʿa," he continues, "determined what *qānūn* was; or, more precisely, when somebody made a claim about what the *qānūn* said about a particular matter, he or she had to do so within the epistemological framework provided by the sharīʿa."[59]

Baldwin's argument about the specific modalities of handling the *qānūn* in the courts of the empire is, constitutionally speaking, significant. The seventeenth century, he argues, saw a transition in which the Ottoman executive was increasingly subjected by the judiciary "to legal checks and oversight," this for him being a *rising conception* of the "rule of law" that "emerged as a model for the relationship between the sultan and the ruling class that exercised his power." He agrees with Tezcan that this change accompanied the increasing influence of non-sultanic forces *within* the ruling class – i.e., the military regiments and provincial notables (*aʿyān*) – who "pushed a legal idiom of governance as a means of consolidating their rising status and protecting their interests and privileges."[60] The sultan's power had thus come to be regulated by higher-order system of rules, external even to the abstract conception of the sultanate as an institution. This process, he asserts, also involved the political empowerment of courts which "became the arbiters of disputes over the interpretation of public law."[61]

There are at least four points to be made here. Both Tezcan and Baldwin seem to presuppose a progressive narrative in which a phenomenon is deemed new (or representing a transformation) if it arises along a linear historical line on which the phenomenon had not existed, or was faintly present, during the immediately preceding period. This kind of understanding is

59 Baldwin, "Deposition of Defterdar," 154.
60 Baldwin, "Deposition of Defterdar," 156.
61 Baldwin, "Deposition of Defterdar," 157.

problematic because it precludes the distinct possibility of cyclical historical motion. Neither Tezcan nor Baldwin, nor for that matter anyone else (as far as I know), specifically asked this kind of question of pre-Ottoman dynastic histories: that is, to what extent have the various sections or factions making up the executive settled their internal disputes by appealing to the Sharīʿa and its legal, procedural, or political precepts? The question and narrative as perceptively formulated by Baldwin in constitutional terms were not, insofar as I can tell, pursued for earlier historical periods. An avid reader of the historical and legal sources written throughout the centuries of Islamic tradition should not, in my opinion, dismiss the possibility that history is not linear, that the Sharīʿa did not consistently evolve in a linear fashion, that there were no ebbs and flows (as patently evidenced in the Circassian Mamlūk period we have discussed at length in the previous chapter). The insistence on the eleventh/seventeenth century (or any Ottoman period or place) as the point in which "the rule of law" arises is suspicious if only because Ottoman historians generally know little about the preceding periods. And when they go beyond the Ottomans, it is the Mamlūk sultanate, and especially its latter half, that becomes the point of comparison. As we have seen in the previous chapter, this comparative point would make for a fatal methodological and substantive error.

The second point to be made is that Baldwin's research has serious implications for Ayoub's and, especially, Burak's theses. His research does not locate itself in a secondary framework of inferences, judging matters from the way the *qānūn externally* regulated a legal hierarchy and administrative practices (Burak); nor does he engage the question of the *qānūn*'s "manipulations" in determining the *fiqh* doctrine through the elevation of minority opinions to a default status in a relatively minuscule number of cases (Ayoub).[62] Rather, what Baldwin shows is the operation of a *structural* feature regulating disputes *within* the executive dynastic power. This type of structural modulation is a litmus test for our constitutional concerns. The conflictual relationship here is not between the executive and the judicial or legislative power; it rather falls within the ranks of the executive itself. In other words, and to appreciate the significance of his findings, the executive power, in all of its inner ranks, divisions, and dynamics, was appealing to the adjudicative force of the law of the land, the Sharīʿa, not to a dynastic law.

62 Although he does so in his *Islamic Law and Empire*, 76-78. It seems to me that Baldwin's article, "Deposition of Defterdar," is methodologically and theoretically quite a few steps ahead of his book.

Nor does it mean, as Baldwin argues, that appeal to a patrimonial model, rather than to Sharīʿa principles, represents the absence of the rule of law. Baldwin judges the matter from a Eurocentric perspective, considering resolution of conflict within executive sultanism by dynastic law an act that is not governed by the rule of law. But, strictly speaking, it is. A proper understanding of Sharīʿa's constitutional configuration obviates such an understanding, for, as we have seen, the domain of *siyāsa sharʿiyya* leaves much unregulated space for the ruler/executive to conduct his/its business as they see fit, as long as this executive management does not infringe or violate the Sharʿī law of the land. In fact, this *siyāsa sharʿiyya* principle is not much different from modern military jurisdictions, including their military courts, military commissions, court-martials, and Courts of Military Appeal. These bodies are not subject to any civil law but claim to themselves a separate and distinct sphere of law and procedure, represented in the United States, for instance, by the Uniform Code of Military Justice.[63] Yet, despite its internal autonomous status, the aggregate body of martial law is embedded *within*, an integral part of, and thus wholly belongs to, the overall structure of the American polity's law.

Furthermore, while it is true that the *qānūn* elevated a relatively few minority opinions to a dominant position, the entirety of its enactments was adjudged in accordance with the procedural law of the Sharīʿa, the same principle that was in operation when the late Mamlūk-era jurists (Ibn Taymiyya, Ibn Farḥūn, et al.) expanded the procedural Sharʿī laws of *taʿzīr* to regulate what was before their time a discretionary (that is, substantively but intentionally unregulated) privilege of the executive within the field of *siyāsa sharʿiyya. One might accurately say that an integral part of the "field" of* siyāsa sharʿiyya *consisted of a non-Sharʿī Sharʿī martial law*. Because the Muslim polity was not a unitary or nation-based phenomenon as the modern state is, there was no fixed national system of military justice, but rather one that was mutative, shifting according to the changes brought about by the varying customary laws brought to the Muslim polity by rotating dynasties (*duwal*). Yet, this dynastic military law was – as we have seen in the Ottoman case – constantly under the scrutiny of the jurists, who relentlessly strove to align it with the procedural requirements of the Sharīʿa, requirements that were part and parcel of the *fiqh*. For at the end of the day, the *fiqh* did

63 See, for instance, the 2019 version of this law, available at: https://jsc.defense.gov/Portals/99/Documents/UCMJ%20-%2020December2019.pdf.

not qualitatively distinguish between procedure and substantive law, as modern law does.

Finally, the fourth and perhaps most fundamental point is this, that Baldwin shows the existence of a robust process of judicial overview over the executive. Subjecting the *qānūn* to the procedural imperatives of the *fiqh* means that the law of the land was ultimately in the hands of the legislative, for the judiciary not only represented the latter's *substantive* legal power over and against what might be called "executive orders," but it was, conversely and by definition, utterly incompetent to exercise its powers of judicial review over and against its moral and epistemological parent, the legislative. A Sharīʿa judge, *qua* judge,[64] could never overturn, even review, a rule of *fiqh* as being invalid on principle (nor could he, as a rule, hear appeals of another *qāḍī*'s decisions).[65] If a court invokes a particular legal opinion as the basis of its decision, it would be a matter of legal choice that would leave all other opinions within the school intact. This is the central constitutional feature against which the writings of Burak and Ayoub, as the most articulate expositions of modern scholarship, attempted to militate but without success.

IV

It is clear from the above that my intention was not to give a full account of modern scholarship on the relationship between *qānūn* and the Sharīʿa, and less on the meager writings on constitutional issues and related concerns about the rule of law. Rather, my aim was to put to the test a part of the most advanced scholarship that may be construed to bear on these issues, if only to show that this scholarship's conclusions on the constitution of Islamic governance are not tenable. In fact, emerging writers, such as Baki Tezcan and Abdurrahman Atçıl,[66] among others, have countered, if only indirectly and by implication, the implausible conclusions of that problematic approach, especially as laid out by Burak and, to some extent, by Ayoub. Here, I meant to confront these

64 The qualification is intended to emphasize the fact that *qāḍī*s had no powers of judicial overview as against the *fiqh* itself, although the *qāḍī* was *also* qualified as a *mujtahid* who would then be reinterpreting the law as such, as a *mujtahid*, not as a *qāḍī*. On the four juristic roles that can exist in the person of one jurist, see Hallaq, *Authority*, 166-235.

65 Powers, "Judicial Review."

66 See bibliography.

writings head-on by means of streamlining their concerns in constitutional terms and then subject them to critique.

Yet, this is not the end of the story. If the basics of a serious constitutional investigation, much less a constitutional field, remains elusive in the field of Islamic studies, then we cannot expect too much in terms of advancing the conversation beyond the preliminaries of conventional constitutional narratives. But the conversation must be developed much further, for the constitutional operation of Islamic governance has profound effects on *a good deal more* than how that culture organized its forms of political management. The ultimate issue in fact is not just rule of law and separation of powers, two concerns that betray a liberal anxiety about freedom and democracy. That "a good deal more" is the concern of the next and last chapter.

Part III

THE HEAVINESS OF BIOPOWER

Chapter 12

Sovereignty and Biopower: Is Constitutionalism Enough?

The study of human-made reality is entirely perspectival. We see and understand it from our particular positions, judging and evaluating it in accordance with the conditions in which we live and by which we are affected. It has been my argument that the Western and colonialist perspective has severely distorted the lens with which Europe, and later Euro-America, saw the constitutional history of Islam, among much else. Even leaving aside the difficult linguistic, epistemic, and ontological hurdles that we, as moderns, encounter in the study of the historical and cultural other and struggle to overcome, we find our feet firmly placed on a thicker sedimentation of colonialist ambition lurking underground. The previous chapter has shown just the tip of the iceberg, since the modern-colonial prejudice has seeped deep even in the psyche of the colonized. In fact, now that the West is beginning to wake up to the severity of the crisis we are facing at multiple levels,[1] the Muslim scholarly contingent across the globe is still in the back

1 On these crises and their epistemic genealogy, see Hallaq, *Restating Orientalism*. I also wager that the Gaza genocide that started in early October 2023 has raised an unprecedented awareness among Western youth that transcends mere political understanding. The new awareness, widespread to remarkable degrees, has been able to connect various phenomena into one whole, bringing together capitalism and politics, corporate greed and war, ethnonationalism and genocide, genocide and education, state terrorism and empire, and, equally important, the virtual collapse of the American constitutional system, including the loss of sovereignty. At the time of writing (summer 2024), social media is crowded with the knowledge that a "foreign power" has "bought off" the American Congress and that popular will and democracy have effectively met their demise. See https://www.manushyafoundation.org/post/the-palestinian-genocide-brought-to-you-by-corporations;

trying to catch up to where Euro-America, with its failing liberal experiment, stood half a century ago.

Yet, legal scholars of Islam of almost every stripe continue to study Islamic political history (while barely grasping at its constitutional component) from within the liberal regime of truth, taking its own idealism to be the normative benchmark that can (or must?) judge Islam and its premodern constitutional history. And it is here, at this juncture, that we can uncover another layer of sedimentation that clouds the modern scholar's vision in studying Islamic constitutionalism, namely, the powerful discursive façade of liberalism and its tenuous connection with liberal practices on the ground.[2]

I do not need to proffer much argument at this moment of writing (summer 2024) to demonstrate how the liberal order has been exposed not only for its duplicity and engagement in genocidal violence (problems I diagnosed several years ago as part of Orientalism and modern forms of knowledge),[3] but also for its constitutional bankruptcy. To say the least, the legislative branch in the United States, as well as, to some extent, in European others, has been mired by the relinquishment of popular will and, effectively, sovereignty in favor of financial benefits and well-nigh foreign domination.[4] Yet, this is just the latest wave of illiberal liberal practices. Constitutional problems inherent in the system, and ensuing cracks, were apparent much earlier, in fact from infancy. Thus, when we study a phenomenon that is quite removed from our current reality (what I have called perpendicular remoteness), we must take care to dive below

https://www.reddit.com/r/changemyview/comments/1aqwncr/cmv_the_us_congress_has_been_bought_out_by_aipac/; https://www.newarab.com/opinion/aipac-has-pro-israel-lobby-bribed-and-bought-us-democracy; https://www.theguardian.com/us-news/2024/jan/10/congress-member-pro-israel-donations-military-support; https://www.opensecrets.org/industries/summary?cycle=All&ind=Q05&recipdetail=S. See also next two notes.

2 See, for instance, the critiques of Losurdo, *Liberalism*; Deneen, *Why Liberalism Failed*; Kahn, *Putting Liberalism in Its Place*; Amin, *Liberal Virus*; Gray, *Liberalism*; Sprangens, *Irony of Liberal Reason*; Nicolacopoulos, *Radical Critique of Liberalism.*

3 See Hallaq, *Restating Orientalism.*

4 This phenomenon of longstanding constitutional crisis, emerging with particular force after the Israel–Hamas conflict of October 2023, has – to my knowledge – thus far not been studied in constitutional terms, although there is no doubt that it is one of the most serious threats to the American constitutional system and the much coveted "democratic rule" in the United States. But the evidence is massive and, indeed, overwhelming. See, for instance, Petras, *Power of Israel*; Mearsheimer and Walt, *Israel Lobby*; Mearsheimer and Walt, "Israel Lobby;" Samuels, "AIPAC Explained." See also "AIPAC Political Achievements Factsheet," as well as "AIPAC", available at: https://www.aipacpac.org/home.

the surface of our ideological liberal façade, not only questioning our own assumptions but also interrogating the fundamentals of the system from whose truth we derive these assumptions in the study of the Other. My point is this: that modern scholars of Islamic legal and political history, whether hailing from White-Christian, Jewish, Brown-Muslim or other backgrounds, have so far lacked sufficient self-consciousness to make their scholarly approaches credible. This last chapter is an attempt to peel off the layers of ideological façade that have masked a Western constitutional reality that unconsciously impels Orientalist constitutional assumptions about Islam. The chapter intends to expose the ideological underpinnings of the scholarly liberal assumptions about constitutionalism while refocusing our gaze on the quality of rule[5] in so-called modern democracies as well as in premodern Islam.

I

Both Western popular belief and liberal constitutional theory[6] advance the narrative that the separation of the three powers or "branches of government" – the legislative, judicial, and executive – constitutes the backbone and foundation of liberty and democratic rule.[7] The vesting of power in three distinct, separate, and independent groups of institutions is said to be indispensable to the constitutional state, the site in which the rule of law is deemed both most sustainable and legitimate. Vital to this concept is the notion that these three powers ought to be exercised by separately staffed departments, each being constitutionally equal and mutually independent. This mutual independence dictates that the legislative branch must not only enjoy total autonomy, but that it also must not delegate its powers, especially to the executive.[8] This ideal has become a universal truism, endlessly repeated by political reform movements

5 In addition, see Introduction and n. 60 therein.

6 This section draws on key paragraphs in chapter 3, sec. 1, of my *Impossible State*, 37-48. There are two reasons for reintroducing this material, now revised and at certain points expanded. The first is that this section goes to the heart of the larger argument that this book is making, and the second is to make this material available to those who have not read *The Impossible State*.

7 On this topic generally, and on Montesquieu and *The Federalist* in particular, see Marrow, *History of Western Political Thought*, 241-47; Carey, "Separation of Powers and the Madisonian Model," 151-53; Vile, *Constitutionalism and the Separation of Powers*.

8 Marshall, *Constitutional Theory*, 100.

around the globe, and enshrined in Article 16 of the Declaration of the Rights of Man and the Citizen: "A society in which the observance of the law is not assured, nor the separation of powers defined, has no constitution at all" – the implication here being that only by clearly defining this separation can a state be constitutional and thus democratic.

As it turns out, however, the doctrine and discourse of the separation of powers not only lacks significant support from the facts on the ground, but also masks a reality in which this separation appears as problematic as the claim that it is the basis of democratic government.[9] F.A. Hayek captures the problem quite accurately: "Because we rightly believe in the basic ideal of democracy we feel usually bound to defend the particular institutions which have been for long accepted as its embodiment, and hesitate to criticize them because this might weaken the respect for an ideal we wish to preserve... It seems to me that the disillusionment with so many experiences is not due to a failure of the principle of democracy as such but to our having tried it in the wrong way."[10]

Constitutional scholarship has thus come to recognize the conceptual and structural problems involved in the theory and practice of separation of powers and, as a result, in the idealistic narrative it has promoted.[11] It has been seen as "most confusing,"[12] "riddled with so many exceptions,"[13] and infected with "notorious difficulties" and "much imprecision and inconsistency."[14] It "may be counted little more than a jumbled portmanteau of arguments for policies which ought to be supported or rejected on other grounds."[15] One scholar declared it a "failure,"[16] while others dismissed it as "unconstitutional"[17] and

9 A point to be argued further in due course. See also Kelsen, *General Theory*, 269, 282. It is also worth emphasizing that a critique of the *practice* of democracy may be leveled from other quarters (not our concern here), including the very process of elections and voting, a process that may be regarded as hampered by the very law that purports to promote democracy. On this see, for instance, Abu El-Haj, "Changing the People."

10 Hayek, *Law, Legislation and Liberty*, III, 1-2, 98.

11 Kelsen, *General Theory*, 269; Calabresi and Prakash, "President's Power to Execute the Law," 544. The idealistic narrative, integral to liberalism's self-legitimation, also hides other aspects of constitutional crisis. See, for example, Loughlin, "The Contemporary Crisis of Constitutional Democracy."

12 Marshall, *Constitutional Theory*, 97.

13 Hansen, "Mixed Constitution," 509.

14 Saunders, "Separation of Powers," 338. Levinson, "Separation of Parties," 2385: "From nearly the start of the American republic, the separation of powers as the Framers understood it, and as contemporary constitutional law continues to understand it, had ceased to exist."

15 Marshall, *Constitutional Theory*, 124.

16 Magill, "Beyond Powers and Branches," 605.

17 Lawson, "Rise and Rise of the Administrative State," 1231.

an unconvincing theory,[18] a mere "page" from Montesquieu.[19] It has been acknowledged as an arena of deep controversy where even the consensus on some of its basic tenets is "confused" and "possibly incoherent," one that "must be abandoned" as "the first important step toward formulating a new set of ideas about separation of powers."[20]

In the United States, constitutional thought and practice have been described as pathological and dangerous.[21] The three branches of government are said to have been effectively reduced to two, if not even one.[22] In this country, "the doctrine about the separation of these powers has been considerably modified by a network of checks and balances, and in Europe the doctrine has been destroyed first by the parliamentary system and after the Second World War by the new constitutional courts."[23] The best argument for it satisfies the minimal and not so hopeful standard that, among all possible ways of rule, it is the "most successful of the twentieth-century State."[24] Yet, many of these scholars argue, often vehemently, that this minimal standard is no sufficient reason for its acceptance.[25]

The difficulties in the concept and practice of separation stem from the structural unity of the nation-state we have described,[26] a unity that premodern Islamic governance never developed. In fact, in the Islamic case, the separation was radical, especially between the legislative and the executive. The modern idea that the three powers should constitute checks upon each other created the dilemma of the *degree* of separation. Since complete separation in the structures of the modern state is obviously impossible, the challenge would then revolve around the determination of that point in the separation where too much or too little of it renders it meaningless or problematic. Obviously, the problem affecting all rule is concentricity of power, and so it is the overlapping, imbalance, and delegation of power between and among the three branches that become the issue.

18 Mansfield, "Separation of Powers," 15.
19 Vanderbilt, *Doctrine of the Separation*, 3.
20 Magill, "Real Separation in Separation of Power," 1129, 1197.
21 Ackerman, *Decline and Fall*, 3: "The pathologies of the existing system are too dangerous to ignore. We can't limit our critique to details. We must ask whether something is seriously wrong – very seriously wrong – with the tradition of government that we have inherited."
22 Edwards, "We No Longer Have Three Branches of Government."
23 Hansen, "Mixed Constitution," 514.
24 Vincent, *Theories of the State*, 8.
25 As evidenced in Posner and Vermeule, *Executive Unbound*.
26 For more on this "unitary" nature of the state in relation to the separation of powers, see Wilson, "Separation of Powers."

Like many critics, Hans Kelsen has vehemently argued the case that the concept of separation is highly inaccurate and that the architecture of the three powers is rather one of distribution,[27] for "one can hardly speak of any separation of legislation from the other functions of the State." The appearance of separation, Kelsen seems to say, is a matter of naming, because the legislature, for example, specializes in legislating but its functions are also "distributed among several [other] organs." If the legislature is referred to as such, this is merely by virtue of a "favored position."[28] The legislative has no monopoly over law-making; it only *specializes* in creating general norms. But even here, in the creation of general legal norms, the legislature is not the only active agency, since this function – i.e., the production of *general* norms – is also delegated to the other two powers. Like many others, Kelsen argues that the label "legislative" is a mere historical convention, given to that branch which specializes in legislation.[29] In both the United States and Europe, there has been such "a merging of legislative and executive functions" that political practice in these regions stands "contrary to the doctrine of the separation of powers,"[30] in effect amounting, particularly in the United States, to a constitutional revolution.[31] As Mogens Hansen aptly put it:

> It is a breach of the separation of functions that a majority in the parliament by a vote of no confidence can force the government to resign or call for an election, and that the government is accountable to the parliament. In these cases it is the legislature that encroaches upon the powers of the executive. Conversely, in many parliamentary democracies the government possesses the right to dissolve the parliament and call for an election. Also the executive has extended its proper sphere

27 Wilson, "Separation of Powers," 486, calls it no more than an "administrative convenience."

28 Kelsen, *General Theory*, 272-73.

29 See next three notes.

30 Hansen, "Mixed Constitution," 514-515, 528.

31 Lawson, "Rise and Rise of the Administrative State," 1233: "Congress frequently delegates ... general legislative authority to administrative agencies, in contravention of Article I [of the Constitution]. Furthermore, those agencies are not always subject to the direct control of the President, in contravention of Article II. In addition, those agencies sometimes exercise the judicial power, in contravention of Article III. Finally, those agencies typically concentrate legislative, executive, and judicial functions in the same institution, in simultaneous contravention of Articles I, II, and III. In short, the modern administrative state openly flouts almost every important structural precept of the American constitutional order."

> of power by arrogating legislative powers to itself. It is a breach of the separation of persons that the prime minister and most of the ministers are members of parliament and at the same time the heads of the executive branch of government. It is a breach of the separation of functions that almost all laws are initiated and drafted by the government and the civil servants working in the various departments of government. The result is that the role of parliament in most cases is restricted to ratifying or rejecting what the government proposes. Furthermore much legislation takes the form of framework laws that leave important details to be filled in by subsidiary government regulations.... There is no longer any separation of powers, each with its own function. Today legislation is divided between *the executive*, namely the government and all the civil servants in the ministries who initiate and prepare almost all new laws, *the legislative*, namely the parliament, which has the power to ratify or reject the bills submitted by the government, and *the judiciary*, namely the constitutional court which in most European democracies has set itself up as a second or third legislative chamber.[32]

Similarly, although much legislation occurs within the judicial and executive branches, they are not named legislative because they specialize in their respective functions. It is an "impropriety" and "particularly unsound" to refer the function of legislation to the judiciary, and especially to the executive.[33] The "progressive breakdown" of the principle of separation is nevertheless particularly "obvious" in the case of the legislative and the executive, where the latter chips away at the prerogatives of the former.[34] For example, the amalgamation of judicial and legislative functions at the hands of American administrative departments, done in the name of "public convenience, interest or necessity," is not only "a standing violation of the separation of powers" but might have in earlier times been struck down "as an abdication of legislative responsibility."[35] This much is in fact openly recognized by American courts

32 Hansen, "Mixed Constitution," 514-15.

33 Kelsen, *General Theory*, 256-57. See also Saunders, "Separation of Powers," 340, where she argues that especially in the UK, the "intermixture of institutions is such that it is almost impossible to describe it as a separation of powers .... This is most obviously the case with the relationship between the legislature and the executive, famously claimed by Walter Bagehot as fusion of powers."

34 Marshall, *Constitutional Theory*, 113-14; Ackerman, *Decline and Fall*.

35 Kelsen, *General Theory*, 114. See also Marshall, *Constitutional Theory*, 113-14; Vanderbilt, *Doctrine of the Separation*, 95.

themselves on the grounds that the modern administrative state might be incapacitated if Congress were required to legislatively oversee all policy and administrative decisions.[36] Nonetheless, it is arguable that "any law that attempts to vest legislative power in the President or in the courts is not 'necessary and proper for carrying into Execution' constitutionally vested federal powers and is therefore unconstitutional."[37]

Furthermore, the emergence of administration and bureaucracy as virtually autonomous entities magnifies the problems of the administrative state and its inherent subversion of the rule of law. As Morton Horwitz argued, the "rise of the administrative state raised the most basic questions about the meaning and continuing viability of the 'rule of law' in situations where unelected officials exercised enormous and unprecedented power to affect the lives and property of citizens."[38] Some constitutional scholars went as far as to declare the post-New Deal administrative state inherently unconstitutional, amounting "to nothing less than a bloodless constitutional revolution.... The destruction of this principle of separation of powers is perhaps the crowning jewel of the modern administrative revolution. Administrative agencies routinely combine all three governmental functions in the same body, and even in the same people within that body."[39]

The administrative state has produced even more problematic effects, at least in the American case. Much vigorous debate – reflecting a state of crisis – has been generated about the fragmentation of the executive, where the president, who is expressly and exclusively mandated by the Constitution – on behalf of "We the People" – to execute and superintend all federal laws, has been shorn of what many view as his unitary capacity. Administrative independence and a lack of presidential control over a considerable portion of the executive is said to have created out of administrative and certain executive agencies a "headless fourth branch of government,"[40] one that appears to possess an autonomous status.[41]

36 Lawson, "Rise and Rise of the Administrative State," 1241: The "majority in Mistretta v. United States declared that 'our jurisprudence has been driven by a practical understanding that in our increasingly complex society, replete with ever changing and more technical problems, Congress simply cannot do it job absent an ability to delegate power under broad general directives.' When faced with a choice between the Constitution and the structure of modern governance, the Court has had no difficulty making the choice."

37 Lawson, "Rise and Rise," 1238.

38 Horwitz, *Transformation of American Law*, 214.

39 Lawson, "Rise and Rise of the Administrative State," 1231, 1248.

40 Calabresi and Prakash, "President's Power to Execute the Law," 559-60, 663; Lawson, "Rise and Rise of the Administrative State," 1242-43.

41 For more on this see Bruff, "Constitutional Status of the Administrative Agencies"; Lawson, "Rise and Rise of the Administrative State."

That the American president is in practical reality far from being the exclusive "Chief Executive magistrate" stipulated in the Constitution is in little doubt, but whether or not this sharing of executive power is constitutional – or whether or not it "distorts" the text of the Constitution[42] – is a controversy that, *ipso facto*, appears to call into question not only the cogency of the American political institution (and "what has gone wrong with it")[43] but also its epistemic structure. However calculated, it must be the case either that the bifurcation in the executive into a presidential branch and a headless fourth branch is right and the Constitution wrong or that the Constitution, in assigning executive power to none other than the president, is right and executive governance is a misapplication and deviation from the Founders' intent. It must be either but it cannot be both.[44]

Furthermore, and still pertaining to the American constitutional arrangement (routinely presented to, and largely accepted by, the world as a model of democracy to be emulated),[45] it is still unclear whether separation of powers has not been "destroyed" under the weight of party politics. As Daryl Levinson has convincingly argued, the notion of political competition built into the structure of American government is "frequently portrayed as the unique genius of the U.S. Constitution, the very basis for the success of American democracy. Yet the truth is closer to the opposite."[46] The dynamics of party politics, Levinson rightly observed, have "overwhelmed the Madisonian conception" of separation of powers nearly from the start of the American republic, preempting the dynamics of that conception, which rests on the presumption that the separation and balance of powers would structurally set off political "ambition" to "counteract ambition." It was Justice Jackson who seems to have been the first to note that only a fanciful observer would overlook the fact that the president heads both a political system as well as a legal system, and that party politics

42 Calabresi and Prakash, "President's Power to Execute the Law," 664.

43 Fisher's review of *Decline and Fall of the American Republic*, 58.

44 Otherwise, the entirety of the vast academic discourse on this and related issues, which attracted some of the best constitutional scholars in the United States, would be both meaningless and a figment of the human imagination.

45 Speaking of the "pathologies of the existing [constitutional] system," which "are too dangerous to ignore," Bruce Ackerman tellingly writes that the "great struggle for constitutional democracy will not be waged in Iraq and Afghanistan or some other distant land. It will be waged closer to home, and it will be a spiritual struggle: Will we continue to celebrate our great tradition in a chorus of self-congratulation? Or will we take a hard look at emerging realities, and rise to the occasion in a movement for constitutional renewal?" *Decline and Fall*, 3, 188.

46 Levinson, "Separation of Parties," 2313.

and interests, "sometimes more binding than law, extend his effective control into branches of government other than his own and he often may win, as a political leader, what he cannot command under the Constitution."[47] Even idealistic and starry-eyed authors like Eric Posner and Adrian Vermeule could not but arrive at the conclusion that the "checks on executive authority ... have eroded considerably over the past two hundred years. Congress has delegated extensive powers to the executive. For new initiatives, the executive leads and Congress follows." In terms of control over independent regulative agencies, Congress has little power, "while presidential control over both the executive and independent agencies is strong and growing stronger."[48]

Thus, politics and its games could override constitutional precepts, including the Madisonian interbranch competition, depending on whether or not the House, Senate and presidency are controlled by a single political party. "Recognizing that these dynamics shift from competitive when government is divided to cooperative when it is unified calls into question many of the foundational assumptions of separation-of-powers law and theory," because when unified, political competition "often tracks party lines more than branch ones" thereby creating in practice at least one more system of separation (a practice that American constitutional theory does not account for in the least).[49] The effects of this duality are numerous, as Levinson and others[50] show, but two such effects are worth noting. First, presidents tend to accumulate too much power and enjoy too free a range on a number of important political issues under unified government. And second, Congress tends to delegate significantly more authority to the executive branch and to further lift constraints designed to curb the discretion of executive agencies when government is unified. In a country where the president's party is traditionally in control of both the House and the Senate most of the time (at least since 1832) this does not make for easy compliance with the Madisonian model.[51]

47 Cited in Levinson, "Separation of Parties," 2314-15; also more generally on the American presidency as a "dangerous branch," see Ackerman, *Decline and Fall.*

48 Posner and Vermeule, *Executive Unbound*, 206.

49 Levinson, "Separation of Parties," 2315: "Recognizing that party competition *can either create or dissolve interbranch competition*, depending on whether government is unified or divided by party, suggests that the United States has not one system of separation of powers but (at least) two." This dynamic has not "received much notice by legal scholars," nor by "the Supreme Court nor any other federal court" (emphasis mine). See also p. 2329.

50 Posner and Vermeule, *Executive Unbound*, 27-28.

51 Levinson, "Separation of Parties," 2322, 2330-31, 2341. From an entirely different angle, it can be furthermore argued, as Hayek did, that "party legislation leads to the decay

But these and other constitutional problems are not exclusively American. Most European states in fact suffer from the adverse effects of party politics on separation of powers.[52]

There is furthermore no nation-state in which the legislative power is the sole organ producing *general* legal norms. Nor, conversely, is there any state in which the executive and judicial branches are expressly barred from creating such norms, which they produce not only on the basis of statutes but also directly on that of the constitution.[53] In most nation-states, and aside from the profound questions that the administrative state raises, the head of the executive is authorized by virtue of his or her office to legislate on a variety of matters related to war, martial law, economic contingency, and much else – all this without implicit or explicit authorization from the legislative. In the United States, for instance, the presidency "was transformed into a kind of plebiscitary principate with despotic tendencies toward arbitrary, ruthless, and self-aggrandizing exploitation of power."[54] Furthermore, in most liberal democracies, the executive frequently performs the function of the courts in that public administration is based on administrative law, which is as coercive as civil and criminal law. Exactly like regular courts, offices of public administration, within their jurisdiction, are exclusively competent to decide infractions and to determine particular sanctions, notwithstanding the fact that one is called "judicial" and the other "executive." What the judiciary and executive powers produce are usually termed "regulations" or "ordinances," but these in effect often possess the same character as general norms created by the legislature.[55] This distribution of power could perhaps be justified if the capacity of the judicial and executive powers to create such general norms were

---

of democratic society. A system which may place any small group in the position to hold a society to ransom if it happened to be the balance between opposing groups, and can extort special privileges for its support of a party, has little to do with democracy or 'social justice'." See his *Law, Legislation and Liberty*, III, 31.

52 Barendt, *Introduction to Constitutional Law*, 149–54.

53 Kelsen, *General Theory*, 270.

54 Dahl, "On Removing Certain Impediments," 249. Dahl continues: "What is more, the other major political actors, including the Congress, the Supreme Court, the parties, the electorate, and the most active and attentive political strata all collaborated in that transformation." See also the prophetic diagnosis of Ackerman, *Decline and Fall*, 15: "But over the course of two centuries, the most dangerous branch has turned out to be the presidency – requiring a fundamental reworking of our thinking and practice, an overhaul that may come too late if it comes at all." It is not entirely fortuitous that Ackerman, on p. 63, capitalizes the expression "Most Dangerous Branch."

55 Kelsen, *General Theory*, 257, 270.

delegated to them by the legislative branch, but it is not always clear that this is case. Nor is it clear, even in the case of presumed delegation, where exactly the lines of separation between the respective competences lie.[56]

Nor is the separation between legislative and judicial powers all that clear.[57] The courts perform a legislative function by virtue of their competence to annul constitutional laws or administrative regulations on a variety of grounds that range from public interest to reasonableness.[58] They can even strike down laws of the legislature on the grounds that these laws are contrary to the law or constitution, although the former is in part created by the legislature itself. The courts also create law through the doctrine of precedent, a law that stands on a par with laws created by the legislative (and executive) powers.

The competence of the courts to review legislation (as well as executive orders) is another patent encroachment upon the principle of separation.[59] What this separation means is that the judges are independent and guaranteed security in discharging their offices, but their role as reviewers of the work of the legislature "invades the principle that each department has an independent sphere of action and a right to take its own review on matters of constitutionality."[60] This competence simply means that courts can and do legislate, and it is precisely here that a certain distrust of the legislative power can be observed.[61]

That the courts may express distrust of the executive is understandable, since history everywhere, and especially in Europe, has taught a universal lesson: an unchecked executive is an arbitrary power on the loose.[62] Historically, the courts during the phase of constitutional monarchy in Europe came to provide an independent check on the executive and legislative powers of the monarch, but when the monarch ultimately lost his legislative power to the parliament, the courts continued to provide such a check as a matter of tradition. But perhaps there is more to this continuity of judicial review than just tradition, for a fuller answer may lie in the absolute sovereign will that itself is the rule over any other rule, including the rule of law. Sovereign will knows only itself, deferring to nothing but itself.[63] When it undergoes a

56 Saunders, "Separation of Powers"; Wilson, "Separation of Powers," 481-86.
57 Lawson, "Rise and Rise," 1246-47.
58 Stewart, "From 'Rule of Law'," 10.
59 Kelsen, *General Theory*, 269.
60 Marshall, *Constitutional Theory*, 103-4.
61 Kelsen, *General Theory*, 281; Waldron, "Core of the Case Against Judicial Review."
62 See the citations in Hansen, "Mixed Constitution," 509.
63 Hallaq, *Impossible State*, 25-28.

change of mind, so does its law.[64] Which is to say that the unity of the state as sovereign will allows this will to be represented even in a potentially arbitrary site, the executive.

This is not all, however. Popular sovereignty can hardly be said to sit well with constitutionalism and a system of separation of powers. Constitutionalism is a system of law and political philosophy that combine to create a public authority governed by an impartial and relatively limited law. That is the point of it. By contrast, popular sovereignty squarely rests on the idea that "the people" hold the unlimited and absolute power to decide on what the law governing them is, making this category, "the people," superior to all other constituted forms of public authority. Daniel Lee raises the good question, "How is it possible for such a doctrine of *unlimited* and absolute sovereignty to be, without contradiction, deployed in a theory intended to realize a state committed to just the opposite goal, *limited* government?"[65] This irresolvable tension has been described as a "paradox of constitutionalism,"[66] one that, I think, undergirds the Paradox of Sovereignty, to be discussed below.

Two main points emerge from the foregoing. First, legislative power does not create all the general norms of the state order (in contradistinction with the Sharīʿa, which does). It is called legislative only because it is an organ which specializes in the creation of general norms. Second, much legislation of general and particular norms originates outside the realm of the legislative power, namely, in the executive and the judiciary. The products of the legislative power are therefore impinged upon by both executive legislation – which often delimits and reinterprets legislative norms – and judicial review, which has just as much power to quash norms created by the legislative branch. That this latter branch is independent in the paradigmatic nation-state is obvious, but its independence must be construed as such in highly relative terms within the context of political structure. If sovereign will is embodied in the law, then the legislative (presumably the organ that legislates the expression

64 It is in this context that Hayek perceptively wrote that "[c]ivilization largely rests on the fact that the individuals have learned to restrain their desires for particular objects and to submit to generally recognized rules of just conduct. Majorities [in Western democracies], however, have not yet been civilized in this manner because they do not obey rules," meaning that there are no rules or law higher than their will. See his *Law, Legislation and Liberty*, III, 7. Hayek's statement carries extraordinary significance for my arguments throughout this book, and provides, along with the Islamic praxis of the technologies of the self, a cognate critical thrust against modern constitutional practices.

65 Lee, *Popular Sovereignty*, 2 (italics in original).

66 Loughlin, *Paradox of Constitutionalism*. From the Islamic perspective, see Iqtidar, "Theorizing Popular Sovereignty," 597 ff.

of this will) is not its mouthpiece in the full sense of the term. For, under this system of sovereign will, the executive, for example, is imbued with an incompatible duality: to legislate and to execute its own legislation. In this respect it shares much with the judicial power, which performs a similar role: it creates norms by precedent and quashes legislation through judicial review (what has been called "negative legislation"),[67] then turns around to adjudicating cases on the basis of law partly of its own making, and proceeding further to issue sanctions.[68]

To sum up: The practice and even theory of liberal separation of powers raise profound questions. If the legislature is the representative of popular sovereignty and of sovereign will, then why can't it be the exclusive legislating organ of the state? Why allow for an organ, whose declared function is to apply the law, to legislate? But perhaps most importantly, why arrogate the power of legislation to an executive organ whose declared function is to execute judicial orders? Even if we accept the standard claim that the separation between the three powers is not so much a separation as a way to prevent concentricity of power in any one of them, how do even satisfactory answers to the questions posed here provide an adequate explanation for the very problem of concentricity? For one, the distribution of legislative power over three organs is a non-solution to this problem. The theory of concentricity-prevention may be deemed incoherent, because by arrogating so much power to the executive, not to mention the judiciary, it promotes the very opposite of its declared intention: it leads to the concentration of too much power in the hands of the executive[69] and a consequent reduction of the powers of the legislative. The fundamental question then is: How can there be a rule of law when an executive and a judiciary are empowered to legislate general norms? At a minimum, the claim for the rule of law must be called into question, and with it the claim for democracy.[70] Hans Kelsen captures this paradox well:

---

67 Marshall, *Constitutional Theory*, 108.

68 Lawson, "Rise and Rise of the Administrative State," 1248-49 and *passim*; Magill, "Real Separation in Separation of Power."

69 Vanderbilt, *Doctrine of the Separation*, 95; Vile, *Constitutionalism and the Separation of Powers*, 385-420; Dry, "Separation of Powers," 82-83; and Schultz, "Congress and the Separation of Powers," 190 and *passim*, despite Schultz's all too charitable approach.

70 Stewart, "From 'Rule of Law'," 6; Hardin, *Constitutional Reform*; Dahl, "On Removing Certain Impediments" (as annotated in the next note).

> The principle of a separation of powers understood literally or interpreted as a principle of division of powers is not essentially democratic. Corresponding to the idea of democracy, on the contrary, is the notion that *all power should be concentrated in the people*; and where not direct but indirect democracy is possible, that all power should be exercised by one collegiate organ the members of which are elected by the people and which should be legally responsible to the people. *If this organ has only legislative functions, the other organs that have to execute the norms issued by the legislative organ should be responsible to the latter, even if they themselves are elected by the people, too.* It is the legislative organ which is most interested in a strict execution of the general norms it has issued. Control of the organs of the executive and judicial functions by the organs of the legislative functions corresponds to the natural relationship existing between these functions. Hence *democracy requires that the legislative organ should be given control over the administrative and judicial organs.* If separation of the legislative function from the law-applying functions, or a control of the legislative organ by the law-applying organs, and especially if control of the legislative and administrative functions by courts is provided for by the constitution of a democracy, *this can be explained only by historical reasons, not justified as specifically democratic elements.*[71]

II

As I noted in the Introduction, however important a robust system of the rule of law and a regime of separation of powers are, they constitute, even together, insufficient conditions for good governance. This basic truism has

71 Kelsen, *General Theory*, 282 (emphasis mine). See also Dunn, "Political Obligation," 24. Speaking of the American constitutional experience, Dahl ("On Removing Certain Impediments," 235–36) states the following: "[T]he elaborate system of checks and balances, separation of powers, constitutional federalism, and other institutional arrangements influenced by these structures and the constitutional views they reflect are both adverse to the majority principle, and in that sense to democracy, and yet arbitrary and unfair in the protection they give to rights.... In their effort to protect basic rights, what the framers did in effect was to hand out extra chips in the game of politics to people who are already advantaged, while they handicapped the disadvantaged who would like to change the status quo. From a moral perspective, the consequences seem arbitrary and quite lacking in a principled justification."

been overlooked by Orientalist scholarship, which has failed to ask the analytical questions that matter most. The defining edge of this scholarship has stopped at the simplistic interrogation of whether or not sultanic administrative law revised or superseded the Sharʿī law of the land. There has been so far no interrogation of the quality of this supposed intervention, its intentions, telos, or overall effects. If our intellectual curiosity about these forms of Islam stem from our knowledge and assumptions about our own modern systems – which has indeed largely and perforce dictated our scholarly agenda – then how does the Islamic system compare with the modern? This is as much a substantive question as it is heuristic, demanding that we put things in perspective whenever we make assumptions in the process of studying the other. At the forefront of such an inquiry into assumptions and, no less, into constitutional effect, stands the central concept of sovereignty.

Sovereignty is located at the heart of the matrix of constitutional structures and rule of law. For this is the highest category of thought and action which determines the form and content, the quality and quantity, the meaning and even teleology of what it means to have, or to speak of, a constitutional structure in a polity, and of a law that rules. Sovereignty is the foundation and vision that bestows on the modalities of rule and governance their existential meaning, their forms, and their quality of life. If it is true that the human is a political animal, then it is also true that the quality of each type of political rule produces its own results, effects, as well as its particular kind of human subject and subjectivity.

In the Introduction to this book, I have stressed the linguistic, conceptual, and philosophical difficulties entailed in the concept of sovereignty, particularly its modernist renderings into Islamic languages. Even without and outside these difficulties, there remains a host of other problems that are well-known to scholars of sovereignty. The concept is so varied and polysemous – if not utterly controversial –[72] that one can discern multiple types of meaning and

72 A radical critique of the concept of sovereignty may be found in Maritain, "Concept of Sovereignty." It must be said that, at several important junctures, Maritain's critique echoes Islamic concerns about the concept. On the contestations surrounding the concept, see Bartelson, "The Concept of Sovereignty Revisited," 463-74. On the virtual denial of the concept of sovereignty, Hans Kelsen proffers an important, though dated, argument. His theory of the *Grundnorm*, which gives rise to and defines all governing legal precepts, and furthermore resolves any contradictions between and amongst them, precludes a notion of sovereignty that means freedom from a binding law. Sovereignty does not stand above the law and cannot therefore be analytically productive as an organizing concept for legal theory. See Dyzenhaus, "Kelsen, Heller and Schmitt."

practices of sovereignty, but not all these are of interest to us here. For instance, none of its connotations and affordances in International Relations is directly relevant to us; nor are the types of so-called divided and partial sovereignties. This is because our concern is with the internal constitutional and legal order of Muslim governance, not with the modalities of political and military relations of inter-Muslim sultanates or between and among Muslim and non-Muslim polities. Likewise, the conceptual ambiguities inherent in partial or divided sovereignties render the concept analytically problematic, if not vacuous, for these types (often arising in times of political crisis and conflict, when questions of whether a region or a ruler is sovereign or not) occlude rather than reveal. A "legal sovereignty" that shares power and competes with "political-cum-military sovereignty" is no sovereignty at all, and so is a political sovereignty severely curbed by the legal imperative; for a power that is confined by a force structurally and systemically external to it is by definition not sovereign.[73] (This is why any reference to Muslim rulers before modernity as sovereign is utterly misplaced. Until the nineteenth century, Islam never had sovereigns on Earth.)

Analytically, and by force of the controversy about the relationship between sultanic law and Sharīʿa we discussed in the previous chapter, sovereignty is a concept whose usefulness will become evident only if we take it to mean what it genealogically signified in its point of origin, namely, the European context which gave rise to it in the first place. Had Europe not existed in the world at all, we most likely would not have known even the term itself, much less the complexities and complications the concept introduced to modern political life around the globe.

The concept of sovereignty is a defining property of the modern state.[74] Politically and ideologically, sovereignty is constructed around the fictitious concept of will to representation. European in origin (which is to say *specifically European conditions of possibility had produced it*), the concept of sovereignty is constituted by the idea that the nation *embodying* the state is the sole author of its own will and destiny.[75] In order for it to come into existence, in order for it to become ontologically conceivable, the will must presuppose a break

73 On Hobbes's concept of sovereignty as absolute yet qualifiable by the rights of citizens to defend their honor and lawful interests against the sovereign, see Nagan and Haddad, "Sovereignty in Theory and Practice," 442-44; Bartelson, "On the Indivisibility of Sovereignty." It is also of interest to us that Hobbes argued for the fundamental right of the citizens to protection by the sovereign; if the sovereign fails to do so, the obligation to obey him no longer holds. See also Maritain, "Concept," 349.

74 Gill, *Nature and Development*, 4-5.

75 Hay, et al., *State*, 4-6; Grosby, "Nationality and Religion," 103.

from an enslaving agency, a tyranny, or some such dominating evil. The break from tyranny – historically, paradigmatically, and narratively exemplified in the American and French Revolutions[76] – represents a quintessential requirement without which sovereignty would then have no meaning.[77] Violence, therefore, is the direct route to sovereignty as an expression of a juridically constituted popular will.[78] In fact, as we will see, violence and death both *structure* the idea of sovereignty and the political, if not of the subject as well.[79]

To speak of the modern state is thus by necessity to speak of sovereignty, and in turn to include perforce popular will as the master of one's own collective destiny. The will, popular and collective, does not presuppose actual and active individual participation,[80] but claims its collective force precisely because it is a fiction.[81] The concept loses none of its force even when non-democratic powers come to rule, for even in the absence of traditional democratic practices, any nation-state comes to expect its sovereign will to be embodied in the acts and speech of its rulers, even when they happen to be a band of devils. That the elision from democratic will to tyranny and vice versa remains protected by sovereignty is an accurate expression of the historical transitions from absolute monarchies to so-called democratic rule under the trenchant concept of the sovereign state.

To come into existence, sovereignty needs not only a state but also the general prerequisite of an imagined construct, the nation.[82] Being sovereign,

---

76 Bolsinger, *Autonomy*, 29.

77 Lee, *Popular Sovereignty*, 3 ff.

78 Iraq under American occupation is an excellent case in point. Even when the dictatorship of Saddam Hussain was removed by the violence of a foreign power, no one was willing to credit "Iraq" with a political voice, much less sovereignty, without and until a government was first constituted on the basis of what was presumed to be an Iraqi constitutional/basic law.

79 Mbembe, "Necropolitics," 15.

80 Nagel, "Ruthlessness in Public Life," 87.

81 On the problematics of constituent power (as exemplified in Hannah Arendt's writings), see Rubinelli, *Constituent Power*.

82 Anderson, *Imagined Communities*. Drawing on Richard Ashley, Finlayson and Martin ("Poststructuralism," 164) argue that the "figure" of the sovereign state "'is nothing more and nothing less than an arbitrary political representation always in the process of being inscribed within history, through practice, and in the face of all manner of resistant interpretations that must be excluded if the representation is to be counted as a self-evident reality.' This is not meant to suggest that the state does not really exist or is a mere charade; only that its existence as a sovereign entity in an international environment is a kind of myth dependent upon ongoing processes that define and redefine its 'inside' and 'outside' through practices of exclusion that create the very environment within and through which the state is then deemed to act."

the nation-state is thus "the product of no subject's actions apart from its own self-creation,"[83] for it is by virtue of the constructed notion of constitutional violence that it both comes into existence and continues to implement its regular law-based practices. The sovereign state is "conceived as the efficient agency of its own construction ... comparable to the divine Creation ex nihilo" and "capable of having or expressing such an act of will." Yet, as Paul Kahn has aptly argued, "we cannot be aware of [the] sovereign without experiencing it as a normative claim that presents itself as an assertion of identity. We understand ourselves as a part, and as a product, of this sovereign. In it, we see ourselves."[84]

The identification of the self with the sovereign amounts to conceiving and fashioning the subject through the sovereign will, in turn conceived as the source of both the law and the nation, which, as a collectivity, is in turn fashioned in the mirror of the law. The law as reflecting sovereign will, and thus the will that creates the subject and fashions him in its own image, is little more than a replacement and substitution for the Christian conception of will. Like a great many modern concepts, pre-Enlightenment, Christian forms of authority are largely retained with a substituted set of sources that are of equal authoritative force.[85] Carl Schmitt cast the matter incisively when he wrote that "[a]ll significant concepts of the modern theory of the state are secularized theological concepts not only because of their historical development – in which they were transferred from theology to the theory of the state, whereby, for example, the omnipotent God became the omnipotent lawgiver – but also because of their systemic structure."[86]

If it is true that the concept of sovereignty, as Suganami correctly argued, is relative and, being European in origin, represents a "historically contingent institutional structure,"[87] then we must be cautious about applying it to a system that was historically constituted by different values, norms, experiences, and structures. As I indicated in the Introduction, Muslims from the beginning of their history and until the second half of the nineteenth century did not recognize human reality, political or otherwise, in terms of political sovereignty. The term itself obviously was not familiar to them (unlike it is today), nor were its

83 Kahn, *Putting Liberalism*, 267.
84 Kahn, *Putting Liberalism*, 267-68.
85 See also Grosby, "Nationality and Religion," 97-104.
86 Schmitt, *Political Theology*, 36; Amin, *Liberal Virus*, 54. For a nuanced analysis of this theme, see Asad, *Formations of the Secular*. But even for Asad, qualifying Schmitt's arguments does not diminish their force in the least.
87 Suganami, "Understanding Sovereignty," 513.

substantive analytical, political, or legal categories. As we have seen in many chapters of this book, Muslims simply spoke a different political language, not only lexically but also, and mainly, conceptually. They viewed the world and articulated its political, legal, and other categories in ways that did not map onto those that Europe happened to produce. And since the very categories that form the conceptual and epistemological background – from which the entire modern discourse about Islamic forms of rule issues – belong to that hegemonic European experience (for any other is naturally inconceivable under the dominion of modern colonialism), then we must be conscious that we are inevitably ruled and subjectively regulated by that "legislated language" that Nietzsche spoke of.[88]

This language was and largely remains Eurocentric, no matter who speaks it. Yet, there is no historical determination dictating that other modes of thinking are inconceivable. We merely *happened* to judge Islamic history of governance along the lines of categories of "rule of law," "separation of powers," "constitutional organization," etc., precisely because of the hegemony of this most crucial colonialist fact. If we must navigate these seas of hegemonic concepts, then we must be clear that we are adjudicating Islamic history in general, and constitutional history in particular, according to Eurocentric standards, norms, values, and, most importantly, conceptual categories. As I declared in setting out the intentions of this book in the general Introduction, the antidote for us is to be constantly aware of our own positions, conceptual categories, and fundamental presuppositions before we speak of what I call Islamic governance. And to do so, we must first understand the historical and political background that gives rise to our own assumptions, both of which – background and assumptions – being unique to our modern world and thus un-universalizable to historical Others, including and especially Muslims and others who flourished in bygone eras. To understand their history, we must first understand ours, including its psycho-epistemic effects on formulating our own *underlying* assumptions. And to do so, we must tackle what is perhaps the most important concept that discolored these assumptions: political sovereignty.

An analytically productive definition of sovereignty must therefore include at least two essential features, both of which stem from the historical European and Euro-American experience that produced the hegemonic and colonizing concepts imposed on our minds. This line of analysis takes into account not only

88 Nietzsche, "On Truth and Lies," 81, 83; Nietzsche, *Human, All Too Human*, 323; See also discussion related to this point in Hallaq, *Sharīʿa*, 1.

the structural outlines of that historical experience but also, and importantly, the general theoretical output of significant political thinkers and intellectuals such as Carl Schmitt, Michel Foucault, and Giorgio Agamben.

The first feature of sovereignty, other than the paradox that plagues it,[89] is the stark fact that it is an "ultimately unauthorized authority" that "continuously authorizes itself as *the* authority and the rest by and large accept this, acquiesce in it, or are made to do so."[90] Central here is the fact that there is neither a prior nor an originative substantive source, nor an independently valid *Grundnorm* that validates this authority. The definition is apt, since it captures the essence of the unauthorized, absolutist monarchical powers that effectively ruled Europe till the end of the eighteenth century, and against which the very notion of popular sovereignty of the unitary modern nation-state arose as a supposed solution and substitute. This state, whose concepts and language we largely take for granted in writing the history of the Other, is precisely that entity that declared itself sovereign without authorization from any source other than itself.

This *ex nihilo* self-authorization is recognizably a colossal migration from the concept of divine sovereignty in European Catholicism. The sovereign God that wills the world into existence *ex nihilo*, and furthermore installs a particular order in it, gets transformed at the hands of the modern state into an anthropocentric axis where the human political sovereign is now regarded as the source of political order. This is the meaning of Schmitt's enduring maxim that all central political concepts of modernity (which is to say a lot about so many socio-political and other interrelated concepts and conceptions) are secularized forms of concepts that dominated and defined European Christianity, however complex the translations may have been.[91]

Yet, sovereignty is much more than an ultimately self-authorized authority. In the very notion of self-authorization there lies the actual historical experience of absolutist rule, which translated, as a matter of fact, into decision over life and death. The sovereign agent is not just he who decides on the

89 On the Paradox of Sovereignty, see Dyzenhaus, "Kelsen, Heller and Schmitt," 343 ff. Agamben aptly defines the paradox thus: "The paradox of sovereignty consists in the fact that the sovereign is, at the same time, outside and inside the juridical order... [T]he sovereign, having the legal power to suspend the validity of the law, legally places himself outside the law. This means that the paradox can also be formulated this way: 'The law is outside itself' or: 'I, the sovereign, who am outside the law, declare that there is nothing outside the law.'" Agamben, *Homo Sacer*, 15.

90 Suganami, "Understanding Sovereignty," 511, 522 (emphasis mine).

91 Schmitt, *Political Theology*, 36. See also Amin, *Liberal Virus*, 54.

exception, but it is also one who decides on *how* to live and die. The point here is not about the mere fact of letting live and making die, but rather *on the modalities and modes* of living and dying, the *qualitative* measure of these modes being of supreme value. This is the second and in fact the most important part of the definition of sovereignty, one that was analytically added to the concept after the integration of popular voice, or popular will, into the business of governing.

As I have argued in *Restating Orientalism*, sovereign power is not a dormant potential waiting to be awakened in times of crisis, when the need "to decide on the exception" arises. Sovereign decision is rather a routine and routinized practice that unfolds through the sequence of infinite atoms constituting social and political life. Just as God perpetually creates the world through the atoms of motion, where He is utterly aware of all particulars, the earthly sovereign likewise decides, through a continuous unfolding of sovereign decision, on the life of the population (that is, those who populate the nation) and how it should be lived. The state of exception is the point of extreme stress, the pivotal moment when crisis raises its monstrous head to threaten the political order. But this cannot and should not obscure the fact that sovereign decision always finds itself in the mode of perennial operation, corralling, directing, and deciding the continuously created atoms of social, economic, and political life of the very society and nation that presumably engendered sovereignty in the state. Like God, therefore, the so-called popular sovereign of the modern state is the ultimate decider on all forms of political and social existence.

III

Central to the idea of sovereignty is its own political location. Sovereignty now is the manifestation of the nation-state, for it cannot arise in any other context. Yet, the ontological order of the nation-state should not hide the fact that it is the self-formation of the state that created the nation, not the other way around. It is the harnessing of the nation in an act of totalization and individuation of its human components that makes up the nation as a quality, the nation being presupposed by the state's imagination of its self-formation. Being an Enlightenment product, the state rested on the conception that the "people" must be first free before they form themselves in a political collectivity, as a distinct nation.[92] Which is to say that integral to the ideological makeup of the state are two fictions: First, that the state is speaking for the people, that is, it represents them and expresses their will, because the "people" as a conceptual category is assumed to be the author of the state. Second, that the freedom of the "people" in coming together as a political body originated in some *post-facto* narrative of liberation from tyranny, from oppressive empire, or some historical or revolutionary march from bondage and subservience onto liberation and independence (precisely mirroring the Kantian "liberation" from minority position, the act making up the Enlightenment). This general narrative, insofar as I know, permeates the educational system of all fully formed modern states, as it does their socio-political cultures and political imagination.

The creation of the nation as an act of resistance or revolutionary eruption against forces that are imagined to have kept it in check (that is, restricting its freedom and thus sovereignty) or wholly under the yoke of oppression meant that the nation paid in blood to constitute itself as a free and sovereign entity. The members of the nation thus owe a debt to their nation, for without its sacrifices, they would not be the citizens they are. If the state is the embodiment of its sovereign citizens as a collectivity, then the citizens see themselves as embodying the state, mirroring it, and thus identifying with it. Each individual, Agamben averred, "becomes subject and object ... of the political order,"[93] further augmenting the unitary nature of the modern state. The debt can go even deeper, in that the members of the nation, the citizens of the state, regard themselves as its nominal children, whose very existence and identity are tied up with the nation in a pastoral relationship that overrides that which they have with their biological parents. For this, after all, explains the "rights" the nation-state has over conscription, intestate citizens, children (against and above their parents), public welfare, among much else. Projecting itself as the site of existential duty, this debt creates a totalistic sense of the will to sacrifice, not only in terms of the state's demand of the citizen to sacrifice himself or herself through military conscription, where the price is the biological life of the willing citizen-body,[94] but, more importantly for our purposes, the *lived*

92 Kahn, *Putting Liberalism*, 260, 261, 265.
93 Genel, "The Question of Power," 58.
94 Kahn, *Putting Liberalism*, 263-64. "Looking at the law [in the liberal order], we will never see the violent character of the modern state. We will never reach the phenomena of killing and being killed for the state. The immense capacity of the nation-state to sacrifice its citizens in war was the great political discovery of the nineteenth century. That discovery begins with Napoleon's armies inheriting the popular enthusiasm of the Revolution; it was

life of the citizens as a quality. Arguably, sacrificing the quality of life is as dear a price, if not dearer, than physical death. Yet, paradoxically, the freedom that is posited as the foundation on which sovereign popular will is erected appears to dissipate, or at least undergo a diminution, by the multiple constraints that are entailed in the creation of the state's political society.

It is this dialectic, padded and propped by ideological paraphernalia (school-sung anthems, parades, national independence discourses, curricular civics, print capitalism, military spectacles, patriotic movies, news, national sports teams, etc.) that delivers the citizen who makes the state and who is made by it. The subjectivation of the nation's child as the site of both politics and the political allows the state to determine the constitution not only of the citizen but the kind and quality of life that he or she lives. This is where the grind lies, for this *subjective constitution* of the citizen is the final and true effect of what Foucault called biopower, where sovereignty is not just the juridical decision over life and death, over who can live and who must die, but, significantly, over the appropriation of the citizen as the object of the political, to be nourished, trained, disciplined, punished, educated, manipulated, taken care of.[95]

Before proceeding, a caveat is in order. Foucault's general language conceives of the "care" that the system of biopower affords the citizen in positive terms,[96] in fact often using the very adjective "positive" to characterize power's influence on life, in the way it "endeavors to administer, optimize, and multiply it [viz., life], subjecting it to precise controls and comprehensive regulations."[97] If Foucault was truly concerned with the quality of subjectivation, asking the fundamental question of "what are we today?" (that is, what are we made of as subjects?),[98] then his conception of the subjectivation of biopower's subject in positive terms betrays a dissonance in his thought, and furthermore supports the claim that his secular (if not latently liberal) politics distorted his vision of his own project.[99] For there is no denying that the alleged "positive effects" on

further revealed in the American Civil War, when the democratic armies based on mass conscription confront each other for the first time. As the conception of citizenship and political participation broadened, so did the conception of the reach of military service. The people's state is supported by people's armies. The end point of this development linking popular sovereignty to popular armies was a breakdown of the distinction between combatants and noncombatants. If all are equal parts of the state, then all can be appropriately sacrificed for the life of the state."

95 For background, see McGushin, *Foucault's Askesis*, 222-41.

96 Foucault, *History of Sexuality*, 137.

97 Foucault, *History of Sexuality*, 137.

98 Foucault, "Subject and Power," 326-27, 331; Hallaq, *Restating Orientalism*, 344, n. 54.

99 Although in a seemingly later lecture, he finds it "puzzling" that the state's machinery

biopower's subject resulted in vicious racism, in killing in the name of nations, in violent nationalism and ethnonationalism, and in genocides, to name but a few political manifestations. We can add to this repertoire yet another trait that has to do with cultivating a comfortable materialist and greedy subject who is raised on self-indulgence and nurtured with a callous disregard toward the environment, this too with devastating consequences. Even if we limit the "positive" effects of biopower to the privileged metropolis, there remains a large question about the global price that must be paid for the attainment of these dubious "positive" effects.

Be that as it may, I have thus far provided a summary of the theoretical analysis of political sovereignty, an analysis that reflects complex developments and massive movements that Europe experienced as a matter of fact in multiple domains of its socio-economic and political life. Perhaps the most monumental fact about Europe's fabrication of the modern project, and its entry into it, is the rise of a bourgeois economy during the so-called age of discovery, largely owing to two factors: the first is the newly emerging secular ways of economic thinking and management that loosened the Christian grip over wealth accumulation; while the second is the colossal flood of gold and silver that was extracted from the native populations of the Americas.[100] To say that these two factors stood in a dialectical relationship with each other is of course to state the obvious.

By the time Bodin and Hobbes were writing, the spread of the new wealth across the many sections of society had become so pervasive that the concept of private property was elevated to a sanctimonious status, it having defined almost all social and economic relations, from family and guild to the larger market. With Locke and Montesquieu, the concept was further democratized by its elevation to a natural right, reflecting the rise of what C. B. Macpherson has aptly called "possessive individualism."[101] What is significant about this

of destruction ("butchery") sits side by side with the "care" the state affords its citizens. Foucault, "Political Technology," 147. A few pages later (152), having elaborated on the rise of the concept of *raison d'état*, he adds that "the individual becomes pertinent for the state insofar as he can do something for the strength of the state.... And sometimes what he has to do for the state is to live, to work, to produce, to consume; and sometimes what he has to do is to die." To give Foucault the benefit of the doubt, he may have meant by "positive" the state's capacity to exercise sovereignty through enhancement of life, however utilitarian that project is. "Positive" would then contrast with sovereignty as a violent, destructive and hence "negative" power.

100 On the first factor, see Grice-Hutchinson, *School of Salamanca*; on the second, see Abad and Nuno Palma, "Fruits of El-Dorado."

101 Macpherson, *Political Theory of Possessive Individualism*. I think the common critique

development is that the protection of private property squarely became one of the most central functions of the sovereign.[102] The result was the rise of wealthy classes whose property was ensured by this protection and who now became dependent on the backing of the sovereign's law. But this was only one side of the dialectic, whereby the now emerging state was also aided by the support it received from these interest classes.

It is not without good reason that Karl Marx saw in this a picture – in which the bourgeoisie set itself up as the effective grouping that constituted the upper echelons of the state itself – a sort of "committee" that manages and protects its own interests.[103] In general outline, and in whatever form or density the bourgeoisie may come, virtually the same situation continues to obtain today, especially as one can easily observe in the United States. Yet, the origins of these effective protections go back to the Glorious Revolution in 1688 England, to be followed by the paradigmatic events of the American Constitution and the French Revolution, in 1787 and 1789, respectively. These paradigmatic shifts were among the first major moves made by the emerging state to cultivate the so-called "popular will." The base of political participation has now widened significantly, because these newly emerging wealthy classes came to increasingly inhabit the domain of sovereignty.

Yet, the base of sovereignty was to widen significantly during the nineteenth century, with the French Revolution marking a significant shift in the structure of politics and the political. The massive but transformative violence unleashed during the first decade of this Revolution was to introduce a new political rationality, a new way of conceiving politics. As one shrewd commentator remarked, the series of events following the 1789 eruption "demonstrated what the mob, provided it was properly aroused and led, could do even to the most powerful and best organized state in history until then."[104] But this mob was relatively new[105] as well. The Industrial Revolution had already begun to reshape social relations and locations, sending huge populations from the

directed at Macpherson's work (namely, that he projected too much onto the early sources and unduly ascribed possessive individualism to an earlier period than he should have) is largely untenable, if only because the trenchant and considerable power of this individualism could not just have appeared in mid or late modernity out of nowhere. Macpherson skillfully detected the potential for this tendency where very few, if any, could see it. For a largely unjustifiable critique of Macpherson, see Hugh Breaky's review in Levy, ed., *Oxford Handbook*.

102 van Creveld, *Rise*, 206-7.

103 Marx, "Manifesto of the Communist Party," 9.

104 van Creveld, *Rise*, 207.

105 See Foucault, "Birth of Social Medicine," 142-45.

countryside to the cities. Given the notorious abuses of this unprecedented industrialization, it was a matter of time, beginning early in the nineteenth century, before the emerging urban population came to present politics with new but hard facts. Without hemming it in, this population would drastically disrupt the sovereign order that had been made of the political elite and the emerging bourgeois classes.

The process of controlling and re-educating this "mob" was made up of stages whose landmarks represented developments that came to constitute the modern state till today. Especially as of the 1790s, a new conception of policing had arisen, expanding police forces and their coercive powers signally. In addition to the considerable budgets allocated to their construction, the new forces were professional, highly bureaucratized, efficiently centralized, and generally organized along military lines.[106] If the regular army was created for the defense of the borders and conquering the external enemy, the modern police force was made to impose internal order and conquer the enemy within – and this was the "unruly mob." As relatively recent scholarship has shown, instilling order was part of the mission, the other part having been to change, through disciplinary education, the mentalities and ways of the newly forming urban populations.[107] Under the pretext of imposing order and discipline on urban quarters and villages, the state set out to conquer their populations "and remake them in its own image."[108]

By the middle of the nineteenth century, the essential steps in the construction of the policing apparatus had become more or less complete. The next stage, beginning around this time, was the introduction of formal institutions of learning, from primary school up to the university. The education of children in these disciplinary institutions became obligatory,

106 Garrioch, "People of Paris," 511.

107 van Creveld, *Rise*, 205-210, speaking not only of Western Europe but also the United States and Russia. See also Garrioch, "People of Paris," 529: "[T]he usual explanations given by historians are either that growing rootlessness and poverty associated with the expansion of capitalism led to a serious problem of social order in the eighteenth century; or that the process of industrialization in the nineteenth and the accompanying shift from small-scale, relatively self-contained, self-policing communities to a more complex, urban, industrial society led to the collapse of older forms of control, rendering a new police force necessary. I think the evidence from Paris suggests that some revision of this is required. While perceptions of social problems were undoubtedly present among property owners, in the case of Paris the new police were imposed on self-policing communities apparently in good health, and themselves helped to change those communities – rather than coming in as a result of their collapse."

108 van Creveld, *Rise*, 210.

with statutory punishments for parents who failed to comply with these state requirements. The family and its inner dynamics would also become the focus of the state's new regulations, now being effectively remade by such administrative regulation (pertaining to education and the like), but also by new regulations and practices of welfare services and constantly amended laws of personal status.[109] All these have come to constitute a systemic machinery of social change, one that is in perpetual operation and production. Wherever and whenever there is a fully formed state, the machinery remains concomitantly in action.

Between the 1780s and 1910s, four or five generations have been gradually trained into obedient denizens on their way to becoming docile citizens. This was the work of coercion and systematic and systemic policing practices, facilitated by networks that tightened the grip of the state over social formations.[110] By the 1910s, two or three generations had been raised in the new schooling system, subjected regularly to the performative power of social services and constant amendments of laws governing the family and its inner and outer relations. By the end of WWI, the proper citizen of the modern state had arrived. This is a tall order of achievements, since this state of affairs meant the paradigmatic absorption of the "populace" – an ideologically indistinct category – into the structured ideology and political apparatus of the state, producing along the way the citizen and society, both of which are entirely the creations of the state. Citizen and society could now see themselves in the state, as much as the state saw itself in them. They arrived because they identified themselves emotively and cerebrally – that is, psycho-epistemically – with the values of the state, its ambitions, programs, policies, and norms. They identified themselves with their nation whose fabric is woven out of and by them. This itself is also the point of arrival of the nation-state, one and the same thing. This is what it means for popular sovereignty to have evolved, and this is why it was the state and its bourgeoisie that created the nation, despite the ups and downs, and conflicts and tensions, that permeated the internal relationship between these two political and economic forces.

The identity of the nation and *its* state has been captured by Foucault, whose following statement is so monumental that it must be recorded here in its entirety:

109 On this, see Hallaq, *Impossible State*, 105-6.

110 See, for instance, Weber, *Peasants into Frenchmen*.

> Another consequence of this development of bio-power was the growing importance assumed by the action of the norm, at the expense of the juridical system of the law. Law cannot help but be armed, and its arm, par excellence, is death; to those who transgress it, it replies, at least as a last resort, with that absolute menace. The law always refers to the sword. But a power whose task is to take charge of life needs continuous regulatory and corrective mechanisms. It is no longer a matter of bringing death into play in the field of sovereignty, but of distributing the living in the domain of value and utility. Such a power has to qualify, measure, appraise, and hierarchize, rather than display itself in its murderous splendor; it does not have to draw the line that separates the enemies of the sovereign from his obedient subjects; it effects distributions around the norm. I do not mean to say that the law fades into the background or that the institutions of justice tend to disappear, but rather that the law operates more and more as a norm, and that the judicial institution is increasingly incorporated into a continuum of apparatuses (medical, administrative, and so on) whose functions are for the most part regulatory. A normalizing society is the historical outcome of a technology of power centered on life. We have entered a phase of juridical regression in comparison with the pre-seventeenth-century societies we are acquainted with; we should not be deceived by all the Constitutions framed throughout the world since the French Revolution, the Codes written and revised, a whole continual and clamorous legislative activity: these were the forms that made an essentially normalizing power acceptable.[111]

It should be stressed, against some tendencies that see Foucault as a somewhat fragmented thinker,[112] that his articulations of the sovereign technologies of

111 Foucault, *History of Sexuality*, I, 144.

112 Or, more accurately, as a thinker whose research themes and writings across his prolific career are not intimately interconnected. In Islamic studies, in particular, the relationship, for example, between his writings on power/knowledge and technologies of the self are not generally understood to constitute two organically interrelated parts of a larger whole. Nor for that matter are his writings on "genealogy" or "archeology" of knowledge, on the one hand, and technologies of the self and sovereign power, on the other. As I interpret him, he was across almost all of his writings preoccupied with the ultimate question of subjective formation, asking questions about the quality of the subject that is cultivated by qualitatively different regimes of truth. Put differently and schematically, his enduring concern was with the Kantian question of "What are we now?" as opposed to the question of "What were we before now?" the latter occupying the bulk of his extensive Collège de

power are not at all separate from his famous theory concerning the intricate relationship between knowledge and power, or his explorations with regard to prisons, social medicine, sexuality, governmentality, and much else. He himself militated against the unidimensional idea that power has the need for certain kinds of knowledge and for certain discoveries in ideas and science in order to increase or intensify power's fields of operation. While he accepted this to be true, it was for him only a part of the story. He wanted to emphasize the other part of the equation, that the practice of sovereignty and the exercise of its power themselves generate certain forms of knowledge, new *objects* of inquiry and understanding, and new constellations or accumulations of particular kinds of knowledge or, as he would have said, epistemic formations. "The exercise of power perpetually creates knowledge and, conversely, knowledge constantly induces effects of power."[113]

This kind of knowledge, however, was mistakenly seen to reside in, and as limited to, what we might call academic knowledge – the human sciences, psychology, sociology, psychoanalysis, criminology, medicine, and the like, fields that Foucault himself studied. But this was not all that he had in mind. For Foucault, these are not just fields of theoretical knowledge (as compared to *ʿilm* vs. *ʿamal*), but rather are *practices* of knowledge that, among other things, went into making the *practices* of sovereignty and its power possible. In other words, and this is my fundamental point, it was not just psychiatry, medicine, criminology, sociology, and the rest of "human sciences" that constituted the desideratum of sovereign power, but also, and as fundamentally, knowledge as constituted by the epistemic and largely *unquantifiable* psychosocial effects generated by such "routine" and ordinary acts as print capitalism, policing discipline (including, e.g., the massive presence of police patrols on the streets of large cities), public statements, parades, national flags, filling application and administrative forms (i.e., the psychologically *performative*[114] effects of bureaucracy), national anthems, national and international sports, national and "folkloric" songs, and even formidable government buildings and their architecture. All these and much more (in fact countless, and often imperceptible forms) were marshaled not only to render the subject knowable and analytically dissectible, but also – through the entire constellation of sovereign power's techniques – to render them amenable to training, manipulation, education,

France lectures he delivered in the last years of his life. Foucault, "Subject and Power," 326-27, 331; Hallaq, *Restating Orientalism*, 344, n. 54.

113 See Gordon's Introduction to Foucault, *Power: Essential Works of Foucault*, xv-xvi.

114 Hallaq, *Restating Orientalism*, 61-63; Austin, "Performative Utterances," 220-40.

supervision, obedience, correction, cooperation, and, no less, state-care. Yet, the ultimate achievement was to coopt the subject as the docile *citizen* of the state, to be controlled and harnessed for labor and economic productivity, and ultimately, for the security of the state itself. This is why life sacrifice-in-conscription became the paradigmatic feature of the modern state – one of the unique characteristics of the modern project.

Now, there is a straight line taking us from Foucault's concept of biopower to the Schmittian-Agambian moment of the political, the former revealing the genealogy and the psycho-epistemic foundations of the latter. In some important ways, the Schmittian-Agambian moment takes off where Foucault's work stops, without articulating the relevance of his work to the substantive rise of the political.[115] This connecting line, too, complicates our understanding of sovereignty and constitutional configurations and exposes the innocent elementariness of the approach so far taken in Islamic studies toward expounding an adequate narrative of Islamic governance. Let me explain.

My interest in Schmitt and Agamben here (particularly in the way they can be read as providing extensions to Foucault's diagnostics of biopower)[116] is deployed to show the quality of the human who stands, as we have seen, at once as subject and object of biopower. This interest is shown on at least three levels.

First, a Schmittian approach would comfortably argue that the "age of the political" – increasingly being marked by the distinction between enemy and friend – would not be possible without corralling the modern state's subject into the technologies of sovereign power, as expressed in the Foucauldian thesis of biopower. The subject and object of the political arrives upon the arrival of the full normalization – i.e., unquestioned conviction – of the necessity for sacrifice-in-conscription. Reaching this point already assumes the individual who has been completely formed as a subject of the state, and perfected as such through its technologies of biopower. We might call this a strong sense of nationalism, and this is partly true; but analytically, it is more meaningful to speak of the efficient agency of the complex biopolitical forms we have enumerated. Nationalism and blind fidelity to the nation are nothing but the

115 This, to my mind, is characteristic of Foucault's style of writing. Almost everywhere he seems to tantalize the reader by leaving concrete conclusions undrawn, often satisfying himself with mere insinuations, intimations, and no more than implied statements of possible consequences.

116 For a different yet complementary approach to the themes I am discussing here, see Chatterjee, *I am the People*, 42-71, especially at 53-59.

effects of the countless assortments of the techniques that manage, control, manipulate, and attend to the welfare and biological life of the subject. In both the Schmittian and Foucauldian logics of modern subject formation, the popular sovereignty that started with integrating the populace and "mob" into the mechanics of rule and political participation culminated in their subjection as the manageable sites of the political (Schmitt) as well as of the operations of biopower (Foucault).

The second, and no less important level, is the arbitrariness of the biopolitical, which by now takes for granted the arbitrariness of politics and the Schmittian political. Max Weber's political sociology allows for the conceptualization of political power as a rational type of domination. As is well known, Weber's concept of rational types regulating a system is that the system does not derive its logic of operation and modus vivendi from a long-standing tradition (supposedly driven by emulation rather than rational considerations) or a charismatic authority, be it religious or not. Rather, rational domination is a deliberate creation ruled by the imperatives of exigency and instrumental calculation; its most distinctive feature, resulting from this logic of exigency, is that it is highly revisable according to circumstance and, furthermore, removable upon the demands of utility. In a rational political organization, state power is the ultimate and final authority. As Bolsinger cogently argued, "[r]ationalism means, therefore, the institutionalization of contingency and arbitrariness in the realm of state and law."[117] Of course there is much more to rational domination than arbitrariness, but arbitrariness is nonetheless an integral and central component of it, however disguised it may be by layers of rationalizing ideological discourse. Yet arbitrariness does not necessarily mean that there are no reasons for action or thought, whether these reasons are tacit or declared, but it does mean that the ultimate posited presuppositions underlying these reasons are founded on sheer will to power, with no fixed end or telos.

While Agamben takes for granted the naturalized Weberian conception of rational types, the idea of bureaucratic domination and rational state management stand central to his modification of biopower as sovereign power. Agamben seems more attentive to what he calls, within the domain of biopower, the "capture of life" than Foucault does, if only because he deems it less innocuous than Foucault thinks. As Katia Genel avers, Agamben's "logic of sovereignty is a logic of capturing life, a logic of isolating 'bare life' as an

117 Bolsinger, *Anatomy*, 130. See also Finlayson and Martin, "Poststructuralism," 164.

exception. This life is exposed not only to the sovereign's violence and power over death but also, more generally, to a decision that qualifies it and determines its value.... The question of biopower, which is not Agamben's central concern, is annexed to another problematic that animates all his writings: *the perpetual definition and redefinition of the human*."[118]

I do not think we need to rehearse the modalities and operations of this perpetual definition and redefinition, since it can be witnessed at all levels of the workings of biopower, be it in law and juridicality, in capitalist discourse and its modus operandi, social work, welfare, education, or what Adorno called "culture industry." If we were to apply the theory of central and peripheral domains[119] to this problematic, then it is safe to say that the central domain of the state's social order, as commanded by biopower, is a domain of perpetually shifting meanings, with all the changing values that they deploy. The peripheral domains, whose modalities and substantive contents are always predicated on the imperatives and priorities of the central domain, are the sites of ambiguity and, often, resistance; but they also constantly remain, by definition, under the constant pressure from the central domain, which decides on the solutions to their problems and determines much of the habitus enveloping them.

Third, there is a crucial level of seemingly paradoxical meaning residing in the heart of biopower, one that is grounded in the first level of meaning adumbrated above. As I have argued in *Restating Orientalism*, the forms of modern knowledge are inextricably connected with the inner structures of the modern state, producing, among other things, racism, nationalism, and genocide, not to mention the constant refinement of the long-standing human activity of warfare. The intertwined phenomena of racism, nationalism, and genocide may even be said to constitute together one of the essences of biopower. Yet, biopower is assumed to consist of the systemic and systematic management, control, education, and correction of the population, all with the supposed intention, nay actual policy, of "increasing life" and "improving" the well-being of the subjects of the state, individually and collectively. This has been characterized by some writers as the "Paradox of Biopower,"[120] but

118 Genel, "Question of Biopower," 43-44 (emphasis mine). On Agamben's central conception of "bare life," see his *Homo Sacer*. It must be said that Genel's subordination of biopower to Agamben's discourse on the perpetual redefinition of the human is not entirely justifiable, for, politically, both go hand in hand. It is undeniable that biopower is the means of choice, if not the only means, to effect this perpetual redefinition.

119 On central and peripheral domains, see Hallaq, *Impossible State*, 6-12.

120 Fiaccadori, "State Racism and the Paradox of Biopower," 151-71; see also Genel, "Question of Biopower," 49.

in view of the inner structures of this power, I do not think a real paradox is entailed. Having historically been preceded by racism, nationalism, and capital oversight,[121] biopower is quintessentially grounded in all three, taking them for granted and using them in its structured forms of management and control. Biopower's effects in the modern state are always nationalist, racist, and ultimately genocidal.[122] Biopower *intends* the cultivation of the population's interests, making it healthier, stronger, and always more productive, but this logic often sits in opposition to other populations (internal or external) who are seen as the enemy. The improvements of one's population therefore implies an attempt to win out against another population, this being again integral to the distinction between enemy and friend.

Nor does this population consist of one hue or a mass of equal subjects. As structurally connected with sovereign power, biopower promotes, necessarily on its own terms (because it is also sovereign), the well-being of certain sections of the population and always harbors, potentially at least, intentions of killing and annihilation for the rest. This explains the alarmingly increasing number of genocides during the last few decades, including some genocides not recognized as such by Western superpowers.

Here therefore lies the intimate structural connection between biopower and sovereign power, the self-authorized right of the modern state to decide which section of the population can live and which must die, even which sections can be classified as humans and which as sub-humans. Essential to this logic remains the consideration of the well-being of the population, that is, the sections that matter in the population. And again, the decision of who "matters" and who does not is a sovereign one. But it is important to realize that this is not "mere decision," or mere arbitrariness of sovereign power. In biopower, this "decision" becomes integral to the other processes of normalization, where the general population comes to accept it as part of the natural state of affairs and thus take it for granted as a truism. This becomes all the more "true" because the structure of discourse expressing racism and genocide is saturated with the articulations of the security and well-being of the population: the elimination of the targeted section of the population is akin to extracting the invasive weeds in one's garden,[123] an act of not just "purify-

121 I say "capital oversight" and not "capitalism" because biopower is common to all modern states, including the socialist and the communist. And all states stand in an intense relationship with capital, whatever their ideological makeup is.

122 As I argue in *Restating Orientalism*, 179-228.

123 As characterized by Bauman, *Modernity and the Holocaust.*

ing the nation" but also of enhancing the "security," "life," and "well-being" of biopower's population.

If sovereign power and biopower inextricably and interconnectedly enmesh themselves in the structures of the modern state, then we may say that they too are ultimately grounded in a system of self-authorization. And if we accept, as we also must, that the state does not know but itself, then we must perforce also accept that the state – along with its biopower – is the final arbiter of what is good in life and what is not. This is the most articulate meaning of *raison d'état*, where there are no reasons higher than the reasons the state sovereignly proffers.

Being of its own making, these reasons are subject to the laws of contingency, without being bound to any high-order principle other than the self-interest and power of the state itself. And if it is true that the state is not in the business of cultivating ethics or making ethical subjects ("making us good"),[124] then its quintessential penchant toward the "perpetual definition and redefinition of the human" becomes perfectly intelligible. The pliable human, arbitrarily defined and redefined at every turn of politics and every consideration of "public good," therefore becomes the means of the state, not its goal or desideratum. There is no assumption here of a natural constitution of the human, one to be taken on its own terms and respected as autonomous or an end unto itself. The very concept of "natural" is diluted into what Alasdair MacIntyre called an interminable disagreement, because the moral values invoked are incommensurable and detached from their context of rational inquiry. If biopower works for the "health of the population," for improving its lot, the workings are not on terms of the human groupings that constitute its "population" boundaries. Rather, the human is what the state says, what the state and its efficient biopower makes and remakes. This explains why the traditional social units of tribe, clan, "extended family," and the like not only disintegrated after the French and Industrial Revolutions, but their residues, represented in the nuclear family, were further fragmented into individualized and atomized units of social existence, all of which are accompanied by a dramatic rise in social crisis and inner psychological disintegration.

The absence of any principle higher than reason-of-state invites us to pursue a genealogical explanation for this arbitrariness, not to mention the destructiveness of racism, genocide, and the like. In *The Impossible State*, I argued that the Euro-American concept and practice of the rule of law does

124 Murdoch, *Metaphysics as a Guide to Morals*, 350.

not measure up to other systems of the rule of law, especially the Islamic, precisely because the law of the modern state – a political entity to its core – is of its own making. I do not mean by this that only the final production of legal codes and regulations are of its own making. This itself is not the real problem. Rather, the structural problem lies in the fact that this law does not hark back to principles higher than what the state legislates as principles. Modern legislation and law in general are self-referential and self-authorizing entities, because their maker is the same.[125]

The phenomena of sovereignty and biopower therefore bring to the fore what I call the Problem of Disanchorage, a problem that is not just epistemological but also ontological. *The analysis of the Problem of Disanchorage investigates the juridico-political effects of a system of government that has abolished cosmology as its ultimate foundation; which is to say, a system that has abolished the very principle of the existence of any principle higher than what the state and its machinery of the political posit and demand as a principle.* The Problem plagues all modern practices of sovereignty because disputes over the final authority behind state decision and rule are inherently irresolvable. This, I think, is the core concern of Maritain's critique of the concept,[126] however much his secular critics may see it as a "Catholic argument."

The Problem of Disanchorage is both ontological and epistemological because the state does not locate itself in a chain of being, where it belongs to a higher order of things (and this is not necessarily "just a religious critique"). Belonging to a world created by a higher intelligence *ipso facto* creates the Weltanschauung of cosmic embodiment, where the human in its bodily, cerebral, and spiritual constitution acts as an expression of its location within the recognized cosmos. This ontological recognition precludes all notions of a cosmic accident, this latter being the epistemological foundation of the state and its scientific craft of biopower. In this picture, the human is subject to no more than the whims of cosmic will through expressions of natural phenomena and an assortment of conjectural myth. These can never perpetually define and redefine humanity, for that concept of humanity is taken for granted because it is largely fixed, or at least remains relatively stable across time. The structure of the human in its social life – family, tribe, social relations, emotive networks of love and care, of familial security and old traditions of value – remains at a premium worth, and never becomes an instrument of attaining an undefined

125 Hence the subtitle of chapter 3 in *The Impossible State*: "Rule of Law or Rule of the State?"

126 Maritain, "Concept of Sovereignty."

telos. While modern constitutional forms and their location in political sovereignty and biopower suffer from severe problems and irresolvable paradoxes,[127] the most significant of these is the Problem of Disanchorage, because the very best of our political forms will continue to drift aimlessly in the ocean of meaninglessness. And because it pertains to the very constitution of our political order, the Problem is much more serious than the generic loss of meaning that so many postmodern critics lament. It is precisely this Problem that induces the kind of political reason that can recognize no telos other than its own will to power, and with it the perpetual definition and redefinition of the human.

IV

The thrust of the foregoing section should by now be clear. The ultimate measure of sovereign power (which encompasses constitutional organization and any concept of separation of power) and biopower is not just the care they afford to the population, ultimately a nationalist grouping. Rather, it is the quality of the human subject that is produced out of the complex processes of the exercise of these powers. The well-being of the nation does not necessarily translate into a "positive" construction of subjectivity, as evidenced in the long list of qualities marshalled earlier, from states of exception and killing-in-conscription to genocides and the destruction of the environment.

But the subject of biopower is not just destructive of the Other, human and insentient, but also of its own being. Which is to say, in simpler words, that the system of governance that manages, manipulates, calculates, and attends to the well-being of its population is not concerned with higher ethical values to which it deems itself subordinate (values that engender in the human respect for the intrinsic value of sentient and insentient beings). Rather, it perpetually defines and redefines "its humans" for no telos other than the perpetuation of its own power, without any *principled* human and humanistic consideration in mind. Of course, the fundamental and perhaps ultimate assumption that drives my critique is that the political power of the nation-state is neither a human achievement nor a desideratum. And, as a matter of critique, it is not only in the very normalization of such achievements and desiderata that the

127 For a summary of these problems, see section I of this chapter as well as Hallaq, *Impossible State*, 37-73.

problem lies. It locates the counter-critique itself in the heart of the system of biopower, making its discourse an integral part of the process by which biopower is produced.

Accordingly, we can confidently insist that the qualitative formation of subjectivity is the highest value of human social existence, for this formation decides the quality of the humans that inhabit a particular system of governance, in its constitutional construction, rule of law, politics, and biopower, among much else. What matters therefore is not just the formal definition of constitutional boundaries, the overreach or restraint of executive power, the independence of the judiciary, or the rule of law. These assuredly constitute necessary conditions for just rule; but they are most certainly insufficient conditions for any type of rule that aims to be just. I have said more than once that many of the genocidal and Apartheid states of the twentieth and twenty-first centuries base themselves squarely in systems of robust rule of law, even in liberal democratic rule. The subjectivities produced by such regimes – bellicose, violent, and distinctly racist, xenophobic and even self-destructive – must therefore be the first analytical priority for the whole range of the human and social sciences. Like all critical thought, the study of constitutionalism and rule of law must always address the fundamental question "What are we now?"[128]

The lack of awareness of such analytical concerns in Islamic studies is not just stunning but also accurately reflects the embeddedness of the entire field itself in the legacies of colonial biopower, by which I mean biopower insofar as the metropolitan colonist is fashioned by its techniques, as well as the colonized subject as its derivative target. In this context, it appears to have escaped Foucault that the notion of "positive effects" of biopower on the population has the very same structure of the construct of *mission civilisatrice*, in the way it reflected and continues to reflect malevolent effects on both the colonizer and the colonized (Foucauldian) "populations."

If the construction of the quality of the subject is the highest measure by which any form of rule and power is judged, then it is of most central importance to ask: What kind of paradigmatic subject did Islamic governance produce? What kind of sovereign power was constructed and practiced in the production of this quality? What is the meaning of sovereignty in the Islamic conception of politics? What was the Islamic political investment in the construction of the subject? Did it compete with the Sharīʿa in regulating

128 Hallaq, *Restating Orientalism*, 175-78.

the life of the population? Was the subject of Islamic governance and politics defined and redefined? If yes, how? By whom? Why?

I ask these questions with a view to framing the upcoming discussion, without intending to answer each question in detail. The synthetic narrative that ensues treats these questions as an interrelated set, an aggregate. Before proceeding, however, I must clarify what I mean by "paradigmatic subject," or "subject" as an analytical category. One of the critiques directed at *The Impossible State* was that I idealize Islamic history and endow it with an unrealistic ethical dimension. There are at least two ways to address this critique. The first is to say that the very critique is engulfed by a theology of progress that refuses to accept that we are not superior to our predecessors, those who are presumed to have inhabited a less developed existence. If human history is a story of progress and development, then we by necessity are more advanced than previous generations.[129] As I have argued in the general Introduction to

129 Integral to what Scheler has termed the Western thought-structure of domination, the idea of progress came to structure history in specifically Euro-centric ways (on Scheler, see Hallaq, *Impossible State*, 75-76; on the idea of progress, see Comte, *August Comte on Positivism*, 33-34, 496-97; Staude, *Max Scheler*, 167-68; Baker, "On Condorcet's '*Sketch*'," 56-64). Condorcet believed that progress is a never-ending process, one that will continue to unfold on European and mainly Revolution-based, French civilizational terms. For him, all societies of the past, irrespective of geography or time, lived and died for the sake of, and in preparation for, modern Europe (Condorcet, *Sketch for a Historical Picture*, 8-13 and *passim*; see also Stark, *Sociology*, 133, for Meinecke's evaluation of Voltaire on this point). Meinecke came to a similar conclusion regarding Voltaire, arguing that the "governing motives of his historiography" were to utilize "the whole of world history for the service of the enlightenment" (Stark, *Sociology*, 133). Hegel predicated individual freedom on his theory of the Spirit (*Geist*): wars, violence, and the horrors of history are in fact conducive to the improvement and refinement of the *Geist*. In Hegel's theory, "there is something distinctive and superior about the period of modernity, a period for which all previous history has been somehow preparatory" (O'Connor, "Philosophy of History," 181; on the British notions of progress within the context of colonialism, see Ferro, *Colonization*, 20-23). The doctrine of progress has been declared "a law of historical development, a philosophy of history, and as a consequence also a political philosophy." (See Stanley's introduction to Sorel's *Illusions of Progress*, xiii; Nisbet, *History of the Idea of Progress*, 4, 7). In his introduction to Bury's important work on this theory, Charles Beard was able to declare that "among the ideas which have held sway in public and private affairs for the last two hundred years, *none is more significant* or likely to exert more influence than the concept of progress" (Bury, *Idea of Progress*, xi [emphasis mine]; an index of this theory's pervasive influence is also to be found in Charles Taylor's work. Despite his recognition of the "barbarism" of modernity and the twentieth century, he still succumbs to a sort of Western civilizational march. See the insightful commentary of Quentin Skinner on Taylor's work, in his essay "Modernity and Disenchantment," 42-43). Being "a receptacle for ideology," the doctrine of progress creates faithful followers "who believe themselves to be absolutely in the right," always finding themselves "confronted by others whom they

the present book, this theology – which inhabits the minds of philologists and historians as much it does laypersons – amounts to epistemic arrogance and hubris. The burden of proof in judging historical depictions as idealistic then shifts to the critic himself or herself, who must now conclusively show that they are free of this theology.

The second way is to argue that there is indeed a subject that we can describe schematically, one who constitutes not just a majority within the relevant population, but also one who is a schematic average of attitudes, perceptions, conceptions, and psycho-epistemic makeup. It should not escape us that throughout the range of fields making up the humanities and social sciences, observers, authors, and commentators almost invariably speak of such averages. People speak of the Enlightenment Man, Enlightenment Reason, the European, Indian, the Maori, Inuit, and the like. Over decades of scholarly production, Foucault used this category in virtually every second paragraph he wrote: "the subject of biopower," "the subject of the techniques of the self," etc. Whether we call it a biopower, a tradition, culture, or habitus, there is always a schematic or representational – even perhaps nominal – subject that is produced by these formations. In a habitus, for instance, no two human individuals are identical, but the subject of habitus is that entity that captures the characteristics of habitus, its tradition-based modes of existence, or its doxastic constitution.

The Muslim/Islamic habitus, being constituted by an ethical and moral subject matter – beginning with the theorization of its heteronomous principles[130] and ending in its social dispensations – strove toward the realization of moral ends. Accordingly, resting on communal ethical foundations, the habitus is characterized by what I call a persistent moral benchmark. Benchmarks do not always fully succeed in implementing their desiderata in the real world (otherwise, society would be ideal); rather, they stand as standards against which reality is not only measured but also, and primarily, pressured and ultimately judged. A persistent benchmark is one whose pressure is greater than those possessed by other benchmarks, especially if its matrix and source of authority stem from a central domain – such as the Sharīʿa and its sister domain Ṣūfism.[131]

regard as absolutely in the wrong" (Bauman, *Intimations of Postmodernity*, xiv; Hayes, *Historical Evolution of Modern Nationalism*, 13-14; Meier, *Greek Discovery of Politics*, 190; Lasch, *Culture of Narcissism*, xvii).

130 See main text of Introduction, at n. 74.

131 I have discussed ethical benchmarks in *Restating Orientalism*, 79 ff. See also Introduction, n. 71.

My argument is that this benchmark is nearly absent in modern structures of life and thus a good philologist must well understand this differential, and how this differential accounts for and structures a philological method, before she can make sense of history.

In chapter 4, I gave a relatively extensive account of the Qur'ānic concept of divine command, expressed as *ʿilm,* knowledge that the Muslim needs in order to live his or her life. As Ibn Idrīs al-Shāfiʿī authoritatively noted some two centuries after the Qur'ān was revealed, and as became commonly accepted throughout the millennium that followed, there is a divine norm for every contingency and occurrence Muslims encounter in their lives.[132] The Sharīʿa evolved with this understanding in mind and was accepted as such as a culture and habitus. All legitimate knowledge, including the high- and low-order principles of law and methods of legal construction, were to be derived, through ethical reason,[133] from the textual indicants and intimations revealed in the Qur'ān and the Sunna. In fact, the very tools and concepts that constituted this ethical reason were likewise derived from the same sources. This conception of law and reasoning is wholly supported by the paradigmatic, authoritative, and only methodology that Islam knew until the nineteenth century: *uṣūl al-fiqh.*

A fundamental feature of *uṣūl al-fiqh* is its ontological situatedness in a chain of being. As an intellectual and ethical formation (that is, as an activity that is at once theoretical and performative of subjectivity),[134] it occupied a place between *kalām* and *fiqh,* that is between the metaphysics of existence (*wujūd*) and the jural regulation of the social world. This was not just an epistemological and logical location, but obviously an ontological one as well. If God, his *al-Lawḥ al-Maḥfūẓ* (the Preserved Tablet), and an ethical structure of divine creation are (pre-)existent realities (*mawjūdāt; wājibat al-wujūd*), and if humans and their social organization are undeniable existents as well, then *uṣūl al-fiqh* is that which also existentially stands between the two. The existential value of this discipline is then precisely to mediate between the First Principles of existence and the earthly priorities and actions in the world of humans. No *uṣūl al-fiqh* could find a place in the world without it resting on the metaphysical and cosmological foundations laid down in *kalām.* God's existence as a prime mover needed to be established first, before one could begin

132 Shāfiʿī, *Risāla,* 14.

133 See ch. 1, sec. II.

134 This is because the study of *uṣūl al-fiqh* is itself an act of *ʿibāda* (i.e., a technology of the self). Thus, the effects of the discipline in terms of reasoning and producing law – which is then applied to social groups and individuals – are techniques producing subjectivities.

to speak of prophethood and religion. And the latter two, in conjunction with God's existence, needed to be equally demonstrated before one could begin to speak of the Qur'ān as the *Speech* of God and therefore the inviolable source of the law. Here the Problem of Disanchorage does not exist.

The study of the law was the most advanced level of instruction in the Islamic system of learning, and the most institutionally established as well. Much else was likewise studied, including Qur'ān, Ḥadīth, linguistics, astronomy, mathematics, geometry, logic, medicine, anatomy, botany, and chemistry. Several schools of thought evolved within these fields of knowledge, some Islamic and some Greek or otherwise, as in the case of medicine and geometry. Yet, all of these, as formations of knowledge, were enveloped by Islamic norms, despite the great variety and diversity in their constitution.

It is also as crucial to note that the subject who is the site of these kinds of knowledge – whether astronomy, mathematics, logic, theology, history, or law – began his or her learning in a fundamentally unified system of education that shared its sources with those of law as well as with all major disciplines. Which is to say that even when a student was taught, say, logic, the discipline remained framed by the paradigms and ordered priorities of *Muslim* education, and in fact seen as "instrumental" for the study of more advanced fields that presuppose it (knowledge of logic, for instance, was a prerequisite for the study of legal theory and *kalām*, among others).

The pupil, from an early age to youth, studied Arabic writing, grammar, syntax, the Qur'ān, Ḥadīth of the Prophet, arithmetic, certain types of *adab*, among possible others.[135] The activity of teaching and learning was not determined by caliphal or sultanic will but rather by the ulama, "the men of the pen." The vast bulk of education took place in private spaces, mainly homes and mosque yards. The rest of it was conducted in *waqf*s which were autonomous endowments whose syllabi were also determined by the ulama.[136] There was no martial discipline, lining up the students every school day to sing the national anthem. There were no political figures, presidents, sultans, or even caliphs[137]

135 Robinson, "Education," 520-22 (to be read, however, with caution).

136 See n. 145, below.

137 Of course, with the exception of the Rāshidūn caliphs. It was by virtue of being the Prophet's Companions that the Rāshidūn caliphs were held in high esteem, not by virtue of being rulers who held a political or military office. They were considered as founding figures. Their authority stemmed from the epistemoral fact that their proximity to the Prophet gave them the highest quality of knowledge that allowed them to lead the Muslim Community in the most exemplary way. Their biographical exemplarity was therefore ethical and thus enshrined in the Muslim ethos, but it was not political, nationalistic, or ideological.

whose exemplarity the pupil was inculcated to appreciate. Nor were there pictures or representations of such figures adorning the walls of the classroom. Students did not study civics and the history of their nation, nor were they subjected to the myths of its glorious past and present, this being simply due to the fact that there was no nation in the first place.[138] The Muslim pupil may have been exposed to some knowledge of tribal genealogies (a specialized science not usually taught at the elementary levels) and may have developed pride in belonging to one or another lineage, but the formation was predominantly grounded in his or her Islamic tradition, anthropologically so defined. The teachings of the Qur'ān and the exemplarity of the Prophetic Sunna were the major sources of pedagogy, inculcation of values, norms, and subjectivation.[139] The Sunna, in particular, constituted the substantive source of embodiment. The challenge of Muslims, across both Sharʿī and Ṣūfī cultures, was to emulate the ethical exemplarity of their Prophet, in deed, word, and even emotively. Customary practices and local convention no doubt constituted an important part of the habitus, but the proactive, constructive, and performative forces stemmed from the Islamic normative sources that bounded these practices and anchored them in the Islamic norms.[140]

If Islam had no states, then it did not have schools and much less societies.[141] Instead, education and upbringing were performed in communal settings, in and by the community, and without disciplinarian structures.[142] The *benchmark* of this education (in contradistinction with its fully formed *effects*, which is not my meaning here[143]) was the cultivation of the ethical and communal subject, one who complied with the sacred values enshrined in the Qur'ān and the Sunna.[144] But we must constantly remember that one of the most fundamental features of this pedagogical discursive tradition (again, meant anthropologically)

138 In fact, it would have been impossible for Islam, without European colonialism and hegemony, to develop the concept of nationalism, and much less a life based on the nation.
139 Robinson, "Education," 524-26. See also in general Marín, "The *'ulamā',*" 682-701.
140 This generalization applies mostly to the central lands of Islam, between Morocco today and Eastern Iran, and from the Hejaz to western Anatolia. In Southeast Asia and Sub-Saharan West Africa, local customary practices were the larger matrix in which partial applications of the Sharīʿa were situated. See, e.g., Trimingham, *History of Islam.*
141 See ch. 1, n. 47.
142 The meaning here is not simple physical punishment, of which teachers no doubt made frequent use. Rather, the reference here is to deep discipline, that which fashions the docile self by "training" both the body and mind. See Foucault, *Discipline and Punish*, 213 ff.
143 On the significance of ethical benchmarks in writing the history of Islam, see Hallaq, *Restating Orientalism*, 80-84 and passim. See also Introduction, n. 71.
144 On the ethics of learning, see Zarnūjī, *Taʿlīm al-Mutaʿallim*, esp. 59-70, 126-29.

is that from a very young age the pupil is inculcated into the techniques of ethical self-cultivation and self-formation. These were integral to all levels of education, from the second quinquennial of life till graduation, if not death.

More complex and intellectually sophisticated, advanced learning followed similar patterns. During the first three centuries of Islam, it was largely disconnected from politics, being limited to what we call today private scholarship which the rulers at times sought to influence in terms of patronage but without much success. Whatever influence was exercised, and even when it was successful, learning and education remained autonomous, institutionally and in terms of curriculum. Even with Sulaymān the Magnificent's presumably effectual reforms in the seventeenth century, and with the unprecedented interference of dynastic rule in the organization of royal *madrasa*s, education – as we have seen in the previous chapter – was and continued to be determined by the Sharīʿa.[145] In terms of curricular substance and content, advanced education in

145 See the significant contribution of Sh. Ahmed and N. Filipovic, "Sultan's Syllabus," 183-218. Significant, because it reveals the limits of the most drastic educational "reforms" in the entirety of Islamic history until the nineteenth century. The authors conclude that "the Süleymānic syllabus is reflective of a process of conservative change in the historical constitution of the scholarly canon in Islam" (217). Their conclusions, judged from the theoretical perspective of this chapter, may be deemed stunted, but the empirical data provided is of tremendous importance. Sulayman's decree lists thirty-nine works, short and long (multi-volume), all of which are authored by "men of religion," so to speak. That they are predominantly Ḥanafī is by now no surprise, the implications of which we have discussed in detail in the previous chapter. It is noteworthy that of the thirty-nine works, twelve are Qur'ān commentaries, including two by Māturīdī and Ṣūfī authors. There are twelve Ḥadīth works, including Bukhārī's compendium, three commentaries on it, and eight more by other Ḥadīth scholars. In the field of substantive law (*fiqh*), the list contains eight works: Marghīnānī's authoritative *Hidāya*, three commentaries on it, as well as four others in the Zaylaʿī-Nasafī *fiqh* line. In addition to two *fatwā* collections and three authoritative lexicons, there is one work on *uṣūl al-fiqh*. Note that none of the works hails from outside the Sharʿī-legislative sociology of knowledge, and no codices of royal *qānūn* or otherwise are included. Sulayman's reforms may have tilted the curriculum in favor of a Ḥanafī perspective, which it did, but the overall thrust of this education remained crucially Sharʿī, through and through. On the other hand, Tunç Şen notably argues the following: "The point this article makes is a rather simple one: that the register Ahmed and Filipovic considered to be a 'clear and detailed syllabus' had far less ambitious aims than imposing a curriculum. This single-page registry was, in fact, not unlike several other extant documents and registers from the periods that mention or list books endowed by the sultans to the royal madrasas they founded or sent ad hoc from the palace to various places, including newly-constructed imperial *madrasas*, the chief physician's office, or even the observatory. *None of these necessarily entailed a dynastic, or specifically sultanic, control over the teaching curriculum.* Seen through the lens that these underused contemporary documents provide, it seems more plausible to argue that the register undergirding Ahmed and Filipovic's analysis was drafted with the mere aim of recording and filing the items sent from the royal

general and legal education in particular were not compromised by any political accommodation or dynastic policies.[146] As we have seen throughout this book, sultanic interventions, even in the more centralized Ottoman Empire, barely touched the surface of substantive law, leaving the *fiqh* almost entirely autonomous.[147] In fact, it was the ruler who – from the beginning of Islam until the middle of the nineteenth century – consistently had to succumb to the dictates of the Sharīʿa's pedagogical and educational imperatives. He, his family members, and non-military personnel were all educated and trained by the ulama, with, *mutatis mutandis*, the same curricular content taught to everyone else.[148]

Sometime during the late fourth/tenth century, the law college – known in Islamic languages as *madrasa/medrese/medresah* – came into being.[149] Established as a charitable trust through the law of *waqf*, the *madrasa* was usually housed in a mosque and mostly for the teaching of law, where the professor and the students were provided, among other things, with stipends, food, a library, a clinic, and dormitories.[150] It is worth emphasizing here the organic connections between and among the Islamic conceptions of charity, piety, and the acquisition of knowledge. Instituted in the Qur'ān as such, charity was a pillar of belief and of being a Muslim. *Waqf*s were acts of charity, and the larger of them were colossuses of public service. The acquisition of knowledge meant the study of many subjects, including language, exegesis, Ḥadīth transmission, logic, mathematics, and astronomy. But the study of law was the queen and king. It was a paradigmatic field of knowledge and a personal and institutional expression of pietistic charity to boot.

The study-circle (*ḥalqa*) differed from the *madrasa* in one crucial respect: it was largely a free scholarly gathering of a professor and his students, without political interference and unfettered by financial patronage. Being an

library to the Süleymaniye madrasas, possibly to enhance the latter's book collection in the designated subject areas. This particular register, and similar other book lists drafted in different periods, no doubt reflect scholarly preferences and delineate 'canonic' contours, *but it would be misleading to take the further step and speak of a 'syllabus' imposed top-down* through these book inventories." Şen, "Sultan's Syllabus Revisited," 202 (emphasis mine).

146 As evidenced in the previous footnote.

147 See previous chapter.

148 See, for example, Maria Eva Subtelny and Anas B. Khalidov, "Curriculum of Higher Learning in Timurid Iran," 210-36. See also Lapidus quotation, main text at n. 160, below.

149 Makdisi, *Rise of Colleges*. On legal education, see also, in general, Lowry, *Law and Education*.

150 On the *waqf* and *madrasa*, see Makdisi, *Rise of Colleges*; Berkey, *Transmission of Knowledge in Medieval Cairo*; Ephrat, *Learned Society in a Period of Transition*.

endowment, the *madrasa* maintained the free scholarly association between professor and student but was bound, within the Shar'ī deed of *waqf*, by the necessary effects of patronage. It was the site in which politics and legal education intersected, since those who founded the largest, most affluent, and most prestigious *madrasa*s were the rulers and their immediate entourage (mothers, wives, daughters, brothers, sisters, viziers, commanders, and less often big merchants, whose endowments tended to be smaller). As we saw in the evaluation of modern scholarship on the Ottoman legal hierarchy,[151] this sultanic intervention was more administrative than legal, affecting none of the curricular content, even for sultanic colleges.[152] Which is to say that whatever "institutional" form education took, its contents, usually quite varied, came from the same pools of Islamic learning, as were its effects on constructing the subject, be that subject's trajectory the juristic field and jurisprudence, the judicial domain, secretarial service, royal chancery, or any other.

More than that, the rulers were in dire need of legitimization, which they found in the circles of the legal and learned profession, and no less in the Ṣūfī orders. Being primarily a securitizing military entity, sultanic authority had no legitimacy by virtue of its sheer might, because it did not control or had no claim over the domain (and culture) of law. It was the Sharī'a that provided both legal and political legitimacy, *because it was entwined with the religious habitus of Muslim social formations*. The Sharī'a was not just a legal system, but the *dominant culture* of Islam properly speaking. Dominant, in the sense that it defined the habitus governing Muslims' lives, including the establishment of parameters for integrating customary "laws" and local forms of knowledge and practice.[153] This also explains the cardinal fact that it was the so-called juristic texts – as those we take to be our primary texts of analysis in this work – that captured the dominant ideas of what politics and rule are and should be. If we know what politics and governance look like in Islam, it is by virtue of the fact that these texts ruled, and were unanimously accepted as the voice of the

151 See the previous chapter.

152 See n. 145, above.

153 To say that the Sharī'a was the dominant legal and cultural system by whose standards and priorities other fields of activity – such as customary law and a wide variety of local practices – were regulated is not to say that the Sharī'a was the only player in the field, as some critics misunderstood. In my understanding and writings, past and present, custom and other local practices were ever-present in Muslim societies, and duly acknowledged as such by both legal theory (*uṣūl al-fiqh*) and substantive law (*fiqh*). But they always stood as peripheral domains vis-à-vis the Sharī'a, which was the central domain. For the theory of central and peripheral domains, see Hallaq, *Impossible State*, 6-12. On the role of custom in the Sharī'a, see Hallaq, "Prelude to Ottoman Reform."

norm and the expression of the habitus. Thus, legitimacy lay in the preserve of religion, erudition, ascetic piety, moral rectitude, and in short, in the *persons* of those men and women who had profound knowledge of, and fashioned their lives after, the example of the Prophet and the exemplary forefathers. There was no other form of legitimacy outside these and associated domains.

The Sharīʿa personnel served as an effective tool for reaching the masses from whose ranks they emerged and whose interests they represented and protected, even largely so under the centralizing and highly pragmatic Ottomans. The jurists, judges, and ulama at large, emerged as the civic leaders who, though themselves products of the masses, found themselves, by the nature of their profession, involved in the day-to-day running of their civic affairs. Jurists and judges felt responsibility toward the common man and woman, and on their own frequently initiated action on behalf of the oppressed without any formal petition being made. And there is no doubt that the *qāḍī*s in particular were not only the judicial and administrative officials who supervised the quotidian life of the masses and, with the local leaders (*shuyūkh*), represented the interests of the populace to the rulers and governors, but they, as foremost administrators, also ensured the application of Sharīʿa values and rules in all segments of society.[154]

As a product of their own social environment and legal training, the ulama's worldview was inextricably intertwined with the interests of their societies. Which is also to say that the regulatory mechanisms that governed the Muslim populations constituted a profoundly bottom-up system of civic governance, standing in sharp contrast to the top-down systems of modern sovereignty and state rule. If we add to this the massive layer of Ṣūfism and Ṣūfī orders, which came to enhance the culture of the Sharīʿa, its discursive tradition, and habitus,[155] then we can appreciate the considerable social power on which the political executive was dependent as a matter of legitimization.

This is why executive sultanism attempted to establish as strong a relationship as it could with the ulama and the Ṣūfīs. The informal financial patronage offered to the jurists during the early period was in due course to change to a relatively more systematic and institutionalized form. It so happened that the *madrasa* became the chief means by which the jurists, and no less the Ṣūfīs,

154 On the centrality of the *qāḍī* for the administration of life in the Muslim city, see the urban historian A. Raymond, *Arab Cities*. On the sway of the *qāḍī*s in the administrative and social life of Ottoman Jerusalem, see ʿAlamī, *Quḍāt al-Quds al-Sharīf*.

155 On habitus and its relationship to "discursive tradition," see Introduction, ch. 1, 2, and 10 (sec. IV).

were brought to serve in the business of constructing dynastic legitimacy. Note here that legitimacy was a one-way street: the civic population as the locus and habitus of the culture of the Sharīʿa, needed no legitimization before the dynastic powers, for it was, as a doxastic phenomenon, legitimate on its own terms. Accordingly, it was on terms of this habitus that political legitimacy was played out. As a legal and educational institution, the *madrasa* continued to operate in ways thoroughly rooted in the pedagogical and hermeneutic tradition that had existed in the study-circle prior to its appearance. The study-circle was the indispensable basic unit and modality of Islamic education until the nineteenth century. The *madrasa* allowed the perpetuation of parts of "urban" Islamic education through permanent material structures, which constituted a fundamental prerequisite for the political elite to garner legitimacy. This may explain why the slave dynasty of the Mamlūks, cultural and ethnic outsiders to Egypt and Syria, constructed some of the most monumental *waqf*s and *madrasa*s in these regions.

Insofar as the quality of the relationship between teacher and student is concerned, Islamic education could not be any more different from modern education. The Muslim shaykh was not just a teacher in the technical sense, but also functioned as a moral educator, an ethical disciplinarian, a companion, a supporter, and a role model. Instilling a deep sense of morality based on the concepts of rectitude and humility, among other qualities, was as much part of the curriculum as any substantive subject. And so was the cultivation of virtue and varied forms of technologies of ethical self-formation. The application of the law as a socially funneled institution presupposed a system of social morality, a system upon which the efficacy of law depended and from which it could not be separated. The teacher, among other instructional agents, cultivated in the student the elements of this moral system. Teacher-student relationship was often akin to that of parent and child, and many students not only resided in, and dined at, the homes of their teachers but married their daughters as well. At the risk of repetition, it is crucial to stress that no caliph, sultan, or governor did or could impose their own conception of what should constitute a "school" curriculum or a *madrasa* text. Even advanced law professors were free to teach the treatises of their choice, a freedom mildly restricted by the appearance of *madhhab*-authorized texts.

I have deliberately entwined the discussion of pedagogy with that of legitimacy because the connections between these two are instructive. One way to cast the matter is to say that the dire search for legitimacy was in part the result of how premodern government was constituted. It was in the nature of premodern rule in general, and Islamic government in particular, to exercise their power through small ruling elites, with a limited sphere of direct influence and minimal bureaucratic control. The rulers could not penetrate the communities, much less form them into "societies" in the manner the modern state has done. And there was no particular national fervor that could be appealed to. In order to be on the good side of the populace, rulers had to show that they heed the Sharīʿa, respect the ulama, and prove their dedication by investing in the religious establishment and the welfare of the communities they ruled.

In this context, it may be worthwhile citing expansively from a mainstream Orientalist historian of Islam, whose account, however theoretically unrefined, is less controversial than perhaps any other.[156] In various places in his vast book, Ira Lapidus states:

> Apart from the residential quarters and the markets, religious congregations or associations were a critical aspect of city communal organization.... The learned and holy men became the leaders of sects, teaching circles, and prayer groups. Local legal scholars, teachers, storytellers, and preachers in the mosques assumed an *independent authority* as Islamic law, theology, and ritual developed largely without state[157] interference. Religious teachers were the social elites, notables in their communities, and assumed authority in all sorts of local matters. As in ancient times, scholarship and education were aligned with social and communal prestige and were connected to tribal chiefs, landowners, merchants, and government officials....[158]
>
> The notables, however, were unable to govern the cities by themselves. They did not have military power, they did not control rural resources, and they did not have the capital to sustain their own cadres and to provide for big urban infrastructure investments – such as walls, canals, mosques and colleges, caravanserais, and shops; for these, they depended on the military elites. Reciprocally, the military did not have the local knowledge, administrative cadres, and legitimacy to govern directly. Although the local units of society remained the same in the

156 See the various reviews of the book floating online.

157 Of course, the author's use of the term "state" should be taken with a grain of salt, since we know that this is an anachronism. Anyone who claims that states existed before the seventeenth century, anywhere in the world, is someone who either does not know what the state is made of, stands for, and means, does not understand the nature of premodern (Islamic) rule, or both.

158 Lapidus, *Islamic Societies*, 190-91 (emphasis mine).

> centuries following the collapse of the ʿAbbasid Empire, a new political elite of nomadic and slave warlords – and the ruin of local landowners and other notables – paved the way for far-reaching changes in the organization of town and village communities. *The crucial change in this period was the widespread diffusion of Muslim identities, the assumption of social leadership by Muslim teachers and holy men,* and the crystallization of Muslim sectarian communities, including Shiʿi sects, Sunni schools of law and theology, and Sufi orders. The creation of an Islamic communal and religious identity ... had already begun in the seventh century.... Popular religious organizations that had their origin in an earlier period became normative and universal throughout the region. In the same period, masses of Middle Eastern peoples converted to Islam and were absorbed into Muslim social bodies. Islam, originally the religion of a political and urban elite, became the religion and social identity of most Middle Eastern peoples....[159]
>
> The crucial feature of this system of states and religious communities was the tacit collaboration of state military, local scholars, and Sufi elites. The foreign origin and the militarization of the ruling elites emphasized the distinction between the state and the religious elites and required their political cooperation. The nomadic and slave military elites needed the collaboration of the scholars in order to govern.... Scribes, finance officials, estate managers, and other technicians were vital. Furthermore, the nomadic and slave elites needed scholars, for both political and psychological reasons, to recognize the rightfulness of their regimes. Scholars were the guardians of tradition and to the Saljuqs – who were at first lacking in technical skills and literary and social knowledge – represented the epitome of a desired way of life. They looked to the scholars to be tutored, educated, and guided in acceptable courses of action. Thus, the conquerors were conquered by their subjects.[160]

Now, as I stressed earlier, premodern polities could not penetrate the societies they ruled, nor could they regulate the internal affairs of their subject populations, even if they wanted to. (It is immeasurably significant to entertain the implications of this last caveat, because consciousness of this possibility, of

159 Lapidus, *Islamic Societies*, 273 (emphasis mine).
160 Lapidus, *Islamic Societies*, 338-39.

this will to power, bears much on the forms and quality of knowledge that undergird power, rule, governance and domination of sorts.)[161]

Another layer of explanation for the "failure" of premodern government to penetrate the societies they governed may be the absence of the mechanisms necessary for them to administer the smallest units of which these societies were made. This is another way of saying that premodern rule lacked the bureaucratic organization that provided the tools for establishing relations of power with the "population," relations that are the cornerstone of all modern political regimes. The very concept of "population" in fact emerges as the product of this very juridico-bureaucratic penetration. Once firmly rooted in a society, impersonal bureaucracy tends to replace personal rule. Unlike bureaucratic rule, therefore, premodern forms of governance depended upon personal loyalty and what might be called institutional habitus rather than obedience to abstract bureaucratic and impersonal regulations.

Yet, to say, as I have, that the premodern rule did not penetrate society because it lacked a system of bureaucratic organization does not and should not mean that only because of this lack of bureaucratic power that the premodern rule failed to so penetrate. For this would amount to misunderstanding the fundamentals of the problem. This "lack" did not represent absence as much as it represented a different modality of cognition and being. The will to power (in both the Schelerian and Nietzschean forms) simply did not exist in the political landscapes of Islam (nor anywhere else other than in Europe, to the best of my knowledge, and Scheler's).[162]

The absence of pervasive bureaucracies from such premodern forms of governance meant that the ruler was navigating at the surface of the "societies" he ruled. Even if he had a staff that could be hierarchically deployed to reach the lowest social strata, loyalty to him progressively dissipated as it traveled away from the center. In other words, in the absence of the modern rule of bureaucracy and the unitary concept of the state, the farther the premodern official found himself from the center of power, the less loyalty he had to the ruler, and, in turn, the more loyalty he had to the social group from which he hailed. Thus, the ruler could neither penetrate nor control or integrate these societies. He merely sat on top of "self-help" groups consisting of linguistic and religious communities, guilds, clans, village assemblies, city councils, and literate elites whose internal ties of loyalty were unsurpassable, and whose

161 On the differentials of this consciousness and the forms of knowledge that undergird politics and modes of living in the world, see Hallaq, *Restating Orientalism*.
162 See Hallaq, "On Orientalism, Self-Consciousness and History," 390-400.

quotidian lives were barely touched by whatever administrative machinery the ruler could muster. This system is anything but unitary, nor is it acculturated by the values of political governance. Local values and local forms of knowledge, heavily colored by Sharīʿa, dominated over political priorities of social, institutional, and other forms of organization.[163]

The bottom line here is that, *genealogically*, law and executive power were not to emerge out of the same sources and could not therefore be made to work in tandem, as if they are two branches of a tree or two hands of the same body. And here lies the colossal difference between the European and Muslim experience of polity. Executive power in Islam remained dispossessed of Sharʿī legislative competence. For it is a truism that bureaucratic domination and sovereign biopower would have been impossible had the modern legislative not been genealogically and organically connected to legislative dominance as well.[164] We can therefore safely conclude that the constitutional order of Islam and its modern counterpart are differentiated not only by the quality[165] of their functioning and operation but also – and this bears on the structure of this quality – by their dramatically different genealogical histories.

This genealogical difference cannot be underestimated, because the implications of the fact that the jurists did not derive their authority or forms of jurisprudential knowledge from political power – however this may have been defined – are of great consequence. Rather, they derived their authority and legitimacy from the law itself, a body of discursive practice hermeneutically constructed and methodologically tied to a transcendental authority that travelled beyond and above any political power. This authority was epistemological-cum-moral, or moral-cum-epistemological, the two conceptions of reality meshing into each other indistinguishably. As such, the legists were the main agents that could represent the foreign ruler and the indigenous subjects to each other, the Ṣūfīs and other ascetics coming a close second and augmenting this representation.

By the fifth/eleventh or sixth/twelfth century, the social backgrounds of the legists had become varied, representing all segments of society. They hailed as much from the lowest strata of tradesmen, artisans, and farmers as from affluent merchant families and politically influential secretarial classes.[166]

163 See Hallaq, *Sharīʿa*, 200-208.
164 See, for example, *The Federalist*, no. 47.
165 See Introduction, n. 60.
166 Throughout the centuries of Islam, the legists tended to increasingly hail from what

Their socio-economic connections – deeply embedded in their own societies but also in relative proximity to the ruling classes – thus allowed them to fulfill a variety of functions in mediating the relationship between the government and the ruled populace. The negotiation of this relationship was thus grounded in the terms of the law, as *culturally conceived*.

It is by now clear that much of education, pedagogy, and subjective formation in Islam occurred through and within the law, this in good part materializing through the agency of the *waqf's madrasa*. While the *madrasa* can be studied separately as an institution of learning in Islam, it would be distortive of its nature and function to treat it in this manner. This is because segregating the *madrasa* in this fashion hides its larger significance within culture, psycho-epistemic formation of the subject, and even its place in the larger scheme of things. We therefore ought to treat the *madrasa* as part of a complex, the *waqf-jāmiʿ* complex that was, in its paradigmatic form, bounded by a multiplicity of mutually supportive and enhancing functions. The epicenter and core of the complex was of course the mosque, itself bearing a multilayered representation of Islam's mission. Here the concept that scholarship is a supreme form of worship (*taʿabbud*) acquires material manifestation in the fact of the college attaching itself to the mosque. Inasmuch as the donor, the founder of the *waqf*, gives away his or her wealth "in the way of God" (*fī sabīl Allāh*), the scholar who is the recipient of the *waqf*'s endowed charity also performs the same function of giving to God as an act of performing public good. Scholarship is not just as virtuous as prayer but ranks higher on the scale of virtue due to the fact that it performs public good. This explains why knowledge in Islam is, on principle, deemed free-for-all, thus invalidating the concept of copyright and intellectual property. The *madrasa* therefore continues, expands on, and implements in social realia one of the most important missions of Islam, namely, the fusion between and among belief, charity, and education. To be a Muslim engaged in the world of Sharʿī learning was an act of engaging the three at once, without any consciousness that they are separable, whether analytically or ontologically. For the Sharīʿa aspirants, to study was to engage

might be roughly called the middle and middle-upper classes. However, during the formation of Islam in the first three or four centuries, when the subject matter of substantive law was formed, they came from modest social origins. On this latter point, see Cohen, "Economic Background," 16–61. It should not escape us that there exists a direct relationship between the phenomenon of humble social backgrounds of the early jurists who formulated substantive law during the first three centuries, on the one hand, and the fact that this law is significantly egalitarian and economically protectionist, on the other.

in charity; and to engage in an intense form of charity was to study. And both were deemed supreme acts of worship.

If we visualize the *madrasa* as a circle intersecting that of the mosque, we must add other circles to complete the schemata of the complex, whose full meaning and significance cannot be understood without them. Integral to the schemata are the library, the public bath, and the cemetery. Enmeshed in the missions of the *madrasa* and the mosque, the public bath fulfills the law's requirements for health practices, just as much as the washing fountains in the mosque's enclosure provide the means to the parallel ritual purity. The library expands on and supports charitable giving, literally spreading knowledge (through lending books) and thus enhancing acts of worship. But none of these supporting functions in the complex is more important than the hospital (*bīmāristān*), which brings within its fold public charity, knowledge, and thus service to God (=worship). Here we see that the same triadic value is reapplied to the domain of health, whereas within the bounds of the *waqf* the same trio applies to the law.

The construction of the hospitals (*bīmāristān*s) was a normal and normative *waqf*ic activity. Whether standing alone or constituting part of a larger *waqf* complex, the *bīmāristān*'s charitable offering was usually made by the powerful and the mighty – caliphs, sultans, queens, princesses, commanders, or big merchants.[167] The charitable offering constituted the relinquishment of royal wealth, via God, to the Community or any sections of it (after all the meaning of "*waqf*" itself). The institution fulfilled several functions, from the pietistic and personal to the pragmatic and the political, at times all of which and more operating in tandem.[168] As I have noted in the case of *madrasa*s, *bīmāristān*s were likewise a means for the ruling dynasty to gain political legitimacy from the civic populace, being a premiere philanthropic domain

167 Asyūṭī, *Jawāhir al-ʿUqūd*, I, 203, 349 ff.; Ragab, *Medieval Islamic Hospital*, 2.

168 From this perspective, Linda Northrup provides exemplary analysis. In her study of the reign of the Mamlūk sultan Qalāwūn, she concludes that "Qalāwūn's deliberate decision to patronize the medical rather than the religious sciences was certainly motivated by a complex of religious, political, social, and personal considerations. These considerations included piety, charity, the preeminent status of Cairo in the Islamic world of the late thirteenth century, legitimation, relations between the religious (and especially the conservative) elite and the Mamlūk ruling class, and possibly the personal benefits accruing to the donor of a *waqf*. Beyond these important, though quite mundane goals, however, the sources hint that Qalāwūn may have aimed at something more: the fostering of medical learning. At the least, it appears that he wished to restore the balance between the spiritual and medical branches of learning. More ambitiously, he may have wished to restore the medical sciences to their former glory." See Northrup, "Qalāwūn's Patronage of the Medical Sciences," 119-40, esp. at 139-140.

that held much popular acclaim. But they also shared with the *madrasa* a similar educational function, namely, the education of students in the science of medicine and pharmacology. The *bīmāristān* therefore often constituted a school of medicine to boot.[169]

There is no doubt that rulers paid special attention to the *bīmāristān*s in the cities under their dominion. They assigned high-ranking officials to audit them, as they did in all other major endowments.[170] As early as the fourth/tenth century, if not earlier, *bīmāristān*s were subject to licensure. Licensing examinations were administered to physicians and licensing boards were set up by the *muḥtasib*, a Sharʿī functionary. Under the latter's watch, the chief physician conducted an examination of the theoretical knowledge and clinical skills of the student, and if the examinee proved successful, the *muḥtasib* administered the Hippocratic Oath and issued a license.[171]

Yet, even the most cynical historian cannot doubt that the royal construction and administration of the *bīmāristān*s were acts that had no ambition further than or beyond those of acquisition of political legitimacy from the masses, enhancement of the personal reputation of the ruler, and even the attainment of closeness to God, this being evident in many cases if not all. A less cynical historian might acknowledge significantly more robust pietistic motivations to engage in these philanthropic projects. For their *raison d'être*, after all, was the health of the Muslim community, including the *dhimmī*s. Because it was a *waqf*, the *bīmāristān* was exclusively seen as a charitable institution, engaged in *khayrāt* and *ḥasanāt*, good deeds that were forcefully commanded by the Qur'ān and elaborated within the bounds of duty in every book of law. Since the highest goal of the *waqf* and its hospital (and colleges and much else) was this sanctified philanthropic thrust, the ruler could not use its operations and modes of being for his own ends. Only by supporting these health institutions as they are endowed by the Sharīʿa *waqf* rules, *and thus on their own terms*, could the ruler gain the political support of the population, the price for his rule and the levy of taxes. Here too, in the realm of medicine, the Sharīʿa ruled. Which is also to say that the human flourishing and well-being of the Community were the telos of governance in all its parts, never constituting an endless dynamic of power that perpetually defined and redefined them.

169 Miller, "Jundi-Shapur," 617; Ragab, *Medieval Islamic Hospital*, 6.
170 See, e.g., Nuwayrī, *Nihāyat al-Arab*, XXXI, 104.
171 Miller, "Jundi-Shapur," 616-17.

V

Be that as it may, government management clearly did not extend to total control of these health institutions, nor could it engage in their constant reconfiguration in a bid to subordinate them to the ultimate end of politics, or, put more precisely, to the imperatives of *raison d'état*. For neither that political and utilitarian "*raison*" nor the insatiable "*l'état*" existed in Islam. It was Europe that effected the most monumental transformation in the history of medicine since Galen. Until the sixteenth century, medicine, even in Europe, remained bound by the imperatives of human health and often intertwined with philanthropic motives. But after this century, and especially during the seventeenth and eighteenth, medicine was to gradually become subsumed under the realm of politics, and put, furthermore, in the service of biopower. As George Rosen argued in his magisterial work about the history of public health:

> [T]he state developed more and more into a centralized national government with a set of political and economic doctrines that in varying degree influenced the administration of public health.... [This] must be seen as part of a scheme of policy and administration whose supreme aim was to place social and economic life in the service of the state.... The welfare of society was regarded as identical with the welfare of the state.... *Raison d'état* was the fulcrum of social policy. For policy makers in all countries, whether in kingdoms or city-states, the important question was: What course must the government pursue to increase the national power and wealth? As the rulers and their advisers saw it, what was required was first of all a large population; second, that the population be provided for in a material sense; and thirdly, that it should be under the control of government so that it could be turned to whatever use public policy required.[172]

Rosen goes on to show how statistics and bookkeeping begin to rise in the context of an increasing attention to public health as part of nation-state building projects, effectively leading to their own development as academic disciplines together with medicine itself.[173] Now emerging as means of control, statistics and bookkeeping came to public consciousness as indispensable tools to

172 Rosen, *History*, 110, 114.

173 Rosen, *History*, 111 ff. For the state-centered context in which many academic disciplines grew, see Hallaq, *Restating Orientalism*, 179-228.

increase the power of the state. At the time, this was called "political arithmetic," and the wily William Petty (d. 1687) was one of the leaders spearheading such a campaign.[174] Among the goals he and others like him set for cultivation of the population was the standardization and centralization of medical practice and medical knowledge. Within less than a century thereafter, new, standardized academic units were created to train physicians, in comparison with the preceding centuries' practice (including in Islam) of leaving such training to individual hospitals and physicians. As Foucault noted, "after standardizing canons, France went on to 'normalize' its professors. The first *écoles normales* designed to offer all professors the same type of training and, consequently, the same level of competence, were created in about 1775.... In Prussia... a special office was assigned the task of collecting the data the doctors conveyed ... and finally, issuing directives based on these centralized data.... It was not the workers' bodies that interested this public health administration but the bodies of individuals insofar as they combined to constitute the state."[175]

Education and the health of the population were not the only sites for the construction of biopower or for making society.[176] There were of course other fields, if not any and all fields, where the state saw a potential for such projects of construction. In fact, the family was a prime target of the same forms of political knowledge. Here, the state was everywhere. It laid claim on the family as a productive political unit, namely, as a unit that produces the citizen, the national subject. Through law, the state's mighty weapon, the family was effectively made and remade. And like education and medicine, the family was redefined to serve the state,[177] a redefinition that was accomplished in the name of a program of legislative priorities pertaining to the interests of the child – interests that nearly always come prior to those of parents.[178] The

174 On William Petty in a larger context of epistemic analysis, see Hallaq, *Restating Orientalism*, 179-190.

175 Foucault, "Birth of Social Medicine," 140-41.

176 See ch. 1, n. 17, above.

177 Bourdieu, *Practical Reason*, 71: "It is indeed clear that in modern societies the main agent of the *construction of the official categories* through which both populations and minds are structured is the state, which, through a whole labor of codification, accompanied by economic and social effects (family allowances, for example), aims to favor a certain kind of family organization, to strengthen those who are in a position to conform to this form of organization, and to encourage, through all material and symbolic means, 'logical conformism' and 'moral conformism' as an agreement on a system of forms of apprehension and construction of the world, of which this form of organization, this category, is without doubt the cornerstone."

178 See Glendon, "Power and Authority," 15-24. On the marginalization of the father in the modern family, see Lasch, *Culture of Narcissism*, 172-76.

child becomes the site in which the authority of the state unfolds as a program of reform inhabited by ideological discourse, juridicality,[179] psychologists, counselors, and technicians. The patriarchy of the family is replaced by that of the magistrate, the school, the psychiatrist, and the social worker.[180] The concurrence of the juridical and the psychiatric professions marks the collaboration of two disciplines that are geared to produce the state subject, the national citizen.

Donzelot characterized the situation of the modern family as one of crisis, having changed from "being a pillar of society to being the place where society constantly threatens to come unglued."[181] By stark contrast, the highest end of the Sharīʿa and of the entire modus vivendi of Islamic polity was to maintain the integrity of social units, be they "extended families," clans, or otherwise. The modern state's inherent modalities of continuously engineering the family – and thus society – would have been Islam's nightmare.

But "ungluing" the family is not merely an unfortunate effect of the state's work, for this work is always cast, as Foucault noted, in the form of "taking care" of the population. The "well-being" and "interests" of society thus require the deliberate disentangling of a social unit whose loyalties resided outside of the state's possessions. Once legislated and reengineered, the family appears fully integrated into the disciplinary apparatus installed by the state, this being a form of nationalist loyalty. Just as the state has given rise to the realm of the political, it has also, through its discipline-based social engineering, created the realm of the social, where society unfolds in the image of the state. As Deleuze has argued, the crisis of the family and the rise of the social are the two-fold political effects of the confluence of discipline-apparatuses of the state.[182] The social has thus become a hybrid domain where the political shapes society, particularly its children, according to a certain model. And the model is that of the national citizen, the citizen of the nation-state, with all the attributes that this identity comprises and implies.[183] And to be a citizen is to be possessed, formed, and produced by the political technology – if not political factory – of the state.[184]

179 Glendon, "Power and Authority."
180 Donzelot, *Policing of Families*, 103-4.
181 Donzelot, *Policing of Families*, 217-19, 227.
182 See his forward to Donzelot, *Policing of Families*, xi.
183 From another perspective, that of Adorno's culture industry, see Johnson, "Social Philosophy," 121 and *passim*.
184 See Foucault, "Political Technology."

If looked at as forms of knowledge, these state fields, in their institutions of coercive surveillance, education, and health (prisons, schools, and hospitals), were neither distinct from each other nor natural or spontaneous in any sense. They each worked in a specialized domain, but they worked on "society" together, having come into existence in the wake of processes that involved rigorous administrative standardization and deep institutional bureaucratization. Hospitals, schools, standing armies, police, and prisons – among much else – constituted systemic manifestations of an elaborate and highly efficient way of doing and ordering things, which explains why the techniques used to implement them spread rapidly from one institution to the next, and from one European country to the other.[185] But we should not forget that biopower was also integral to the production of the docile body. Extensive regulations, shaped by calculative and statistical methods, were applied to these institutions for the purpose of disciplining the operations of the body. They reflected the two major concerns of submission to the regulating techniques and utility as a materially productive performance. The body, the site of the new citizen, thus becomes colonizable and as such amenable to analysis and capable of manipulation, all of which for the purpose of rendering it useful for carrying out the state's projects.[186]

Notable here is that the will sustaining the operation of the techniques of subjective production did not issue from the internal volition of the subject or the local community (a characteristic of the premodern world, notably in Islam), but rather from an external force, a political will that located itself outside it. As Foucault noted, the "human body was entering a machinery of power that explores it, breaks it down and rearranges it. A 'political anatomy,' which was also a 'mechanics of power', was being born; it defined how one may have a hold over others' bodies, not only so that they may do what one wishes, but so that they may operate as one wishes, with the techniques, the speed and the efficiency that one determines."[187]

This external agency is none other than "the great Leviathan, the modern state, whose outlines slowly appear out of the storm sea of politics like a whale coming to the surface."[188] But it is crucial for our constitutional concerns to understand that this is a new kind of politics that no longer recognizes any

185 Tallett, *War and Society*, 39-44.

186 This is partly the meaning of my argument in *Restating Orientalism*, 213 ff., namely, that Europe had already colonized itself before it colonized the rest of the world.

187 Foucault, *Discipline and Punish*, 138.

188 Rosen, *History*, 109.

principle other than those that it itself decides to adopt, when and where it likes. As Viroli has aptly argued, a downright revolution had to take place in the sixteenth century in order to give birth to this new species of politics. This famously goes by the name of "reason of state," *raison d'état*, a fundamentally ontological doctrine that asserts that "the preservation of the state – understood simply as dominion (legitimate or illegitimate) – can be pursued by any means, just or unjust. The emergence of this conception was a revolution in the sense of representing a profound change in the meaning and scope of the concept of politics as well as that of political man and political science."[189] The revolution had moved politics from the domain of political reason of equity and justice to pure will to power. Political reason of justice and equity had indeed allowed for violations of the letter of the just law, but it did not recognize as legitimate any violation of the aim of the law as an expression of the higher principle of common good. As Viroli shows, many influential voices from as early as the seventeenth century insisted that the new conception violated the general understanding of what politics consists of, and deemed the new concept tantamount to the "invention of tyrants ('*inventio tyrannorum*') that justifies the violation of civil, natural, divine, and international laws in the interests of whomsoever is in power."[190] It is with this understanding that Agamben saw in this unprincipled type of power a machinery that is always in the business of *the perpetual definition and redefinition of the human*. The absence of any telos other than the sheer will to power marks the fundamental structure not only of the unprecedented modern state but also its biopower.

The methodological, theoretical, and historical ramifications of this recognition are grave, for we must qualitatively segregate the history of the modern from that which preceded it. We can no longer assume even the basic modes of cognition to be common to the two. Here, there are two different thinking animals, two highly distinguishable rational creatures who see the world with two diametrically opposed and distinct rational faculties. Conceived as such, biopower's sovereignty never existed in Islam, as it, by definition, could never exist as whole in any "religion" or culture that subordinates itself to, and strives to live by, higher moral principles. The conscription of Man in the laboratory of the modern state, its biopower, and the enveloping Schmittian political are perhaps the most profound transformations that occurred in the conception of the human since its appearance on Earth.

---

189 Viroli, "Revolution," 473; Foucault, "Political Technology," 147-53.
190 Viroli, "Revolution," 474.

By massive contrast, Islam in general and the Sharīʿa and Ṣūfism in particular worked hard to create the human in its best ethical form, to improve the lot of the Muslim Community, the *Umma*, in whatever form this Community manifested itself (whether North African, Anatolian, Keralan, Javanese, or otherwise). After all, Muslims universally recognized the truth of the maxim that the Sharīʿa was sent to them with the aim of improving their lot on Earth (*al-Sharīʿa ursilat li-maṣāliḥ al-ʿibād*).[191] The trajectory of improvement was driven by principles of justice, these latter marking themselves as different from biopower in an important way; namely, that the Sharīʿa was bound and bounded by first-order principles of thought and action, and that these principles were strongly marked by their ethical and moral thrust. Variety, pluralism, and difference no doubt colored Muslim life across the social, economic, and political spectra, but commitment to these higher principles could fix a teleology that never loses sight of the human as the premium value. Biopower, in sharp contrast, never claims ethics as its basis of action, precisely because it has in the first place negated the very possibility of sticking to any principle higher than itself. Its justifications for thought and action appeal to national and political considerations whose telos shifts as its calculus of power fluctuates from one state to another. This is why the human inhabiting the arena of biopower is perpetually and arbitrarily defined and redefined.

191 One of the most comprehensive and exhaustive philosophical-legal treatments of what one might call *raison du la vie* in Islam (in sharp contrast to *raison d'état*), is to be found in Shāṭibī's four-volume *Muwāfaqāt*. See also Hallaq, *History of Islamic Legal Theories*, 162-206, esp. at 168.

Conclusion: Past, Present, Future

I

In the opening chapters of this book, we saw how some of the most important texts in the Islamic tradition speak to the fundamental components of the political system. Having "read" these texts and expounded their relevant concepts through chapter 11, it was not entirely clear how the meaning of "politics" has fundamentally changed from the premodern to the modern. But the previous chapter, along with chapters 1 and 2, have drawn a sharp line of difference between the logic and ontology of *raison d'état* and its integral mechanics of biopower, on the one hand, and those of the premodern conceptions of politics, on the other. The "separation between fact and value" reemerges once again[1] as being as fundamental to politics as it was to everything else, and perhaps more so in the domains of the political and biopower. The separation has become ideologically so pervasive in modern thinking that the vast majority of modern scholars continue to apply their presuppositions – heavily overlaid by biases of the logic of *raison d'état* – to the Islamic conception of politics and (anachronistically) so-called "state" in Islam.[2]

1 On this crucial separation, and as relevant to different contexts, see Hallaq, *Impossible State*, 75-89; Hallaq, *Restating Orientalism*, 91-98, 148-50, 206-207, and passim.

2 This is where such writings as those of Marina Rustow and Jo van Steenbergen exaggerate the similarities between the premodern forms of governance and the modern state, the latter writer in fact betraying especially complex forms of anachronism. These and similar writings reveal a deep misunderstanding of the nature of the modern state, its techniques of power and biopower (not to mention the modern bureaucratic systems) that the modern state possesses and that the Muslim sultanates did not know. See Rustow, *Lost Archive*, 470, n. 47 and passim; and van Steenbergen, "Appearances of *Dawla*." Such substantive claims in Rustow's and van Steenbergen's writings dwarf the more innocent and generally vague conceptual conflation of the descriptor *dawla* with state, as appears,

The entrenchment of what I call the Greco-Islamic conception of politics is so evident that the entire range of political, juristic, and quasi-political literatures were saturated by it across Muslim lands and centuries. I call this Greco-Islamic (or, as comfortably, Sassano-Islamic) without meaning to say that Muslims owed their political conceptions to Greece (or to the Sassanids). In fact, this book deliberately omits a discussion of the manifestations of Greek political thought in Islam (Fārābī et al.),[3] deeming them, despite their general importance, irrelevant for the structural history I want to proffer.[4] The "Greco-Islamic" sense of politics I employ here is intended to convey the idea that up to the eighteenth century, the ethical form of politics was a West Asian phenomenon, where Greco-Roman, Sassanid, and Muslim cultures constituted variants of a larger cultural constellation that unified more than separated them.[5]

In our account, the first theoretician accorded a status of epistemic privilege was Māwardī. The reason for this act of privileging is certainly not just because he was the distinguished jurist who wrote *AS*, but rather because he was the first to compile and synthesize the political and constitutional components that were spread out through the literature. His project of compiling acquired lasting authoritativeness because it expressed the mainstream conception of the political and the constitutional. Which is to say that his work represented a constitutional synthesis of what Sunni Islam had arrived at in the world of political management during the preceding decades. The force of his synthesis was enhanced and in fact propped by his magisterial *ADD*, which articulated a theory of political society. Māwardī's *AS* was also conceived by later political writers and executive administrators as a founding text, one that became *the textbook* of political administration and *dīwān*ic practices for centuries to come. It was effectively the blueprint of good governance, but one that also

---

for instance, in Black's characterization of the early and middle Ottoman dynasty. See his *History of Islamic Political Thought*, 199 and passim.

3 For a survey of these philosophies of rule, see Black, *History of Islamic Political Thought*, 57-65.

4 See also the reservations that Ibn Khaldūn makes in his *Muqaddima*, 238.

5 My argument here is grounded in a conception of history that refuses to see Greece as historically integral to Europe and as foreign to Islam or West Asia. The Greco-Sassanid world was an essential part of the cultural terrain which Islam inherited and which it molded in the most innovative ways to produce its own ways of seeing and being in the world. The Greco-Roman cultural constellation was appropriated by Europe after the sixteenth century, as evidenced by the considerable scholarship and discourse generated by the Black Athena controversy, among others. See Bernal, *Black Athena*; Moore, *Black Athena Writes Back*; and sources cited in Hallaq, "Use and Abuse of Evidence," 81-82, nn. 16-17. On the test of "cultural genealogy" and determination of origins, see Hallaq, *Origins*, 25-28.

implicated a certain division and configuration of power in the structures of that form of governance.

The act of compiling and synthesizing was undoubtedly of monumental importance, no less crucial and significant for us than "original" authorship. An "original" author or work conveys to us a unique voice that may not be representative. Māwardī's *oeuvre* is significant because what he offered was a general representation – positive and normative at once – of what we might call the "mainstream" ways of thinking and acting in the world of governance. In reading Māwardī the way we did, we can confidently claim that we uncovered through his treatises, especially *ADD*, an outline of the Muslim habitus, in its sociological and political modus vivendi. His works also constitute a representation of the political discursive tradition that was Islam.

An integral part of this representation is the epistemoral genealogy of the Islamic political conception. The Muslim conception of *ʿaql* ("reason") is one that is intrinsically tied up with the comprehension of divine command, a comprehension that contains all the necessary ingredients that enable the bearer of this *ʿaql* to distinguish between what is beneficial and what is not, and ultimately between good and evil. Knowledge (*ʿilm*) is thus the result (*natīja*) of this *ʿaql*, which is to say that knowledge is defined and corralled by the same ethical considerations which *ʿaql*, when complete and mature, will take into full account.

It is at this juncture that Māwardī supplements his theory of ethical reason with an account of social association. The human was created as an imperfect being, needy, and dependent on multiple sources and resources. He needs sustenance – which can never be taken for granted – as much as he needs the support and help of his own kind. This need for cooperation is thus the lynchpin of association, and this association by its nature demands the competence to organize the social body and control its modalities of operation. In their cooperation, people will misinterpret transactions and will behave in ways that others may not find acceptable, this giving rise to disputes. The body politic initially arises in this site, the core assumption about it being that a ruler is needed to adjudicate these disputes.

At this point, the political function of resolving disputes ties back to ethical knowledge since the question that instantaneously emerges is the manner in which this adjudication takes place, what constitutes its regulating principles, governing laws and rules. The answer was easy to find, because the sources that would ultimately result in this distinctly legal knowledge were taken for granted. The Sharīʿa being the result, it would not then be too difficult to posit that living by this knowledge is living by the Sharīʿa, across all human acts conceivable, and living by the Sharīʿa is therefore to live in, and be constituted by, a polity. Once this polity comes into existence, it would by the nature of things be subject to the ambitions of other polities, a fact that generates the other major duty of the polity's ruler: the defense of the realm against external attacks. Therefore, the laws and principles that govern the Islamic polity, from beginning to end, originate in ethical reason and are interpreted and applied according to this reason. This is anything but *raison d'état*.

This is not all, however. The genealogy that begins with *ʿaql*-rationality and travels to ethics and politics through *ʿilm*-knowledge carries with it two other consequences. First, that politics is not grounded in ethics only genealogically, having a free reign once it departs from its epistemic source. In Islam past and even present, there has been no movement of any kind which allowed the human mediation of God's power, as Europe's deistic movement had done, where God's role was deemed limited to a creator who leaves the world by design for human beings to run and who has no knowledge of the particulars of Man's lived experiences. The origination of knowledge in ethical reason and the grounding of the particulars of the lived life in this knowledge meant that politics, constitutional divisions, and all that which has to do with running the affairs of government are in turn grounded in that knowledge. This was the habitus, with its doxastic praxis, a fact which explains why our authors, from beginning to end, took it for granted that their proffered counsel to kings and sultans, whether political or ethical-cum-legal, was one of the most natural things to do. And counsel was not just *words* of advice but effectively a representational act.

Second, and of even more crucial consequence, is the constitutional effect of this ethical grounding. In the Islamic constitutional tradition, the Paradox of Sovereignty is *ab initio* impossible, and this for two conspicuous reasons: If the Paradox of Sovereignty is caused by the fact that the modern state is both inside and outside the juridical order at the same time ("I, the sovereign, who am outside the law, declare that there is nothing outside the law"),[6] that is, that the state makes the law yet it stands as subject to it, then none of these conditions obtained in the Islamic political traditions prior to the nineteenth century. The Islamic system of governance, in the totality of its political power, was not the author of the Law of the Land. This, on its own, is a crucial and

6 See ch. 12, n. 89, above.

monumental fact. Yet, there was a second consideration that bolstered this legal autonomy. Both the foundations of the law and its substantive products were ethically anchored and furthermore enshrined in a system of knowledge whose hermeneutics and logic were tightly woven from and around an ethical thread. Politics was law, admittedly of the most pragmatic kind, but even this law remained an expression of a profoundly ethical system that is ruled by the laws of habitus.

As important is the consideration of the historical background and origins of the Islamic political and legal experience. In Europe, as we have already seen, the rise of the state along with its various divisions, departments, and organs was in good measure the direct result of the French Revolution and Enlightenment movements which themselves were reactions to the brutish life that absolutism and Church abuses had caused. The modern state arose from this environment, grounding itself in political sovereignty and the logic of *raison d'état*.[7] Significantly, it was precisely against the religious and monarchic background of oppression that the modern state developed as a substitute, but one that is secular and materialist. Neither religion nor ethics were allowed to partake in the causality giving rise to the state – hence the rise of secularism; if anything, it was precisely against these that the state, as a constitutional order, worked and finally reared its head to take them over. But no matter what this takeover involved, it was one that grounded itself in the operative logic of *raison d'état*.

By sharp contrast, the rise of Islamic governance was entirely the product of what law meant in Islam from the dawn of the Qur'ānic moment. As we have seen in chapters 1, 2, and 4, the constitution of knowledge as an ethical endeavor was clearly marked as a divine act. And it was this knowledge that determined the political practices of the early Muslims, resulting rather quickly in the determination that whatever form of rule Muslims chose to adopt, it would always be anchored and thoroughly determined by the ethics of the *dīn*, which, in the practice of life, is also known as the Sharīʿa, including its ethical benchmarks.[8]

This historical divergence also explains another difference in the nature of the separation of powers in the two systems. It is quite a distinctive political vision to deem justice and fairness impossible without the executive being separated from the legislative and these two from the judicial. In this narrative,

7 Foucault, "What is Critique?"; Foucault, "Political Technologies."
8 See Introduction, n. 71.

the need for this separation takes on an *a priori* conception, if not an axiomatic status; it assumes an adversarial system, populated by selfish and intrinsically unfair human beings who are constantly aggressing one another. The Hobbesian presumption of an evil human nature rules the day, giving rise to the now doxastic conception that the rationale for the separation of powers is to ensure that greed combats greed and ambition confronts ambition[9] – these being the preconditions for such a system to hold. But there is nothing natural about such an assumption or perception of reality.[10] One could wager that had Europe not made this constitutional conception the standard norm in the world through its aggressive colonialist ventures and hegemonic discourses, this model of separation would have largely been seen as an anomaly or at least a curious way of seeing reality.

Because the Islamic constitutional system is grounded in ethics, deriving its configuration from the constellation of caliphal functions, the separation in no way reflects a traumatized fear of tyranny. The main consideration for

9 James Madison in the *The Federalist*, No. 51 (p. 268).

10 For, among other things, this runs counter to the Islamic conception of human nature, which is viewed as fundamentally ethical *by nature*. The Islamic conception of nature cannot be understood without or outside the central concept of *fiṭra*, which means several interrelated things, depending on the context. At a basic level, it is an inborn original disposition through which humans perceive things in the world. Intelligence and stupidity, and anything in between, are attributes determined by *fiṭra*, which is to say that *fiṭra* is relative, with some people having a sharper "disposition" than others. For Fārābī as well as for Ghazālī, as Frank Griffel argues, it also meant a natural ability or talent. For Ibn Sīnā, *fiṭra* is a judgment or proposition that all human beings possess in common and are able to form irrespective of their education or upbringing. Thus, *fiṭra* is "distinct from the rational capacity to derive theoretical knowledge from earlier [judgments/propositions] by the use of arguments." It is thus "a stock of judgments that are considered primary [that is, innate to the human; WH].... Therefore, the true judgments of the *fiṭra* enable the individual to develop accurate knowledge about the world. For al-Ghazālī as well as Ibn Sīnā such knowledge remains descriptive [but] once the human reaches into the field of moral judgments he or she has left the ground of truth that the judgments of the *fiṭra* help to build. This is where Islam comes in, because, according to Ghazālī, true moral judgments can only come from revelation." Yet, Ghazālī seems to have believed that "judgments of the *fiṭra* contain knowledge of God's existence." See Griffel, "Al-Ghazālī's Use of 'Original Human Disposition'," 28, 30. See also Hallaq, "Ibn Taymiyya on the Existence of God." *Fiṭra* thus denoted an ethical feeling, a moral sentiment with which humans are born. It is not a cultivable trait, nourished by upbringing or education, but a naturally ingrained instinct that has the competence to evaluate theoretical and practical affairs of the world in moral terms. This is consistent, as we saw in chapter 1, with the Islamic view of *ʿilm* ("knowledge"), which is intrinsically ethical because the *ʿaql* (reason) is likewise by definition that which restrains the passions while arriving at the moral truth of things. The comprehension and knowledge of things are precisely those acts that express this arrival at the moral truth of phenomena.

the rule of law in Islam was that no man shall rule another, for God is the only ruler. *With him and him alone lies sovereignty.* It was a foundational tenet and a theological consideration that sought justice and relief from no lesser than God. The quest for justice was one pertaining to all life, not limiting itself to the forms of political rule. It was as much economic and social as it was spiritual, emotive, and what we call today "environmental." There was no *systemic problem* of politics to be solved. It was in fact the possibility of the absence of politics that was a source of anxiety, when anarchy and civil war could break out. The Islamic forms of rule, even in their sectarian versions, originated in a wider cultural, legal, and socio-political context, one that was not specifically dominated by considerations of tyranny – which explains why and how the separation of powers as caliphal functions worked.

Just as much as the running and management of human life was and remains forever the business of God, so was the mandate and function of Muhammad's Prophethood. And by delegation and proxy were likewise the tasks assigned to the caliphal office. In other words, God's rule in all of its aspects was to be implemented by the Prophet, and by proxy, by the caliph whose name precisely captures his encompassing mandate. There is no aspect of human life that escapes the concerns and jurisdictions of the caliph because the caliphate itself was the carbon-copy register of all that God wanted to achieve on Earth through the Messenger. It turned out that this was not just theory but a constitutional practice that began in the first century of the Hijra, reaching its full discursive maturity some three centuries later and continuing to operate by the same general principles – notwithstanding the changes and mutations[11] – until the total structural destruction of these institutions in the nineteenth century.

But we must be careful to distinguish caliphal and, later, sultanic functions. To say that the caliph was the Prophet's legatee and proxy is not to arrogate to him powers of legislation, for even the Prophet himself was no more than a messenger and spokesman of God's decree, a fallible human. The comprehensive mandate of the caliphate – that is, to govern the *Umma* and administer its life and procure its security – stems from a suppositional logic where "enforcing" the law presupposes that there is a prior law, historically and logically, to enforce. This was the *ʿilm* of the law, resulting in the *fiqh* and its commanding system of the Shariʿa. Because "legislation" in Islam was an epistemoral conception and practice, it could not have been instituted within a corporate

11 See, e.g., ch. 10.

body, a synod, an assembly, or a collective body of any kind. This was because the basis of the discovery of God's ethical thinking was from the beginning a matter of productive piety, belief being the foundation of knowledge. This is the proper meaning of ethical reason in the Islamic tradition.

The locus of productive piety was the thinking, erudite individual whose relationship to the sacred texts is the product of his conscience. Precisely because knowledge grounded itself entirely in ethics, the individual was the only possible site of ethico-legal responsibility, accountability, and liability. Law and all its associated rules of life (=the Sharīʿa) were thus to constitute the project of individual pious persons who made the study of "what-Muslims-must-do-in-every-detail-of-life" the center of their inquiry. In other words, because of its ethical substrate and its individualistic ethical accountability that was to shoulder juristic activity, no government body or collective assembly could take on this burden. Collective decision on the norm governing any given legal question/case was inconceivable, partly due to the pietist-individualistic nature of knowledge that the Qur'ān prescribed and partly because in corporate functioning ethical accountability tends to be diluted (which explains why the Sharīʿa did not develop juristic personality and the notion of corporation).[12] And most certainly, no single individual, jurist or not, could authoritatively pronounce what the law applicable to one and all is. For even within the domain of law, sovereignty of a singular source of authority never existed. This, as we have seen, was a Qur'ānic doctrine.[13]

The individuation of "legal" and "legislative" duty constituted doxastic knowledge, to be taken for granted, which is why the caliphs and sultans from the first year after the Prophet's death and until late Ottoman times never claimed a legislative prerogative and always recognized the individual jurist, *with his* madhhab, as the ultimate authority on the law. The old dictum that the Sharīʿa is a jurists' law holds a timeless truth. But what is most significant for our concern is that this truth has enormous constitutional effects.

We should also remember that there is no "legal"/Sharʿī knowledge that could originate in a caliphal office or, for that matter, any human being, since the source of this knowledge is always God, the Omniscient. Human beings can only guess through their disciplined, agreed-upon hermeneutical methods of *ijtihād* what the "law" might be. And even when the caliph, the sultan, or any government official attempted to partake in this endeavor – which at

12 On this theme, see Hallaq, *Restating Orientalism*, 79 ff.
13 See ch. 4.

times they did – theirs was simply yet another *individual* "attempt" (=*ijtihād*), standing along a series of juristic others, and effectively evaluated by them. No caliph could claim special authority in backing up his "opinion" (and it could never be more than a legal opinion) outside of the general rules of hermeneutics. If some of ʿUmar I's opinions were deemed particularly authoritative, *it was not because he was a caliph* but rather because his opinion was seen to be backed by either a strong line of reasoning or due to his (epistemic) proximity to the Prophet as a Companion, or both. The significance of the qualifier "Rāshidūn" ("Rightly-Guided") in the title of the first four caliphs is precisely this, epistemic.

The individuated conception of "legislative" activity – that is, attempting to find out or "guess," through rigorous hermeneutics, what God's "law" on a particular issue *might be* – was therefore a direct line of authorization from God to the Prophet and from the Prophet to the pious men of learning, *including the caliphs*. That the caliphs were wholly responsible for guarding and enforcing the Sharīʿa does not mean – and it bears repetition – that they were to take on the charge of determining it substantively on their own. No caliph could or did pretend to such an ambition. As we have seen in the writings of many of our authors, the caliphate *assumes and presupposes* the Sharīʿa as the expression of the "legal" will of God, which is to say that it comes as the logical and ontological consequence of the divine legislative will. It is therefore this stark fact that marks the *radical* separation of the two most important "powers" in Islam, namely, the legislative and the executive; the Sharīʿa and its culture, on the one hand, and the *dawla*, on the other.[14]

We must insist therefore that the declaration "The ulama are the Heirs of the Prophets" is not a mere rhetorical utterance but one that carries with it thick constitutional bearings. The corridor of legislative authority is therefore historically, genealogically, epistemically, and ontologically separate from the corridor through which God delegated his powers for the enforcement of his Sharʿ on Earth.[15] The caliphs sat *alongside* the ulama in receiving, as deputies, the functions of the prophethood. To say that they were the heirs of the prophets amounts to the claim that their legislative authority did not flow through the caliph. Yet, though they were *ab initio* separate, both ontologically and epistemologically, they were also partners in carrying out the Message.

---

14 On my meaning of radical, see main text in ch. 7, at n. 58.

15 Although, as we have seen earlier, there was a debate in early Islam about whether the *qadī*s may be regarded as the deputies of God rather than of the Prophet. See Ibn Māza, *Sharḥ Adab al-Qāḍī*, I, 163. See also ch. 5, n. 3.

The partnership manifested itself in several domains but none more obvious or important than in the judicial field (*qaḍā'*), a partnership that gave rise to what we nowadays call "judicial power." It was precisely within the larger definition of this judicial province that constitutional questions and problems needed to be answered and solved; for there was neither overlap nor ambiguity in the boundaries that separated the executive from the legislative. But it was the judiciary that brought the two on the same estate. The personnel populating the judiciary were exclusively ulama, legists, and prominent jurists whose training and disciplinary culture were located squarely within the Sharīʿa,[16] which is also to say that their ultimate loyalties were first to the Sharīʿa and only second to the sultan and the executive-*dawla* culture.

Yet, as we have seen, in the domain of executive administration there were other quasi-judicial functions, such as the *maẓālim*, that represented tribunals often run by Sharʿī *qāḍī*s themselves. The constitutional grind in Islam lay precisely here, within the boundaries that lay between the *qāḍī*s' Sharʿī province and the *dawla*tic administration of *siyāsa* tribunals. We need no longer emphasize that *siyāsa* is not necessarily *siyāsa sharʿiyya*, for the former preceded the latter by some three centuries (and had already thrived for long under Sassanid rule). But the succession, the diachronic development from *siyāsa* to *siyāsa sharʿiyya*, tells the most complex constitutional story in Islam, because the greatest bulk of the constitutional grind happened precisely here, in the transformation of the former to the latter. There were of course ebbs and flows, but the increasing domestication of executive extra-judicial modalities at the hands of the Sharīʿa came to showcase itself in the long history of the Ottomans and their immediate predecessor, the Circassian Mamlūk *dawla*.

As intimated, historically speaking, when the Sharīʿa was being formed during the first three or four centuries of Islam, and long before then, *siyāsa* had already stood as a recognized and well-established practice in Sassanid Iran and probably Byzantium. In this early phase, *siyāsa* was neither systematic nor well-defined, and was noticeably unconstrained by Sharʿī-mindedness.[17] When the Sharīʿa came to full maturity during the fourth/tenth and early fifth/eleventh centuries, *siyāsa* was brought along the side of Sharīʿa to share and cooperate in the business of executive governance; which is to say that bringing the two together was a mutual act of concession: The *siyāsa* retained

16 As I have shown in *Authority, Continuity and Change*, it was the case that the same jurist would often function as both *qāḍī* (judiciary) and *muftī* (legislative) at the same time, simultaneously wearing two "hats," so to speak.

17 Yücesoy, *Disenchanting the Caliphate.*

its effective powers as the coercive hand of the sultan but the Sharīʿa came to envelop it, curb it – or surround it from the outside, so to speak – as a matter of constitutional organization. The Sharīʿa's constitutional sway could not reduce the effective powers of the *maẓālim* as an extra-judicial organ, but it brought it under a regime of law that defined its functions and jurisdictions. The *maẓālim*, on the other hand, retained these effective powers but lost its freedom of action outside of the limits set by the Sharīʿa. Māwardī's *al-Aḥkām al-Sulṭāniyya* is the most eloquent depiction of this symbiotic relationship.

Some three centuries after Māwardī wrote, and due to complex and multi-pronged developments under the Mamūk sultanate, the *maẓālim* were being gradually absorbed within the Sharʿī judicial domain. The *qāḍī* now begins to adjudicate matters of *siyāsa* as much as the executive official does. By the end of the Mamlūk sultanate, this process was brought to fruition, and when the Ottomans expanded their domains in the tenth/sixteenth century, they incorporated the *maẓālim* within the office of the *qāḍī*,[18] the most important judicial and administrative unit in the empire prior to the thirteenth/nineteenth century. *This act of incorporation was not an executive Ottoman initiative as much as it was a Sharʿī process of absorption that had already begun in the seventh/thirteenth century.* Indeed, during the last decades of their rule, the Mamlūks attempted to restrict the jurisdiction of *siyāsa* governance, thereby preparing the grounds to streamline the justice system *within* the boundaries of the Sharīʿa.[19] The Ottomans completed this doctrinal and institutional transformation which was accomplished over the haul of two or three centuries by jurists of all four schools. It was their *madhhab*ic structure and its powerful constitutional effect that allowed the Sharīʿa to envelop and finally contain the *maẓālim* tribunals. The appointment of Shaykh al-Islām in Istanbul was the hallmark of this cardinal development. One of the top two or three most influential figures in the empire was no other than the spokesman of the Sharīʿa.

II

Throughout this book, we have encountered, directly or by implication, the fundamental differentiation between a cosmic-moral order of politics and the

18 Fuess, "*Ẓulm* by *Maẓālim*?" 141; Jennings, "Kadi, Court, and Legal Procedure," 148 f.
19 See Rapoport, "Royal Justice," 98-99.

secular conception of *raison d'état*. It is crystal clear by now that the order of politics – represented in the Islamic experience under study – stood below the law, and had no powers of repeal or amendment, precisely because its political habitus took it for granted that law is an integral part of *dīn* ("religion"), which in turn is not only inspired by divine moral-cum-legal powers but was in charge of making legible the chain of being as a matter of practice, not just one of theology and philosophical ontology. Put differently, the Islamic model of polity was bounded by a cosmic hierarchy that placed the polity not only within a larger, ontologically meaningful, and overpowering context; it also, *ipso facto*, determined the location of the very act of envelopment within a universal "legal" order that is at once governed by a supreme divine law, above and beyond any earthly power.

Within the logic of *raison d'état*, by contrast, the political order is itself seen as the source of the law, which the order itself legislates. This is not a mere paradox or a logical inexplicability that we observe before going on to live our lives as if all is well. The ramifications of this phenomenon have defined the inextricable layers of the modern human experience, with effects that reverberate throughout the many fields of human endeavor lying outside, but ultimately connected with, the political field. From the destruction of the environment down to the collapse of communal ties and the inner psyche of the individual, from severe inequalities to genocides and much else – all this has been intimately connected with, if not the direct result of the various practices of this unhinged type of polity – by which I mean that this polity acutely suffers from the Problem of Disanchorage.[20]

Yet, it was precisely this model of polity that came to colonize the Muslim world, starting, without much success, in the seventeenth century but finally succeeding in the nineteenth. This success was not the result of a triumph of rational argument or cultural superiority. Rather, it was the effect of much hard work by this polity to organize life around power and violence, marshalling its "population" and shaping it in accordance with the new values of the machinery of biopower. This explains why it is that in human history there existed no premodern polity (= "state") that could accumulate so much generally destructive power as the modern state can, with its highly disciplined and bellicose armies, military bases, nuclear arsenal, devastating chemical weapons, and much else of this ruinous sort. The "population" is therefore the pool of investment that produces the necessary economy,

20 On the Problem of Disanchorage, see ch. 12, sec. III.

wealth, science, organization, discipline, and whatever is needed in order to build the state. This is why biopower's logic revolves around the perpetual production and reproduction of the human, because the reproduced human subject becomes the means through which the modern state realizes itself, notwithstanding the fact that it does so as a paradoxical entity and without a teleology.

It is this state then that came to colonize the Muslim world in the nineteenth century, perforce upending Muslim social and political existence. In other writings,[21] I have given detailed accounts of the institutional and epistemological devastation that Europe wrought on nineteenth-century Islam. The essential outline of this history is the following: (1) Through military effect and financial loans and debts, Europe forced Muslim rulers to begin dismantling the major *waqf* foundations, perhaps the most important institutional prop for the Sharīʿa as a social and educational phenomenon; (2) Wholesale displacement and replacement of legal ordinances meant that by 1917 even the law of personal status was reproduced in the image of the rising modern state. Criminal law, land law, civil law, procedural law, and much else had been replaced by European codes between the 1850s and 1870s. By about the 1880s, the very modes of writing as expressions of Sharʿī reasoning and articulations of the world (and as deep epistemological markers) effectively ceased to exist, this likewise constituting another realm of displacement and replacement; and (3) During roughly the same period, new schools, institutes, colleges, and universities, constructed on the European model, came to replace the Islamic educational system, essentially decapitating the Sharīʿa as a sociology of knowledge and thus increasingly marginalizing the ulama as the leaders and protectors of the Community. By the 1930s at the latest, the Sharīʿa and the ulama class were reduced to a marginality, having already been subordinated to the modern state bureaucracy and legal imperatives.

The decimation of the Sharīʿa as a tradition, habitus, and culture was necessitated by many considerations and goals, not least of which was to break the protectionist and relatively egalitarian form of economics and property rights that the Sharīʿa insisted on. Among the most important goals of Europe's project of colonization was the exploitation of the markets and through them the natural resources of Muslim lands. Prying these markets open to European investment and exploitation would not have been possible

21 Hallaq, *Sharīʿa*, 357-550; Hallaq, *Restating Orientalism*, 65-137.

without first destroying the Sharīʿa (including the vast *waqf*-land holdings), which provided age-old protections against abusive practices that European capitalism deemed essential for its own operations and growth (think of hoarding, for example). Furthermore, and directly pertinent to our concerns, the new logic of the European state and its penchant for political domination could not tolerate – much less coexist with – the Sharīʿa because this latter had been an autonomous entity that refused, throughout the twelve preceding centuries, to allow any executive to take over the legislative domain, even insisting that the judiciary must be run in accordance with its own imperatives. There was therefore an unresolvable contradiction between these two logics: The Sharīa could not exist as culture and habitus (i.e., as what it had in reality been for twelve hundred years) without defining the boundaries and limits of political power and the executive, whereas the modern state's "legislative power" has been structurally unable to hem the executive in (this in fact being historically the source of constitutional problems in the liberal order in the first place).

Put in yet other words, the modern state and the Sharīʿa are conceptually and institutionally entirely incompatible because both belong to the same genus in that they equally are law-givers, however much they markedly differ from each other as specific technologies of governance and in terms of their teleology.[22] Both are designed to organize their respective "populations" (whether it is "society" or Community) and to resolve disputes that threaten their orders. In sum, therefore, their coexistence as fully operational entities is inconceivable. This is why the most important mission of the European colonialists, aided by their Orientalist platoons, was to destroy the Sharīʿa, and destroy it they did.[23] And with this mission accomplished, a strengthened but unrestrained executive became itself the state. That this new state retains the name of *dawla* is not without irony. That it was foisted on Muslims by European political machinery and its logic of domination is not at all surprising.

The massive power of the European colonialist state, with its military organization, materialist wealth, and technologies of violence – among several

22 For a list of the structural differences between the modern state and Sharīʿa governance, see Hallaq, *Sharīʿa*, 361-66.

23 This consideration alone renders Edward Said's work, *Orientalism*, paradoxical in the extreme since it was entirely silent on the law as the major component of both colonialist ambitions and Orientalist "scholarship." For more on this, see Hallaq, *Restating Orientalism*, 18, 112-37, and passim.

other components – has not only ensured the destruction of the Sharīʿa and Muslim traditional institutions (by which I mean the institutions that were the conduits of Muslim habitus and discursive tradition) but also succeeded in installing itself, or its replica, in Muslim lands. The Muslim world would accordingly inherit from Europe a political machine and techniques of rule that not only sat on top of the ruins of *tradition and habitus*, but also a machine that transported to the Muslim world all the constitutional problems inherent in the concept of the separation of powers (discussed in the previous chapter). More than that, Muslims – elite and laypersons alike – were the recipient of a political machine that they understood no more than did the Europeans themselves, the exporters of the project. Arguably, Western academia and political science still struggle with understanding the state,[24] and Muslims seem to lag far behind in this sphere.[25]

It is abundantly clear that the exportation of the European state to the Muslim world effected an acute ecological imbalance in the Muslim political order. This is because there were two processes that occurred at once: the first was the destruction of Sharīʿa's institutions (as summarized above), and second, a simultaneous replacement of the Sharīʿa by the various departments of the modern state.

We must remember that the European state colonizing the Muslim world began to replicate itself in those lands as it stood during – or as it was developed by – the second half of the nineteenth century, which means that the effects of this replication were even more devastating to the Muslim colonies, especially in light of their Sharʿī political history. There were at least three considerations involved here: First, the modern state's executive power exported to the Muslim world was manifold stronger than the sultanic executive in Islam, a new experience that on its own constituted a major political problem that created further imbalance in the ecology of governance.

Second, the colonial powers, by the nature of things, exported a weak notion of the legislative, and a weaker institution to implement it. We should recall that parliaments and representative popular assemblies had barely appeared in Europe itself, with many countries (including Germany, Denmark, Italy, and Sweden) acquiring parliamentary institutions as late as the middle

24 See, e.g., Abrams, "Notes on the Difficulty of Studying the State;" Pierre Bourdieu, "Rethinking the State." I believe that the situation has not changed since Abrams and Bourdieu wrote these articles.

25 As I have attempted to argue in *The Impossible State*.

of the nineteenth century, effectively when colonization had attained an advanced level.

And, third, even if we assume that parliamentary systems were already entrenched in Europe, a colonial power was not about to install a system of genuine popular representation in a colony, whose very *raison d'être* is precisely to be exploited. Europe, and later the United States, did their best to militate against both legislative and judicial independence, because these were obviously both legal and political means of ascertaining national will or else advocating the interests of the indigenous populations. The history of colonialism in Asia and Africa, including nearly all lands of Islam, is also the history of the indigenous struggle to build representative bodies that acted for the best interests of the people, not the colonial governments at home or in the Western Metropolis. The suppression of popular will, as is well known, remains the hallmark of American hegemony in Muslim countries, where democratically elected politicians and parties continue to be crushed in order to maintain the grip the US has over these countries' resources.

All this is to say that the new political model imposed on Muslim lands by colonialism has strengthened the executive disproportionately and weakened the legislative inordinately, and this for either structural reasons (the inherently problematic constitutional history of Europe) or for reasons of political expediency (exploitative colonialist policy), or, more often, both. The result has been a virtually hollow legislative power in the body of modern Muslim polities. No wonder then that constitutional scholars are in general agreement that constitutions in the Muslim world have served many functions, almost none having to do with so-called democratic reform and much to do with augmentation of public executive power and even with undermining political oppositions that challenge the dominance of the ruling elites, nearly always backed by Western powers. And even when partially independent courts have been created in some Muslim states, it has been for the purpose of creating rule by law rather than rule *of* law.[26]

If this dismal state of affairs traces its causes to the destruction of indigenous Sharʿī culture, habitus, traditions, institutions, and forms of knowledge, and if their colonialist replacements were a dominating executive and an atrophied legislative, then we can begin from here to reconceptualize possible solutions. As I argued more than a decade ago, the modern state is not an exclusively

26 Moustafa, *Struggle for Constitutional Power*; Lust-Okar, *Structuring Conflict in the Arab World.*

Muslim problem. In fact, if anything, it is a problem that arose in Europe and for which Europe and the West must find a solution. But understanding Islamic constitutional history properly can shed light on the ways in which we can begin to think about and articulate solutions. This book has been an extended exercise in critical philology, where lived experiences and inhabited worlds of the past can teach us much about the quality of problems we are facing today.

Bibliography

In classifying entries, no account is taken of the letter *ʿayn*, the *hamza*, and the English definite article.

SOURCES IN ARABIC

ʿAbbās, Makram. *Al-Islām wal-Siyāsa fil-ʿAṣr al-Wasīṭ* (Beirut: Markaz Nuhūḍ lil-Dirāsāt wal-Nashr, 2020).

ʿAbd al-Jabbār, Abū al-Ḥasan al-Qāḍī. *Al-Mughnī fī Abwāb al-Tawḥīd wal-ʿAdl*, ed. Amīn al-Khūlī, 17 vols. (Cairo: al-Dār al-Miṣriyya lil-Taʾlīf wal-Nashr, 1963).

ʿAbd al-Munʿim, Fuʾād. "Introduction" in *Al-Siyāsa al-Sharʿiyya* by Dāda Afandī (Alexandria: Muʾassasat Shabāb al-Jāmiʿa, n.d.).

ʿAbd al-Rāziq, ʿAlī. *Al-Islām wa-Uṣūl Al-Ḥukm*, ed. Mamdūḥ Ḥiqqī (Beirut: Maktabat al-Ḥayāt, 1966).

Abū al-Baqāʾ, Ayyūb b. Mūsā al-Kafawī. *Kulliyyāt*, ed. ʿAdnān Darwīsh and Muḥammad al-Miṣrī (Beirut: Muʾassasat al-Risāla, 1992).

Abū Shāma, Shihāb al-Dīn ʿAbd al-Raḥmān b. Ismāʿīl. *Tarājim Rijāl al-Qarnayn al-Sādis wal-Sābiʿ* (Beirut: Dār al-Jīl, 1974).

Abū Yaʿlā. *See under* Farrāʾ.

Abū Yūsuf, Yaʿqūb b. Ibrāhīm. *Kitāb al-Kharāj* (Beirut: Dār al-Maʿrifa, n.d.).

ʿAdlān, ʿAṭiyya. "Muʾassasat Bayt al-Māl fil-Niẓām al-Islāmī," *Egyptian Institute for Political and Strategic Studies* (Jan. 2017), 1-13.

Afandī, Dada. *See under* Dede Jöngi Efendī.

Aḥmadnagarī, ʿAbd al-Nabī ʿAbd al-Rasūl. *Jāmiʿ al-ʿUlūm fī Iṣṭilāḥāt al-Funūn al-Mulaqqab bi-Dustūr al-ʿUlamā'*, 4 vols. (Repr. Beirut: Mu'assasat al-Aʿlamī lil-Maṭbūʿāt, 1975).

Alūsī, Shihāb al-Dīn al-. *Rūḥ al-Maʿānī fī Tafsīr al-Qur'ān al-ʿAẓīm wal-Sabʿ al-Mathānī*, ed. Maḥmūd Shukrī al-Alūsī, 30 vols. (Beirut: Dār Iḥyā' al-Turāth al-ʿArabī, n.d.).

ʿĀmirī, Muḥammad b. Aḥamd al-. *Bahjat al-Nāẓirīn ilā Tarājim al-Muta'akhkhirīn*, ed. ʿAbd Allāh al-Hundurī (Beirut: Dār Ibn Ḥazm, 2000).

ʿAskarī, Abū Hilāl al-. *Mā Iḥtakama bi-hi al-Khulafā' ilā al-Quḍāt*, ed. and trans. Mathieu Tillier, *Abū Hilāl al-ʿAskarī, Le Livre des califes qui s'en remirent au jugement d'un cadi*. In *Cahier des Annales Islamologiques, Institut Français d'Archéologie Orientale*, 30 (2011).

ʿAsqalānī, Aḥmad b. ʿAlī Ibn Ḥajar al-. *Al-Durar al-Kāmina fī Aʿyān al-Mā'a al-Thāmina*, 4 vols. (Hyderabad: Dā'irat al-Maʿārif, 1350/1931).

Asyūṭī, Shams al-Dīn Muḥammad b. Aḥmad al-. *Jawāhir al-ʿUqūd wa-Muʿīn al-Quḍāṭ wal-Muwaqqiʿīn wal-Shuhūd*, ed. Muḥyī al-Dīn al-ʿUtaybī, 2 vols. (Beirut: Dār Yūsuf lil-Ṭibāʿa wal-Nashr, n.d.).

ʿAṭṭār, Farīd al-Dīn al-. *Manṭiq al-Ṭayr*. *See under* Attar, sec. 2.

Baghdādī, Abū Bakr Aḥmad b. ʿAlī al-Khaṭīb al-. *Tārīkh Baghdād aw Madīnat al-Salām*, ed. Muṣṭafā ʿAbd al-Qādir ʿAṭā, 24 vols. (Beirut: Dār al-Kutub al-ʿIlmiyya, 1425/2004).

Baghdādī, Abū Manṣūr ʿAbd al-Qāhir b. Tamīm al-. *Uṣūl al-Dīn* (Istanbul: Maṭbaʿat al-Dawla, 1346/1928).

Bāqillānī, Abū Bakr Muḥammad b. al-Ṭayyib al-. *Kitāb Tamhīd al-Awā'il wa-Talkhīṣ al-Dalā'il*, ed. ʿImād al-Dīn Ḥaydar (Beirut: Mu'assasat al-Kutub al-Thaqāfiyya, 1987).

_____. *Al-Taqrīb wal-Irshād* (*al-Ṣaghīr*), ed. ʿAbd al-Ḥamīd Abū Zunayd, 3 vols. (Beirut: Mu'assasat al-Risāla, 1418/1998).

Bilqzīz, ʿAbd al-Ilāh. *Al-Nubuwwa wal-Siyāsa* (Beirut: Markaz Dirāsāt al-Waḥda al-ʿArabiyya, 2005).

Buhūtī, Manṣūr b. Yūnus b. Idrīs al-. *Kashshāf al-Qināʿ ʿan Matn al-Iqnāʿ*, ed. Muḥammad ʿAdnān Darwīsh, 6 vols. (Beirut: Dār Iḥyāʾ al-Turāth al-ʿArabī, 1999-2000).

_____. *Sharḥ Muntahā al-Irādāt*, 5 vols. (Riyadh: Maktabat Nizār Muṣṭafā al-Bāz, 1997).

Bukhārī, ʿAlāʾ al-Dīn ʿAbd al-ʿAzīz al-. *Kashf al-Asrār*, 4 vols. (Beirut: Dār al-Kutub al-ʿIlmiyya, 1997).

Bukhārī, al-Ḥāfiẓ Abū ʿAbd Allāh Muḥammad b. Ismāʿīl al-. *Ṣaḥīḥ*, ed. Muḥammad Quṭb and Hishām al-Bukhārī, 5 vols. (Beirut: al-Maktaba al-ʿAṣriyya, 1999).

Bukhārī, Ṭāhir b. Aḥmad b. ʿAbd al-Rashīd al-. *Khulāṣat al-Fatāwā* (Lahore: Amjad Akādīmī, 1977).

Bustānī, Buṭrus al-. *Nafīr Sūriyyah* (Beirut: Dār al-Fikr lil-Abḥāth wal-Nashr, 1990).

Dede Jöngi Efendī. *al-Siyāsa al-Sharʿiyya*, ed. Fu'ād ʿAbd al-Munʿim (Alexandria, Egypt: Mu'assasat Shabāb al-Jāmiʿa, 1411/1991).

Farrā', Abū Yaʿlā Muḥammad b. al-Ḥusayn, al-. *Al-Aḥkām al-Sulṭāniyya*, ed. Muḥammad Ḥāmid al-Faqī (Beirut: Dār al-Kutub al-ʿIlmiyya, 1403/1983).

Ghazālī, Abū Ḥāmid Muḥammad ibn Muḥammad al-. *Al-Adab fil-Dīn*, printed with *al-Munqidh min al-Ḍalāl* (Beirut: al-Maktaba al-Shaʿbiyya, n.d.).

_____. *Faḍā'iḥ al-Bāṭiniyya*, ed. ʿAbd al-Raḥmān Badawī (Repr. Kuwait: Mu'assasat Dār al-Kutub al-Thaqāfiyya, 1964).

_____. *Iḥyā' ʿUlūm al-Dīn*, 5 vols. (Beirut: Dār Ibn Ḥazm, 2005).

_____. *Al-Tibr al-Masbūk fī Naṣīḥat al-Mulūk*, ed. Aḥmad Shams al-Dīn (Beirut: Dār al-Kutub al-ʿIlmiyya, 1988).

Hadhlūl, Ṣāliḥ b. ʿAlī al-. *Al-Madīna al-ʿArabiyya al-Islāmiyya: Athar al-Tashrīʿ fī Takwīn al-Bī'a al-ʿImrāniyya* (Riyadh: Al-Jamʿiyya al-Saʿūdiyya li-ʿUlūm al-ʿImrān, 2010).

Ḥaḍramī Abū Bakr Muḥammad b. al-Ḥasan al-Murādī al-. *Kitāb al-Siyāsa aw al-Ishāra fī Tadbīr al-Imāra*, ed. Muḥammad Ismāʿīl, et al. (Beirut: Dār al-Kutub al-ʿIlmiyya, 2003).

Harrāma, Abd al- Ḥamīd al-. "Introduction." In Ibn Farḥūn, *al-Dībāj al-Mudhahhab*, ed. Ma'mūn al-Jannān and ʿAbd al-Ḥamīd al-Harrāma (Beirut: Dār al-Kutub al-ʿIlmiyya, 1996).

Hilāl al-Ṣābī, Abū al-Ḥusayn. *Rusūm Dār al-Khilāfa*, ed. Mikhā'īl ʿAwwād (Beirut: Dār al-Rā'id al-ʿArabī, 1406/1986).

Hujwīrī, ʿAlī b. Uthmān al-. *Kashf al-Maḥjūb*, ed. and trans. Isʿād Qindīl (Alexandria: Maktabat al-Iskandariyya, 1974).

Ibn ʿAbd al-Barr, Abū ʿUmar Yūsuf. *Jāmiʿ Bayān al-ʿIlm wa-Faḍlihi*, 2 vols. (Beirut: Dār al-Kutub al-ʿIlmiyya, n.d.).

Ibn Abī al-Baqā', Ayyūb b. Mūsa al-Kafawı. *Al-Kullıyat: Muʿjam fil-Muṣṭalaḥāt wal-Furūq al-Lughawiyya*, ed. ʿAdnān Darwīsh and Muḥammad al Miṣrī (Beirut: Mu'assasat al-Risāla, 1419/1998).

Ibn Abī al-Damm, Ibrāhīm b. ʿAbd Allāh. *Adab al-Qaḍā' aw al-Durar al-Manẓūmāt fī al-Aqḍiya wal-Ḥukūmāt*, ed. Muḥammad ʿAṭā' (Beirut: Dār al-Fikr, 1399/1979).

Ibn ʿĀbidīn, Muḥammad Amīn. *Radd al-Muḥtār ʿalā al-Durr al-Mukhtār Sharḥ Tanwīr al-Abṣār*, ed. ʿĀdil ʿAbd al-Mawjūd et al., 6 vols. (Riyad: Dār ʿĀlam al-Kutub, 2003).

Ibn ʿAqīl, Abū al-Wafā' ʿAlī b. Aḥmad. *Kitāb al-Funūn*, vol. 1 (Damanhūr: Maktabat Līna, 1411/1991).

_____. *Al-Wāḍiḥ fī Uṣūl Al-Fiqh*, ed. George Makdisi (Wiesbaden: Franz Steiner Verlag, 1996).

Ibn ʿArabī, Muḥyī al-Dīn. *Al-Insān al-Kāmil*, ed. Maḥmūd al-Ghurāb (Damascus: n.p., 1990).

_____. *Al-Quṭb al-Ghawth al-Fard Ṣāḥib al-Waqt*, printed with *Al-Insān al-Kāmil*, ed. Maḥmūd al-Ghurāb (Damascus: n.p., 1990).

_____. *Al-Tadbīrāt al-Ilāhiyya fī Iṣlāḥ al-Mamlaka al-Insāniyya* (Beirut: Dār al-Kutub al-ʿIlmiyya, 2003).

Ibn al-Athīr. *Al-Kāmil fil-Tārīkh.* 12 vols. (Beirut: Dār Ṣādir, 1965-1967).

Ibn al-Jazarī, Shams al-Dīn Muḥammad b. Ibrāhīm. *Ḥawādith al-Zamān wa-Anbā'ih wa-Wafayāt al-Akābir wal-Aʿyān min Abnā'ih*, ed. ʿUmar Tadmurī, 3 vols. (Beirut: al-Maktaba al-ʿAṣriyya, 1419/1998).

Ibn Farḥūn, Burhān al-Dīn Abū al-Wafā' Ibrāhīm b. Muḥammad. *Al-Dībāj al-Mudhahhab*, ed. Ma'mūn al-Jannān and ʿAbd al-Ḥamīd al-Harrāma (Beirut: Dār al-Kutub al-ʿIlmiyya, 1996).

_____. *Tabṣirat al-Ḥukkām fī Uṣūl al-Aqḍiya wa-Manāhij al-Aḥkām*, ed. Shaykh Jamāl Marʿashlī, vol. 2 (Riyadh: Dār ʿĀlam al-Kutub, 2003).

Ibn Ḥazm, ʿAlī b. Aḥmad b. Saʿīd. *Marātib al-Ijmāʿ* (Beirut: Dār Ibn Ḥazm, 1998).

Ibn Iyās, Abū al-Barakāt Muḥammad. *Badā'iʿ al-Zuhūr fī Waqā'iʿ al-Duhūr* (Cario: al-Maktabah al-Tawfīqiyya, 1992).

Ibn Jamāʿa, Badr al-Dīn Abū ʿAbd Allāh Muḥammad. *Taḥrīr al-Aḥkām fī Tadbīr Ahl al-Islām*, ed. Fu'ād ʿAbd al-Munʿim Aḥmad (Qatar: Al-Maḥākim al-Sharʿiyya wal-Shu'ūn al-Dīniyya, 1985).

Ibn al-Jawzī, Abū al-Faraj ʿAbd al-Raḥmān b. ʿAlī b. Muḥammad. *Al-Muntaẓam fī Tārīkh al-Mulūk wal-Umam*, 9 vols. (Haidarbad: Dā'irat al-Maʿārif al-ʿUthmāniyya, 1359/1940).

Ibn Kathīr, Ismāʿīl b. 'Umar. *Al-Bidāya wal-Nihāya*, 14 vols. (Beirut: Maktabat al-Maʿārif, 1990).

_____. *Tafsīr al-Qur'ān al-ʿAẓīm*, ed. Ḥusayn Zahrān, 4 vols. (Cairo: Bābī al-Ḥalibī, n.d.).

Ibn Khaldūn, ʿAbd al-Raḥmān. *Al-Muqaddima* (Beirut: Dār al-Kutub al-ʿIlmiyya, 2000).

Ibn al-Mamātī, Asʿad. *Kitāb Qawānī al-Dawānīn*, ed. ʿAzīz Sūryāl ʿAṭiyya (Cairo: Maṭbaʿat Madbūlī, 1411/1991).

Ibn Manẓūr, Jamāl al-Dīn Muḥammad. *Lisān al-ʿArab*, ed. ʿĀmir Aḥmad Ḥaydar and ʿAbd al-Munʿim Ibrāhīm, 15 vols. (Beirut: Dār al-Kutub al-ʿIlmiyya, 2009).

Ibn Māza, Burhān al-Dīn Ṣadr al-Sharīʿa al-Bukhārī. *Al-Muḥīṭ al-Burhānī li-Masāʾil al-Mabsūṭ wal-Jāmiʿayn wal-Siyar wal-Ziyādāt wal-Nawādir wal-Fatāwā wal-Wāqiʿāt, Mudallala bi-Dalāʾil al-Mutaqaddimīn*, ed. Naʿīm Aḥmad, 25 vols. (Karachi: Idārat al-Qurʾān wal-ʿUlūm al-Islāmiyya, 2004).

Ibn Māza, ʿUmar b. ʿAbd al-ʿAzīz al-Ḥusām al-Shahīd. *Sharḥ Adab al-Qāḍī*, ed. Abū al-Wafā al-Afghānī and Muḥammad al-Hāshimī, 3 vols. (Beirut: Dār al-Kutub al-ʿIlmiyya, 1414/1994).

Ibn al-Mibrad, Yūsuf b. Ḥasan b. ʿAbd al-Hādī al-Maqdisī. *Īḍāḥ Ṭuruq al-Istiqāma fī Aḥkām al-Wilāya wal-Imāma* (Damascus: Dār al-Nawādir, 2011).

Ibn al-Muqaffaʿ, ʿAbdullāh. *Risāla fil-Ṣaḥāba*, in Ibn al-Muqaffaʿ, *Āthār Ibn al-Muqaffaʿ* (Beirut: Dār al-Kutub al-ʿIlmiyya, 1409/1989), 309-23.

Ibn al-Qāṣṣ, Aḥmad b. Abī Aḥmad al-Ṭabarī. *Adab al-Qāḍī*, ed. Ḥusayn al-Jabūrī (Ṭāʾif, KSA: Maktabat al-Ṣiddīq, 1989).

Ibn Qayyim al-Jawziyya, Shams al-Dīn Abū ʿAbd Allāh Muḥammad. *Iʿlām al-Muwaqqiʿīn ʿan Rabb al-ʿĀlamīn*, ed. Muḥammad ʿAbd al-Ḥamīd, 4 vols. (Beirut: al-Maṭbaʿa al-ʿAṣriyya, 1407/1987).

_____. *Al-Ṭuruq al-Ḥukmiyya fil-Siyāsa al-Sharʿiyya*, ed. Muḥammad al-Zuḥaylī and Bashīr Muḥammad ʿUyūn (Beirut: Maktabat al-Muʾayyad, 1989).

Ibn Qudāma, Muwaffaq al-Dīn al-Maqdisī. *Rawḍat al-Nāẓir wa-Junnat al-Munāẓir*, ed. Sayf al-Dīn al-Khaṭīb (Beirut: Dār al-Kitāb al-ʿArabī, 1981).

Ibn al-Rāmī al-Bannāʾ, Abū ʿAbd Allāh. *Al-Iʿlān bi-Aḥkām al-Bunyān*, ed. Farīd b. Sulaymān (N.P.: Markiz al-Nashr al-Jāmiʿī, 1999).

Ibn Rushd, Muḥammad b. Aḥmad (al-Ḥafīd). *Bidāyat al-Mujtahid wa-Nihāyat al-Muqtaṣid*, 2 vols. (Beirut: Dār al-Maʿrifa, 1986); trans. Imran Ahsan Khan Nyazee, *The Distinguished Jurist's Primer*, 2 vols. (Reading: Garnet Publishing, 1994).

Ibn Sallām. *See under* Qāsim b. Sallām.

Ibn al-Ṣayrafī, Abū al-Qāsim ʿAlī b. Munjib. *Al-Ishāra ilā man Nāla al-Wizāra*, ed. ʿAbd Allāh al-Mukhliṣ (Cairo: Maṭbaʿat al-Maʿhad al-ʿIlmī al-Faransī, 1923).

Ibn Shāhīn, Zayn al-Dīn ʿAbd al-Bāṣit b. Khalīl. *Nayl al-Amal fī Dhayl al-Duwal*, ed. ʿUmar Tadmurī, 2 vols. (Beirut: al-Maktaba al-ʿAṣriyya, 1422/2002).

Ibn Ṭaghrībirdī, Abū al-Maḥāsin Jamāl al-Dīn. *Ḥawādith al-Duhūr fī Madā al-Ayyāmi wal-Shuhūr*, ed. Muḥammad ʿIzz al-Dīn, 2 vols. (Riyadh: ʿĀlam al-Kutub, 1990).

_____. *Al-Nujūm al-Zāhira fī Mulūk Miṣr wal-Qāhira*, 16 vols. (Cairo: Maṭbaʿat Dār al-Kutub al-Miṣriyya, 1929).

Ibn al-Ṭaḥḥān, Yaḥyā b. ʿAlī b. Ibrāhīm, *Tārīkh ʿUlamāʾ Ahl Miṣr*, ed. Maḥmūd al-Ḥaddād (Riyadh: Dār al-ʿĀṣima, 1408/1988).

Ibn Taymiyya, Taqiyy al-Dīn. *Darʾ Taʿāruḍ al-ʿAql wal-Naql*, ed. ʿAbd al-Laṭīf ʿAbd al-Raḥmān, 5 vols. (Beirut: Dār al-Kutub al-ʿIlmiyya, 2009).

_____. *Al-Khilāfa wal-Mulk*, ed. Ḥammād Salāma (Zarqā, Jordan: Maktabat al-Manār, 1414/1994).

_____. *Naqd Marātib al-Ijmāʿ*, printed with Ibn Ḥazm, *Marātib al-Ijmāʿ*.

_____. *Qāʿida fil-Ḥisba*, in Ibn Taymiyya, *Majmūʿat al-Fatāwā li-Shaykh al-Islām Taqiyy al-Dīn Aḥmad Ibn Taymiyya al-Ḥarrānī*, vol. 28 (Manṣūra: Dār al-Wafāʾ, 2005).

_____. *Al-Siyāsa al-Sharʿiyya fī Iṣlāḥ al-Rāʿī wal-Raʿiyya*, ed. ʿAlī Muḥammad al-ʿUmrān (Jadda: Dār ʿĀlam al-Fawāʾid, n.d.).

Ibn al-Tilmisānī, ʿAbd Allāh b. Muḥammad. *Sharḥ al-Maʿālim fī Uṣūl al-Fiqh*, ed. ʿĀdil ʿAbd al-Mawjūd and ʿAlī Muʿawwaḍ, 2 vols. (Beirut: ʿĀlam al-Kutub, 1999).

Ibn al-Wardī, Abū Ḥafṣ Zayn al-Dīn ʿUmar. *Tarīkh*, 2 vols. (Najaf: al-Maṭbaʿa al-Ḥaydāriyya, 1969).

_____. *Tatimmat al-Mukhtaṣar fī Akhbār al-Bashar*, ed. Aḥmad Rifʿat al-Badrāwī, 2 vols. (Beirut: Dār al-Maʿrifa, 1970).

Jaʿfar, Khadīja Yūsuf. "Naẓariyyat al-Imāma ʿInda al-Bāqillānī," *al-Ḥayāt* (13 September 2014).

Jahshayārī, Abū ʿAbd Allāh Muḥammad b. ʿAbdūs al-. *Kitāb al-Wuzarāʾ wal-Kuttāb*, ed. Muṣṭafā al-Saqqā, et al. (Cairo: Muṣṭafā Bābī al-Ḥalabī, 1938).

Jāsim, Khālid Muḥammad. "Ṣalāḥiyyāt Waliy al-Amr fil-Taṣarruf fī Bayt al-Māl," *Majallat Kulliyyat al-Tarbiyya al-Asāsiyya*, 67 (2011), 23-29.

Jurjānī, al-Sharīf Abū al-Ḥasan ʿAlī b. Muḥammad al-. *Al-Taʿrīfāt*, ed. Muḥammad Bāsil ʿUyūn al-Sūd (Beirut: Dār al-Kutub al-ʿIlmiyya, 2003).

Juwaynī, Imām al-Ḥaramayn al-. *Al-ʿAqīda al-Niẓāmiyya fil-Arkān al-Islāmiyya*. ed. Muḥammad Zāhid al-Kawtharī. (Cairo: al-Maktaba al-Azhariyya, 1992). See also under Klopfer, section 2, below.

_____. *Ghiyāth al-Umam fī Iltiyāth al-Ẓulam*, ed. Muṣṭafā Ḥilmī and Fu'ād ʿAbd al-Munʿim (Alexandria: Maṭābiʿ Jarīdat al-Safīr, 1979).

_____. *Al-Irshād*, ed. J. D. Luciani (Paris: Librairie Ernest Lecroux, 1938).

Kāshānī, 'Abd al-Razzāq. *Iṣṭilāḥāt al-Ṣūfiyyah*, ed. 'Abd al-Laṭīf Muḥammad al-'Abd (Cairo: Dār al-Nahḍah al-ʿArabiyya, 1977).

Khālidī, Maḥmūd. *Qawāʿid Niẓām al-Ḥukm fil-Islām* (Irbid, Jordan: n.p., 1983).

Khaṭīb, Muʿtazz al-. "Al-ʿAdl fil-Tafkīr al-Islāmī: al-Mafāhīm wal-Siyāqāt," *Tafāhum*, 47 (Winter 1436/2015), 11-34.

Kūnākātā, Ḥasan. *Al-Naẓariyya al-Siyāsiyya ʿInda Ibn Taymiyya* (Dammām and Riyāḍ: Dār al-Ikhlā' lil-Nashr wal-Tawzīʿ, 1415/1994).

Kurdarī, Muḥammad b. Muḥammad b. Shihāb Ibn al-Bazzāz al-. *Al-Fatāwā al-Bazzāziyya al-Mawsūma bil-Jāmiʿ al-Wajīz*, printed on the margins of *al-Fatāwā al-Hindiyya*, IV-VI (Beirut: Dār Iḥyā' al-Turāth al-ʿArabī, 1980).

Maqrīzī, Taqiyy al-Dīn Abū al-ʿAbbās Aḥmad al-ʿUbaydī al-. *Al-Sulūk li-Maʿrifat Duwal al-Mulūk*, 8 vols. (Beirut: Dār al-Kutub al-ʿIlmiyya, 1997).

Mārdīnī, Muḥammad b. ʿUthmān al-. *Al-Anjum al-Zāhirāt fī Ḥall Alfāẓ al-Waraqāt*, ed. ʿAbd al-Karīm al-Namla (Riyad: Maktabat al-Rushd, 1996).

Marwazī, Abū ʿAbd Allāh Naʿīm b. Ḥammād al-. *Kitāb al-Fitan*, ed. Samīr al-Zuhayrī (Cairo: Maktabat al-Tawḥīd, 1412/1991).

Māwardī, ʿAlī b. Muḥammad b. Ḥabīb al-. *Adab al-Dīn wal-Dunyā* (Jedda: Dār al-Minhāj, 2013).

_____. *Adab al-Dunyā wal-Dīn* (Beirut: Dār al-Kutub al-ʿIlmiyya, 2005).

_____. *Adab al-Qāḍī*, ed. Muḥyī Hilāl Sarḥan, 2 vols. (Baghdad: Maṭbaʿat al-Irshād, 1971).

_____. *Adab al-Wazīr al-Maʿrūf bi-Qawānīn al-Wizāra wa-Siyāsat al-Mulk*, ed. Ḥasan Ḥusayn (Cairo: Maktabat al-Khanjī, 1994).

_____. *Al-Aḥkām al-Sulṭāniyya wal-Wilāyāt al-Dīniyya* (Cairo: al-Fikr, 1983).

_____. *Aʿlām al-Nubuwwa*. (Beirut: Dār al-Kutub al-ʿIlmiyya, 1986).

_____. *Al-Amthāl wal-Ḥikam*, ed. Fu'ād ʿAbd al-Munʿim Aḥmad (Riyadh: Dār al-Waṭan, 1999).

_____. *Al-Ḥāwī al-Kabīr fī al-Furūʿ*, ed. Maḥmūd Maṭarjī et al., 24 vols. (Beirut: Dār al-Fikr, 1994).

_____. *Al-Nukat wal-ʿUyūn*, ed. Sayyid b. ʿAbd al-Maqṣūd b. ʿAbd al-Raḥīm, 6 vols. (Beirut: Dār al-Kutub al-ʿIlmiyya, n.d.).

_____. *Tashīl al-Naẓar wa-Taʿjīl al-Ẓafar fī Akhlāq al-Malik wa-Siyāsat al-Mulk*, ed. Muḥyī Hilāl Sarḥān et al. (Beirut: Dār al-Nahḍa al-ʿArabiyya, 1981).

Al-Mawsūʿa al-Fiqhiyya, 45 vols. (Kuwait: Dār al-Ṣafwa lil-Ṭibāʿa wal-Nashr, 1990-2006).

Miṣrī, Ibn Naqīb al-. *ʿUmdat al-Sālik*, ed. and trans. N. H. M. Keller, *The Reliance of the Traveler* (Evanston, IL: Sunna Books, 1991).

Muḥāsibī, al-Ḥārith b. Asad al-. *Kitāb Mā'iyyat al-ʿAql wa-Maʿnāh wa-Ikhtilāf al-Nās Fī-hi*, in *Al-ʿAql wa-Fahm al-Qur'ān*, ed. Ḥusayn al-Quwwatlī (Beirut: Dār al-Fikr, 1391/1971).

Muslim, Abū al-Ḥusayn b. al-Ḥajjāj. *Ṣaḥīḥ*, ed. Ayman Zāmilī et al., 5 vols. (Beirut: ʿĀlam al-Kutub, 1998).

Nasafī, ʿAbd Allāh b. Aḥmad al-. *Tafsīr al-Qur'ān al-Jalīl al-Musammā bi-Madārik al-Tanzīl wa-Ḥaqā'iq al-Ta'wīl*, ed. Sharaf al-Dīn al-Khaṭṭāb and M. al-Batrāwī, 3 vols. (Cairo: al-Maṭa'a al-Amīriyya, 1939-43).

Nawawī, Muḥyī al-Dīn Sharaf al-Dīn b. Yaḥyā al-. *Al-Majmūʿ: Sharḥ al-Muhadhdhab*, 23 vols. (Jedda: Maktabat al-Irshād, 1980).

_____. *Rawḍat al-Ṭālibīn*. ed. ʿĀdil ʿAbd al-Mawjūd and ʿAlī Muʿawwaḍ, 8 vols. (Beirut: Dār al-Kutub al-ʿIlmiyya, n.d.).

Nīsābūrī, ʿAlī b. Aḥmad al-Wāḥidī al-. *Asbāb al-Nuzūl* (Beirut: Dār al-Kutub al-ʿIlmiyya, 1991).

Nīsābūrī, al-Ḥasan b. Muḥammad al-. *Tafsīr al-Gharā'ib wa-Raghā'ib al-Furqān*, ed. Zakariyyā ʿUmayrāt, 6 vols. (Beirut: Dār al-Kutub al-ʿIlmiyya, 1996).

Niẓām al-Mulk. *Siyar al-Mulūk aw Siyāsat Nāmeh*, trans. Yūsuf Bakkār (Beirut: Dār al-Manāhil, 2007).

Nuwayrī, Shihāb al-Dīn Aḥmad b. ʿAbd al-Wahhāb al-. *Nihāyat al-Arab fī Funūn al-Adab*, 31 vols. (Cairo: Maṭbaʿat Dār al-Kutub al-Miṣriyya, 1926).

Qāḍīkhān, Maḥmūd Fakhr al-Dīn al-Ūzajandī. *Al-Fatāwā al-Khān*iyya, 6 vols. (Būlāq: al-Maṭbaʿa al-Amīriyya, 1310/1893).

Qānūnnāma Miṣr, trans. Aḥmad Fu'ād Mitwallī (Cairo: Maktabat al-Anglo-Miṣriyya, 1986).

Qarāfī, Shihāb al-Dīn al-. *Al-Dhakhīra*, ed. Muḥammad Būkhubza, 10 vols. (Beirut: Dār al-Gharb al-Islāmī, 1994).

Qāsim, ʿAbduh Qāsim. *ʿAṣr Salāṭīn al-Mamālīk* (Cairo: Dār al-Shurūq, 1415/1994).

Qāsim b. Sallām, Abū ʿUbayd al-. *Kitāb al-Amwāl*, ed. Sayyid b. Rajab, 2 vols. (Manṣūra, Egypt: Dār al-Hudā, 2007).

Qasṭalānī, Aḥmad b. Muḥammad al-. *Al-Mawāhib al-Laduniyya bil-Minaḥ al-Muḥammadiyya*, ed. Ṣāliḥ Aḥmad al-Shāmī, 4 vols. (Beirut: al-Maktab al-Islāmī, 2004).

Qudāma Ibn Jaʿfar, Abū al-Faraj b. Ziyād. *Al-Kharāj wa-Ṣināʿat al-Kitāba*, ed. Muḥammad Ḥusayn al-Zabīdī (Baghdad: Dār al-Ḥurriyya lil-Ṭibāʿa, 1981).

Al-Qur'ān al-Karīm (Kuwait: Wizārat al-Awqāf wal-Shu'ūn al-Islāmiyya, 1402/1981).

Al-Qur'ān al-Karīm (Madina: Majma' al-Malik Fahd li-Ṭibā'at al-Muṣḥaf al-Sharīf, 1407/1987).

Qurṭubī, Muḥammad b. Aḥmad al-Ansārī al-. *Tafsīr*, ed. Sālim Muṣṭafā al-Badrī, 21 vols. (Beirut: Dār al-Kutub al-'Ilmiyya, 2005).

Qushayrī, Abū Qāsim al-. *Al-Risāla*, ed. 'Abd al-Ḥalīm Maḥmūd et al. (Cairo: Maṭābi' Dār al-Sha'b, 1989).

Quṭb, Sayyid. *Fī Ẓilāl al-Qur'ān*, 6 vols. (Cairo: Dār al-Shurūq, 1968).

Ramlī, Muḥammad Shams al-Dīn b. Shihāb al-Dīn al-. *Ghāyat al-Ma'mūl fī Sharḥ Waraqāt al-Uṣūl*, ed. 'Uthmān Yūsuf Aḥmad (Beirut: Risālah Publishers, 2005).

Rāzī, Fakhr al-Dīn Muḥammad b. 'Umar al-. *Al-Maḥṣūl fī 'Ilm al-Uṣūl*, 2 vols. (Beirut: Dār al-Kutub al-'Ilmiyya, 1988).

_____. *Al-Tafsīr al-Kabīr*, 32 vols. (Cairo: al-Maṭba'a al-Bahiyya al-Miṣriyya, 1934-62).

Riḍā, Rashīd. *Al-Khilāfa* (Cairo: Mu'assasat al-Hindāwī lil-Ta'līm wal Thaqāfa, 2015).

Ṣābī, Abū al-Ḥusayn Abū Hilāl b. Muḥsin al-. *Rusūm Dār al-Khilāfa*, ed. Mikhā'īl 'Awwād (Beirut: Dār al-Rā'id al-'Arabī, 1406/1986).

Sam'ānī, Abū Muẓaffar al-. *Tafsīr al-Qur'ān*, ed. Ghunaym b. Ghunaym, 6 vols. (Riyadh: Dār al-Waṭan, 1997).

Samarqandī, Naṣr al-Dīn b. Muḥammad al-. *Baḥr al-'Ulūm*, ed. 'Alī Mu'awwaḍ and 'Ādil 'Abd al-Mawjūd, 3 vols. (Beirut: Dār al-Kutub al-'Ilmiyya, 1993).

Sarrāj, Abū Naṣr al-. *Kitāb al-Luma'* (Cairo: Dār al-Kutub al-Ḥadītha, 1960).

Shāfi'ī, Muḥammad Ibn Idrīs al-. *Al-Risāla* (Cairo: Bābī al-Ḥalabī, 1969).

Sha'rānī, 'Abd al-Wahhāb b. Aḥmad b. 'Alī al-. *Al-Mīzān al-Kubrā*, ed. 'Abd al-Wārith 'Alī (Beirut: Dār al-Kutub al-'Ilmiyya, 1418/1998).

_____. *Mukhtaṣar Irshād al-Mughaffalīn min al-Fuqarā' ilā Shurūṭ Ṣuḥbat al-Umarā'*, ed. Sayyid Ḥusnī Shākir (Cairo: Dār al-Karaz, 2011).

Shāṭibī, Abū Isḥāq Ibrāhīm. Al-*Muwāfaqāt fī Uṣūl al-Aḥkām*, ed. Muḥyī al-Dīn 'Abd al-Ḥamīd, 4 vols. (Cairo: Maṭba'at 'Alī Ṣubayḥ, 1970).

Shawkānī, Muḥammad b. 'Alī al-. *Al-Badr al-Ṭāli' bi-Maḥāsin man Ba'd al-Qarn al-Sābi'*, ed. Muḥammad Ḥasan Ḥallāq, 2 vols. (Damascus: Dār Ibn Kathīr, 2006).

Shaybānī, Muḥammad b. al-Ḥasan al-. *Kitāb al-Aṣl al-Ma'rūf bil-Mabsūṭ*, ed. Abū al-Wafā al-Afghānī, 5 vols. (Beirut: 'Ālam al-Kutub, 1990).

Shayzarī, ʿAbd al-Raḥmān b. ʿAbd Allāh b. Naṣr al-. *Al-Nahj al-Maslūk fī Siyāsat al-Mulūk*, ed. Muḥammad Ḥasan Ismāʿīl et al. (Beirut: Dār al-Kutub al-ʿIlmiyya, 2003).

_____. *Nihāyat al-Rutba fī Ṭalab al-Ḥisba*, ed. Muḥammad Ḥasan Ismāʿīl et al. (Beirut: Dār al-Kutub al-ʿIlmiyya, 2003).

Shīrāzī, Abū Isḥāq Ibrāhīm. *Al-Muhadhdhab fī Fiqh al-Imām al-Shāfiʿī*, ed. Muḥammad al-Zuḥaylī, 6 vol. (Damascus: Dār al-Qalam, 1966).

Subkī, Tāj al-Dīn b. Taqiyy al-Dīn al-. *Ṭabaqāt al-Shāfiʿiyya al-Kubrā*, 10 vols. (Cairo: Maṭbaʿat Bābī al-Ḥalabī, 1964-76).

Surūjī, Abū al-ʿAbbās Shams al-Dīn al-. *Adab al-Qaḍā'*, ed. Shams al-ʿĀrifīn Yāsīn (Beirut: Dār al-Bashā'ir al-Islāmiyya, 1418/1997).

Suyūṭī, Jalāl al-Dīn ʿAbd al-Raḥmān al-. *Mā Rawāhu al-Asāṭīn fī ʿAdam al-Majī'i ilā al-Salāṭīn*, ed. Majdī al-Sayyid (Ṭanṭa, Egypt: Dār al-Ṣaḥāba lil-Turāth, 1991).

_____. *Al-Durr al-Manthūr fil-Tafsīr bil-Ma'thūr*, ed. ʿAbd Allāh al-Turkī, 16 vols. (Cairo: Markaz Hajar lil-Buḥūth wal-Dirāsāt al-ʿArabiyya wal-Islāmiyya, 2003).

_____. *Ḥusn al-Muḥāḍara fī Tārīkh Miṣr wal-Qāhira*, ed. Muḥammad Ibrāhīm, 2 vols. (Cairo: Muṣṭafā Bābī al-Ḥalabī, 1967).

Ṭabarī, Abū Jaʿfar Muḥammad b. Jarīr. *Tafsīr al-Ṭabarī al-Musammā Jāmiʿ al-Bayān fī Ta'wīl al-Qur'ān*, 13 vols. (Beirut: Dār al-Kutub al-ʿIlmiyya, 1426/2005).

_____. *Tārīkh*, 13 vols. (Beirut: Dār al-Fikr, 1418/1998).

Tahānawī, Muḥammad Aʿlā b. ʿAlī. *Kashshāf Iṣṭilāḥāt al-Funūn*, 5 vols. (Beirut: Dār al-Kutub al-ʿIlmiyya, 2006).

Ṭarābulsī, ʿAlā' al-Dīn Abū al-Ḥasan ʿAlī b. Khalīl. *Muʿīn al-Ḥukkām fī-mā Yataraddadu bayna al-Khaṣmayni min al-Aḥkām* (Cairo: al-Maṭbaʿa al-Maymaniyya, 1310/1892).

Ṭarkhān, Ibrāhīm ʿAlī. *Miṣr fī ʿAṣr Dawlat al-Mamālīk al-Jarākisa 1382-1517* (Cairo: Maktabat al-Nahḍa al-Miṣriyya, 1959).

Ṭāshkuprīzādeh, Muḥammad b. Muṣṭafā b. Khalīl. *Al-Shaqā'iq al-Nuʿmāniyya fī ʿUlamā' al-Dawla al-ʿUthmāniyya* (Beirut: Dār al-Kitāb al-ʿArabī, 1395/1975).

Tilmisānī, ʿAbd Allāh b. Muḥammad al-. *Sharḥ al-Maʿālim fī Uṣūl al-Fiqh*, ed. ʿĀdil ʿAbd al-Mawjūd and ʿAlī Muʿawwaḍ, 2 vols. (Beirut: ʿĀlam al-Kutub, 1999).

Tinbaktī, Aḥmad Bābā al-. *Nayl al-Dībāj bi-Taṭrīz al-Dībāj*, ed. ʿAbd al-Ḥamīd al-Harrāma (Tripoli, Libya: Dār al-Kātib, 2000).

Tirmidhī, Abū ʿĪsā Muḥammad b. ʿĪsā. *Al-Jāmiʿ al-Ṣaḥīḥ wa-huwa Sunan al-Tirmidhī*, ed. Muṣṭafā al-Dhahabī, 6 vols. (Cairo: Dār al-Ḥadīth, 1419/1999).

Tirmidhī, al-Ḥakīm Muḥammad b. ʿAlī al-. *Bayān al-Farq Bayna al-Ṣadr wal-Qalb wal-Fu'ād wal-Lubb*, ed. Aḥmad al-Sāyiḥ (Cairo: Markiz al-Kitāb lil-Nashr, n.d.).

Ṭūghān Shaykhul-Muḥammadī. *Al-Muqaddima al-Sulṭāniyya fil-Siyāsa al-Sharʿiyya*. Manuscript, Istanbul, Sulaymaniyya, no. 3519. Microfilm no. 4542

Ṭurṭūshī, Muḥammad b. al-Walīd al-. *Sirāj al-Mulūk* (Jadda: Dār al-Minhāj lil-Nashr wal-Tawzīʿ, 2016).

Ṭūsī, Abū Jaʿfar. *ʿUddat al-Uṣūl*, ed. Muḥammad Riḍā al-Anṣārī, 2 vols. (Qumm: Setāreh, 1417/1996).

Udfawī, Abū al-Faḍl Kamāl al-Dīn b. Thaʿlab al-. *Al-Ṭāliʿ al-Saʿīd al-Jāmiʿ Asmā' Nujabā' al-Ṣaʿīd*, ed. Saʿd Ḥasan (Cairo: Al-Dār al-Miṣriyya lil-Ta'līf wal-Tarjama, 1966).

ʿUmar, Aḥmad Mukhtār. *Muʿjam al-Lugha al-ʿArabiyya al-Muʿāṣira*, 2 vols. (Cairo: ʿĀlam al-Kutub, 1429/2008).

Wāḥidī al-Nīsābūrī, Abū al-Ḥassan ʿAlī b. Aḥmad al-. *Asbāb al-Nuzūl* (Beirut: Dār al-Kutub al-ʿIlmiyya, 1991).

Wakīʿ, Muḥammad b. Khalaf b. Ḥayyān, *Akhbār al-Quḍāt*, 3 vols (Beirut: ʿĀlm al-Kutub, n.d.).

Zabīdī, Muḥib al-Dīn Abū al-Fayḍ al-Sayyid al-Husaynī Murtaḍā al-. *Tāj al-ʿArūs min Jawāhir al-Qāmūs*, ed. ʿAlī Shīrī, 14 vols (Beirut: Dār al-Fikr, 1994).

Zamakhsharī, Jār Allāh Maḥmūd b. ʿUmar al-. *Tafsīr al-Kashshāf ʿan Ḥaqā'iq Ghawāmiḍ al-Tanzīl*, ed. Muḥammad Shāhīn, 4 vols. (Beirut: Dār al-Kutub al-'Ilmiyya, 2006).

Zarnūjī, Burhān al-Islām. *Taʿlīm al-Mutaʿallim Ṭarīq al-Taʿallum*, ed. Marwān Qabbānī (Beirut: al-Maktab al-Islāmī, 1981).

Ziyāda, Khālid. *Kātib al-Sulṭān: Ḥirfat al-Fuqahā' wal-Muthaqqafīn* (London: Riad El-Rayyes Books, 1991).

———. *Al-Ṣūra al-Taqlīdiyya lil-Mujtamaʿ al-Madanī* (Tripoli: Maʿhad al-ʿUlūm al-Ijtimāʿiyya, 1983).

SOURCES IN OTHER LANGUAGES

Abad, Leticia A. and Nuno Palma. "The Fruits of El-Dorado: The Global Impact of American Precious Metals," in *Economics Discussions Paper Series*

(Manchester: University of Manchester Economics Discussions Paper Series, 2021), available at: https://hummedia.manchester.ac.uk/schools/soss/economics/discussionpapers/EDP-2003.pdf

Abdel Meguid, Ahmed. "Reversing Schmitt: The Sovereign as a Guardian of Rational Pluralism and the Peculiarity of the Islamic State of Exception in al-Juwaynī's Dialectical Theology," *European Journal of Political Theory*, 19, 4 (2020), 489-511.

Abisaab, Rula. *Converting Persia: Religion and Power in the Safavid Empire* (London: I.B. Tauris, 2004).

Abou El Fadl, Khaled. "The Centrality of Sharīʿah to Government and Constitutionalism in Islam," in *Constitutionalism in Islamic Countries: Between Upheaval and Continuity*, ed. Rainer Grote et al. (Oxford: Oxford University Press, 2012).

_____. *Rebellion and Violence in Islamic Law* (Cambridge: Cambridge University Press, 2001).

Abou-El-Haj, Rifaʿat Ali. "Power and Social Order: The Uses of the *Kanun*," in *The Ottoman City and its Parts: Urban Structures and Social Order*, ed. Irene Bierman et al. (New Rochelle, NY: A.D. Caratzas, 1991), 77-99.

Abrams, Philip. "Notes on the Difficulty of Studying the State," *Journal of Historical Sociology*, 1, 1 (1988), 58-89.

Abu El-Haj, Tabatha. "Changing the People: Legal Regulation and American Democracy," *New York University Law Review*, 86, 1 (2011), 1-68.

Abu-Lughod, Janet. *Before European Hegemony: The World System A.D. 1250-1350* (Oxford: Oxford University press, 1989).

Abu-ʿUksa, Wael. *Freedom in the Arab World: Concepts and Ideologies in Arabic Thought in the Nineteenth Century* (Cambridge: Cambridge University Press, 2016).

Ackerman, Bruce. *The Decline and Fall of the American Republic* (Cambridge, Mass.: Belknap Press, 2010).

Afsaruddin, Asma. "Obedience to Political Authority: An Evolutionary Concept," in *Islamic Democratic Discourse: Theory, Debates and Philosophical Perspectives*, ed. M. Muqtedar Khan (Lanham: Lexington Books, 2006), 37-60.

Agamben, Giorgio. *Homo Sacer: Sovereign Power and Bare Life* (Stanford: Stanford University Press, 1998).

Ahmed, Asad Q. *The Religious Elite of the Early Hijaz* (Oxford: Prosopographica et Genealogica, 2011).

AIPAC, available at: https://www.aipacpac.org/home

AIPAC Political Achievements Factsheet, available at: https://aipacorg.app.box.com/s/3bnlheso6zkiicp3znpbrqqdqhku698j

Akarli, Engin Deniz. Review of Colin Imber. *Ebu's-Su'ud: The Islamic Legal Tradition* (Stanford: Stanford University Press, 1997). In *Islamic Law and Society*, 6, 2 (1999), 284-88.

Alam, Muzaffar. *The Languages of Political Islam in India*, 1200-1800 (New Delhi: Permanent Black, 2004).

_____. "Shari'a and Governance in the Indo-Islamic Context," in *Beyond Turk and Hindu: Rethinking Religious Identities in Islamicate South Asia*, ed. David Gilmartin et al. (Gainsville: University Press of Florida, 2000), 216-45.

Al-Azami, M. M. *The History of the Qur'ānic Text* (Riyadh: Azami Publishing House, 2003).

Al-Azem, Talal. *Rule-Formulation and Binding Precedent in the Madhhab-Law Tradition: Ibn Quṭlūbughā's Commentary on the Compendium of Qudūrī* (Leiden: Brill, 2016).

Al-Azmeh, Aziz. *Muslim Kingship: Power and the Sacred in Muslim, Christian, and Pagan Politics* (New York: I. B. Tauris, 2001).

Al-Hibri, Azizah Y. "Islamic Constitutionalism and the Concept of Democracy," *Case Western Reserve Journal of International Law*, 24, 1 (1992), 1-29.

Al-Qadi, Wadad. "The Term 'Khalifa' in Early Exegetical Literature," *Die Weit des Islams* (1988), 392-411.

American Civil Liberty Union. "Unleashed and Unaccountable: The FBI's Unchecked Abuse of Authority" (September 2013), available at: https://www.aclu.org/sites/default/files/assets/unleashed-and-unaccountable-fbi-report.pdf

Amin, Samir. *The Liberal Virus* (New York: Monthly Review Press, 2004).

Amnesty International. "Fatal Flaws: Innocence and the Death Penalty in the USA" (November 1988); available at: https://www.amnesty.org/en/wp-content/uploads/2021/06/amr510691998en.pdf

Angier, Tom. "Alasdair MacIntyre's Analysis of Tradition." *European Journal of Philosophy* 22, no. 4 (2011): 540-72.

Anidjar, Gil. "The Idea of an Anthropology of Christianity," *Interventions*, 11, 3 (2009), 367-93.

Anjum, Ovamir. *Politics, Law, and Community in Islamic Thought: The Taymiyyan Moment* (New York: Cambridge University Press, 2012).

Annas, Julia. "MacIntyre on Traditions." *Philosophy and Public Affairs* 18, no. 4 (1989): 388-404.

Anooshahr, Ali. The *Ghazi Sultans and the Frontiers of Islam: A Comparative Study of the Late Medieval and Early Modern Periods* (London: Routledge, 2009).

Anscombe, G. E. M. "Modern Moral Philosophy," *Philosophy*, 33, 124 (1958), 1-19.

Asad, Talal. *Formations of the Secular: Christianity, Islam, Modernity* (Stanford: Stanford University Press, 2003).

_____. "The Idea of an Anthropology of Islam." *Qui Parle*, 17, 2 (2009), 1-30.

Ashtor, E. *A Social and Economic History of the Near East in the Middle Ages* (London: Collins, 1976).

Atçıl, Abdurrahman. *Scholars and Sultans in Early Modern Ottoman Empire* (Cambridge: Cambridge University Press, 2016).

Attar, Farid. *The Conference of the Birds*, trans. Afkham Darbandi and Dick Davis (London: Penguin Books, 1984).

Austin, J. L. "Performative Utterances," in *Philosophical Papers*, ed. J. O. Urmson et al., 3rd ed. (Oxford: Clarendon Press, 1979), 220-40.

Ayalon (Neustadt), David. "Studies on the Structure of the Mamluk Army, I," *Bulletin of the School of Oriental and African Studies* 15, 2 (1953): 203-28.

_____. "The Circassians in the Mamlūk Kingdom," *Journal of the American Oriental Society*, 69, 3 (1949), 135-47.

_____. "The Plague and Its Effects Upon the Mamlûk Army," *Journal of the Royal Asiatic Society* (1946), 67-73.

Aykan, Yavuz. "A Legal Concept in Motion: The 'Spreader of Corruption' (*sā ʿī bi'l-fesād*) from Qarakhanid to Ottoman Jurisprudence," *Islamic Law and Society* (2018), 1-19.

_____. "Review of Guy Burak, *The Second Formation of Islamic Law: The Ḥanafī School in the Early Modern Ottoman Empire* (New York: Cambridge University Press, 2015), in *International Journal of Middle East Studies*, 48 (2016), 793-95.

Ayoub, Samy A. *Law, Empire, and the Sultan: Ottoman Imperial Authority and Ḥanafī Jurisprudence* (Oxford: Oxford University Press, 2020).

_____. "'The Sulṭān Says': State Authority in the Late Ḥanafī Tradition," *Islamic Law and Society*, 23 (2016), 239-78.

Bagley, Nicholas. "The Procedure Fetish," *Michigan Law Review*, 118, 3 (2019), 345-401.

Baldwin, James E. "The Deposition of Defterdār Aḥmad Pasha and the Rule of Law in Seventeenth-Century Egypt," *Journal of Ottoman Studies*, 46 (2015), 131-61.

_____. *Islamic Law and Empire in Ottoman Cairo* (Edinburgh: Edinburgh University Press, 2017).

Banister, Mustafa. "'Naught Remains to the Caliph but his Title': Revisiting Abbasid Authority in Mamlūk Cairo," *Mamlūk Studies Review*, 18 (2015), 219-45.

Barendt, Eric. *Introduction to Constitutional Law* (Oxford: Oxford University Press, 1998).

Bartelson, Jens. "The Concept of Sovereignty Revisited," *European Journal of International Law*, 17, 2 (2006), 463-74.

_____. "On the Indivisibility of Sovereignty," *Republics of Letters: A Journal for the Study of Knowledge, Politics, and the Arts*, 2, 2 (June 2011), 85-94.

Bauman, Zygmunt. *Intimations of Postmodernity* (London: Routledge, 1992).

_____. *Modernity and the Holocaust* (Ithaca: Cornell University Press, 1989).

Belhaj, Abdessamad. "Law and Order According to Ibn Taymiyya and Ibn Qayyim al-Jawziyya: A Re-examination of *Siyasa Shar'iya*," in *Islamic Theology, Philosophy and Law: Debating Ibn Taymiyya and Ibn Qayyim al-Jawziyya*, ed. Birgit Krawietz et al. (Berlin and Boston: De Gruyter, 2013), 400-21.

Ben Hammed, Mohamed Wajdi. "Contesting the Empty Time of Modernity: Sufi Temporalities in Postcolonial Arab Thought and Literature" (Ph.D. Dissertation: Columbia University, 2022).

Berkey, Jonathan. *The Transmission of Knowledge in Medieval Cairo: A Social History of Islamic Education* (Princeton: Princeton University Press, 1992).

Berlin, Isaiah. "Two Concepts of Liberty," in *Liberty*, ed. Henry Hardy (Oxford: Oxford University Press, 2008), 166-217.

Bernal, Martin. *Black Athena: The Asian Roots of Classical Civilization*, 3 vols. (New Brunswick, N.J.: Rutgers University Press, 2020).

Berriah, Mehdi and Mohamad El-Merheb (eds.), *Professional Mobility in Islamic Societies (700-1750): New Concepts and Approaches* (Leiden: Brill, 2021).

Black, Antony. *The History of Islamic Political Thought: From the Prophet to the Present* (Edinburgh: Edinburgh University Press, 2001).

Bodice, Rob. "History of Emotions: Past, Present, Future," *Revista de Estudios Sociales*, 62 (2017), 10-15.

Bolsinger, Eckard. *The Anatomy of the Political: Carl Schmitt's and Lenin's Political Realism* (Westport, Conn.: Greenwood Press, 2001).

Bori, Caterina. "Istanbul, Süleymaniye Kütüphanesi MS Şehid Ali Paşa 1553: A Neglected Version of Ibn Taymiya's *al-Siyasa al-Shar'iya* and Its Manuscript," in *History and Society During the Mamluk Period, 1250-1517*, ed. Bethany J. Walker and A. El Ghouz, III (Göttingen: V&R unipress, 2021), 9-60.

Born, Lester Kruger. "The Perfect Prince: A Study in Thirteenth- and Fourteenth-Century Ideals," *Speculum*, 3, 4 (October 1928), 470-505.

Borsch, Stuart. "Nile Floods and the Irrigation System in Fifteenth-Century Egypt," *Mamlūk Studies Review*, 4 (2000): 131-45.

_____. "Plague Depopulation and Irrigation Decay in Medieval Egypt." *The Medieval Globe*, 1, no. 1 (2016): 125-56.

Borsch, Stuart and Tarek Sabraa. "Plague Mortality in Late Medieval Cairo: Quantifying the Plague Outbreaks of 833/1430 and 864/1460," *Mamlūk Studies Review* 19 (2016), 115-48.

Bosworth, C.E. "The Political and Dynastic History of the Iranian World," in *The Cambridge History of Iran*, ed. J.A. Boyle (Cambridge: Cambridge University Press, 1968), 68-83.

Bourdieu, Pierre. *Outline of a Theory of Practice*, trans. Richard Nice (Cambridge: Cambridge University Press, 1977).

_____. *Practical Reason: On the Theory of Action* (Cambridge: Polity Press, 1998).

_____. "Rethinking the State: Genesis and Structure of the Bureaucratic Field," in *State/Culture: State Formation After the Cultural Turn*, ed. George Steinmetz (Ithaca: Cornell University Press, 1999), 53-75.

Breaky, Hugh. Review of C. B. Macpherson, *The Political Theory of Possessive Individualism: Hobbes to Locke* (New York: Oxford University Press, 1962), in J. T. Levy, ed., *The Oxford Handbook of Classics in Contemporary Political Theory* (Oxford: Oxford University Press, 2015).

Broadbridge, Anne F. *Kingship and Ideology in the Islamic and Mongol Worlds* (Cambridge: Cambridge University Press, 2008).

Bruff, Harold. "On the Constitutional Status of the Administrative Agencies," *American University Law Review*, 36 (Winter 1987), 491-517.

Burak, Guy. *The Second Formation of Islamic Law: The Ḥanafī School in the Early Modern Ottoman Empire* (New York: Cambridge University Press, 2015).

Bury, J. B. *The Idea of Progress* (Westport, Conn.: Greenwood Press, 1982).

Butterworth, Charles. "Prudence versus Legitimacy: The Persistent Theme in Islamic Political Thought," in *Islamic Resurgence in the Arab World*, ed. Ali Dessouki (New York: Praeger, 1982), 84-114.

Cahen, Claude. "The Turkish Invasion: The Selchükids," in *A History of the Crusades, Volume I: The First Hundred Years*, ed. Kenneth M. Setton and Marshall W. Baldwin (Madison, Milwaukee, and London: University of Wisconsin Press, 1955), 135-76.

Calabresi, Steven G. and Saikrishna Prakash, "President's Power to Execute the Law," *Yale Law Journal*, 104 (December 1994), 541-65.

Carey, George W. "Separation of Powers and the Madisonian Model: A Reply to the Critics," *The American Political Science Review*, 72, 1 (March 1978), 151-64.

Chatterjee, Partha. *I am the People: Reflections on Popular Sovereignty Today* (New York: Columbia University Press, 2020).

Chemerinsky, Erwin. *Constitutional Law: Principles and Policies* (New York: Aspen Law & Business, 1997).

Chevigny, Paul. *Edge of the Knife: Police Violence in the Americas* (New York: New Press, 1995).

Cohen, H. J. "The Economic Background and Secular Occupations of Muslim Jurisprudents and Traditionists in the Classical Period of Islam (Until the Middle of the Eleventh Century)," *Journal of the Economic and Social History of the Orient* (January 1970), 16-61.

Comte, August. *August Comte on Positivism: The Essential Writings*, ed. G. Lenzer (New Brunswick, N.J.: Transaction, 1998).

Condorcet, Marquis de. *Sketch for a Historical Picture of the Progress of the Human Mind* (London: Weidenfeld and Nicolson, 1955).

Crone, Patricia. *God's Rule: Government and Islam* (New York: Columbia University Press, 2004).

Crone, Patricia, and Martin Hinds. *God's Caliph: Religious Authority in the First Centuries of Islam* (Cambridge: Cambridge University Press, 2003).

Cuno, Kenneth M. "Reorganization of the Sharia Courts of Egypt: How Legal Modernization Set Back Women's Rights in the Nineteenth Century," *Journal of the Ottoman and Turkish Studies Association*, 2, 1 (2015), 85-99.

Dahl, Robert. "On Removing Certain Impediments to Democracy in the United States," in *Moral Foundations of the American Republic*, ed. Robert H. Horwitz, 3rd ed. (Charlottesville: University Press of Virginia, 1986), 230-52.

Darling, Linda T. *A History of Social Justice and Political Power in the Middle East: The Circle of Justice from Mesopotamia to Globalization* (London: Routledge, 2013).

_____. "Political Literature and the Development of an Ottoman Imperial Culture in the Fifteenth Century," *Journal of the Ottoman and Turkish Studies Association*, 1, 1-2 (2014), 57-69.

_____. "'The Vicegerent of God, from Him We Expect Rain': The Incorporation of the Pre-Islamic State in Early Islamic Political Culture," *Journal of the American Oriental Society*, 134, 3 (2014), 407-29.

Decosimo, David. "The Umma of Accountability: Al-Ghazālī Against Domination," *Soundings*, 98, 3 (2015), 260-88.

Deneen, Patrick J. *Why Liberalism Failed* (New Haven and London: Yale University Press, 2018).

Dodman, Thomas. "Theories and Methods in the History of Emotions," in *Sources for the History of Emotions: A Guide*, ed., Katie Barclay et al. (London: Routledge, 2020), 15-25.

Dols, Michael. *Black Death in the Middle East* (Princeton: Princeton University Press, 1977).

DPIC Special Report: "The Innocence Epidemic" (Feb. 18, 2021). Available at: https://deathpenaltyinfo.org/facts-and-research/dpic-reports/dpic-special-reports/dpic-special-report-the-innocence-epidemic

Dry, Murray. "The Separation of Powers and Representative Government," *Political Science Reviewer*, 3 (Fall 1973), 43-83.

Dussel, Enrique. "Anti-Cartesian Meditations: On the Origin of the Philosophical Anti-Discourse of Modernity," *Journal for Culture and Religious Theory*, 13, 1 (Winter 2014), 11-52.

Dyzenhaus, David. "Kelsen, Heller and Schmitt: Paradigms of Sovereignty Thought," *Theoretical Inquiries in Law*, 16, 2 (2015), 337-66.

Edwards, Mickey. "We No Longer Have Three Branches of Government," Politico (February 27, 2017). Available at: https://www.politico.com/magazine/story/2017/02/three-branches-government-separation-powers-executive-legislative-judicial-214812/

Elbendary, Amina. *Crowds and Sultans: Urban Protest in Late Medieval Egypt and Syria* (Cairo: The American University in Cairo Press, 2015).

El-Merheb, Mohamad. *Political Thought in the Mamluk Period: The Unnecessary Caliphate* (Edinburgh: Edinburgh University Press, 2022).

El-Merheb, Mohamad, et al. (eds.), *Professional Mobility in Islamic Societies (700-1750): New Concepts and Approaches* (Leiden: Brill, 2021).

El-Tobgui, Carl Sharif. *Ibn Taymiyya on Reason and Revelation: A Study of Darʾ Taʿāruḍ Al-ʿAql Wa-l-Naql* (Boston: Brill, 2019).

Emon, Anver M. "Shariʿa and the Rule of Law," in *Shariʿa Law and Modern Muslim Ethics*, ed. Robert Hefner (Bloomington: Indiana University Press, 2016), 37-64.

Ephrat, Daphna. *Learned Society in a Period of Transition: The Sunni Ulama of Eleventh-Century Baghdad* (Albany: State University of New York Press, 2000).

Evans, Jennifer C. "Hijacking Civil Liberties: The USA PATRIOT Act of 2001," *Loyola University Chicago Law Journal*, 33, 4 (2002): 933-90.

Fadel, Mohammad. "Islamic Law and Constitution-Making: The Authoritarian Temptation and the Arab Spring," *Osgoode Hall Law Journal*, 53, 2 (Winter 2016), 472-507.

Farahat, Omar "Generality and Exception in Islamic Legal Theory: Intent, Language, and the Jurist's Role," *American Journal of Comparative Law*, 20 (2024), 1-32.

_____. "Peace to Those of Faith: Political Affiliation and Belonging in Classical Islamic Thought," in *Routledge Handbook of Citizenship in the Middle East and North Africa*, ed. Roel Meijir et al. (London and New York: Routledge, 2021), 19-32.

Federalist (*The Federalist Papers*). The Gideon Edition, ed. George W. Carey and James McClellan (Indianapolis: Liberty Fund, 2001).

Fiaccadori, Elisa. "State Racism and the Paradox of Biopower," *Foucault Studies*, 19 (June 2015), 151-71.

Finlayson, Alan and J. Martin. "Poststructuralism," in *The State: Theories and Issues*, ed. C. Hay et al. (New York: Palgrave, 2006), 155-71.

Fisher, Louis. "Review of Bruce Ackerman, *The Decline and Fall of the American Republic*," *Federal Lawyer*, 58 (June 2011), 56-58.

Fleischer, Cornell. "Royal Authority, Dynastic Cyclism, and 'Ibn Khaldûnism' in Sixteenth-Century Ottoman Letters," *Journal of Asian and African Studies*, XVIII, 3-4 (1983), 198-220.

Foisneau, Luc. "Sovereignty and Reason of State: Bodin, Botero, Richelieu, and Hobbes," in *The Reception of Bodin*, ed. Howell Lloyd (Leiden: Brill, 2013), 323-42.

Foucault, Michel. "The Birth of Social Medicine," in M. Foucault, *Power: Essential Works of Foucault*, 134-56.

_____. *Discipline and Punish: The Birth of the Prison*, trans. Alan Sheridan (New York: Vintage, 1979).

_____. *Hermeneutics of the Subject: Lectures at the Collège de France, 1981-82*, ed. F. Gros (New York: Palgrave Macmillan, 2005).

_____. *History of Sexuality*, trans. Robert Hurley, vol. 1 (New York: Pantheon Books, 1978).

_____. "The Political Technology of Individuals," in *Technologies of the Self: A Seminar with Michel Foucault*, ed., Luther H. Martin et al. (London: Tavistock Publications, 1988), 145-62.

_____. *Power: Essential Works of Foucault, 1954-1984*, ed. James Faubion (New York: The New Press, 1973).

_____. "The Subject and Power," in *Power: Essential Works of Foucault*, 326-48.

_____. "What is Critique?" in M. Foucault, *The Politics of Truth*, ed. Sylvere Lotringer; trans. Lysa Hochroth et al. (Los Angeles: Semiotext(e), 2007), 41-82.

Frier, Bruce. *The Rise of the Roman Jurists* (Princeton: Princeton University Press, 1985).

Fuess, Albrecht. "*Ẓulm* by *Maẓālim?* The Political Implications of the Use of *Maẓālim* Jurisdiction by the Mamluk Sultans," *Mamlūk Studies Review*, 13 (2009), 121-42.

Garden, Kenneth. *The First Islamic Reviver: Abu Hamid al-Ghazali and His Revival of the Religious Sciences* (Oxford: Oxford University Press, 2013).

Garrioch, David. "The People of Paris and their Police in the Eighteenth Century: Reflections on the Introduction of a 'Modern' Police Force," *European History Quarterly*, 24 (1994), 511-35.

Gee, Graham and G. C. N. Webber, "What is a Political Constitution?" *Oxford Journal of Legal Studies*, 30, 2 (2010), 273-299.

Genel, Katia. "The Question of Biopower: Foucault and Agamben," *Rethinking Marxism*, 18, 1 (January 2006), 43-62.

Gibb, H. A. R., "Constitutional Organization," in *Law in the Middle East*, ed. Majid Khadduri et al. (Washington: Middle East Institute, 1955), 3-27.

_____. "The Schools of Law and Later Developments of Jurisprudence," in *Law in the Middle East*, ed. Majid Khadduri et al. (Washington: Middle East Institute, 1955), 57-84.

Giddens, Anthony. *Central Problems in Social Theory: Action, Structure and Contradiction in Social Analysis* (Houndsmill and London: Palgrave, 1979).

_____. *The Constitution of Society: Outline of the Theory of Structuration* (Cambridge: Polity Press, 1984).

Ginio, Eyal. "The Administration of Criminal Justice in Ottoman Selânik (Salonica) During the Eighteenth Century," *Turcica*, 30 (1998), 185-209.

Goitein, S.D. "Attitudes Toward Government in Islam and Judaism," in S.D. Goitein, *Studies in Islamic History and Institutions* (Leiden: Brill, 2010), 197-213.

_____. "The Birth-Hour of Muslim Law? An Essay in Exegesis," *Muslim World*, 50, 1 (1960): 23-29.

_____. "On the Origins of the Term Vizier," *Journal of the American Oriental Society*, 81 (1961), 425-26.

Gordon, Colin. "Introduction," in Foucault, *Power: Essential Works of Foucault*, xi-xli.

Gray, John. *Liberalism* (Minneapolis: University of Minneapolis Press, 1986).

Grice-Hutchinson, Marjorie. *The School of Salamanca: Readings in Spanish Monetary Theory 1544-1605* (Oxford: Clarendon Press, 1952).

Griffel, Frank. "Al-Ghazālī's Use of 'Original Human Disposition' (*Fiṭra*) and Its Background in the Teachings of Fārābī and Avicenna," *Muslim World*, 102 (January 2012), 1-32.

Grosby, Steven. "Nationality and Religion," in *Understanding Nationalism*, ed. Montserrat Guibernau et al. (Cambridge: Polity Press, 2001), 97-119.

Hadot, Pierre. *The Inner Citadel: The Meditations of Marcus Aurelius* (Harvard University Press, 1998).

_____. *Philosophy as a Way of Life*, trans. Michael Chase (Malden, MA: Blackwell, 1995).

Haider, Najam. "How to Make a Zaydi Imam: Zaydi Reports on the Revolt of Ṣāḥib Fakhkh Ḥusayn b. ʿAlī (d. 169/786)," *Journal of the American Oriental Society*, 144, 1 (January-March 2024), 1-22.

Hallaq, Wael. *A History of Islamic Legal Theories: An Introduction to Sunnī Uṣūl al-fiqh* (Cambridge: Cambridge University Press, 1999).

_____. *An Introduction to Islamic Law* (Cambridge: Cambridge University Press, 2009).

_____. "The Authenticity of Prophetic Ḥadīth: A Pseudo-Problem," *Studia Islamica*, 89 (1999), 75-90.

_____. *Authority, Continuity and Change in Islamic Law* (Cambridge: Cambridge University Press, 2001).

_____. "Caliphs, Jurists, and the Saljūqs in the Political Thought of Juwaynī," *Muslim World*, 74, 1 (1984), 26-41.

_____. "Considerations on the Function and Character of Sunnī Legal Theory." *Journal of the American Oriental Society*, 104, 4 (1984): 679-89.

_____. "From *Fatwās* to *Furū*ʿ: Growth and Change in Islamic Substantive Law," *Islamic Law and Society*, 1, 1 (1994): 29-65.

_____. "From Geographical to Personal Schools?: A Re-evaluation," *Islamic Law and Society*, 8, 1 (2001), 1-26.

_____. "'God Cannot be Harmed': On Ḥuqūq Allāh/Ḥuqūq al-ʿIbād Continuum," in *Routledge Handbook of Islamic Law*, ed. Khaled Abou El Fadl, et al. (London: Routledge, 2019), 67-81.

_____. "Groundwork of the Moral Law: A New Look at the Qur'ān and the Genesis of Sharīʿa." *Islamic Law and Society* 16, 3/4 (2009): 239-79.

_____. *Ibn Taymiyya Against the Greek Logicians* (Oxford: Oxford University Press, 1993).

_____. "Ibn Taymiyya on the Existence of God," *Acta Orientalia*, 52 (1991): 49-69.

_____. "*Iftā'* and *Ijtihād* in Sunnī Legal Theory: A Developmental Account," in *Islamic Legal Interpretation: Muftis and Their Fatwas*, ed. Muhammad Khalid Masud, Brinkley Messick, David Powers (Cambridge, Mass.: Harvard University Press, 1996), 33-43.

_____. *The Impossible State: Islam, Politics, and Modernity's Moral Predicament* (New York: Columbia University Press, 2013).

_____. "Juristic Authority vs. State Power: The Legal Crises of Modern Islam," *Journal of Law and Religion*, 19:2 (2003-2004): 243-58.

_____. "Model *Shurūṭ* Works and the Dialectic of Doctrine and Practice." *Islamic Law and Society* 2, 2 (1995): 109-34.

_____. "Murder in Cordoba: *Ijtihād*, *Iftā'* and the Evolution of Substantive Law in Medieval Islam," *Acta Orientalia* (Oslo), 55 (1994), 55-83.

_____. "Non-Analogical Arguments in Sunni Juridical *Qiyās*," *Arabica*, 36 (1989), 286-306.

_____. "Notes on the Term *Qarīna* in Islamic Legal Discourse," *Journal of the American Oriental Society*, 108, 3 (1988), 475-80.

_____. "On Inductive Corroboration, Probability, and Certainty in Sunni Legal Thought," in *Islamic Law and Jurisprudence*, ed. Nicholas Heer (Seattle: University of Washington Press, 1990), 3-31.

_____. "On Orientalism, Self-Consciousness and History," *Islamic Law and Society* 18, 3-4 (2011), 387-439.

_____. "On the Origins of the Controversy about the Existence of *Mujtahids* and the Gate of *Ijtihād*," *Studia Islamica*, 63 (1986): 129-41.

_____. *Origins and Early Evolution of Islamic Law* (Cambridge: Cambridge University Press, 2005).

_____. "A Prelude to Ottoman Reform: Ibn ʿĀbidīn on Custom and Legal Change," *Histories of the Modern Middle East: New Directions*, ed. I. Gershoni et al. (Boulder & London: Lynne Rienner, 2002): 37-61.

_____. "The 'Qāḍī's *Dīwān* (*Sijill*)' before the Ottomans," *Bulletin of the School of Oriental and African Studies*, 61, 3 (1998), 415-436.

_____. "The Quest for Origins or Doctrine? Islamic Legal Studies as Colonialist Discourse," *UCLA Journal of Islamic and Near Eastern Law*, 2, 1 (2002-03), 1-31.

_____. "Qur'ānic Constitutionalism and Moral Governmentality: Further Notes on the Founding Principles of Islamic Society and Polity." *Comparative Islamic Studies* 8 (2014): 1-52.

_____. *Reforming Modernity: Ethics and the New Human in the Philosophy of Abdurrahman Taha* (New York: Columbia University Press, 2019).

_____. *Restating Orientalism: A Critique of Modern Knowledge* (New York: Columbia University Press, 2018).

_____. *Sharīʿa: Theory, Practice, Transformations* (Cambridge: Cambridge University Press, 2012).

_____. "*Takhrīj* and the Construction of Juristic Authority," in *Studies in Islamic Legal Theory*, ed. Bernard G. Weiss (Leiden: Brill, 2002), 317-35.

_____. "A Tenth-Eleventh Century Treatise on Juridical Dialectic," *Muslim World*, 77 (1987), 197-228.

_____. "The Use and Abuse of Evidence: The Question of Provincial and Roman Influences on Early Islamic Law," *The Journal of the American Oriental Society*, 110, 1 (1990), 79-91.

_____. "*Uṣūl al-Fiqh* and Shāfiʿī's *Risāla* Revisited," *Journal of Arabic and Islamic Studies*, 19 (2019), 129-83.

_____. "Was al-Shāfiʿī the Master Architect of Islamic Jurisprudence?" *International Journal of Middle East Studies* 25, 4 (1993), 587-605.

_____. "Was the Gate of *Ijtihād* Closed?" *International Journal of Middle East Studies* 16, 1 (1984), 3-41.

Hamid, Eltigani Abdulqadir. "Al-Mawardi's Theory of State: Some Ignored Dimensions," *The American Journal of Islam and Society*, 18, 4 (2001), 1-18.

Hanna, Nelly, "The Administration of Courts in Ottoman Cairo," in Nelly Hanna, *The State and Its Servants: Administration of Egypt from Ottoman Times to the Present* (Cairo: The American University in Cairo Press, 1995), 44-59.

Hansen, Mogens H. "The Mixed Constitution Versus the Separation of Powers: Monarchical and Aristocratic Aspects of Modern Democracy," *History of Political Thought*, 31, 3 (2010), 509-31.

Hardin, Charles M. *Constitutional Reform in America: Essays on the Separation of Powers* (Ames: Iowa State University Press, 1989).

Hassan, Mona. *Longing for the Lost Caliphate: A Transregional History* (Princeton: Princeton University Press, 2016).

Hayek, F. A. *Law, Legislation and Liberty, A New Statement of the Liberal Principles of Justice and Political Economy*, 3 vols. (London: Routledge, 1982).

Heck, Paul. *The Construction of Knowledge in Islamic Civilization: Qudāma b. Ja'far and his Kitāb al-Kharāj wa-Ṣinā'at al-Kitāba* (Leiden: Brill, 2002).

Henry, Paul, "Wittgenstein and Contemporary Linguistics," in *Wittgenstein and Contemporary Theories of Language*, ed. Paul Henry et al. (Bergen: Bergen University Press, 1992), 3-19.

Heyd, Uriel. "Some Aspects of the Ottoman Fetva," *Bulletin of the School of Oriental and African Studies*, 32, 1 (1969), 35-56.

_____. *Studies in Old Ottoman Criminal Law* (Oxford: Clarendon Press, 1973).

Hillenbrand, Carole. "Nizām al-Mulk: A Maverick Vizier?" in *The Age of the Saljūqs*, ed. Edmond Herzig and Sarah Stewart, vol. VI (London: I.B. Tauris, 2015), 29-37.

Holt, P. M. *The Age of the Crusades: The Near East from the Eleventh Century to 1517* (London: Routledge, 1986).

Horkheimer, Max and Theodor Adorno, *Dialectic of Enlightenment: Philosophical Fragments* (Stanford: Stanford University Press, 1987).

Horwitz, Morton. *Transformation of American Law, 1870-1960: The Crisis of Legal Orthodoxy* (Oxford: Oxford University Press, 1992).

Houtsma, Martijin, "Malikshāh," *Encyclopaedia of Islam*, 1st ed. (Brill: Leiden, 1913-1936).

Huda Lutfi, "A Study of Six Fourteenth Century *Iqrārs* from Al-Quds Relating to Muslim Women," *Journal of the Economic and Social History of the Orient* 26, 3 (1983), 246-94.

Hurvitz, Nimrod. "Competing Texts: The Relationship Between Al-Mawardi's and Abu Ya'la's *Al-Ahkam Al-Sultaniyya*," *Occasional Publications*, no. 8, Harvard Law School (2007), 1-53. Available at: https://pil.law.harvard.edu/wp-content/uploads/2019/12/ Competing_Texts_by_Minrod_Hurvitz.pdf

Ibn Rushd, *The Distinguished Jurist's Primer. See under* Ibn Rushd, *Bidāyat al-Mujtahid.*

Imber, Colin. *Ebu's-Su'ud: The Islamic Legal Tradition* (Stanford: Stanford University Press, 1997).

_____. "Review of Guy Burak, *The Second Formation of Islamic Law: The Ḥanafī School in the Early Modern Ottoman Empire* (New York: Cambridge University Press, 2015)" in *Journal of Islamic Studies*, 27 (2016), 392-94.

İnalcik, Halil. "Application of the Tanzimat and its Social Effects." *Archivum Ottomanicum*, 5 (1973), 97-127.

_____. "Ḳānūn," *Encyclopaedia of Islam*, 2nd ed., IV (Leiden: Brill, 1978).

_____. "Review of Uriel Heyd, *Studies in Old Ottoman Criminal Law* (Oxford: Clarendon Press, 1973)," in *Bulletin of the School of African and Oriental Studies*, 37, 3 (1974), 696-98.

_____. "Suleiman the Lawgiver and Ottoman Law," in H. İnalcik, *The Ottoman Empire, Conquest, Organization and Economy* (London: Variorum, 1978), 105-38.

Iqtidar, Humeira. "Theorizing Popular Sovereignty in the Colony: Abul Aʿla Maududi's 'Theodemocracy'," *Review of Politics*, 82 (2020), 595-617.

_____ and Oliver Scharbrodt. "Sovereignty, Morality and the State: Maududi and His Influence," *Journal of the Royal Asiatic Society*, series 3 (2021), 1-17.

Irwin, Robert. "The Privatization of 'Justice' under the Circassian Mamluks," *Mamlūk Studies Review* 6 (2002), 63-70.

Jackson, Sherman A. *Islamic Law and the State: The Constitutional Jurisprudence of Shihāb al-Dīn al-Qarāfī* (Leiden: E. J. Brill, 1996).

János, Jany. "The Four Sources of Law in Zoroastrian and Islamic Jurisprudence," *Islamic Law and Society*, 12, 3 (2005), 291-332.

Jennings, Ronald. "Kadi, Court, and Legal Procedure in 17th C. Ottoman Kayseri: The Kadi and the Legal System." *Studia Islamica*, 48 (1978), 133-72.

Johansen, Baber. "Legal Literature and the Problem of Change: The Case of Land Rent," in *Islam and Public Law*, ed. Chibli Mallat (London: Graham & Trotman, 1993), 29-47.

_____. "Signs as Evidence: The Doctrine of Ibn Taymiyya (1263-1328) and Ibn Qayyim al-Jawziyya (d. 1351) on Proof," *Islamic Law and Society* 9, 2 (2002), 168-93.

Johnson, Pauline. "Social Philosophy," in *Theodor Adorno: Key Concepts*, ed. Deborah Cook (Stocksfield: Acumen, 2008), 115-29.

Jomaa, Katrin A. *Ummah: A New Paradigm for a Global World* (Albany: SUNY Press, 2021).

Kahn, Paul W. *Political Theology: Four New Chapters on the Concept of Sovereignty* (New York: Columbia University Press, 2011).

_____. *Putting Liberalism in Its Place* (Princeton: Princeton University Press, 2005).

Kaiser, Thomas. "The Evil Empire? The Debate on Turkish Despotism in Eighteenth-Century French Political Culture," *The Journal of Modern History*, 72, 1 (2000), 6-34.

Kant, Immanuel. "An Answer to the Question: What is Enlightenment?" in *Immanuel Kant*, ed. Mary J. Grego (Cambridge: Cambridge University Press, 1996), 17-22.

Kelsen, Hans. *General Theory of Law and State*, trans. A. Wedberg (New York: Russell and Russell, 1961).

Khalidi, Tarif. *See under Qur'ān.*

Khan, Ahmad. *Heresy and the Formation of Medieval Islamic Orthodoxy: The Making of Sunnism from the Eighth to the Eleventh Century* (Cambridge: Cambridge University Press, 2023).

Kia, Mana. "Lingering with *Adab* before Rushing to Literature," *History of Humanities*, 9, 1 (Spring 2024), 65-79.

Klopfer, Helmut. *Das Dogma des Imam al-Haramain al-Djuwaini* (Cairo-Wiesbaden: Otto Harrassowitz, 1958).

Korsgaard, Christine M. *Self-Constitution: Agency, Identity, and Integrity* (Oxford: Oxford University Press, 2009).

Koselleck, Reinhart. *Futures Past: On the Semantics of Historical Time*, trans. Keith Tribe (New York: Columbia University Press, 2004).

Kuhn, Thomas S. *The Structure of Scientific Revolutions* (Chicago: University of Chicago Press, 1970).

Lambton, Ann A.K.S. "Justice in the Medieval Persian Theory of *Studia Islamica*, 17 (1962), 91-119.

_____. *State and Government in Medieval Islam* (London: Routledge, 2004).

Lange, Christian. *Justice, Punishment and the Medieval Muslim Imagination* (Cambridge: Cambridge University Press, 2008).

Lapidus, Ira. *Islamic Societies to the Nineteenth Century: A Global History* (Cambridge: Cambridge University Press, 2012).

Lawson, Gary. "The Rise and Rise of the Administrative State." *Harvard Law Review*, 107 (1994), 1231-54.

Lee, Daniel. *Popular Sovereignty in Early Modern Constitutional Thought* (Oxford: Oxford University Press, 2016).

Levinson, Daryl J. "Separation of Parties, Not Powers," *Harvard Law Review*, 119 (June 2006), 2311-86.

Levy, Kenneth N. et al. "A Historical Review of Narcissism and Narcissistic Personality," in *Handbook of Narcissism and Narcissistic Personality Disorder: Theoretical Approaches, Empirical Findings, and Treatments*, ed. W. Keith Campbell et al. (Hoboken, N.J.: John Wiley & Sons, 2011), 3-13.

Lewin, Micah. "Liberal Conception of Justice," in *The Cambridge Rawls Lexicon*, ed. Jon Mandle et al. (Cambridge: Cambridge University Press, 2014), 440-41.

Liew, Han Hsein. "The Caliphate of Adam: Theological Politics of the Qur'ānic Term 'Ḫalīfa'," *Arabica*, 16, 63 (2016), 1-29.

Little, Donald P. "The Nature of the *Khānqāhs*, *Ribāṭs*, and *Zāwiyas* under the Mamlūks," in *Islamic Studies Presented to Charles J. Adams*, ed. Wael B. Hallaq et al. (Leiden: Brill, 1991), 91-105.

Lloyd, Christopher. *The Structures of History* (Oxford: Blackwell, 1993).

London, Jennifer A. "The Circle of Justice," *History of Political Thought*, 32, 3 (Autumn 2011), 425-47.

Losurdo, Domenico. *Liberalism: A Counter-History*, trans. Gregory Elliott (London: Verso, 2011).

Loughlin, Martin. "The Contemporary Crisis of Constitutional Democracy," *Oxford Journal of Legal Studies*, 39, 2 (2019), 435-54.

Loughlin, Martin and Neil Walker (eds.), *The Paradox of Constitutionalism: Constituent Power and Constitutional Form* (Oxford: Oxford University Press, 2008).

Lowry, Joseph, et al. (eds.), *Law and Education in Medieval Islam* (Chippenham, UK: E. J. W. Gibb Memorial Trust, 2004).

Lust-Okar, Ellen. *Structuring Conflict in the Arab World: Incumbents, Opponents, and Institutions* (New York: Cambridge University Press, 2005).

Machiavelli, Niccolo. *The Prince*, Harvard Classics, Vol. 36 (New York: P. F. Callier & Son, 1910).

MacIntyre, Alasdair. *After Virtue: A Study in Moral Theory* (Notre Dame, Ind.: University of Notre Dame Press, 1981).

_____. *Whose Justice? Which Rationality?* (Notre Dame, Ind.: University of Notre Dame Press, 1988).

Macpherson, C. B. *The Political Theory of Possessive Individualism: Hobbes to Locke* (New York: Oxford University Press, 1962).

Magill, Elizabeth M. "Beyond Powers and Branches in Separation of Powers Law," *University of Pennsylvania Law Review*, 150, 2 (Dec., 2001), 603-60.

_____. "The Real Separation in Separation of Powers Law," *Virginia Law Review*, 86 (September 2000), 1127-98.

Makdisi, George. *Ibn ʿAqīl et la Resurgence de l'Islam Traditionaliste au Xe Siècle* (Damas: Institut Français, 1963).

_____. *The Rise of Colleges: Institutions of Learning in Islam and the West* (Edinburgh: Edinburgh University Press, 1981).

Mann, Michael. *The Sources of Social Power*, vol. 1 (Cambridge: Cambridge University Press, 1986).

Mansfield, Harvey C. "Separation of Powers in the American Constitution," in *Separation of Powers and Good Government*, ed. Bradford P. Wilson et al. (London: Rowman and Littlefield, 1994), 3-15.

March, Andrew. "Constitutional Authority," *Ashgate Research Companion to Islamic Law*, ed. P. Bearman et al. (London: Routledge, 2014), 179-92.

Marín, Manuela. "Law and Piety: A Cordovan Fatwā," *British Society for Middle Eastern Studies Bulletin*, 17, 2 (1990), 129-36.

_____. "The *'ulamā'*," in *The New Cambridge History of Islam*, vol. 2, ed. Maribel Fierro (Cambridge: Cambridge University Press, 2010), 682-701.

Maritain, Jacques, "The Concept of Sovereignty," *American Political Science Review*, 44, 2 (June 1950), 343-57.

Marmura, Michael. "Some Aspects of Avicenna's Theory of God's Knowledge of Particulars," *Journal of the American Oriental Society*, 82 (1962): 299-312.

Marrow, John. *History of Western Political Thought* (London: Palgrave Macmillan, 2005).

Marshall, Geoffrey. *Constitutional Theory* (Oxford: Clarendon Press, 1971).

Marsham, Andrew. *Rituals of Islamic Monarchy: Accession and Succession in the First Muslim Empire* (Edinburgh: Edinburgh University Press, 2009).

Marx, Karl. "Manifesto of the Communist Party," in *Marx and Engels: Basic Writings on Politics and Philosophy*, ed. Lewis Feuer (New York: Anchor, 1959).

Mauss, Marcel. "Techniques of the Body," *Economy and Society*, 2, 1 (1973), 70-88.

Mbembe, Achille. "Necropolitics," *Public Culture*, 15, 1 (2003), 11-40.

McGushin, Edward. *Foucault's Askesis: An Introduction to the Philosophical Life* (Evanston: Northwestern University Press, 2007).

Mearsheimer, John and Stephen M. Walt. "The Israel Lobby and U.S. Foreign Policy," *Middle East Policy*, vol. XIII, 3 (Fall 2006), 29-87.

_____. *The Israel Lobby and U.S. Foreign Policy* (Toronto: Viking Canada, 2007).

Melchert, Christopher. *The Formation of the Sunni Schools of Law, 9th-10th Centuries C.E.* (Leiden: Brill, 1997).

Miller, Andrew C. "Jundi-Shapur, Bimaristans, and the Rise of Academic Medical Centers," *Journal of the Royal Society of Medicine*," 99 (December 2006), 615-17.

Misri, Ibn Naqib. *See under* Ibn Naqīb, sec. 1, above.

Moin, A. Azfar. *The Millennial Sovereign: Sacred Kingship and Sainthood in Islam* (New York: Columbia University Press, 2012).

Moore, David Chioni (ed.). *Black Athena Writes Back: Martin Bernal Responds to his Critics* (Durham: Duke University Press, 2001).

Morimoto, Kosei. "What Ibn Khaldūn Saw: The Judiciary of Mamluk Egypt," *Mamlūk Studies Review* 6 (2002), 109-131.

Moustafa, Tamir. *The Struggle for Constitutional Power: Law, Politics, and Economic Development in Egypt* (New York: Cambridge University Press, 2007).

Murdoch, Iris. *Metaphysics as a Guide to Morals* (London: Random House, 2003).

Nagan, Winston P. and Aitza M. Haddad, "Sovereignty in Theory and Practice," *San Diego International Law Journal*, 429 (2011-12), 429-519.

Nagel, Tilman. *Staat und Glaubensgemeinschaft im Islam: Geschichte der politischen Ordnungsvorstellungen der Muslime* (Zürich: Artemis, 1981).

Najib, Aseel. "Common Wealth: Land Taxation in Early Islam" (Ph.D. Dissertation: Columbia University, 2023).

Naturalization Oath of Allegiance to the United States of America. At: https://www.uscis.gov/citizenship/learn-about-citizenship/the-naturalization-interview-and-test/naturalization-oath-of-allegiance-to-the-united-states-of-america.

Neustadt, David. *See under* Ayalon.

Nicolacopoulos, Toula. *The Radical Critique of Liberalism: In Memory of a Vision* (Melbourne: Re-Press, 2008).

Nietzsche, Friedrich. *Human, All Too Human*, trans. R. J. Hollingdale (Cambridge: Cambridge University Press, 1996).

_____. "On Truth and Lies in a Nonmoral Sense," in *Philosophy and Truth: Selections from Nietzsche's Notebooks of the Early 1870's*, ed. and trans. Daniel Breazeale (Atlantic Highlands, NJ: Humanities Press, 1979).

Nisbet, Robert. *History of the Idea of Progress* (New York: Basic Books, 1980).

Northrup, Linda. "Qalāwūn's Patronage of the Medical Sciences in Thirteenth-Century Egypt," *Mamlūk Studies Review*, 5 (2001), 119-40.

O'Connor, Brian. "Philosophy of History," in *Theodor Adorno: Key Concepts*, ed. D. Cook (Stocksfield: Acumen, 2008), 179-95.

Opwis, Felicitas. "Shifting Legal Authority from the Ruler to the *'Ulamā'*: Rationalizing the Punishment for Drinking Wine During the Saljūq Period," *Der Islam*, 86, 1 (2011), 65-92.

Ottaway, A. K. C. "The Educational Sociology of Émile Durkheim," *British Journal of Sociology* 6, 3 (1955), 213-27.

Peirce, Leslie. *Morality Tales: Law and Gender in the Ottoman Court of Aintab* (California: University of California Press, 2003).

Peters, Rudolph. *Crime and Punishment in Islamic Law* (Cambridge: Cambridge University Press, 2005).

_____. "What Does it Mean to be an Official *Madhhab*? Ḥanafīsm and the Ottoman Empire," in *The Islamic School of Law: Evolution, Devolution, and Progress*, ed. P. Bearman, et al. (Cambridge: Harvard University Press, 2005), 147-58.

Petras, James. *The Power of Israel in the United States* (Atlanta: Clarity Press, 2006).

Pfeifer, Helen. *Empire of Salons: Conquest and Community in Early Modern Ottoman Lands* (Princeton: Princeton University Press, 2022).

Pickthall, Mohammed Marmaduke. *The Meaning of the Glorious Koran* (New York: Mentor Religious Classic, 1955).

Posner, Eric and Adrian Vermeule, *The Executive Unbound: After the Madisonian Republic* (Oxford: Oxford University Press, 2010).

Powers, David. "On Judicial Review in Islamic Law," *Islamic Law and Society*, 26 (1992), 315-41.

Quraishi-Landes, Asifa. "Islamic Constitutionalism: Not Secular, Not Theocratic, Not Impossible," *Rutgers Journal of Law and Religion*, 16 (2015), 553-79.

Qur'ān. See under Pickthall.

Qur'ān, The. Trans. Tarif Khalidi (London: Penguin, 2008).

Qur'ān: Arabic Text with Corresponding English Meanings (Riyadh: Abulqasim Publishing House, 1997).

Ragab, Ahmed. *The Medieval Islamic Hospital: Medicine, Religion, and Charity* (New York: Cambridge University Press, 2015).

Rapoport, Yossef. "Royal Justice and Religious Law: *Siyāsah and Sharīʿah* under the Mamluks," *Mamlūk Studies Review*, 16 (2012), 71-102.

Rawls, John, *Political Liberalism* (New York: Columbia University Press, 2005).

Raymond, André. *Arab Cities in the Ottoman Period: Cairo, Syria and the Maghreb* (London and New York: Routledge, 2002).

Reid, Megan H. *Law and Piety in Medieval Islam* (Cambridge: Cambridge University Press, 2013).

Reinstein, Robert J. "The Limits of Executive Power," *American University Law Review*, 59, 2 (December 2009), 259-337.

Robinson, Francis. "Education," in *The New Cambridge History of Islam*, vol. 4, ed. R. Irwin (Cambridge: Cambridge University Press, 2010), 497-531.

Rosen, George. *A History of Public Health* (New York: MD Publications, 1958).

Rosenthal, Erwin I. J. *Political Thought in Medieval Islam: An Introductory Outline* (Cambridge: Cambridge University Press, 1958).

Rubiés, Joan-Pau. "Oriental Despotism and European Orientalism: Botero to Montesquieu," *Journal of Early Modern History*, 9, 1-2 (2005), 109-80.

Rubin, Avi. *Ottoman Nizamiye Courts: Law and Modernity* (New York: Palgrave Macmillan, 2011).

Rubinelli, Lucia. *Constituent Power: A History* (Cambridge University Press, 2020).

Rustow, Marina. *The Lost Archive: Traces of a Caliphate in a Cairo Synagogue* (Princeton: Princeton University Press, 2020).

Said, Edward W. *Orientalism* (New York: Vintage Books, 1979).

Saito, Natsu Taylor. "Whose Liberty? Whose Security? The USA PATRIOT Act in the Context of COINTELPRO and the Unlawful Repression of Political Dissent," *Oregon Law Review*, 82 (2002), 1051-1132.

Saleh, Walid. "Ibn Taymiyya and the Rise of Radical Hermeneutics: An Analysis of An Introduction to the Foundations of Qur'ānic Exegesis," in *Ibn Taymiyya and His Times*, ed. Y. Rapaport et al. (Karachi: Oxford University Press, 2010).

Salmone, Habib. *An Advanced Learner's Arabic-English Dictionary* (1889), available at: http://arabiclexicon.hawramani.com/?p=16904#d38cad

Samuels, Ben. "AIPAC Explained: The Inside Story of America's Powerful and Divisive Pro-Israel Lobby," *Ha'aretz* (Feb. 28, 2024), available at: https://www.haaretz.com/us-news/2024-02-28/ty-article-magazine/.premium/aipac-explained-the-inside-story-of-americas-powerful-and-divisive-pro-israel-lobby/0000018d-e4ac-d972-a5bf-efaf96c60000

Saunders, Cheryl. "Separation of Powers and the Judicial Branch," *Judicial Review*, 11 (2006), 337-47.

Sapiro, Gisèle. "Habitus: History of a Concept," in *International Encyclopedia of the Social & Behavioral Sciences*, 2nd ed., ed. James D. Wright, vol. 10 (Oxford: Elsevier, 2015), 484-89.

Schacht, Joseph. *Introduction to Islamic Law* (Oxford: Clarendon Press, 1964).

_____. *The Origins of Muhammadan Jurisprudence* (Oxford: Oxford University Press, 1950).

______. "Problems of Modern Islamic Legislation," *Studia Islamica*, 12 (1960), 99-129.

Schmitt, Carl. *Political Romanticism*, trans. Guy Oakes (New Brunswick, N.J.: Transaction, 2011).

_____. *Political Theology: Four Chapters on the Concept of Sovereignty*, trans. G. Schwab (Chicago: University of Chicago Press, 1985).

_____. *The Concept of the Political*, trans. G. Schwab (Chicago: University of Chicago Press, 2007).

Schultz, Peter L. "Congress and the Separation of Powers Today: Practice in Search of a Theory," in *Separation of Powers and Good Government*, ed. B. P. Wilson et al. (Lanham, MD: Rowan and Littlefield, 1994), 185-200.

Şen, Tunç A. "The Sultan's Syllabus Revisited: Sixteenth-Century Ottoman Madrasa Libraries and the Question of Canonization," *Studia Islamica*, 116 (2021), 198-235.

Şentürk, Recep. "Between Traditional and New Forms of Authority in Modern Islam," in *Tradition and Modernity: Christian and Muslim Perspectives*, ed. David Marshall (Washington, D.C.: Georgetown University Press, 2013), 45-55.

Sewell, William H. *Logics of History: Social Theory and Social Transformations* (Chicago and London: Chicago University Press, 2005).

Shaikh, Sa'diyya. *Sufi Narratives of Intimacy: Ibn 'Arabi, Gender, and Sexuality* (Chapel Hill: University of North Carolina Press, 2012).

Shils, Edward. *Tradition* (Chicago: University of Chicago Press, 1981).

Shoshan, Boaz. "Notes sur les épidémies de peste en Egypte," *Annales de démographie historique* (1981), 387-404.

Siddiqui, Sohaira Z. M. *Law and Politics under the Abbasids: An Intellectual Portrait of al-Juwayni* (Cambridge: Cambridge University Press, 2019).

_____. "Power Vs. Authority: Al-Juwaynī's Intervention in Pragmatic Political Thought," *Journal of Islamic Studies*, 28, 2 (2017), 193–220.

Sinai, Nicolai. "Qur'ānic Self-Referentiality as a Strategy of Self-Authorization," in *Self-Referentiality in the Qur'ān*, Diskurse der Arabistik, no. 11, ed. Stefan Wild (Wiesbaden: Otto Harassowitz, 2006), 103-34.

Skinner, Quentin. *The Foundations of Modern Political Thought*, 2 vols. (Cambridge: Cambridge University Press, 1978).

_____. "Modernity and Disenchantment: Some Historical Reflections," in *Philosophy in an Age of Pluralism*, ed. James Tully (Cambridge: Cambridge University press, 1994), 37-48.

Sprangens, Thomas A. Jr. *The Irony of Liberal Reason* (Chicago: University of Chicago Press, 1981).

Stark, Werner. *Sociology of Knowledge: An Essay in Aid of a Deeper Understanding of the History of Ideas* (London: Routledge and Kegan Paul, 1960).

Staude, John Raphael. *Max Scheler* (New York: The Free Press, 1967).

Steinmetz, George, "Bourdieu, History, and Historical Sociology," *Cultural Sociology*, 5, 1 (2011), 45-66.

Stewart, Iain. "From 'Rule of Law' to 'Legal State': A Time of Reincarnation?" *Macquarie Law* (November 2007), 1-11.

Stilt, Kristin. "Constitutional Islam: Genealogies, Transmissions and Meanings," in *On the Ground: New Directions in the Middle East and North African Studies*, ed. B. T. Edwards (Qatar: Akkadia Press, 2014).

Subtelny, Maria Eva and Anas B. Khalidov, "The Curriculum of Higher Learning in Tīmurid Iran in the Light of the Sunnī Revival under Shāh-Rukh," *Journal of the American Oriental Society*, 115, 2 (1995), 210-36.

Suganami, Hidemi. "Understanding Sovereignty Through Kelsen/Schmitt," *Review of International Studies*, 33 (2007), 511-30.

Tallet, Frank. *War and Society in Early Modern Europe, 1495-1715* (London: Routledge, 1992).

Tazi Hemida, Doha. "A Sufi Conception of Order: Ibn ʿArabī's Discourse on Governance," *Journal of Islamic Studies*, 35, 1 (2024), 46-81.

_____. "The Problem of God's Sovereignty in Classical Islamic Thought" (Ph.D. Dissertation: Columbia University, in progress).

Tezcan, Baki. "The Ottoman 'Mevali' as 'Lords of the Law'," *Journal of Islamic Studies*, 20, 3 (September 2009), 383-407.

_____. "The Second Empire: The Transformation of the Ottoman Polity in the Early Modern Era," *Comparative Studies of South Asia, Africa and the Middle East*, 29, 3 (2009): 556-72.

_____. *The Second Ottoman Empire: Political and Social Transformations in the Early Modern World* (Cambridge: Cambridge University Press, 2010).

Toft, Amir. "Review of Guy Burak, *Second Formation of Islamic Law*," *Journal of Near Eastern Studies*, 77, 2 (2018), 333-36.

Tor, D. G. "Sovereign and Pious: The Religious Life of the Great Seljuq Sultans," in *The Seljuqs: Politics, Society, and Culture*, ed. Christian Lang et al. (Edinburgh: Edinburgh University Press, 2011), 39-62.

Trimingham, J. S. *A History of Islam in West Africa* (Oxford: Oxford University Press, 1970).

Tucker, Judith E. "Revisiting Reform: Women and the Ottoman Law of Family Rights, 1917," *The Arab Studies Journal*, 4, 2 (1996), 4-17.

U.S. Government. "Executive Overreach in Domestic Affairs (Part II) – IRS Abuses, Welfare, Reform, and Other Issues," *Hearing Before the Executive*

Overreach Task Force of the Committee on the Judiciary House Representatives (April 19, 2016), available at: https://www.govinfo.gov/content/pkg/CHRG114hhrg99839/pdf/CHRG-114hhrg99839.pdf

Vakalopoulos, Konstantinos. "Shedding Some (More) Light on Bourdieu's Habitus and Doxa: A Socio-Phenomenological Approach," *Journal for the Theory of Social Behaviour*, 53, 2 (September 2022), 255-70.

van Creveld, Martin. *The Rise and Decline of the State* (Cambridge: Cambridge University Press, 1999).

Vanderbilt, Arthur. *The Doctrine of the Separation of Powers and Its Present-Day Significance* (Lincoln: University of Nebraska Press, 1953).

van Steenbergen, Jo. "Appearances of *Dawla* and Political order in Late Medieval Syro-Egypt. The State, Social Theory, and the Political History of the Cairo Sultanate (Thirteenth-Sixteenth Centuries)," in *History and Society During the Mamluk Period, 1250-1517*, ed. S. Conermann (Göttingen: V&R unipress, 2016), 51-85.

van Vleet, John Anton. "Tactical Military Deception" (Thesis; Monterey: Naval Postgraduate School, 1985).

Vile, M. J. C. *Constitutionalism and the Separation of Powers* (Indianapolis, Ind.: Liberty Fund, 1998).

Viroli, Maurizio. "The Revolution in the Concept of Politics," *Political Theory*, 20, 3 (August 1992), 473-95.

Vogel, Frank. "Tracing Nuance in Māwardī's *Al-Aḥkām al-Sulṭāniyyah*: Implicit Framing of Constitutional Authority," in *Islamic Law in Theory: Studies on Jurisprudence in Honor of Bernard Weiss*, ed. A. Kevin Reinhart et al. (Leiden: Brill, 2014), 331-59.

Vogelsang, Kai. "Conceptual History: A Short Introduction," *Oriens Extremus*, 51 (2012), 9-24.

Waldron, Jeremy. "The Core of the Case Against Judicial Review," *Yale Law Journal*, 115 (2006), 1346-1406.

Weber, Eugen. *Peasants into Frenchmen: The Modernization of Rural France, 1870-1914* (Stanford: Stanford University Press, 1976).

Wehr, Hans. *A Dictionary of Modern Written Arabic* (Beirut: Librarie du Liban, 1980).

Weiss, Bernard. "Knowledge of the Past: The Theory of Tawātur According to Ghazālī," *Studia Islamica*, 61 (1985), 81-105.

Wilson, Charles H. "Separation of Powers under Democracy and Fascism," *Political Science Quarterly*, 52, 4 (1937), 481-503.

Wittgenstein, Ludwig. *The Blue and Brown Books* (Oxford: Basil Blackwell, 1964).

Wolff, J. *Roman Law* (Norman: University of Oklahoma Press, 1951).

Wolfson, Harry Austryn. *The Philosophy of the Kalam* (Cambridge, MA: Harvard University Press, 1976).

Yilmaz, Hüseyin. *Caliphate Redefined: The Mystical Turn in Ottoman Political Thought* (Princeton: Princeton University Press, 2018).

_____. "Containing Sultanic Authority: Constitutionalism in the Ottoman Empire before Modernity," *Journal of Ottoman Studies*, XLV (2015), 231-64.

Young, Walter. *The Dialectical Forge: Juridical Disputation and the Evolution of Islamic Law* (Bonn: Springer, 2017).

Yücesoy, Hayrettin. "Caliph and Caliphate up to 1517," *Encyclopedia of Islam*, 3rd Ed., available at: https://referenceworks.brill.com/display/entries/EI3O/COM-25459.xml?rskey=rEp7tR&result=2

_____. *Disenchanting the Caliphate: The Secular Discipline of Power in Abbasid Political Thought* (New York: Columbia University Press, 2023).

_____. "Justification of Political Authority in Medieval Sunni Thought," in *Islam, the State, and Political Authority: Medieval Issues and Modern Concerns*, ed. Asma Afsaruddin (New York: Palgrave, 2011), 9-33.

Zaman, Qasim M. "The Caliphs, the Ulama, and the Law: Defining the Role and Function of the Caliph in the Early Abbasid Period," *Islamic Law and Society*, 4, 1 (1997), 1-36.

_____. *Religion and Politics under the Early ʿAbbāsids* (Leiden: Brill, 1997).

Index

Note: References to notes show both the page number and the note number (19 n. 36).